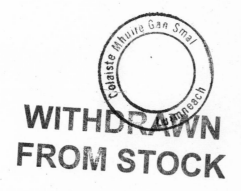

Concepts in Art and Education

CONCEPTS
in Art and Education

AN ANTHOLOGY OF CURRENT ISSUES

George Pappas

UNIVERSITY OF SOUTH FLORIDA

THE MACMILLAN COMPANY

COLLIER-MACMILLAN LIMITED, LONDON

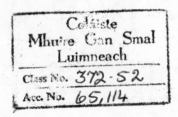
First Printing

Library of Congress catalog card number: 75–87894

THE MACMILLAN COMPANY
COLLIER-MACMILLAN CANADA, LTD., TORONTO, ONTARIO

Printed in the United States of America

For Tom and Jane

Preface

The readings in this anthology represent a sampling of works selected to give the student or teacher of art, education, or art education an opportunity to gain critical insight into the problems and major issues involved in teaching art in today's tumultuous society. Through this presentation of concepts, methods, and theories based on the interrelated areas of the visual arts, aesthetics, psychology, sociology, and anthropology, it is hoped the student will be motivated to engage in a challenging intellectual self-dialogue by objectively examining his own thoughts and feelings, thus arriving at a personal attitude and a commitment to the teaching of art.

Many prospective teachers may be surprised to find that art education has developed as a result of some sound basic theories and concern with scientific methodology. Today the new climate of art education, based on the reassessment and advancement of earlier achievements, has made the study of this important and ever-widening area an exciting challenge.

Only through direct confrontation with the diverse concepts and current methods of teaching art will the student or teacher be in a position to deepen his understanding of the intimate relationship between concept and method. Needless to say, there is subtle conflict and strong controversy within American art education today. The problem of developing art concepts and curriculum, the strategies of art action through student-teacher relationships, the

vii

aesthetic evaluation of art products, and the role of research in art are issues that are constantly being reevaluated and revised.

These complexities that are characteristic of art education in today's society should stimulate in the reader the need and desire to discover an initial position, to seek a new position, or to become more flexible in an established position. Because this desire is anticipated, no attempt has been made to present these readings as a panacea for the problems of art and education. Their purpose is to generate and extend thinking—to inspire into action the involvement with basic theory and innovative ideas as a result of careful and critical analysis of each of the readings. Because of the limitations of space, it is impossible to present every point of view related to all the issues. However, an attempt has been made to give a representative sampling of a variety of issues within the working structure of the anthology. The book presents six basic areas: background, foundation, attitudes, practice, critical analysis, and research.

In Chapter 1 the readings focus on the major historical developments that have played an important role in shaping the character of contemporary theory and methodology. This knowledge is essential in tracing the growth of art education and establishing a pertinent contrast between past and present.

Chapter 2 is organized around the concepts and theories of leading educators, art educators, philosophers, and aestheticians whose contributions can be regarded as having established and shaped the core of currently accepted art education thought. The readings in this chapter are presented under the title "Foundation," as their study and assimilation become preparatory to any knowledgeable course of action.

The political, economic, and social mainstreams of our society also have to be considered before establishing a course of action, and Chapter 3 attempts to develop an identity with the current pulse of our environment. The demands of youth as the consumer of education provide vital insight and direction. The unique problems of the disadvantaged, as dramatically illustrated in Jonathan Kozols' *Death at an Early Age*, reflect an extreme in attitude that many art educators have neither confronted nor considered.

Chapter 4 includes readings organized around two strongly interrelated themes in educational practice. The first deals with current practice in teaching art; the second is concerned with the innovative insights that unquestionably pave the way for the future of art education. *Creative and innovative thought* must become the life blood of art education methodology if it is to have a future. Teachers who have developed a secure confidence in the guaranteed traditional methods and materials of the past must begin to extend their thinking to include the impact of the new image in art and the knowledge gained through experimental educational research.

Art experiences developed in the classroom are not complete until responsible and critical analysis has occurred. Chapter 5 presents the writings of educators who are concerned with this difficult aspect of the total involvement in art. Evaluative objectives must be developed by each teacher in relationship to formulated goals, the nature of student art, and the developmental level of the students themselves. An understanding of the intimate and complex nature of aesthetics is valuable as a prerequisite to the development of any logical system of analysis and evaluation and especially as a source for guiding the practice of art.

The concern with research which makes up the final chapter of this anthology has been misunderstood and looked upon with suspicion by many educators, especially in the area of fine arts. The romantic notion that portrays the art experience and process as a divine and unobservable emotional action is no longer valid. No discipline can survive without meaningful research. The processes of inquiry are at times quite slow and seemingly superfluous. However, the careful and discriminating selection of these bits of research information can help immeasurably in developing and extending previously learned dimensions of education. The reader will have an opportunity to evaluate the role of research in art and education and become informed of some significant models of current research.

The editor is especially grateful for the approval of authors and publishers for permission to include their important works in this volume. The generosity of educators in contributing information, time, and energy in the interest of adding additional knowledge to educational literature is unparalleled in any other field.

Tampa, Florida   G. P.

Contents

PART I
BACKGROUND AND FOUNDATIONS:
INITIAL INVOLVEMENT

1. Background

Selections from Historical Writings on Art Education

ROBERT J. SAUNDERS   4

Some Historical Developments in Art Education

ELLIOT W. EISNER / DAVID W. ECKER   12

The Plastic Arts, History of Art and Design—Three Currents Toward Identifying Content for Art Education

JEROME J. HAUSMAN   26

2. Foundation

Does Philosophy Have a Future?

SIDNEY HOOK   46

The Meaning of Creative Activity for Elementary Education

VIKTOR LOWENFELD   53

Experience and Thinking

JOHN DEWEY   62

xi

Society, Art, and Education

JUNE KING MC FEE   71

The Act of Discovery

JEROME S. BRUNER   90

Sketches Toward a Psychology of Learning in Art

KENNETH R. BEITTEL   101

Meditations on a Hobby Horse or the Roots of Artistic Form

E. H. GOMBRICH   156

Expressiveness

SUSANNE K. LANGER   168

The Inert and the Frenetic

MAX KOZLOFF   175

PART II
ATTITUDES AND PRACTICE:
CUES FOR DIRECTION

3. Attitudes

The Teacher in the World

HAROLD TAYLOR   194

Death at an Early Age

JONATHAN KOZOL   202

Youth, Change and Violence

KENNETH KENISTON   206

The Liberal Tradition and Art Education

RALPH A. SMITH   220

The School as a Model of Society

JOSEPH GRANNIS   229

A Revision of Purposes for Art Education

GUY HUBBARD   246

4. Practice

The Contexts of Teaching Art

IRVING KAUFMAN   256

Advancing Art in U.S. Public Schools

JOHN GOODLAD   274

Quality Education and Aesthetic Education

HARRY S. BROUDY   280

Light as a Creative Medium

GYORGY KEPES   290

Newer Media and the Teaching of Art

VINCENT LANIER   296

The Science of Art

ROBERT E. MUELLER   303

Meaning of Crafts

EDWARD MATTIL 306

Happenings In and Out of School—
An Interview with Allan Kaprow

DAVID ECKER 311

The Mass Media as an Educational Institution

HERBERT J. GANS 319

Teacher as Artist and Artist as Teacher

JEROME J. HAUSMAN 333

✕ Summary of Development Stages

VIKTOR LOWENFELD / LAMBERT BRITTAIN 341

PART III
CRITICAL ANALYSIS AND RESEARCH:
CONTRIBUTORS TO COMPLETE ART EDUCATION

5. Critical Analysis
Engaging Art in Dialogue

EDMUND B. FELDMAN 352

Criticism and Its Premises

HAROLD ROSENBERG 360

Systems Esthetics

JACK BURNHAM 375

Evaluating Children's Art

ELLIOT W. EISNER 386

The Problem of Objectivity in Esthetic Value

IRVIN L. CHILD 390

✕ Aesthetic Criticism: The Method of Aesthetic Education

RALPH A. SMITH 404

6. Research
Limitations of Research in Teaching Art

IRVING KAUFMAN 423

Basic and Applied Research in Education:
Definitions, Distinctions, and Implications

JOHN B. CARROLL 433

A Reconsideration of the Problem of Introspection

DAVID BAKAN 445

Research Trends in Art Education

DONALD JACK DAVIS 458

Three Bases for Research and Teaching in the Arts:
Subjective, Objective, and Projective

HUGH W. STUMBO 465

Concepts in Art and Education

Part I

Background and Foundation:
Initial Involvement

It becomes an almost impossible task to singularly trace the history of any movement in art education without considering the varied sources from which it has developed. The history of art education reflects not only a relationship to general education but also the influences from the social sciences, advances in technology, and the conceptual and visual changes inherent in the art object itself.

Looking at the distant past through contemporary eyes has always been a major problem for the historian. The ability to identify meaningfully with the past becomes an initial concern and a necessary requisite for complete understanding. Because the history of art education in the public schools is involved with the relatively recent past, it may be possible to grasp more readily the historical flavor and the philosophical essence of its development. By establishing a relationship between the past and the complexity of our present active culture, we add yet another dimension to our need for finding meaning in the historical order of art education, identifying its current philosophical foundations, and considering the role it is to play in the future.

In the eighteenth century men like Benjamin Franklin and Thomas Jefferson took an active interest in the American educational system and strongly recommended that art instruction become an important part of the education of all children. However, it was not until the later part of the nineteenth century that the first step toward organized public school art education was taken by the Massachusetts Board of Education. Instruction in drawing was justified and became a required part of the public school curriculum. Thus, this important step initiated the role of art education into the public school system. It is both surprising and unfortunate that after such an early introduction the need to justify the teaching of art in the schools continues to this day.

In Chapter 1, "Background," the complete development of art in American public education is concisely outlined in a review by Ecker and Eisner. Their thorough approach traces the stages of growth in art education with explicit references to political, social, economic, and intellectual developments in American Society.

Hausman takes a somewhat broader view by tracing three major currents from which theory and practice will develop. These currents are "the studio production of art, the history of art (to include the whole range of man-made things involving beauty and intrinsic value) and the emerging of design disciplines." From this historical structure he proceeds to outline some important operational implications related to the teaching of art in the public schools.

These essays and others form the prologue for Chapter 2, "Foundation." The understanding of the historical logic of art education and its many facets forms a substantial base from which to explore the varied and exciting philosophical concepts that follow.

The term *foundation* very aptly underscores the work of Viktor Lowenfeld whose essay is reprinted from his classic first edition of *Creative and Mental Growth*, published in 1949. He was one of the first art educators to deal with the psychological development of children and their art. The influence of his writing has continued throughout the years, presenting a strong, sound basis for the humanistic process-centered approach to teaching art.

In a much more specialized investigation, the research of Beittel begins to focus in on the isolated act of sequential drawing, in an attempt to structure an inquiry into a psychology of learning in art. Although, by his own admission, his population is limited, the implications of his work and its philosophical import extends well beyond the scope of the investigation.

McFee's work in identifying the relationship between fields as complex as society, art, and education is most important at a time when the entire moral and organizational structure of our society is being critically reviewed. The role of the art educator in this crisis must also be examined. McFee states:

Most of us would agree, I think, that this country is in a period of intense social change. Increased consciousness of minority groups and their emergence are challenging stereotypes of prejudice. Automation and population increase are affecting our concepts of leisure and of work. Social organization and human behavior are affected by the increase of megapolis and changes in urban and rural environs. World problems, with the accelerating speed of communication and transportation, become community problems. Art educator's individual reactions to change probably run the gamut of those found among diverse groups in the larger society. We may be retreating from the changes by refusing to recognize them, or we may be trying to solve the conflicts they present with old solutions to old problems.

The challenge for today's art educator is to identify both the old and the new problems and to face them with new solutions.

Other important works in this section, by Bruner, Dewey, Gombrich, and Langer, move beyond the immediate sphere of teaching art in the schools but subsequently broaden the foundational base from which art education has developed. The influence these educators have had on the development of a sound foundation for art and educational thought is universally recognized.

A final and important contribution to Chapter 2 is an article by Kozloff. His thoughts on contemporary visual art help focus attention toward the ultimate relationship that must be established between educational theory and the complex, unorthodox approaches of today's professional artists. Where a classic certainty of this relationship once existed, there are now some elements of doubt and confusion brought about by the very nature of contemporary art. However, without seeking the virtues of the art of one's own time and establishing them as an integral part of current teaching philosophy and methodology, the term "art education" loses both its impact and meaning.

The articles, loosely categorized in this book under the title "Foundation" are not to be studied as a panacea for the problems of art and education. Rather, they should be viewed as a base for the extension and exploration, on a significant level, of the ideas of others in an attempt to ultimately arrive at a personally innovative approach to teaching art in the schools.

1

Background

Selections from Historical Writings on Art Education
Compiled and annotated by

ROBERT J. SAUNDERS

ARISTOTLE

Selected from The Basic Works of Aristotle, edited by Richard McKeon *(New York: Random House, 1941), "Politics," Bk. VIII, Chap. 3, pp. 1306– 1308.*

In "Politics," Aristotle (384–22 B.C.) wrote about the ideal state. In the last book, Book VIII, he observes that the goal of the ideal state is leisure. He differentiates between leisure, which is spent in pursuit of those activities which have no other purpose than the enjoyment of them, and the enrichment of a virtuous life and recreation, the opposite of work. The Greek word for leisure was skole, from which we get the word school. At the beginning of chapter 3, Book VIII, Aristotle observed:

Reprinted by permission from Art Education: Journal of the National Art Education Association, Vol. 19, No. 1, January 1966.

The customary branches of education are in number four; they are—(1) reading and writing, (2) gymnastic exercises, (3) music, to which is sometimes added, (4) drawing. Of these, reading and writing and drawing are regarded as useful for the purposes of life in a variety of ways, and gymnastic exercises are thought to infuse courage. Concerning music a doubt may be raised—in our own day most men cultivate it for the sake of pleasure, but originally it was included in education, because nature herself, as has been said, requires that we should be able, not only to work well, but to use leisure well; for, as I must repeat once again, the first principle of all action is leisure. . . .

It is evident, then, that there is a sort of education in which parents should train their sons, not as being useful or necessary, but because it is liberal or noble. . . . Thus much we are now in a position to say, that the ancients witness to us; for their opinion may be gathered from the fact that music is one of the received and traditional branches of education. Further, it is clear that children should be instructed in some useful things—for example, in reading and writing—not only for their usefulness, but also because many other sorts of knowledge are acquired through them. With a like view they may be taught drawing, not to prevent their making mistakes in their own purchases (of paintings or sculpture), or in order that they may not be imposed upon in their buying or selling of articles, but perhaps rather because it makes them judges of the beauty of human form. To be always seeking after the useful does not become free and exalted souls. Now it is clear that in education practice must be used before theory, and the body be trained before the mind; and therefore boys should be handed over to the trainer, who creates in them the proper habit of body, and to the wrestling-master, who teaches them their exercises.

RABELAIS

Selected from The Histories of Gargantua and Pantagruel *by Francois Rabelais (Baltimore: Penguin Books, Ltd., 1957), Translated by J. M. Cohen, p. 89.*

It does not require much of a reference for an educational historian to latch onto a phrase, and say the teaching of a subject was mentioned by so-and-so in his work published sometime-or-other. Usually it is the entire context of the reference which is important, and in the various references to the education of Gargantua in Rabelais' Gargantua and Pantagruel (1535), it is his satirizing of the abuse of Scholasticism by the humanists to which the historians refer. Be that as it may, it is this work along with the essays of Montaigne, "On Pedantry" and "Of the Institution and Education of Children: to the Lady Diana of Foix, Countess of Gurson" (1580), and The Great Didactic of John Amos Commenius (1592–1670) that we find the beginning of recommendations that drawing be taught as an accomplishment for gentlemen. We offer here, the earlier reference by Rabelais: it is not as

*loud as a school bell, or as wide as a school door, but it is enough to establish
an historical precedent. It occurs in the Chapter 23 of Book I, "How Gargantua was so disciplined by Ponocrates that he did not waste an Hour of
the Day." After studying reading, writing, Holy Writ, and Greek scholars
since four in the morning, and having reviewed his lessons, he had lunch,
reviewed the lessons again, learned numbers by playing dice and cards, studied
mathematical sciences, geometry, and astronomy. Mid-afternoon, Gargantua
studied the art of lettering:*

After this they amused themselves by singing music in four or five parts or
on a set theme, to their throats' content. With regard to musical instruments,
he learned to play the lute, the spinet, the harp, the German flute, the nine-
holed flute, the viol, and the trombone. After spending an hour in this way,
his digestion being complete, he got rid of his natural excrements, and then
returned to his principal study for three hours or more, during which time
he repeated the morning's reading, went on with the book in hand, and also
practiced writing, drawing, and shaping the Gothic and Roman letters.

LOCKE

Selected from Some Thoughts Concerning Education *by John Locke, Introduction and Notes by R. H. Quick (Cambridge: University Press, 1934),
pp. 136–137.*

*In March of either 1692, or 1693, John Locke after being much prevailed
upon by friends to do so, published his essay "Some Thoughts Concerning
Education." Originally the essay was a series of letters sent to Locke's friend,
Edward Clarke, of Chipley, Esq., and were concerned with the education
of Clarke's son. We find in the following passage, a continuation of drawing
in the training of a gentleman, which began with the previously selected
passage from Rabelais, and perhaps influenced Benjamin Franklin later, in
his "Proposals Relating to the Education of Youth in Pensilvania (1749),"
to the effect that with writing, "may be learnt something of Drawing, by
Imitation of Prints, and some of the first Principles of Perspective."*

161. *Drawing.* When he can write well and quick, I think it may be convenient not only to continue the Exercise of his Hand in Writing, but also
to improve the Use of it farther in *Drawing;* a Thing very useful to a Gentleman in several Occasions; but especially if he travel, as that which helps a
Man often to express, in a few Lines well put together, what a whole Sheet
of Paper in Writing would not be able to represent and make intelligible.
How many Buildings may a Man see, how many Machines and Habits meet
with, the Ideas whereof would be easily retain'd and communicated by a little
Skill in *Drawing;* which being committed to Words, are in danger to be lost,
or at best but ill retained in the most exact Descriptions? I do not mean that
I would have your Son a *perfect painter;* to be that to any tolerable Degree,

will require more Time than a young Gentleman can spare from his other Improvements of greater Moment. But so much Insight into *Perspective* and Skill in *Drawing*, as will enable him to represent tolerably on Paper any thing he sees, except Faces, may, I think, be got in a little Time, especially if he have a Genius to it; but where that is wanting, unless it be in the things absolutely necessary, it is better to let him pass them by quietly, than to vex him about them to no Purpose: And therefore in this, as in all other things not absolutely necessary, the Rule holds, *Nil invita Minerva.* [*Note: R. H. Quick interprets this phrase, "Nil invita Minerva" to mean, "Do nothing without the consent of Minerva," against the natural bent, against the grain.*]

FROEBEL

Selection from The Education of Man *by Frederick Froebel, translated by W. N. Hailman (New York: D. Appleton and Co., 1826).*

Although educational practices which seem respectable during one period of time may no longer be so during another, knowing the source of them can aid in understanding how they entered into common practice. The following passage from, The Education of Man *by Frederick Froebel (1826) may well be the beginning of coloring books. If this is true, then their introduction into the public school system may have resulted from the concepts of the Kindergarten movement. In view of the following selection, and what we know of the spread of Froebellean methods throughout Germany during the last century, it is possible to understand what Viktor Lowenfeld meant, when, while discussing the effects of coloring books on children's ability to think, he said to his students at Penn State: "Nazism began in the kindergartens of Germany." We also find how even the best intended methods of education can, through misuse, become among the worst methods of education.*

About a dozen boys of suitable age are gathered around their teacher like sheep around their shepherd. As the shepherd leads his sheep to green pastures, so the teacher is to lead the boys to joyous activity. It is Wednesday afternoon, when there is no ordinary school instruction; but to-day there is no call for other activity. It is fall, and the desire to paint has often been expressed by each one of these active boys. Perhaps fall invites the boys most urgently to paint, because the colors in nature are most varied and massive in the latter part of fall; and each one has probably tried in his own way to obey the summons.

"Come, let us paint," the teacher says. "It is true, you have painted a great deal; but painting itself and the things you painted did not seem to please you long for you did not paint in distinct and pure colors. Come, let us see if we can not do better together. Now, what shall we paint? What is easy enough for us? For we are to learn, and what we paint should be simple, and of one color if possible."

Teacher and pupils decide quickly that it is easiest to paint leaves, flowers, or fruits. Leaves are chosen; for the beautiful, bright red, yellow, etc., trees, and the gorgeous leaves which in perfect fall days float with a gentle rustle from branches, and deck the ground with a brilliant carpet, have been keenly noticed by the boys, and often they have bound them in wreaths and brought home.

"Here are outlines of leaves [the teacher had prepared them for the purpose]; how will you paint them?" "Green," "Red," "Yellow," "Brown." "Which leaves will you paint green, red, etc.? Why?"

The teacher then distributes the paints, properly prepared. First, the colors are correctly designated. It need, however, scarcely be mentioned that— inasmuch as the representation of the object is secondary, and the knowledge and treatment of the colors primary consideration—we can not expect to do more than to give the leaves approximately exact coloring. For the present, even distribution of the color, keeping within the lines, etc., are as yet the most important concerns; the proper position of the body, in order to insure free movement of arm, hand, and finger, is a matter to be attended to, of course.

Inasmuch as each pigment requires its own treatment, we do not pass from one color to the next until the pupil has attained proficiency in the use of the former.

MANN

Selected from "Seventh Annual Report to The Board of Education of the Commonwealth of Massachusetts," from Common School Journal, *April 15, 1844, pp. 132–135.*

Horace Mann's tour of Europe, and the "Seventh Annual Report" and his discussion of drawing in the Prussian schools which resulted from it, are standard reference points in nineteenth century art education history. However, there is confusion about the dates. In one instance, the tour has been placed in 1839 (Logan[1]), and the date of the report for 1843 (Bennett[2]). We clarify. On May 1, 1843, Horace Mann, and his bride since that morning, Mary Peabody Mann, sailed for Europe on the tour which was also their honeymoon. Horace visited schools, prisons, hospitals, and asylums. Although Mary accompanied him many places, she did not go with him to the dangerous parts of the cities. She preferred country houses, palaces and their gardens, and art museums. They visited parts of England, Scotland, the German states, Belgium, Holland, Switzerland, and France. They returned November 15, 1843.

Horace had a stronger sense of moral justice and human need than he had

---

[1] Frederick Logan, *Growth of Art in American Schools* (New York: Harper and Bros. Co., Inc., 1955), p. 19.

[2] Charles Bennett, *History of Manual and Industrial Education up to 1870* (Peoria, Ill., Chas. A. Bennett Co., 1926), p. 421.

*a sense of the aesthetic. After he and Mary had visited the cathedral at York,
he wrote in his journal: "To me the sight of one child educated to understand
something of his Maker, and of that Maker's works, is a far more glorious
spectacle than all the cathedrals which of the art of man ever reared. . . ."*

*Years later, Mary, in her biography of her husband, wrote "In Germany
alone he met with any true comprehension of what he regarded as moral
and religious instruction." Mann's now famous report on drawing in the
Prussian schools, was quite concerned with the relation between good penmanship and the teaching of drawing. Mann usually published his annual
reports through the "Common School Journal," of which he, as Secretary
of Education for the Commonwealth of Massachusetts, was editor. "The
Seventh Annual Report" was published in a series of issues. The section on
"Drawing and Writing" occurred in the April 15, 1844 issue (pp. 132–135).
We present an excerpt here:*

Such excellent hand-writing as I saw in the Prussian schools, I never saw
before. I can hardly express myself too strongly on this point. In Great Britain,
France, or in our own country, I have never seen any schools worthy to be
compared with theirs in this respect. I have before said that I found all
children provided with a slate and pencil. They write or print letters, and
begin with the elements of drawing, either immediately or very soon after
they enter school. This furnishes the greater part of the explanation of their
excellent hand-writing. A part of it, I think, should be referred to the peculiarity of the German script, which seems to me to be easier than our own.
But after all due allowance is made for this advantage, a high degree of
superiority over the schools of other countries remains to be accounted for.
This superiority cannot be attributed in any degree to a better manner of
holding the pen, for I never saw so great a proportion of cases in any schools
where the pen was so awkwardly held. This excellence must be referred in
a great degree to the universal practice of learning to draw, contemporane-
ously with learning to write. I believe a child will learn both to draw and
to write sooner and with more ease, than he will learn writing alone;—and
for this reason:—the figures or objects contemplated and copied in learning
to draw, are larger, more marked, more distinctive one from another, and
more sharply defined with projection, angle or curve, than the letters copied
in writing. In drawing there is more variety, in writing more sameness. Now
the objects contemplated in drawing, *from their nature*, attract attention
more readily, impress the mind more deeply, and of course will be more
accurately copied than those in writing. And when the eye has been trained
to observe, to distinguish, and to imitate, in the first exercise, it applies its
habits with great advantage to the second.

Another reason is, that the child is taught to draw things with which he
is familiar, which have some significance and give him pleasing ideas. But
a child who is made to fill page after page with rows of straight marks, that
look so blank and cheerless though done ever so well, has and can have no

pleasing associations with his work. The practice of beginning with making inexpressive marks, or with writing unintelligible words, bears some resemblance, in its lifelessness, to that of learning the alphabet. Each exhales torpor and stupidity to deaden the vivacity of the worker.

. . . In the course of my tour, I passed from countries where almost every pupil in every school could draw with ease, and most of them with no inconsiderable degree of beauty and expression, to those where less and less attention was paid to the subject; and, at last, to schools where drawing was not practiced at all; and after many trials, I came to the conclusion that, with no other guide than a mere inspection of the copy-books of the pupils, I could tell whether drawing were taught in the school or not;—so uniformily superior was the hand-writing in those schools where drawing was taught in connection with it. On seeing this, I was reminded of that saying of Pestalozzi,—somewhat too strong,—that "without drawing there can be no writing."

But suppose it were otherwise, and that learning to draw retarded the acquisition of good penmanship, how richly would the learner be compensated for the sacrifice. Drawing, of itself, is an expressive and beautiful language. A few strokes of the pen or pencil will often represent to the eye what no amount of words, however well chosen, can communicate. For the master-architect, for the engraver, the engineer, the pattern-designer, the draughtsman, moulder, machine-builder, or head mechanic of any kind, all acknowledge that this art is essential and indispensable. But there is no department of business or condition in life, where the accomplishment would not be of utility. Every man should be able to plot a field, to sketch a road or a river, to draw the outlines of a simple machine, a piece of household furniture or a farming utensil, and to delineate the internal arrangement or construction of a house.

But to be able to represent by lines and shadows what no words can depict, is only a minor part of the benefit of learning to draw. The study of this art develops the talent of observing, even more than that of delineating. Although a man may have but comparatively few occasions to picture forth what he has observed, yet the power of observation should be cultivated by every rational being. The skillful delineator is not only able to describe far better what he has seen, but he sees twice as many things in the world as he would otherwise do. To one whose eye has never been accustomed to mark the form, color or peculiarities of objects, all external nature is enveloped in a haze, which no sunshine, however bright, will ever dissipate. The light which dispels this obscurity must come from within. Teaching a child to draw, then, is the development in him of a new talent,—the conferring upon him, as it were, of a new sense,—by means of which he is not only better enabled to attend to the common duties of life, and to be more serviceable to his fellow-men, but he is more likely to appreciate the beauties and magnificence of nature, which everywhere reflect the glories of the Creator into his soul. When accompanied by appropriate instruction of a moral and religious character, this accomplishment becomes a quickener to devotion.

EDGEWORTH

Selected from Essays in Practical Education *by Maria and Richard Edgeworth (London: printed for J. Johnson, St. Paul's Church Yard, by J. Crowder, Warick Sq. Second Edition in Three Volumes, 1801), Vol. III, pp. 8–10.*

In the same way that Locke prescribed how drawing should be taught to the young gentleman, Maria and Richard Edgeworth, in "Essays in Practical Education" (1799, 1801), discuss the nature of drawing as a "Female Accomplishment":

Those who have excelled in drawing do not appear to abandon the occupation so suddenly; it does not demand such an inordinate quantity of time (as music) to keep up the talent; the exertion of the imitative powers is agreeable; the employment is progressive, and therefore the mind is carried on to complete what has been begun. Independently of all applause, which may be expected for the performance, there is a pleasure in going on with the work. By setting aside enthusiasm and habit, the probability that any sensible person will continue to pursue a given employment, must depend, in a great measure, upon their own conviction of its utility, or of its being agreeable to those whom they wish to please. The pleasure, which a lady's friends receive from her drawings, arises chiefly from the perception of their comparative excellence. Comparative excellence is all to which gentlewomen artists usually pretend, all to which they expect to attain; positive excellence is scarcely attained by one in a hundred. Compared with the performances of other young ladies of their acquaintance, the drawings of Miss X or Y may be justly considered as charming! admirable! astonishing! But there are few drawings by young ladies which can be compared with those of a professed artist. The wishes of obliging friends are satisfied with a few drawings in handsome frames, to be hung up for the young lady's credit; and when it is allowed amongst their acquaintance that she draws in a *superior* style, the purpose of this part of her education is satisfactorily answered. We do not here speak of those few individuals who really *excel* in drawing, who have learnt something more than the common routine which is usually learnt from a drawing-master, who have acquired an agreeable talent, not for the mere purpose of exhibiting themselves, but for the sake of the occupation it affords and the pleasure it may give to their *friends*.

Some Historical Developments in Art Education

ELLIOT W. EISNER

AND

DAVID W. ECKER

SOME HISTORICAL DEVELOPMENTS IN ART EDUCATION

In order to understand what art education is today, it would be useful to examine some of the developments which have occurred in its history. By becoming familiar with the major developments of art in American public education, the character of present-day theories and practices can be seen more clearly because a basis for comparison will have been established. With a clearer view of the present, those responsible for art education programs will be better prepared to make intelligent decisions regarding its future.

Art education, like all other subject areas in the curriculum, functions in at least two contexts. One of these contexts is that of the school and the other the society within which the school functions. Although what happens in the school has some influence upon society, the rapid and dramatic changes in American society have greatly influenced the school. These changes have incurred new and evolving expectations of the school and of the various subject areas that constitute its curriculum. We shall see as the chapter proceeds that the teaching of art has been affected by these changing expectations and that the goals which art educators have tried to attain have been shaped, in large measure, by developments—political, social, economic, and intellectual—in society. Indeed, the very facts that one seeks and the moral ends one hopes to attain through education cannot be understood or realized apart from the milieu in which one lives.

The Introduction of Art in the Schools

Although instruction in art was advocated as early as 1770 by Benjamin Franklin,[1] the formal introduction of art in the public schools of America begins with the nineteenth century. During the first half of the nineteenth century art was taught in public and private schools when individual teachers elected to do so. During this period no national organizations of art teachers existed, no state laws requiring the teaching of art were in force, and the type of art instruction that did occur was based upon the personal views and aspirations of individual teachers.[2]

Those teachers who taught art in their classes, such as William Minifie[3]

Reprinted by permission of the publisher, from Elliot Eisner and David Ecker, *Readings in Art Education*. Blaisdell Publishing Company, a division of Ginn and Company, Waltham, Massachusetts, 1966.

12

of Philadelphia and William Bently Fowle [4] of Boston, conceived of art as drawing: to engage in the teaching of art was to engage in the teaching of drawing. This conception of drawing as art and art as drawing continued well into the twentieth century in many of the nation's schools. For Minifie, art was valuable because it was an aid to industry, and in the Baltimore Boys High School in which he taught in 1848–49, he based his teaching of drawing on geometric principles. As the students developed skill in geometric or mechanical drawing Minifie thought that they would be better able to meet the industrial demands of an increasingly industrial society. And Fowle, in addition to using geometric drawings as a basis for his teaching, also used monitorial techniques, a method whereby groups of students seated around large tables could be taught by a student monitor who in turn was instructed by the headmaster.[5] Thus, one headmaster might instruct twenty monitors who in turn would instruct ten students each, an arrangement which when first initiated promised to be highly effective as well as economical.

In addition to the teaching of art through monitorial methods and through the practice of having students copy geometric designs, drawing was also taught because some teachers thought that it contributed to better writing habits. After all, in order to draw well one needed to control the pencil, to develop skill of hand and eye; weren't the same skills necessary for writing legibly, and couldn't, therefore, drawing be used as an aid in developing a graceful and legible penmanship?

These were not the only functions art performed in the schools during the first half of the nineteenth century; art was also taught in some schools as a mark of refinement, as a social nicety.[6] In private schools, especially for upper class young ladies, art was seen as a cultural accomplishment, something to symbolize the finer things of life, and in such schools art included more than drawing. Art also included fancy stitching and painting on velvet and on glass. As these young, future debutantes were to learn the social graces, the proper way to dance, to sit and to eat, so were they to learn to create pretty things, to engage in the cultivated arts of painting and sketching.

With the growing industrialization of America in the 1850's and the 1860's the vocational value of drawing instruction was emphasized even further. Although the methods of instruction remained much the same as when Minifie taught it as geometric drawing in Baltimore in the 1840's, the justification for art as a subject to be taught in the school—especially in the industrial states in New England—was that it was necessary for the development and prosperity of American industry. Minifie himself pointed out that in 1852 Americans had imported $36,000,000 worth of textiles from Great Britain alone and $11,000,000 worth from France.[7] If America as an industrial nation was to compete with the nations of Europe she needed craftsmen and designers who could produce products that were attractive to people abroad as well as to those in this country. And in 1864 drawing became a required subject in the Boston Public Schools: slates and tablets for drawing were provided at the primary grades, drawing books at the grammar grades, and special teachers of art at the high school level. By 1874 a U. S. Bureau of Education Bulletin [8] stated:

In addition to the increased competition arising from steam-carriage, new and cheaper methods of manufacture, and increased productiveness, another element of value has rapidly pervaded all manufacturers, an element in which the United States has been and is woefully deficient—the art element. The element of beauty is found to have pecuniary as well as aesthetic value. The training of the hand and of the eye which is given by drawing is found to be of the greatest advantage to the worker in many occupations and is rapidly becoming indispensable. This training is of value to all the children and offers to girls as well as boys opportunity for useful and remunerative occupations, for drawing in the public schools is not to be taught as a mere "accomplishment." The end sought is not to enable the scholar to draw a pretty picture, but to so train the hand and eye that he may be better fitted to become a bread-winner.

Owing to the economic changes of the nation, art took on an unprecedented significance. Art was placed in the service of industry, and competence in drawing was seen as an important vocational skill. Thus, one of the most significant episodes in the historical development of art education in this country occurred when the State of Massachusetts, under pressure from the leading industrialists of the state, passed a state law requiring that art be taught to boys over 15 years of age living in cities over 10,000.

To find leadership for the newly founded state program, the legislature sent to England in 1871 to invite Walter Smith—a teacher of Industrial Drawing and Crafts at the time at the South Kensington School—to come to America to direct the program. After a short visit, Smith accepted the post—an unenviable one which entailed being not only Director of Art for the State of Massachusetts but also Supervisor of Art for the City of Boston and principal of the Art Normal School, a school designed to prepare teachers of art. In his contractual arrangements Smith was to devote three-fifths of his time to the city of Boston and two-fifths of his time to the state. Like most academic part-time jobs, his probably turned out to be three full-time jobs. But Smith was an energetic and imaginative man who not only managed to oversee the teaching of art in the state and to establish new curricula for the training of art teachers; he also managed to write several books on the teaching of art which had an influence well beyond the borders of Massachusetts.[9]

To Smith drawing and writing had certain parallels. As writing has its alphabet and its grammar, so too does drawing have its alphabet—the straight and the curved line—and its form. To teach the student to write, he believed, one should progress from the simple to the complex so that the student would gradually be able to arrange the individual units together to create a sentence; so too in the teaching of art must one move from the simple to the complex, making sure that the student first masters the single straight and curved lines and then their combinations until he is able to construct a well-proportioned design. For Smith the objective of drawing was practical:

the acquisition of a useful vocational skill; and the methods were clear-cut: a highly systematic and prescribed curriculum which teachers were to follow scrupulously. The creation of art was not essentially a matter of talent but of training, and if effective training methods could be developed (which Smith didn't question for a moment), students could be trained to produce art.

Needless to say, Walter Smith, an Englishman with definite and clear-cut ideas about art education in an America not yet one hundred years old, made an impact. The Art Normal School, of which he was the head, opened in 1873 and by the time of the Philadelphia Centennial Exposition of 1876, at which his course of studies was displayed, his reputation was well established. But his relationship to the State legislature did not remain satisfactory and, for reasons that are not altogether clear, he was relieved in 1885 of the three posts he had worked so hard to develop and returned to his native land to take up the role of headmaster in a large English art school.

The direction and emphasis that Walter Smith provided in art education lasted a great many years. Indeed, even today in some schools in both rural and urban areas art is taught in a copybook manner similar to Smith's, and drawing is the sole or dominant mode of activity used for instruction. But America in the eighties and nineties was changing rapidly. New ideas were crossing the seas from Europe, immigration increased, and industrialization continued at an even faster pace.

The Growth of Professional Education Movements

There developed, therefore, in the 1880's forces both social and intellectual which began to change the general character of art education in the United States. It was during the 1880's that the Child Study Movement got underway under the leadership of the eminent American psychologist G. Stanley Hall.[10] As a movement within psychology and education its main concerns were with the child and his development both mental and physical. Its work, building upon the ideas of Pestalozzi, Herbart, and Froebel, developed a new conception of the child. It was a conception which saw the child as being an individual who had particular and even unique needs and whose mind differed qualitatively from that of an adult. To many in education the child was still viewed as a miniature adult and hence expectations were set for children that they could not possibly attain. Indeed, Walter Smith described his own daughter's performance in drawing this way: [11]

. . . a young lady of the mature age of three . . . [with] the advantage of being quite unprejudiced in the matter of style of execution and perfectly fearless in the expression of what she believes to be the truth, whilst the firmness of her natural touch is something tremendous. . . . Her mental disadvantages arise from an altogether too exalted opinion of her own works causing a self-satisfaction which hinders her progress and blinds her to defects in style, and her imperfect execution; and she is wildly indignant with me at any faults I point out, and simply turns round and thrashes me if I point out a faulty line.

Unless references to a "mature young lady of three," "her mental disadvantages," "too exalted opinion" and "defects in style" be an attempt at gentle irony, by current standards Mr. Smith had quite inappropriate expectations for his young daughter! Yet with the Child Study Movement and with what was to develop in the field of education through the work of John Dewey, a newer and quite different view of the child emerged. It was a view which began to take an interest in not only what could be *im*pressed upon the child through instructional methods, but also what the child had to *ex*press. The Child Study Movement and the developments which were to follow liberalized the art curriculum, initiated an interest in the role of imagination, and paid greater attention to the stages through which children normally develop in their visual expression. These concerns, buttressed by the availability of inexpensive crayons and water colors, dramatically changed the general character of art education, all within a twenty-year period. By the turn of the century *The Applied Arts Book, The Voice of the Applied Arts Guild of Worcester, Massachusetts* (which was later to become *School Arts* magazine) could state as its doctrine that it advocated "taste in all matters relating to Applied Arts. It stands for beauty in American life." But more, it also urged teachers to have students draw from *nature*, to draw objects in their environment, to study color, and to learn the principles of art, e.g., "harmony—Nature's use of straight lines for strength and curved lines for beauty." [12] Although such exhortations seem quaint by today's standards they were a far cry from the geometrically inspired directions prescribed by Smith.

In addition to the Child Study Movement and the availability of new art media in America, education itself was expanding. And with this expansion came the growth of educational organizations, education journals, and art magazines. The National Education Association formed an art department with Langdon S. Thompson as its first president; the manual training movement gained even greater impetus and later developed as an independent organization; and these, together with the Columbia Exposition of 1893, boosted interest in the art of the child by displaying hundreds of portfolios of art work produced by American schoolchildren.

Thus, by the turn of the century art education had developed another type of concern. As it once was concerned solely with enabling students to develop manual skills useful in industrial vocations, art education now became concerned about helping children "appreciate beauty." Where is beauty found? These men and women had the answer—in nature and in art. Thus began that aspect of art education known as *picture study*.

Art Education for Art Appreciation
In picture study the students were shown "masterpieces" painted by the world's "greatest" artists and were encouraged to familiarize themselves with the lives of these artists and with the story depicted in each painting. It should be noted that the paintings that the students studied, even as late

as 1927, were not those of the Impressionists, the Cubists, or those of the then contemporary American artists. They were, more often than not, the works of the Renaissance artists, those of the genre school of painters in France and those Victorians who told interesting tales in their paintings. *"Picture Study in the Grades,"* wrote its author Oscar Neale in 1927, "aims primarily to develop in the children of our schools an appreciation of the great masterpieces of art so that they may know the joy that comes from such an appreciation and so that their ideals may be influenced by the patriotism, the sympathy, the courage, the piety, and the beauty which the great artists of different ages have given to the world." [13] Thus, not only were the significant modern artists of the age—who by 1927 had already established themselves—absent from picture study, but the study itself was directed to issues that present-day art educators would be inclined to call extraneous to the concerns of art. If picture study was designed to teach something about art history, it was mostly used to inculcate certain ethical values the paintings were believed to reflect.

It is important to mention here that until very recently art education as a field has been quite unresponsive to contemporary developments in the world of art. Even as late as the 1940's the styles of art work held in high esteem in art education were the genre paintings of Millet and Dupre and the works of the Florentine and Venetian masters, especially those which had some sort of visual narrative. That art educators were receptive to such work rather than to the contemporary art of their time is evidenced not only in the paintings selected for picture study but also in the type of art work displayed in the schools and the type of art work published in school art journals. Art education until as late as the middle of the twentieth century was more a reflection of lay artistic tastes than it was a leader in shaping those tastes and in enabling students to experience the work on the artistic frontiers of their day.

Art Education for Art Production
The turn of the century not only brought picture study but also brought a number of men to the fore who had a profound effect on art education. Arthur Wesley Dow, Professor of Fine Arts at Columbia University, was such a man. Dow was concerned with trying to understand the principles which were incorporated in successful works of art. What were their ingredients? What needed to be considered in constructing an art product that displayed harmony and beauty? Dow found an answer and it was *composition.*[14] To construct a composition that was successful—and to be successful the composition was to display harmony—three elements must be considered: (1) Line, (2) Value, and (3) Color. Line referred to the contour of drawn objects, value to lights and darks, and color to the hues incorporated in the picture. To obtain harmony in composition five principles were to be employed: (1) Opposition, (2) Transition, (3) Subordination, (4) Repetition, and (5) Symmetry. By identifying the elements that con-

stituted successful works of art Dow believed he was in a position to teach such principles systematically, thus enabling students to produce harmonious compositions.

Dow was not alone in his efforts to understand the nature of art and to formulate a systematic way in which it could be taught. But as Dow focused on the finished work of art in order to identify the order it seemed to possess, Walter Sargent, Professor of Aesthetic and Industrial Education at the University of Chicago, focused upon the process through which children learned to draw. Sargent was interested in the psychology of children's art and in the methods that would help them produce art. To Sargent, "Drawing is a language, a mode of reproducing ideas, and as such is a means of forming and developing these ideas. . . . Drawing thus becomes a tool with which to think." And again, "Drawing an object means translating one's perceptions into terms which have been evolved by the race, and which demand careful selection. It means organizing one's sensations so as to determine what produces the impression and the modes in which that impression can be interpreted. To draw an object requires a mental activity comparable to that which occurs when a thought is translated from one language into another." [15]

The tenor of Sargent's discourse about art and the process through which art is created places him very close to the field of psychology. His conception of drawing as a language and as a *tool with which to think* is a remarkable conception considering the historical context in which it was made. And it should be recognized that even today the idea that art is a cognitive activity is not widely recognized or well understood. Walter Sargent, through his work in *Fine and Industrial Arts in Elementary Schools* [16] and in *How Children Learn to Draw* [17] developed a level of sophistication about art that has since then been matched too rarely. According to his theory, three factors influence children in their ability to learn to draw. First, the child must want to say something, he must have some idea or image he wants to express through drawing. Second, the child needs to use devices such as three-dimensional models or pictures to work from in making his drawings. And finally, he claimed that children often learn to draw one thing well but not others, so that skill in drawing is specific; a person could be good at drawing houses or boats and not good at drawing other things.

Walter Sargent's inquiry grew out of an interesting intertwining of two important but distinct branches of American psychological thought.[18] One branch in psychology stems from the work done by German psychologists and scientists such as Gustav Fechner, Hermann Von Helmholtz, and Wilhelm Wundt, an orientation which emphasized laboratory methods, the significance of the mental event and the mind. The other branch stems from the English, from the work of John Locke, Charles Darwin, Francis Galton, and Herbert Spencer, and emphasizes the importance of natural observation and of the environment in shaping human behavior. The German experimental orientation with its concern for the mind and introspection is perhaps best exemplified by the work of G. Stanley Hall, who studied with Helmholtz, Fechner, and Wundt. The English tradition is reflected in greater degree in the work of such psychologists as Edward Lee Thorndike and John Watson, the latter interested in purging psychology from the German interest in introspection and in replacing it with objective methods for the study of human behavior. These traditions were in the air, in modified American form, when Sargent was writing, and his concern with both the mind and its product, thought, and with the use of objective methods for teaching art suggest the influence of these two historical traditions.

Art Education for Creative Development and Mental Health

The work in psychology by Hall and by the Child Study Movement, with its interest in children's development and the factors that affect it, found support from two major forces, each of which influenced art education in the first half of the twentieth century. One of these influences emanated from the writings of John Dewey and the other from the writings of Sigmund Freud.

Dewey, influenced by the work of Charles Darwin and William James, saw man's nature as being biological.[19] For Dewey man was an organism that not only lived *in* but *through* an environment. And since that environment was not always friendly, since it did not automatically meet the organism's needs, the organism needed to control the environment or to adjust to it. Man's basic need, for Dewey, was to come to terms with his environment, to attain equilibrium, and to grow. In order to grow and to cope with the problematic situations that arose during one's life, the organism needed to behave intelligently. And since human intelligence was based, in large measure, upon the experience and past resolutions to problems the individual had achieved, the role of experience in education became a crucial issue for Dewey.

What Dewey saw when he viewed the schools in the 1880's and 1890's were institutions that made little provision for the individual experiences of the child. He saw institutions that did not provide for the child's needs nor for the child's unique view of the world. Schools, Dewey thought, were pervaded by a formalism that was inappropriate for meaningful learning. In these schools children were considered miniature adults who were to pay attention and be still. They were arranged in rows, seated in immovable desks, and restrained from both the psychological and physical freedom that they needed in order to develop into intelligent human beings. Schools were bookish, teachers dogmatic and pedantic, and instruction was crammed with inert ideas unconnected with the lives of the children.

In developing his conception of man's nature, the nature of knowledge and how it was achieved, Dewey concerned himself with education and conceived of education as a process of expanding human intelligence, thereby increasing its capacity to experience. For him schools needed to provide physical, emotional, and intellectual freedom for the pupil, freedom that could be attained only if the student had the opportunity to exercise his intelligence on problems that were meaningful to him. Not only this, but the child could not be thought of as part mind and part body; the child is whole, a thinking and feeling organism that could not be artificially carved into neat categories.

Dewey's thinking represents one of the major influences on art education in the twentieth century because it provided the ideological leadership for the Progressive Education Association. Dewey's ideas, although carried at times to extremes he never intended, encouraged educators to reconsider the means and ends of education. Dewey's interest in helping educators provide for the uniqueness of the child and the significance of experience in his life grew into a movement which eventually considered self-expression and noninterference by the teacher an important tenet of its program. Indeed, many of the practices advocated in the journals of the Progressive Education Association and in other progressive publications were exaggerated to such a degree that Dewey felt compelled, in 1938, to write a book, *Experience and Education*,[20] which was intended to clarify his views regarding the nature of education. Art education shifted from a concern with correct drawing, picture study, and hand-eye coordination to an emphasis upon unlocking the *creative* capacities of children. Creativity, a concept seldom found in the literature prior to the twenties, now became one of art education's major organizing ideas. If a child, by nature, had the capacity for creative intelligent action, perhaps art education could be instrumental in helping the child realize his latent creativity.

A number of progressives writing on art education articulated the role of creativity in art and education. Margaret Mathias,[21] Bell Boas,[22] Florence Cane,[23] and, later, Victor D'Amico[24] pointed to the creative abilities of the child and to the unique cognitive world which he possessed. Art, they claimed, could unlock these latent creative capacities and what is more, once developed, these abilities could be applied to areas other than the arts. Thus, art education was important not only because it developed creativity in art but also because it developed creativity in general. That was a most significant shift. With this subtle but crucial shift the teaching of art became an instrumentality for creative development in all walks of life; it was to be a process-oriented activity which was to have as one of its major goals the development of children's creative thinking. "Creative self-expression" was soon to become the watchword of the new art education that emerged during this priod.

With the concern for the creative development of the child there developed an interest in the relationship of art to the other subject areas of the curriculum. The progressives, concerned as they were with meaningful learning and with eliminating the artificial dichotomies of the traditional curriculum, tried to build their program around problems or projects. The project method developed by William Heard Kilpatrick,[25] a disciple of Dewey and a Professor of Education at Columbia, was a means whereby students would investigate a problem area by bringing to bear upon it the tools and methods of a host of disciplines. If students studied the Middle Ages, they were encouraged not only to understand the social arrangements between the master and his serfs but were encouraged also to build a castle or to construct figures of knights and their armor. Here, art had an important function to perform. Through art the students could learn more clearly about the practices and ideas that animated the medieval period. Art was to be a correlated activity and not "cubby-holed" as an independent subject area unrelated to the projects in which children engaged. With this conception of the role and function of art, art was again used as an instrumentality, but this time not so much a means for developing the general creative abilities of the child as a means of teaching important ideas. With this view of educational method, art was in the service of concept formation.

There was still another type of emphasis that characterized art education during the twenties and thirties; this was an emphasis on the therapeutic aspects of work in art. Freud, whose *On the Interpretations of Dreams* was published in 1900, had a slow but growing influence on American intellectuals concerned with education.[26] This influence grew steadily from the turn of the century on and was given an important thrust forward when Hall, as President of Clark University in 1909, invited Freud to come to America to lecture on his work. By a decade or so later the intellectuals in the East were quite familiar with his concepts of ego, id, and superego. In art education people such as Margaret Naumberg [27] saw the relationship between the art of the child and the unconscious needs and desires that underlie his behavior. To the child experiencing stress under the rigors of growing up and in the confines of the school, the visual arts could serve as a form of release. Art could, if used intelligently, contribute to the mental health of the child by giving him an opportunity to alleviate those tensions and communicate those meanings that he could not articulate in discursive language. Art in the schools could be a type of therapy, a preventive medicine that contributes to the psychological comfort of the child. On this view, art was in the service of mental health.

The Recognition of Modern Art, Technology, and Scientific Inquiry

Developments in art education since the thirties have been various. The trends initiated in the twenties and early thirties continued as did some of the practices that were begun before the turn of the century. But two developments stand out as being especially important. One of these was the slow but growing recognition of those artists who worked in the modern idiom and the second was the writing and stature of Viktor Lowenfeld.

The date of the birth of the modern movement in art is a disputed issue. Whether it started with Delacroix and the practice of going directly to nature for one's subject matter or with the Impressionists and their concern with light, with Cézanne and his emphasis on form, or with Kandinsky and the abstract movement has not been settled. This dispute need not concern us here. If it is recognized that artists working in Europe in the 1880's and 1890's developed a style and approach to visual art that differed radically from the realism of the middle of the nineteenth century, this will be sufficient. The work of the Post-Impressionists, the Fauves, the Cubists, and the Expressionists was not new by the thirties. Indeed, in 1913 the famous Armory Show, held in New York, Chicago, and Boston, displayed paintings by the foremost moderns. Yet art education in both its aesthetic tastes and its practices seems to have been well insulated from the then current (and not so current) artistic movements. If one is to judge the type of aesthetic values held in art education by the kinds of projects advocated and the type of work displayed in art education journals, art education's insulation from the mainstream of modern art did not change from its neo-Victorian character until the late forties. Puppetry, egg coloring, leather tooling, and stencil designs were characteristically advocated and displayed on the pages of the most widely circulated art education journals. But the influence of the modern artist could not be held back. By the early fifties art educators began to recognize the "new," sixty-year-old aesthetic, and the influence of Cubism, Surrealism, and Expressionism began to affect the type of instruction taking place in the schools and the type of work which the students were producing.

The use of varied materials in the classroom, well beyond standard art media, was now being advocated. The materials approach to art was seen as a device for furthering the creative capacities of students and developing their sensitivity to texture, form, and design. The ideas generated in the Bauhaus,[28] a school of design in Germany which attempted to prepare designers to meet the needs of a technological society, began by the fifties to affect some art education programs in the schools of the United States. Explorations to determine the constructive possibilities of new, "non-art" materials were advocated, the construction of purely formal or abstract three-dimensional sculpture was introduced, and the experimental treatment of visual qualities in two-dimensional media was pursued. Modern art began its slow but steady advance into the art curriculum, and the present-day character of art instruction in the public schools of America had found its beginning. Art education not only attempted to develop the creative capacities of students through the use of novel visual problems, but it could also sensitize them to a host of media previously considered outside the scope of the field of art.

The work of Viktor Lowenfeld in American art education is significant for several reasons: first, because through the three of his four books that were printed in English he, more than any other, laid a psychological foundation for the way in which children develop in and through art; second, because he crystallized much of the teaching about art education that had developed through the progressive era; and third, because his system became one of the major psychological systems in which teachers of art were trained during the late forties and fifties in the United States and Europe. *The Nature of*

Creative Activity [29] and *Creative and Mental Growth* [30] are hallmarks in the literature of art education, the latter having been translated into several languages and having undergone three revisions by the time of Lowenfeld's death in 1960. It is difficult to summarize the work of a man in a few sentences, yet the major thesis of Lowenfeld's work is clear-cut. He was interested in the creative and mental growth of the child and saw art as a vehicle for facilitating this growth. Although art was important to him in his own life, and although he valued it for students, his primary concern was in the growth of the child as a seeing, thinking, and feeling human being—concerns that were not alien to those who were brought up on the educational philosophies of Dewey and Kilpatrick. Art education, as Lowenfeld saw it and as he encouraged teachers to view it, should not lose sight of the child and what was happening to him in the *process* of working with art media. The child was paramount, the art instrumental. Copying and using coloring books were forbidden, and art contests for children were deemed inappropriate if not downright harmful.

Lowenfeld's ideas, contained in his widely read books, articles and speeches, set the stage for current practices and assumptions among art educators in the fifties. Creative activity and self-expression in art gained a new stature through his publications, and the significance of the child was again re-emphasized in the programs that prepared teachers of art.

Lowenfeld influenced art education not only through his writing but also because he provided a model for careful, scholarly inquiry in art education. Much of Lowenfeld's work as an art educator was scientific, and he was one of the few who published in psychological journals. Furthermore, in his position as chairman of one of the largest graduate programs in art education, he was in a position to influence future art educators who themselves would be responsible for the education of teachers of art. In short, Lowenfeld not only wrote two of the most significant books in the field of art education and provided a model for scholarly inquiry into the field, but also worked directly with those who were later to become professors of art education in the colleges and universities in the United States and in Europe.

What we have seen in this overview of some of the significant developments in the history of art education is a past characterized by a variety of practices, theories, and objectives. As American society has changed, new responsibilities have been placed upon the school. Art education as one of the instrumentalities within the school has, as a consequence, changed with the institutions. If society saw education as a means of creating an individual of culture, art was seen as a tool for developing cultured tastes and cultural accomplishments. If schools were to prepare citizens to contribute to the economic welfare of the nation, art was to be taught as an important vocational skill. If the schools' major task was to develop man's creative intelligence, art became a means for unlocking the child's potential creativity. Art education, inescapably, operates within the context of the school and within the context of the society. We can expect that as American society changes in the future, new and different objectives and practices for art education will be advocated.

One of the crucial tasks for art educators is not one of finding ways to resist change but, rather, to employ critical procedures by which wise choices may be made among competing proposals for change. In matters of fact the body of conclusions provided by research in the behavioral sciences may be the most appropriate resource to consult. But where critical answers to factual problems relevant to art education are not available, art educators must themselves engage in scientific research. Likewise, in matters of value, art educators must pursue philosophic research. Art education, especially since the early fifties, has considered a part of its task the provision of relevant data through empirical research. But to determine with any clarity the ends worth pursuing is not a problem to be solved by the massing of scientific data. However important such data may be, the problem of what ends are worth pursuing is reasonably managed by philosophic inquiry. Indeed, the extent to which *this* inquiry should or should not, can or cannot, employ various scientific procedures is itself a philosophic problem. So we can see that neither scientific nor philosophic inquiry should be considered alien to the field of art education. When art educators engage in research into both factual and value problems, they more firmly establish—and even enlarge—the traditional domain of art education.

REFERENCES

1. See *Writings of Franklin,* A. H. Smyth, ed. New York: The Macmillan Co., 1905.
2. For a competent treatment of the history of art education see Frances Bland Belshe's unpublished dissertation, "A History of Art Education in the Public Schools of the United States," Yale University, 1946.
3. William Minifie. *A Text Book of Geometrical Drawing.* Boston: Hilliard, Gray, Little, and Williams, 1830.
4. William Bently Fowle. *The Eye and the Hand; Being a Series of Practical Lessions in Drawing, for the Training of These Important Organs, Adapted to the Use of Common Schools.* Boston: W. B. Fowle, 1847, 94 pp.
5. For a discussion of Fowle's work on monotorial schools see William Russell. *Manual of Mutual Instruction: Consisting of Mr. Fowle's Directions.* Boston: Wait, Greene, and Co., 1826.
6. For a history of the arts in American life see Holger Cahill, ed. *American Folk Art.* New York: Museum of Modern Art, 1932.
7. F. B. Belshe, *op. cit.*
8. "The Relation of Art to Education," *Circulars of Information of Bureau of Education,* No. 2. Washington: Government Printing Office, 1874, pp. 86, 88.
9. Perhaps the most influential was Walter Smith. *Teachers Manual of Free Hand Drawing and Designing.* Boston: Charles Osgood and Co., 1873.
10. For an excellent treatment of Hall's work as it related to the child study

movement see Lawrence Cremin. *The Transformation of the School*. New York and London: D. Appleton and Co., 1911.

11. Quoted from Frederick M. Logan. *The Growth of Art in American Schools*. New York: Harper and Bros., 1955, p. 70.

12. *The Applied Arts Book, The Voice of the Applied Arts Guild of Worcester, Massachusetts*, Vol. 1, No. 1 (September 1901), p. 4.

13. Oscar Neale. *Picture Study in the Grades*. Milwaukee: O. W. Neale Publishing Co., 1927. From the preface.

14. Arthur W. Dow. *The Theory and Practice of Teaching Art*. New York: Teachers College, Columbia University, 1908.

15. Walter Sargent. *Fine and Industrial Arts in Elementary Schools*. Boston: Ginn and Co., 1912, pp. 5–7.

16. *Ibid.*

17. Walter Sargent and Elizabeth Miller. *How Children Learn To Draw*. Boston: Ginn and Co., 1916.

18. For a history of European and American psychology see Gardner Murphy. *An Historical Introduction to Modern Psychology*. New York: Harcourt, Brace and Co., 1932.

19. The books and articles written by John Dewey are too numerous to list. *The School and Society, Democracy and Education, Logic: The Theory of Enquiry*, and *Art as Experience* are a few of his more important works.

20. John Dewey. *Experience and Education*. New York: The Macmillan Co., 1938.

21. Margaret Mathias. *The Teaching of Art*. New York: Scribner, 1932.

22. Bell Boas. *Art in the School*. New York: Doubleday, 1924.

23. Florence Cane, "Art—The Child's Birthright," *Childhood Education*, Vol. 7 (May 1931), pp. 482–485.

24. Victor D'Amico. *Creative Teaching in Art*. Scranton, Pennsylvania: International Textbook Co., 1942.

25. William Heard Kilpatrick. *The Project Method: The Use of the Purposeful Act in the Educative Process*. New York: Teachers College, Columbia University, 1919.

26. Sigmund Freud. *The Interpretation of Dreams*. New York: The Macmillan Co., 1933.

27. Margaret Naumberg. *The Child and the World*. New York: Harcourt, Brace and Co., 1928.

28. For a history of the Bauhaus see Herbert Bayer, and Walter and Ise Gropius, *Bauhaus 1919–33*. New York: Museum of Modern Art, 1938.

29. Viktor Lowenfeld. *The Nature of Creative Activity*, First Edition. New York: The Macmillan Co., 1939.

30. Viktor Lowenfeld. *Creative and Mental Growth*, First Edition. New York: The Macmillan Co., 1949.

The Plastic Arts, History of Art and Design—Three Currents Toward Identifying Content for Art Education

JEROME J. HAUSMAN

There is a continuing theme that runs through my thinking about the problems of content development for art education—the need to conceive of the teaching of art within a context of twentieth century dynamics. For just as the contemporary artist must deal with the realities of his "present," the art educator must conceive of his role as part of the dynamics that mold and shape contemporary ideas and values. How simple it would be if facts and values in our experience were "fixed" and could remain stationary. Teaching in a relatively "closed" society with fixed values assumes clearly defined goals and procedures. Teachers can go forth with such confidence that questions of value and direction need not concern them. This circumstance, however, is not to be our lot. Today's reality (with which teachers *must* contend) is characterized by dramatic and continuous change. There is little security afforded by a world of indeterminate value. Fixed "truths" eventually give way to new concepts and dimensions for thought and action. Change and anticipation of change have themselves become the fixed ideas for dealing with our world. For many people, the difficulty in adjusting to continuous change is the cause of their creating more rigid conceptual and operational structures. It is as if some would say, "Stop the world, I want to get off!" Theirs is a longing for "basic" and "fundamental" truths that provide stability and confidence for dealing with the future. Such attempts to act as if we could bring things to a halt, as if the factor of transformation was not upon us, only serve to heighten a sense of frustration and failure. Things keep changing anyway.

Changes that can be seen in art and art education are not isolated phenomena. There are dramatic and far reaching changes in present day science and technology. Our most dramatic changes have occurred since the nineteenth century. Nineteenth century science was founded on the ideas of Newton and Descartes. Fixed categories in our concepts of time, space, and causality enabled man's projecting and establishing knowledge about this world. Today's discoveries have outstripped the ability of any individual to synthesize and internalize all of knowledge. Contemporary man experiences a strange uneasiness as he views the advances of scientific knowledge. The changes that are brought to our attention on political, social, and economic fronts give pause as to our movements toward the future.

Reprinted by permission from *A Seminar in Art Education for Research and Curriculum Development*, Cooperative Research Project No. V-002, The Pennsylvania State University, 1966 Copyright. University Park, Pa.

For the "man in the street" and the parents of the children who are in our schools, the drama of our times is very real. One has but to look at population statistics: about twenty-five per cent of all human beings who have ever lived are now alive. It is projected that our world population will double itself within the next forty years. I can only observe along with Harold Rosenberg "that vast shiftings of population, both geographically (through migrations, exiles, displacements) and vertically (through revolutions, mass education, equalization of opportunity), have destroyed the historically stabilized character of individuals and introduced the problem of identity, personal and collective as a dominant theme of contemporary cultural forms." Add to this the impact of computer technology. Computers are now available to perform many of the tasks previously performed by men. Devices can carry on functions involving the storage and retrieval of information (memory), the organization and sorting of information (analysis), the relating of information to possible actions (decision-making), and the carrying out of specific actions (operations). Automation and computers have had a profound effect upon our work force. For the first time in human history there is a prospect for a society able to shrug off the need for manual labor—machines can do the work for us.

The impact of science and technology upon the ways we think and act is great. It is staggering to contemplate the implications of this shift upon human perceptions, aspirations, and values. Alvin Toffler addressed himself to this point in a recent article, "Even our conceptions of self will be transformed in a world in which the line between man and machine grows increasingly blurred. It is now almost certain that within a matter of years the implantation of artificial organs in human bodies will be a common medical procedure. The human 'body' in the future will often consist of a mixture of organic and machine components. What happens to the definition of man when one's next-door neighbor or oneself may be equipped with an electronic or mechanical lung, heart, kidney, or liver, or when a computer system can be plugged into a living brain? How will it 'feel' to be part protoplasm, part transistor? What new possibilities will it open? What limitations will it place on work, play, sex, intellectual or aesthetic responses? How will it feel to have information transferred electronically between computer and brain? What happens to mind when body is changed?" (Alvin Toffler, "The Future as a Way of Life," *Horizon*, Summer, 1965, p. 112.)

There have always been the alarmists, those who would offer prophesies of doom and disaster. Moreover, there have always been those who would place their own training and concerns at the front in offering solutions for larger and more pervasive problems than could properly be undertaken by their disciplines. I trust that I shall not be placed in either of these groups. Neither doctors, lawyers, biologists, physicists, religionists, and yes, art educators can do the job alone. Nevertheless, it does seem to me that art educators cannot avoid the obligation of conceiving of their role and function as part of the many forces that can help shape human life in the years to come.

Anyone viewing the range and diversity of human ideas and achievements is faced with such multiplicity as to approximate infinity. Through mass media and communications involving the past and present we can be made instantaneously aware of ideas and images the world over. The unique differences in settings, chronology, and circumstance (to say nothing of individual differences in people) are such as to give one a sense of humility, a sense of being part of a vast and complex scheme of things in which each man is, in the end, faced with his own limitations. At the same time, there is the fact of existence, the potential for wonder, excitement, and unique insight. There is the sense in which men may join together, in the sharing of insights, in furthering knowledge and understanding, in making possible a more informed and disciplined basis for human thought, understanding and action. I take this to be the central concern for the education enterprise.

At the risk of gross oversimplification, I shall approach the problems of art education by stating the obvious: one of the factors that distinguishes man from all other animals is his capacity to project ideas and feelings in symbolic form. The forms that are created serve to embody and reflect, indeed sometimes to modify these ideas and feelings. They serve as the means by which people communicate with themselves and others; they serve as the mechanisms for establishing and transcending knowledge and tradition.

Visual signals have always been critical to man's thought processes. As was stated by Kepes, "Every properly functioning human being transforms the visual signals that he receives from outside into structured, meaningful entities. Without the perceptual ordering of his sense responses into images of things in space, man cannot orient himself. Without shaping his physical environment in accordance with these images, he cannot survive. His capacity to structure his environment according to his needs—that is, his ability to work out a rapport with his world—determines the quality of his life." (G. Kepes, Introduction, *Education of Vision*, p. 1.) In today's world we are witnessing a dramatic shift toward visual imagery as a means for conveying and realizing ideas. Modern technology has made it possible to reproduce and convey our symbolic images with greater speed and intensity than ever before.

The field of art education concerns itself with educating people for greater control and understanding of visual images and forms broadly conceived as art. Usually this involves education in studio practice as well as historical and critical study of art (to include architecture and design). As I conceive of the field, it seeks to educate for knowledge, understanding and application of aesthetic dimensions in the visual forms we experience.

Study of human achievements must seek out the resultant forms of human thought and activity; put more simply, what man *is* is reflected and revealed by what he *does*. Our earliest records of symbolic activity are man's images.

There is still some conjecture about the first attempts at art being born of accident. However, it is clear that what may have started as random and uncontrolled markings led to those physical and conceptual controls that suggested resemblance between movement, form and reality. Men were able to take the step of consciously abstracting images from the materials and forms about them; they were able to exercise controls over these forms. Their images became the embodiment of their environment; controls exercised over their images provided a sense of control over that environment.

The forms of art have changed from era to era, so has the role of the artist. Anyone viewing the broad traditions of art is forced to the inescapable conclusion that there are no single, fixed properties for establishing a particular form appropriate for all art. Artists engage in the creation of new forms; these forms, in turn, provide a basis for continuing evaluations and definitions. Explanations of art must deal with particular objects in particular contexts. Any attempt to view the broad area of art, past, present, and future, must account for the open-ended and metaphoric nature of aesthetic forms. For example, through painting and sculpture, some artists have devoted themselves to the exploration of "pure" form, faithful to an almost Pythagorian ideal of geometric harmony; others have courted the expressive and random qualities of a spontaneous, unplanned utilization of materials. Some painters and sculptors have sought to embody a lyrical and serenely poetic content; others have tried to communicate a sense of violence, tragedy, and despair. Some art forms were created as part of a clearly established tradition; other art forms have been shaped in periods encouraging and supportive of dramatic innovation and change.

Obviously, art is not produced in a vacuum; no man is independent of his predecessors. Artists, like all other men, are born into a stream of traditions and events. In part, the culture's language, images, and customs structure his values and expectations; in part, each man is unique. No two persons or events can be found on the precise coordinates of time, space, and action. No event ever repeats itself in precisely the same terms. People put together their structure of understanding and concepts (their "reality") by relating the variety of events (real and imagined) with their knowledge and expectations. In this transactional setting, timing and circumstance combine as key factors in shaping individual abilities and directions. Artists, indeed, all men, are in tension with their environment—in part, shaped by its circumstances; in part, driven by human capacities to transcend these circumstances. Actions become inventive by departing from the forms of preceding actions. The degree, extent, and significance of these departures vary in relation to the individuals themselves as well as their time, setting, and value patterns. Utilizing such an "evolutionary model" to account for the artist, "the variations or innovations tend to be almost imperceptible in stable cultures and to be more abrupt and radical in fluid cultures. Some innovations are incorporated into traditional styles, and others become the root of new styles which often grow alongside the older ones. Poorly adapted innovations either are summarily rejected or, if they are potentially viable, lie dormant to act upon a later, more congenial environment. So while the individual imagination generates change, society, including artists, guides its rate and direction; but only by post-facto selectivity; the environment can prompt imaginative solutions by posing challenging problems, but cannot itself formulate solutions." (James Ackerman, "Art and Education," *The Nature and Art of Motion,* edited by Gyorgy Kepes, p. 39.) (Also see George Kubler, *The Shape of Time.*)

Given our time of rapid innovation, there are those who have come to equate "change" with progress. Having done so, they proceed to talk about changes in a field as necessarily constituting "progress" in that field. There is, however, no reason to believe that special conditions exist today that make for "progressively better" art forms than have been created in the past. At all times, the artist has engaged in the creation of form. In varying degrees, this has involved the exploration of reality—the shaping of ideas and feelings in a medium in relation to the values and purposes of his time. In the end, that which makes it art is that which makes the form an organized expression and realization of value. "For although man is not the master of the elements imposed on him by life, which presses on him from all sides and molds his own nature, he is the master of the value he ascribes to these elements in his capacity as spectator, or of the value with which he endows them in his capacity as creator. Whatever the pressures to which he may be subjected, he always preserves his capacity to judge them, to determine their value, aesthetic or moral, and by this token he remains indomitably free.

"The more insight the history of art gives us into the necessities that form the artist, the more nearly it liberates us from the temptation of formulas, theories, and fashions, because it shows us that these things, being subject to perpetual change, are relative and vain. The only permanent thing is quality, which cannot be reduced to a formula or a definition." (R. Huyghe, *Ideas and Images in World Art,* p. 438.)

What I have attempted to do thus far is set forth some very broad generalizations as we contemplate the more specific issues of developing theory and practice in the field of art education. The key points, that I trust I have made, give emphasis to the environmental dynamics of twentieth century living, the continuity and pervasiveness of visual forms as expressions and realizations of human thought and feelings, and the changing nature of art forms themselves. The content of our art programs should be conceived with these points in view. The resources for establishing "content" can be drawn from the disciplines of artists and designers as they shape visual forms, art historians as they study art forms of the past, and critics as they elucidate art forms of the present. Art should be seen as a basic human activity requiring sensitivity and understanding in the visual choices we make. Given this attitude and point of view, our schools would become centers for a vital and active confrontation of works of art. Our studio classes would be conceived as laboratories for the exploration of ideas, materials and techniques within the student's symbolic framework. Works of art could then be removed from the necessity of being "masterpieces," of somehow being given a stamp of approval by someone or something apart from life that makes them "worthy" of being seen. While I do not agree with it in full, I am much attracted to George Kubler's supposition, "Let us suppose that the idea of art can be expanded to embrace the whole range of man-made things, including all tools and writing in addition to the useless, beautiful, and poetic things of the world. By this view the universe of man-made things simply coincides with the history of art." (G. Kubler, *The Shape of Time*, p. 1.) It then follows that the universe of man-made things can become the resource for study and speculation; the focus of such study would be understanding those factors that pertain to the aesthetic and artistic qualities inherent in these objects.

In some degree, each student is himself a symbol-maker; he brings some background of choice and discrimination in his visual world. One can observe certain general factors in the development of a child's image-making capacities. There is, at first, an undifferentiated and uncontrolled "marking" that results from a child's developing sense of movement and touch. What begins in a rather haphazard fashion soon leads to the exercising of physical controls over these "markings"; children's scribbles take on qualities of controlled repetition and clearer definition of form. Of equal importance, children learn to relate their movement and markings to ideas. They become aware of the power of symbolization for projecting and realizing ideas and feelings. Beginning from simple and uncontrolled motor projection, children move toward image-making as a means for invention and communication. As part of their language they develop schematic representations of their reality. The writings of Viktor Lowenfeld, Dale Harris and others have documented the developmental aspects of children's drawings. What is important to note is that children, like artists, can be seen as entering the stream of traditions and events. Their capacities and drives are combined with factors of setting, timing, and circumstance in shaping their abilities and directions. Like artists, children are in tension with their environment—in part shaped by its circumstances; in part, driven by their capacities to transcend these circumstances.

In the process of a child's forming an image, the emerging form takes on an identity of its own. The artifact suggests its own form and meaning. The form being created can be said to be the expression of an idea; it is also the means by which the creator (student and/or mature artist) realizes and is shaped by the artifact itself. This thought has been expressed by Henri Focillon: "As for me, I separate hands neither from the body nor from the mind. But the relationships between mind and hand are not, however, so simple as those between a chief accustomed to obedience and a docile slave. The mind rules over the hand, hand rules over mind. The gesture that makes nothing, the gesture with no tomorrow, provokes and defines only the state of consciousness. The creative gesture exercises a continuous influence over the inner life. The hand wrenches the sense of touch away from its merely receptive passivity and organizes it for experiment and action. It teaches man to conquer space, weight, density and quantity. Because it fashions a new world, it leaves its imprint everywhere upon it. It struggles with the very substance in metamorphoses and with the very form it transfigures." (H. Focillon, *The Life of Forms in Art*, p. 78.)

Obviously, the overall problem of identifying what is to be "taught" in art education programs involves us in different kinds of specifics. For example, the four or five year old who has moved through stages of undifferentiated markings to the development of simple schema to represent man, sun, house, tree, etc., is still operating from an egocentric vantage point. The problem for him is still the relatively simple and personal task of inventing symbols that convey generalized meaning. His concerns are focused upon his own involvement with the image he creates. When new forms (or schema) are "invented," they are repeated and reinforced until such time as the schema are no longer adquate to embody and reflect active meanings with which the youngster is involved. Children then seek to change and enlarge upon their repertoire of images for the drawings they make. Given the growing complexity of ideas and feelings that they face as well as their increasing social awareness, the problems attendant to artistic expression become much more complicated. The inner-directed and ego-centered beginnings of visual expression soon are merged with forces external to the youngster. Environmental factors, traditions, and values gradually exert their force upon the growing child. Factors of reinforcement and reward as well as the structure of language and other means of communication impose themselves upon him. Indeed, our institutions (the school, the church, etc.) exist as formalizations of these values and directions.

Thus, I trust that I have now brought two other generalizations to the broad outlines against which I am attempting to discuss the problems identifying content in art education: (1) children make images as part of their normal and natural growth and development. Image-making is intimately related to developing their capacities for symbolization and thought; (2) making images is the resultant of complex forces within and external to the individual. To the degree that a child is actively involved in the shaping of his ideas and feelings through image making, he is also involved with a complex of purposes, values, and motives.

Just as one might observe changing styles and purposes in the creation of artifacts, one can also observe changes in the roles accorded to and assumed by artists. In the Middle Ages, an "art" was a technique; those persons who engaged in the making of painting or sculpture were seen as engaging in a lower level of mechanical activity. Painting and sculpture were considered as being merely sensuous and manual. Art served to represent the Divine; the artist was only the medium through which this representation was made visible. Given these circumstances, there could be no interest in the autonomy of the object or the individuality of the artist. Hence, it is no wonder that archaeologists and historians have great difficulty in identifying individual artists of the Middle Ages in relation to the artifacts they produced. It was not until the Renaissance that the concept of the artist as an individual and the work of art as the resultant form of human sensory, intellectual, and practical faculties appeared. Gradually the painters and sculptors began their ascent from the role of craftsman and artisan to a position more closely aligned to that of the humanist: the poet and scholar. This change had (and continues to have) its impact upon the forms of art; it also has had broad implications for the role of the artist. The change should be seen as part of a larger development involving the growth of individualism and the dramatic forces that were to develop in the Industrial Revolution. The displacement of artisans by machines and the popularization of ideas of freedom characterized a new stream of cultural change in whose force we still live. By the nineteenth century, artists saw their role as part of a larger declaration of independence against the ordinary life of their times. Theirs was an affirmation of the integrity and strengths of the mythical free individual who had become their ideal. They abandoned the strictures and limitations of the guilds and the seeming security of patronage to turn toward a more personal cause. As part of this role, they endured the material hardships of poverty and neglect; they did so in order that their art grow from individualized and personal directions. (See Geredline Pelles, *Art, Artists, and Society*.)

The late nineteenth century marks a critical point of origin for many of the problems and developments we face in art education today. As the artists turned from the crafts and those elements of commonly defined values, there was still another development in scholarly and humanistic study involving works of art. At that time historical analysis and the interpretation of artifacts was a comparatively recent addition to the academic disciplines. As Professor Taylor has indicated, while artists turned toward their own inner subjective feelings as a basis for their work, art historians tended towards a greater belief in objectivity and analytical systems for dealing with works of art. For the most part, the beginnings of art history as we know it can be found in Germany. There are those who contend that the resultant "Teutonic" methods and early institutionalization of the discipline served to create rigid and unecessary limitations for the field. What is generally agreed, however, is that art history as it has developed in the United States was strongly influenced by the work of German scholars and of art historians that had come to the field from classical archaeology, theology, philosophy, literature, architecture, and other fields. As was described by Erwin Panofsky: "At the beginning, the new discipline had to fight its way out of an entanglement with practical art instruction, art appreciation, and that amorphous monster 'general education.' The early issues of the *Art Bulletin*, founded in 1913 and now recognized as the leading art-historical periodical of the world, were chiefly devoted to such topics as 'What Instruction in Art Should the College A.B. Course Offer to the Future Layman?'; 'The Value of Art in a College Course'; 'What People Enjoy in Pictures'; or 'Preparation of the Child for a College Course in Art.' Art history, as we know it, sneaked in by the back door, under the guise of classical archaeology, evaluation of contemporary phenomena and, characteristically, book reviews. It was not until 1919 that it was permitted to lift its ugly head in large print. But in 1923, when the *Art Bulletin* carried ten unashamedly art-historical articles and only one on art appreciation, and when it was found necessary to launch a competing periodical, the short-lived *Art Studies*, the battle was won." (E. Panofsky, *Meaning in the Visual Arts*, p. 324–325). It is however, the larger issue of the "war" (not the "battle") that concerns me. I shall return to this point later. Presently, I only want to observe that there was (and continues to be) a current toward specialized and objective scholarly inquiry in the history of art.

There is still another large stream of development against which present day art education needs to conceive of its role and function: the developments in contemporary design. Just as there have been dramatic changes in the concept of the artist, there have also been changes in the concept of the designer. The notion of a designer is a relatively new idea growing from the Industrial Revolution. Prior to industrialization, the designer was not seen as being set apart from the producer; indeed, it is only the consequences of specialization and mass production that has brought him into being. In the nineteenth century, John Ruskin and William Morris set into motion the idea that the artist and craftsman had central roles to play in the making of useful objects. Theirs was a reaction against the standardization and impersonalization of the machine. This reaction led to the decorative flamboyance of the Art Nouveau Movement; the movement was short lived because of its inability to adapt to the new requirements of the industrial age. What was set in motion, however, was an increased awareness of growing technology and the aesthetic and functional needs of man.

In 1919, the Bauhaus was established at Weimar. Its stated purpose was to unify the arts and crafts toward future synthesis with architecture. At that time, the terms "industrial designer" or "planner" did not exist. It was the Bauhaus that gave emphasis and direction to the concept that the production of products and architecture needed not only the insights and understandings of engineers but the imagination and sensitivity of artists. In general, the school represented a movement away from the romantic tendencies of the nineteenth century toward the rationalist current of the twentieth century. Neoplasticism, constructivism, and photography tended to replace the decorative emphases of the arts and crafts as well as the classical and romantic stylistic tendencies of the plastic arts. A rationalist aesthetic for industrial production began to take form. However, in retrospect, there are those who point to the Bauhaus as having fostered another kind of formalism.

What is important to note is the development of a design discipline that, in many ways, is separate and distinct from that of the artist: the painter, sculptor, and potter. To be sure, artists and designers deal with the organization of visual and plastic elements; they each require aesthetic insights. Designers, however, assume responsibilities in a more immediate and functional context. "It is the organization of materials and processes in the most productive, economic way, in a harmonious balance of all elements necessary for a certain function. It is not a matter of façade, of mere external appearance; rather it is the essence of products and institutions, penetrating and comprehensive. Designing is a complex and intricate task. It is the integration of technological, social and economic requirements, biological necessities, and the psychophysical effects of materials, shape, color, volume, and space: thinking in the relationships." (L. Moholy-Nagy, *Vision in Motion*, p. 42.)

Given the three directions stemming from the nineteenth century in the plastic arts, the history of art, and the design disciplines, it would be interesting to make brief note of what was happening in our schools with regard to an emerging field of art education. From the time of Walter Smith's arrival in the 1870's, the focus of art education was upon the training of skills in drawing and the crafts. A nation involved in the "important business of growing up"—expanding and developing its frontiers, and building its industry and agriculture had little or no time for the fine arts. Education was tied to utilitarian principles; education in the fine arts could be only part of our leisure time activity or, at best an activity of moral enlightenment. It was not until the 1920's that John Dewey and the Progressive Education Movement started to formulate a viewpoint of art forms as the resultants of a creative process and the centrality of such process to educational goals. It is easy to see how the many factors operating to shape programs in art education then led to considerable confusion and disarray. On the one hand, there were the dramatic changes taking place in the plastic arts themselves. The paintings of the post-Impressionists—Van Gogh, Gauguin and Lautrec; the works of artists such as Monet and Cézanne; the Fauve outburst; and the birth of Cubism all seemed to reach America's shores at once. These forms excited our artists; they opened a new realm of possibility; and created another image for art. This new "image" carried with it considerable confusion and distrust. For example, one need only look at the public's negative response to the Armory Show in 1913. Make no mistake about it, many of our "art teachers" responded in a similar manner. Then there were the forces from an emerging field of art history. Art historians struggling for their own identity within a community of humanistic scholars could only look with disdain upon programs in art education that focused on technique and utilitarian values. Moreover, the rapidly changing art forms of the time did not lend themselves to their systems of objective categorization. Hence, art historians seemed to cast aside their concerns for the present and turned more and more toward unassailable but limited techniques for describing the past. The design disciplines created still other forces. On the one hand there was a growing academism from the Bauhaus tradition, a stylistic centered tendency rather than the initial intent of men such as Gropius or Moholy-Nagy; on the other hand there was the massive intrusion of the values and needs of commerce and advertising upon design programs. Students in our design schools were then trained as "commercial artists," "stylists," or decorators. Ironically, public school programs were able to grow in so mixed a soil. That is, there were growing numbers of art teachers, schools with art programs, and money and materials devoted to their efforts. It might even be said that art programs grew because of their very lack of clarity. Art programs became "all things to all people." However, as one moves about our schools today, it is apparent that some of the elements of confusion and contradiction stemming from the turn of the century are still with us. Given the prospect of continued change (and doubtless, greater challenge) it is essential that we take stock of the current status and directions for the field.

Let me be clear about one point: I do not see the need to clarify our contradictions and confusion in order that there be greater regimentation in what art teachers do in their classrooms. I see no panacea of a single established national curriculum or methodology for teaching. Indeed my proposal is that we actively seek multiple directions in our research and inquiry. However, to do so involves *the willingness and obligation to be informed and knowledgeable about a range of factors that contribute to establishing content in art education.* Recognizing that the fields of the plastic arts, art history and design provide changing referents, there is the obligation that any specific inquiry be in constant tension with the larger ground in which it exists. In this paper I have sought to establish a larger ground against which we need to conceive of and develop the content of our art programs. The particular cues that I have taken are man himself, his symbols, his art and those larger tendencies in the plastic arts, the history of art, and design stemming from the turn of the century. I would also observe that these tendencies have taken still another turn in more recent years. These changes can and should have a great impact upon art education.

The changes that have come about as a result of scientific and technological accomplishments have had a profound effect upon men. As I stated at the outset, today's images are conveyed instantaneously: they are enlarged and made more pervasive. The "realities" of Viet Nam, a college course in Botany, the United Nations, and the Miss Universe competition are made available to us by a flick of a knob. We are made symbolically aware of the drama of a world in conflict and turmoil. This has had a tremendous effect upon artists. In his paper prepared for this conference, Harold Rosenberg points to the problems of identity as an issue of personal and collective life. "Art movements in the twentieth century have tended to swing back and forth between extreme affirmations of individual self-consciousness and self-negation through efforts at anonymous production or group identification. The values of expressionist art, on the one hand, and of the neo-realistic and science-derived modes, on the other, have been related to this dialectic or identity." He then points out that "failure to see modern art against the background of the politico-cultural crises and revolutions of our time results in emptying contemporary painting and sculpture of content. Critical discussion is deprived of serious intellectual reference and tends to be reduced to recitals of the history of formal development presented as arguments in support of personal tastes." Anyone viewing the art of our time must view it for its ideational meaning, its significance as an act of man apart from the craft or beaux arts traditions of the nineteenth century. Contemporary art faces man with decision and action in relation to its own intrinsic drama and meaning. This, it seems to me, was the great breakthrough of Abstract Expressionism. As Rosenberg put it: "In that it dared to be subjective, to affirm the artist as an active self, Action Painting was the last 'moment' in art on the plane of dramatic and intellectual seriousness. The painters in this current have kept to the tradition of the human being as the ultimate subject of painting." (H. Rosenberg, *The Anxious Object*, pp. 46–47.)

Given a greater sense for the changing forms and styles in the traditions of art, made more aware of the changing purposes and values motivating the creation of art, and conscious of new materials and images, today's artist is, at once, faced with an infinity of possibility and the responsibility of *his* own choice. This is the same problem faced by artists of the past. As Ad Reinhardt put it: "The next revolution in Art will be the same, old, one Revolution." Nevertheless, today's artist is faced with the relatively new problem of being aware and motivated by so much that he is forced to greater awareness of himself and his actions; today's artist is (in Allan Kaprow's world) "a man of the world." Operationally this change is reflected by the many artists now actively participating in our colleges, universities, and museum educational programs. It seems to me that it is no accident that artists are more involved with institutions of education rather than the church. Their concerns are of a social nature. Ironically, this concern can best be fulfilled by being "themselves." Thus it is possible for Ad Reinhardt to say: "Art-as-Art is a concentration on Art's essential nature. The nature of art has not to do with the nature of perception or with the nature of light or with the nature of space or with the nature of time or with the nature of mankind or with the nature of society or with the nature of the universe or with the nature of creation or with the nature of nature." Yet in the same article he asserts: "The next revolution will see the fading away of old unschooled, 'school of hard knocks' artists telling young artists they need not go to school" . . . "the next revolution will see the emancipation of the university-academy of art from its marketplace-fantasies and its emergence as a 'center of consciousness and conscience'." (A. Reinhardt, "The Next Revolution in Art," *Art News*, February, 1964, p. 49.)

Many have referred to schools as the emerging patrons of the arts. A more realistic view is that they may emerge as centers for artistic activity. Presently, it must be said that the arts are still "uncomfortable guests" in a burgeoning household. They are told that they are "welcome"; but, "in their hearts," they are not certain it is so. There is, however, a growing positive note, namely, that our schools (in particular our colleges and universities) can provide a viable alternative to the commercial gallery world. More and more, one can hear the leaders in education speaking out in behalf of the artist. One of the more eloquent of such statements was made by James A. Perkins, President of Cornell University: "Artist beware, but university prepare. Let the artist learn where his real talent lies and how it can be most effectively adjusted into a university environment and protected from what is inimical to its development. And at the same time, let the university recognize the need for the special treatment required for creative talent whether working in the field of the arts or in other fields.

"And, although the idea may be startling, it is by no means certain that in this process the artist on the campus may not make a greater contribution to the future of the university than the university can make to the future of the artist." (J. Perkins, "Should the Artist Come to the Campus," *Saturday Review*, July 17, 1965, p. 71.)

In sum, the picture as I see it is that of the contemporary artist faced with and aware of the dynamics of the twentieth century. Like today's scientists, he is interested in relationship functions. The nature of the challenge and his commitments are such as to draw him closer to educational efforts. Unlike our preceding century, his primary contribution is not seen as teaching a craft in an isolated context. The art of today places its emphases upon visual form as an *idea* (as that form which structures the many facets of sensibility and imagination).

Lest I have presented an overly optimistic view of artists marching en masse toward the "good of man," let me hasten to remind you that there are still questions as to who "declares" himself to be an "artist." In a period when the elements of craftsmanship have given way to the lure of ideational fluency and the resultant art forms are more inviting of diversity, problems of value judgment become even more critical. Above all, we should not hold forth any naive assumptions about necessary relationships between the declared "artist," values in critical judgments, and moral and/or ethical values of man. Given the dynamics of our time, critical judgments are more difficult to make. What I have noted is that the concerns and contributions of artists are becoming part of the valuing process in our educational institutions. These concerns, however, need to be seen in relation to the traditions and nature of the discipline. In this regard, I would note some hopeful developments in the history of art.

Earlier, I referred to the beginnings of the history of art and efforts to establish the discipline in this country. It is easy to see the rationale for using a European model of the discipline as a basis for developing the field in this country. As has been pointed out by Professor Taylor, there was an initial press for "objectivity" and analytical method at the very time that contemporary art moved toward more subjective and dynamic values. James Ackerman described this state of affairs: "The Philosophy of art history of the last generation could be called antiphilosophical; it taught nonintervention, not only in the sense of avoiding value judgments, but in the sense of minimizing the factor of creativity in historical scholarship." (J. Ackerman, *Art and Archaeology*, p. 142.)

While efforts were being made to emulate the European model of Art History, there were also forces that contributed to deviation from that model.

I will not reiterate the dramatic changes that have taken place in the forms and styles of art since the turn of the century. Suffice to say, historians have had to review and revise their categories for dealing with these forms. In so doing, there has been a growing awareness of the creative component in their discipline. This change was part of a larger change in historicism itself: The subject matter of history became human life in its totality and multiplicity. It was the historian's aim "to portray the bewildering, unsystematic variety of historical forms—people, nations, cultures, customs, institutions, songs, myths, and thoughts—in their unique, living expressions and in the process of continuous growth and transformation. This aim is not unlike the artist's; at any rate, it differs from the systematic, conceptual approach of the philosopher." (Hans Meyerhoff, *The Philosophy of History in Our Time*, p. 10.)

Art objects provide the primary data for the art historian. Inevitably, conflicting opinions and interpretations come into play as historians attempt to illuminate a particular work. This is especially the case in that art objects are valued for their intrinsic qualities rather than their functional rationale (if any). Cultural change and the passage of time do more to alter the context in which a work of art exists and the way it is perceived than does any change such as wearing or deterioration in the work itself. The object stands as a primary datum for hypothesizing about the past. Works of art can also provide some of the distance for developing insights into our own times. Inevitably, engaging in such inquiry and speculation involves critical and evaluative judgments. Any attempts to separate "fact" from "feeling" about works of art only lead to limited frames of reference. This kind of separation fosters thinking that arbitrarily separates the work of art from the observer. What is neglected is the fact that our perceptions of objects are "colored" by our values, training, and expectations. The observer affects the definition of that which is being observed. Objectivity and subjectivity as factors in visual perception are not that easily pulled apart.

Changes in the history of art have moved the field toward greater awareness of the dynamics involved in historical method. This has resulted in the possibility for a different kind of communication between art historian and artist. The basis for such communication is not that of adversaries trying to "capture" the work of art; rather it is the communication of men who engage in separate disciplines where each might inform the other.

Design as a discipline is perhaps the most recent of the three tendencies I have identified as providing a basis for establishing the content of our art programs. I would observe, however, that it poses an educational problem of equal complexity and significance. As I have viewed the disciplines of studio production and historical inquiry as being separate, I would also view design as a unique discipline embracing a great variety of human activities. As relative "new-comers" among faculties in our colleges and universities, designer-teachers do not fit most of our existing patterns. Among some, design is seen as nothing more than an extension of a beaux-arts or craftsman's tradition.

Product design then becomes a functionally oriented sculptural form; visual communication is no more than a category of the problems engaged in by painters and printmakers. Among others, design need be no more than an extension of engineering and other technological solutions. Design can then be relegated to a styling or decorative function. My contention is that neither role is appropriate. Design is both an art and a science in that it involves responsibilities for the functional and aesthetic planning of our man-made environment. To "design" involves the synthesizing of conscious and deliberate controls with intuitive and felt needs. Design is a dynamic process by which men seek rational and aesthetic solutions. Designers, architects, and planners must assume a primary responsibility for projecting our mass-produced and functional forms—from visual images to small products to shelter and community requirements. Whereas our schools of design were conceived as vehicles for training craftsmen or advertisers (indeed, many schools are still organized for these ends), the direction that I want to identify is that of a design field moving toward a more significant challenge, one that will involve greater responsibility and discipline. Given the tremendous developments in mass media and production technology, given our pressing social and aesthetic problems, it is essential that the ideas undergirding the training of designers be above a crass commercial level and beyond the more limited concerns of the craftsman. Designers need to be trained to assume responsibilities in governmental as well as educational agencies; they need to participate in the shaping of aesthetic and social conscience as well as functional forms. In short, we will need to educate people to assume a major responsibility for developing initiative in advancing the art and science of conscious choice where products, physical facilities, shelter, and communications are concerned.

The overall challenge that I envision for art education involves developing theory and practice (including the challenge of content development) for educating for our world of vision and form. The three major currents I have projected are the studio production of art, the history of art (to include the whole range of man-made things involving beauty and intrinsic value) and the emerging design disciplines. In viewing these themes I have referred to the dynamics that gave them their character around the turn of this century. In each instance, one can identify the uniqueness of the disciplines as well as a growing interdisciplinary tendency, a greater awareness of relationships among disciplines. My view is that the field of art education (as it conceives its role in developing programs in our elementary and secondary schools and as it proceeds in the training of teachers) needs to pay attention to the distinctive as well as the related aspects of these disciplines.

Others at this conference will deal with the specific tasks of curriculum development and teaching methodologies. There are, however, a number of general considerations that occur to me as I contemplate the operational implications of what I have said.

The task for art educators in our elementary schools involves encouraging that which young children can do naturally—the creation of symbols that express their ideas and feelings. Human beings are essentially "symbolic" organisms; they learn to select information and "construct" it into a uniquely human world. Initial emphases should be on developing predispositions toward learning. Media and materials ought to be chosen with a view toward their potentials for being formed and shaped in terms of ideas to be expressed. Above all, the emphasis cannot be upon "expression" alone; nor should it be upon limited descriptive values. A youngster's expression or stereotyped form must not be conformed with understanding and communication. Children should develop a sense for recognizing their own power in giving shape to their ideas and feelings; they need to learn that what they do suggests other possibilities; they need to become aware of the poetry in their vision, of the drama in their lives. The basis for such learning should draw upon ideas and experiences that are part of the child's life—the people he knows, the places he has seen, the ideas he has. As his intellectual and experiential horizons expand, the potential for ideas and forms is thus enlarged. Above all, the structure of teaching art, at any level, must be done with a sense for a larger body of knowledge and insight that can be generated. The concept of what constitutes an "artistic" problem—its limitations and possibilities—is central to what is taught. What the teacher does is, of course, related to the student's larger vision and insight about his field. In this regard, art teachers can do much to provide a broadened base for understanding the world of vision and form by bringing their students in contact with artists, scholars, and designers. The opportunity to talk with an artist in his studio; to visit with museum, gallery, and library personnel; and to see first hand, the working spaces of architects, planners, and designers cannot help but broaden their conceptions of these fields of human endeavor. The subject matter of art can thus be taken out of the realm of the "remote" and the "unreal." Generalizations about what artists, historians, and designers do would then have a more operational referent.

Whenever possible, children should be confronted with original works of art. I agree with Professor Taylor that they can be helped to recognize and realize their own abilities to make visual judgments and talk about these judgments. My own bias for using original works of art as teaching referents is related to the feeling that children need to manipulate and deal with tangible realities. So much in their lives is lived out of a "can"; our mass culture provides an imbalance of predigested stimuli. Just as we would want children to develop confidence and skills for shaping their own ideas, we should seek opportunities for them to come to grips with the primary data of art. This is not to say that slides, photographs, and reproductions of art cannot be used in the teaching of art. Quite the contrary, these images can be used to expand and enrich the visual learning in the classroom. What should be avoided, however, is the exclusive use of "reproduced images" and the idea that paintings and sculpture can only be seen by their being projected on a screen. In the long run, the challenge is that of developing values and attitudes for dealing with all aspects of our visual experience. It is my supposition that young children can best develop these values by first hand contact with their own symbols and original artistic forms of others.

As children move through our schools, we should seek to develop increasingly sophisticated levels of sensitivity, insights, and skills about visual forms. Teachers need to help students approach problems at their own level; they need to assist them in projecting and testing their own personal criteria and standards of excellence against the standards and criteria that the teacher helps to evolve. In the elementary school it should be possible to develop a range of skills and techniques; it should also be possible to develop a sense for the broad traditions of art. In this latter regard the emphases need not be upon chronology, the memorization of dates and names, or the isolation of art from the broad areas of human concern. Children can be shown the many ways that artists have shaped forms dealing with the same or similar themes; they can be made aware of the many meanings contained within a single work of art; and they can become aware of how the same artist may have handled a particular subject in different ways. Professor Taylor's examples of a "sculptured T'ang horse and one by Remmington, a Lascaux painting and a race horse by Stubbs, a mobile by Calder and an energetic construction by Tinguely" could be extended endlessly by a resourceful and knowledgeable teacher. Artists have dealt with an infinity of themes for their work—man, work, play, life, death, nature, etc. Even the simplest of themes such as the "moon" or the "sun" can open tremendous visual and conceptual possibilities when one looks to the traditions of art. From the Celtic sun worship remains of Stonehenge to the Egyptian Sun-God Ra to the Sun-Temple of Konarak to Sun Gods in Aztec Culture to thirteenth and fourteenth century images of the sun to modern conceptions of the same subject as seen in the works of Rousseau, Klee, Max Ernst, Miro, and Lippold, the teacher of art can draw upon a theme such as "the subject matters that concern the students. Naturally some geographical areas will have greater advantage than others in the art forms that are available in local museums and galleries; some locations will have a greater concentration of artists and craftsmen. In all cases, however, imaginative art teachers can do a great deal in bringing together the available resources to expand upon the student's knowledge and insight about visual forms. In short, I would see the primary focus of art education in our elementary schools to be that of developing greater knowledge and awareness of our visual environment; building attitudes of discovery and invention in the expression and realization of visual forms; and encouraging conscious aesthetic choice and evaluation of these forms.

Beyond our elementary schools there are many possibilities for rethinking and reformulating our programs. The need for change that I see ahead involves the identification and development of knowledge and techniques to enable greater ideational fluency and aesthetic awareness. The forming of "ideas" (or "image") in any significant way is not possible without knowledge and control of technique. Every discipline has its techniques. What warrants possible criticism is not the teaching of techniques, but its narrow viewing as an end into itself.

Whatever biases and experiences I have lead me to the conclusion that studio learning should continue into the junior high school education of all students. Opportunities should be provided for students to become involved with materials and tools that provide greater physical and intellectual challenge. The primary datum of one's own experience is important in grasping the significance of visual forms. This is a period when attitudes toward discovery, abilities to court mystery and tolerate ambiguity are formed. It is also a period where more structured learnings are possible. Students should become more aware of the limits and possibilities for their tools and media; they can consciously seek inventive, aesthetic, and craftsmanlike solutions to the problems they undertake. At a minimal level, studio learnings should continue through the junior high school for all students and beyond the junior high school for those with expressed interests and aptitudes. I am, however, in essential agreement with Professor Taylor in his observation that there comes a point in the experience of most people when intellectual capacities for understanding and appreciation outstrip abilities to actually create the forms of appreciation. By the secondary school, those factors that differentiate the capacities and interests of one individual from another become more apparent. Youngsters start to "sort" themselves in terms of personal directions and tendencies.

Alongside or part of programs of study with studio emphases, there is an important place for the study of art as part of our broad humanistic traditions. Currently, many of our secondary schools are developing required courses of study in which the history and criticism of art play vital roles. In some instances, there is instruction that includes contemporary film, mass produced images and products, or architecture as resources for study. To be sure, these programs differ in accordance with the strengths of the particular staff members involved. What is becoming apparent, however, is that the full content of our secondary school art programs can rarely be covered by one man. The knowledge and skills to be imparted are too diverse. Most secondary school programs (and their budgets) are conceived with a single art teacher in mind. Indeed, the present state of affairs is that all too many schools have not even reached this point; they do not have provision for a single art teacher. Our programs for the training of art teachers have, for the most part, sought to train generalists—persons competent to teach at all levels of the junior and senior high school (many carry this one step further through certification to teach art in grades one through twelve). My contention is that there is a need for greater depth and understanding in areas of content for our secondary school art programs. Our failure to achieve this depth and understanding has resulted in a generalized and vague image of the field.

As I have indicated, works of art can be seen as objects that illuminate history; works of art also exist apart from history with meanings to be derived in the present. Students in our secondary schools should be introduced to historical and critical method. We are also living in an exciting world of vision and form. Our students need to be made consciously aware of visual communications, products, architectural forms, and community and regional planning problems. All of this is to say nothing of developing their own capacities for the organization and expression of ideas through imagery.

The task ahead for art educators is overwhelming in its proportions. That is, it will be overwhelming if it is approached from points of view based upon a nineteenth century outlook. A beaux arts tradition, a "fixed objective base" for categorizing art historical data, or an arts and crafts approach—each had its rationale developed in another time. If we are to meet the challenge ahead, it will be necessary to reorient our thinking to present day knowledge and dynamics. There is a great deal to be done in clarifying concepts and developing instructional materials and strategies appropriate for educating students in the broad areas represented by the visual arts. No single "model" of what the art teacher should be like will suffice to meet this challenge. The field of art education will have to be made up of persons with differing strengths and interests that bear upon the larger problems of art education. A great deal will need to be done in areas not alluded to in this paper: teaching strategies, communication and learning problems, philosophical inquiry, and curriculum development. In this paper I have set forth some of our sources for content. The nature of the three currents described poses a special problem. The fields of the plastic arts, the history of art, and the design disciplines are themselves in flux, each reaching for broader ideational and operational significance. Our fields of knowledge and content will not stand still for us to fix rigid boundaries. Indeed, it is only as one moves with a field that the motion is not as disturbing. Secondary school art teachers will have to be persons who are themselves involved and motivated by the dynamics of their work. As they "move" with a sense for the scope and breadth of what artists, art historians, critics, and designers are about, they can convey some of this same sense to their students. As they "move" with the confidence of their own discipline and knowledge, they can help students to develop that same disciplined sense for facing the future that only they can make.

REFERENCES

1. James S. Ackerman, "Art and Evolution," *The Nature and Art of Motion*, G. Kepes, ed., George Braziller, 1965, p. 32–39.
2. James S. Ackerman and Rhys Carpenter, *Art and Archaeology*. Prentice-Hall, 1963, p. 241.
3. Henri Focillon, *The Life and Forms in Art*, George Wittenborn, Inc., 1948, p. 94.

4. Rene Huyghe, *Ideas and Images in World Art*, Harry N. Abrams, Inc., 1959, p. 447.
5. Allan Kaprow, "Should the Artist Become a Man of the World?," *Art News*, October, 1964, pp. 34–37, 58–59.
6. Gyorgy Kepes, Introduction, *Education of Vision*, George Braziller, 1965, pp. i–vii.
7. George Kubler, *The Shape of Time. Remarks on the History of Things*, Yale University Press, 1962, p. 136.
8. Hans Meyerhoff, *The Philosophy of History in Our Time*, Doubleday & Co., Inc., 1959, p. 350.
9. L. Moholy-Nagy, *Vision in Motion*, Paul Theobald, 1947, p. 371.
10. Erwin Panofsky, *Meaning in the Visual Arts*, Doubleday & Co., Inc., 1965, p. 362.
11. Gereldine Pelles, *Art, Artists, and Society*, Prentice-Hall, Inc., 1963, p. 180.
12. James A. Perkins, "Should the Artist Come to the Campus?," *Saturday Review*, July, 1965, pp. 54–56, 71.
13. Ad Reinhardt, *"The Next Revolution in Art,"* Art News, February, 1964, pp. 48–49.
14. Harold Rosenberg, *The Anxious Object*, Horizon Press, 1964, p. 270.
15. Alvin Toffler, *"The Future as a Way of Life,"* Horizon, Summer 1965, Vol. VII, No. 3, pp. 109–115.

2

Foundation

Does Philosophy Have a Future?

SIDNEY HOOK

In periods of world and national crisis, such as we are passing through, many individuals are wont to turn to philosophy and philosophers in hope of finding a faith to sustain them in time of troubles. If God is dead, is philosophy still alive? They usually discover that philosophers are not agreed on any particular faith, and that what they are commonly concerned with is the meaning of faith. Those who ask questions find that the answer which the philosopher gives them is an invitation to inquiry, not a conclusion or credo. Philosophy, they are sometimes told, is not so much an activity that offers definite answers to questions as one that questions answers. But surely philosophy does not question answers to anything or everything.

This failure to get a specific answer sometimes leads to frustration and to a series of other questions. What is philosophical inquiry as distinct from other forms? What is philosophy, after all? What has it to say? Why study it?

I propose to discuss briefly some of the uses of philosophy without offering a formal definition of it, because any definition presupposes some conception not likely to be shared by all philosophers. Further, it seems possible to convey a notion of what philosophy is by describing its common uses.

The first and most obvious use of the study of philosophy is that it helps us to understand the nature and history of our civilization. We cannot grasp the pattern of its events and the character of its institutions without some knowledge of the ideas of Plato, Aristotle, Plotinus, Aquinas, Kant, Hegel, and Marx. We cannot understand the political history of the United States without some appreciation of the philosophy of Locke. We cannot appreciate the recent history of Europe and Asia without a grasp of the social philosophy of Marx. I am not saying that the philosophical ideas of these thinkers alone are the forces which entered into the determination of history. Obviously, economic and national interests as well as outstanding personalties played a large role, too; but I am saying that philosophical conceptions of the nature of man, of the nature of justice, of social welfare, of human personality, of freedom, had some influence upon events, and that without reference to them we cannot explain the shape of the past.

Ideas—philosophical ideas—also have a direct relevance to present-day religious, social, and political movements. They are not merely a part of the heritage of the West. They are the means by which we seek to preserve and defend the West. That is why ideas are among the most practical things in the world. Whoever wants to understand our world, and the world of the past out of which it grew, must therefore pay some attention to philosophical ideas. The study of philosophy, in other words, gives us a perspective upon our human history and our present-day experience. It reveals, in John Dewey's words, "the predicaments, the prospects, and aspirations of men."

But philosophy has an even more important use. It has a bearing not only on the shape of the past, but on the shape of things to come. To the extent that fundamental ideas determine our actions, they flow from our basic commitments. Philosophy is a mode of thought which analyzes our presuppositions and assumptions in every field of action and thought. It enables us to make explicit our allegiances to the ideals in behalf of which we are prepared to live, to fight, sometimes even to die. Its primary concern here is with meaning, not truth, and it aims to produce an awareness of what we are about. This awareness or self-consciousness is not easy to achieve. The fruit of ancient wisdom was expressed in the Greek injunction, "Know thyself," but this is a difficult task. Very few of us can answer the questions: "What do we really want?"; What do we really mean by the large terms which play a role in human discourse?" We inherit a large mass—usually a mess—of traditional beliefs. Some of these we call first principles. Others, who do not share them, dub them prejudices. How do we sort them out?

This suggests the third use of philosophy. Awareness and self-consciousness do not come about by revelation. For the revelations—"the moments of truth," as the phrase goes—which overtake us are themselves in need of understanding. This can be reliably achieved only by the activity of logical analysis. A person may utter statements that are true or false and yet not be clear about their meaning or their justification or relevance. Whatever else philosophy is, it is an activity of logical analysis which seeks to locate issues in dispute and to help clarify them. When properly pursued, philosophy gives a methodological sophistication that can be achieved by no other discipline. It is not a mere matter of reasoning from premises to conclusion, as in mathematics or chess, because it scrutinizes the premises and basic terms which all subjects take for granted. It enables us to distinguish between statements of fact and disguised definitions, between hypotheses which may be true or false and resolutions which are adequate or inadequate. It is always prepared to consider alternatives to the familiar. William James actually defines philosophy as a quest for alternatives and their investigation. In summary, then, philosophy consists of an analysis of concepts and ideas in an attempt to cut through slogans to genuine issues and problems.

Let us consider a few simple illustrations:

1. The most fashionable slogan in intellectual and educational circles during recent years has been "Down with conformity and conformism." The conformist is the yes man, the man who agrees. He is at the bottom of the cultural ladder. But everyone who denounces conformism can be made to realize that one of the greatest nonconformists of the twentieth century was Adolf Hitler. Would that he had conformed to the accepted decencies of his time! To make a fetish of nonconformity won't do at all—especially when we run into a lunatic who refuses to conform to the traffic laws and rams our car, or a man who shortchanges us and tosses our complaint off with the observation that he is an arithmetical nonconformist. It is or should be obvious that conformism is a relational term. Conformity or nonconformity is no virtue in itself. Unless we know what we are conforming with or not conforming with, the term is meaningless. What we sometimes have in mind when we praise nonconformity is intellectual independence, the intelligence and courage to agree or disagree on the basis of evidence.

2. Another illustration is the slogan which originated in high places and which has been often repeated: "There are no alternatives to peace!" How many who mouth this sentence are aware that it commits them to unconditional surrender if an enemy threatens attack? What those who utter this sentence mean to say is that peace is desirable. The meaning of what they actually said is that peace at any price, even at the cost of freedom, is desirable. People who speak this way don't say what they really mean.

More important—and this is not the same thing—they don't mean what they really say.

3. Another confusion is the belief that the equality or inequality of races necessarily has a bearing on the question of segregation or integration in housing, transportation, schooling. The view which condemns discrimination against human beings on the basis of religion or race is primarily a moral view. It flows from our belief in the validity of the democratic ideal which rests upon an equality of concern for all human beings to develop their personality to their highest potential. Some facts may have a bearing on this policy, but not the discovery that there is a greater distribution of natural capacity in one race or group than another. Whatever be the facts about the distribution of capacity in group A or B, each member of that group is morally entitled to the rights and privileges which flow from the obligation of a democratic community to all its citizens.

Consider a family which has several children with varying natural capacities —very bright, normal, and dull. Would any responsible parent deprive any of these children of food, clothing, and shelter because of difference in their capacities? If the question of their schooling arose, their educational opportunities would be commensurate with their educational capacities. So with the educational opportunities for the children of members of different groups. The question is not whether the distribution of capacity is inherently the same or different among them, but whether they are to be given educational opportunities on the basis of their capacities or on the basis of their color. This would mean that children, white or nonwhite, Christian or Jewish, would find themselves in the same class in the same school if their educational capacities were the same. Once this analysis is made we can see where the issue lies. It lies in the field of social morality. It is not a question of physical anthropology at all, but rather of the extent to which we accept democracy.

I could have taken other illustrations for analysis from popular philosophy, such as the vulgar notion that because all human action is interest, everyone therefore acts for his own interests, that willy-nilly everyone is selfish. I wanted, however, to show how a little elementary logical analysis has relevance to practical affairs.

But a word about that old chestnut of adolescent cynicism—everyone is selfish, everyone acts for his own pleasure. If I say that all men have two eyes, I am saying something which is confirmed by universal observation. Were I to ask, however, under what possible circumstances one could show that this statement were false, you would be able to describe a state of affairs I could observe—the presence of only one natural eye or three; or, if the mother, when pregnant, had taken thalidomide, none. But suppose you could not describe any possible state of affairs which would invalidate your position; what meaning could be assigned to not having two eyes? Obviously, none. Now suppose I ask: Under what circumstances would you be prepared to say that a person is unselfish; how would he have to behave for you to count him as unselfish? As soon as you indicated the specifiable respects, observation of which would lead you to the conclusion, you could know what to do to put it to a test. But if you can't describe the behavior which you are prepared to describe as unselfish, then you are using the term "selfish" in such a way that it has no empirical meaning. You are claiming that the statement, "Everyone is selfish," is true no matter what the facts are or will be—and, therefore, you are not making a statement of fact at all.

4. There is a further use of philosophy. It concerns itself with the place of man in the universe from the point of view of certain large and perennial questions which all reflective men at some time or another ask. These questions are not raised or answered in any of the special sciences, but to answer them intelligently one must be familiar with the best science and theology of the day, and approach them in a rational spirit. These are questions such as: In what sense, if any, does the universe show a design? Does this design imply a designer or a God or a Friend behind the phenomena? Is man a tenement of clay inhabited by an immortal soul or a handful of wonderful salts in a solution of water? Are human beings responsible for their actions? If they are, does this mean that they have free wills? If the will is free, does this mean that the will is uncaused? If the will is uncaused, does this mean that actions are a matter of chance, and if so, in what sense are men morally responsible for their conduct?

This leads on to all sorts of exacting and intricate questions. What do we mean by a cause? Can there be a first cause? Are these questions answerable? What is a genuine question anyhow? Does every sentence which has the form of a question possess the sense of one? Concerning these questions there is dogmatic belief and often dogmatic disbelief. Philosophy is the discipline which considers the fundamental questions in such a way that no matter what answers one makes to them, one can give reasons or grounds for belief or disbelief.

5. Finally, I come to what I regard as the most important use of philosophy, to which all the other uses of philosophy are ancillary—philosophy as the quest for wisdom. Everyone knows that there is a difference between knowledge and wisdom, but not everyone can tell in what this difference consists. We are aware that a man can have a great deal of knowledge about many things and still be a learned fool. We sometimes say he has been educated beyond his capacities. We also know there are wise men who are not encyclopedias of learning, and that wise men of the past often lacked the knowledge of present-day schoolboys. This has led some thinkers to contrast knowledge and wisdom as if they belonged to entirely different orders or dimensions of insight. But if we speak of a wise man, we are entitled to ask: "What is he wise about?" If he were ignorant of everything, he couldn't be wise.

Consequently, we must conclude that wisdom is a species of knowledge— it is knowledge of the origin, careers, interrelations, and reliabilities of human values in our experience. Wisdom is an affair of values, and of value judgements. It is intelligent conduct of human affairs. It is knowledge of what is of most worth in our experience, of the ends which we can justifiably pursue, of the good, the better, and the best, the bad, the worse, and the worst in those concrete situations in which, confronted by alternatives of policy or action, we ask: "What shall I do?"

This raises a very large question. How can we be wise or even rational about our values or our ends? What does it mean to be rational or reasonable about them? The term "rational," or "reasonable," has many meanings, but some eminent thinkers claim that they can all be reduced to variations of one meaning, viz, the appropriate or economical use of means to achieve ends. They assert that once we have an end we can be rational about the means of realizing it, but that it makes no sense to speak of ends being rational or reasonable. This suggests that ultimately all ends are on the same plane and that no good reason or rational ground can be given for accepting one or rejecting others. If one accepts Gandhi's ends, one can be rational about achieving them. If one accepts Hitler's ends, one can be rational about achieving them. But we cannot be rational in choosing between Gandhi's and Hitler's ends.

This is the position of Bertrand Russell, who says, "There is no such thing as an irrational end except one impossible of realization." Now, this is false on its face because in one sense there are many ends which are impossible of realization, but are not irrational to pursue because of the desirable consequences of our pursuit of them. Suppose I take all knowledge as my province. It is impossible to achieve literal mastery of the whole of knowledge, but it may not be irrational to pursue it as a goal, because I may thereby acquire more knowledge in this fashion than if I had taken a more restricted end. Or, suppose I take as my end kindness in all circumstances to everyone. This, too, given men as we know them, is impossible, but the world would be a far better place if I try to be invariably kind than if I take as my ideal a more restricted sort of kindness or an ideal of indifference.

One might retort that what Russell means is still valid, for in these cases what I am really taking as my end are those consequences which are realizable. The problem then is: How can you rationally decide concerning alternative ends, all of which are equally realizable?

The answer, it seems to me, is suggested by analyzing how we proceed in any concrete situation in which we must make a choice between ends. If we have only one end, we have no moral problem. It is only a question of means. But the obvious truth is that we always have more than one end—usually a cluster of ends or values—to which we are committed. Our problem is, which end should we commit ourselves to? Now, the answer I suggest is that we always proceed by checking the alternative possible ends in terms of the consequences of the means used to achieve them and in the light of all the other ends which, on the basis of past experience, we have accepted as having prima facie validity. Of course, every one of these other ends may itself be questioned. Every end in human experience is also a means to some other end. How do we test them? By the same process. But does this not set up an infinite regress? No, not if we take our problems one at a time.

Consider a simple example. A student comes to me in distress and wants to know whether he should remain in school or exploit some opportunity for remunerative employment. I point out the relative advantages and disadvantages of both, stressing the fact that in the modern world he is more likely to find a creative vocation through continuing his schooling. Now, this assumes that a creative vocation is a good thing to have. How do we know that? Suppose it is denied. Again, we point to the alternative used of the concrete goals or possibilities of living. A creative vocation is a center around which to organize experience; it is a source of satisfaction and delight; it also provides occasions for companionship and friendship. But are these worthwhile? To which I reply that they enrich living. Yes, comes the rejoinder, but is life worthwhile? Now, at this point we can very well question the validity of the process. A student who wants to know whether life is worth living. That is a legitimate question, too, in its context. But it is out of context here.

What I have been trying to illustrate is the general method by which we do, in fact, seek to answer specific moral questions. They are much more complicated, of course, when they concern other human beings. (I am not giving any answers here or claiming to be wise. A philosopher in his own life need be no more wise than a physician need be healthy.) I am particularly concerned to challenge the view that all our values are ultimate values that are inarbitrable. Indeed, I question whether it is true that any value in a speicfic context is an ultimate value rather than a penultimate one which is tested by its successive consequences. At any rate, I believe I have shown that we can be wise or foolish about the ends of action, that it makes good sense to undertake rational criticism of our ends, and that the originally desired end may sometimes appear in the light of our reflective analysis as undesirable.

Although the philosopher does not himself have to be a wise man, at his best he knows more than the methods and techniques by which the process of reflection is carried out. He has vision of possibilities. He is not only a critic but a seer. His vision is often expressed as a glimpse into what can make our society better for our time, into what can most enrich our life and give it abiding worth, an insight into human possibilities and how to realize them. When the philosopher is a man of vision, he leaves his mark upon the experience of others, whose ordinary life acquires new dimensions of significance.

Of such philosophers, Santayana says: "It is not easy for him to shout or to address a crowd; he must be silent for long periods; for he is watching stars that move slowly and in courses that it is possible though difficult to see; and he is crushing all things in his heart as in a winepress, until his life and their secret flow out together."

The Meaning of Creative Activity in Elementary Education

VIKTOR LOWENFELD

If children developed without any interference from the outside world, no special stimulation for their creative work would be necessary. Every child would use his deeply rooted creative impulse without inhibition, confident in his own kind of expression. We find this creative confidence clearly demonstrated by those people who live in the remote sections of our country and who have not been inhibited by the influences of advertisements, funny books, and "education." Among these folk are found the most beautiful, natural, and clearest examples of children's art. What civilization has buried we must try to regain by recreating the natural base necessary for such free creation. Whenever we hear children say, "I can't draw that," we can be sure that some kind of interference has occurred in their lives. No Eskimo child would express such lack of confidence. These interferences might come from anywhere. To provide children with the kinds of stimulation necessary for their creative growth, it is important to examine some of the interferences that thwart such growth.

For the child, art is not the same as it is for the adult. Art for the child is merely a means of expression. Since the child's thinking is different from that of the adult's, his expression must also be different. Out of this discrepancy between the adult's "taste" and the way in which a child expresses himself arise most of the difficulties and interferences in art teaching. I have seen and heard educators, intrigued by the beauty of children's drawings and paintings, asking for the "right" proportions and "good" color schemes. The child sees the world differently from the way he draws it. Precisely from our analysis of this discrepancy between the representation and the thing represented do we gain insight into the child's real experience. Therefore it is easy to understand that *any* correction by the teacher which refers to reality, and not to the child's experience interferes greatly with the child's own expression. This interference starts perhaps when children scribble and eager parents expect to see something that fits their own adult conception. How ridiculous to overpower these little children's souls!

The seriousness of the problem of providing the appropriate stimulation every child needs for his work is illustrated by two typical case histories which follow:

The first is an example of the youngster who says, "I can't draw." The boy was completely incapable of (or better, inhibited from) producing any kind of picture. He did not want to draw a line. Under no circumstances could he be brought to use visual percepts. The child made a very nervous and unfree impression. His mother told me that he usually came home from school without speaking or telling anything of his experiences. He was very inhibited in his bodily movements. He had no friends at all.

Since nothing else availed, it occurred to me to try to distract his attention altogether from visual impressions, and I asked him to control his images by bodily feelings, which I emphasized by the choice of the topics. The stress was laid upon what the boy was doing and what he felt while doing it. The boy began to draw, and the more he drew, the more he drew out of proportion. He emphasized his experiences in proportions of value rather than in proportions of actual physical objects. At the same time, his mother reported that the boy had changed considerably, that he had begun to speak freely, that he was no longer shut in, that his nervousness had diminished, and that even his body movements were freer.

I investigated this case more closely and found that this child, the child of a teacher, had been influenced repeatedly to copy nature, to draw "beautifully" in correct proportions. Such an influence, which came in this case from the father, who wanted to see "good" and "nice" pictures and not the drawings of a child, had stifled the imagination of the child and diverted it into personal, rather than visual experiences. As the child learned that he could not draw as his father required (mothers usually have more instinct), he lost confidence in his creations and stopped his work. This loss of self-confidence inhibited the child as a whole. Encouraged to return to his own individual way of expression through the stimulation of his bodily feelings, the child found again his confidence in his own creations and his whole personality. What can we learn from this case? Don't impose your own images on a child! All modes of expression but the child's own are foreign to him. We should neither influence nor stimulate the child's imagination in any direction which is not appropriate to his thinking and perception. The child has his own world of experiences and expression.

The second case illustrates another way in which family influences upon art education may be unfortunate—the case of a brother and sister. The girl was very gifted; the boy just average. The girl, who was a very bright child, was always the favorite in the family; the boy was neglected. The girl drew very well. The boy, who could not draw as well as his sister, began to imitate her by taking over the same kind of representation his sister used in her drawings. He hoped this could be a way of getting the attention of his parents, as his sister got it with the same means. The boy became more and more bound up with a kind of representation that was not at all in accord with his own experience. It was as though he tried to speak a language that he was not able to understand. Whereas his sister was happy in creating new forms and thoughts, his anxiety to copy his sister prevented him from living his own life. So the child grew more and more sick mentally as well as emotionally. When he came home, he would throw himself on his bed and cry. His mother could not discover the reason. The child became extremely introverted. In this stage his mother brought the child to me. With my help, the boy returned to his former kind of expression and found again his own manner of representation, which I appreciated in the same way as I did that of his sister. Having found self-confidence in his own creations, the child grew happier, lost all the signs of disturbance, and was quite changed. The parents, very happy about this result (which required seven months to achieve) learned the correct way of showing their appreciation for both children.

What can we learn from this case? We see that through the efforts this boy made to compensate for his feelings of inferiority, he grew more and more fixed on a kind of representation that was not the expression of his own experiences. This fixation on strange expressions finally stopped the whole mental development of the child! Therefore, never prefer one child's creative work over that of another! Never give the work of one child as an example to another! Never let a child copy anything! This case exposes also the very devastating effect of the numerous color books which our children still get in school for the sake of "developing a sense of color," but which in reality inhibit their free creative development.

After this short introduction, the double function of art in the elementary-school classroom as self-expression and as a means of self-adjustment appears evident.

Self-Expression

The term "self-expression" has been misunderstood so often that I feel it necessary to clarify this term before using it. It would be wrong to think that self-expression means the expression of thoughts and ideas in general terms of content. This is the greatest mistake made in the use of this word. Thoughts and ideas can also be expressed imitatively. If one finds himself truly and originally occupied in any kind of medium, the outcome of this occupation and the mode of its expression are of decisive importance. What matters then is the mode of expression, not the content; not the "what" but the "how." That is why "scribbling" or, in another field of expression, "babbling," can be a means of self-expression as well as a potential high form of art creation. It can even happen that scribbling or babbling is a truer means of self-expression than a higher form of art, when the work of art moves from the sincere mode of expression to a form which is based upon the dependency on others, on imitation. In this connection it seems important to point out that the more primitive the stage of creative activity, the weaker the effect of such formal influences or interferences. The explanation of this fact seemingly lies in the nature of the more complex expression of art. Rarely can there be found a scribbling or babbling that is not a direct expression of an adequate mental and emotional state. However, more complex forms of art expression can be influenced easily by stronger personalities. This influence often grows to such an extent that complex forms of art, even in spite of technical perfection, lack completely the inner spirit or the adequate mental and emotional state of the "creator." They are, then, façades without substance, masks without life, condemned to die. However, this condemnation holds not only for the single art work, but also for the "creator," who cannot live because he cannot breathe with strange lungs. In the same way that a babbling child is unable to pronounce words correctly, even if urged to do so, a scribbling child if forced to draw "reality" can neither understand nor conceive what he is supposed to draw. Both would express themselves by strange means, which would not only inhibit them but would block their further development. This applies to all stages and all levels of creative activity. Such an education toward truth is one of the highest and deepest meanings of self-expression. This development toward freedom of expression, this great experience of individuals in finding themselves rests upon the knowledge of what truth is in art education. This knowledge cannot be achieved without a thorough study of what we can expect in modes of expression in the different age groups and on the different mental levels.

Self-Adjustment

Any work that is forced upon a person creates tension and dissatisfaction. When the individual feels unable to perform a task, he becomes conscious of his own insufficiencies and develops lack of confidence, or even feelings of inferiority. All this, as we have seen in the Introduction, can happen if art education is applied improperly and if children are urged to do something not appropriate to their development, or even if their work is criticized in a way that is not adjusted to the level of the child's ability to understand.

For instance, when a scribbling child, whose control of body movements is not developed to the extent that he can corrrelate them with his visual experiences, is forced to represent something "real," he not only would be unable to perform a task which depends upon ability to achieve such correlation, but the child may also lose confidence in his own means of expression (scribbling). The child might even become aware of the fact that he does not represent anything real. A child who expresses the importance of an object by overemphasizing it—like the Egyptians who drew the king larger than the servants—would become confused by criticism based on our visual sense of proportion. The child not having another means to determine the importance of the object, would first become aware of the inadequacy of his expression, would then lose confidence in his own experiences, and would finally start to measure proportions rigidly until blocked in his further development. Inhibited by such a stimulation, the child would then stop expressing himself altogether. "I can't draw it" would be the known indication for such a discouragement.

However, if the child expresses himself adequately and freely by repeating his motions during scribbling with ever greater certainty, by expressing importance with his own adequate means, by feeling and expressing his space experience (contradicting that of adults), the satisfaction from such creative work documents itself in the profound feelings of a great achievement. And we all know how achievements create confidence. Since it is an established fact that nearly every emotional or mental disturbance is connected with a lack of self-confidence, it is easily understood that the proper stimulation of the child's creative abilities will be a safeguard against such disturbances.

Besides this natural adjustive effect, there is another way of using creative activity as a type of therapy. A special chapter deals with this approach for the abnormal individual. Here I would like to point out the principles in the use of creative ability as a therapy for merely retarded or maladjusted children, who can be found everywhere. Three points will be of especial interest. (1) How can such deficiencies be recognized? (2) What is their nature? (3) What means for adjustment can be used?

Two characteristics in particular make it possible to recognize deficiencies from children's drawings:

1. If there is an abnormal discrepancy between chronological age and the development stage, which average periods of duration are given in our discussion, the existence of a mental retardation can be accepted as a certainty. For instance, if a child of seven years still scribbles, we can say that he is still concerned with the primitive experiences of uncontrolled kinesthetic feelings when he should feel the desire to represent something. The lower the mentality, the greater these discrepancies, and the greater will be the differences between chronological and mental age. Creative developmental stages, however, are always characterized by wide ranges in chronological age and in variety of forms of expression. Therefore, it is important to be flexible in the evaluation of creative products.

2. If a child is emotionally blocked, his rigid repetitions demonstrate his inability to express experiences. In both cases, I have found that the stimulation of body experiences leads to an adjustment of these deficiencies in a rather short time, if the deficiencies are not too deeply rooted. As an example, I would like to discuss a case of an exceedingly shy girl who could approach her playmates only with great difficulty and who showed in her representations a great deal of such rigid repetitions. I asked this girl to catch a ball which I had thrown high into the air, and I said, "Who can catch it sooner, you or I?" This competitive stimulus aroused in her a greater

insight into what she was doing. Then I asked her to draw this event. With repeated individual stimulation, she found such enjoyment in the newly gained correlation between her actions and her representations that she started to introduce all kinds of experiences as her own contribution. Thus, she gained, through this constant correlation between herself and her drawings, a more conscious and free relationship to the world around her, which finally helped her completely to overcome her shyness. Although this analysis does not pretend to be scientific (such an analysis would require a more specific treatment of this special question beyond the limits of this textbook) the success which results from using this method of therapy makes it worth mentioning even in this very concise way. In the last chapter of this book questions of this kind are treated in more detail. In summary, it seems important to point out the contrasting effects upon the child's development of creative activity as a means of self-expression and as a means of mere imitation.

Self-expression we have defined as the appropriate mode of expression according to the age level of the child. Imitation, however, is expression according to adult, or at least foreign, levels. If the child expresses himself according to his own level, he becomes encouraged in his own independent thinking by expressing his own thoughts and ideas by *his own* means. The child who imitates becomes dependent in his thinking, since he relies for his thoughts and expressions upon others. The independent, thinking child will not only express whatever comes into his mind but will tackle any problem, emotional or mental, that he encounters in life. Thus his expression serves also as an emotional outlet.

Dependent thinking, however, restricts the child in his choice of subject matter as well as in his mode of expression. Since the imitative child cannot give expression to his own thoughts and emotions, his dependency leads directly to feelings of frustration. The child who uses creative activity as an emotional outlet will gain freedom and flexibility as a result of the release of unnecessary tensions. However, the child who feels frustrated develops inhibitions and, as a result, will feel restricted in his personality. The child who has developed freedom and flexibility in his expression will be able to face new situations without difficulties. Through his flexible approaches toward the expression of his own ideas, he will not only face new situations properly but will adjust himself to them easily. The inhibited and restricted child, accustomed to imitating rather than expressing himself creatively, will prefer to go along set patterns in life. He will not be able to adjust to new situations quickly but will rather try to lean upon others as the easiest way out. Since it is generally accepted that progress, success, and happiness in life depend greatly upon the ability to adjust to new situations, the importance of art education for personality growth and development can easily be recognized.

The following diagram depicts clearly what has been said in the foregoing summary:

Self-Expression	contrasted with	Imitation
Expression according to child's own level	———————	Expression according to strange level
Independent thinking	———————	Dependent thinking
Emotional outlet	———————	Frustration
Freedom and Flexibility	———————	Inhibitions and restrictions
Easy adjustment to new situations	———————	Going along set patterns
Progress, success, happiness	———————	Leaning toward others, dependency, stiffness

THE TEACHER'S NEED FOR KNOWING DEVELOPMENTAL STAGES

As has been pointed out, the need for properly stimulating the child derives from the basic psychological connection between the child's emotional experience, his mental level, and his creative expression. It is this psychological connection which we have to study. Since subject matter in creative activity has such a different meaning from that in other fields, a thorough clarification of the relationships between developmental stages and subject matter is necessary. In arithmetic, for instance, only a gradual increase in the difficulty and amount of subject matter will allow the child to grasp it properly. According to the child's mental development, the amount and difficulty of subject matter is thoroughly balanced. The child starts by learning the single symbols for numbers. Then he learns to count, to add, to subtract, to multiply, and so forth.

How does subject matter relate to creative expression and how is subject matter in creative activity related to the mental stages of the child? Before answering these important questions, it is necessary to clarify the meaning of subject matter in creative activity.

Whereas subject matter in other fields is almost exclusively related to content, in creative expression it is quite different. The content, the "what" we represent, are trees, houses, plants, flowers, men, and so forth. In creative activity there is no changing subject matter which must be taught, because the same subject matter is used in all the various age levels. There is no orderly sequence of subject matter, as in arithmetic or other fields. A man can be drawn by a five-year-old child or by a sixteen-year-old youth. What then can be expected to be the difference in teaching a five-year-old child or a sixteen-year-old youth? The difference in teaching of arithmetic is evident. There, the child may first learn to distinguish between one and two, and later he will study the higher forms of mathematics. Subject matter in creative art, as stated above, does not change during the different age levels. It is determined by "man and environment" throughout elementary-school levels and beyond. "Man and environment" do not change. *What changes is our subjective relationship with man and environment.* It is this subjective relationship between the world and ourselves that has to be studied in order to know how to stimulate a child properly according to his age level. A "man" to a five-year-old child means mainly the self, the ego, which needs a head for thinking and eating and two legs for running (head-feet representation). For a ten-year-old child, a "man" still means mainly a projection of the self. However, consciously aware of the variety of man's actions, movements, and body parts, the ten-year-old represents "man" accordingly. A sixteen-year-old youth, however, has already discovered that man is a part of environment and he represents "man" with conscious consideration of size and proportions in comparison to what surrounds him. So changes a tree—for a five-year-old child the tree is something undifferentiated, a trunk and something indefinite on top; for a ten-year-old, the tree is a trunk with branches to climb on; and for a sixteen-year-old youngster, a tree is a part of the environment, with which he is acquainted in detail. The subjective relationship of these young people to the tree has changed entirely, though it is still the same tree—the same subject matter. This makes it clear that it would be entirely wrong to teach how to draw a tree or a man. Moreover it would be beyond the comprehension of a five-year-old child to perceive or understand a tree in all its details as a part of environment. He would not even be able to take in an explanation of the realistic meaning of a tree. Accordingly a "perfect" drawing of a tree with all its details would be entirely out of place. "Perfect" is a relative value judgment, and in creative activity it means "perfect" in relationship to the child's experience. "Perfect" for a five-year-old child is a representative symbol for tree. It would be unnatural if the child drew it realistically with all details. Hence, it is clear that "subject matter" must be more confined to the "how" than to the "what." In creative activity subject matter is based upon *the subjective experience of man and environment according to the various age levels.* A proper application of subject matter in creative activity requires the study of the change of the subjective relationship of the child to man and environment throughout the age levels. There is no subject matter "tree," only the different ways a tree is experienced in the various years of life. However, since there are so many possible ways of drawing a tree in each school grade and since there are besides trees, an almost unlimited number of things in the environment, it will be necessary to investigate the common base of children's experiences. This investigation will lead to the understanding of all the various forms of expression used in their representations.

The answer to the question, "What makes the child express one and the same thing differently at different age levels?" will be of essential importance for the understanding of the child's creative work. It also will be significant for the nature of stimulation on the part of the teacher. What makes a child of four or five years express a man by drawing only a head and two legs? Does this really represent the child's knowledge of a human being? Certainly, every four- or five-year-old child knows that we have a body, two arms, hands, and even fingers. He even knows that we have fingernails if his attention is directed towards them. But no child of this age would ever draw such details. *What the child draws is his subjective experience of what is important to him during the act of drawing.* Therefore, the child only draws what is *actively* in his mind. Thus in such a drawing of a "man" we get only a report of the *active knowledge* the child has of a man while he was drawing. *In other words, the drawing gives us an excellent record of the things which are of especial mental or emotional importance to the child.*

Still another factor has to be taken into consideration as an important means for the proper stimulation of a child's creative activity. The change of the child's *relationship* to environment involves *emotional* as well as *mental* growth. This is one of the most important facts in the child's emotional and social adjustment. The child, depending upon the help and care of others (at the beginning on the parents), does not feel the necessity of cooperating or collaborating with others. His most important experience is the experience of the self. That is why his spatial correlations are very indefinite in the beginning. The growing interdependence between the child and his environment is expressed in his drawings. If, in this emotional experience, the experience of perceiving environment sensually (bodily, kinesthetically, or visually) is included, the investigation of the child's relationship to what surrounds him is placed on a broader base. This investigation still lacks an important part if size, dimensions, distance, and relative proportions of the self to environment are not also included. The differences in the concept of size and distance of children and adults point clearly to the psychological importance of these questions. Distances and sizes which appeared large in childhood appear different to the adult. But since these psychological questions of the child's relationship to outside experiences can scarcely come under the heading "environment," all these experiences are put together under "space"—experiences in space or of space. To simplify matters, *all experiences that refer to things outside of our body will be regarded as experiences of space.*

As a result of this discussion, it can be understood why no proper stimulation of the child's creative activity can be given without a thorough knowledge of what changes may be expected, at the various developmental stages, in the child's subjective relationship to man and environment.

Experience and Thinking

JOHN DEWEY

1. The Nature of Experience

The nature of experience can be understood only by noting that it includes an active and a passive element peculiarly combined. On the active hand, experience is *trying*—a meaning which is made explicit in the connected term experiment. On the passive, it is *undergoing*. When we experience something we act upon it, we do something with it; then we suffer or undergo the consequences. We do something to the thing and then it does something to us in return: such is the peculiar combination. The connection of these two phases of experience measures the fruitfulness or value of the experience. Mere activity does not constitute experience. It is dispersive, centrifugal, dissipating. Experience as trying involves change, but change is meaningless transition unless it is consciously connected with the return wave of consequences which flow from it. When an activity is continued *into* the undergoing of consequences, when the change made by action is reflected back into a change made in us, the mere flux is loaded with significance. We learn something. It is not experience when a child merely sticks his finger into a flame; it is experience when the movement is connected with the pain which he undergoes in consequence. Henceforth the sticking of the finger into flame *means* a burn. Being burned is a mere physical change, like the burning of a stick of wood, if it is not perceived as a consequence of some other action.

Blind and capricious impulses hurry us on heedlessly from one thing to another. So far as this happens, everything is writ in water. There is none of that cumulative growth which makes an experience in any vital sense of that term. On the other hand, many things happen to us in the way of pleasure and pain which we do not connect with any prior activity of our own. They are mere accidents so far as we are concerned. There is no before or after to such experience; no retrospect nor outlook, and consequently no meaning. We get nothing which may be carried over to foresee what is likely to happen next, and no gain in ability to adjust ourselves to what is coming—no added control. Only by courtesy can such an experience be called experience. To "learn from experience" is to make a backward and forward connection between what we do to things and what we enjoy or suffer from things in consequence. Under such conditions, doing becomes a trying; an experiment with the world to find out what it is like; the undergoing becomes instruction—discovery of the connection of things.

Two conclusions important for education follow. (1) Experience is primarily an active-passive affair; it is not primarily cognitive. But (2) the *measure of the value* of an experience lies in the perception of relationships or continuities to which it leads up. It includes cognition in the degree in which it is cumulative or amounts to something, or has meaning. In schools, those under instruction are too customarily looked upon as acquiring knowledge as theoretical spectators, minds which appropriate knowledge by direct energy of intellect. The very word pupil has almost come to mean one who is engaged not in having fruitful experiences but in absorbing knowledge directly. Something which is called mind or consciousness is severed from the physical organs of activity. The former is then thought to be purely intellectual and cognitive; the latter to be an irrelevant and intruding physical factor. The intimate union of activity and undergoing its consequences which leads to recognition of meaning is broken; instead we have two fragments: mere bodily action on one side, and meaning directly grasped by 'spiritual' activity on the other.

It would be impossible to state adequately the evil results which have flowed from this dualism of mind and body, much less to exaggerate them. Some of the more striking effects, may, however, be enumerated. (*a*) In part bodily activity becomes an intruder. Having nothing, so it is thought, to do with mental activity, it becomes a distraction, an evil to be contended with. For the pupil has a body, and brings it to school along with his mind. And the body is, of necessity, a wellspring of energy; it has to do something. But its activities, not being utilized in occupation with things which yield significant results, have to be frowned upon. They lead the pupil away from the lesson with which his 'mind' ought to be occupied; they are sources of mischief. The chief source of the 'problem of discipline' in schools is that the teacher has often to spend the larger part of the time in suppressing the bodily activities which take the mind away from its material. A premium is put on physical quietude; on silence, on rigid uniformity of posture and movement; upon a machine-like simulation of the attitudes of intelligent interest. The teachers' business is to hold the pupils up to these requirements and to punish the inevitable deviations which occur.

The nervous strain and fatigue which result with both teacher and pupil are a necessary consequence of the abnormality of the situation in which bodily activity is divorced from the perception of meaning. Callous indifference and explosions from strain alternate. The neglected body, having no organized fruitful channels of activity, breaks forth, without knowing why or how, into meaningless boisterousness, or settles into equally meaningless fooling—both very different from the normal play of children. Physically active children become restless and unruly; the more quiescent, so-called conscientious ones spend what energy they have in the negative task of keeping their instincts and active tendencies suppressed, instead of in a positive one of constructive planning and execution; they are thus educated not into responsibility for the significant and graceful use of bodily powers, but into an enforced duty not to give them free play. It may be seriously asserted that a chief cause for the remarkable achievements of Greek education was that it was never misled by false notions into an attempted separation of mind and body.

(b) Even, however, with respect to the lessons which have to be learned by the application of 'mind,' some bodily activities have to be used. The senses—especially the eye and ear—have to be employed to take in what the book, the map, the blackboard, and the teacher say. The lips and vocal organs, and the hands, have to be used to reproduce in speech and writing what has been stowed away. The senses are then regarded as a kind of mysterious conduit through which information is conducted from the external world into the mind; they are spoken of as gateways and avenues of knowledge. To keep the eyes on the book and the ears open to the teacher's words is a mysterious source of intellectual grace. Moreover, reading, writing, and figuring—important school arts—demand muscular or motor training. The muscles of eye, hand, and vocal organs accordingly have to to trained to act as pipes for carrying knowledge back out of the mind into external action. For it happens that using the muscles repeatedly in the same way fixes in them an automatic tendency to repeat.

The obvious result is a mechanical use of the bodily activities which (in spite of the generally obtrusive and interfering character of the body in mental action) have to be employed more or less. For the senses and muscles are used not as organic participants in having an instructive experience, but as external inlets and outlets of mind. Before the child goes to school, he learns with his hand, eye, and ear, because they are organs of the process of doing something from which meaning results. The boy flying a kite has to keep his eye on the kite, and has to note the various pressures of the string on his hand. His senses are avenues of knowledge not because external facts are somehow 'conveyed' to the brain, but because they are *used* in doing something with a purpose. The qualities of seen and touched things have a bearing on what is done, and are alertly perceived; they have a meaning. But when pupils are expected to use their eyes to note the form of words, irrespective of their meaning, in order to reproduce them in spelling or reading, the resulting training is simply of isolated sense organs and muscles. It is such isolation of an act from a purpose which makes it mechanical. It is customary for teachers to urge children to read with expression, so as to bring out the meaning. But if they originally learned the sensory-motor technique of reading—the ability to identify forms and to reproduce the sounds they stand for—by methods which did not call for attention to meaning, a mechanical habit was established which makes it difficult to read subsequently with intelligence. The vocal organs have been trained to go their own way automatically in isolation; and meaning cannot be tied on at will. Drawing, singing, and writing may be taught in the same mechanical way; for, we repeat, any way *is* mechanical which

narrows down the bodily activity so that a separation of body from mind—
that is, from recognition of meaning—is set up. Mathematics, even in its
higher branches, when undue emphasis is put upon the technique of
calculation, and science, when laboratory exercises are given for their
own sake, suffer from the same evil.

(c) On the intellectual side, the separation of 'mind' from direct
occupation with things throws emphasis on *things* at the expense of *relations* or connections. It is altogether too common to separate perceptions
and even ideas from judgments. The latter are thought to come after the
former in order to compare them. It is alleged that the mind perceives
things apart from relations; that it forms ideas of them in isolation from
their connections—with what goes before and comes after. Then judgment
or thought is called upon to combine the separated items of 'knowledge'
so that their resemblance or casual connection shall be brought out. As
matter of fact, every perception and every idea is a sense of the bearings,
use, and cause, of a thing. We do not really know a chair or have an idea
of it by inventorying and enumerating its various isolated qualities, but only
by bringing these qualities into connection with something else—the purpose
which makes it a chair and not a table; or its difference from the kind of chair
we are accustomed to, or the 'period' which it represents, and so on. A wagon
is not perceived when all its parts are summed up; it is the characteristic
connection of the parts which makes it a wagon. And these connections
are not those of mere physical juxtaposition; they involve connection with
the animals that draw it, the things that are carried on it, and so on.
Judgment is employed in the perception; otherwise the perception is mere
sensory excitation or else a recognition of the result of a prior judgment, as in
the case of familiar objects.

Words, the counters for ideas, are, however, easily taken for ideas. And
in just the degree in which mental activity is separated from active concern
with the world, from doing something and connecting the doing with
what is undergone, words, symbols, come to take the place of ideas. The
substitution is the more subtle because *some* meaning is recognized. But
we are very easily trained to be content with a minimum of meaning, and
to fail to note how restricted is our perception of the relations which confer
significance. We get so thoroughly used to a kind of pseudo-idea, a half
perception, that we are not aware how half-dead our mental action is,
and how much keener and more extensive our observations and ideas
would be if we formed them under conditions of a vital experience which
required us to use judgment: to hunt for the connections of the thing
dealt with.

There is no difference of opinion as to the theory of the matter. All
authorities agree that that discernment of relationships is the genuinely
intellectual matter; hence, the educative matter. The failure arises in
supposing that relationships can become perceptible without *experience*—
without that conjoint trying and undergoing of which we have spoken.

It is assumed that 'mind' can grasp them if it will only give attention, and that this attention may be given at will irrespective of the situation. Hence the deluge of half-observations, of verbal ideas, and unassimilated 'knowledge' which afflicts the world. An ounce of experience is better than a ton of theory simply because it is only in experience that any theory has vital and verifiable significance. An experience, a very humble experience, is capable of generating and carrying any amount of theory (or intellectual content), but a theory apart from an experience cannot be definitely grasped even as theory. It tends to become a mere verbal formula, a set of catchwords used to render thinking, or genuine theorizing, unnecessary and impossible. Because of our education we use words, thinking they are ideas, to dispose of questions, the disposal being in reality simply such an obscuring of perception as prevents us from seeing any longer the difficulty.

2. Reflection in Experience

Thought or reflection, as we have already seen virtually if not explicitly, is the discernment of the relation between what we try to do and what happens in consequence. No experience having a meaning is possible without some element of thought. But we may contrast two types of experience according to the proportion of reflection found in them. All our experiences have a phase of 'cut and try' in them—what psychologists call the method of trial and error. We simply do something, and when it fails, we do something else, and keep on trying till we hit upon something which works, and then we adopt that method as a rule of thumb measure in subsequent procedure. Some experiences have very little else in them than this hit and miss or succeed process. We see *that* a certain way of acting and a certain consequence are connected, but we do not see *how* they are. We do not see the details of the connection; the links are missing. Our discernment is very gross. In other cases we push our observation farther. We analyze to see just what lies between so as to bind together cause and effect, activity and consequence. This extension of our insight makes foresight more accurate and comprehensive. The action which rests simply upon the trial and error method is at the mercy of circumstances; they may change so that the act performed does not operate in the way it was expected to. But if we know in detail upon what the result depends, we can look to see whether the required conditions are there. The method extends our practical control. For if some of the conditions are missing, we may, if we know what the needed antecedents for an effect are, set to work to supply them; or, if they are such as to produce undesirable effects as well, we may eliminate some of the superfluous causes and economize effort.

In discovery of the detailed connections of our activities and what happens in consequence, the thought implied in cut and try experience is made explicit. Its quantity increases so that its proportionate value is very different. Hence the quality of the experience changes; the change is so significant that we may call this type of experience reflective—that is, reflective *par excellence*. The deliberate cultivation of this phase of thought constitutes thinking as a distinctive experience. Thinking, in other words, is the intentional endeavor to discover *specific* connections between something which we do and the consequences which result, so that the two become continuous. Their isolation, and consequently their purely arbitrary going together, is cancelled; a unified developing situation takes its place. The occurrence is now understood; it is explained; it is reasonable, as we say, that the thing should happen as it does.

Thinking is thus equivalent to an explicit rendering of the intelligent element in our experience. It makes it possible to act with an end in view. It is the condition of our having aims. As soon as an infant begins to *expect* he begins to use something which is now going on as a sign of something to follow; he is, in however simple a fashion, judging. For he takes one thing as *evidence* of something else, and so recognizes a relationship. Any future development, however elaborate it may be, is only an extending and a refining of this simple act of inference. All that the wisest man can do is to observe what is going on more widely and more minutely and then select more carefully from what is noted just those factors which point to something to happen. The opposites, once more, to thoughtful action are routine and capricious behavior. The former accepts what has been customary as a full measure of possibility and omits to take into account the connections of the particular things done. The latter makes the momentary act a measure of value, and ignores the connections of our personal action with the energies of the environment. It says, virtually, 'things are to be just as I happen to like them at this instant,' as routine says in effect 'let things continue just as I have found them in the past.' Both refuse to acknowledge responsibility for the future consequences which flow from present action. Reflection is the acceptance of such responsibility.

The starting point of any process of thinking is something going on, something which just as it stands is incomplete or unfulfilled. Its point, its meaning lies literally in what it is going to be, in how it is going to turn out. As this is written, the world is filled with the clang of contending armies. For an active participant in the war, it is clear that the momentous thing is the issue, the future consequences, of this and that happening. He is identified, for the time at least, with the issue; *his* fate hangs upon the course things are taking. But even for an onlooker in a neutral country, the significance of every move made, of every advance here and retreat there, lies in what it portends. To *think* upon the news as it comes to us is to attempt to see what is indicated as probable or possible regarding an outcome. To fill our heads, like a scrapbook, with this and that item as a finished and done-for thing, is not to think. It is to turn ourselves into a piece of registering apparatus. To consider the *bearing* of the occurrence upon what may be, but is not yet, is to think. Nor will the reflective experience be different in kind if we substitute distance in time for separation in space. Imagine the war done with, and a future historian giving an account of it. The episode is, by assumption, past. But he cannot give a thoughtful account of the war save as he preserves the time sequence; the meaning of each occurrence, as he deals with it, lies in what was future for *it*, though not for the historian. To take it by itself as a complete existence is to take it unreflectively.

Reflection also implies concern with the issue—a certain sympathetic identification of our own destiny, if only dramatic, with the outcome of the course of events. For the general in the war, or a common soldier, or a citizen of one of the contending nations, the stimulus to thinking is direct and urgent. For neutrals, it is indirect and dependent upon imagination. But the flagrant partisanship of human nature is evidence of the intensity of the tendency to identify ourselves with one possible course of events, and to reject the other as foreign. If we cannot take sides in overt action, and throw in our little weight to help determine the final balance, we take sides emotionally and imaginatively. We desire this or that outcome. One wholly indifferent to the outcome does not follow or think about what is happening at all. From this dependence of the act of thinking upon a sense of sharing in the consequences of what goes on, flows one of the chief paradoxes of thought. Born in partiality, in order to accomplish its tasks it must achieve a certain detached impartiality. The general who allows his hopes and desires to affect his observations and interpretations of the existing situation will surely make a mistake in calculation. While hopes and fears may be the chief motive for a thoughtful following of the war on the part of an onlooker in a neutral country, he too will think ineffectively in the degree in which his preferences modify the stuff of his observations and reasonings. There is, however, no incompatibility between the fact that the occcasion of reflection lies in a personal sharing in what is going on and the fact that the value of the reflection lies upon keeping one's self out of the data. The almost insurmountable difficulty of achieving this detachment is evidence that thinking originates in situations where the course of thinking is an actual part of the course of events and is designed to influence the result. Only gradually and with a widening of the area of vision through a growth of social sympathies does thinking develop to include what lies beyond our *direct* interests: a fact of great significance for education.

To say that thinking occurs with reference to situations which are still going on, and incomplete, is to say that thinking occurs when things are uncertain or doubtful or problematic. Only what is finished, completed, is wholly assured. Where there is reflection there is suspense. The object of thinking is to help *reach* a conclusion, to project a possible termination on the basis of what is already given. Certain other facts about thinking accompany this feature. Since the situation in which thinking occurs is a doubtful one, thinking is a process of inquiry, of looking into things, of investigating. Acquiring is always secondary, and instrumental to the act of *inquiring*. It is seeking, a quest, for something that is not at hand.

We sometimes talk as if "original research" were a peculiar prerogative of scientists or at least of advanced students. But all thinking is research, and all research is native, original, with him who carries it on, even if everybody else in the world already is sure of what he is still looking for.

It also follows that all thinking involves a risk. Certainty cannot be guaranteed in advance. The invasion of the unknown is of the nature of an adventure; we cannot be sure in advance. The conclusions of thinking, till confirmed by the event, are, accordingly, more or less tentative or hypothetical. Their dogmatic assertion as final is unwarranted, short of the issue, in fact. The Greeks acutely raised the question: How can we learn? For either we know already what we are after, or else we do not know. In neither case is learning possible; on the first alternative because we know already; on the second, because we do not know what to look for, nor if, by chance, we find it can we tell that it is what we were after. The dilemma makes no provision for *coming* to know, for learning; it assumes either complete knowledge or complete ignorance. Nevertheless the twilight zone of inquiry, of thinking, exists. The possibility of *hypothetical* conclusions, of *tentative* results, is the fact which the Greek dilemma overlooked. The perplexities of the situation suggest certain ways out. We try these ways, and either push our way out, in which case we know we have found what we were looking for, or the situation gets darker and more confused—in which case, we know we are still ignorant. Tentative means trying out, feeling one's way along provisionally. Taken by itself, the Greek argument is a nice piece of formal logic. But it is also true that as long as men kept a sharp disjunction between knowledge and ignorance, science made only slow and accidental advance. Systematic advance in invention and discovery began when men recognized that they could utilize doubt for purposes of inquiry by forming conjectures to guide action in tentative explorations, whose development would confirm, refute, or modify the guiding conjecture. While the Greeks made knowledge more than learning, modern science makes conserved knowledge only a means to learning, to discovery.

To recur to our illustration. A commanding general cannot base his actions upon either absolute certainty or absolute ignorance. He has a certain amount of information at hand which is, we will assume, reasonably trustworthy. He then *infers* certain prospective movements, thus assigning meaning to the bare facts of the given situation. His inference is more or less dubious and hypothetical. But he acts upon it. He develops a plan of procedure, a method of dealing with the situation. The consequences which directly follow from his acting this way rather than that test and reveal the worth of his reflections. What he already knows functions and has value in what he learns. But will this account apply in the case of the one in a neutral country who is thoughtfully following as best he can the progress of events? In form, yes, though not of course in content. It is self-evident that his guesses about the future indicated by present facts, guesses by which he attempts to supply meaning to a multitude of disconnected data, cannot be the basis of a method which shall take effect in the campaign. *That* is not *his* problem. But in the degree in which he is actively thinking, and not merely passively following the course of events, his tentative inferences will take effect in *a* method of procedure appropriate to *his* situation. He will anticipate certain future moves, and will be on the alert to see whether they happen or not. In the degree in which he is intellectually concerned, or thoughtful, he will be *actively* on the lookout; he will take steps which although they do not affect the campaign, modify in some degree *his* subsequent actions. Otherwise his later "I told you so" has no intellectual quality at all; it does not mark any testing or verification of prior thinking, but only a coincidence that yields emotional satisfaction—and includes a large factor of self-deception.

The case is comparable to that of an astronomer who from given data has been led to foresee (infer) a future eclipse. No matter how great the mathematical probability, the inference is hypothetical—a matter of probability.[1] The hypothesis as to the date and position of the anticipated eclipse becomes the material of forming a method of future conduct. Apparatus is arranged; possibly an expedition is made to some far part of the globe. In any case, some active steps are taken which actually change *some* physical conditions. And apart from such steps and the consequent modification of the situation, there is no completion of the act of thinking. It remains suspended. Knowledge, already attained knowledge, controls thinking and makes it fruitful.

So much for the general features of a reflective experience. They are (*i*) perplexity, confusion, doubt, due to the fact that one is implicated in an incomplete situation whose full character is not yet determined; (*ii*) a conjectural anticipation—a tentative interpretation of the given elements, attributing to them a tendency to effect certain consequences; (*iii*) a careful survey (examination, inspection, exploration, analysis) of all attainable consideration which will define and clarify the problem in hand; (*iv*) a consequent elaboration of the tentative hypothesis to make it more precise and more consistent, because squaring with a wider range of facts; (*v*) taking one stand upon the projected hypothesis as a plan of action which is applied to the existing state of affairs: doing something overtly to bring about the anticipated result, and thereby testing the hypothesis. It is the extent and accuracy of steps three and four which mark off a distinctive reflective experience from one on the trial and error plane. They make *thinking* itself into an experience. Nevertheless, we never get wholly beyond the trial and error situation. Our most elaborate and rationally consistent thought has to be tried in the world and thereby tried out. And since it can never take into account all the connections, it can never cover with perfect accuracy all the consequences. Yet a thoughtful survey of conditions is so careful, and the

---

[1] It is most important for the practice of science that men in many cases can calculate the degree of probability and the amount of probable error involved, but that does not alter the features of the situation as described. It refines them.

guessing at results so controlled, that we have a right to mark off the reflective experience from the grosser trial and error forms of action.

Summary
In determining the place of thinking in experience we first noted that experience involves a connection of doing or trying with something which is undergone in consequence. A separation of the active doing phase from the passive undergoing phase destroys the vital meaning of an experience. Thinking is the accurate and deliberate instituting of connections between what is done and its consequences. It notes not only that they are connected, but the details of the connection. It makes connecting links explicit in the form of relationships. The stimulus to thinking is found when we wish to determine the significance of some act, performed or to be performed. Then we anticipate consequences. This implies that the situation as it stands is, either in fact or to us, incomplete and hence indeterminate. The projection of consequences means a proposed or tentative solution. To perfect this hypothesis, existing conditions have to be carefully scrutinized and the implications of the hypothesis developed—an operation called reasoning. Then the suggested solution—the idea or theory—has to be tested by acting upon it. If it brings about certain consequences, certain determinate changes, in the world, it is accepted as valid. Otherwise it is modified, and another trial made. Thinking includes all of these steps—the sense of a problem, the observation of conditions, the formation and rational elaboration of a suggested conclusion, and the active experimental testing. While all thinking results in knowledge, ultimately the value of knowledge is subordinate to its use in thinking. For we live not in a settled and finished world, but in one which is going on, and where our main task is prospective, and where retrospect—and all knowledge as distinct from thought is retrospect—is of value in the solidity, security, and fertility it affords our dealings with the future.

Society, Art, and Education

JUNE KING MC FEE

The purpose of this paper is to stimulate further inquiry into the relationships between society, art, and education for possible directives for curriculum development in art. Identifying relationships among fields as complex as contemporary society, the broad aspects of the visual arts, and present day education is a nebulous undertaking. The materials that follow are based upon one individual's selection and analysis from the research and study

Reprinted by permission from *A Seminar in Art Education for Research and Curriculum Development*, Cooperative Research Project No. J-002, The Pennsylvania State University, 1966 Copyright. University Park, Pa.

that are available, and can only be presented to you within this qualifying framework.

Most of us would agree, I think, that this country is in a period of intense social change. Increased consciousness of minority groups and their emergence are challenging stereotypes and prejudice. Automation and population increase are affecting our concepts of leisure and of work. Social organization and human behavior are affected by the increase of megapolis and changes in urban and rural environs. World problems, with the accelerating speed of communication and transportation, become community problems. Art educators' individual reactions to change probably run the gamut of those found among diverse groups in the larger society. We may be retreating from the changes by refusing to recognize them, or we may be trying to solve the conflicts they present with old solutions to old problems. Others of us may be overwhelmed into inaction by the complexities presented, or isolate ourselves by believing that our area of education or profession is not involved, that social problems belong to political scientists and sociologists but certainly not to individuals in the arts.

Our reaction depends in part on our concepts of the nature of art and its relationship to humanity. We cannot begin to explore the relationships between art and society without assessing our basic assumptions about art, for these assumptions condition our inquiry.

If we believe that art is to be produced and enjoyed only by an aesthetic and intellectual elite or subculture of our total society, then we might have reason for believing in social isolation of the arts. If, on the other hand, we consider art as a phenomenon of human behavior to be found wherever form, line, color are used to create symbols for communication and to qualitatively change the nature of experience, then art is related in some degree to all of society. If we accept this definition we, as art educators, become involved in problems of society and social change; we recognize art as one of the major communication systems of social interaction and of society in transition.

Definitions

The word art is often used to both denote and to qualify. We compare two objects by saying one is, but the other is not, *art*, when in actuality they may have many characteristics in common. Cultural anthropologists tend to identify most examples of visual symbolism and embellishment as art. This is a denoting, identifying function and does not necessarily make a value judgment about the quality of the art form. Much of commercial illustration is often derided as "non-art," yet form, line, color, and texture are used in some kind of composition or design to express ideas, conditions, or feelings. In our so-called "popular culture" we find myriad examples, where the elements and principles of art are used. The anthropologist would identify them as art. Further, the like-dislike behavior of a large majority of our students is learned within the context of the art in popular culture. As educators, we need a better structure of our terminology, so denoting and qualifying are not confused. We need other concepts and criteria for evaluating all the visual arts, fine, commercial, applied, to identify and evaluate their quality—integrity, impact, improvisation, organization or design quality and use of media. If we continue using art both to denote and to qualify we will deprive students of the aesthetic criteria they need to evaluate all phases of art.

As this thesis is developed it will become clearer, I hope, why the denotative concept of art is necessary if art education is to respond to the social demands of the day. Specifically, in contemporary society art is used in the full range from the sentimental to the profound, the superficial to the intrinsic, the commonplace to the unique, the repetitious to the divergent, the tawdry to the refined. Examples from each stage of these continua can be found in all of the major visual communication systems:

those traditionally called the fine arts,
in all product design including the handcrafted to the mass produced,
in all advertising, display, and packaging,
in architecture, city planning, and urban renewal,
in television, publications, and moving pictures,
in interiors and costume design.

Further, art exists in the present conditions of our cities and towns, representing many periods and copies of periods, in assorted states of preservation or decay. The whole broad face of America expresses values and attitudes through art forms and their condition. The art quality ranges from the sublime to the odious, and *students must have qualifying concepts to evaluate the whole range* if they are to make aesthetic discriminations as citizens in a democracy.

The Functions of Art

Art has varying functions in the lives of mankind which need to be considered as we develop curricula in art for students from various subcultures as they in turn are affected by social change. Some degree and combination of these functions of art are found in all cultures past and present.[1] Art is used to maintain the values, attitudes, and sense of reality from one generation to another. It is used to give character, identity and status to groups of people, individuals, institutions through mutually understood symbols—the styles of architecture and costume. Almost all religions use art forms to create their effective environment and stimulate the essence of worship. Political systems use non-verbal symbols to encourage recall of the values upheld. A symbol may have many meanings depending upon its variation. People with different backgrounds bring somewhat different sets of concepts into play when seeing it. The cross, for example, has pre- and post-Christian meanings and many derivations—a Maltese cross, a Latin cross and a burning cross stimulate recall of different concepts and emotions.

Some cultures use art for "group-self-reflection" as in social criticism and satire; for education to identify patterns of behavior, eras of history, significant ideas. Finally, art is used in more subtle, but often more immediate emerging expressions of the essence of being and direct interaction, using less literate symbols of form and composition.

Culture and Society

The concepts culture and society have, like most terms, evolved with usage. They are sometimes used differently in the different social disciplines. In this paper society is used to mean an organization of people whose interaction patterns cluster them as a group. The United States is a large society that, through a system of government and interaction, separates it from other national governments. *Culture* is used to identify the values, attitudes, and acceptable behavior of people from a common heritage. A classroom can be considered a society as it has a pattern of interrelations among its members. Within the classroom there may be many cultures represented, children who have backgrounds that have influenced the development of quite different values, belief systems, and concepts of acceptable behavior. Cultures vary with different socio-economic classes, religions, ethnic backgrounds, urban or rural environment, and geographic area. Our overall American society may have a broad identifiable culture, but it has many subcultures, large and small sub-societies.

Social class is identified by studying the ways groups of people relate themselves to other people, to economic level, and in some degree to behavioral patterns. Class stratification in this country is a reality that is often ignored by our idealism. Though there is considerable overlapping, shifting in an open society, there are identifiable differences between groups. They tend to share that which is called American culture, but they have distinct subcultural characteristics. Each ethnic group within a socio-economic class tends to vary in cultural pattern. Though social classes have general likenesses throughout the country, there are also regional differences, and differences if the groups are living in rural or urban areas.

A new term used by the sociologist Milton M. Gordon is particularly useful.[2] It is *ethclass*. He finds it necessary in describing the ethnic groups within the different economic strata of society. As more and more members of minority groups move into the middle and upper middle class, ethnic identification alone becomes inadequate to describe them, for they identify increasingly with mores of their social status. As this takes place more cultural diversity will be found within economic groups.

Gordon finds two conflicting trends in America. One is a pressure for conformity, due to middle class oriented education and the extent and intensity of mass communications.[3] *The other* trend is that subcultures of race, religion, national origin, and economic level are much stronger than has been assumed.[4] This is in-group cohesion and persistence of cultural values and attitudes shows signs of increase. Most people's primary group interaction is within their subculture, while their secondary group activities tend to be within the larger society. Gordon finds that most of the professional and business leadership of the country comes from the middle class core culture, and from those members of other groups who have learned this core culture.[5] Another interesting trend which he identifies is the development of an intellectual subculture which includes some members of the academic community, the arts, and some of the upper levels of journalism, law, and medicine. Within this group ethnic differences are maintained by some, but there are also those who leave their ethnic subculture to become mainly part of the intellectual community.[6]

To those trained in education with the melting pot as an ideal, this pluralistic-culture with multiple value systems may seem paradoxical. Even if we decide that the core culture or middle class culture should be the focus of public school education for all American youth, we need to re-evaluate our goals in terms of the ethnic and cultural diversity of society. As art educators our problem is complicated by the fact that the middle class generally has not embraced the arts as central to its culture. It still has the stigma of being for an economic and cultural elite, and done by somewhat marginal people. Another contradiction emerges with the recognition of social class as a social reality by an educational system devoted to the preservation of an open society. The concept of the open society itself appears to exist within a middle class framework; that is, open from the middle class standpoint, and the school an institution for helping everyone become middle class.

MAJOR AREAS OF SOCIAL CHANGE IN AMERICA OF THE SIXTIES

Now that we have discussed briefly some of the concepts describing the structure of American society, we should look at some of the major changes that are taking place which influence and affect all the segments in varying degrees and suggest some possible implications for art education.

Emergence of Minority Groups

Probably the most obvious single force in American society is that of desegregation of public institutions and services for the American Negro. Public desegregation and serious questioning of the rights of the states to dictate interpersonal relations between races have brought the question of the rights of all minority groups to the fore. The provisions of the civil rights bill open the door to more opportunity for many others besides the Negro; this means far-reaching social change affecting most of the society.

A correlative of the civic rights of the Negro is his transition from a rural to an urban resident. In 1900, 90 per cent of the Negroes lived in the South and in rural areas. In 1960, only five out of every nine remained in the South. In 1960, 73 per cent of the Negroes were urban dwellers; outside of the South 90 per cent of the Negro population was urban.[7] Some of these people are definitely middle and upper middle class. They have the same goals for themselves and their children that other middle class people have. They take excellent care of property, their children are very carefully trained. But there are many Negroes among the new urban population who have little or no awareness of the complexities of urban life, little ability to interact effectively within it, nor the skills needed to improve their living situations. The absentee landlord who continues to allow decaying slums to exist does little to help these people learn to help themselves. The magnitude of the problem of decaying living conditions with respect to the sense of identity and self-respect in the personality development of children can only be guessed.

The dynamic effect of the civil-rights movement on minority groups that range from those who still live in degrading situations, whether they be Negro, Mexican-American, American Indian, or white, to those who have achieved the education and work opportunities to live with some dignity, portends to be one of our most serious problems. Some of these people will profit from civil rights so much sooner and in so much greater degree that the discrepancy between different Negro classes could cause even more volatile conflicts. Giving civil rights without giving economic opportunity and meaningful education could compound the social problem. All three are imperatives.

Economic Deprivation

The second change in American society is our recognition of the economically and socially deprived—the estimated 20 per cent of our population who have less than $3,000 a year income per family. A large majority of these people are the undereducated members of the minority groups. Their young people are entering the labor market during the period when the childern born during the post-World War II baby boom are also entering the labor market. At the same time, automation is decreasing at a compounding rate the number of jobs that were most often done by the less educated people. These three factors—automation, increased population among those entering the labor market, which creates increased competition and the need for more education—decrease the chances of many economically deprived persons and those in the social minorities from ever emerging from this depressed state. A very real question for the educator is: "How effective are middle-class oriented curricula in helping these children and youth deal with their immediate problems so they can work for the future?" Is education broadening the gap even with the limited education many of these students are receiving?" Is this the reason that the drop-out rate among them is so great—the gap between their immediate needs, their view of society, and that of the schools too great? Are they overwhelmed that the society that demands that they go to school really has no place for them when they finish?

If the stability of ethnic identification and ethclass as identified by Gordon continues, and if little progress is made from the economically deprived in the next decades, then grouping and stratification in our society may be on the increase rather than the decrease. The openness of our society in terms of upward social mobility may be more limited, at least for those who are now in the deprived segment of society.

The group of citizens most involved in developing school policy—the local school boards—tends to represent the white middle class core. If the needs of the students in our multicultural society are to be met, this leadership should include representatives of these groups. In many parts of the country this would mean that more Spanish-speaking people, more Indians, and more Negroes should be active members of school boards. It rarely happens now, and when it does the individuals are those who are an elite of their group, or have moved out of their background culture.

Implications for Art Education

In thinking of the functions of art in culture, and the social trends among minority peoples, what directives can we gain for art education? The *first directive*, to be sure, is that we need to do a great deal of research of the field of art, of the social functions and behaviors involved, as a basis for evaluating what might be possible to help these people. A study of the function of art in societies other than our own should give us insight into the way art forms, no matter how humble, operate in people's lives *right now*. We may have to be willing to look at these art forms with a new sensitivity to see how they function to give a sense of continuity and belonging to a community. If their art forms are making this contribution, then our introduction of art to members of these groups should include their symbolism. If not, we are in some degree teaching their children to devalue their own background. But one cannot make stereotyped judgments about children's ties to their background without knowing their *ethclass* as well, and the degree that they already accept or reject their background culture.

The American Negro is unique in his cultural heritage. Unlike the American Indian or Mexican-American who has a long-standing art background that may have meaning and remnants of meaning, the Negro has only the art forms that he has created in his more immediate past. He carried music forms from Africa, but his visual art forms were cut off. It appears that today's educated Negro's interest in African art tends to be intellectual rather than a culturally transmitted art form, available to those who have an opportunity to learn.

To understand the function of art for all urban people we need to become familiar with the cultural complex of our cities to identify the varied ethclasses represented. We need to make extensive study of the differences in values and attitudes toward art held by these various groups. Our sampling needs to include those who are working toward middle class assimilation, those who are middle class but desire to maintain ethnic identification. We need to identify the widely different segments of lower class society, to see what art might mean to them. This does not mean necessarily seeing how they react to the fine arts *as we know them*, but rather finding out how they may or may not use art in its broadest sense, which of mass media art forms are getting through to them. Attitude analysis will tell us what we need to recognize in beginning to make art experience of value, to relate it to what already has meaning for them.

Second, we need to take a long look at what we are teaching them about art. Are we helping children of these various groups preserve and develop symbols that help them preserve their cultural continuity, to identify and communicate with others in their same culture? Are we able to help them retain and respect their own culture at the same time that we give them the choice of accepting and appreciating all the visual arts? If we accept the concert of the pluralistic society—that it produces a richer, more varied national culture—then our art programs need to be developed at both the diverse and the universal levels.

Third, if we accept the function of the schools as an instrument for providing social mobility, are we including in our curricula opportunities for students to learn the discriminations and aesthetic sensitivity needed by people who do not learn them in their home environment. If we accept the assumption that the school has the further function of improving the environment, improving the standards of the core culture as well, then skills in art criticism need to be developed in language understandable to all age levels, and to encompass the broad uses of art.

Fourth, we need to look at cultures far removed from our own to gain perspectives for looking with more discrimination at the functions of art in our culture.

Ronald and Catherine Berndt are two Australian anthropologists who have made a comparative study of the diverse culture patterns of the Australian minority—the aborigines. They stress the importance of recognizing that these are contemporary cultures that have developed in different patterns from the white Australian, but not necessarily "different in quality or degree." [8]

Art forms and motives vary in the different groups. They range from naturalism to highly conventionalized symbols that can be understood only by those who know the meanings. Within a cultural group distinguishing individual artistry is apparent, yet a group pervasive is clearly recognizable. As groups vary in their art forms, a commonality of quality that distinguished Australian aboriginal art persists. [9]

Each art form has some degree of meaning. Some serve as a partial check on forgetting of complex verbal literature that is handed down for many generations. [10] Others reinforce religious faith by giving the participants a means of expressing their own religious experience. Religious ideology may be represented by series of key symbols of their belief system. [11]

The aborigine today ranges from the full-blood living very much as their forefathers did, in a slowly changing culture. Others have only a few words and memories of their past culture with which to identify but are separated from full participation in their new, learned culture by their physical appearance.

If these seemingly homogenous peoples have this much diversity, we should gain insights into the vast cultural variety and symbolic meanings that may be found in our own country. The American Indian, the Mexican-American, the Negro, the Oriental, the New England white Anglo-Saxon, the religious and/or cultural Jew, the Irish, the Italian, the Eastern, Northern, and Southern European, and Southern American, the Southwesterner, the peoples of the newly cosmopolitan Pacific Coast all represent multiple social classes, cultural, economic, and social subgroups; and men's culture, women's culture, teenage culture all see symbolic meaning in somewhat different and changing ways.

As we analyze each of the major social forces we find that they are interdependent and *interfluential*. The implications for art education that appear important for one often apply to the others. It is only for the sake of clarification that they are separated.

Population and Urban Increases

The third major change in American society is the increase of population, compounded in its impact by the increase in urbanization and shifts of people within cities. In 1963 it was estimated that in three years there would be 10,000,000 more people in this country—and we are well on our way. If current projections materialize, there will be 225,000,000 people in the United States in 1975—ten years from now. In 1963 there were 50 per cent more teenagers age 16 than there were in 1962; now they are 18 years old.[12] Think what this means to population trends when these young people become parents, even if the present slow decrease in birth rate continues.

The size of cities during the ten-year period from 1950 to 1960 has varied throughout the country, but the national average is very high. From an analysis of 216 metropolitan areas the national average is estimated at 26.6 per cent.[13] This figure represents the global area of a central city with its suburbs, whether under one government or not. Such growth puts tremendous strains on city governments to uphold standards for the overall city when the demands for expansion are so immediate, the money to be made from mushrooming housing developments so lush, and the tendency to crowd low income groups into less and less space per individual in the decaying parts of the cities so prevalent. In all cases, increase in population puts a strain on all existing facilities—schools, hospitals, care for the aged, transportation, law enforcement, and recreational facilities.

All these pressures of immediate problems to be solved tend to direct less and less attention to the aesthetic quality of our cities. The value on expediency, getting things done as quickly as possible, that is so much a part of our expanding economy, allows little time for the solving of the practical problems of city growth in terms of the long range *visual effect* of the cities themselves.

These trends all point to the critical necessity of educating more people in the visual arts, so that this period of what may become the *greatest growth of cities* will not result in more and more ugly monotony as slums are renewed, in bland and impersonal areas that have little color or cultural meaning. When the problem of the increased numbers moving into cities is compounded by the percent of these people who are ill-prepared for living in urban areas of complex and diverse cultures, we see how important art becomes as a means of developing a sense of community through variation in meaningful design and symbolic communication.

The complexities of city planning often leave the human dimension with much less attention than it deserves. Planning is often concerned with the acute problems that are easily measurable—traffic congestion, the need for better access to services and goods, housing in terms of statistical averages. Real estate boards and vested interest groups often live within their own economic and social group cultures and tend not to think in terms of the whole city and the diverse cultural groups within it. Though leading architects and urban designers are often social architects as well, many magnificent plans for urban renewal do not consider the cultural or the aesthetic needs of people. Even the aesthetic needs are often in terms of an educated elite, not the population who will use the housing.

I do not propose that our levels of taste would be reduced to some common denominator, but rather than designers and architects be aware of the cultural diversity and plan so that the life patterns of people are not needlessly destroyed, rather that they are maintained, enhanced, and developed. At the turn of the century the emergent new plans for developing our cities had the *"melting pot"* as a basic assumption. Plans for renewal after World War II were based on the assumption that population would stabilize, and were made for a much smaller population than was actually born or migrated into the cities.

Henry S. Churchill, the architect, in his well-titled book, *The City Is The People*, pleads with city planners to review the old plans of the last fifty years, to see how inadequate they have been in effectively dealing with the situation as it actually exists. He is among those architects who are concerned with the social and psychological life-space of the people who make up the city. He asks for preservation of areas of color and imagination, as well as opening space, for diversity rather than planning by averages which don't really fit any group's way of life.[14]

In part, a long-standing tradition needs to be broken. The architect has traditionally been a designer for the elite or large organizations which were responsible for other parts of society. Today this is exemplified by architects working for metropolitan districts, for large insurance companies that invest in what has been planned to be slum clearance. European city planning, because of the necessary rebuilding due to World War II, has included more effective housing for low-income groups. In this country no one bombed out our slums, there is money to be made in perpetuating them, so our renewal trails far behind in terms of our capacity to produce.

Another American tradition—the rights of the individual—has been distorted into a callous disregard of society's natural and aesthetic resources. Our air and our countryside have been treated as *private* domain to serve the cause of monetary progress, irrespective of the visual consequences in the *public* domain. *To stress each citizen's responsibility, to evaluate the quality of his aesthetic contribution to the public view, in the face of the tradition of socially irresponsible individualism, may be crying in the dark.* But the public reaction to air and stream pollution, The President's plea for a beautiful America, the progress made by responsible industries, may encourage public support for art education in helping students gain the capacity for critical aesthetic judgment as part of their civic responsibility.

Another shift that needs to be made in our thinking is the idea that something that is well-designed according to our tastes will have meaning to other people as well. We are extremely egocentric as a people, seeing the world only through our own eyes and through our own ethclass values. It seems to me that art educators must take responsibility for a much wider curriculum. Certainly, our long standing goal of helping individual children and youth acquire an open avenue of expression through art is as important as ever. As we have less geometric space in which to live, the development of self-direction and expression is important, but understanding design as communication, and its myriad application and use in creating rich and meaningful environments in our multifaceted and increasingly complex society is needed as well. We cannot allow people to grow up as visual and aesthetic illiterates and expect them to be aware of their aesthetic responsibilities as citizens.

Automation and the Increase of Leisure

Programmed production and the decreased work week, somewhat independently of each other, are influencing a fourth area of change in American society. Automation is increasingly accelerating the long range decrease of working time that has been going on during this century.

The Darnell Corporation survey of 342 United States and Canadian companies points out a recent and decided trend toward the reduced work week, particularly when vacation time is included in yearly work patterns. Prior to World War II only one worker in four got a paid week's vacation. Between the two decades of 1940 to 1960, the total working time for the average worker dropped the equivalent of four weeks. In the last five years, a great increase in vacation time has developed, with half the salaried workers getting a month's vacation sometime in their career. Paid holidays have increased in 25 years from an average of two to over seven. Now if a person works on a new job six months he gets a week's vacation, a year's work qualified for two weeks, after three to five years the period is three weeks, and after ten years, a month. At present, one in four workers in this sample works between 32 and 40 hours a week.[15] The main trend indicates that there will be more people with leisure time than ever before in the history of mankind. Now the machine is freeing vast numbers for leisure that they have neither cultural pattern nor cultural training to use. Decrease in work creates both leisure and unemployment, but the unemployed have no leisure if it is defined as the time one has beyond gainful work.

One of the most crucial problems of automation is what it does to the new worker, the young man or woman with or without a high school education. Automation is cutting down most drastically in those kinds of unskilled jobs in which young people got the experience they needed to move up in the labor market. As the 1947 war baby population enters the labor market, this will probably increase the percentages of unemployed youth.[16] These same unemployed youth, if these conditions continue, will have fewer opportunities for a first job. It was reported in the winter of 1965 by the Population Reference Bureau that over ¼ of the 1947 baby boom, now aged 17, are out of school and looking for work.[17]

The Negro and the under-educated are most affected. In 1962, 11 per cent of the non-white members of the working force were not working, compared to only 4.9 per cent of the white members. It still remains twice as high. Among all groups, ⅔ of the unemployed had not finished high school. The overall percentage was 9 per cent for those who had not finished 9th grade, 7 per cent for those who had not finished high school, but only 2 per cent for those with some college education.

One of the long standing concepts that has underlain much of our past history has been that those who work have a right to income, and income is necessary to life. We have assumed that we could carry a certain number of people on relief. Now we are faced with a revolution in the nature of work in which the machine replaces people. We are faced with having to decide whether or not we will change our concepts of what work is, what would be repaid by society for service to it, or whether we shall consign more and more people to lives of inaction and poverty.

In a succinct publication of the Center for the Study of Democratic Institutions, Gerard Piel and Ralph Helstein discuss the relation of work to income as follows:

Helstein:

I accept the fact that full employment at this juncture in time is a misleading goal if by full employment is meant the traditional kind of jobs in the private market—a market that has failed in the last five years to produce the kind and number of jobs necessary. A revision of our concept of work is required. After all, work is only what society says it is. There is no reason why we cannot start redefining our notions of what work is and in this way provide full employment. . . .[18]

Piel:

The underlying scandal of what we are talking about here is that the market economy offered and promoted kinds of work that were sanctioned by the values of the market and the profit system. The function we are talking about, the people-to-people function, is notably not conducted for profit or market-generated. . . . We are talking in terms of fundamental changes in our society that go beyond the emergency measure of providing an income for everybody, to building a society with an entirely different set of values about *what qualifies as socially useful work*.[19]

As we reflect on what these men have said, and think about the arts, we may gain some insight. The arts and the artist have long been outside the mainstream of American life. Though gaining in prominence, the stereotype of the artist is still not an ideal personality type to which young people may be motivated. As this change in the concept of work takes place, will we in the visual arts be ready to provide the impetus and education so that the arts can become central activities in socially useful work—improving our cities and our homes, and the quality of our experience, as well as contributing to the quality of production; *in creating new dimensions for communication which have symbolic and aesthetic meaning in our diversified society?* Can we help more people contribute to society through art, who are now denied admission to the market economy?

As concepts of work and play change, our evaluation of leisure will of necessity change. One possible explanation of the reticence found in American education against accepting education for leisure in the elementary and high schools has been our Puritanical tradition that non-work is somehow related to sin. Though the social structure of American life is changing, the concept of a college education as a doorway to the good life, which includes the right to leisure, has preserved the liberal arts in higher education. To educate for leisure below that level has somehow seemed unimportant because we have assumed that only the elite have the right to leisure. The further stereotype that the arts are the play of the leisure elite, and the artist a social deviant, because he participates little in the mainstream of economic gain, have contributed to the peripheral position of the arts in public school education.

As art educators we have felt the need, and in part rightly so, to defend the artistic dimension as vital to good economy, long range planning in cities, the development of significant communities, and necessary for improved production. At the same time, the nation as a whole must recognize that increased population, automation, and the decreased work week mean that a majority rather than a minority of society will be in the leisure class. So we must educate the public to recognize that education in the visual arts is vital to the development of citizens in our society because it is one of the primary communication systems, and that it is also a means of individual and collective development during leisure.

MASS MEDIA AND ITS EFFECTS ON SOCIAL CHANGE

Mass media is a major factor to be considered in social change. It accentuates the differences between its general standard of mediocrity and commonalty and the diversity of cultures and economic levels. It purports, through advertising, to identify the so-called good life which anyone can achieve if they are just able to buy the right products. Paul Hoffman identifies rising expectations, as a result of increased communication and transportation, as one of the most crucial factors in international affairs. He writes: ". . . rising expectations" are ". . . one of the most powerful forces affecting the future of mankind." He cautions that one face of the movement is a desire for progress which we must help or we will have ". . . the other face turned upon us. This is the ugly face of violence and even chaos, born from hopeless frustration and despair. . . ." [20]

At the same time that the open door to opportunity seems to be closing due to increased automation and population, these same people in *this* country are able to see at least a distorted picture of the affluent society. We need careful content analysis of the values being projected through mass media, as well as continued study of the diversity of values in American society, to be able to understand the conflicts, the anxieties and frustrations that television, for instance, may produce among children from deprived segments of society. There has been extensive concern over the violence on television, but little for this more subtle influence with its distorted picture of "the good life" in creating hostility and frustrations among the economically deprived.

In another report of the Center for the Study of Democratic Institutions on the nature of the American Character, Jack Gould, Television Critic of the New York Times, analyzes the power structure of American television, and the decision-making that goes into the selection of programs. He states: ". . . the real control rests with the sponsor. By the act of not purchasing certain kinds of programs the sponsor exercises a tremendous force on television programming. The sponsor's negative power is enormous . . . he has a power of veto over what the public sees; he simply does not buy that program." [21] News and public affairs programming are the two areas where, as he says, "Sponsors, to their credit, have kept their hands off." It is in the area of creative writing for television that Gould finds the greatest disaster, both to the arts and to society. Nothing controversial that is to be found on the contemporary scene can be used. Only those writers survive who are well-trained "in the taboos of the business." Further, the uncreative, plot-repeating westerns, situational comedy, horror and gangster programs come when the greatest viewing takes place, from eight to eleven at night. Sunday mornings and late evenings provide the main alternatives. Any book shop, any news stand, any record store provides the consumer with a far greater choice. But for many the window on the good life, the advertising that accompanies their diversion, is not only a farce on life, but is also unattainable. [22]

The major question which the impact of television and mass media on society raises for us is whether we do, or can, give students the tools with which to evaluate the obvious and the subtle messages of this one-way communication system. *We have the obligation to try to offer students more alternatives.* This requires that we be aware of what they are receiving; that we analyze the art forms being used so that we may help them develop and use aesthetic criteria in their evaluations.

ANOMY

The final social force is "anomy" in American society. Merton defines it as a "breakdown in the cultural structure, occurring particularly when there is an acute disjunction between the cultural norms and goals and the socially structured capacities of members of the group to act in accord with them," or to put it in other words, situations where the indvidual cannot relate himself to his perceptions of the norms of society, resulting, among other feelings, in a sense of isolation. What happens to individuals also appears to happen to groups of individuals.

Sociologists and social and personality psychologists disagree as to whether or not anomy is increasing. Durkheim and Merton deal with social conditions and their relationships to deviant behavior. Others, mainly psychologists, are concerned with the kinds of personalities which, in response to certain kinds of social situations, become more deviant in behavior. Those who study personality factors in anomy feel that one cannot evaluate the trend of the overall society as being more or less anomic unless one identifies the point of view of the observer.

McClosky and Schaar, in a review of the literature and their own study of national and Minnesota samples, report that anomy is found mostly among old people, widowed, divorced, and separated; under-educated, persons with low incomes or with low prestige positions; people moving downward socially; Negroes, foreign-born, and non-city dwellers and farmers.[23]

They feel that these people have less opportunity to interact and communicate within the dominant society, and thus have less opportunity to "see and understand how the society works and what its goals and values are."

Anomic feeling may come from the social situation for some people, from their own personalities in others, or can be a combinate from both sources.

In a comprehensive series of tests, administered to random national and Minnesota samples, these researchers find the following trends. *Low anomy* correlated highly with high education, intellectuality, high tolerance for ambiguity and those who took social responsibility. *High anomy* was correlated most with low education and intellect, *intolerance* of the ambiguous, dependence on black and white answers, and low social responsibility. Using the totals for their figures on tolerance (Table 9), I found the following percentages of persons high in anomy: 35 per cent of the people in the national sample and 28 per cent of those in the Minnesota sample were high in anomy.

Some percentages of these people were found in all economic and educational levels, though predominantly found among the under-educated, underprivileged, the rigid and anxious who have less opportunity for social interaction with the dominant society through "communication, interaction, and learning. . . ."

Whether these figures represent an increase or not, they do represent a serious situation which should concern educators, for it apparently concerns one in three students. The big question for the art educator, it would seem, is: how can art experience and symbolic communication contribute to the sense of identity and social participation of these people? Many of them will be found among our new urbanites, certainly among the economically and socially deprived. This dimension of psycho-social behavior, like the "eth-class" becomes a confounding but useful tool if we are really concerned about developing art curricula that can have meaning to all American children and youth.

These are the key issues as I see them. What do they mean to us? Some investigators of American society feel that this is the era of greatest rapidity of change in human history. This means that we need greater flexibility in our use of categories, more awareness of the possible alternatives to our assumptions, than ever before. At this point, we may feel we have opened a Pandora's box by looking so briefly at complex social factors that are acting and reacting upon each other to change our way of life. A caution is needed here:

Culture does persist, attitudes and values sometimes remain beyond their usefulness, but in our haste to meet the challenge of change, we may heed-lessly throw out values that have continuing importance: For example, when some of us plead for the use of more intellect in art education to solve aesthetic problems in modern society, we should not negate the use of *intuition, improvisation,* or even *personality projection through art.* Because we believe that art has a place in the lives of all people does not deny the right, and society's need for, an *aesthetic-creative elite* to break the barriers of artistic discovery. The recognition and encouragement of the best in the fine arts does not necessarily have to negate, as non-art, the ethnic and popular arts that have meaning to large segments of society. *We need only to ask that the students develop evaluative criteria for responding to all the visual arts.*

REVIEW AND IMPLICATIONS FOR ART EDUCATION

In summary, the big forces in social change that have implications for art education are as follows:

First, we find that American culture, as studied by sociologists interested in social diversity, is much more complex than we may have imagined. Sub-cultures appear to maintain their characteristics even when they change socio-economic levels.

Second, minority groups are emerging into fuller citizenship roles through increased civil rights, but within these groups the opportunities to utilize these rights vary significantly.

Third, the plight of the economically and socially deprived is not helped by automation, population increase, and the decrease of jobs, even though civil rights may give them more right to opportunity.

Fourth, the increase in population that is centering in urban areas, the increase of megapolis, is bringing many people to cities who know little of the ways of city culture. Urban renewal without some education and con-tinuity from past culture may create new problems of anomy, and new slums.

Fifth, automation is decreasing the number of jobs, particularly for the under-educated. The chances of entering the labor force are decreasing for the under-educated minority youth. Further, automation is decreasing the need for working hours. More people will have more time for leisure than they need to earn a living.

Sixth, mass media, at present, is making shallow use of the arts to present a picture of the good life which centers around the use of its products. The pressure to enter the so-called good life through acquisition of the proper products comes at the same time that automation and increased population, in combination, decrease the purchasing power of approximately one-fifth of our people. At the same time, there are combinations of factors; automation, increased population, that appear to be decreasing opportunity in our society, as society as a whole is beginning to be aware of its social responsibility to all members.

Seventh, anomy, social isolation, operates to compound the problems. Those who are most separated may be the most easily affected by society's lack of recognition of its diversity, and by decreased opportunity to operate in the dominant society.

Our question then becomes: what can we as art educators do to begin to deal with these problems as we try to cope with the education of all children and youth? What follows is only my own attempt to try to identify the kinds of behaviors requiring aesthetic judgments that appear to be needed by the members of our society, and then to postulate some directives for art education.

The first deals with rural people learning to live in crowded cities, and slum dwellers moving into urban renewal.

1. Preserving, through their own creation, the symbolism of their background culture if it has meaning for them.
2. Developing independent judgment in evaluating what is presented to them in the city.
3. Learning to take responsibility for their contribution to the public view.
4. Learning basic skills in production and maintenance of what they do possess.
5. Becoming aware of the differences between order and disorder, and the difference in impact these have upon themselves.
6. Learning ways to make order and variation through groupings of color, of forms, of line and textures, etc. with minimal materials.
7. Developing new avenues of socially useful work through art.

Teachers who attempt this will need to be prepared to understand cultural, economic, and personality differences among groups of children so that the initial comparisons are with things that have meaning to them. In some way the goals of the teacher will have to be related to the goals the students have for themselves—which in many cases will be the goals given them by mass media. By attempting to start where they are, with what is important to them, a beginning can be made. If art is not related to their own past experience, to their own goals, the beginning experiences upon which further learnings in art can be built will not take place. This is as true in teaching middle class children, where art is not respected in the home, as those whose folk art or lack of art has not prepared them for using art in their civic and social responsibilities.

A question I can see being raised by some of us is: "Lots of kids from most deprived backgrounds are very expressive once they get a chance to use some art material. Why all this emphasis on differences in background?" My answer to this is to agree in part. I've had the exciting experience of watching hostile, rejected students pour out their feelings with paint. I wouldn't discourage this kind of communication. But does this help these youngsters make aesthetic judgments to improve the quality of their experience? Does it help them preserve their own unique background and still help them contribute to the life of those around them? Does it help those who don't open up in this kind of experience, to find art operative and useful in their own lives? Will self-projection alone open up avenues for art in the new dimensions of what is to be called work, that some of our sociologists see as necessary in the immediate future?

Some of these behaviors we have discussed are needed by all children in this mobile society where people change their residence so often. The following are some aesthetically based behaviors I believe should be considered in all art education:

1. Helping students see the functions of art in culture as it transmits values and attitudes, and identifies cultural meanings.
2. Helping students respect and understand cultural pluralism in our society by becoming aware of the functions of art in our many subcultures.
3. Helping students recognize the importance of the aesthetic dimension in the economic and political decisions of civic affairs, in urban and rural renewal, conservation, city planning, and neighborhood development.
4. Helping students discriminate and evaluate the symbolic communication of mass media to preserve independent judgment.
5. Helping students understand the uses of intuition and creativity so that the arts can become avenues for self-directed use of leisure.
6. Helping students understand the multifaceted interaction of the elements of design so that they may develop a basis for aesthetic discrimination.
7. Helping students to differentiate between social aesthetic responsibility and individual divergent creativity; to develop and preserve the uniqueness of the individual while increased population and decreased space require more cooperative planning and social responsibility.
8. Helping the artistically gifted to recognize their responsibilities to society as designers, artists, and architects.

To further develop these objectives, we in art education face several tasks. We need to know a great deal more about the functions of design, its structure, so that we can teach it to people of widely divergent backgrounds. We need to study the differences in values and attitudes about art and about the life of many more groups of people. Certainly this includes becoming aware of our own basic assumptions about art and its relation to life as we understand our own unique backgrounds. Finally, we need to do considerable classroom research in means and methods of making design meaningful and useable in all segments of American life.

We must become increasingly aware of the political, economic, cultural realities of our cities today as they affect the rapidly changing society, if we wish to make the aesthetic dimension felt. We need to teach art in general education so that all concerned with the city and its development—its managers, planners, economists, and its electorate—are keenly aware of the aesthetic impact of their decisions on the lives of people. Further, we must so understand the cultural diversity of students so that art will have meaning in the lives of more and more people, to preserve culture, to enhance their day-to-day living, and preserve their group uniqueness and their individual identity.

We in art education can probably contribute only a small part to the solution of our nation's monumental problems, but we cannot even begin unless we are more aware of the complexities and dynamics of change which we face. In teacher training, in curriculum development, in research, our best creative efforts, based on a broad awareness, would help us give American youth the aesthetic tools they need.

Art education as I understand it is multifaceted. Its content is drawing, painting, sculpture, etc.; it is design in its broad ramifications; it is art as historical impact, it is art criticism, it is *also* cultural communication. It requires the art of teaching based on highly developed understandings of individual and cultural diversity and their relationship to learning. The art teacher can then *become* a central figure in cultural transmission and development.

REFERENCES

1. McFee, June K. *Preparation for Art.* Belmont, Wadsworth Publishing Co., 1961, Chapter XX.
2. Gordon, Milton M. *Assimilation in American Life: The Role of Race, Religion, and National Origins.* New York, Oxford University Press, 1964, pp. 51–54.
3. *Ibid.,* pp. 74–76.
4. *Ibid.,* p. 34.
5. *Ibid.,* p. 73.
6. *Ibid.,* pp. 254–257.
7. Lee, Everett, "Internal Migration and Population Redistribution in the

United States," Freedman, Ronald, ed. *Population: The Vital Revolution.* Garden City, Doubleday & Company, 1964.

8. Berndt, Ronald and Catherine. *The First Australians.* New York, The Philosophical Library, 1954, p. 12.
9. *Ibid.,* p. 104.
10. *Ibid.,* p. 80.
11. *Ibid.,* p. 75.
12. Cook, Robert. Population Reference Bureau, Washington, D. C. Population Growth Symposium, Palm Springs, California, November 11, 1964.
13. Statistical Abstract of the United States, 1964, 85th Ed., "Metropolitan Growth."
14. Churchill, Henry S. *The City Is The People.* New York, W. W. Nuton, Inc., 1962, pp. 198–202.
15. Porter, Sylvia. "New Trends in Vocations" (Syndicated News Column), Prepublication Review of Darnell Corporation publication, New York, June 2, 1965.
16. Brandwein, Seymour. U. S. Dept. of Labor, "Manpower, Automation and Training" in *Britannica Book of the Year 1964.* Chicago, Encyclopedia Britannica, Inc., p. 343.
17. Cook, Robert. *Loc. cit.*
18. Helstein, Ralph, Piel, Gerard and Theobald, Robert. *Jobs, Machines, and People.* Santa Barbara, Center for the Study of Democratic Institutions, The Fund for the Republic, Inc., p. 15.
19. *Ibid.,* p. 20.
20. Hoffman, Paul. "The Future of Mankind in a Shrinking World," *Views and Ideas on Mankind.* Council for the Study of Mankind, Bulletin No. 15; Dec., 1963, p. 2.
21. Gould, Jack. "Television: One of a Series of Interviews on the American Character." Center for the Study of Democratic Institutions, The Fund for the Republic, Inc., Santa Barbara, 1961, p. 3.
22. *Ibid.,* pp. 4–6.
23. McClosky, Herbert and Schaar, John H. "Psychological Dimensions of Anomy," *American Sociological Review,* Vol. 30, No. 1, Feb. 1965, pp. 14–40.

The Act of Discovery

JEROME S. BRUNER

Maimonides, in his *Guide for the Perplexed,*[1] speaks of four forms of perfection that men might seek. The first and lowest form is perfection in the acquisition of worldly goods. The great philosopher dismisses such perfection on the ground that the possessions one acquires bear no meaningful relation

Reprinted by permission from Jerome S. Bruner, "The Act of Discovery," *Harvard Educational Review,* Vol. 31, Winter 1961, pp. 21–37. Copyright © 1961 by the President and Fellows of Harvard College.

[1] Maimonides, *Guide for the Perplexed* (New York, Dover Publications, 1956).

to the possessor: "A great king may one morning find that there is no difference between him and the lowest person." A second perfection is of the body, its conformation and skills. Its failing is that is does not reflect on what is uniquely human about man: "he could [in any case] not be as strong as a mule." Moral perfection is the third, "the highest degree of excellency in man's character." Of this perfection Maimonides says: "Imagine a person being alone, and having no connection whatever with any other person; all his good moral principles are at rest, they are not required and give man no perfection whatever. These principles are only necessary and useful when man comes in contact with others." "The fourth kind of perfection is the true perfection of man; the possession of the highest intellectual faculties. . . ." In justification of his assertion, this extraordinary Spanish-Judaic philosopher urges: "Examine the first three kinds of perfection; you will find that if you possess them, they are not your property, but the property of others. . . . But the last kind of perfection is exclusively yours; no one else owns any part of it."

It is a conjecture much like that of Maimonides that leads me to examine the act of discovery in man's intellectual life. For if man's intellectual excellence is the most his own among his perfections, it is also the case that the most uniquely personal of all that he knows is that which he has discovered for himself. What difference does it make, then, that we encourage discovery in the learning of the young? Does it, as Maimonides would say, create a special and unique relation between knowledge possessed and the possessor? And what may such a unique relation do for a man—or for a child, if you will, for our concern is with the education of the young?

The immediate occasion for my concern with discovery—and I do not restrict discovery to the act of finding out something that before was unknown to mankind, but rather include all forms of obtaining knowledge for oneself by the use of one's own mind—the immediate occasion is the work of the various new curriculum projects that have grown up in America during the last six or seven years. For whether one speaks to mathematicians or physicists or historians, one encounters repeatedly an expression of faith in the powerful effects that come from permitting the student to put things together for himself, to be his own discoverer.

First, let it be clear what the act of discovery entails. It is rarely, on the frontier of knowledge or elsewhere, that new facts are "discovered" in the sense of being encountered as Newton suggested in the form of islands of truth in an uncharted sea of ignorance. Or if they appear to be discovered in this way, it is almost always thanks to some happy hypotheses about where to navigate. Discovery, like surprise, favors the well prepared mind. In playing bridge, one is surprised by a hand with no honors in it at all and also by hands that are all in one suit. Yet all hands in bridge are equiprobable: one must know to be surprised. So too in discovery. The history of science is studded with examples of men "finding out" something and not knowing it. I shall operate on the assumption that discovery, whether by a schoolboy going it on his own or by a scientist cultivating the growing edge of his field, is in its essence a matter of rearranging or transforming evidence in such a way that one is enabled to go beyond the evidence so reassembled to additional new insights. It may well be that an additional fact or shred of evidence makes this larger transformation of evidence possible. But it is often not even dependent on new information.

It goes without saying that, left to himself, the child will go about discovering things for himself within limits. It also goes without saying that there are certain forms of child rearing, certain home atmospheres that lead some children to be their own discoverers more than other children. These are both topics of great interest, but I shall not be discussing them. Rather, I should like to confine myself to the consideration of discovery and "finding-out-for-oneself" within an educational setting—specifically the school. Our aim as teachers is to give our student as firm a grasp of a subject as we can, and to make him as autonomous and self-propelled a thinker as we can—one who will go along on his own after formal schooling has ended. I shall return in the end to the question of the kind of classroom and the style of teaching that encourages an attitude of wanting to discover. For purposes of orienting the discussion, however, I would like to make an overly simplified distinction between teaching that takes place in the *expository mode* and teaching that utilizes the *hypothetical mode*. In the former, the decisions concerning the mode and pace and style of exposition are principally determined by the teacher as expositor; the student is the listener. If I can put the matter in terms of structural linguistics, the speaker has a quite different set of decisions to make than the listener: the former has a wide choice of alternatives for structuring, he is anticipating paragraph content while the listener is still intent on the words, he is manipulating the content of the material by various transformations, while the listener is quite unaware of these internal manipulations. In the hypothetical mode, the teacher and the student are in a more cooperative position with respect to what in linguistics would be called "speaker's decisions." The student is not a bench-bound listener, but is taking a part in the formulation and at times may play the principal role in it. He will be aware of alternatives and may even have an "as if" attitude toward these and, as he receives information he may evaluate it as it comes. One cannot describe the process in either mode with great precision as to detail, but I think the foregoing may serve to illustrate what is meant.

Consider now what benefit might be derived from the experience of learning through discoveries that one makes for oneself. I should like to discuss these under four headings: (1) The increase in intellectual potency, (2) the shift from extrinsic to intrinsic rewards, (3) learning the heuristics of discovering, and (4) the aid to memory processing.

1. Intellectual potency.

If you will permit me, I would like to consider the difference between subjects in a highly constrained psychological experiment involving a two-choice apparatus. In order to win chips, they must depress a key either on the right or the left side of the machine. A pattern of payoff is designed such that, say, they will be paid off on the right side 70 per cent of the time, on the left 30 per cent, although this detail is not important. What is important is that the payoff sequence is arranged a random, and there is no pattern. I should like to contrast the behavior of subjects who think that there *is* some pattern to be found in the sequence—who think that regularities are discoverable—in contrast to subjects who think that things are happening quite by *chance*. The former group adopts what is called an "event-matching" strategy in which the number of responses given to each side is roughly equal to the proportion of times it pays off: in the present case R70: L30. The group that believes there is no pattern very soon reverts to a much more primitive strategy wherein *all* responses are allocated to the side that has the greater payoff. A little arithmetic will show you that the lazy all-and-none strategy pays off more if indeed the environment is random: namely, they win seventy per cent of the time. The event-matching subjects win about 70 per cent on the 70 per cent payoff side (or 49 per cent of the time there) and 30 per cent of the time on the side that pays off 30 per cent of the time (another 9 per cent for a total take-home wage of 58 per cent in return for their labors of decision). But the world is not always or not even frequently random, and if one analyzes carefully what the event-matchers are doing, it turns out that they are trying out hypotheses one after the other, all of them containing a term such that they distribute bets on the two sides with a frequency to match the actual occurrence of events. If it should turn out that there is a pattern to be discovered, their payoff would become 100 per cent. The other group would go on at the middling rate of 70 per cent.

What has this to do with the subject at hand? For the person to search out and find regularities and relationships in his environment, he must be armed with an expectancy that there will be something to find and, once aroused by expectancy, he must devise ways of searching and finding. One of the chief enemies of such expectancy is the assumption that there is nothing one can find in the environment by way of regularity or relationship. In the experiment just cited, subjects often fall into a habitual attitude that there is either nothing to be found or that they can find a pattern by looking. There is an important sequel in behavior to the two attitudes, and to this I should like to turn now.

We have been conducting a series of experimental studies on a group of some seventy school children over the last four years. The studies have led us to distinguish an interesting dimension of cognitive activity that can be described as ranging from *episodic empiricism* at one end to *cumulative constructionism* at the other. The two attitudes in the choice experiments just cited are illustrative of the extremes of the dimension. I might mention some other illustrations. One of the experiments employs the game of Twenty Questions. A child—in this case he is between 10 and 12—is told that a car has gone off the road and hit a tree. He is to ask questions that can be answered by "yes" or "no" to discover the cause of the accident. After completing the problem, the same task is given him again, though he is told that the accident had a different cause this time. In all, the procedure is repeated four times. Children enjoy playing the game. They also differ quite markedly in the approach or strategy they bring to the task. There are various elements in the strategies employed. In the first place, one may distinguish clearly between two types of questions asked: the one is designed for locating constraints in the problem, constraints that will eventually give shape to an hypothesis; the other is the hypothesis as question. It is the difference between, "Was there anything wrong with the driver?" and "Was the driver rushing to the doctor's office for an appointment and the car got out of control?" There are children who precede hypotheses with efforts to locate constraint and there are those who, to use our local slang, are "pot-shotters," who string out hypotheses non-cumulatively one after the other. A second element of strategy is its connectivity of information gathering: the extent to which questions asked utilize or ignore or violate information previously obtained. The questions asked by children tend to be organized in cycles, each cycle of questions usually being given over to the pursuit of some particular notion. Both within cycles and between cycles one can discern a marked difference on the connectivity of the child's performance. Needless to say, children who employ constraint location as a technique preliminary to the formulation of hypotheses tend to be far more connected in their harvesting of information. Persistence is another feature of strategy, a characteristic compounded of what appear to be two components: a sheer doggedness component, and a persistence that stems from the sequential organization that a child brings to the task. Doggedness is probably just animal spirits or the need for achievement —what has come to be called *n-ach*. Organized persistence is a maneuver for protecting our fragile cognitive apparatus from overload. The child who has flooded himself with disorganized information from unconnected hypotheses will become discouraged and confused sooner than the child who has shown a certain cunning in his strategy of getting information—a cunning whose principal component is the recognition that the value of information is not simply in getting it but in being able to carry it. The persistence of the organized child stems from his knowledge of how to organize questions in cycles, how to summarize things to himself, and the like.

Episodic empiricism is illustrated by information gathering that is unbound by prior constraints, that lacks connectivity, and that is deficient in organizational persistence. The opposite extreme is illustrated by an approach that is characterized by constraint sensitivity, by connective maneuvers, and by organized persistence. Brute persistence seems to be one of those gifts from the gods that make people more exaggeratedly what they are.[2]

---

[2] I should also remark in passing that the two extremes also characterize concept attainment strategies as reported in A *Study of Thinking* by J. S. Bruner *et al.* (New York: J. Wiley, 1956). Successive scanning illustrates well what is meant here by episodic empiricism; conservative focussing is an example of cumulative constructionism.

Before returning to the issue of discovery and its role in the development of thinking, let me say a word more about the ways in which information may get transformed when the problem solver has actively processed it. There is first of all a pragmatic question: what does it take to get information processed into a form best designed to fit some future use? Take an experiment by Zajonc [3] as a case in point. He gives groups of subjects information of a controlled kind, some groups being told that their task is to transmit the information to others, others that it is merely to be kept in mind. In general, he finds more differentiation and organization of the information received with the intention of being transmitted than there is for information received passively. An active set leads to a transformation related to a task to be performed. The risk, to be sure, is in possible overspecialization of information processing that may lead to such a high degree of specific organization that information is lost for general use.

I would urge now in the spirit of an hypothesis that emphasis upon discovery in learning has precisely the effect upon the learner of leading him to be a constructionist, to organize what he is encountering in a manner not only designed to discover regularity and relatedness, but also to avoid the kind of information drift that fails to keep account of the uses to which information might have to be put. It is, if you will, a necessary condition for learning the variety of techniques of problem solving, of transforming information for better use, indeed for learning how to go about the very task of learning. Practice in discovering for oneself teaches one to acquire information in a way that makes that information more readily viable in problem solving. So goes the hypothesis. It is still in need of testing. But is it an hypothesis of such important human implications that we cannot afford not to test it—and testing will have to be in the schools.

2. Intrinsic and extrinsic motives.

Much of the problem in leading a child to effective cognitive activity is to free him from the immediate control of environmental rewards and punishments. That is to say, learning that starts in response to the rewards of parental or teacher approval or the avoidance of failure can too readily develop a pattern in which the child is seeking cues as to how to conform to what is expected of him. We know from studies of children who tend to be early over-achievers in school that they are likely to be seekers after the "right way to do it" and that their capacity for transforming their learning into viable thought structures tends to be lower than children merely achieving at levels predicted by intelligence tests. Our tests on such children show them to be lower in analytic ability than those who are not conspicuous in over-achievement.[4] As we shall see later, they develop rote abilities and depend upon being able to "give back" what is expected rather than to make it

[3] R. B. Zajonc (Personal communication, 1957).

[4] J. S. Bruner and A. J. Caron, "Cognition, Anxiety, and Achievement in the Pre-adolescent," *Journal of Educational Psychology* (in press).

into something that relates to the rest of their cognitive life. As Maimonides would say, their learning is not their own.

The hypothesis that I would propose here is that to the degree that one is able to approach learning as a task of discovering something rather than "learning about" it, to that degree will there be a tendency for the child to carry out his learning activities with the autonomy of self-reward or, more properly by reward that is discovery itself.

To those of you familiar with the battles of the last half-century in the field of motivation, the above hypothesis will be recognized as controversial. For the classic view of motivation in learning has been, until very recently, couched in terms of a theory of drives and reinforcement: that learning occurred by virtue of the fact that a response produced by a stimulus was followed by the reduction in a primary drive state. The doctrine is greatly extended by the idea of secondary reinforcement: any state associated even remotely with the reduction of a primary drive could also have the effect of producing learning. There has recently appeared a most searching and important criticism of this position, written by Professor Robert White,[5] reviewing the evidence of recently published animal studies, of work in the field of psychoanalysis, and of research on the development of cognitive processes in children. Professor White comes to the conclusion, quite rightly I think, that the drive-reduction model of learning runs counter to too many important phenomena of learning and development to be either regarded as general in its applicability or even correct in its general approach. Let me summarize some of his principal conclusions and explore their applicability to the hypothesis stated above.

I now propose that we gather the various kinds of behavior just mentioned, all of which have to do with effective interaction with the environment, under the general heading of competence. According to Webster, competence means fitness or ability, and the suggested synonyms include capability, capacity, efficiency, proficiency, and skill. It is therefore a suitable word to describe such things as grasping and exploring, crawling and walking, attention and perception, language and thinking, manipulating and changing the surroundings, all of which promote an effective—a competent—interaction with the environment. It is true of course, that maturation plays a part in all these developments, but this part is heavily overshadowed by learning in all the more complex accomplishments like speech or skilled manipulation. I shall argue that it is necessary to make competence a motivational concept; there is *competence motivation* as well as competence in its more familiar sense of achieved capacity. The behavior that leads to the building up of effective grasping, handling, and letting go of objects, to take one example, is not random behavior that is produced by an overflow of energy. It is directed, selective, and persistent, and it continues not because it serves primary drives, which indeed it cannot serve until it is almost perfected, but because it satisfies an intrinsic need to deal with the environment.[6]

[5] R. W. White, "Motivation Reconsidered: The Concept of Competence," *Psychological Review*, LXVI, 1959, pp. 297–333.
[6] *Ibid.*, pp. 317–18.

I am suggesting that there are forms of activity that serve to enlist and develop the competence motive, that serve to make it the driving force behind behavior. I should like to add to White's general premise that the *exercise* of competence motives has the effect of strengthening the degree to which they gain control over behavior and thereby reduce the effects of extrinsic rewards or drive gratification.

The brilliant Russian psychologist Vigotsky [7] characterizes the growth of thought processes as starting with a dialogue of speech and gesture between child and parent; autonomous thinking begins at the stage when the child is first able to internalize these conversations and "run them off" himself. This is a typical sequence in the development of competence. So too in instruction. The narrative of teaching is of the order of the conversation. The next move in the development of competence is the internalization of the narrative and its "rules of generation" so that the child is now capable of running off the narrative on his own. The hypothetical mode in teaching by encouraging the child to participate in "speaker's decisions" speeds this process along. Once internalization has occurred, the child is in a vastly improved position from several obvious points of view—notably that he is able to go beyond the information he has been given to generate additional ideas that can either be checked immediately from experience or can, at least, be used as a basis for formulating reasonable hypotheses. But over and beyond that, the child is now in a position to experience success and failure not as reward and punishment, but as information. For when the task is his own rather than a matter of matching environmental demands, he becomes his own paymaster in a certain measure. Seeking to gain control over his environment, he can now treat success as indicating that he is on the right track, failure as indicating he is on the wrong one.

In the end, this development has the effect of freeing learning from immediate stimulus control. When learning in the short run leads only to pellets of this or that rather than to mastery in the long run, then behavior can be readily "shaped" by extrinsic rewards. When behavior becomes more long-range and competence-oriented, it comes under the control of more complex cognitive structures, plans and the like, and operates more from the inside out. It is interesting that even Pavlov, whose early account of the learning process was based entirely on a notion of stimulus control of behavior through the conditioning mechanism in which, through contiguity a new conditioned stimulus was substituted for an old unconditioned stimulus by the mechanism of stimulus substitution, that even Pavolv recognized his account as insufficient to deal with higher forms of learning. To supplement the account, he introduced the idea of the "second signalling system," with central importance placed on symbolic systems such as language in mediating and giving shape to mental life. Or as Luria [8] has put it, "the first signal system [is] concerned with

[7] L. S. Vigotsky, *Thinking and Speech* (Moscow, 1934).
[8] A. L. Luria, "The Directive Function of Speech in Development and Dissolution," *Word*, XV, 1959, pp. 341–464.

directly perceived stimuli, the second with systems of verbal elaboration." Luria, commenting on the importance of the transition from first to second signal system, says: "It would be mistaken to suppose that verbal intercourse with adults merely changes the contents of the child's conscious activity without changing its form. . . . The word has a basic function not only because it indicates a corresponding object in the external world, but also because it abstracts, isolates the necessary signal, generalizes perceived signals and relates them to certain categories; it is this systematization of direct experience that makes the role of the word in the formation of mental processes so exceptionally important." [9, 10]

It is interesting that the final rejection of the universality of the doctrine of reinforcement in direct conditioning came from some of Pavlov's own students. Ivanov-Smolensky [11] and Krasnogorsky [12] published papers showing the manner in which symbolized linguistic messages could take over the place of the unconditioned stimulus and of the unconditioned response (gratification of hunger) in children. In all instances, they speak of these as *replacements* of lower, first-system mental or neural processes by higher order or second-system controls. A strange irony, then, that Russian psychology that gave us the notion of the conditioned response and the assumption that higher order activities are built up out of colligations or structurings of such primitive units, rejected this notion while much of American learning psychology has stayed until quite recently within the early Pavlovian fold (see, for example, a recent article by Spence [13] in the *Harvard Educational Review* or Skinner's treatment of language [14] and the attacks that have been made upon it by linguists such as Chomsky [15] who have become concerned with the relation of language and cognitive activity). What is the more interesting is that Russian pedagogical theory has become deeply influenced by this new trend and is now placing much stress upon the importance of building up a more active symbolical approach to problem solving among children.

To sum up the matter of the control of learning, then, I am proposing that the degree to which competence or mastery motives come to control behavior, to that degree the role of reinforcement or "extrinsic pleasure" wanes in shaping behavior. The child comes to manipulate his environment more actively and achieves his gratification from coping with problems. Symbolic

[9] *Ibid.*, p. 12.

[10] For an elaboration of the view expressed by Luria, the reader is referred to the forthcoming translation of L. S. Vigotsky's 1934 book being published by John Wiley and Sons and the Technology Press.

[11] A. G. Ivanov-Smolensky, "Concerning the Study of the Joint Activity of the First and Second Signal Systems," *Journal of Higher Nervous Activity*, I, 1951, p. 1.

[12] N. D. Krasnogorsky, *Studies of Higher Nervous Activity in Animals and in Man*, Vol. I (Moscow, 1954).

[13] K. W. Spence, "The Relation of Learning Theory to the Technique of Education," *Harvard Educational Review*, XXIX (1959), pp. 84–95.

[14] B. F. Skinner, *Verbal Behavior* (New York: Appleton-Century-Crofts, 1957).

[15] N. Chomsky, *Syntactic Structure* (The Hague, The Netherlands: Mouton & Co., 1957).

modes of representing and transforming the environment arise and the importance of stimulus-response-reward sequences declines. To use the metaphor that David Riesman developed in a quite different context, mental life moves from a state of outer-directedness in which the fortuity of stimuli and reinforcement are crucial to a state of inner-directedness in which the growth and maintenance of mastery become central and dominant.

3. Learning the heuristics of discovery.

Lincoln Steffens,[16] reflecting in his *Autobiography* on his undergraduate education at Berkeley, comments that his schooling was overly specialized on learning about the known and that too little attention was given to the task of finding out about what was not known. But how does one train a student in the techniques of discovery? Again I would like to offer some hypotheses. There are many ways of coming to the arts of inquiry. One of them is by careful study of its formalization in logic, statistics, mathematics, and the like. If a person is going to pursue inquiry as a way of life, particularly in the sciences, certainly such study is essential. Yet, whoever has taught kindergarten and the early primary grades or has had graduate students working with him on their theses—I choose the two extremes for they are both periods of intense inquiry—knows that an understanding of the formal aspect of inquiry is not sufficient. There appear to be, rather, a series of activities and attitudes, some directly related to a particular subject and some of them fairly generalized, that go with inquiry and research. These have to do with the *process* of trying to find out something and while they provide no guarantee that the *product* will be any *great* discovery, their absence is likely to lead to awkwardness or aridity or confusion. How difficult it is to describe these matters—the heuristics of inquiry. There is one set of attitudes or ways of doing that has to do with sensing the relevance of variables—how to avoid getting stuck with edge effects and getting instead to the big sources of variance. Partly this gift comes from intuitive familiarity with a range of phenomena, sheer "knowing the stuff." But it also comes out of a sense of what things among an ensemble of things "smell right" in the sense of being of the right order of magnitude or scope or severity.

The English philosopher Weldon describes problem solving in an interesting and picturesque way. He distinguishes between difficulties, puzzles, and problems. We solve a problem or make a discovery when we impose a puzzle form on to a difficulty that converts it into a problem that can be solved in such a way that it gets us where we want to be. That is to say, we recast the difficulty into a form that we know how to work with, then work it. Much of what we speak of as discovery consists of knowing how to impose what kind of form on various kinds of difficulties. A small part but a crucial part of discovery of the highest order is to invent and develop models or "puzzzle forms" that can be imposed on difficulties with good effect.

---

[16] L. Steffens. *Autobiography of Lincoln Steffens* (New York: Harcourt, Brace, 1931).

It is in this area that the truly powerful mind shines. But it is interesting to what degree perfectly ordinary people can, given the benefit of instruction, construct quite interesting and what, a century ago, would have been considered greatly original models.

Now to the hypothesis. It is my hunch that it is only through the exercise of problem solving and the effort of discovery that one learns the working heuristic of discovery, and the more one has practice, the more likely is one to generalize what one has learned into a style of problem solving or inquiry that serves for any kind of task one may encounter—or almost any kind of task. I think the matter is self-evident, but what is unclear is what kinds of training and teaching produce the best effects. How do we teach a child to, say, cut his losses but at the same time be persistent in trying out an idea; to risk forming an early hunch without at the same time formulating one *so* early and with so little evidence as to be stuck with it waiting for appropriate evidence to materialize; to pose good testable guesses that are neither too brittle nor too sinuously incorrigible, etc., etc. Practice in inquiry, in trying to figure out things for oneself is indeed what is needed, but in what form? Of only one thing I am convinced. I have never seen anybody improve in the art and technique of inquiry by any means other than engaging in inquiry.

4. Conservation of memory.

I should like to take what some psychologists might consider a rather drastic view of the memory process. It is a view that in large measure derives from the work of my colleague, Professor George Miller.[17] Its first premise is that the principal problem of human memory is not storage, but retrieval. In spite of the biological unlikeliness of it, we seem to be able to store a huge quantity of information—perhaps not a full tape recording, though at times it seems we even do that, but a great sufficiency of impressions. We may infer this from the fact that recognition (i.e., recall with the aid of maximum prompts) is so extraordinarily good in human beings—particularly in comparison with spontaneous recall where, so to speak, we must get out stored information without external aids or prompts. The key to retrieval is organization or, in even simpler terms, knowing where to find information and how to get there.

Let me illustrate the point with a simple experiment. We present pairs of words to twelve-year-old children. One group is simply told to remember the pairs, that they will be asked to repeat them later. Another is told to remember them by producing a word or idea that will tie the pair together in a way that will make sense to them. A third group is given the mediators used by the second group when presented with the pairs to aid them in tying the pairs into working units. The word pairs include such juxtapositions as "chair-forest," "sidewalk-square," and the like. One can distinguish three styles of mediators

---

[17] G. A. Miller, "The Magical Number Seven, Plus or Minus Two," *Psychological Review*, LXIII (1956), pp. 81–97.

and children can be scaled in terms of their relative preference for each: *generic mediation* in which a pair is tied together by a superordinate idea: "chair and forest are both made of wood"; *thematic mediation* in which the two terms are imbedded in a theme or little story: "the lost child sat on a chair in the middle of the forest"; and *part-whole mediation* where "chairs are made from trees in the forest" is typical. Now, the chief result, as you would all predict, is that children who provide their own mediators do best— indeed, one time through a set of thirty pairs, they recover up to 95% of the second words when presented with the first ones of the pairs, whereas the uninstructed children reach a maximum of less than 50% recovered. Interestingly enough, children do best in recovering materials tied together by the form of mediator they most often use.

One can cite a myriad of findings to indicate that any organization of information that reduces the aggregate complexity of material by imbedding it into a cognitive structure a person has constructed will make that material more accessible for retrieval. In short, we may say that the process of memory, looked at from the retrieval side, is also a process of problem solving: how can material be "placed" in memory so that it can be got on demand?

We can take as a point of departure the example of the children who developed their own technique for relating the members of each word pair. You will recall that they did better than the children who were given by exposition the mediators they had developed. Let me suggest that in general, material that is organized in terms of a person's own interests and cognitive structures is material that has the best chance of being accessible in memory. That is to say, it is more likely to be placed along routes that are connected to one's own ways of intellectual travel.

In sum, the very attitudes and activities that characterize "figuring out" or "discovering" things for oneself also seems to have the effect of making material more readily accessible in memory.

Sketches Toward A Psychology of Learning in Art

KENNETH R. BEITTEL

I am forced to admit from the outset that I cannot accomplish in this paper what I would like to—namely, the groundwork for a theory of learning in art. It would be a challenging work of the imagination to suggest what kind of person armed with what kind of knowledge would be needed for this job. But I have not chosen this route.

When I speak of a psychology of learning in art, I mean to indicate,

Reprinted by permission from A *Seminar in Art Education for Research and Curriculum,* Cooperative Research Project No. V-002, The Pennsylvania State University, 1966 Copyright. University Park, Pa.

modestly, the beginning development of only one of several possible theories with some of the likely axioms and theorems that would pertain to it. Considering that the entire notion of a psychology of art is a fairly recent and novel idea, my erstwhile objective is nothing short of chancy. Yet the climate is assuredly right, if I read the intellectual signs of the times, for trespassing from both sides across the boundaries between psychology and art.

The ferment within psychology concerning learning theory I leave to more able analysts within that discipline, feeling it unseemly to speak of the squabbles and reconciliations in another family. Instead, I have set myself the more realistic task of selective trespassing and selective neglect of the vast eye- and brain-taxing literature on learning itself. The sketchbook idea comes in because I borrow garments from psychology in which to dress characters from art and art education. This might be dubbed the "Mrs. Siddons as the Tragic Muse" approach to the problem. As in a sketchbook, the ideas will have to be more suggestive than conclusive, for while they might be judged as ends in themselves, I would prefer that they be judged for what they may lead to later.

The scope of even this more realistic task is frightening enough to make me fumble my five-by-eight cards nervously. Let me, therefore, box myself in by setting still further limits to my inquiry, this time making my approach vulnerable to the charge of inconsequence in my own field. I propose to focus on the adult (college) level, on individuals working alone, and on learning in the context provided by sequential drawings. The possible irrelevance of this focus comes from my ignoring vast areas of meaning in child development, group processes and interaction, other kinds of art production, appreciation and art criticism, and to a great extent aesthetic perception itself. I am forced into this posture by the scope and logical incoherence of the broader field of art education, by the necessity to draw upon content from my own research interests, and by my very real need to have a locus from which to depart and to which to return on my excursions into psychology. Otherwise I would produce a mere catalogue of the unconnected. Here, if I succeed at all, I would like to provide much that can be criticized, extended, and even disproved outright.

Still another reason why I will not attempt a coherent theory, apart from the simple fact that I cannot, lies in the eclectic nature of what I will select from the psychological literature, since I am not consciously partisan to any one viewpoint in psychology. Rather what I select or neglect will be determined by two simple criteria, in nature functional and aesthetic. The questions these will pose are: "Can the connection be made?" and "Is there cogency and fruitfulness in the translation?" Although I could cite numerous warnings on the procedure I am about to follow, other learning theorists would support me. Postman,[1] for example, in duscussing knowledge on learning in relation to education says that ". . . the analysis of the process of . . . education does not call for the formulation of special principles;

it calls for the application and elaboration of the general laws of human learning." It is to attempt a partial test of this assumption that this paper is written.

It is from time to time put forth that we are undergoing a kind of Copernican revolution in the life sciences.[2] In the psychology of learning, there is an ascendancy of cognitive theory, which ". . . in its baldest form . . . differs from the other approaches in its insistence upon the elementary fact that we cannot fully understand an individual's reaction to situation A until we know how A appears to him." [3]

This premise of cognitive theorists is superficially most appealing to me. Yet, by and large, I have found no writers harder to follow into battle than these same cognitive theorists. It becomes patent that it is hard to know who or where the enemy is and what kinds of arms are being borne. One of the reasons why this is so is brought out in a statement by Estes: [4]

. . . no convergence is imminent between the educator's and the laboratory scientist's approaches to learning. The latter is interested, not in "learning as a dynamic process" but in learning as a system of relationships among operationally definable concepts; not in the "totality of learning" but in the aspects that may usefully be abstracted and generalized; not in "focus on the learner" but in the formulation of predictive, and preferably quantitative theories.

In the same article, Estes points out that the connection between psychology and education is like that between physiology and medicine.

All in all, it seems defensible to say that the language of the cognitive theorist, who talks bigger and sees man more "from above," and the methods of the functionalist or neobehaviorist, who speaks littler pieces and sees man in specific and controllable context, need to be merged in my task. This is like urging one to be a "hard-nosed soft-head," but I know of no better advice than that of trying to resolve this "cognitive dissonance" by some "transcendence" of these polemical schools of thought. I have elsewhere [5] averred my faith that "larger or molar units of structure and properly-sized molecular units need not be seen as incompatible. The implication is that neither 'fat' gestaltism nor thin atomism will do."

One of my problems is certainly that of language. The earlier quotations from Postman and Estes suggest, first, that communication will be enhanced between psychology and education if the same construct families can be used in each, and, secondly, that the big statements concerning learning by educators are unacceptable to psychologists. Again, the cognitive theorists may supply a bridge. In still another way, fuzzy phrases such as Robers' "internal locus of evaluation" may find an objective or operational counterpart in the findings of experimental research.[6]

On the topic of language usage, signs in the wind endorse the proposed acts of trespassing. As Barkan [7] recently pointed out, it is now widely admissible that the methods of the behavioral sciences can be profitably applied to the understanding of many facets of art education. Consider the following neologisms [8] as testimony of this point: stylometrics, iconology, linguistics of fine arts, iconic sign, iconic mode of representation, the psychology of art, the psychoanalysis of art, art strategies, aesthetic morphology, and the biology of art. You will not find any of these in a standard psychology of learning text, but they can be uncovered with relative ease.

There are still a few more points to my rambling preamble. The current literature in our field abounds with references to the "is ought" distinction,[9] or the difference between descriptive and prescriptive uses of language in research reports. Usually the instances singled out are those where correlational or configurational studies have been followed by a charge on what "must" be done in art education. This point in criticism is well taken and should lead us in research to the point where our reporting is not so naive. On the other hand, the issue in the study of learning is infinitely more subtle. Here we more likely deal with plain old "is-ain't," and the frustrating variant "can't tell." The "ought" is hidden within the very design of our experiments, in the assumptions behind our controls and our dependent and independent variables. The critical eye of the philosopher and the researcher must focus on this much more difficult to criticize problem itself.

A still more subtle and hidden assumption may be found in the cognitive theorist's belief that experimentation has the major function of "revealing" structure and processes working, as Bruner [10] puts it, from the "inside out." Still, there is no reason why "naturalistic studies" and experiments cannot go on hand in hand. In animal studies, the researches of ethologists such as Tinbergen and Lorenz [11] suggest that this may be the case. In education, a recent review [12] of "Educational Programs: Early and Middle Childhood" contains a chapter heading "Naturalistic Studies of Classroom Learning." This orientation suggests that one formulation of the learning problem might be "what is actually being learned?" while another might be "what conditions affect a representative kind of learning?" The interdependence of these two questions should be obvious, especially when we consider the state of knowledge about learning in art. Prematurely plucked theory may hinder empirical observation, but, on the other hand, the constraints of experimentation are a stable frame for the interpretation of observations.

Geiger,[13] clarifies the point of view of the researcher toward any such implied conflict:

> . . . the scientist has consistently refused to be impressed by a problem of knowledge. His content of knowing or inquiry is fixed by a particular problem or set of problems (whether theoretical or applied), and therefore the most fruitful assumptions in science are designed to integrate, not to separate, problem and solution. There are problems of knowledge, of course, but they are not "epistemological," that is, not those of trying to get an already separated subjective knower and objective world together again; they are contextual problems, those concerned with initiating and directing a series of inquiries called into existence by difficulties to be overcome.

Having presented these introductory ideas, I nevertheless know that I struggle with certain unexpressed and possibly inexpressible doubts in my own mind. Earlier Lanier [14] thought to detect in my stance a certain inconsistency—a kind of "empirical mysticism," if you please. Blackmur [15] put his finger on this deep source of discontent in an essay on Yeats, when after arguing for a "stiffer intellectual exercise" in the interpretation of myth and magic in Yeats, he capitulates by saying ". . . that magic, in the sense we all experience it, is nearer the represented emotions that concern us in poetry than psychology, as a generalized science, can ever be. We are all, without conscience, magicians in the dark." To this lack of overlap between art as experienced and knowledge of art, I do obeisance. The concerted disciplines gathered here may hit their limits from other directions, but just as drastically. And I cannot share the hope [16] that ". . . humanistic research in what is perhaps the most human of man's endeavors" will advance us even as far as the kind of inquiries here proposed.

In any event, I must write as an art educator, not a psychologist, positioned between an eclectic, derivative, or applied learning theory, and a slowly sharpening image of institution and learning in art, the latter being contingent on the "structure of knowledge" of a particular discipline or body of knowledge, conceived in the fashion of Bruner's writings on this subject.[17] The work "structure" is extremely troublesome and elusive, as later usages may illustrate.[18]

Change and Learning in Sequential Drawings Where Instruction is Absent

Claude Monet [19] thought young artists should:

. . . paint as they can, as long as they can, without being afraid of painting badly. If their painting doesn't improve by itself, it means that nothing can be done—and I wouldn't do anything.

Hidden in this simple advice from an artist is a key assumption underlying my presentation. This is that from the simplest first scribbles of the child to the drawings of the most advanced artist, change across drawings has typically the features of a "learning automation" about it. What artist has not had the experience of looking back on earlier work and seeing it as, possibly, shrunken, simple, direct, naive, or whatever, but within a history of continuous change, still, inescapably connected to present products? Many cases of primitives showing continual improvement without "instruction" also come to mind. I mention these instances, not to discredit instruction, for my aim is to eventually clarify its proper and facilitative function, but rather to point to certain features in a series of uninstructed drawings, stretched over time, which might help us to conceptualize what change and learning in drawing are like. I do not limit myself to any kind of drawing, such as representational drawing; nor do I deny the many, many influences that affect drawing. Kris [20] has ably stated the broad nature of these:

. . . art is not produced in an empty space . . . no artist is independent of predecessors and models . . . he no less than the scientist and the philosopher is part of a specific tradition and works in a structured area of problems.

Yet there is something about this section of my paper that makes it hard to state, even though my aim is to make it disarmingly simple by making little of the aesthetic and symbolic properties of drawings and focusing on the act of drawing itself. Arnheim [21] begins to make the point I am after, when he suggests that the act of drawing has its own constraints and reality about it, whatever is brought to it.

In terms of a single drawing, the artist is in effect an operating organism (system) regulated by feedback of his own acts or traces. The "cybernetic principle" which describes a "regulated system" as one guided by feedback of its own output comes closest to what I mean.[22] Of course, in a broad sense all conscious action, all speech, etc., conform to this model, but in the case of a drawing, the field boundaries of the page, the lingering trace made by hand and marking tool, the clearly sequential and cumulative nature of the traces, and the fact that a terminal product results set drawing apart as a prime example of a regulated system in operation.

In earlier research,[23] Burkhart and I tried to describe drawings done in a series in much the same way as a single drawing has been here described— that is, where conditions of theme and medium are relatively constant, and especially where prior drawings are present to influence direction, the drawings themselves become larger "feedback" units regulating subsequent drawings (we said that an evaluative phase of self-reflective feedback led to goal-setting, self-correction, and an eventual reformulation in the next drawing).

The gist of all this, to paraphrase Monet, is that "the very art of drawing and stringing out your complete drawings in time will improve your next drawings." Of course he was addressing "young artists" (a possible qualification) and seemed to feel that if nothing improved the case was hopeless or "unnatural." I do not believe either qualification to be necessary. In fact, I would assert that the paraphrased statement applies to any sequential (free) drawing situations and to any age from scribbling on (and can even be extended to chimpanzees [24]).

According to Nelson: [25]

Emotive, motivational and cognitive dimensions . . . enter (into drawing) but find perceptual motor-expression. They are of greater significance in free drawing situations than in those where demand is well structured. And even though drawing has this duplex character, perceptual components seem of overriding importance. They are the limiting factor ordinarily.

What I take Nelson to be saying is that "perceptual components" (whatever they are), even in "free drawing situations" precede "emotive, motivational and cognitive dimensions" of drawings. An important quality of "perceptual components" is that they are not at all static, as the following statement by Gibson [26] well illustrates:

As things become identifiable, and as we learn to notice the differences between them, our perceptions of the world become differentiated. Formerly indefinite qualities become definite. . . . the progress of learning is from indefinite to definite, not from sensation to perception. We do not learn to have percepts but to differentiate them.

If we take these "perceptual components" to mean "differentiated perceptions," then I believe it possible to speak of "learning to see" in the visual field of drawings and to suggest that this is quite closely tied to learning to "differentiate" in drawing "components" as well. I feel that this is a transactional process and that the two processes are in fact one process. In a basic sense, we do not learn to draw but rather, in the context of this section, we "learn to learn to draw" as we differentiate and redirect components, and sequences in our own drawings. A "good" drawing, however realized, is a high level of performance, but learning in drawing involves interdrawing change. There are good reasons why a systematic attack on my topic is difficult. Gibson,[27] again, states these well:

For linguistic meaning . . . systematic definitions of signs and symbols can be worked out on the basis of logical and psychological theory. . . . But visual meaning has so far defied systematic analysis and the whole subject, including art-criticism, is notoriously speculative.

If this be so, and we reflect how little we know of the child's learning to use language (which Whitehead considered the most amazing learning of a human's lifetime), even though we are beginning to handle the syntactics and semantics of language logically and psychologically, how much more difficult of comprehension is what takes place in learning to draw which is part of a "whole subject" which is "notoriously speculative." As indicated, studies are progressing in the acquisition, use, and understanding of language syntax. The acquisition of syntax is seen,[28] as "a gradual and extended learning process that is comparable to other forms of meaningful learning and retention." Braine [29] has done preliminary analyses of two-work utterances of children which follow "one-word sentences" and precede "primitive sentences." In the two-word sentences he finds the child manipulating a "pivotal construction" based on his knowledge of certain key (pivot) words.

Language acquisition studies are mentioned because Kellogg,[30] Alexander,[13] Arnheim,[32] and Morris [33] make similar claims for the acquisition of drawing component "vocabularies" and "syntax" in the young child. I have been most impressed with this congruence of opinion on the emergence of prepictorial and early pictorial formal properties in the young child. By ending where art education, usually begins,[34] that is, with "pictorials," Kellogg has, as Morris points out, performed a valuable descriptive service in recording and labelling stages in "prepictorial" drawing. These she terms, in order, scribbles, diagrams, combines, aggregates, and, lastly, pictorials. The latter are constructed out of the progressively differentiated forms of the earlier stages (each of which

she has further classified into developing form units). These logically consistent basic stages of Kellogg are in need of further verification, but as they
stand they are provocative and useful concepts for reconstructing "perceptual and graphic differentiation" as observable in drawings.

Alexander [35] brings to bear a cognitive theorist's viewpoint on change and
"power" in children's drawings. A key viewpoint of his is that:

> . . . the rule-boundedness of drawing does not consist of externally imposed
> rules, but of constraints which are implicit in the act of drawing.

To Alexander, any particular individual's drawing is "generated under constraint," that is by a set of rules. Further, to define these rules, he states
that:

> . . . The schemata of the drawing were invented before the drawing; most of
> the basic forms which appear in a drawing were known before the drawing was
> done, and it is this set of available schemata which constitute the rules within
> which drawing can take place.

He postulates that there is a schematic base to all art, agreeing with
Gombrich [36] who sees all art as "conceptual." Where do the schemata come
from? He would agree with Kellogg that they come not from other children
or adults or from the world directly, but from the act of drawing itself. To
explain this emergence into differentiation, Alexander [37] presents three "postulates."

1. The child frequently reproduces his own previously established motor acts.
2. These acts are modified during execution by random variation.
3. They are also modified by a highly systematic built-in process of levelling
and sharpening.

In the first postulate on how schemata develop, we find traces of Lowenfeld's [38] "repetition for self-confidence," or Piaget's [39] "function pleasure,"
coinages which seem to interpret as well as label. In the second postulate,
repetition is seen as never the same because freedom, elision, variation, errors,
and automatism creep in. Whichever the more plausible explanation, repeated
elements undergo "random variation," apparently mostly on the motor side.
Postulate three, however, brings in the perceptual differentiation earlier
cited, but ties it directly to "sharpening," a procedure whereby the figure
or form is strengthened into "versions which are easier to encode perceptually."
What was almost something now becomes that something and extraneous
elements are left out, for ". . . it is not the passive side of memory which
obscures the detail, but the creative act of reproduction." [40]

Alexander goes even further than this, purporting to show how these
postulates help to explain not only the origin of schemata and their change
across drawings, but how organization and integration occur in drawings—
namely, as a result of "the child's developing ability to force the forms
apart from one another." [41]

Morris,[42] in his study of picture-making behavior in the great apes, concludes his book *The Biology of Art*, with six "biological principles of picture-making." Space will not permit much more than their names here, except where they extend the viewpoints (notice I have not called these "findings") of Kellogg and Alexander. Morris's principles, "which apply to picture-making as a whole and cover everything from Leonardo to Congo" (the latter the best of his ape-painters) are:

1. *The principle of self-rewarding activation.*
This was seen in Alexander's pleasurable repetition, Piaget's "function pleasure" and Lowenfeld's "repetition for self-confidence." The importance of this principle is so pervasive and it is so simple that it can easily be ignored as an essential theoretical building block. In Morris's [43] words:

All pictures, whether by young apes or adult humans, must have a self-rewarding element involved as all or part of the motivation of the picture-maker. Other sociological or materialistic motives may or may not be operating at the same time, but if the production of the picture is not also a reward in itself, then its aesthetic value will be impaired. This particular point has been discussed frequently, but judging by the fact that it is so clearly illustrated by the apes, it would appear basic enough.

In passing, it should be stated that Morris experimentally manipulated bribery with a food reward with his apes, who as soon as they came to associate drawing with the reward took less and less interest in picture-making itself so that any old scribble would do. Morris even refers to this as "commercial art" among apes!

2. *The principle of compositional control.*
This principle is confined largely to placement, filling of space, repetition, etc. Animals and young children, by the way, seem to prefer the stable "complexibility" of regular patterns (geometric, nested, etc.). Preference for asymmetry and complexity as Barron [44] uses these terms, is apparently a later development. The amount of figural "uncertainty," to use a variant of an information theory term, which can early be tolerated, seems to be slight. McWhinnie [45] and other students of McFee are presently investigating learning of the preference for these more difficult figures and arrangements which are a part of the vocabulary of contemporary art and appear to increase with art training.

3. *Calligraphic differentiation.*
This principle is akin to Alexander's "sharpening" postulate, since it refers to a process of clarification and differentiation of "details and component units of a picture, as opposed to the inter-relations of these units."

4. *Thematic variation.*
"There are two factors involved here: the finding of a theme and the subsequent variation of it. Sometimes the basic theme (will) itself be

completely replaced, but more often (the artist will) simply find some way of making a slight enough change to produce a variation without completely obscuring the original theme on which it (is) based.[46]

Morris gives an example from Congo, one of his chimpanzee picture makers, showing how Congo took a simple fan pattern and varied this theme into: Split fan, centrally-spotted fan, stippled fan-bundle, curved fan, and reversed fan. In the child, thematic variation usually proceeds via differentiation, where one theme grows out of the preceding in increasing complexity. In adults, complex and simple phases may follow each other, as a reaction one to the other. The dynamics of thematic variation will be subsumed under the learning set "directionality" in later discussion, whereas change of theme will be subsumed under "uniqueness, novelty, or innovation" learning set.

5. *Optimum heterogeneity.*

Morris sees a Scale stretching between "maximum heterogeneity (a mass of fussy detail)" and "maximum homogeneity (blank space)." The decision as to what constitutes "optimum heterogeneity" is apparently subjectively determined, by ape and human. Morris admits that there are transitional stages—as between "multiple scribble" and "blot out" when this principle seemed to get lost, but not for long. This principle, being largely unjudgable, is a difficult one to operate with and brings one to the much debated "when is a picture finished" question. Beardsley [47] gives the answer, although one weak in explanatory power and operational meaning. A picture is finished, he says, when the painter runs out of things to do next.

6. *Universal imagery.*

The source of universal imagery need be seen as neither mystical nor unconscious in nature. Morris makes a convincing case for muscular, optical, and psychological factors as parameters for universality of forms. On the ape-child-adult artist continuum, the shift is progressively from the muscular and the optical to the psychological. "As there are much greater individual differences in personal psychology than in arm musculature, or optical structure, it is not surprising that it is amongst the professional adult picture-maker, where the muscular and optical factors are most suppressed by the intellect, that one gets the greatest pictorial variation, and the weakest universality of imagery. In the pictures, of young children, or untrained adults, the universality is greater, owing to the levelling effect of muscular limitations and also the (as yet unobliterated) legacy of the strong pre-representational domination by optical influences over the image precursors." [48]

In recapitulation, Kellogg gives us the clearest description and taxonomy of pre-pictorial graphic development and differentiation, specifying its interdrawing or sequential drawing base. Alexander gives us the broadest explanation of forces bringing about such progressive differentiation and organization while Morris gives us the most far-reaching principles of picture-making as content within Alexander's scant repertoire, replacing, for example, "levelling and sharpening" by "compositional control, calligraphic differentiation, thematic variation, and optimum heterogeneity. As was true in the understanding of children's drawings near the turn of the century, the valuable insights are largely being generated from outside the art teaching profession, just as perspective on the existing literature on children's drawings is currently best analyzed and organized by a psychologist, Dale Harris.[49]

The above authors, much like Piaget, are non-experimental, though, they are, to varying degrees, logical and pre-theoretical. If the focus on sequential drawing as a learning automation has any merit, it must lead to fruitful questions and be submitted itself to checks and self-corrections. For example, Smedslund's [50] experiments with children on trainability of the "conservation" principle as described by Piaget, seem to suggest that stable mastery of such stages in thought may indeed proceed without much benefit of "formal instruction," as apparently is Piaget's position. Within "pictorials," the mastery of schematic detail, proportion and articulation depicting the concept "man" appears to have, overall, according to Goodenough and Harris, similar stability. Representational three dimensional space in "pictorials" has a like history of development, to all accounts.

It is, however, with the more difficult and central aesthetic and psychological ends of art that profound difficulties arise. I can hope to do no more than expose to your eyes the weight of my massive burden of confusion on the topics.

Unlike language, which if Bruner is correct can move toward progressive arbitrariness away from enactive and iconic modes of representation, graphic images and symbols are neither as completely arbitrary nor social.[51] Part of this confusion is historical and cultural, for to call a symbol non-social is, at least on the common sense plane, a contradiction of terms. Yet I am convinced that the degrees of freedom within graphic images and symbols is far in excess of those in language. To begin with, let us hark back to Gibson's charge that no logic or psychologic can be worked out as yet, and that the whole field is "speculative." L. L. Whyte [52] makes the same claim in his introduction to a book of essays from science and art on "Aspects of Form" when he says that art ". . . though for many the noblest of human activities, is still so obscure that Gombrich can provide, just for good measure in this volume, a new and intriguing interpretation, perhaps as useful as any yet."

Let us consider the difficult concept of visual meeting and dwell a bit upon its less directly aesthetic components. Visual symbols, in common with all symbols, are at the apex of complexity in the hierarchy of "meaning." Symbols ". . . mediate knowledge, as distinguished from perception, and they are the basis for reasoning, creative imagination, invention and discovery." Further, symbols as commonly used ". . . are completely determined by culture." [53] And to the psychologist "drawings not resembling anything familiar are called nonsense forms and, along with nonsense syllables, are employed in experiments on memorizing" or in studies of "rote" as opposed to "meaningful" learning.[54] But even here, it appears that in drawing non-sense forms from memory, recall does not occur until the senseless form gains sense.[55] Further, research on learning to recognize aircraft "suggests that when a nonsense form becomes identifiable it also becomes meaningful." [56] As I interpret these words whereas symbols may be "completely determined by culture," a so called nonsense form is imprinted with sense or meaning by a human being who has any commerce with it, and the resulting tincture of meaning might run the whole spectrum of meaning from simple use- or need-meanings to symbols themselves, which "mediate knowledge."

In our time, our shared visual symbols are singularly chaotic and impotent. To have all myths and symbol systems possible, is to have none. The great freedom thus provided us as artists must indeed exist in the aesthetic and psychological functions of art, as Morris [57] suggests, the religious and communicative functions being essentially dormant in our present culture. Before I get over my head in unprovable assertions, let me state that this condition exists not only for the visual artist, but all artists. To be sure, we have all that past cultures symbolized to rummage among, and indeed perhaps pictures owe more to other pictures, as Wölfflin, Malraux, and Cezanne insist, than to nature, and, I suppose I am saying, to even myths and symbol systems in themselves. Lest it seem that I am lamenting of being robbed of my religion, as Yeats did, by the science of the day, let me be quick to correct that impression. I speak of a general problem of inbalance in modern man which need not be lamented but described. I am inclined to the notion, as expressed by Adams [58] in an essay on Yeats, that any war between art and science is a false one:

Each presents its own meaningful fiction. One is essentially a fiction of human passivity, a world of mechanical forces in which man is contained. In its great systematic statements it is a supremely beautiful fiction, but its truth demands a counter-truth, another fiction. The fiction of literature provides an active human intelligence with the power to contain the world in his own imagination rather than allowing it to contain him.

(I cannot, in passing, resist saying that it is logically possible, though strange, that the one "fiction" can make the other its subject.)

But there is a reason why a great poet like Yeats writes as strange a book as his A Vision.[59] Lacking a meaning system, a symbol system, a myth, he set out to invent one. He wanted ". . . . a world larger than himself to live in; for the modern world as he saw it was, in human terms, too small for the human spirit, though quantitatively large if looked at with the scientist." [60] However outlandish A Vision may seem, Yeats wanted something which would stand toward his poetry in the relationship that Dante's Divine

Comedy stood toward the Christian Myth. Both poets ". . . strove for a visible structure of action which is indeed necessary to what they said, but which does not explain what they said." What Yeats created was not a mythology but "an extended metaphor . . . which permits him to establish relations between the tag-ends of myths eclectically gathered from all over the world." [61]

I leave to the anthropologist whether in *homo sapiens* there is a "biological universal" to be called "need: myth." Notice that Yeats is not thought to have needed the myth for the sake of his poetic craft but for his expressed desire for necessity or, if you please, symbolic meaning to his act of creation.

Gombrich,[62] in a recent talk to psychologists, suggests, following Pope, that "the sound must seem an echo to the sense." My simplest point, then, is that when discussing visual meaning and symbols as they come into art, "detachable meanings" which exist in symbols "as completely determined by culture" are more or less absent from our lives, so that the sense which the sound must seem to echo is either chimerical, extraordinarily abstract or esoteric, or idiosyncratic. I will now get into trouble, for sounds in themselves take on meaning in commerce with them. Further, as Gibson [63] acknowledges:

. . . any scene begins to appear strange when the eyes are fixated long enough. The attempt to observe one's visual field leads in this direction as does . . . the painter's intent view of something which interests him.

In brief, I am leading to the notion that "aesthetic" meanings are "non-detachable," belonging more to what Gibson would call the "visual field" as opposed to the "visual world," to the "echo" and not directly to the "sense." (I might just as well use Langer's "symbolic transformation" concept now that I've said all this.)

But the point of greater significance here has to do with the idiosyncratic sense or meaning that the drawing echoes, in which our attention shifts from "sense" to the picture-maker's perception of "sense," whether from what is culturally nonsense or from symbol is somewhat irrelevant. It is this which is really echoed, or eventually "matched," to borrow a construction from Gombrich.[64]

Polanyi [65] suggests there is a meaning to any context, but man-made ones, including drawings, are "contrived" and thus have a "message." This means, I feel, that the "context" or the "non-detachable meanings of the visual field" stand in some relation to the detachable, contrived meaning. The one side would appear to be more "aesthetic," or more "enactive and iconic" (these terms, in turn, match Morris's [66] "psychological, motoric, and optical").

The next point is that these contrived meanings are today mostly outside any myth. The earliest meanings "contrived" are apparently motoric and perceptual, locked in drawing itself. Later the contrived messages aid "creative and mental growth" [67] but, in my analysis, may often focus on sense at the expense of the echo, the non-detachable contextual or aesthetic component becoming subservient to socialized or logical perception of three-dimensional space, it being forgotten how hard-earned the smudges, lines, perspectives, etc. were when "illusion" was under conquest in the service of other myths or in the effort at mastering "illusion" itself.[68]

Wickiser [69] has expressed the question I am skirting as follows:

We discover that classifying or establishing . . . stages of development assumes all children want to do realistic art. This may have been a valid assumption prior to the modern art movement, but during the last fifty years many non-realistic types of art expression have developed, which seem to be more natural modes of expression. Add to this the fact that the greatest art periods of the past have been more Symbolic than Realistic, and suddenly we can no longer assume each child is striving to move out of the Symbolic stage into the Realistic.

Harris,[70] from a different vantage point, however, states that ". . . graphic ability which achieves representative drawing of esthetic or artistic merit cannot be discerned in young children; such appears only after certain psychological (cognitive) processes have run their course, and the child has mastered techniques appropriate to the medium. Much the same can be said of graphic traditions other than the representative."

Are these positions both reasonable and are they antithetical? I propose that if there are motor and perceptual determinants of drawings, assuredly there are psychological (I know all of these terms fall within psychology, but am following Morris's usage) or cognitive deeterminants of still greater scope. Otherwise we are in the untenable position of suggesting that the aesthetic meaning of drawings falls off with "the naming of Scribbling" and must be recaptured after representational drawing is mastered or after "certain psychological (cognitive) processes have run their course."

In a time when Piaget's considerable contributions to child development are being applied willy nilly to everything and everywhere, it may indeed be appropriate to consider his system of thought more closely for what it has to say about art (which is very little). Piaget [71] himself has said:

. . . very often, the young child appears more gifted than the older child in the fields of drawing, of symbolic expression such as plastic representation, participation in spontaneously organized collective activities, and so on, and sometimes in the domain of music. If we study the intellectual functions or the social sentiments of the child, development appears to be more or less a continuous progression, whereas in the realm of artistic expression, on the contrary, the impression gained is frequently one of retrogression.

In the same essay, he contrasts "social reality" with the "life lived by the ego" as follows:

On the one hand, there is the material or social reality to which the child must adapt himself and which imposes upon him its laws, its rules, and its means of expression; that reality determines the child's social and moral sentiments, his conceptual or socialized thought, with the collective means of expression constituted by language and so on. On the other hand, there is the life lived by the ego with its conflicts, its conscious or unconscious desires, its interests, joys, and anxieties; these form individual realities, often unadapted and always incapable of being expressed solely by the collective instruments of communication, for they require a particular means of expression. Symbolic play is nothing more than this method of expression; created almost out of nothing by each individual, thanks to the use of representative objects and mental images, all of which supplement language; its function is to permit the fulfillment of wishes, to compensate for reality, to allow free satisfaction of subjective needs, in short, to permit the fullest possible expansion of the ego as distinct from material and social reality.[72]

I quote Piaget at length because he speaks most cogently against the application of his work on social, moral, and logical development to matters aesthetic, and because his peculiar use of "symbolic" is one which I wish to borrow; to avoid confusion however, I will turn his usage into "idiosyncratic symbol," because that is precisely and simply what he means by it, though this usage contradicts convention.[73] There will be commonality (a further contradiction) in an "idiosyncratic symbol" by dint of some residue from our common life or from some "biological universals" (which I leave to the anthropologists) wherever man is socialized. Gombrich [74] comes close to this meaning when, "meditating on a hobby horse" in search of the "roots of artistic form" he sees aesthetic creation as not ". . . representation, image-forming, or abstraction, but simply the *making of a functional substitute*, an object which can serve in place of an original (or desired) experience in respect of some function or need of the individual." The formulation is very simple, like saying in this context "shaping freely something seeming like an echo for some idiosyncratic sense." Thus, we deal not just with the "relation of man and his environment" but as Lowenfeld [75] well knew with the relation between man and himself as celebrated in "symbolic play."

The difficulty is that some kind of nativism is apt to be inferred when unintended. There is no intent to make these processes other than "natural," rationally describable, and acquired. Yet ". . . the very logic of an education based upon intellectual authority tends to eliminate or, at least, to weaken" the aesthetic life of which we speak.[76]

In the same volume from which the quotations from Piaget were drawn, Ott [77] speaks of the similarity between children and artists (as I am trying to do only with respect to learning to learn to draw):

Children, like artists, are influenced by the effects they create as their work proceeds and they change their concepts accordingly. With increasing experience they add to their fund of shapes and sounds, each of which can be submitted to infinite interpretations.

But Ott is indeed a nativist in his references to "racial archetypes" and other, to me, unnecessary and nonexplanatory assumptions. Perhaps like many great art teachers (Cizek for example, who wanted his own island on which to raise child-artists) Ott either denies that these powers are capable of instruction or else implies they may be amenable only to his personal methods. He says [78] that children's

. . . aesthetic impulses should not be limited or constrained by any aesthetic formula based on historical, modern, or popular art. Children learn absolutely nothing from art teaching. They only develop of themselves.

I am going to comment on this viewpoint, for I trust that though I may appear to be a romantic I am looking less like a mystic.

There are still several more points about the "idiosyncratic symbols" or sense echoed in drawings. It is only because we do not have a duplex culture, where art and science instead of art or science, the conjunctive not the disjunctive, exists, that verbal processes are often seen as inimical to visual art. Certainly words can echo the sense as well as images; but from Pavlov [79] to Bruner [80] the relative inferiority of "iconic modes" of representation is pointed out, and for the ends these men have in mind, they are undoubtedly right. For "idiosyncratic symbols," however, the non-arbitrary, non-systematic properties of visual images and of sounds may be unexcelled, just because of their relative lack of syntactic and semantic properties (or whatever the visual equivalents of these terms would be).

Gombrich [81] describes a game of "multiple matrix matching" in which the symbol is revealed through "the choice from a given set of matrices of what is least unlike the referent to be represented." He illustrates his meaning by a parlor game in which an acquaintance is to be revealed through such questions as: "If he were a flower, what would he be? Or what would be his emblem as an animal, his symbol among colors, his style among painters? What would he be if he were a dish?" In this freer field, it is the pile up of hunches that counts. It is a "refusal to gate," using the phrase Gombrich borrows from Bruner, who uses it to describe perceptual economy where we either cannot derive more information or do not need it. But the game is different when the differentiated forms and organizational schemas we have won from the acts of drawing constitute the matrices from which to construct our "hobby horse."

The layman may wonder whether Giotto could have painted a view of Fiesole in sunshine, but the historian will suspect that, lacking the means, he would not have wanted to, or rather that he could not have wanted to. We like to assume, somehow, that where there is a will there is also a way, but in matters of art the maxim should read that only where there is a way is there also a will.[82]

What is won from drawing itself can aid us in the next drawing. This is almost a tautology, but seems far from being acknowledged. Language and logic have taught us that images and other sensory elements are useless, except, in the modern view, as steps in the acquisition of language and logic.

It can hardly be conjectured what might correct this departure from the idiosyncratic symbol (which comes into Bruner's system when language and logic fail or are blocked even as elsewhere "personal metaphor" is a source of "ideas" and "intuitions." [83]) Reid [84] advised us to "abolish the use of articulated sounds and writing for a century, for then every man would become a painter, actor, or orator."

I know of no more poignant way to get at the tendency of words to hide us from ourselves in modern times than in a passage from Proust: [85]

The great difference there is between the actual impression we received from something and the artificial impression we create for ourselves when we endeavor by an effort of the will to bring the object before us again, I did not pause to consider; remembering only too well the comparative indifference with which Swann used to be able to speak of the period of life when he was loved (because the expression suggested something so different to him) and the sudden pain caused by Vinteuil's little phrase (of music), which brought to mind those days themselves just as he had felt them. . . .

I believe I am drawn to sequential drawings as my focus because of the long swath cut from early childhood to the mature artist. The fact that drawing schemata are developed to a certain degree for all of us provides a beginning "structural" base from which to study change.

The case is not greatly different, however, for a more arbitrary and later acquired art, like that of throwing on the potter's wheel. Once the rudimentary skills are learned (and here instructional methods can cause marked improved speed of acquisition of these skills), the potter can only throw what he masters from pot to pot. I often think I should speak within the context of learning as seen in sequential pots made on the potter's wheel, for it might be clearer and less arguable, because in comparison to drawing, potting has constraints or rules which have more intersubject commonality. The residue of pre-pictorial schemata and idiosyncratic symbols from earlier years would not work their subtle interference with newer learning—there would be less "proactive inhibition." While many styles and directions and paradoxes abound in potting, the time-honored skills still demand respect from layman and artist alike, even though the language of pots is closed to many and even though it speaks in many dialects. There is no such issue as "potting and illusion," for example. Where there is clarity of goals from level to level of the art, there can be clarity of knowledge about methods of learning related to them.

But it is precisely because drawing will not be forced into such arbitrary intersubjective external rules and because the goals are in our century extraordinarily debatable that it is challenging, for it typifies the crisis of "knowledge" and learning in art and renders real and problematic what it is indeed to "think like an artist." Potting might do the same, to a degree, but it would have to be on a more exclusive and sophisticated plane.

My main points sketched to here need recapitulation:

1. Changes as seen in sequential drawings in the absence of instruction constitute a prototype of learning in art, occurring as they do in the works of primitive, untrained adult, and mature artist.

2. Sequential drawings are lawful across picture-makers on an appropriate level of generalization which considers:

   a. Motoric and perceptual differentiation of forms

   b. Sharpening of calligraphic components and their interrelations

   c. Sequential thematic development and search for novelty, seen in adult artists as alternations between complex and simple phases, interacting with sets toward novelty and directionality.

3. Sequential drawings are at the minimum, lawful within picture-makers in continuity, elaboration, and search for idiosyncratic symbolic themes to which drawing schemata stand in a matched but non-detachable relationship, or seem like an echo (in context of the medium) to (what seems like) a sense (or is contrived by the picture-maker).

4. This entire viewpoint has been termed a "learning automation," to suggest that, par excellence, a person involved in sequential drawings is illustrative of the cybernetic description of a regulated open system, as extended to organisms—that is, a system directed by feedback of its own output.

THE DESCRIPTION OF CHANGE AND CONDITIONS FOR CHANGE IN SEQUENTIAL DRAWINGS

It follows that no organism is directed, even in sequential drawings, by feedback of its own output exclusively. Even the statement that art owes more to other art than to nature implies this to be so.

The interdependence of context in the medium and what is or can be contrived has been suggested. When the child masters what Kellogg calls aggregates, and even combines, diagrams, and scribbles, rudimentary pictorials are possible. When the potter can center, open, and draw his clay into an even cylinder, rudimentary non-cylindrical shapes are possible. When through random variation, sharpening, or "meaningful imitation" of our external schemata (we know very little about these things), a matrix of forms is extended, new contrived messages can arise from the next context.

I know I have observed this latter process again and again in adult picture-makers. One instance may illustrate this point. A girl, not trained in art, had chosen, on her own volition, the theme "nature" for a series of drawings. Later an interview revealed that by this she apparently meant certain idiosyncratic symbols representative of an island beach, a country garden, etc., stemming from her childhood memories and environment. She began with a tree which, even to her, seemed stiff and stereotyped. Dissatisfied, she observed trees between drawings and drew a more "real" tree. Though it was different, it was obviously not illusionistic or meaningful enough to please her. In disgust or from aimlessness she made curved "tired" lines. These suggested how she felt and she developed this curved axis first into figures, then into a tree with "gesture." She felt some relation between herself, her theme, and the lines and refined this relationship over several subsequent drawings.

There is intended to be nothing spectacular or conclusive about this simple report. How does it fit under the topic of "conditions?" Well, it springs out of the basic viewpoint toward change in sequential drawings. More particularly, "no condition" here is a condition, in that it was under certain controls.

At this point a deviation into other assumptions is required. Burkhart and I [86] tried to make explicit several assumptions underlying our "self-reflective learning experiments" in drawing. In a sense, to coin a phrase, we tried to construct a model of the "structure of practice" (rather than knowledge) underlying the artist's (and to a degree even the chimpanzee's) picture-making. Our assumptions were simple but crucial:

1. Drawing is a "dialogue" between artist and drawing
2. As such, drawing is essentially a private affair
3. Reformulation, self-correction, and self-direction are facilitated by minimizing change in:
   a. Medium
   b. Theme or stimulus
   c. Procedure for self-evaluation
   d. General working environment
4. A "value neutral field" surrounding the picture-maker, removing extrinsic rewards, emphasizes the "principle of self-rewarding activation" Morris finds basic to picture-making.

Since these assumptions are delineated elsewhere [87] I will not dwell on their rationale here. The notion that art is a "dialogue" or a "crazy game of strategy" is commonplace in art writing. "Crazy" means that there are rules but that they are free to change in process and are somewhat particular to each "game." The idea of strategy and dialogue are exemplified in this statement of Black's.[88]

There is . . . in all artistic creation a characteristic *tension* between the man and the material in which he works . . . the artist literally *wrestles* with his material, while it both resists and nourishes his intention. . . . He finds himself constantly excited by the qualities objectively present in the material which it is his aim progressively to discover.

In like manner, Santayana [89] speaks of structure in the person and structure in the material and of their necessary tension and interaction.

In a very real sense, there is no "natural" condition for picture-making, but the artist's habits as abstracted have been a general guide. In addition, several research studies [90] suggested some support for "depth" or continuity of medium and theme and for specific evaluative activity on the part of the picture-maker.

The "self-reflection" learning experiment [91] Burkhart and I carried out under these broad general assumptions established the superiority of several further conditions for learning:

1. The strong facilitative effect of what we called "process feedback." Operationally, process feedback means giving the subject regularly sampled photographs of stages in the development of his prior drawing before he undertakes his next drawings—this is the most potent condition we uncovered. It bespeaks the importance previously ascribed to the drawing activity itself. It might be expressed thus: nothing seems to improve drawing like drawing and paying attention to how one draws.
2. The merit of what Rogers [92] calls an "internal locus of evaluation." In operational terms this meant that the subject "discovered for himself" what criteria he should use to evaluate his drawings.
3. The feasibility of carrying out the evaluation of one's drawings by a program (written instructions), this appearing to work as well as through mediation by another person (teacher surrogate).
4. The likelihood that the teacher surrogate or mediator and the internal locus or self-discovery evaluative setting instills in the picture-maker perceptions of himself as more creative, confident, independent, and worthy.

I know I have slipped a lot over on you, because I have not explained what it means to "improve" drawings. This is the subtle and important criterion for learning problem which is under constant study [93] but which cannot be studied profitably out of the context specific to the given research problem.

I had intended to borrow much more from psychological learning theory than I have to this point, but my many references seem largely foreign to this setting so I have not forced them into the discussion. There was indeed a "learning set" established in the case of the girl who drew the trees in the earlier example. She knew the conditions under which she would work, what would be supplied and what not, that she would have to initiate the theme and its development, that she would see photographs of how she drew, and that she would evaluate these according to her own goals. She knew that while I did not give her direction, I projected "interest" and "confidence" in her direction as she perceived these. She engaged in "trials" or practice-distributed "practice." I guess a psychologist would call it, with task criterion unspecified externally. "Process feedback" appears equivalent to "delayed knowledge of results" or, at the least, "information" through "stimulated recall" of how results were obtained. Evaluation of this process information led to the development of "concepts" and "principles," probably "advance organizers" and "internally mediated or induced learning sets" for later drawings.

I do not believe it requires a stretch of the imagination to talk logically and objectively about conditions fitting an activity of which the main parameters are "idiosyncratic symbols" and "drawing schemata" (and drawing strategy, soon to enter the discussion). We will disagree to the extent that these basic parameters cause disagreement. I mean to make them extraordinarily abstract, pervasive, and basic to all free drawing serving simultaneously aesthetic and psychological functions for the picture-maker—that is, all settings where sense and its seeming echo, contrived message and context meaning, functional substitute for an internal state, or symbolic transformation involving images and forms is involved.

Bruner [94] has argued, even with children, that it is best not to mess up a person's method (or strategy) of processing information. What does "processing information" mean in the act of drawing and in sequential drawings? What, in fact, is a drawing strategy? To what degree can we speak of drawing as problem-solving? Do the terms used in the psychology of learning fit the drawing act? For example, is there anything to be gained by the distinction rote—meaningful, reception-discovery, visual-verbal; or classical and operant conditioning, discrimination learning, concept formation, principle and rule learning, and problem-solving? I have pondered many writings on these matters and taken many notes where I thought to discern parallels or possible translations, but while I may draw upon these, I have decided that this is not the time or the place to treat the possible correspondences systematically. After all, this is a sketchbook. Furthermore, the very effort strikes me as both pretentious and premature. It is a time to imitate selectively, but not to incorporate.

In returning to information processing, I have uncovered an interesting lead in pilot work on learning in sequential drawing now in progress. In working intensively with a small group of untrained (non-art major) college students, taking them one at a time and carefully sampling photographic data on their drawing processes, I have uncovered an interesting lead in pilot work on learning in sequential drawing now in progress. In working intensively with a small group of untrained (non-art major) college students, taking them one at a time and carefully sampling photographic data on their drawing processes, I have observed clear differences between drawing schemata and strategy when working from "mental themes" on the one hand and from a physically present complex still life on the other. In some subjects the two kinds of drawings would be quite hard to put together without further clues. Untrained subjects usually automatically assume a representational or illusionist set toward the physical stimulus but feel no compulsion to do so from a mental theme (I sometimes refer to these conditions as outside- and inside-the-head-junk stimuli). Further, about twice as long, on the average, is spent on working from the physical stimulus (which is, to be sure, rather complex). This suggests the simple notion that with these subjects more "information" is being processed for inclusion or translation into drawing when more time is taken. Further indication of this is suggested by the fact that when I give some subjects twice as much process feedback as others, they also seem to take more time on their subsequent drawings, whether from mental theme or still-life. The combination of still-life and increased process feedback, thus, keeps my untrained subjects at a drawing longer. When I shift subjects after four periods from one of these stimulus conditions to the other, there seems to be some transfer of time conditions to the new setting for those going from still life to mental theme, but a big shift occurs with the opposite group.

I well know that time spent on a drawing in a free drawing setting is not in itself important as related to learning or change, but it is certainly a factor of possible explanatory significance where information processing and strategy are considered.

One of our doctoral students [95] studying the effect of "highly structured visual and highly structured memory approaches to drawing" has this to say:

Hale repeatedly points out that most of the "great drawings" have been done from memory and not from life, but that the storehouse was full before the memory could be tapped. At whatever point in the education system the student undertakes to develop his drawing skill, he is in need of a background of visual concepts that can be drawn upon by memory. Some would say that this storehouse can be supplied only by direct contact with objects.

From the base supplied by the parameters of idiosyncratic symbol and drawing schemata, and in the perspective of this century, I see no necessary superiority for Hale's viewpoint. A contrary case could be made even more cogently focusing on the two parameters of drawing. If indeed all drawing is conceptual (or, at the least, more or less conceptual), the conceptual base need not be limited to "representation," especially as construed in the illusionistic tradition. It would seem that any approach which extended and enriched the symbols and schemata of drawing would fulfill this function. I rather sense that what Britsch and his followers Schaeffer-Simmerin and Arnheim call "visual conceiving" is not the mysterious thing it is made out to be, but merely the result of continual (sequential) drawing, and that the similarities seen, for example, in Schaeffer-Simmerin's book,[96] are a simple outcome of students working in proximity with each other and with a master or teacher, so that schemata and symbols are common property and receive fairly consistent reinforcement. Any teacher of a studio, or any scholar who has advisees, who has not seen this happen has not kept his eyes open.

Unexpected support for the idea that drawing schemata do not "naturally" incline toward representational illusion, comes from recent studies in the psychology of perception. Hochberg [97] claims that outline pictures are not a learned visual language, and that what learning there is, if any, "occurs very early in life in consequence of our normal commerce with spatial objects." Whereas Bruner [98] speaks of how it is to the child's advantage to "denature" his representations of knowledge into the arbitrary symbols of language and number as quickly as possible, it appears that "denatured" images or schemata much precede those later illusionistic ones which conceal their artistically speaking arbitrary nature from us. As Hochberg [99] puts it

". . . the characteristics of a given object may be communicated better as the representational fidelity of the surrogate deteriorates." But, as Gibson [100] points out, this is not to say that all perception is "schematic" or based on the misperceptions of observers because of subjective factors. Ordinary life and ambiguous or improverished stimuli in the laboratory lead to "schematic" perception, as in the famous study of Bartlett [101] where "nonsense" figures were altered in keeping with characteristics of the individual. It appears, says Gibson, that "literal perception" can also occur and be remarkably accurate according to stimuli presented.

More important for the story here, however, is the argument for "tertiary qualities" or "physiognomic qualities" which are increasingly felt to be, in large part, more a function of "in the object" variables than "in the observer" variables. Pratt [102] summarizes this viewpoint and I repeat his summary:

Tertiary qualities permeate and suffuse all perception, and in art reveal a heightened expression which becomes the very essence of artistic enjoyment and appreciation. Writers who have been influenced by this newer outlook tend to agree on at least three points: (a) Tertiary qualities can only be described by words which also connote subjective moods, but they themselves are not subjective; (b) they are intrinsic properties of visual and auditory perception, not borrowed from any other modality; and (c) they are probably correlated with higher-order stimulus variables. This last conviction awaits proof. If some Gibsonian global psychophysics can eventually produce it, the demise of empathy, at least in the fine arts, will be unavoidable.

The argument suggested by these references is that, though perception is often "misperception" in ordinary life, the "literal" perception of art does not depend on this schematic tendency, for there are tertiary or physiognomic qualities matching that to which we give expression-laden and subjective-sounding names in the art object itself. It is no contradiction to hint that the sense that seems to be echoed in the sound of the drawing schemata that seem to stand in some relation to an idiosyncratic symbol are actually made up of these very physiognomic or tertiary qualities alluded to. That these concepts can be logically combined, a kind of paradoxical "objective subjectivity," is suggested by Gombrich's [103] sweeping statements:

The growing awareness that art offers a key to the mind . . . has led to a radical change of interest on the part of artists . . . The language of forms and colors . . . that explores the inner recesses of the mind has come to be looked upon as being right by nature. Our nature.

To the artist the image in the unconscious is as mythical and useless an idea as was the image on the retina. There is no short cut to articulation. Wherever the artist turns his gaze he can only make and match, and out of a developed language select the nearest equivalent.

Whether such a growing tendency to resort to "formalism" will, in fact, offer those of us studying art some refuge from the accidents of both neoassocianism and ultra subjective relativism or not remains to be seen. But it is still a cognitive fact of life that such formal properties are "formed" into context and "stand in relation" to contrived sense.

At this point, against the rambling backdrop supplied by this paper, I would like to introduce the process emphasis raised by the term "drawing strategy." I have already labored at defining further certain consistent differences in drawing behavior that Burkhart and I earlier described,[104] but this work is just begun.

Psychologists have by and large used the term strategy to describe consistent modes of processing information. The very term "processing information" fits the productive side of art quite poorly. The broader terms used by Miller, Galanter, and Pribram,[105] "image, plan, strategy, and tactics" have greater appeal to one in the arts. Further, the analogies to computer strategies advanced by Newell, Shaw, and Simon [106] for use in simulating certain kinds of problem solving are attractive, perhaps because both of these sources reflect more global and eclectic positions which, nevertheless, have a behavioral or functional ring to them in that they deal with input-output relations and with feedback in a somewhat mechanistic manner. The computer simulation programs in particular use:

> . . . a substantive view of the nature of information as well as the cybernetic principle of a control system that is both (a) sensitive to feedback indicative of behavioral error or discrepancy between existing and desired states of affairs, and (b) differentially responds to such feedback in ways that correct the existing error or discrepancy.[107]

The difficulty in speaking of a strategy in drawing is that the entire set of actions involved in making a drawing, described as a dialogue between artist and work are covertly mediated. "Inputs" can only to a general degree be manipulated without distortion of the process. A simple example of manipulation was given in the case of physical still-life or mental theme as beginning stimulus for a drawing. The "drawing-cognitive structure" of the learner, in terms of the kinds of "idiosyncratic symbols" and "drawing schemata" in his experience at the outset, seem especially important bits of knowledge for understanding what will ensue. For surely no S-R mediational chain, a horizontal left-to-right concatenation of antecedent and subsequent conditions in time, will suffice even for the understanding of the pre-pictorial child, although we need such attempted studies, even like the simple studies of Morris when he structured the drawing field for the chimpanzee by placement of stimuli within it. But the drawing act then changes from that where no such structuring or external stimuli are applied.

Rather, it would appear that certain "drawing operations" and "drawing transformations" are at the command or in the repertoire of the picture-maker, and that it might be preferable to use this more dynamic language in preference to the term "drawing schemata." The latter term, "schemata," suggests a repertoire of forms, while the former, "transformations," suggests ways of forming and of relating forms. Probably both ideas are involved. Bruner and Olver [108] speak of concepts as being formed by imposing "transformations" on data, and, interestingly, feel that these constitute strategies that grow with age and allow for progressively *simpler* processing of information.

Because human memory and consciousness can manipulate only a few items at a time, and thus resort to "chunking" of information,[109] the energy of the organism or system is distributed between encoding "chunked" input (to include in my beginning thinking or fuzzy aspects of the "image," in which symbol and schemata are already brought into tension), and selecting and applying "transformations" on this output, and for this reason, simple and clear strategies or systems of operations are important. Too many techniques and ways to operate and too many beginning ideas of nearly equal importance would effectively forestall action. When my subjects "stop to think" a minute or two about what they will draw next, I assume that they are reviewing symbolic material and schematic operations by means of "mediating verbal processes" [110] and other mediating processes. Actually, I can only infer this from what subjects can tell me of this process. Will it suffice to merely conclude that an "image" and "plan" are emerging which, following Miller, Galanter, and Pribram,[111] will eventuate in a strategy with its tactics for carrying it out?

Actually, even language on this global level becomes excessively restraining for talking about drawing. Even if there is a vague "image" for a drawing, to what degree is there an overall plan? Burkhart and I [112] sensed that operationally speaking on a high level of abstraction, there were coherent strategies covering temporal, spatial, and hierarchical (evaluative) kinds of order.

But before discussing these kinds of order, I would like to deal with drawing as problem-solving behavior. As though it were not enough that this kind of behavior gives psychologists a most difficult time, I must express my conviction that drawings are more complex behaviorally than what I find in discussions of problem-solving. In Gagne's [113] discussion of "learning types," problem solving is "type 8," at the top of the hierarchy of learning types (the other seven being "prerequisites" to it). Gagne says of problem-solving that it ". . . is a kind of learning that requires the internal events usually called thinking. Two or more previously acquired principles are somehow combined to produce a new capability that can be shown to depend on a 'higher-order' principle."

Although the number "eight" is not a mystical one, Getzels [114] further subdivides problems into eight kinds, defining them along four dimensions: presented-discovered problems requiring convergent-divergent thinking, involving secondary-primary process thought, and having a stimulus reducing-stimulus seeking quality for the organism. For Getzels, the highest order of problems is one in which ". . . the problem itself exists but remains to be identified or discovered, and no standard method for solving it is known to a problem-solver or to others."

Simon [115] has recently said that "problem-solving involves selective trial-and-error search in a vast space of possibilities." "Selective search" means in the case of humans usually less than 100 alternatives and not the 10^{120} choices that would have to be considered in playing chess, for example, if an algorithm were involved. Therefore some "heuristic" hunch about short cuts is invoked. Creative problem-solving is near the "blind-search end of the continuum." Further, for Simon, the "novel" arises for a number of reasons: the subject has a superior intelligence, a new problem, observes a new phenomenon, has a new instrument or a new analytic tool, or is utilizing a mixture of cues from different fields. "Depth" in problem-solving is revealed through a tremendous preoccupation with the problem and "a long term tolerance for ambiguity."

Ecker [116] has spoken of "art as qualitative problem-solving," and thus has inserted an important qualifier setting art problem-solving, to a degree, off from other kinds. But the question remains whether it is helpful to consider drawing as problem-solving at all. It may, to be sure, be a kind of "discovered, divergent, stimulus-seeking, primary process" activity directed toward "qualitative" or aesthetic ends, and lying near the "blind search end of the continuum." But is this formulation of any virtue in the explanatory sense? Apparently there are "rules," but drawing still appears, though lawful, as a kind of qualitative crazy process game of strategy, in which the medium talks back and the rules can keep shifting until the very end.

At this point, it is tempting to turn to the more obscure or analogical language often used by artists and art critics in speaking about art. Instead I prefer another source, which while still unsatisfactory, has a certain heuristic function in my own blind search. Ehrenzweig [117] has recently spoken of creative thought as seen in drawing as a gradual advance in successive stages, each opening into new possibilities, unforeseen to a degree, then closing into clarity; thence into subsequent stages, and into integration through combinations made in progress. If I drop out the psychoanalytic constructs which Ehrenzweig leans upon (and which I think are unnecessary as explanations), this simple formulation is consistent with what I have gained from Alexander, Morris, and Gombrich on the one hand, and from Miller, Galanter, and Pribram, Bruner, and Newell, Shaw, and Simon on the other—especially if we restrict our attention to what Simon calls "creative problem solving." In common with Ehrenzweig, Bruner [118] speaks of appropriately open and appropriately closed phases to ideation, and of "retreat" to personal metaphor or lower levels of representational modes for knowledge when blocked. In like fashion, Beardsley [119] analyzes "preconscious" processes (apparently the seedbed for intuitive and illuminative ideas), into gestalt strengthening and associative components which, taken together, become the preconscious and inventive phase of the creative process, alternating with a conscious and selective phase, the latter being critical or evaluative. Rhythmical cycles thus emerge, in which the entire process of making a drawing would consist of stages, each gradually advancing through "preconscious and conscious" phases, which would find their equivalent in still more molecular structural units composed of the actual transformations or operations sought, selected, applied, and compared or evaluated. I get the image of a fugue which gives the impression of great detail and order in retrospect but was not at all that way in its actual parts and organization, in prospect. Or this checks with Alexander's and Morris' notion that an attempt to clarify or differentiate components of drawings leads naturally to component relations and larger organization. Such formulations are in a pre-explanatory phase, with a heavy component of "hope" in them, or at least a big leap from one level to another of the problem.

Just what the preconscious is, no one has helped me to understand. It is perhaps a retreat into the strangeness of perception that Gibson speaks of (the "visual field"), or Fiedler's lingering at the stage of "pure perception," or Ehrenzweig's cross-eyed "unconscious scanning" or "diffused attention" which is thought to lead to "or-or" structures (disjunctives, or mutually exclusive variations of a theme), or James' "consciousness" which cannot be attended to directly.

Perhaps the entire notion of a "preconscious" phase is unparsimonious. McKellar [120] speaks of an "authorship-editorship" relation which holds between "autistic" or free-association thinking and directed thinking.[121] And Berlyne, who has, as an "integrative neoassociationist," taken pains to set up autistic as distinct from directed thought, and stresses the dependence of the latter on "transformational chains" (see footnote 121) nevertheless states that ". . . transformational and free-associative thinking must usually interact and collaborate in practice." The way an artist or thinker recognizes an appropriate route or heuristic is not known. Progress may have some relation to "conflict reduction." [122] Even problem-solving simulated in computers alternates between running through lists and selecting or applying an operation.[123]

Berlyne [24] further states: "Symbolic structures must . . . store information in at least three forms which are at the disposal of directed thinking; transformational chains, free-associative chains of situational thoughts, and free-associative chains of transformational thoughts." Beardsley [125] believes that the psychological dispute about what goes on in the preconscious can be resolved by stating that both "associative processes" and "closure or strengthening of gestalts" are involved, or a work of art would not get done. To a great degree, both Berlyne and Beardsley are admitting that, in terms of the arguments in this paper, there is a circulation or scanning of "idiosyncratic symbolic" stuff, or "sense," and of schemata or schematic drawing operations. Thus, it is possible to surmise that "implicit drawing" takes place to make actual drawing operations possible and to scan freely alternatives for resolving subjective uncertainty or arousal or what we sometimes in art education call "motivation."

Certain conditions within the organism are now felt to be related to exploratory behavior, and to what Getzels [126] earlier called the "stimulus-seeking" side of the organism. Berlyne [127] defines two kinds of exploratory behavior.

. . . specific exploration is occasioned by an aversive condition that may be called "perceptual curiosity" . . . brought on by incomplete perception of a sector of the stimulus field, which leaves the subject with some uncertainty regarding its characteristics. . . . *Diversive* exploration . . . has the function of introducing stimulation from any source that is "interesting" or "entertaining." It is exemplified by the various activities through which human beings seek "amusement," "diversion," or "aesthetic experience."

Berlyne then goes on to relate "specific exploration" to "directive thinking," and "diversive exploration" to "autistic thinking," thereby tending to take "aesthetic experience" out of the "problem-solving" field reserved for directed thinking.

It is now clear that a resolution to my own conflict and uncertainty becomes possible. As stated, I feel there is no useful function served by calling the production of a drawing a problem. This is the schoolman's distortion of a process to fit instructional language and control, and those of us who teach art know that our instructional "problem" often arises from the fact that we have structured a problem for the performer. In this context, I am inclined to follow the reasoning of Beardsley: [128]

What is the problem? It might be: "How can I make a good drawing using these lines I've already drawn?" or, "How can I make a good sculpture out of this block of marble?" But these are queer things to call problems: they are really tasks, the terms of which are voluntarily accepted by the artist. The main question involved in each of these is simply: "What do I do next?"

But across a series of drawings or works, something like directed thinking, learning to learn, or in the case of the young child and chimpanzee, unfolding or differentiated development occurs. In the instructional setting, therefore, and in developing a sketchy theory of learning in art, the process-product argument can be resolved, and the problem or product of learning made that of the sequence itself, of the series of directional processes. The child and the mature artist alike face this problem, though on differing levels of complexity and consciousness. Learning-to-learn, therefore, whether conscious or not, becomes the problem in art, and the term directed thinking can be applied to it.

The individual work, in contrast, has more in common with diversive exploratory behavior where the goal is unclear and the subjective uncertainty or conflict the prime mover. At times a "classic work" for each subject will occur, the nature of which is, in a sense, a verification of a nearly fully intuited transformational chain arising out of the series of works of which it is a part and made possible by the "feel" of the series. Thus the potter or draughtsman will often sense he is about to make the "real thing" because his submersion in production has permitted him to project the most satisfying resolution of his natural uncertainty as to what he is after.

But, more often, the individual work, especially in the school setting, will reflect a much less clear image of what the person is after. The danger of the one good work which is not in a series (where the series itself can be an instructional and subjective problem) is that it is a "performance" and can take attention away from learning. We therefore often house good performers in school who are good to show off but may be learning little or at least nothing they might not have learned better drawing by themselves.[129]

Thus, I am trying to present a clear distinction between the individual drawing and the sequential drawing context. The latter yields us a problem and direction, which has been called "learning to learn" and which has its reasonable base in uninstructed sequential drawings. Four out of Morris's six "biological principles of picture-making" require sequential works to be meaningful. The first, "the self-rewarding activation," does not. It suggests that the individual work may pick up its uncertainties or conflicts or sub-goals (if any), from its place in a series, but that its character is still more esthetic or like that of "diversive exploration." Further it may be defined with learning terms as meaningful or intelligent and not mechanical or rote, as discovery and not reception, and as involving some directed thinking and specific exploration as well as autistic thinking and diversive exploration. Continued drawing experience, therefore, should enable the student to handle more appealing, complex, or novel kinds of uncertainty and conflict because he has available a growing store of idiosyncratic symbolic material and schematic drawing operations with which to resolve that conflict. The language commits me to a more problem-solving sound than I intend, because I still feel that, apart from getting the work started, the problem is of a more pervasive quality, namely in the context of sequential works.

It appears, thus, that a work of art is only in this broader sense qualitative problem-solving. Even if I take a more so-called functional and obviously formal art, such as pottery, this is so. If, for example, I were to set out to make a stoneware cup for my ceremonial daily office-coffee, the latitude for variation in clay, form, thickness, lip, balance, foot, handle, decoration, glaze, and firing is virtually endless, even admitting, as I must, that I will work within my own "cup schemas." To be sure, there is the general and persisting problem of throwing a cup. Also, I generally throw a "run" of cups to get a "good" one (but cannot specify ahead of time what "good" will be). If I had never thrown a cup, I would not only have a problem but problems, and in this sense the word has some educational utility. In the example given, even with my expressed goal, if I felt a good cup for cool water on the desert was emerging, instead of one for my ceremonial office coffee, I would not be dismayed because if that is the reality that sense and context take, so be it.

Note that we are not plunged into a "crisis of meaning" where a cup or any craft object is involved, in anything like the manner where we deal with picture-making. This is true to a degree even though the boundaries between craft, painting, and sculpture are breaking down, and even though some "pots" could not possibly hold anything and were not intended to.

Another important point concerning the general topic of art strategies in the context of sequential drawings, is that of specifying what takes place in a strategy, or better, in a drawing itself. There is an interest in specifying operations in problem-solving and thinking converging from many sources. "Operations" are foremost in the system of Piaget [130] in his discussion of the development of thought and logic in the child. In computer simulation of problem-solving it is necessary to define the operations to be performed to transform information in one form into another closer to the solution. Berlyne speaks of "transformational chains" as the key to "directed thinking." Since they are "derivatives of overt responses that regularly result in particular kinds of environmental change" (p. 123), it would appear that the earlier formulation stating that drawings come from drawings is not at all erroneous, providing allowance is made for both the symbolic and operational side of drawings. As in directed thought, any one transformational chain in producing a drawing must ". . . on the whole . . . depend on the information contained in the subject's symbolic structures and cannot rely on periodic replenishments of information from the outside world." [131]

Just what are the components of a transformational chain in drawing or of a drawing strategy? (By the way, I must agree with Berlyne that the phrase "transformational chain" has certain advantages over the fuzzier "strategy," in that it embarrassingly asks one to "put up or shut up." "Strategy," however, suggests the cognitive structure of the subject better, in its emphasis on hierarchy, or verticality, as well as in order, or horizontality. I will thus retain both terms, and attempt to speak of the transformational chain of a drawing strategy.) As a first step toward answering the question about the contents and dynamics of the transformational chain of a drawing strategy, it is necessary to clearly re-establish the dialogue which is drawing.

Each time the artist . . . takes a step, he adds something to what is already there (A), and makes another and different object (B). If he judges B worse than A, he must go back. If B is better than A, the question is whether it is good enough to stand alone as a work of art. If not, the question is whether B can be transformed into still another and better object, C. If this is impossible, if every attempt to improve it only makes it worse, then the whole project is left unfinished, for it is unfinishable.[132]

The first step taken Beardsley calls the "incept," and feels may be any sort of thing: ". . . the first sentence of a story or the last, a simple plot situation, a character, theme, scene, figure of speech, or tone or style" (p. 297). Any sort of thing of esthetic or psychological appeal will do for the first step because ". . . the crucial controlling power at every point is the particular stage or condition of the unfinished work itself, the possibilities it presents, and the developments it permits." [133] In support of this position, the same author presents a revealing passage from Valéry [134] who feels that poetry proceeds by means of ". . . word combinations, not so much through the conformity of the meaning of these groups to an idea or thought that one thinks should be expressed, as, on the contrary through their effects once they are formed, from which one chooses." In similar vein, I could cite many examples of the larger transformations a work has gone through before its completion. Often this process material is lost, but where it is retained, many revealing changes occur. In Yeats' Byzantium poems where a record of their development has been preserved,[135] many of the meanings are completely reversed from earlier to later versions. And it is common in the visual arts nowadays to allow for Picasso's dictum that a painting may be the result of a sum of destructions. Some years back at Ohio State University, process photographs of certain painters were spoken of as indecipherable as to directionality if time clues to order were concealed. The stages, in other words, were large and startling transformations. In drawings, however, with an essentially additive medium, this will be less likely in the larger sense but completely likely in the chain sense. Why this should be so requires discussion.

In symbolic behavior as in overt behavior ". . . the associations that a subject possesses may link up to produce a chain that he has never used before. In directed thinking, this may take the form of inference or of the random reshuffling to which a subject may resort when his established hierarchies leave him at a loss." [136] In addition, as Alexander, Morris, and I have tried to suggest, drawing changes drawing by differentiation, sharpening, thematic variation, idiosyncratic symbolic inputs, and general lap-over from one work in a series to the next.

Two further concepts strike me as appropriate to the drawing incept and process: the first is that of "recursive anchoring," the second "adventurous thinking." "Recursive anchoring" has been compared by Berlyne [137] to the technique by which a person is rescued who has fallen through a hole in the ice on a pond. A human chain is formed. "As long as the first member of the chain has a solid foothold on land, his security is transmitted throughout the chain until it ultimately reaches the victim, who is therefore prevented from sinking." Analogies are suggested to Gombrich's "schema and correction" formula for drawing. In fact, it is suggested, as Beardsley stated, that any beginning will do that serves the artist's purpose to engage himself in the chain. An "as if," or something taken "for the sake of argument" or an "improvised theme" will also fill this definition. In my own research, where I deal with "inside-the-head" and "outside-the-head junk," these labels are intended to designate no more than the broadest control of conditions for purposes of studying their motivational effects, for in each the appropriate point of "recursive anchorage" is seen as necessarily mediated through the subject's perception and choice. This choice, in fact, is part of the reality of this very learning, and many subjects must learn to establish some idiosyncratic symbolic or drawing base anchorage in their incept. This is one simple point of what "to think like an artist means" to me. In this I differ slightly from Lowenfeld, for the "what" is as holy as the "how." The "what," in fact, is the "how" of the incept.

The label "adventurous thinking" used by Bartlett [138] is a poor one for this next point, but his research comes closest to what I wish to communicate. Structural analysis in scientific study of forms in nature designates the "branched structure," or "dendritic form," illustrated by the common tree, as that of an "individual," which occurs "whenever a protuberance has an advantage over adjacent areas in getting more matter, heat, light, or other requisite for growth. . . . All these branching structures start from a point and grow lineally, but they eventually stop as the branches interfere with others already present" (or some "extraneous obstacle"). An "inverse mechanism" is seen in the example of "the successive joining of many small streams to form a single large river." [139] I dwell on these analogies for a reason, soon to become apparent.

"Adventurous thinking" in Bartlett's [140] example, is in a problem-solving context. He states that:

> . . . when a thinker is working in an open, or relatively open system . . . he inclines to prefer the evidence which releases the greater rather than the smaller number of possibilities . . . The working, though not the formulated, rule seems to be that it is better to explore along the line of the greater number of possibilities, because it is more likely that the one sought will be found when there are a lot of chances than when there are only a few.

Thus, returning to Ehrenzweig's [141] earlier point describing the creative process as a gradual advance through unpredictable stages, I see a connection in that one can get into the drawing through a beginning stage, or subjective recursive anchoring, which then fans out through tree-form possibilities intellectually unforeseeable as "lists" of symbolic and transformational branches are evoked or stumbled upon in context. Unlike the solution-bound logic of problem-solving, we literally, as in the instructions to the Goodenough-Harris test, "draw the best man" that we can at the time, putting this, that, and the other thing in. For there is no reason to feel that a search of the branches at a node means that only one will be followed to the exclusion of other alternatives, in the drawing case, for indeed selected but opposed alternatives generate their own aesthetic and psychological appeal. Thus, in drawing, as in autistic thinking or diversive exploration, we may deal simultaneously with what Gombrich (1965) calls "the consonance and the dissonance of multiple meanings that interlink in the structure of artistic symbols" but we denied expression in our ordinary directed thinking, discursive logic, or problem-solving behavior. This revelation of the route and this clatter of symbols and schemata across matrices has always been a part of art, and all creative thought, but is apparently a conscious part of contemporary art.

Also, unlike problem-solving and much directed thinking, drawings run their course. As I recently put it: "We *can draw*, no matter how well or how badly. When we get there, the cupboard somehow isn't bare." Because diversive exploration and an esthetically directed transformational chain toward no clear solution but completion of its course, is involved, there are degrees of subjective success or failure only. Drawings are more rarely blocked and left unfinished or rebegun than might be supposed. In the last 100 drawings I have recorded processes on, only has this happened in one or two instances. Even admitting the possible effect of the research context, this is different from problem-solving as typically construed. In short, whether art educators quiver or not when it is said, free drawing is "serious fun" (or at least "self-rewarding activation," following Morris).

It is now time to return to the concept of strategies of drawing. Since Burkhart and I [142] have presented this concept elsewhere, I will not sketch in its origin here or draw from these sources except as points from them clarify my purpose in this paper. The main position is that the shift from a product to a process focus, from qualities in the work to patterns in its production, is helpful in the conception of change in sequential drawings (in itself a process viewpoint). Emphasis on "process realities" is not new in education. According to Brownell,[143]

. . . we need infinitely more process studies, for such studies yield the data and give rise to the insights that can affect teaching most directly. Process studies are not to be taken lightly. They are time-consuming, and they are especially susceptible to the charge of yielding unreliable, if not invalid, measures.

Schulz [144] questions the usefulness of process-tracing:

Process-tracing experiments, in which the experimenter analyzes peoples' responses to see what they do in achieving a solution to a problem, are argued to have limited usefulness because such experiments seem to assume that events observable during problem solving are themselves the causes of problem solving behavior.

In another passage, Anderson [145] comes even closer to a critique of the strategy concept:

What is alleged to *happen* when a person "executes a step in a strategy?" Does the essential part of a "step" consist of "thinking" certain words, that is, saying the words to one's self? If so, what for any particular "step," are these words and what accounts for their efficacy? If "steps" are nonverbal or not necessarily verbal, how then are they to be conceived? Or, perhaps we are *not* to imagine that there are actual events inside the person that constitute the strategy, but merely that the person behaves *as if* he were executing a strategy.

My own opinion is that it is too early to answer such questions and certainly much too early to discard the "drawing strategy" concept. So far, it has proved fruitful in research and generated a number of hypotheses. Recently, for example, Wise [146] has shown that students classified before experimentation as using what Burkhart and I called the spontaneous and divergent drawing strategies performed significantly better on expressive qualities linked conceptually with their strategies, suggesting a matching tendency within a strategy between the symbolic and schematic poles earlier discussed. Using drawing strategy terminology, a superior performance in expressing "inter-

action" is predictable for such spontaneous strategy "components" as movement within shapes; erratic, wandering fine lines; action gestures; and direct,
abrupt, quick motions. On the opposite side, the divergent strategy can
better match the expressive theme "isolation," by utilizing such strategy components as elimination of non-essentials (less cluttered), single element focus;
static, spatial suspension, floating (no base line implied); and fine line control
(the clearly "isolated" line). This finding would tend to support Gombrich's
thesis that one expresses well only what can be constructed or "matched"
from one's existing artistic means.

Another instance of the usefulness of the strategy concept is in judging
itself, where it appears that a judge is inclined to bias his judgment of
aesthetic quality in drawings toward his own drawing strategy.[147] This bias,
however, does not extend to his ability to discriminate between the strategies
themselves, for he can do this very well.

My third argument for the usefulness of the strategy concept is that it has
brought into question the earlier emphases in research on the relationships
between art and personality, which were lop-sided, overdrawn, and value-
laden. In this context, I refer to research in which I, Burkhart, and others [148]
were engaged, where we sought for the creative personality. There are undoubtedly general personality correlates of drawing strategies, but these are
not qualitatively important, but historically. Kagan [149] has recently pointed
to some of those characteristics in the young child that suggest a match
with strategy selection (or learning):

It has been established that the tendency to be impulsive or reflective in
selecting ideas for action is an extremely stable trait that generalizes across a
wise variety of tasks.

Kagan then attempts to relate this "stable trait" to educational methods
and concludes that:

. . . the method of discovery is most appropriate for highly motivated older
children who might have high dependency conflict and who are inclined to
use a reflective strategy. This method is least appropriate for younger children
. . . who do not have high motivation to master intellectual tasks and who tend
to be impulsive.

Recent evidence, however, including a number of theses underway, the
earlier study by Burkhart and me,[150] and my current research,[151] indicated
convincingly that, overwhelmingly, the incidence of the spontaneous strategy
as identifiable in drawings, is dependent on the amount of art training a
person receives. The higher the level of training, the more the instances of
spontaneous strategy. Therefore, personality correlates are not sufficient to
suggest possible explanations of strategies. Superficially, it would thus appear
that in art training the reversal of the "strangling of the preconscious," which
Kubie [152] equates with most education occurs.

A digression is here required. Kagan, in the quotations presented, seems to match the discovery method to the reflective child, which suggests a connection with the divergent strategy. A recent study by Getzels [153] with art students, however, indicated, through observational records of the students at work in a "structured" setting where their choices of objects and general art behavior could be observed, that a high correlation existed between judgments of their art on originality and what was called a "discovered problem-solving process" score (.90, with aesthetic quality and craftsmanship held constant) but negatively with their capability in a "present problem-solving process" (−.30). Further, craftsmanship (with aesthetic quality and originality held constant) correlated negatively (−.53) with "discovered problem-solving process" but positively with "presented problem-solving process" (.47). Overall aesthetic quality, however, when originality and craftsmanship were held constant, did not relate to either the "discovered" or "presented" problem-solving process. Further, the "high discoverers" had significantly more shows or exhibits to their credit.

Getzels' study is provocative in that it suggests that the trained and exhibiting art student is likely to combine aesthetic quality with a drive for originality and novelty and that the behaviors he has learned may not relate highly to abilities for solving "presented" problems, whereas those combining aesthetic quality and craftsmanship may, conversely, do poorly on "discovered" problem-solving. The difficulty here, however, is that we may equate these relationships with strategies and personalities and not with art training, experience, and drive for recognition. While strategies are correlated with art experience, the divergent strategy (in a strong form) seems to emerge with greater frequency in the moderate range of art experience whereas the spontaneous strategy progressively increases over the art experience continuum. Confusion enters perhaps, in applying the term at all to lesser levels of training, even though such an application, as in the study of Wise at the college level with untrained subjects, has demonstrated the value of doing so. Drawing-wise, it makes sense; personality-wise and quality-wise, I feel confusion arises. I am inclined to the view of Huyghe,[154] which rises above accident and fashion (although I do not support his use of "inner determinism," "fated," etc.):

> There are, on the one hand, vitalists eager to express themselves passionately, and on the other, formalists bent upon working out constructions. The art historians, to whom this dichotomy is familiar, see it as epitomized in the contrast between the Baroque and the Classical artists . . . For what we have here are not two aesthetic theories, freely chosen and developed, but an inner determinism, as a result of which some artists are fated to express themselves only in terms of intensity and others in terms of harmony . . . This particular instance shows that even where a physiological imperative seems to determine man's course, art maintains its freedom, for its value is equal in either conception . . . the only consideration that counts being the creative quality.

Another European writer [155] claims that these distinctions hold even in the art of children:

Each of the two worlds has its own particularities. One is dominated by the mechanism of separation, of what Bleuler called "Spaltung"; the other, by that of joining or connection. The first world tends to immobility and compensates through precision for what it loses in dynamism. The other, oriented toward movement, often errs through impreciseness of form.

It seems to me that personality correlates and shifting cultural fashions are to be discounted in the study of drawing strategies in favor of the view that ". . . art maintains its freedom, for its value is equal in either conception." My own natural reaction, presently, is to "push" the divergent strategy, since it is misunderstood and less frequent in its complex and higher form than the spontaneous strategy. But even this tendency toward a corrective emphasis is to be resisted. My role is to describe, and it cannot matter directly whether the frequency of high exemplars is low in one strategy or not.

Lowenfeld suffered somewhat from the corrective emphasis he placed on "haptic" as opposed to "visual"—terms he felt happiest about applying, by the way, from adolescence on. In this later life [156] he spoke out quite frequently against "cubby-holing" people. Gombrich has described the general habit of mind created by typologies: [157]

It was the intellectual fashion in German art history to work with contrasting pairs of concepts such as haptic-optic (Riegl), paratactic-hypotatic (Coellen), abstraction-empathy (Worringer), idealism-naturalism (Dvorak), physioplastic-ideoplastic (Verworn), Multiplicity-Unity (Wölfflin), all of which could probably be expressed in terms of "conceptual" and "less conceptual" art. While the heuristic value of this method of antithesis is not in doubt it often tends to introduce a false dichotomy. . . . I have attempted to stress the continuity of tradition and the persistent role of the conceptual image.

Indeed, as Gombrich also says, "all art is 'image-making' and all image-making is rooted in the creation of substitutes." The trap of typology is just that of creating a "false dichotomy." I often muse that if three clear strategies could be defined, this would not occur. (In addition, three is a mystical number.) I constantly point out to my students that the strategies of drawing are not bipolar and should not be subjected to either-or thinking, even though judges making comparative judgments on these dimensions often act so. The strategies, in many ways, are unrelated, not negatively related. I base this conclusion, which flies in the face of a number of negative correlations between them, on the factor analysis of the forty criteria with which Burkhart and I originally defined them. In factor analysis, very few bipolar factors emerge, mostly there is a cluster of spontaneous or divergent criteria forming a factor by themselves. At any rate, even though strategy judgments typically intercorrelate highly negative, a bipolar continuum or typology is, in my opinion, not justified on logical grounds. The first reason I say this, is that there is strategy change or mobility over time. This change has not, so far, been directly related to treatment conditions, but then neither have conditions to modify strategy been studied. Secondly, a subject cannot use two unrelated strategies simultaneously. Thus, where conditions to effect change of strategy are not manipulated, and the majority continue to develop (not just utilize) a strategy over a "run" of drawings, a negative relationship between strategy judgments is a natural outcome. The fact that individual strategy components (such as "direct flowing strokes" in the spontaneous strategy and "strong black-white contrasts" in the divergent) correlate significantly with aesthetic quality in those cases where these strategies are being used verifies their qualitative independence of each other.

In short, it is to prevent the researcher from making value judgments outside a problem context that strategies are important. Further, they provide precision and content for the difficult task of describing temporal (chainlike) and hierarchical (vertical structure) order to what unfolds in a drawing. Thus an abstract language of words that match actual drawing operations and their flow may result. Nothing can be described in processes until systematic differences of an abstract nature can be perceived.

That strategies are accessible and conceptual to a degree is suggested by my present research. These are hunches only, for the study is in progress. With untrained college subjects, the more their previous art experience, the more they report that the stages they used could be changed *but*, importantly, the *less* they report that the overall effect of the work they were doing was clear before the last stage (of stages they themselves designate from process photographs of their drawing). In other words, stage manipulation or order and final effect seem to be inversely related with growing art experience. A person who sees his stages as invariant and also knows where he is going before the last stage, has his schemata at the mercy of predetermined and imposed symbols, and the dialogue turns into a lecture. It is, in this sense, that a drawing may be described as too much conceptual and too little aesthetic. The process stages and the meaning are held on to as relatively invariant. It would appear that the more complex and differentiated the strategy, the more its process components are manipulable as to selection and order and as to matching and meaning.

What, indeed are the components of a strategy? Can we borrow Miller, Galanter and Pribram's [158] "image-plan-strategy-tactics" terminology? Or should we borrow the language of computer simulation of problem-solving as developed by Newell, Shaw and Simon: [159] "Task environment, systems of heuristics, object and operator, vocabulary for task environment, vocabulary for organization of processes, and goal types?" Are broader usages of terms helpful? Polya [160] for example, speaks of "problems to prove" and "problems to find." Bruner [161] and Pettigrew [162] speak of "category width or narrowness." Piaget [163] uses the concepts "operation selecting" and "operation applying" and Spearman [164] of "education of relations" and "education of correlates." Various degrees of clarification come from all these sources, but it is my opinion that the computer studies take us farthest.

Newell, Shaw, and Simon [165] speak of "two very general systems of heuristics—*means-ends analysis* and *planning*." They also develop the very useful language of "goal-types" and of "methods" of achieving them within each strategy. But we can follow them only so far, for there is no "problem" to solve in the sense they are using the term, nor is there an invariant and arbitrary system of symbols, but the general utility and clarity of this approach is inviting.

Space will not permit development and analysis of these possibilities here, nor can I logically determine how helpful this attempt would be beforehand. The aim would not be to simulate drawing on a computer, though if I could do so I would put the computer to this use, but rather to put leverage on the process-language problem in art. What I would like to do here is compare the heuristic systems of these researchers with the drawing strategies.

Means-ends analysis (equivalent to the divergent drawing strategy), classifies things "in terms of the functions they serve" and oscillates "among ends, functions required, and means that perform them." It has three basic methods:

1. Transforming one object into another (desired one) by detecting the difference and producing a new or modified object which can be transformed into the desired one.
2. Application of an operator to eliminate differences between objects to which they are applied and the desired ones. Some operators make more changes than others, but all are likely to leave some features unchanged.
3. Some differences between given and desired states are more difficult to bring about than others. "Difficult" differences are eliminated even if this results in new differences of lesser difficulties, and so on, as long as progress occurs.

Interestingly enough, the diagrammatic structure of "means-ends analysis" created a series of horizontal transformational chain images.

The planning method (equivalent to the spontaneous strategy) is designed to:

construct a proposed solution in general terms before working out the details. It acts as an antidote to the limitation of means-ends analysis in seeing only one step ahead. It also provides an example of the use of an auxiliary problem in a different task environment to aid in the solution of a problem. This . . . method consists in (a) *abstracting* by omitting certain details of the original objects and operators, (b) forming the corresponding problem in the abstract task environment, (c) when the abstract problem has been solved, using its solution to provide a plan for solving the original problem, (d) translating the plan back into the original task environment and executing it. The power of the method rests on two facts . . . because of the suppression of detail there is a simpler problem (having fewer steps) than the original one. Second, the subproblems that make up the plan are severally simpler (each having fewer steps) than the original problem . . . Like the other heuristics, the planning heuristic offers no guarantees that it will always work. It may generate no plan, a simple plan, or several plans. More serious, a plan may turn out to be illusory—it may prove impossible to carry it out.[166]

There is but one method associated with the planning heuristic and this is given above. It proceeds to abstract properties of the problem, searches for a plan, specifies a sequence of operators, if successful applies these to the original problem to arrive at the desired object. The diagrammatic structure of this strategy produces a single vertical, hierarchical image.

I have dwelled upon these computer heuristics systems because they may lead to greater insight into drawing strategies. I wish to emphasize that programmers make use of both kinds of systems, for it is clear that each has its advantages and its deficiencies. While we have not observed great flexibility in their interchange-ability in a drawing series, experimentation toward studying the effects of their mutual accessibility may be fruitful. In human learning there may be storage, retrieval, and interference problems involved, but this is not known. The mutually facilitative and complementary nature of the two strategies has been elsewhere suggested, and, to a degree, demonstrated.[167]

It is certain that work on sorting, defining, labeling, and judging strategy components must continue before experimentation can be satisfactorily analyzed. The forty names Burkhart and I called, what we saw merge together, beginning or attack components (big organic statement devoid of detail at start; begins with single element, early inclusion of detail); perceiving-selecting or focusing components (fused solidification across objects, movement across forms and contours; only single element, single element focus, change in size or internal scale alteration); kinesthetic or empathic components (action gestures; formal distortion-static, elongated, abstract); calligraphic and speed components (erratic wandering fine lines, open and broken contours, movement within shapes; fine line control); organizational components (central emphasis, balancing out of dynamic elements, spatial network through voids surrounded by dynamic dark forms; edge contrast-edge to edge, off center composition-off balance); sequence of plan components (progressive development as an organic unit, medium overlays; variation of same element, theme and variation, carry over of pictorial theme); novelty components (incorporation of accidental forms; unexpected organizational progression); finish operations (reliance on suggestion for completeness; decorative patterns); style elements (direct forceful, flowing movements, abrupt movements, enrichment through diversity; fine line control, black-white contrasts, flatness, black-white negative reversals); etc. Thus a process taxonomy with greater logic than now apparent needs to be developed. A language specifying factors of speed, linear-painterly coverage, placement, detail, organizational plan or syntax, value and black-white range as related to coverage, form differentiation or fusion, form development, etc., is not beyond the realm of possibility. Description of stages and the operations appropriate to them, the sub-goals they serve, and their manipulation within a given "task environment" may then be possible.

It is time to leave this concept, after saying that the drawing strategies provide the best base into a process language. Having stated my belief in change as the usual outcomes of the sequential drawing context, especially where output becomes feedback to regulate the "system," I am committed to "naturalistic" studies of these processes as they are observed under minimal constraints.

The constraints on the sequential drawing context which I think would yield most in advancing a theory of learning in art, possibly transposable into instructional terms, would deal with context or "task environment," feedback, evaluation, and transfer. Under "context" I would include: learning set (induced or implicit); structure of physical stimuli or verbal structure for eliciting mental themes; specific task environment (working alone or in groups instructed or uninstructed, observed or unobserved, non-verbal communications, kinds of external constraints; the "frame"—that is, how fluid or relatively static the conditions are from drawing to drawing; the "value field"— that is, presence or absence of external and authoritative evaluation, external incentives or their absence); and because of their importance in school learning, verbal instructions and verbal evaluations deserve to be mentioned by themselves.

I would like to elaborate further on examples of the above variables. Currently I am distinguishing between "implicit learning set" and "induced learning set." It might be argued that individual differences in the form of previous art experience, dominant drawing strategy at the beginning of experimentation, and motivational and personality states in themselves suggest some "implicit learning set." This, I believe, is true; but only to the extent the researcher classified subjects according to these can he observe their possible relevance. Thus, in the study by Wise earlier mentioned, beginning dominant drawing strategy was a powerful factor related to the differential expressive capability of the student. I have found, in addition, that there are interactions between individual differences and stimuli for drawing. Untrained subjects, for example, typically assume for some time that the learning set appropriate to a physically present still-life is that of representational drawing. They do not assume this to be as true, or else cannot cope with such a set, when they draw from "mental themes." The variability observed from such drawing stimuli is much greater with art trained subjects, but they do not show as much change attributable to the two kinds of stimuli for drawings. My main point here is that the context or task environment often evokes a learning set in the student which is partly a function of the environment but also partly a function of the students' individual differences. Because this learning set is largely mediated by the student himself, I have called it "implicit."

An "induced learning set," in contrast, is predominantly mediated through verbal instruction, goal descriptions, explicit "desirable model" (this could also be a class of pictorials or a pictorial concept), what Ausubel calls "advance organizers" [168] or even a carry-over from a previous highly or loosely structured task environment. The structure and form of stimuli conveying an "induced learning set" is in itself an important research topic, since it relates so closely to school instruction. The general importance of this emphasis is underscored by McDonald,[169] who says that it is ". . . reasonably clear that task instructions, task expectation, or set, is a potentially powerful form of task control. This effect has been demonstrated repeatedly."

It is an assumption of mine that, apart from the acquisition of certain specific skills—such as centering, opening, etc., for throwing on the potter's wheel—the kinds of induced learning sets appropriate to drawing need to be of sufficient abstractness to suggest the kind of general model and differentiation appropriate but not the specifics. Further, such learning sets should be consonant with "how an artist thinks," even though a certain artificiality adheres to making this thinking explicit in even a general sense.

"Style" and "innovation" are two such elusive concepts, in my opinion. The former suggests "sustaining" one's base into elaboration and differentiation, with or without an explicit "desirable model." The latter suggests designed "entry" of the new, and the breaking rather than the extension of established habits and associations. Both of these concepts are important in drawing, and both can be operationally defined and manipulated in a task environment, even as in our earlier study (1964) "entry" and "sustaining" questions were experimentally manipulated by teachers during the evaluative stages of a sequential drawing series. There sets, beginning evidence suggests, may to a degree interact in a complementary fashion with one's habitual drawing strategy. The person working one step ahead in the "means-ends control" heuristic appears to profit from sustaining, or from a bigger image of his stages. The person working under the "planning" heuristic seems to profit from divergent or new material. "Isolation" and "sophistication" may be further dimensions to this problem. The "flora and fauna" that can grow on an isolated island as opposed to the "latest things" from the big city hothouse. Malraux [170] illustrates the isolation concept with his statement that had El Greco remained in Venice instead of going to Toledo he might have become a second-rate Titian or Tintoretto. On the other hand, certainly the "tradition of the new," to borrow Rosenberg's phrase, suggests a somewhat conscious grasp of what has been already achieved. I will not burden this report with further operational definers of these sets as they might be introduced into the sequential drawing context, but I am convinced they can be experimentally studied and refined.

"Feedback" is a broad appellation in psychological literature,[171] but I propose to give it a specific meaning for this discussion. "Process Feedback" is its clearer designation, for this operationally means displaying to the subject at a specified time after his drawing performance and under stipulated conditions some defined sample of that performance. For research purposes, I have favored the use of still photographs of the drawing taken without interrupting the subject at designated time intervals. Thus the amount of process "information" becomes a manipulable independent variable, the significance of which can be objectively studied. "Learning feedback" is a term I reserve for information, usually in the form of verbal evaluations or judgment scales, concerning the status of a drawing with respect to an induced goal or learning set.

A digression on "learning feedback" is in order. Annett and Kay [172] feel that it is the subject's perception of "knowledge of results" that is important. But one could go even further, and assume that in drawing it is the subject's perception of the learning set itself that really counts and that "learning feedback" should serve the function of helping him decide how he is doing on his goal, as perceived. Therefore, ratings of his goal on some neutral instrument, such as Osgood's [173] semantic differential scales, could provide a base against which his later ratings of his sequential drawings could be objectively matched. On the other hand, an equally objective external rating of before and after position could be supplied by the same means. Thus variations on internal and external "learning feedback" constitute another important independent variable of the feedback family. What Kagan [174] calls "the motivation to maximize similarity to a desirable model" could well constitute a less verbal "learning set." As art educators we only need to rise above our traditional distaste for external models to see that this motive is a natural one in art, if we can believe Malraux,[175] and therefore necessary to our theories. Kagan [176] says:

It may seem inconsistent to state that the child has a strong motive for differentiation and an equally strong motive for maximizing similarity to an adult model . . . Psychological development has a spiral form in which a child identifies with a group commanding desirable goals and, after maximizing similarity to that group, differentiates from it and passes on to the next identification, in an almost never ending seesaw struggle between maximizing similarity to one model and differentiating from another.

Identification-differentiation cycles could be submitted to systematic study in the sequential drawing context if "desirable models" were made available.

Under "evaluation," I will limit myself to a consideration of some systematic procedure whereby the subject responds to "process feedback" and "learning feedback." The response is typically verbal, pitched in terms of projected changes that the subject feels will help his progress toward his goal.[177] There is no reason, however, why the evaluation response could not be pictorial-productive, as in thumbnail sketches or simplified, abstract pictorial plans or images; or why the subject could not choose from pictorials-perceptual material (which have the experimental advantage of being structured in various ways by the experimenter) samples which would help him visualize his next drawing.

Finally, by "transfer" I mean a test of the power and retention of any learning under scrutiny. One simple test is that of learning in a related but different "task environment." Thus in my current research, I intend to look at the change from the physical still-life stimulus to the mental theme stimulus and vice versa. In the general sense, however, I follow Bruner's [178] statement that ". . . it is indeed a fact that massive general transfer can be achieved by appropriate learning, even to the degree that learning properly under optimum conditions leads one to 'learn to learn.' " Among proofs to be sought from the sequential drawing base would be the greater and quicker learning evidenced in later sequences where learning constraints are internally selected and manipulated by the subject himself. Thus would be demonstrated "learning to learn to learn." A possible qualification is suggested by Stebbins [179] who says:

> Whereas changes in motivation tend to bring about widespread changes in behavior irrespective of the stimulus situation, behavioral change as a function of variation in amount of reinforcement would appear to be limited to the specific stimulus condition under which the reinforcement prevails.

This may presage a blow against transfer in my "learning theory" experiments, but I perceive the subjects' motivation as stronger than the constraints. I prefer to take the easier and possible position espoused by psychologists; [180] and assume that if the subject attends to the task and to the information presented, he is likely to learn something. It follows from my massive assumption about learning taking place in sequential drawings without instruction that a large part of my design is to keep the subject at this task, observe what I can, and study the variation of a few factors at a time. Thus I have, in present studies, thought more of individual differences (three factors are included) than of manipulating conditions (two factors are included).

Quite important under the topic of transfer is a test of how the subject operates in a slightly changed context when controls on induced learning set, process and learning feedback, and evaluation are relaxed. In this way the researcher would observe whether the subject's implicit capability to learn to learn over a series of drawings has been improved.

Criteria for Learning to Learn in Art

Although it may appear obvious and like circular logic, an experiment should include criteria for evaluation which match its experimental conditions. Thus where "directionality" and "uniqueness" are present as "indiced learning sets," criteria oriented toward these are essential. "Directionality," further, has an intraindividual connotation to it, which suggests that variation and differentiation from the subject's own beginning benchmark is a proper focus. "Uniqueness" suggests, on the other hand, a comparative interindividual frame of reference, for my convention what is unique is rare in a sample. For the first time, to my knowledge, we can attempt to judge "directionality" through drawing strategy criteria, observing their increased differentiation, complexity, and ordering from one drawing process to another. Whether "uniqueness" or "originality" can be functionally separated from global "aesthetic quality" judgments is unclear, it having been done successfully at some times and not others. The recent study of Getzels,[181] in which he partialled out the part played by "aesthetic quality" and "craftsmanship" from "originality" may be a desirable model to follow.

I have commented elsewhere [182] on the "criterion problem" in art and will not reopen the entire issue here. Suffice it to say that structural and gestalt phenomena are at operation in the "physiognomic" or "tertiary" and "contextual" properties of the aesthetic in art, and that these are partially sieved and distorted by the art training and personality of the judge. It is the researcher's responsibility to face and account for these phenomena to the best of his ability. It would not make sense to exercise control over individual differences of subjects and over task variables and ignore those attributable to judges and judgment variables. I am indebted to a doctoral student for this quotation from Hume.[183]

. . . but where are such expert critics to be found? By what marks are they to be known? How distinguish them from pretenders? One person is more pleased with the sublime; another with the tender; a third with raillery. One has a strong sensibility to blemishes, and is extremely studious to correctness; another has a more lively feeling of beauties, and pardons twenty absurdities and defects for one elevated or pathetic stroke. The ear of this man is entirely towards conciseness and energy; that man is delighted with a copious and harmonious expression. Simplicity is affected by one; ornament by another.

Or, if one is inclined to irresponsibility or humor as well as to despair, consider from Proust [184] the

. . . fantastic formula of Swann's which used to mislead people who take everything literally: "One-fourth is the interpreter's own invention, one-fourth is sheer madness, one-fourth makes no sense and the remainder is La Fontaine."

Suffice it to make the simple-minded statement that those who weary at the labor of facing the criterion problem in learning in art are not made for the task, but it is my conviction that the task is far from impossible and its very difficulties are among the greatest challenges in the psychology of art. Nor are we to be mislead by psychologists such as Michael [185] who panic at the very term "aesthetic quality." Psychologists will not solve our criteria problem; they can only help us with our methods of investigation and control.

We can deploy our attack by checking, as indicated, what we set out to influence *as well as* aesthetic quality, and we can become more purely descriptive as befits a young field of study. Progress has been made in "breaking the aesthetic atom," even though this success is a temporary defeat, since we suffer from what I have called "humpty-dumptyism"—we don't how to combine the separated components, so that "global" judgments are more sensitive in recording change and learning than are discrete or differentiated ones. But, then, what person in a drawing tries to achieve pervasively one differentiated descriptive criterion, such as "ragged edges?" Nevertheless, studies [186] like those of Bernheim and Rouse and, in processes, the drawing strategy components singled out by Burkhart and me, are of great importance. The structural interdependence of drawing strategy components makes them more readily combinable, for they are more an organic part of the subject's own "aesthetic heuristics." Yet, we know little about whether we have named the right criteria or about how they combine. We have merely been lucky enough to find that they seem to combine as simple additive parts. How they emerge and combine and whether these are the best units remains in question.

SUMMARY AND CRITIQUE

In brief, I have attempted to set a more or less intact base for the study of learning in art upon "learning to learn" to draw as it is exemplified in the sequential drawing context in the absence of instruction. I have thus thought to protect myself from excessive generalities or an excessive catalogue of the atomistic, by seeking some vision of dynamic wholeness which still does not rely on vitalism or lapse into nominalism. Thus all experiments dealing with this context have a "naturalistic" aspect to them complementing the desire to control for individual differences and to manipulate the learning environment. The studies of Kellogg, Alexander and Morris have aided me in examining descriptive and explanatory aspects of change in this context. They have also been focused on drawing itself and suggest the cybernetic image of a regulated open system directed by feedback of its own output. This system is seen as changing under form differentiation, perceptual sharpening, and calligraphic and thematic variation. Idiosyncratic symbolic material, entering conceptually with the advent of pictorials in the young child, early set the tension between sense and seeming echo, or contrived message and contextual meaning, or evoke the concept of symbolic transformation, or the making of a functional substitute for some individual needs. In early life these symbolic forms are "created almost out of nothing by each individual, thanks to the use of representative objects and mental images, all of which supplement language . . . to permit the fullest possible expansion of the ego as distinct from material and social reality." [187] With growing age, idiosyncratic symbols and drawing schemata and operations are in continual interplay in making-matching and matching-making, through extension and correction of the drawing schemata themselves.

Drawing is not seen as a problem in the sense typically implied in discussions of learning and problem-solving. It is closer to autistic thinking and diversive exploration than to the directed thinking illustrative of most problem-solving process. In a given drawing, what some writers term preconscious activity is directed thinking, and involved. These appear to occur in problem-solving also, but the emphasis is different. The concept of stages of creative thought which gradually advance without a clear perception of stage to stage beforehand appears to fit drawing, where the basic question is taken to be "What do I do next?" More trained subjects maintain their suspense and surprise concerning the outcome of their drawings, but do not see their stages as invariant or inflexible in their order. Nevertheless, the possibilities in drawing are so endless that more or less conscious heuristic systems or strategies are developed and manipulated by experienced subjects. Over time or within a drawing series, these strategies appear to differentiate themselves into increasingly complex systems of drawing transformations and plans. These strategies are not so much opposed to each other as unrelated, and each has its virtues and limitations. Though there are personality and experience correlates of strategies, such relationships are more historical than logical and necessary. The language of computer-simulations of problem-solving appears to hold promise for further elaboration of drawing strategies.

When a sequence of drawings occurs within a controlled contex, something more akin to direct thinking and conscious inner-mediation of learning occurs. The constraints that appear fruitful to the topic of learning in art were classified according to four key concepts. Under *context* or *task environment, learning set* was the central term, further divided into *implicit* and *induced* learning set. Under *feedback, process feedback* and *learning feedback* were defined. *Evaluation* was defined as the subject's action upon the two kinds of feedback. It was further suggested that this action could be verbal, pictorial-perceptual, pictorial-enactive, or combinations of these. Under *transfer* it was advanced that in addition to applications where constraints on learning are applied, a true test of capability to learn to learn occurs where such mediation is implicit in the subject's self-direction and shows improvement over a pre-treatment series.

Finally the criterion problem as related to sequential drawing changes was discussed, with the simple recommendation for the use of learning criteria which match the learning constraints under scrutiny as closely as possible. Induced learning sets for style or directionality and uniqueness or originality were taken as illustrations. It was further recommended that control of individual differences and learning constraints be balanced by control of judge differences and judgment constraints. The problem of analytically separable or discrete criteria as opposed to contextual global or gestalt criteria continues unresolved despite recent progress.

I have tried not to conceal the fact that a discussion of learning in art, even in a context such as I have chosen, is highly speculative. It may even turn out to be in some ways a work of fiction (and therefore art more than science).

It is now time to attempt a critique of what I have attempted. The word "automation" in describing sequential drawing as "a learning automation" is obviously wrong, but I wished to make a point through this crude metaphor. The process is of course dynamic and, as any artist knows, change, value, direction, and learning are not always attendant on one another in the continual practice of one's art. They are, however, more the case than not, and they provide an on-going context removing our gaze from static and single works to flow and change-even decomposition, if it occurs—and therefore to learning or its inhibition.

Though Gombrich [188] says that all art is "conceptual," or at least "more or less conceptual" (a significant qualification), and though Harris's [189] extensive reviews lead him to similar conclusions on the art of the child, art is certainly not completely conceptual in our ordinary usage of the word, though its production may be mediated by concepts. The "aesthetic" as opposed to the "artistic" leaves us with the impression, however hard to formulate, that the former deals with the "sensuous" as "immediately given" in our experience. It may be argued that even this is conceptual, but the opposite point is worth the making.

Art is not the expression or the embodiment of experience which is mediated by means of concepts. Such expression of experience is reserved for language. Art is the only form of expression devised by man to embody the immediate sensuousness of his living experiences.[190]

My only qualification would be that even this quality is conceptually manipulated in the open-closed, symbolic-schematic cyclical business which is drawing. Aesthetic and artistic "thinking," diversive exploration, specific exploration, and directed thinking all occur in a drawing series and all process "mental stuff" and lead to selective arts, even when such mental contents "represent" what it is in immediate experience to "color," to "form," and to "move." If by dint of practice and time I "no longer think" as certain operations are applied in throwing a pot, and even when a particular "habit family" or "transformation family" is so elided that it seems to occur between my fingertips and the clay alone, this I consider only "less conceptual." As Piaget has argued, thinking preceded and is broader than language, and, at base, includes those symbolic products "created almost out of nothing" from mental stuff which "supplements language."

I find schools (and the general culture) devastatingly foreign to the lore of art; I find art devastatingly foreign to life; and I find psychology devastatingly estranged from school, art, and life. Research on learning in art is in a pinch. Borrowing, applying, and translating the theoretical stance of psychology, I have had to guard against any easy purity achieved at the expense of art, school, and life. It will not surprise me if the art and the psychology I project will not soon date themselves, if they are indeed not already dated.

I now see that instead of completing my sketches according to the "Mrs. Siddons as the Tragic Muse" approach, I have taken a nude and given her a scanty motley indeed. As Malraux and Gombrich observed about painters, regardless of what I said I would do, in practice I have to do what I can. The "schemata in the cupboard" echoed what they could as the "meaning matrices" were shuffled around. I invite your best energies, especially you younger participants, to this speculative game.

REFERENCES

1. Postman, Leo. "Human Learning and Audiovisual Education," AV *Communication Review*, Vol. 9, No. 5, Supplement 4, 1961, p. 78.
2. For a lucid description of modern biological and scientific thought see Ludwig von Bertalanffy's *Problems of Life*, London: C. A. Watts, 1952.

BACKGROUND AND FOUNDATION

3. Quoted from a personal letter to the writer from Dr. Ray Human, Department of Psychology, The University of Oregon, Eugene, Oregon.
4. Estes, William K. "Learning," *Encyclopedia of Educational Research*, Third Edition; New York: Macmillan, 1960, p. 767.
5. This statement of the writer's appears in the Spring, 1965 issue of The Pennsylvania State University Art Education Graduate Club's Newsletter.
6. The term "internal locus of evaluation" is described by Carl Rogers in "Toward a Theory of Creativity," etc. A *Review of General Semantics*, Summer 1954, Vol. II, No. 4; pp. 249–260. An operational form of this concept proved superior when compared with an "external locus" in a recent study by the writer and Burkhart: See Beittel, K. R. "Effect of Self-Reflective Training in Art on the Capacity for Creative Action," Cooperative Research Project No. 1874, The Pennsylvania State University, 1964.
7. Barkan, Manual. "Viktor Lowenfeld: His Impact on Art Education." Paper delivered at the 1965 National Art Education Association Conference; Philadelphia, Pennsylvania, April 8, 1965.
8. Examples of the use of these neologisms is given here in condensed form. *Stylometrics*: Newman, Ernst. "Beethoven: The Last Phase." *The Atlantic*, March, 1953. *Iconology*: Gombrich, E. H. "Meditations on a Hobby Horse, or the Roots of Artistic Form," in *Aspects of Form*. London: Humphries, 1951. *Linguistics of Fine Arts*: Yamamoto, Kaoru. "Et Cetera—Linguistics of Fine Arts," paper read at UCLA Developmental Conference to Assay the Potential Promise of Longitudinal Study of Creative Behavior in the Arts, Santa Monica, February 18–20, 1965. *Iconic Sign*: Morris, C. R. *Signs, Language and Behavior*. New York: Prentice-Hall, 1946. *Iconic Mode of Representation*: Bruner, Jerome S. "The Course of Cognitive Growth." *American Psychologist*, Vol. 19, No. 1, January 1964; pp. 1–15. *The Psychology of Art*: Malraux, Andre. *La Psychologie d'Art*. Vols. I, II. Geneva, 1947–48; Vol. III: Paris, 1950. *The Psychoanalysis of Art*: Kris, Ernst. *Psychoanalytic Explorations in Art*. New York and London, 1952. *Art Strategies*: Beittel, K. R. and Burkhart, R. C. "Strategies of Spontaneous, Divergent, and Academic Art Students." *Studies in Art Education*, Vol. 5, No. 1, Fall 1963; pp. 20–41. *Aesthetic Morphology*: Huyghe, Rene. *Ideas and Images in World Art*. New York: Abrams, 1959. *The Biology of Art*: Book of the same name by Desmond Morris, New York: Knopf, 1962.
9. See Ecker, David W. "Some Inadequate Doctrines in Art Education and a Proposed Resolution." *Studies in Art Education*, Autumn 1963, Vol. 5, No. 1. Also see Chapman, Laura H. "Some Comments on 'Spontaneous, Divergent, and Academic Art Students.'" *Studies in Art Education*, Autumn 1964, Vol. 6, No. 1, pp. 25–29.
10. Bruner, Jerome S. "The Act of Discovery," *Harvard Educational Review*, 1961, 31, pp. 21–32.
11. Lorenz, Konrad Z. "The Role of Gestalt Perception in Animal and Human Behavior," in *Aspects of Form*, L. L. Whyte, ed. London: Humphries, 1951; pp. 157–178.
12. "Educational Programs: Early and Middle Childhood." *Review of Educational Research*, April 1965, Vol. XXXV, No. 2.
13. Geiger, George R. "An Experimentalist Approach to Education." *In Mod-*

ern Philosophies and Education, Nelson B. Henry (ed). Fifty-fourth Yearbook of The N.S.S.E., Part I.

14. Lanier, Vincent. Reply to the writer's "Some Viewpoints on Research in Art Education," *Art Education*, December 1957.

15. Blackmur, R. P. "The Later Poetry of W. B. Yeats." *Southern Review*, Autumn, 1936, Vol. II, No. 2, pp. 339–362.

16. Marantz, Kenneth. "Indecent Exposure." *Studies in Art Education*, Autumn, 1964, Vol. 6, No. 1; pp. 20–24.

17. Bruner, Jerome S. *The Process of Education*. Cambridge, Massachusetts: Harvard University Press, 1961. See also the same author's "Some Theorems on Instruction Illustrated with Reference to Mathematics." Chapter 13 in *Theories of Learning and Instruction*, E. Hilgard (ed.), 63rd Yearbook, N.S.S.E., Chicago: University of Chicago Press, 1964; pp. 306–335.

18. When the writer mentioned this seminar to a woman from a related applied field of education, she said, "Oh, *our* 'concepts' are done and are currently being printed up in Washington."

19. Goldwater, R. and Treves, M. *Artists on Art*. New York: Pantheon Books, 1945, p. 313.

20. Kris, Ernst. *Psychoanalytic Exploration in Art*. New York and London, 1952.

21. Arnheim, Rudolph. *Art and Visual Perception*. London: Faber & Faber, 1956.

22. Wiener, Norbert. *Cybernetics*. New York: Wiley, 1948. See also Maccia, E. S.; Maccia, G. S.; and Jewett, R. C., *Construction of Educational Theory Models*. Cooperative Research Project No. 1632, The Ohio State University, 1963.

23. Beittel, Kenneth R. "Effect of Self-Reflective Training in Art on the Capacity for Creative Action." Cooperative Research Project No. 1874, The Pennsylvania State University, 1964.

24. Morris, Desmond. *The Biology of Art*. New York: Knopf, 1962.

25. Nelson, Thomas M. and Flannery, Merle E. "Instructions in Drawing Techniques as a Means of Utilizing Drawing Potential of Six and Seven Year Olds." Unpublished manuscript.

26. Gibson, James J. *The Perception of the Visual World*. Boston: Houghton Mifflin Company, 1950, p. 222.

27. Gibson, James J. *op. cit.*, p. 202.

28. Anderson, R. C. and Ausubel, D. P. *Readings in the Psychology of Cognition*. New York: Holt, Rinehart, and Winston, 1965, p. 224.

29. Braine, Martin D. S. "The Ontogeny of English Phrase Structure: The First Phase." *Language*, Vol. 39, 1963, 1–13.

30. Kellogg, Rhoda. *What Children Scribble and Why*. Palo Alto, California: N-P Publications, 1955.

31. Alexander, Christopher. "The Origin of Creative Power in Children." *Brit. J. of Aesthetics*, Vol. 2, No. 3, July 1962; pp. 207–226.

32. Arnheim, Rudolph. "Visual Thinking." In *Education of Vision*, Gyorgy Kepes (ed.). New York: George Braziller, 1965, pp. 1–11.

33. Morris, Desmond. *op. cit.*

34. In art education there is need for some systematic taxonomy of early pictorials of children. Representational spatial properties of drawings have so far received the clearest description.

35. Alexander, Christopher. *op. cit.*, p. 208.
36. Gombrich, E. H. *Art and Illusion.* New York: Pantheon Books, 1960.
37. Alexander, Christopher. *op. cit.*, pp. 220–221.
38. Lowenfeld, Viktor. *Creative and Mental Growth.* New York: Macmillan, 3rd Ed., 1957.
39. The term "function pleasure" comes from Bühler, K. "Displeasure and Pleasure in Relation to Activity." In M. L. Reymert (ed.), *Feelings and Emotions: The Wittenberg Symposium.* Worcester, Massachusetts: Clark University Press, 1928; Chapter 14.
40. Alexander, Christopher. *op. cit.*, p. 222.
41. Alexander, Christopher. *op. cit.*, p. 225.
42. Morris, Desmond. *op. cit.*
43. Morris, Desmond. *op. cit.*, p. 158.
44. Barron, Frank, and Welsh, G. S. "Artistic Perception as a Factor in Personality Style: Its Measurement by a Figure Preference Test," *Journal of Psychology*, Vol. 33, 1952, pp. 199–203. See also Barron, Frank. *Creativity and Psychological Health.* New York: Van Nostrand, 1963.
45. McWhinnie, Harold James. "The Effects of a Learning Experience upon the Preference for Complexity and Asymmetry." San Fernando Valley State College, Northridge, California, 1964.
46. Morris, Desmond. *op. cit.*, p. 162.
47. Beardsley, Monroe C. "On the Creation of Art," *Journal of Aesthetics and Art Criticism*, Vol. XXIII, No. 3, Spring 1965, pp. 291–304.
48. Morris, Desmond. *op. cit.*, pp. 167–168.
49. Harris, Dale B. *Children's Drawings as Measures of Intellectual Maturity.* New York: Harcourt, Brace & World, 1963.
50. Smedslund, Jan. "The Acquisition of Conservation of Substance and Weight in Children." *Scandinavian Journal of Psychology*, 1961, Vol. 2, pp. 71–84 and 85–87.
51. Bruner, Jerome S. "The Course of Cognitive Growth," *American Psychologist*, Vol. 19, No. 1, January 1964, pp. 1–15.
52. Whyte, L. L. (ed.). *Aspects of Form.* London: Humphries, 1951.
53. Gibson, James J. *op. cit.*, p. 199.
54. Gibson, James J. *op. cit.*, p. 202.
55. Woodworth, R. S. *Experimental Psychology.* New York: Henry Holt, 1938, Chap. 4.
56. Gibson, James J. *op. cit.*, p. 202.
57. Morris, Desmond. *op. cit.*
58. Adams, Hazard. "Symbolism and Yeats A Vision." *Journal of Aesthetics and Art Criticism*, Vol. XXII, No. 4, Summer 1964, p. 427.
59. Yeats, W. B. *A Vision.* New York: Macmillan Paperbacks Edition, 1961. (A Reissue of the 1938 book with the author's final revisions.)
60. Tate, Allen. "Yeats's Romanticism: Notes and Suggestions," *The Southern Review*, Vol. II, 3, Winter 1942, pp. 591–600.
61. Tate, Allen. *op. cit.*
62. Gombrich, E. H. "The Use of Art for the Study of Symbols." *American Psychologist*, Vol. 20, No. 1, January 1965, pp. 34–50.
63. Gibson, James J. *op. cit.*, p. 204.
64. Gombrich, E. H. *op. cit.*, (1960).

65. Polanyi, Michael. *Personal Knowledge*. Chicago: University of Chicago Press, 1958.
66. Morris, Desmond. *op. cit.*
67. Lowenfeld, Viktor. *op. cit.*
68. Gombrich, E. H. *op. cit.*, (1960).
69. Wickhiser, Ralph L. *An Introduction to Art Education*. New York: World Book Company, 1957, p. 202.
70. Harris, Dale B. *op. cit.*
71. Piaget, Jean. "Art Education and Child Psychology," in *Education and Art*. Edwin Ziegfeld (ed.), UNESCO, 1953, p. 22.
72. Piaget, Jean. *op. cit.*, p. 22.
73. Notice that we fall into the trap of saying that a child "draws a symbol for a house," when it were better for art if we spoke of "drawing a house for a symbol."
74. Gombrich, E. H. *op. cit.* (1951), p. 6.
75. Lowenfeld, Viktor. *op. cit.*
76. Piaget, Jean. *op. cit.*, p. 23.
77. Ott, Richard. "Children as Artists," in *Education and Art*. Edwin Ziegfeld, (ed.), UNESCO, 1953, p. 23.
78. Ott, Richard. *op. cit.*, p. 24.
79. Pavlov says that ". . . under certain unfavorable conditions, when the nervous system is weakened, . . . phylogenetic division of the brain takes place anew; then probably one individual will use predominantly the first signaling system while the other will use predominantly the second signaling system (language), and it is this that divides men into artistic natures and purely intellectual abstract natures." The "artistic nature" is "analogous and close to that of animals." Pavlov, I. P., *Experimental Psychology and Other Essays*. New York: 1957.
80. Bruner, Jerome S. *op. cit.*, (January 1964).
81. Gombrich, E. H. *op. cit.*, (1965).
82. Gombrich, E. H. *op. cit.*, (1960).
83. Bruner, Jerome S. "What Social Scientists Say About Having an Idea." *Printers' Ink Magazine*, Vol. 260, 1957, pp. 48–52. Also see *op. cit.*, January 1964.
84. Reid, Thomas. Cited in Rene Huyghe's *Ideas and Images in World Art*, p. 35.
85. Proust, Marcel. *The Past Recaptured*.
86. Beittel, K. R. *op. cit.*, (1964; CRP No. 1874).
87. Beittel, K. R. *op. cit.*, (1964; CRP No. 1874).
88. Black, Max. "Education as Art and Discipline," *Ethics*, Vol. 54, July 1944, pp. 290–291.
89. Santayana, George. *Reason in Art*. New York, 1922.
90. Mattil, E. L., *et al.*, "The Effect of a 'Depth' vs. a 'Breadth Method' of Art Instruction at the Ninth Grade Level," *Studies in Art Education*, Vol. 3, No. 1, Fall, 1961; pp. 75–87. See also: Schwartz, Bernard. "The Effect of Working Time and Instruction in Art upon the Process Characteristics and Aesthetic Quality of Art Performance," unpublished doctoral thesis, The Pennsylvania State University, 1964.
91. Beittel, K. R. *op. cit.*, (1964; CRP No. 1874).

92. Rogers, Carl. *op. cit.*
93. For recent references on the art criterion problem see the following: Bernheim, Gloria D. "The Dimensionality of Differential Criteria in the Visual Art Product," *Studies in Art Education*, Vol. 5, No. 1, Fall 1964; pp. 31–48. Beittel, K. R. *op. cit.*, (1964; CRP No. 1874); Burkhart, Robert C. "Evaluation of Learning in Art," *Art Education*, Vol. 18, No. 4, April 1965, pp. 3–5. Rouse, Mary J. "Development and Validation of a Descriptive Scale for Measurement of Art Products," Cooperative Research Project No. S-077, Indiana University, Bloomington, Indiana, 1965.
94. Bruner, Jerome S. *op. cit.*, ("The Act of Discovery").
95. Thesis proposal of Edward L. Longley, July 1965, The Pennsylvania State University. The reference is to Hale's *Drawing Lessons from the Great Masters*.
96. Schaeffer-Simmern, H. *The Unfolding of Artistic Activity*. Berkeley, California: University of California, 1950.
97. Hochberg, Julian. "The Psychophysics of Pictorial Perception," *AV Communication Review*, Vol. 10, No. 5, 1962, pp. 22–54.
98. Bruner, Jerome S. *op. cit.*, (1964 NSSE 63rd Yearbook).
99. Hochberg, Julian. *op cit.*, p. 30.
100. Gibson, James J. *op cit.*
101. Bartlett, F. C. *Remembering, a Study in Experimental and Social Psychology*. Cambridge: Cambridge University Press, 1932.
102. Pratt, C. C. "Aesthetics," in *Annual Review of Psychology*. Palo Alto, California, 1961, p. 76.
103. Gombrich, E. H. *op cit.* (1960), p. 360, p. 358.
104. Beittel, K. R. and Burkhart, R. C. "Strategies of Spontaneous, Divergent, and Academic Art Studies," *Studies in Art Education*, Vol. 5, No. 1, Fall 1963; pp. 20–41.
105. Miller, G. A., Galanter, E., and Pribram, K. H., *Plans and the Structure of Behavior*. New York: Henry Holt and Company, 1960.
106. Newell, A., Shaw, J. K., and Simon, H. A. "Report on a General Problem-Solving Program." *Proceedings of the International Conference on Information Processing*, Paris, 1959, pp. 256–264. See also by the same authors: "The Process of Creative Thinking." Chapter 3, in Gruber, *et al.*, eds., *Contemporary Approaches to Creative Thinking*. New York: Atherton, 1962, pp. 63–119.
107. Anderson, R. C. and Ausubel, D. P. *op cit.*, p. 11.
108. Bruner, Jerome S. and Olver, Rose R. "Development of Equivalence Transformations in Children," *Monograph for the Society for Research in Child Development*, 1963, Vol. 28, pp. 125–141.
109. Miller, George A. "The Magical Number Seven, Plus or Minus Two: Some Limits on Our Capacity for Processing Information," *Psychological Review*, 1956, Vol. 63, pp. 81–97.
110. For a discussion of mediating verbal processes in problem-solving see: Cofer, Charles N. "Reasoning as an Associative Process: III. The Role of Verbal Responses in Problem Solving," *Journal of Gen. Psychol.*, 1957, Vol. 57, pp. 55–68.
111. Miller, G. A., Galanter, E., and Pribram, K. H. *op. cit.*

112. Beittel, K. R., and Burkhart, R. C. *op. cit.* (1963). Also see: Beittel, K. R., *op cit.*, 1964; CRP No. 1874.

113. Gagne, Robert M. *The Conditions of Learning.* New York: Holt, Rinehart and Winston, Inc., 1965, pp. 58–59.

114. Getzels, J. W. "Creative Thinking, Problem-Solving, and Instruction." Chapter 10, in *Theories of Learning and Instruction*, E. Hilgard (ed.), 63rd Yearbook, NSSE, Chicago: University of Chicago Press, 1964; pp. 240–267.

115. Simon, Henry A. "Understanding Creativity," *Carnegie Review*, No. 2, 1964/1965.

116. Ecker, David W. "The Artistic Process as Qualitative Problem Solving." *Journal of Aesthetics and Art Criticism*, Vol. 21, No. 3, Spring 1963, pp. 283–290.

117. Ehrenzweig, Anton. "Conscious Planning and Unconscious Scanning." In Kepes, Gyorgy, Ed., *Education of Vision*, New York: Braziller, 1965, pp. 27–49.

118. Bruner, Jerome S. *op. cit.* (1957, "On Having an Idea").

119. Beardsley, Monroe C. *op cit.*

120. McKellar, P. *Imagination and Thinking: A Psychological Analysis.* New York: Basic Books, 1957.

121. Berlyne, D. E. *Structure and Direction in Thinking.* New York: Wiley, 1965. In this book Berlyne defines "directed thinking" as a process ". . . that involves a chain (that is, a sequence of two or more members) of symbolic responses . . . whose function is to convey us to solutions of problems." (p. 19) The kinds of thinking involved in drawing, he would say, is "transformational thought." Such thoughts ". . . are conceived as derivatives of overt responses that regularly result in particular kinds of environmental change. Their possession enables the subject to represent to himself, and communicate to others, the stimulus situation that would result from a series of transformations, even when the transformations are not actually effected." (p. 123)

122. Berlyne, D. E. *op. cit.*, pp. 310–311.

123. Green, B. F. *Digital Computers in Research.* New York: McGraw-Hill, 1963.

124. Berlyne, D. E. *op. cit.*, p. 312.

125. Beardsley, Monroe C. *op. cit.*, pp. 300–301.

126. Getzels, J. W. *op. cit.*

127. Berlyne, D. E. *op cit.*, p. 244.

128. Beardsley, Monroe C. *op cit.*, p. 295.

129. In an earlier study, it was found that the best performers in a group of general education college students in an art studio did their best work outside of class. See Beittel, K. R. "Predictors and Settings Relating to the Capacity for Creative Action in the Visual Arts," Progress Report, NSF GL-17984, The Pennsylvania State University, 1962, pp. 24–25.

130. Piaget, Jean and Inhelder, Barbel. *The Growth of Logical Thinking.* Basic Books, 1958.

131. Berlyne, D. E. *op cit.*, p. 117.

132. Beardsley, Monroe C. *op. cit.*, p. 299.

133. Beardsley, Monroe C. *op. cit.*, p. 297. Gombrich, *op. cit.*, 1960 in like fashion feels that any schema will suffice to get a drawing started or supply the be-

ginning "hunch" for perception, further operations or cues then extending, confirming, or disconfirming this base, which, further, succeeds when it is simple enough to be easily disproved and modified. Herein may reside some of the "confidence" seen in a child's drawing and certainly, to the adult, much of its "charm."

134. Valery, Paul. "Poetry and Abstract Thought," in *The Art of Poetry*. New York, 1961.
135. Bradford, Curtis. "Yeats's Byzantium Poems: A Study of Their Development," *PMLA*, Vol. 75, March 1960, pp. 110–125.
136. Berlyne, D. E. *op. cit.*, p. 117.
137. Berlyne, D. E. *op cit.*
138. Bartlett, F. C. *Thinking*. London: Methuen, 1958.
139. Smith, Cyril Stanley, "Structure, Susstructure, Superstructure," in Kepes, Gyorgy (ed.), *Structure in Art and Science*. New York: Braziller, 1965, pp. 29–41.
140. Bartlett, F. C. *op. cit.*
141. Ehrenzweig, Anton. *op cit.*
142. Beittel, K. R. and Burkhart, R. C. *op cit.* (1963), and Beittel, K. R. *op. cit.*, (1964, CRP No. 1874).
143. Brownell, William A. "The Study and Guidance of Learning in Children," in *Education 2000 A.D.* Syracuse: Syracuse University Press, 1956, pp. 123–140.
144. Schultz, Rudolph W. "Problem Solving Behavior and Transfer," *Harvard Education Review*, 1960, 30, pp. 61–77. Quotation is from Anderson, R. D. and Ausubel, D. P., *op cit.*, p. 542.
145. Anderson, R. D., and Ausubel, D. P. *op cit.*, p. 399.
146. Wise, James. "The Effects of Sex, Working Conditions, Style and Art Process Strategy on Ability to Incorporate Expressive Qualities into Drawings," doctoral thesis, The Pennsylvania State University, in progress.
147. Beittel, K. R. *op. cit.* (1964, CRP No. 1874).
148. For an overview of this literature see the writer's "On the Relationship between Art and General Creativity: A Biased History and Projection of a Partial Conquest," *The School Review*, Vol. 72, No. 3, Autumn 1964, pp. 272–288.
149. Kagan, Jerome. "Personality and the Learning Process," *Daedalus*, Vol. 94, No. 3, Summer 1965, p. 559.
150. Beittel, K. R. *op. cit.* (1964, CRP No. 1874).
151. Beittel, K. R., "Selected Psychological Concepts as Applied to the Teaching of Drawing," Current Cooperative Research Project, 1965–66.
152. Kubie, Lawrence S. "Unsolved Problems of Scientific Education," *Daedalus*, Vol. 94, No. 3, Summer 1965, pp. 564–587.
153. Getzels, J. W. and Csikszentmihalyi, M., "Creative Thinking in Art Students: The Process of Discovery." Cooperative Research Project No. S-080, 1965, The University of Chicago.
154. Huyghe, Rene. *op. cit.*, (1959), pp. 394–96.
155. Minkowska, F. *De Van Gogh et de Seurat aux Dessins d'Enfants*. Paris, 1949. Cited in Hughe, Rene, *op. cit.*
156. Lectures and speeches given by Lowenfeld in his last years give repeated examples of his feeling that the visual haptic typology was being misused.

Tapes in possession of Department of Art Education, The Pennsylvania State University.

157. Gombrich, E. H. *op. cit.*, (1951), p. 224.

158. Miller, G. A.; Galanter, E.; and Pribram, K. H. *op. cit.*

159. Newell, A.; Shaw, J. C.; and Simon, H. A. *op. cit.* (1959).

160. Polya, G. *How to Solve It.* Princeton: Princeton University Press, 1945.

161. Bruner, Jerome S. and Tajfel, Henri. "Cognitive Risk and Environmental Change," *Journal of Abnormal and Soc. Psychol.*, Vol. 62, 1961, pp. 231–241.

162. Pettigrew, Thomas F. "The Measurement and Correlates of Category Width as a Cognitive Variable," *Journal of Personality*, Vol. 26, 1958, pp. 532–44.

163. Piaget, Jean and Inhelder, Barbel. *op. cit.*

164. Spearman, C. *The Nature of "Intelligence" and the Principles of Cognition.* London: MacMillan, 1923.

165. Newell, A.; Shaw, J. C.; and Simon, H. A. *op. cit.* (1959).

166. Newell, A.; Shaw, J. C.; and Simon, H. A. *op. cit.* (1959).

167. Beittel, K. R. *op. cit.* (1964; CRP No. 1874); *op. cit.*, (1964; *School Review*).

168. Ausubel, David P. "Cognitive Structure and the Faciliation of Meaningful Verbal Learning," *Journal of Teacher Education*, 1963, Vol. 14, pp. 217–221.

169. McDonald, Frederick J. "Meaningful Learning and Retention: Task and Method Variables," *Review of Educational Research*, Vol. 34, No. 5, December 1964, pp. 530–544.

170. Malraux, Andre. *The Voices of Silence.* New York: Doubleday, 1953.

171. For a review of meanings of this term see Bilodeau, E. A. and Bilodeau, I., "Motor-Skills Learning," in *Annual Review of Psychology*, Vol. 12, 1961, pp. 243–280.

172. Annett, J., and Kay, H., "Knowledge of Results and Skilled Performance." *Occupational Psychology*, Vol. 31, pp. 69–79.

173. Osgood, Charles, *et al. The Measurement of Meaning.* Urbana: University of Illinois, 1957.

174. Kagan, Jerome. *op. cit.*, p. 554.

175. Malraux, Andre. *op. cit.*, (1953).

176. Kagan, Jerome. *op. cit.*, p. 555.

177. Beittel, K. R. *op. cit.* (1964; CRP No. 1874).

178. Bruner, Jerome S. *The Process of Education.* Cambridge: Harvard University Press, 1961.

179. Stebbins, W. C. "Relation of Amount of Primary Reinforcement to Discrimination and to Secondary Reinforcement Strength," *J. Comp. Physiol. Psychol.*, Vol. 52, pp. 721–26, 1959.

180. For example, see Kagan, Jerome. *op. cit.*, p. 553.

181. Getzels, J. W. and Csikszentmihalyi, M. *op. cit.*

182. See Beittel, K. R. *op. cit.*, (1964; CRP No. 1874); *op. cit.*, (1964; *School Review*); "Factor Analyses of Three Dimensions of the Art Judgment Complex: Criteria, Art Objects, and Judges," *J. of Exp. Ed.*, Vol. 32, No. 2, 1963, pp. 167–174; "Art," in *Encyclopedia of Educational Research*, 3rd ed., 1960; "Meeting or Molesting the Muse: A Look at Research on the 'Crea-

tivity' in the Visual Arts," *Studies in Art Education*, Vol. 1, 1, 1959, pp. 26–37.

183. Schorer, Mark (ed.). *Criticism: The Foundations of Modern Literary Judgment*. New York: Harcourt, 1948.

184. Proust, Marcel. *op. cit.*

185. Michael, William B. "A Short Evaluation of the Research Reviewed in Language Arts and Fine Arts," *Review of Educational Research*, Vol. 34, No. 2, April 1964; pp. 249–256.

186. See footnote 93 for reference cited.

187. Piaget, Jean. *op. cit.* (1953).

188. Gombrich, E. H. *op. cit.* (1951).

189. Harris, Dale B. *op. cit.*

190. Madenfort, Wellington. "A Phenomenology of the Aesthetic in Art Education," unpublished doctoral thesis, The Pennsylvania State University, University Park, Pennsylvania, 1965.

Meditations on a Hobby Horse or the Roots of Artistic Form

E. H. GOMBRICH

The subject of this article is a very ordinary hobby horse. It is neither metaphorical nor purely imaginary, at least not more so than the broomstick on which Swift wrote his meditations. It is usually content with its place in the corner of the nursery and it has no aesthetic ambitions. Indeed it abhors frills. It is satisfied with its broomstick body and its crudely carved head which just marks the upper end and serves as holder for the reins. How should we address it? Should we describe it as an 'image of a horse'? The compilers of the *Pocket Oxford Dictionary* would hardly have agreed. They defined *image* as 'imitation of object's external form' and the 'external form' of a horse is surely not 'imitated' here. So much the worse, we might say, for the 'external form', that elusive remnant of the Greek philosophical tradition which has dominated our aesthetic language for so long. Luckily there is another word in the *Dictionary* which might prove more accommodating: *representation*. To *represent*, we read, can be used in the sense of 'call up by description or portrayal or imagination, figure, place likeness of before mind or senses, serve or be meant as likeness of . . . stand for, be specimen of, fill place of, be substitute for'. A portrayal of a horse? Surely not. A substitute for a horse? Yes. That it is. Perhaps there is more in this formula than meets the eye.

This essay was originally written as a contribution to *Aspects of Form, A Symposium on Form in Nature and Art*, L. L. Whyte, ed. London, 1951. Reprinted by permission from Phaidon Press Ltd.

I

Let us first ride our wooden steed into battle against a number of ghosts which still haunt the language of art criticism. One of them we even found entrenched in the *Oxford Dictionary*. The implication of its definition of an image is that the artist 'imitates' the 'external form' of the object in front of him, and the beholder, in his turn, recognizes the 'subject' of the work of art by this 'form'. This is what might be called the traditional view of representation. Its corollary is that a work of art will either be a faithful copy, in fact a complete replica, of the object represented, or will involve some degree of 'abstraction'. The artist, we read, abstracts the 'form' from the object he sees. The sculptor usually abstracts the three-dimensional form, and abstracts *from* colour; the painter abstracts contours and colours, and *from* the third dimension. In this context one hears it said that the draughtsman's line is a 'tremendous feat of abstraction' because it does not 'occur in nature'. A modern sculptor of Brancusi's persuasion may be praised or blamed for 'carrying abstraction to its logical extreme'. Finally the label of 'abstract art' for the creation of 'pure' forms carries with it a similar implication. Yet we need only look at our hobby horse to see that the very idea of abstraction as a complicated mental act lands us in curious absurdities. There is an old music hall joke describing a drunkard who politely lifts his hat to every lamp-post he passes. Should we say that the liquor has so increased his power of abstraction that he is now able to isolate the formal quality of uprightness from both lamp-post and the human figure? Our mind, of course, works by differentiation rather than by generalization, and the child will for long call all four-footers of a certain size 'gee-gee' before it learns to distinguish breeds and 'forms'! [1]

II

Then there is that age-old problem of universals as applied to art. It has received its classical formulation in the Platonizing theories of the Academicians. 'A history-painter,' says Reynolds, 'paints man in general; a portrait-painter a particular man, and therefore a defective model.' [2] This, of course, is the theory of abstraction applied to one specific problem. The implications are that the portrait, being an exact copy of a man's 'external form' with all 'blemishes' and 'accidents', refers to the individual person exactly as does the proper name. The painter, however, who wants to 'elevate his style' disregards the particular and 'generalizes the forms'. Such a picture will no longer represent a particular man but rather the class or concept 'man'. There is a deceptive simplicity in this argument, but it makes at least one unwarranted assumption: that every image of this kind necessarily refers to something outside itself—be it individual or class. But nothing of the kind need be implied when we point to an image and say 'this is a man'. Strictly speaking that statement may be interpreted to mean that the image itself is a member of the class 'man'. Nor is that interpretation as farfetched as it may sound. In fact our hobby horse would submit to no other interpretation. By the logic of Reynolds's reasoning it would have to represent the most generalized idea of horseness. But if the child calls a stick a horse it obviously means nothing of the kind. The stick is neither a sign signifying the concept horse nor is it a portrait of an individual horse. By its capacity to serve as a 'substitute' the stick becomes a horse in its own right, it belongs in the class of 'gee-gees' and may even merit a proper name of its own.

When Pygmalion blocked out a figure from his marble he did not at first represent a 'generalized' human form, and then gradually a particular woman. For as he chipped away and made it more lifelike the block was not turned into a portrait—not even in the unlikely case that he used a live model. So when his prayers were heard and the statue came to life she was Galatea and no one else—and that regardless of whether she had been fashioned in an archaic, idealistic, or naturalistic style. The question of reference, in fact, is totally independent of the degree of differentiation. The witch who made a 'generalized' wax dummy of an enemy may have meant it to refer to someone in particular. She would then pronounce the right spell to establish this link—much as we may write a caption under a generalized picture to do the same. But even those proverbial replicas of nature, Madame Tussaud's effigies, need the same treatment. Those in the galleries which are labelled are 'portraits of the great'. The figure on the staircase made to hoax the visitor simply represents 'an' attendant, one member of a class. It stands there as a 'substitute' for the expected guard—but it is not more 'generalized' in Reynolds's sense.

III

The idea that art is 'creation' rather than 'imitation' is sufficiently familiar. It has been proclaimed in various forms from the time of Leonardo, who insisted that the painter is 'Lord of all Things',[3] to that of Klee, who wanted to create as Nature does.[4] But the more solemn overtones of metaphysical power disappear when we leave art for toys. The child 'makes' a train either of a few blocks or with pencil on paper. Surrounded as we are by posters and newspapers carrying illustrations of commodities or events, we find it difficult to rid ourselves of the prejudice that all images should be 'read' as referring to some imaginary or actual reality. Only the historian knows how hard it is to look at Pygmalion's work without comparing it with nature. But recently we have been made aware how thoroughly we misunderstand primitive or Egyptian art whenever we make the assumption that the artist 'distorts' his motif or that he even wants us to see in his work the record of any specific experience.[5] In many cases these images 'represent' in the sense of being substitutes. The clay horse or servant, buried in the tomb of the mighty, takes the place of the living. The idol takes the place of the god. The question whether it represents the 'external form' of the particular divinity or, for that matter, of a class of demons is quite inappropriate. The idol serves as the substitute of the God in worship and ritual—it is a man-made god in precisely the sense that the hobby horse is a man-made horse; to question it further means to court deception.[6]

There is another misunderstanding to be guarded against. We often try instinctively to save our idea of 'representation' by shifting it to another plane. Where we cannot refer the image to a motif in the outer world we take it to be a portrayal of a motif in the artist's inner world. Much critical (and uncritical) writing on both primitive and modern art betrays this assumption. But to apply the naturalistic idea of portrayal to dreams and visions—let alone to unconscious images—begs a whole number of questions.[7] The hobby horse does not portray our idea of a horse. The fearsome monster or funny face we may doodle on our blotting pad is not projected out of our mind as paint is 'ex-pressed' out of a paint tube. Of course any image will be in some way symptomatic of its maker, but to think of it as of a photograph of a pre-existing reality is to misunderstand the whole process of image-making.

IV

Can our substitute take us further? Perhaps, if we consider how it could become a substitute. The 'first' hobby horse (to use eighteenth-century language) was probably no image at all. Just a stick which qualified as a horse because one could ride on it. The *tertium comparationis*, the common factor, was function rather than form. Or, more precisely, that formal aspect which fulfilled the minimum requirement for the performance of the function—for any 'ridable' object could serve as a horse. If that is true we may be enabled to cross a boundary which is usually regarded as closed and sealed. For in this sense 'substitutes' reach deep into biological functions that are common to man and animal. The cat runs after the ball as if it were a mouse. The baby sucks its thumb as if it were the breast. In a sense the ball 'represents' a mouse to the cat, the thumb a breast to the baby. But here too 'representation' does not depend on formal similarities, beyond the minimum requirements of function. The ball has nothing in common with the mouse except that it is chasable. The thumb nothing with the breast except that it is suckable. As 'substitutes' they fulfill certain demands of the organism. They are keys which happen to fit into biological or psychological locks, or counterfeit coins which make the machine work when dropped into the slot.

In the language of the nursery the psychological function of 'representation' is still recognized. The child will reject a perfectly naturalistic doll in favour of some monstrously 'abstract' dummy which is 'cuddly'. It may even dispose of the element of 'form' altogether and take to a blanket or an eiderdown as its favourite 'comforter'—a substitute on which to bestow its love. Later in life, as the psychoanalysts tell us, it may bestow this same love on a worthy or unworthy living substitute. A teacher may 'take the place' of the mother, a dictator or even an enemy may come to 'represent' the father. Once more the common denominator between the symbol and the thing symbolized is not the 'external form' but the function; the mother symbol would be lovable, the father-image fearable, or whatever the case may be.

Now this psychological concept of symbolization seems to lead so very far away from the more precise meaning which the word 'representation' has acquired in the figurative arts. Can there be any gain in throwing all these meanings together? Possibly: for anything seems worth trying, to get the function of symbolizing out of its isolation.

The 'origin of art' has ceased to be a popular topic. But the origin of the hobby horse may be a permitted subject for speculation. Let us assume that the owner of the stick on which he proudly rode through the land decided in a playful or magic mood—and who could always distinguish between the two?—to fix 'real' reins and that finally he was even tempted to 'give' it two eyes near the top end. Some grass could have passed for a mane. Thus our inventor 'had a horse'. He had made one. Now there are two things about this fictitious event which have some bearing on the idea of the figurative arts. One is that, contrary to what is sometimes said, communication need not come into this process at all. He may not have wanted to show his horse to anyone. It just served as a focus for his fantasies as he galloped along— though more likely than not it fulfilled this same function for a tribe to which it 'represented' some horse-demon of fertility and power.[8] We may sum up the moral of this 'Just So Story' by saying that substitution may precede portrayal, and creation communication. It remains to be seen how such a general theory can be tested. If it can, it may really throw light on some concrete questions. Even the origin of language, that notorious problem of speculative history,[9] might be investigated from this angle. For what if the 'pow-wow' theory, which sees the root of language in imitation, and the 'pooh-pooh' theory, which sees it in emotive interjection, were to be joined by yet another? We might term it the 'niam-niam' theory postulating the primitive hunter lying awake through hungry winter nights and making the sound of eating, not for communication but as a substitute for eating—being joined, perhaps, by a ritualistic chorus trying to conjure up the phantasm of food.

V

There is one sphere in which the investigation of the 'representational' function of forms has made considerable progress of late, that of animal psychology. Pliny, and innumerable writers after him, have regarded it as the greatest triumph of naturalistic art for a painter to have deceived sparrows or horses. The implication of these anecdotes is that a human beholder easily recognizes a bunch of grapes in a painting because for him recognition is an intellectual act. But for the birds to fly at the painting is a sign of a complete 'objective' illusion. It is a plausible idea, but a wrong one. The merest outline of a cow seems sufficient for a tsetse trap, for somehow it sets the apparatus of attraction in motion and 'deceives' the fly. To the fly, we might say, the crude trap has the 'significant' form—biologically significant, that is. It appears that visual stimuli of this kind play an important part in the animal world. By varying the shapes of 'dummies' to which animals were seen to respond, the 'minimum image' that still sufficed to release a specific reaction has been ascertained.[10] Thus little birds will open their beak when they see the feeding parent approaching the nest, but they will also do so when they are shown two darkish roundels of different size, the silhouette of the head and body of the bird 'represented' in its most 'generalized' form. Certain young fishes can even be deceived by two simple dots arranged horizontally, which they take to be the eyes of the mother fish, in whose mouth they are accustomed to shelter against danger. The fame of Zeuxis will have to rest on other achievements than his deception of birds.

An 'image' in this biological sense is not an imitation of an object's external form but an imitation of certain privileged or relevant aspects. It is here that a wide field of investigation would seem to open. For man is not exempt from this type of reaction.[11] The artist who goes out to represent the visible world is not simply faced with a neutral medley of forms he seeks to 'imitate'. Ours is a structured universe whose main lines of force are still bent and fashioned by our biological and psychological needs, however much they may be overlaid by cultural influences. We know that there are certain privileged motifs in our world to which we respond almost too easily. The human face may be outstanding among them. Whether by instinct or by very early training, we are certainly ever disposed to single out the expressive features of a face from the chaos of sensations that surrounds it, and to respond to its slightest variations with fear or joy. Our whole perceptual apparatus is somehow hypersensitized in this direction of physiognomic vision [12] and the merest hint suffices for us to create an expressive physiognomy that 'looks' at us with surprising intensity. In a heightened state of emotion, in the dark, or in a feverish spell, the looseness of this trigger may assume pathological forms. We may see faces in the pattern of a wallpaper, and three apples arranged on a plate may stare at us like two eyes and a clownish nose. What wonder that it is so easy to 'make' a face with two dots and a stroke even though their geometrical constellation may be greatly at variance with the 'external form' of a real head? The well-known graphic joke of the 'reversible face' might well be taken as a model for experiments which could still be made in this direction. It shows to what extent the group of shapes that can be read as a physiognomy has priority over all other readings. It turns the side which is the right way up into a convincing face and disintegrates the one that is upside down into a mere jumble of forms which is accepted as a strange headgear.[13] In good pictures of this kind it needs a real effort to see both faces at the same time, and perhaps we never quite succeed. Our automatic response is stronger than our intellectual awareness.

Seen in the light of the biological examples discussed above there is nothing surprising in this observation. We may venture the guess that this type of automatic recognition is dependent on the two factors of resemblance and biological relevance, and that the two may stand in some kind of inverse ratio. The greater the biological relevance an object has for us the more will we be attuned to its recognition—and the more tolerant will therefore be our standards of formal correspondence. In an erotically charged atmosphere the merest hint of formal similarity with sexual functions creates the desired response and the same is true of the dream symbols investigated by Freud. The hungry man will be similarly attuned to the discovery of food—he will scan the world for the slightest promise of nourishment. The starving may even project food into all sorts of dissimilar objects—as Chaplin does in *Gold Rush* when his huge companion suddenly appears to him as a chicken. Can it have been some such experience which stimulated our 'niam-niam' chanting hunters to see their longed-for prey in the patches and irregular shapes on the dark cave walls? Could they perhaps gradually have sought this experience in the deep mysterious recesses of the rocks, much as Leonardo sought out crumbling walls to aid his visual fantasies? Could they, finally, have been prompted to fill in such 'readable' outlines with coloured earth— to have at least something 'spearable' at hand which might 'represent' the eatable in some magic fashion? There is no way of testing such a theory, but if it is true that cave artists often 'exploited' the natural formations of the rocks,[14] this, together with the 'eidetic' character of their works,[15] would at least not contradict our fantasy. The great naturalism of cave paintings may after all be a very late flower. It may correspond to our late, derivative, and naturalistic hobby horse.

VI

It needed two conditions, then, to turn a stick into our hobby horse: first, that its form made it just possible to ride on it; secondly—and perhaps decisively—that riding mattered. Fortunately it still needs no great effort of the imagination to understand how the horse could become such a focus of desires and aspirations, for our language still carries the metaphors moulded by a feudal past when to be chival-rous was to be horsy. The same stick that had to represent a horse in such a setting would have become the substitute of something else in another. It might have become a sword, sceptre, or—in the context of ancestor worship—a fetish representing a dead chieftain. Seen from the point of view of 'abstraction', such a convergence of meanings onto one shape offers considerable difficulties, but from that of psychological 'projection' of meanings it becomes more easily intelligible. After all a whole diagnostic technique has been built up on the assumption that the meanings read into identical forms by different people tell us more about the readers than about the forms. In the sphere of art it has been shown that the same triangular shape which is the favourite pattern of many adjoining American Indian tribes is given different meanings reflecting the main preoccupations of the peoples concerned.[16] To the student of styles this discovery that one basic form can be made to represent a variety of objects may still become significant. For while the idea of realistic pictures being deliberately 'stylized' seems hard to swallow, the opposite idea of a limited vocabulary of simple shapes being used for the building up of different representations would fit much better into what we know of primitive art.

VII

Once we get used to the idea of 'representation' as a two-way affair rooted in psychological dispositions we may be able to refine a concept which has proved quite indispensable to the historian of art and which is nevertheless rather unsatisfactory: that of the 'conceptual image'. By this we mean the mode of representation which is more or less common to children's drawings and to various forms of primitive and primitivist art. The remoteness of this type of imagery from any visual experience has often been described.[17] The explanation of this fact which is most usually advanced is that the child (and the primitive) do not draw what they 'see' but what they 'know'. According to this idea the typical children's drawing of a manikin is really a graphic enumeration of those human features the child remembered.[18] It represents the content of the childish 'concept' of man. But to speak of 'knowledge' or 'intellectual realism' (as the French do [19]) brings us dangerously near to the fallacy of 'abstraction'. So back to our hobby horse. Is it quite correct to say that it consists of features which make up the 'concept' of a horse or that it reflects the memory image of horses seen? No—because this formulation omits one factor: the stick. If we keep in mind that representation is originally the creation of substitutes out of given material we may reach safer ground. The greater the wish to ride, the fewer may be the features that will do for a horse. But at a certain stage it must have eyes— for how else could it see? At the most primitive level, then, the conceptual image might be identified with what we have called the minimum image— that minimum, that is, which will make it fit into a psychological lock. The form of the key depends on the material out of which it is fashioned, and on the lock. It would be a dangerous mistake, however, to equate the 'conceptual image' as we find it used in the historical styles with this psychologically grounded minimum image. On the contrary. One has the impression that the presence of these schemata is always felt but that they are as much avoided as exploited.[20] We must reckon with the possibility of a 'style' being a set of conventions born out of complex tensions. The man-made image must be complete. The servant for the grave must have two hands and two feet. But he must not become a double under the artist's hands. Image-making is beset with dangers. One false stroke and the rigid mask of the face may assume an evil leer. Strict adherence to conventions alone can guard against such dangers. And thus primitive art seems often to keep on that narrow ledge that lies between the lifeless and the uncanny. If the hobby horse became too lifelike it might gallop away on its own.[21]

VIII

The contrast between primitive art and 'naturalistic' or 'illusionist' art can easily be overdrawn.[22] All art is 'image-making' and all image-making is rooted in the creation of substitutes. Even the artist of an 'illusionist' persuasion must make the man-made, the 'conceptual' image of convention his starting point. Strange as it may seem he cannot simply 'imitate an object's external form' without having first learned how to construct such a form. If it were otherwise there would be no need for the innumerable books on 'how to draw the human figure' or 'how to draw ships'. Wölfflin once remarked that all pictures owe more to other pictures than they do to nature.[23] It is a point which is familiar to the student of pictorial traditions but which is still insufficiently understood in its psychological implications. Perhaps the reason is that, contrary to the hopeful belief of many artists, the 'innocent eye' which should see the world afresh would not see it at all. It would smart under the painful impact of a chaotic medley of forms and colours.[24] In this sense the conventional vocabulary of basic forms is still indispensable to the artist as a starting point, as a focus of organization.

How, then, should we interpret the great divide which runs through the history of art and sets off the few islands of illusionist styles, of Greece, of China, and of the Renaissance, from the vast ocean of 'conceptual' art?

One difference, undoubtedly, lies in a change of function. In a way the change is implicit in the emergence of the idea of the image as a 'representation' in our modern sense of the word. As soon as it is generally understood that an image need not exist in its own right, that it may refer to something outside itself and therefore be the record of a visual experience rather than the creation of a substitute, the basic rules of primitive art can be transgressed with impunity. No longer is there any need for that completeness of essentials which belongs to the conceptual style, no longer is there the fear of the casual which dominates the archaic conception of art. The picture of a man on a Greek vase no longer needs a hand or a foot in full view. We know it is meant as a shadow, a mere record of what the artist saw or might see, and we are quite ready to join in the game and to supplement with our imagination what the real motif undoubtedly possessed. Once this idea of the picture suggesting something beyond what is really there is accepted in all its implications—and this certainly did not happen overnight—we are indeed forced to let our imagination play around it. We endow it with 'space' around its forms which is only another way of saying that we understand the reality which it evokes as three-dimensional, that the man could move and that even the aspect momentarily hidden 'was there'.[25] When medieval art broke away from that narrative conceptual symbolism into which the formulas of classical art had been frozen, Giotto made particular use of the figures seen from behind which stimulates our 'spatial' imagination by forcing us to imagine the other side.

Thus the idea of the picture as a representation of a reality outside itself leads to an interesting paradox. On the one hand it compels us to refer every figure and every object shown to that imaginary reality which is 'meant'. This mental operation can only be completed if the picture allows us to infer not only the 'external form' of every object represented but also its relative size and position. It leads us to that 'rationalization of space' we call scientific perspective by which the picture plane becomes a window through which we look into the imaginary world the artist creates there for us. In theory, at least, painting is then conceived in terms of geometrical projection.[26]

The paradox of the situation is that, once the whole picture is regarded as the representation of a slice of reality, a new context is created in which the conceptual image plays a different part. For the first consequence of the 'window' idea is that we cannot conceive of any spot on the panel which is not 'significant', which does not represent something. The empty patch thus easily comes to signify light, air, and atmosphere, and the vague form is interpreted as enveloped by air. It is this confidence in the representational context which is given by the very convention of the frame, which makes the development of impressionist methods possible. The artists who tried to rid themselves of their conceptual knowledge, who conscientiously became beholders of their own work and never ceased matching their created images against their impressions by stepping back and comparing the two—these artists could only achieve their aim by shifting something of the load of creation on to the beholder. For what else does it mean if we are enjoined to step back in turn and watch the coloured patches of an impressionist landscape 'spring to life'? It means that the painter relies on our readiness to take hints, to read contexts, and to call up our conceptual image under his guidance. The blob in the paintings by Manet which stands for a horse is no more an imitation of its external form than is our hobby horse. But he has so cleverly contrived it that it evokes the image in us—provided, of course, we collaborate.

Here there may be another field for independent investigation. For those 'privileged' objects which play their part in the earliest layers of image-making recur—as was to be expected—in that of image-reading. The more vital the feature that is indicated by the context and yet omitted, the more intense seems to be the process that is started off. On its lowest level this method of 'suggestive veiling' is familiar to erotic art. Not, of course, to its Pygmalion phase, but to its illusionist applications. What is here a crude exploitation of an obvious biological stimulus may have its parallel, for instance, in the representation of the human face. Leonardo achieved his greatest triumphs of lifelike expression by blurring precisely the features in which the expression resides, thus compelling us to complete the act of creation. Rembrandt could dare to leave the eyes of his most moving portraits in the shade because we are thus stimulated to supplement them.[27] The 'evocative' image, like its 'conceptual' counterpart, should be studied against a wider psychological background.

IX

My hobby horse is not art. At best it can claim the attention of iconology, that emerging branch of study which is to art criticism what linguistics is to the criticism of literature. But has not modern art experimented with the primitive image, with the 'creation' of forms, and the exploitation of deep-rooted psychological forces? It has. But whatever the nostalgic wish of their makers, the meaning of these forms can never be the same as that of their primitive models. For that strange precinct we call 'art' is like a hall of mirrors or a whispering gallery. Each form conjures up a thousand memories and after-images. No sooner is an image presented as art than, by this very act, a new frame of reference is created which it cannot escape. It becomes part of an institution as surely as does the toy in the nursery. If—as might be conceivable—a Picasso would turn from pottery to hobby horses and send the products of this whim to an exhibition, we might read them as demonstrations, as satirical symbols, as a declaration of faith in humble things or as self-irony—but one thing would be denied even to the greatest of contemporary artists: he could not make the hobby horse mean to us what it meant to its first creator. That way is barred by the angel with a flaming sword.

NOTES

1. In the sphere of art this process of differentiation rather than abstraction is wittily described by Oliver Wendell Holmes in the essay 'Cacoethes Scribendi', from *Over the Teacups* (London: 1890): 'It's just the same thing as my plan . . . for teaching drawing. . . . A man at a certain distance appears as a dark spot—nothing more. Good. Anybody . . . can make a dot. . . . Lesson No. 1. Make a dot; that is, draw your man, a mile off. . . . Now make him come a little nearer. . . . The dot is an oblong figure now. Good. Let your scholar draw an oblong figure. It is as easy as to make a note of admiration. . . . So by degrees the man who serves as a model approaches. A bright pupil will learn to get the outline of a human figure in ten lessons, the model coming five hundred feet nearer each time.'
2. *Discourses on Art* (Everyman Edition, p. 55). I have discussed the historical setting of this idea in 'Icones Symbolicae', *Journal of the Warburg and Courtauld Institutes*, XI (1948), p. 187, and some of its more technical aspects in a review of Charles Morris, *Signs, Language, and Behavior* (New York: 1946) in *The Art Bulletin*, March, 1949. In Morris's terminology these present meditations are concerned with the status and origin of the 'iconic sign'.
3. Leonardo da Vinci, *Paragone*, edited by I. A. Richter (London: 1949), p. 51.
4. Paul Klee, *On Modern Art* (London, 1948). For the history of the idea of *deus artifex* cf. E. Kris and O. Kurz, *Die Legende vom Künstler* (Vienna: 1934).
5. H. A. Groenewegen-Frankfort, *Arrest and Movement: An Essay on Space and Time in the Representational Art of the Ancient Near East* (London: 1951).

6. Perhaps it is only in a setting of realistic art that the problem I have discussed in 'Icones Symbolicae', loc. cit., becomes urgent. Only then the idea can gain ground that the allegorical image of, say, Justice, must be a portrait of Justice as she dwells in heaven.

7. For the history of this misinterpretation and its consequences cf. my article on 'Art and Imagery in the Romantic Period.' . . .

8. This, at least, would be the opinion of Lewis Spence, *Myth and Ritual in Dance, Game, and Rhyme* (London: 1947). And also of Ben Jonson's Busy, the Puritan: 'Thy Hobby-horse is an Idoll, a feirce and rancke Idoll: And thou, the *Nabuchadnezzar* . . . of the *Faire*, that set'st it up, for children to fall downe to, and worship'. (*Bartholomew Fair*, Act. III, Scene 6).

9. Cf. *Géza Révész, Ursprung und Vorgeschichte der Sprache* (Berne: 1946).

10. Cf. Konrad Lorenz, 'Die angeborenen Formen möglicher Erfahrung', *Zeitschrift für Tierpsychologie* V (1943), and the discussion of these experiments in E. Grassi and Th. von Uexküll, *Vom Ursprung und von den Grenzen der Geisteswissenschaften und Naturwissenschaften* (Berne: 1950).

11. K. Lorenz, loc. cit. The citation of this article does not imply support of the author's moral conclusions. On these more general issues see K. R. Popper, *The Open Society and Its Enemies*, esp., I, pp. 59 ff. and p. 268.

12. F. Sander, 'Experimentelle Ergebnisse der Gestaltpsychologie', *Berichte über den 10. Kongress für Experimentelle Psychologie* (Jena: 1928), p. 47, notes experiments that show the distance of two dots is much harder to estimate in its variations when these dots are isolated than when they are made to represent eyes in a schematic face and thus attain physiognomic significance.

13. For a large collection of such faces cf. Laurence Whistler, *Oho! The Drawings of Rex Whistler* (London: 1946).

14. G. H. Luquet, *The Art and Religion of Fossil Man* (London: 1930), pp. 141 f.

15. G. A. S. Snijder, *Kretische Kunst* (Berlin: 1936), pp. 68 f.

16. Franz Boas, *Primitive Art* (Oslo: 1927), pp. 118–28.

17. E.g., E. Löwry, *The Rendering of Nature in Early Greek Art* (London: 1907), H. Schaefer, *Von aegyptischer Kunst* (Leipzig: 1930), M. Verworn, *Ideoplastische Kunst* (Jena: 1914).

18. Karl Bühler, *The Mental Development of the Child* (London: 1930), pp. 113–17, where the connection with the linguistic faculty is stressed. A criticism of this idea was advanced by R. Arnheim, 'Perceptual Abstraction and Art', *Psychological Review*, LVI, 1947.

19. G. H. Luquet, *L'Art primitif* (Paris: 1930).

20. The idea of avoidance (of sexual symbols) is stressed by A. Ehrenzweig, *Psycho-Analysis of Artistic Vision and Hearing* (London: 1953), pp. 22–70.

21. E. Kris and O. Kurz, loc. cit., have collected a number of legends reflecting this age-old fear: thus a famous Chinese master was said never to have put the light into the eyes of his painted dragons lest they would fly away.

22. It was the intellectual fashion in German art history to work with contrasting pairs of concepts such as haptic-optic (Riegl), paratactic-hypotactic (Coellen), abstraction-empathy (Worringer), idealism-naturalism (Dvořák), physioplastic-ideoplastic (Verworn), multiplicity-unity (Wölfflin), all of which could probably be expressed in terms of 'conceptual' and 'less conceptual' art. While the heuristic value of this method of antithesis is not in doubt it often

tends to introduce a false dichotomy. In my book *The Story of Art* (London: 1950) I have attempted to stress the continuity of tradition and the persistent role of the conceptual image.

23. H. Wölfflin, *Principles of Art History* (New York: 1932).

24. The fallacy of a passive idea of perception is discussed in detail by E. Bruns-wik, *Wahrnehmung und Gegenstandswelt* (Vienna: 1934). In its application to art the writings of K. Fiedler contain many valuable hints; cf. also A. Ehrenzweig, loc. cit., for an extreme and challenging presentation of this problem.

25. This may be meant in the rather enigmatic passage on the painter Parrhasius in Pliny's *Natural History*, XXXV, 67, where it is said that 'the highest subtlety attainable in painting is to find an outline . . . which should appear to fold back and to enclose the object so as to give assurance of the parts behind, thus clearly suggesting even what it conceals'.

26. Cf. E. Panofsky, 'The Codex Huygens and Leonardo da Vinci's Art Theory', *Studies of the Warburg Institute*, XIII (London: 1940), pp. 90 f.

27. Cf. J. v. Schlosser, 'Gespräch von der Bildniskunst', *Präludien* (Vienna: 1927), where, incidentally, the hobby horse also makes its appearance.

Expressiveness

SUSANNE K. LANGER

When we talk about "Art" with a capital "A"—that is, about any or all of the arts: painting, sculpture, architecture, the potter's and the goldsmith's and other designers' arts, music, dance, poetry, and prose fiction, drama and film—it is a constant temptation to say things about "Art" in this general sense that are true only in one special domain, or to assume that what holds for one art must hold for another. For instance, the fact that music is made for performance, for presentation to the ear, and is simply not the same thing when it is given only to the tonal imagination of a reader silently perusing the score, has made some aestheticians pass straight to the conclusion that literature, too, must be physically heard to be fully experienced, because words are originally spoken, not written; an obvious parallel, but a careless and, I think, invalid one. It is dangerous to set up principles by analogy, and generalize from a single consideration.

But it is natural, and safe enough, to ask analogous questions: "What is the function of sound in music? What is the function of sound in poetry? What is the function of sound in prose composition? What is the function of sound in drama?" The answers may be quite heterogeneous; and that is itself an important fact, a guide to something more than a simple and sweeping theory. Such findings guide us to exact relations and abstract, variously exemplified basic principles.

At present, however, we are dealing with principles that have proven to be the same in all the arts, when each kind of art—plastic, musical, balletic, poetic, and each major mode, such as literary and dramatic writing, or painting, sculpturing, building plastic shapes—has been studied in its own terms. Such candid study is more rewarding than the usual passionate declaration that all the arts are alike, only their materials differ, their principles are all the same, their techniques all analogous, etc. That is not only unsafe, but untrue. It is in pursuing the differences among them that one arrives, finally, at a point where no more differences appear; then one has found, not postulated, their unity. At that deep level there is only one concept exemplified in all the different arts, and that is the concept of Art.

The principles that obtain wholly and fundamentally in every kind of art are few, but decisive; they determine what is art, and what is not. Expressiveness, in one definite and appropriate sense, is the same in all art works of any kind. What is created is not the same in any two distinct arts—this is, in fact, what makes them distinct—but the principle of creation is the same. And "living form" means the same in all of them.

A work of art is an expressive form created for our perception through sense or imagination, and what it expresses is human feeling. The word "feeling" must be taken here in its broadest sense, meaning *everything that can be felt*, from physical sensation, pain and comfort, excitement and repose, to the most complex emotions, intellectual tensions, or the steady feeling-tones of a conscious human life. In stating what a work of art is, I have just used the words "form," "expressive," and "created"; these are key words. One at a time, they will keep us engaged.

Let us consider first what is meant, in this context, by a *form*. The word has many meanings, all equally legitimate for various purposes; even in connection with art it has several. It may, for instance—and often does—denote the familiar, characteristic structures known as the sonnet form, the sestina, or the ballad form in poetry, the sonata form, the madrigal, or the symphony in music, the contredance or the classical ballet in choreography, and so on. This is not what I mean; or rather, it is only a very small part of what I mean. There is another sense in which artists speak of "form" when they say, for instance, "form follows function," or declare that the one quality shared by all good works of art is "significant form," or entitle a book *The Problem of Form in Painting and Sculpture*, or *The Life of Forms in Art*, or *Search for Form*. They are using "form" in a wider sense, which on the one hand is close to the commonest, popular meaning, namely just the *shape* of a thing, and on the other hand to the quite unpopular meaning it has in science and philosophy, where it designates something more abstract; "form" in its most abstract sense means structure, articulation, a whole resulting from the relation of mutually dependent factors, or more precisely, the way that whole is put together.

The abstract sense, which is sometimes called "logical form," is involved in the notion of expression, at least the kind of expression that characterizes art. That is why artists, when they speak of achieving "form," use the word with something of an abstract connotation, even when they are talking about a visible and tangible art object in which that form is embodied.

The more recondite concept of form is derived, of course, from the naive one, that is, material shape. Perhaps the easiest way to grasp the idea of "logical form" is to trace its derivation.

Let us consider the most obvious sort of form, the shape of an object, say a lampshade. In any department store you will find a wide choice of lampshades, mostly monstrosities, and what is monstrous is usually their shape. You select the least offensive one, maybe even a good one, but realize that the color, say violet, will not fit into your room; so you look about for another shade of the same shape but a different color, perhaps green. In recognizing this same shape in another object, possibly of another material as well as another color, you have quite naturally and easily abstracted the concept of this shape from your actual impression of the first lampshade. Presently it may occur to you that this shade is too big for your lamp; you ask whether they have *this same shade* (meaning another one of this shape) in a smaller size. The clerk understands you.

But what is *the same* in the big violet shade and the little green one? Nothing but the interrelations among their respective various dimensions. They are not "the same" even in their spatial properties, for none of their actual measures are alike; but their shapes are congruent. Their respective spatial factors are put together in the same way, so they exemplify the same form.

It is really astounding what complicated abstractions we make in our ordinary dealing with forms—that is to say, through what twists and transformations we recognize the same logical form. Consider the similarity of your two hands. Put one on the table, palm down, superimpose the other, palm down, as you may have superimposed cut-out geometric shapes in school —they are not alike at all. But their shapes are *exact opposites*. Their respective shapes fit the same description, provided that the description is modified by a principle of application whereby the measures are read one way for one hand and the other way for the other—like a timetable in which the list of stations is marked: "Eastbound, read down; Westbound, read up."

As the two hands exemplify the same form with a principle of reversal understood, so the list of stations describes two ways of moving, indicated by the advice to "read down" for one and "read up" for the other. We can all abstract the common element in these two respective trips, which is called the *route*. With a return ticket we may return only by the same route. The same principle relates a mold to the form of the thing that is cast in it, and establishes their formal correspondence, or common logical form.

So far we have considered only objects—lampshades, hands, or regions of the earth—as having forms. These have fixed shapes; their parts remain in fairly stable relations to each other. But there are also substances that have no definite shapes, such as gases, mist, and water, which take the shape of any bounded space that contains them. The interesting thing about such amorphous fluids is that when they are put into violent motion they do exhibit visible forms, not bounded by any container. Think of the momentary efflorescence of a bursting rocket, the mushroom cloud of an atomic bomb, the funnel of water or dust screwing upward in a whirlwind. The instant the motion stops, or even slows beyond a certain degree, those shapes collapse and the apparent "thing" disappears. They are not shapes of things at all, but forms of motions, or dynamic forms.

Some dynamic forms, however, have more permanent manifestations, because the stuff that moves and makes them visible is constantly replenished. A waterfall seems to hang from the cliff, waving streamers of foam. Actually, of course, nothing stays there in mid-air; the water is always passing; but there is more and more water taking the same paths, so we have a lasting shape made and maintained by its passage—a permanent dynamic form. A quiet river, too, has dynamic form; if it stopped flowing it would either go dry or become a lake. Some twenty-five hundred years ago, Heraclitus was struck by the fact that you cannot step twice into the same river at the same place—at least, if the river means the water, not its dynamic form, the flow.

When a river ceases to flow because the water is deflected or dried up, there remains the river bed, sometimes cut deeply in solid stone. That bed is shaped by the flow, and records as graven lines the currents that have ceased to exist. Its shape is static, but it *expresses* the dynamic form of the river. Again, we have two congruent forms, like a cast and its mold, but this time the congruence is more remarkable because it holds between a dynamic form and a static one. That relation is important; we shall be dealing with it again when we come to consider the meaning of "living form" in art.

The congruence of two given perceptible forms is not always evident upon simple inspection. The common *logical* form they both exhibit may become apparent only when you know the principle whereby to relate them, as you compare the shapes of your hands not by direct correspondence, but by correspondence of opposite parts. Where the two exemplifications of the single logical form are unlike in most other respects one needs a rule for matching up the relevant factors of one with the relevant factors of the other; that is to say, a *rule of translation*, whereby one instance of the logical form is shown to correspond formally to the other.

The logical form itself is not another thing, but an abstract concept, or better an *abstractable* concept. We usually don't abstract it deliberately, but only use it, as we use our vocal cords in speech without first learning all about their operation and then applying our knowledge. Most people perceive intuitively the similarity of their two hands without thinking of them as conversely related; they can guess at the shape of the hollow inside a wooden shoe from the shape of a human foot, without any abstract study of topology. But the first time they see a map in the Mercator projection—with parallel lines of longitude, not meeting at the poles—they find it hard to believe that this corresponds logically to the circular map they used in school, where the meridians bulged apart toward the equator and met at both poles. The visible shapes of the continents are different on the two maps, and it takes abstract thinking to match up the two representations of the same earth. If, however, they have grown up with both maps, they will probably see the geographical relationships either way with equal ease, because these relationships are not *copied* by either map, but *expressed,* and expressed equally well by both; for the two maps are different *projections* of the same logical form, which the spherical earth exhibits in still another—that is, a spherical—projection.

An expressive form is any perceptible or imaginable whole that exhibits relationships of parts, or points, or even qualities or aspects within the whole, so that it may be taken to represent some other whole whose elements have analogous relations. The reason for using such a form as a symbol is usually that the thing it represents is not perceivable or readily imaginable. We cannot see the earth as an object. We let a map or a little globe express the relationships of places on the earth, and think about the earth by means of it. The understanding of one thing through another seems to be a deeply intuitive process in the human brain; it is so natural that we often have difficulty in distinguishing the symbolic expressive form from what it conveys. The symbol seems to be the thing itself, or contain it, or be contained in it. A child interested in a globe will not say: "This means the earth," but: "Look, this is the earth." A similar identification of symbol and meaning underlies the widespread conception of holy names, of the physical efficacy of rites, and many other primitive but culturally persistent phenomena. It has a bearing on our perception of artistic import; that is why I mention it here.

The most astounding and developed symbolic device humanity has evolved is language. By means of language we can conceive the intangible, incorporeal things we call our *ideas,* and the equally inostensible elements of our perceptual world that we call *facts.* It is by virtue of language that we can think, remember, imagine, and finally conceive a universe of facts. We can describe things and represent their relations, express rules of their interactions, speculate and predict and carry on a long symbolizing process known as reasoning. And above all, we can communicate, by producing a serried array of audible or visible words, in a pattern commonly known, and readily understood to reflect our multifarious concepts and percepts and their interconnections. This use of language is *discourse;* and the pattern of discourse is known as *discursive form.* It is a highly versatile, amazingly powerful pattern. It has impressed itself on our tacit thinking, so that we call all systematic reflection "discursive thought." It has made, far more than most people know, the very frame of our sensory experience—the frame of objective facts in which we carry on the practical business of life.

Yet even the discursive pattern has its limits of usefulness. An expressive form can express any complex of conceptions that, via some rule of projection, appears congruent with it, that is, appears to be of that form. Whatever there is in experience that will not take the impress—directly or indirectly—of discursive form, is not discursively communicable or, in the strictest sense, logically thinkable. It is unspeakable, ineffable; according to practically all serious philosophical theories today, it is unknowable.

Yet there is a great deal of experience that is knowable, not only as immediate, formless, meaningless impact, but as one aspect of the intricate web of life, yet defies discursive formulation, and therefore verbal expression: that is what we sometimes call the *subjective aspect* of experience, the direct feeling of it—what it is like to be waking and moving, to be drowsy, slowing down, or to be sociable, or to feel self-sufficient but alone; what it feels like to pursue an elusive thought or to have a big idea. All such directly felt experiences usually have no names—they are named, if at all, for the outward conditions that normally accompany their occurrence. Only the most striking ones have names like "anger," "hate," "love," "fear," and are collectively called "emotion." But we feel many things that never develop into any designable emotion. The ways we are moved are as various as the lights in a forest; and they may intersect, sometimes without cancelling each other, take shape and dissolve, conflict, explode into passion, or be transfigured. All these inseparable elements of subjective reality compose what we call the "inward life" of human beings. The usual factoring of that life-stream into mental, emotional, and sensory units is an arbitrary scheme of simplification that makes scientific treatment possible to a considerable extent; but we may already be close to the limit of its usefulness, that is, close to the point where its simplicity becomes an obstacle to further questioning and discovery instead of the revealing, ever-suitable logical projection it was expected to be.

Whatever resists projection into the discursive form of language is, indeed, hard to hold in conception, and perhaps impossible to communicate, in the proper and strict sense of the word "communicate." But fortunately our logical intuition, or form-perception, is really much more powerful than we commonly believe, and our knowledge—genuine knowledge, understanding—is considerably wider than our discourse. Even in the use of language, if we want to name something that is too new to have a name (e.g., a newly invented gadget or a newly discovered creature), or want to express a relationship for which there is no verb or other connective word, we resort to metaphor; we mention it or describe it as something else, something analogous. The principle of metaphor is simply the principle of saying one thing and meaning another, and expecting to be understood to mean the other. A metaphor is not language, it is an idea expressed by language, an idea that in its turn functions as a symbol to express something. It is not discursive and therefore does not really make a statement of the idea it conveys; but it formulates a new conception for our direct imaginative grasp.

Sometimes our comprehension of a total experience is mediated by a metaphorical symbol because the experience is new, and language has words and phrases only for familiar notions. Then an extension of language will gradually follow the wordless insight, and discursive expression will supersede the non-discursive pristine symbol. This is, I think, the normal advance of human thought and language in that whole realm of knowledge where discourse is possible at all.

But the symbolic presentation of subjective reality for contemplation is not only tentatively beyond the reach of language—that is, not merely beyond the words we have; it is impossible in the essential frame of language. That is why those semanticists who recognize only discourse as a symbolic form must regard the whole life of feeling as formless, chaotic, capable only of symptomatic expression, typified in exclamations like "Ah!" "Ouch!" "My sainted aunt!" They usually do believe that art is an expression of feeling, but that "expression" in art is of this sort, indicating that the speaker has an emotion, a paint, or other personal experience, perhaps also giving us a clue to the general kind of experience it is—pleasant or unpleasant, violent or mild—but not setting that piece of inward life objectively before us so we may understand its intricacy, its rhythms and shifts of total appearance. The differences in feeling-tones or other elements of subjective experience are regarded as differences in quality, which must be felt to be appreciated. Furthermore, since we have no intellectual access to pure subjectivity, the only way to study it is to study the symptoms of the person who is having subjective experiences. This leads to physiological psychology—a very important and interesting field. But it tells us nothing about the phenomena of subjective life, and sometimes simplifies the problem by saying they don't exist.

Now, I believe the expression of feeling in a work of art—the function that makes the work an expressive form—is not symptomatic at all. An artist working on a tragedy need not be in personal despair or violent upheaval; nobody, indeed, could work in such a state of mind. His mind would be occupied with the causes of his emotional upset. Self-expression does not require composition and lucidity; a screaming baby gives his feeling far more release than any musician, but we don't go into a concert hall to hear a baby scream; in fact, if that baby is brought in we are likely to go out. We don't want self-expression.

A work of art presents feeling (in the broad sense I mentioned before, as everything that can be felt) for our contemplation, making it visible or audible or in some way perceivable through a symbol, not inferable from a symptom. Artistic form is congruent with the dynamic forms of our direct sensuous, mental, and emotional life; works of art are projections of "felt life," as Henry James called it, into spatial, temporal, and poetic structures. They are images of feeling, that formulate it for our cognition. What is artistically good is whatever articulates and presents feeling to our understanding.

Artistic forms are more complex than any other symbolic forms we know. They are, indeed, not abstractable from the works that exhibit them. We may abstract a shape from an object that has this shape, by disregarding color, weight and texture, even size; but to the total effect that is an artistic form, the color matters, the thickness of lines matters, and the appearance of texture and weight. A given triangle is the same in any position, but to an artistic form its location, balance, and surroundings are not indifferent. Form, in the sense in which artists speak of "significant form" or "expressive form," is not an abstracted structure, but an apparition; and the vital processes of sense and emotion that a good work of art expresses seem to the beholder to be directly contained in it, not symbolized but really presented. The congruence is so striking that symbol and meaning appear as one reality. Actually, as one psychologist who is also a musician has written, "Music sounds as feelings feel." And likewise, in good painting, sculpture, or building, balanced shapes and colors, lines and masses look as emotions, vital tensions and their resolutions feel.

An artist, then, expresses feeling, but not in the way a politician blows off steam or a baby laughs and cries. He formulates that elusive aspect of reality that is commonly taken to be amorphous and chaotic; that is, he objectifies the subjective realm. What he expresses is, therefore, not his own actual feelings, but what he knows about human feeling. Once he is in possession of a rich symbolism, that knowledge may actually exceed his entire personal experience. A work of art expresses a conception of life, emotion, inward reality. But it is neither a confessional nor a frozen tantrum; it is a developed metaphor, a non-discursive symbol that articulates what is verbally ineffable —the logic of consciousness itself.

The Inert and the Frenetic

MAX KOZLOFF

Classification has always bothered people interested in visual art. It has become a human problem far more than an academic one, for the reason that if one can know where a work of art "belongs," one can diminish its challenge to the imagination and to the emotions. When a critic triumphantly claims that an artist fits into no category, that he is, in fact, his own man, we are invited to applaud, as if that artist deserved special praise for having demonstrated meritorious conduct in being individual. No less of a cliche is it to say that an artist does fit into a style, or a movement, as if it were somehow a virtue to affirm the known, and the tested, or even the avant-garde. Both these thought-saving processes reveal an extreme self-consciousness about the identity of art, at least when they cease being descriptive, and become evaluative. And in this instance, neither is very valuable because based on a cor-

Reprinted by permission from *Art Forum*, Vol. IV, No. 7, March 1966. This essay is a revised version of a lecture given at Bennington College, Vermont, on November 29, 1965.

rupted romanticism on one hand, and a coarse historical theorizing, on the other.

Especially is this true of the pluralistic situation we have today, where it seems possible only to add idioms together, rather than to forge conceptual analogies, in order to arrive at some comprehensive picture of what is going on. It is, of course, out of the question to "organize" the immediate scene; but the recent past beckons. It tempts synthesis. Yet here one generally tends to relate material by its surface—iconographical, stylistic, social, or ideological determinants being the most obvious, but not necessarily the most profound or decisive. One thing, however, we know. The great, mythic distinctions that have been applied to art even as recent as our own modern tradition, have outlived their usefulness, or rather, their suggestiveness. Thus, Apollonian-Dionysian, Classic-Romantic, Representational-Abstract, all these are dead issues, false polarities which merely schematize a content becoming ever more elusive and ambiguous. The same thing goes for a goodly number of more specific, seemingly technical terms: Post-Painterly, hard edge or soft edge, geometric or biomorphic. How boring to depend on these super-annuated expressions, so imprecise, and so demeaning—to ourselves and to our experience.

It is in an attempt to do a slightly different justice to that experience that I propose an approach which, to a certain extent, may be self-evident, but also neglected. I want to examine what might be called the esthetic "beat" of a work; how, figuratively speaking, we "hear" the visual composition. The main hypothesis here is that there are units, "beats," which make up the perceptible visual or spatial accents by which the work appears to compose itself. Thus, for instance, the "tempo" is the rate of "speed" at which these beats occur. And the visual "rhythm" is the particular flow or pattern of beats existing at various tempi. Needless to say, all these are inter-relating ideas, often very difficult to settle out in any one instance. Just as obvious, "beat" is merely one consideration when analyzing works of art, and then, not by any means the most immediately helpful. Other, more measurable factors play the dominant role: image, texture, or, to borrow once again from musical terminology, pitch, timbre, registration, as well as shading, density, volume and scale. Yet, to give a notion of how such features may intersect with "beat," it is only necessary to indicate that color may be, and often is, used rhythmically. So may any of the other elements. Like notes, they can be put together in various ways, one of which is by rhythmic emphasis. Such a "sonic" approach, therefore, alludes to the almost animal state of excitation of the work more than it does to the conventions (although it is itself a convention) by which the visual information is imparted. It is a tool by which to approach content, not a key that will unlock it.

Moreover, one's general impression of a painting, that is, its effect, may not be explained by one's perception of its beat. It would be an untenable deduction, for example, to say that because they are equivalently "fast" works of art, a Cubist Braque of 1911 and a Kandinsky improvisation of the same era must have a similar meaning. For all that they may have comparable ranges of small arcs, broken intersections, contrasts, aggregations and dis-aggregations, no one will confuse their expressive intentions. Kandinsky's loosened skeins, wiry scratches and radiant color contrast with Braque's axial-pendular structure, and greyed, faceted transparencies. Forces expand outward in the Kandinsky where entanglement is only a foil for explosion, whereas in the French painter, there is a subtly perceived, lost, and reperceived equi-librium of energies.

Conversely, much the same caution applies to comparisons between nom-inally "slow" paintings. Looking at a post-World War I Mondrian, and, say, a primer type, compartmented Magritte, the eye discerns even, gridded, self-contained, harmoniously arranged pictures. But the Mondrian elicits a sense of bodily and optical tensions reduced to an armature and held in rigid, vivid suspension, while the Magritte will show that the realm of knowl-edge and of observation can play tricks on one another, and that the outer world is made up of material that irrationally betrays one's notion of what it is thought to be. Clearly artists can work in entirely different areas, and make points antithetical to each other even when the inner "metabolism" of their art reveals a great kinship. All this is obvious enough.

The moment in the history of twentieth century art when this kind of differentiation was minimized was Abstract Expressionism. Combining Cub-ism, Surrealism, and Expressionism in a convulsive tumult, this movement was the most radical in equating a physiological frenzy with an artistic aim. It might be said to have exploded its abstract legacy—value oriented towards a coherently structured, schematically presented vision of interior forces—by means of Dada and Surrealist subversions, involved with the probing of un-conscious and even absurd impulses which questioned the nature of that legacy, and, in fact, the whole vision. Out of this tumult emerged an art holding on to its potentialities only by having stripped itself down to its own pulse. Perhaps, in the strictest sense, this is what the kinesthetic supposition amounts to. A drip Pollock, for instance, is a veritable layered tissue of rapid rhythms to which line, color and texture have been subsumed. Yet here, too, Abstract Expressionism had a calming systole to its diastolic image of passion. If in de Kooning, there is a kind of divine tantrum, a staggered multiplicity of beats, conscripting all pictorial elements, in Rothko, there are only two or three beats, fatalistically hushed within each other, but with such a wealth of over and undertones that the experience is compounded of a chromatic and luminous resonance even more than of that which emits it. Abstract Expressionism, surely, identified raw energy with an appropriate rhythmic existence. To apprehend the one is instantly to have felt the other. Ultimately, one finds a homogeneous, even a synoptic merging of form and content in the whole style, no matter how much internal conflict was necessary to distill it.

The situation today is totally altered out of all recognition from what it once was. For one thing, there is no field theory of what art should be, and

Jack Tworkov. PD #. Charcoal on paper 14" x 12", 1962. Courtesy of Leo Castelli Gallery. Photograph by Rudolph Burckhardt.

no comprehensiveness of esthetic scope. The relationship of general ideas to individual sensations, such as it was, has broken down. The sacrifices made by Abstract Expressionism in the interests of emotional unity no longer have to be made; nor is emotional unity itself a goal. Secondly, tempi have been riotously stepped up, or outrageously decelerated, not so much to concur with, but to dominate, most other pictorial circumstances. Finally, the notion of rhythm is perverted. It seems almost to work against itself. A viewer is stymied by this rhythmic insubordination. Instead of his experience pleasurably unfolding in a kind of mimetic discovery of beat relationships in Abstract Expressionist painting and sculpture, bodily empathy is now assaulted and disjointed. But to the extent that it becomes increasingly difficult to follow through the rhythmic function of a current work, the more that work asserts its own weird contemporaneity.

Present art, therefore, thoroughly rejects the belief of the post-war period that there could ever be a direct correlation between rhythm and intention. If the matter is superficially considered, what we have today is the establishment of two quite opposed camps, which might be summarized as the inert and the frenetic. Pop art and its related idioms, for instance, might qualify as a belated successor to Surrealism, as it rushes merrily and garrulously to ever more feverish entanglements. Conversely, present abstraction might be thought of as the excessive amplification of the tendency towards rigid and ultrastabilized statements in Constructivism and de Stijl. On one hand, then, a kind of hyper-mobility, and on the other, an immobility bordering on paralysis.

So much for the basic postulate. How well does it apply to one's encounters in the galleries? In Rauschenberg's works of any vintage from the last five years, the orientation of images is such that one no longer knows what is "up" or "down," or more, what are the rates of speed by which one assimilates the composite, montaged elements. The Rosenquists that one can see now, or remember from the past, look like so many billboard Magrittes, jostling with each other. They appear to be pictures composed only of other pictures, many pictures within one, all operating at different tempi, and, needless to say, with different rhythms. Or, one can think of Oyvind Fahlstrom's extraordinary painting "Dr. Livingstone," in which the plane is overgrown with a kind of inky vegetation that immediately oversaturates the powers of attention. What at first glance might be mistaken to be a Pollock-like labyrinth turns out to be the most microscopically articulated carpet of unnameable, but sharply defined "incidents," each demanding to be read as a separate (but curiously unbounded) episode. Something of the kind also pertains to Edward Kienholz's "Barney's Beanery," in which the proliferation of details and the compression of the space in which the spectator intimidatedly enters, produce a state of affairs never more calm than frantic, and often dissipating into hysteria. Other non-abstract artists whose natural realm seems to be the frenetic are Peter Saul, Jasper Johns (the last five years), Robert Hudson, R. J. Kitaj, Jean Tinguely, Larry Rivers, and Eduardo Paolozzi. They have in common only their acknowledgement that art is a non-agreement of part with whole, a communion of dissimilarities and discords. Whether it be through existential differences, or illustrational conflicts, their work bodies forth an almost pathologically awry, gratuitously adrenalized condition of awareness.

In opposition to these smatterings of chaos and mental dissolution are the rarified and recalcitrant offspring of the color-field painting that came up after the war. It is not merely that abstraction of this persuasion rejects nerv-

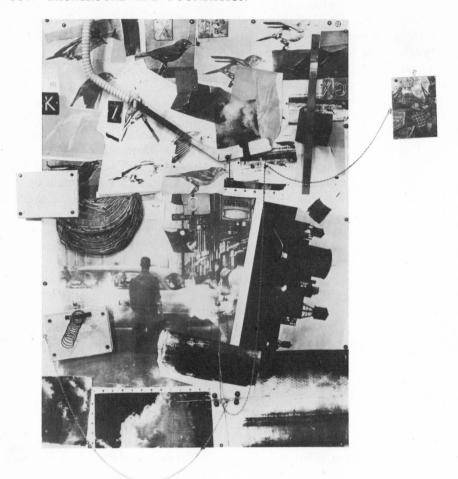

Robert Rauschenberg. New York Bird Calls for Ovyind Fahlstrom. *Combine 84" x 69", 1965. From the collection of Mr. and Mrs. John Murchison. Photo courtesy of Leo Castelli Gallery.*

ousness, complexity and virtuosity. Rather, it is inimical to any but the most trivial or hairsplitting differentiations of form itself. A painting by Ellsworth Kelly may present only two shapes or areas, uniform in color saturation, and ambiguous only insofar that each may substitute for figure or ground. Ad Reinhardt manifests a vision in which distinguishable units tremble on the brink of invisibility, making any interpretation of rhythm problematical. Jules Olitski, in his latest work, gives over the whole pictorial façade exclusively to the chromatic palpitation of undertones, the aftermath of a physical event or contact seemingly absent from the canvas itself. That his pigment is now sprayed on has something to do with this curious effect. As for Kenneth Noland, the transfer of imagery evidenced by his earlier concentric circles to

James Rosenquist. Nomad. *84" x 210", 1963. Albright-Knox Art Gallery, Buffalo, New York. Photo by Eric Pollitzer.*

his present chevrons and wedges only reaffirms the more or less obvious stasis that is at the heart of symmetry and the equilateral triangle. For his part, Frank Stella has confined himself to frozen, modular systems of parallel stripes whose orientation and scale is determined only by the external shape (and width!) of the stretcher. These artists are hardly isolated figures. They belong to a list which would also include Barnett Newman, Ludwig Sander, Lyman Kipp, Robert Morris, Dan Flavin, Donald Judd, and Edward Avedesian: all quite distinct as artists, but sharing the belief that perception can be enhanced by a certain obvious lifelessness (reductiveness), a certain refusal to deal with "relationships" in any normative sense of the word. More accurately, their work purveys tautological or redundant structures, brought into finical, opaque adjustment with a tradition of abstract art whose eloquence now seems a little blatant.

The co-existence of these idiomatic polarities in current art offers a sharp rebuke to those who see history prescriptively, and who have an idea of the avant-garde as something holistic and unitary. Such a view disregards the underground reinforcement these polarities give each other, if only through being thrust into relief. And it also misses that concept, all appearances to the contrary, which they mutually partake. The clue here, it seems to me, is

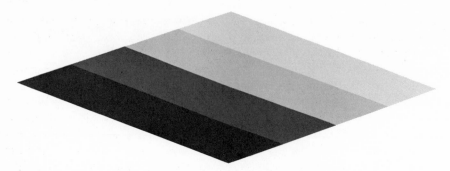

Kenneth Noland. Up Cadmium. Acrylic paint on canvas, 6' x 8', 1966. Collection of the artist. Photo by Rudolph Burckhardt. Courtesy of Andre Emmerich Gallery, Inc.

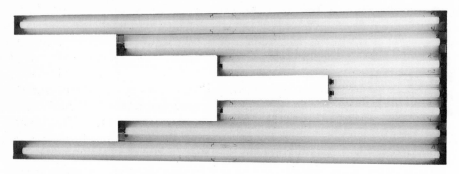

Dan Flavin. Monument #IV for V. Tatlin. Flourescent light, 23" x 96", 1968. Photo courtesy of Dwan Gallery.

mechanism, implacably transforming the rate at which artistic experience can be comfortably assimilated by the spectator. When we listen to a long-playing record, no matter what the tempi of the music, they are transcribed by a disc which revolves at 33⅓ revolutions per minute. But if its speed is moved up to 78 rpm or lowered to 16, all musical timbre and sequence is altered shrilly or lugubriously by the ungeared-for distortion. I am not suggesting that the supposed "content" of the two tendencies sketched above might be "restored" or "exchanged" if only they could be modified to act at their "proper" speed. That speed, or lack of it, is built in from the beginning, and is absolutely essential to the comprehension of the experience. It is for this reason that I am suggesting, however, that mechanism, or a mechanistic attitude, in the form of some arbitrary, seemingly extra-human agency, functions as an obstacle to understanding the otherwise clear-cut strategies of recent art. For it appears that either by straining or belittling one's powers of attention, the artist hopes to gain a further durability for his work in our consciousness. This would imply that the really fruitful areas for artistic invention are exactly those in which it becomes increasingly difficult, and altogether more necessary, for the spectator to make subtle "temporal" discriminations. Evidently, it might be inferred that sluggishness and simple-mindedness generate an unexpected drama the longer objects characterized by those qualities are contemplated. Conversely, a deadpoint, or a coldly static condition of experience can sometimes be discerned in the midst of a confused swirl of sensations. Be that as it may, the beat of a work of art is just as integral to its intention as in the past, but it is more likely now to act as a kind of psychological feint that would block too easy a conclusion about the nature of the esthetic message. Works of art now ostentatiously run their own visual interference.

If one can accept this premise provisionally for paintings and sculptures, one will grant it easily in its definition of certain aspects of contemporary film and literature. Among those representative film makers who have given new life to their medium, two groups might be distinguished. On one hand, there are Fellini, Richardson, Mekas, Truffaut, Lester and Resnais, to name but a few of the hectic echelon. On the other hand one has Bergman, Antonioni, much of Godard (of whom more later), Ray, and Bresson, all of whose work can be far more excruciatingly time-consuming to view than seems warranted by its length. Similarly, there are picaresque, feverish authors like Barth, Borges, Gadda, and Heller contrasting with such as Becket and Robbe-Grillet. (Comparable parallels can be drawn in music.) The pseudo-manic or inhuman atmosphere often evoked in the films and books created by these men fulfills an anti-naturalistic, and often an anti-narrative role, for it expels the organic dimension and temporal expectations in which reality is generally, and passively, received. Furthermore, the more ambitiously refractive the medium of perception, the more, inevitably, it begins to subvert its own "nature," and works against the notion of medium purity. The directors of stasis, for instance, are criticized for being banal symbolists in a heavy-handed literary way, while the practitioners of the "nouveau roman" are accused of giving in words only such information which would be more graphically conveyed by images. But it is, of course, the very harassment which these artists visit on our conventional notions of literary and filmic form that brings the shock of discovery. Events that crowd into ever smaller spatial or temporal intervals, but which do not build up (e.g. Mekas' astonishing "The Brig"); tiny incidents which spread out into enormously disproportionate time spans, denying the factor of beat, and introducing a note of impersonal panic into boredom itself (Warhol's alienating filmed "stillies"): such are the inverted rhythms of the modern sensibility.

These provocative inversions eventually put a considerable strain on the lines of an argument which seeks to give Pop art and its related idioms a frenetic cast, and the inert mold to abstraction. The number of cross-overs in each mode jeopardizes the general idea. But it is also one of the most fascinating areas of the whole problem to explore. Warhol's early arrays of

Campbell Soup cans, his Brillo boxes, and many of his serial image canvases, like the dollar bills, all convey multiple, limitless standardized beats, having no discernible rhythm, and no tempo—and yet they incarnate themselves in specific Pop imagery and technique. Jasper Johns' painting "Grey Rectangles" is neither abstract nor representational. Its drawer units do not act as beats, its paint strokes are equivocal in their minimally articulated monotony, and its overall aspect as a field painting "manque" yields a very haunting situation. Meanwhile, all of current so-called "retinal painting" is obviously a species of abstract frenetic which yolks the spectator as a passive receptor of optical poppings, blips, after-images and moire curves that constantly prevent apprehension of the nature of their forms. In this respect, too, it is anti-relational, but more through reluctance to consider the problem of relations, than through the structurally felt necessity to undermine them. Additionally, if one turns to one of the most prominent and extraordinary Pop artists, Claes Oldenburg, the thesis has to be re-defined once again. In his "Large Light Switch," for example, wooden forms of the utmost geometric simplicity mimic an absurdly larger than life domestic artifact. As in so many of his other magnifications and environments, this three-dimensional Magritte demonstrates the abstract inert possibilities of Pop art. So do Roy Lichtenstein's series of "ben-day" screened landscape paintings. Yet, if both are calculatedly frozen or languid, in the manner of current abstract art, they also inevitably question the abstractness of abstraction. Oldenburg, in fact, sees reality as consisting of just so many mutually transmutable, or rather, equivalent materials: "Newspaper equals drawing. Food equals painting. Furniture equals sculpture." (*Artforum*, January 1966, p. 33.) It is, perhaps a more up-to-date, and social reformulation of Dubuffet's "anything can come from anything."

Such existential laissez-faire, of course, is at loggerheads with the hopefully non-referential, ferociously separatist philosophy of what Barbara Rose has called "ABC" art. For Stella, or Judd, or Morris, nothing equals anything else, and, above all, nothing can be projected into a work of art, which must resist interpretation at all costs. One of the best explanations of this point of view actually comes from a novelist and theorist rather than a painter, Alain Robbe-Grillet:

Instead of this universe of "signification" (psychological, social, functional), we must try to construct a world both more solid and more immediate. Let it be first of all by their presence that objects and gestures impose themselves.

To describe things, in point of fact, requires that we place ourselves deliberately outside them. We must neither appropriate them to ourselves nor transfer anything to them . . . Henceforth we refuse all complicity with objects. (Quoted from *The Modern Tradition*, edited by Richard Ellman and Charles Feidelson Jr., pp. 364, 377.)

I submit that the main technique utilized by the ABC artists in structuring both the distance and the intractable presence of their created objects, is

Roy Lichenstein. Study for Preparedness. Oil and magna on canvas, 56" x 100", 1968. From the collection of Ludwig, Aachen. Photo by Rudolph Burckhardt. Courtesy of Leo Castelli Gallery.

that of choking rhythm. Typically, their work presents itself as a pokerfaced monolith—a beam, an hermetic rectangle or a bent pole are examples—which petrifies all movement, literal or implied. As the slow film is anti-narrative, so their sculptures are anti-formal, despite the extremely "willed" and controlled look of each composition. In fact, they find a kind of derangement of order precisely in the self-contained. As it comes forth in recent efforts by Donald Judd and Robert Morris, their art is ostensibly abstract and geometric

Donald Judd. Untitled. Painted galvanized iron, 5″ x 40″ x 9″, 1967. From the collection of Mr. and Mrs. S. Carter Burden. Photo by Eric Pollitzer. Courtesy of Leo Castelli Gallery.

in origin. But, to the extent that there is no visual dialogue, or at most an extremely inconsequential one, within their parts—often even the notion of parts is terribly atrophied—one is compelled to see them as real, circumstantial, if non-descript objects of the actual world. We are familiar with the concept of the "found object"; these, as one critic has pointed out, are "lost sculptures." That minute quiver between abstraction and concretion, obtained by eliminating practically all rhythmic interplay from the work, becomes its justifying ambiguity. No quietude could be more aggressive. Naturally, in the works I am discussing, a great deal of this stems from the Dada legacy, and it is interesting to note the conflict between Dadaistic appropriation and annexation of significance in real life, and the Robbe-Grillet impulse to fight it off. Even when there is a modular or repeated exposition of forms, as in some of Judd's recent structures, the effect is of a dumb show, than which nothing could be more recalcitrant or non-allusive. All this is reminiscent of Duchamp's and Picabia's "forays in demoralization," only much more sensitized to examine the suddenly hyper-conscious changes—psychological or physiological—that may occur in himself, as he is given a startling option to fill in the vacancy, and to color the blandness which these algid works present. Here the experience becomes the challenge to change a desperate, unappetizing option into an esthetic opportunity.

If the difficulty of inert art is that it refuses to motivate the spectator, the quality of frenetic painting or sculpture consists in perversely over-motivating him. The encounter is so fretted and stressed with mutually interfering signals, that if he ventures forth into any number of false paths, the viewer eventually must retire in confusion in order to gain some inner poise. Out from the welter of chromatic, tactile, and scale differentiations, the chronic unevenness and rapidity of beat, he flees in pursuit of a suddenly alluring stillness. In

Rauschenberg's "Express," a movie-like, newsreel montage of silk-screen transferred photographs extends in space (as Vanderbeek's or Conner's compilation films exfoliate in time), without, however, any apparent principles to isolate, cause, or relate the sequence of images. And yet, an overall conception can still be found within an apparent anarchy. Of his "F-111," for instance, Rosenquist made the following comment in an interview:

> The ambience of the painting is involved with people who are all going toward a similar thing. All the ideas in the whole picture are very divergent, but I think they all seem to go toward some basic meaning.
> Going towards what? (he was asked).
> Some blinding light, like a bug hitting a light bulb. I think of the picture as being shoveled into a boiler . . . I gather myself up to do something in a specific time, to produce something that could be exposed as a human idea of the extreme acceleration of feelings. (Italics mine.) (G. R. Swenson: "An Interview with James Rosenquist," *Partisan Review*, Fall, 1965, p. 590.)

Such sentiments are not dissimilar from those expressed by Jean Tinguely in his Dusseldorf Manifesto of 1962:

> Everything moves continuously. Immobility does not exist. Live in time. Be static with movement. Movement is static because it is the only immutable thing —the only certainty, the only unchangeable. (Calvin Tomkins: *The Bride and the Bachelors*, pp. 162, 165.)

It was Tinguely, also, who once opened a show called "Pure Speed and Monochrome Stability," which consisted of Yves Klein's monochrome blue paintings whirled and "dematerialized" by the sculptor's motors. Unlike the Futurists, the frenetic artists of today apparently attach a nihilistic rather than an optimistic value to a 20th-century dynamicism that increasingly grows out of hand.

Again unlike the Futurists, space in recent art is not a product of the action, but is displaced by the action. And the simultaneity of actions or incidents is not a tribute of some inherent principle of vitality which infuses and penetrates all things, but a usurping of continuity and energy. Always, one feels the presence and even the involvement of the artist outside the object he creates, self-consciously funnelling and sublimating his relations to the world by the use of some slightly altered raw material, instead of re-creating them directly by new formal metaphors. Both processes, naturally, can be, and have been, innovational, but their differences are fairly obvious.

Eventually, of course, art cannot escape metaphor. Since painting and sculptures are generally immobile to begin with, that is, objects which simply stay in their place, they permit a threshold of sheer busyness that temporal media and performed arts cannot sustain. This, after all, may be the resistance that is offered a spectator who is free to return and re-examine puzzling physical evidence at his leisure. It is at this point that the pile-up of simultaneous sensations in frenetic art compels one to recreate his own viewing time as a freshly investigated, yet constantly shifting entity. Whereas, in, say, Robert

Morris' grey fiberglass blocks, one wants to diminish even more the negligible period in which the work can be visually consumed—that is, to escape from time itself, as an experiential container. One mode sees a stupifying complicity in all things and sensations; its opposite number encounters a mindless and isolated palpability in every presence. One rages coldly against its own discreteness and finiteness, and the other wants to make something impossibly more mobile than the immobilized. To the extent that visual metaphor resists and yet can still encompass these aims, both tendencies have opened up extraordinary possibilities.

It only remains to be said that there are a few artists who deliberately combine these possibilities, or who are in the act of transcending them. One recalls the paintings of Larry Poons, consisting of straight, mono-hued fields sprinkled with dots which chromatically modify their immediately adjacent areas as well as startle by their almost musical activation as beats. That Poons was a student of the Mondrian of the late "Broadway Boogie-Woogie" series, themselves a frenetic version of his earlier harmonious grids, is an interesting fact. Another artist who started out prophetically paralyzed, but has gradually moved to an increasingly more dynamic position, is Frank Stella, who now galvanizes his shaped stop-start canvas perimeters into hyper-active (because wall-contrasted) foils for the frozen systems within. On a different level, Larry Bell's new chrome-framed glass boxes, precious metals smokily annealed to their surfaces, permit just so much penetration of the eye before one's own reflection is bounced back. And perhaps the most singular instance of this bi-focal vision is Roy Lichtenstein's last show: a series of canvases depicting the most juicy and violent, dripping and splattering "action" paint strokes in comic strip style. Here an artist mockingly refrigerates the very ideogram of spontaneity. In the art of all these men, there develops an acrostic of motion, whose planned abortiveness runs a poignant tangent to life in the sixties.

Ultimately, a theory that concerns itself with the tempi and rhythms of visual art cannot avoid the obvious conclusion that the act of looking has a past. For beats resound through the memory, the somatic as well as the visual memory. Regarding this, current art has become extremely complex. For, as it is represented in Rauschenberg's Dante drawings, or Johns' "According to What," or Kitaj or Kienholz, the visual units themselves are mnemonic patches, scenes whose data is made up of even smaller visual units. Seeing their work is actually a process of recalling, of repatriating the microcosm into the macrocosm. With a sculpture by Donald Judd, however, there is no rootedness in the present (which would allow rumination in time), but neither is there complexity to force one to consider what has happened, or may happen to oneself in the past or future. From this indeterminacy, once one has the bravery to consider it, there is no real escape: time is shown to be unilateral, basically undifferentiated, our habitual divisions of it merely arbitrary. In that visual art which is explicitly temporal, the film (let us exclude Happenings and dance for the moment), the most extraordinary

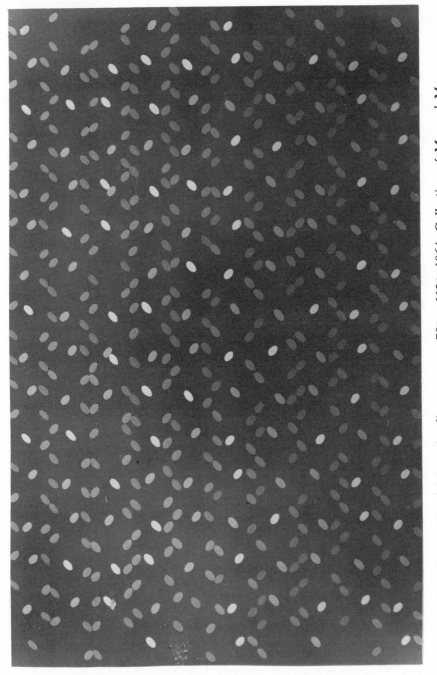

Larry Poons. Nixes' Mate. Acrylic on canvas, 70" x 112", 1964. Collection of Mr. and Mrs. Robert C. Scull. Photo by Eric Pollitzer. Courtesy of Leo Castelli Gallery.

Frank Stella. Hagmatana III. *Flourescent acrylic on canvas, 120" x 180",
1967. From the collection of David Whitney. Photo courtesy of Leo Castelli
Gallery.*

statements of these problems have come forth in Resnais' "Muriel" and
Godard's "The Married Woman" and "Alphaville." If these movies are
compositions that have a distinct beginning and end, separated by time (as
the confines of a painting or sculpture are separated by space), the material
they contain perpetually transforms itself into something open-ended, unbounded. For the personae of "Muriel," as well as its viewers, the past is
always overwhelming the thought and action of the present. Remembering,
often involuntary, eats up all duration, and hence transforms itself into the
present, becomes the present. In "The Married Woman" Charlotte speaks
of the present as the only meaningful experience, and yet it constantly eludes
her (becomes the past?), and is beyond understanding. As for the Lemmy
Caution character, he could be a man of the past transplanted into the Alphaville of the present, or a man of the present displaced in a city of the future.
Both characters are Proustian waifs, glimpsed in a cinematic matrix combining the subliminal and the stilted with such calculated pressure, that one's
whole nervous system is perspicuously jolted. As a result, our own present
is revealed to be far more chaotic and yet hypnotic than it had been ever
thought to be. None of this, of course, solves the problem of classification.
But then, it was not a worthwhile problem. It is better to know this: that
to penetrate modern visual art, not only must the eye and the mind have
memory, but now the ears and the glands as well.

Part II

Attitudes and Practice:
Cues for Direction

Although art education has had a comparatively short history in relationship to other areas in higher education, in the course of twenty years it has made substantial progress in establishing itself as an important and vital educational force. The sharp criticism of its formative years, in which it was characterized as a disorganized, chaotic, completely intuitive operation, has lessened considerably. The past decade has seen the development of a number of strong, sound art-education programs especially on the university level.

However, the public schools have not been the beneficiaries of this progress. The intense involvement of justifying the existence of art education to university administrators and the development of new courses and programs, have left art educators with a minimal amount of time for serious consideration of their responsibility to the public schools. It is not sufficient to simply graduate more art teachers each year. The university and its graduates must take a leadership role in establishing art as an important and respected part of the public school curriculum. A strong, determined, innovative reform movement in art, similar to those occurring in science and mathematics, has not materialized. Goodlad's research in school curriculum supports a reason for this.

There is not yet an innovative curricular thrust in the field (art). The curricular movement that began in math and science was spurred and financed out of threat to our national status. I have not known any national crisis that led to a renaissance in the arts. Consequently, we cannot look to national crisis as a basis for curriculum reform and curriculum change in the art field.

Unfortunately, many situations still live with or under the shadow of the educational reforms of the late nineteenth or early twentieth century. The "factory schools" that Grannis describes in his essay introduced instructional experiences identical for all children who were expected to produce work that met the demands of the teacher, "and to be rewarded or punished according to the outcomes."

Because theory and practice have not been extended to meet the demands of a changing social environment, these approaches still exist at all levels of our less enlightened school systems. Kozol describes such a situation:

The Art Teacher's most common technique for art instruction was to pass out mimeographed designs and then to have the pupils fill them in according to a dictated or suggested color plan. An alternate approach was to stick up on the wall or on the blackboard some of the drawings on a particular subject that had been done in the previous years by predominantly white classes. These drawings, neat and ordered and very uniform, would be the models for our children.

These rigid, traditional practices which divide content, process, and outcomes into neat, easily administered, teacher-conceived segments are not satisfactory approaches to teaching in our more sophisticated and complex society. The total reliance on these kinds of packaged educational practices has led to the encouragement and development of countless numbers of packaged texts, workbooks, manuals of "successful motivations," how-to-do-it books, and a variety of standardized educational curricula. Most of them lose touch completely with the individual needs and differences of students.

The review of art-education history and theory in Chapters 1 and 2 of this book indicates that art educators were among the first to embrace theoretically the concepts of innovative, individualized instruction and in a limited way break with the tradition of the factory school system. To move forward and out of this restricting system would be an initial step toward adding immediate, maximum flexibility to our art-education practices and initiating curriculum reform in the public schools. Coupled with this move is the need to understand the attitudinal changes of today's youth, and present to them concepts and motivational content with which they can identify. Kenniston states:

We often feel that today's youth are somehow "different." There is something about today's world that seems to give the young a special restlessness, an increased impatience with the "hypocrisies" of the past, and yet an open gentleness and a searching honesty more intense than that of youth in the past.

If the necessity for change is recognized and the need for new approaches to teaching is desired, the questions arise as to where and how these new directions are to be discovered and implemented. Perhaps the most logical approach for gaining insight into the problem is to seek answers from those who are to be educated. The prevailing attitude among most educators in the past has been that "kids can't help because they don't know what's good for them." Unfortunately they were never given a chance. Today, educators are listening to the young on all levels and accepting their educational challenge to change the status quo, to become more deeply involved on a personal basis, and to take risks related to in-depth investigation of concepts rather than superficial involvement with surface exercises.

The art teacher, working with the art student, should take the initiative in the development of new dimensions in art instruction through the extension of existing philosophical foundations and careful consideration of major changes in practice designed to meet the demands of this "new" youth and the contemporary epoch in which they are involved. A closer relationship between the "ivory tower" attitudes of the university and the action-centered involvement of the public schools must ultimately occur if the long awaited renaissance in public school art is to become a reality.

Chapters 3 and 4 of this book, concerning attitudes and practice, will give the reader an opportunity to seek ties between history and theory of art education and the current school situation. Every attempt has been made to avoid "packaged solutions" in the chapter on Practice, as vital educational practices should be developed individually and in relationship to one's immediate situation. Rather, a variety of concepts are presented and explored that hopefully will become cues for direction and the ultimate extension of the frame of reference from which we are currently operating.

3

Attitudes

The Teacher in the World

HAROLD TAYLOR

The education of teachers lies at the heart of everything that matters in the life of the world's people. We who are teachers have a chance we have never had before to teach and learn on a world scale, and to join forces with a world community of those who have the good of humanity at heart. For the principal fact of the modern world is not its massive unrest, although that is its most visible characteristic, but its growing and necessary unity— the inter-penetration of all lives by every other, the coming-together of peoples, cultures, and societies to accomplish common purposes. We are groping toward something named by Adlai Stevenson just before his death, "impartial protection for the whole wide society of man."

A transformation is under way, partly through blind and unavoidable impulses in contemporary history, partly through conscious changes in the thinking of those with political, social, and intellectual power. The interna-

Reprinted by permission from *The Humanist*, Vol XXVIII, No. 1, January/February 1968, Copyright: The Humanist 1968.

tional social and political systems are now affecting each other in fundamental ways. So are the educational systems. Secular and religious beliefs are finding new accommodations; the great religions are in the process of discovering, through a world-wide ecumenical movement, a set of shared truths which have to do, not with theological dogma, but with what Pope John in *Pacem in Terris* called, "the common good of the entire human family."

It is with this common good that I am concerned; this is the heart of the matter. There exists beneath the surface of the visible world society an inner community of persons—peasants, teachers, doctors, scientists, poets, lawyers, architects, men of religion, writers, readers, students, lovers, composers and others linked together intuitively by common concerns and interests, and reaching out to each other across the divisions of the world and its governments. That community has within it a kind of power, a growing sense of unity, a common culture coalescing into new forms which add the flavor of regional differences to a newly developing heritage of man.

The teacher and the student are at the center of this new community. They share, in whatever country they live, a common interest in the advancement of learning for human benefit. In the United States, a new generation of students has created a national community among themselves, with national and international interests, of which the problems of peace and war, human rights, the politics of change and the reform of education are central. The solutions they propose and act upon, their unifying beliefs, are based on the idea that the older generation and the established order in any society cannot assume the right of authority and control over the younger generation. The young have equal rights as citizens; they have their own ideas about how to run a society and its educational system. Since they are the ones education is done to, they have special qualifications for knowing what it is.

Elsewhere around the world there is a comparable constituency—the young Indonesians who have united against Sukarno, the Korean youth who opposed the dictatorship of Rhee, the Spanish students who reject educational control by Franco, the Soviet young who question, through poetry, the politics of their elders. In international and world education, here is where we must start—with the living reality of the world community of students and teachers. We must bring that community together, put it in touch with itself. The education of the teacher and the student (the two are inseparable) must now draw upon the cultural and intellectual resources of the entire world, no matter to which part of it the teacher's habitat confines him. For the American teacher and his students, the cultural and intellectual resources of the world are at his feet, and if he does not find them there, he can go to the places where they are.

At this point in history, we in America *are* the world's most powerful economic, social, military and political force. We are also the ones who have mastered the technique of mass communication, the ones with the most technology, the most educational institutions, museums, art galleries, science laboratories, television stations, cultural centers, educational programs.

Whether we like it or not, we are the forerunners of what mass societies will some day be. Despite our Western geography, we live in the middle of the world. The world has come to us, we travel into it by the millions every year, we serve as a point of linkage between the thousands of elements which make up the cultural and social fabric of world society. What is at stake now is the question of how we use the power at this center, with what degree of imagination and good will we can enter the lives of the rest of the world's people.

We have not yet come to terms with the fact that we have a latent cultural power of fantastic proportions, and that we could very well fritter it away. A large part of this power lies in the sheer amount of interest the rest of the world has in us. We are watched and listened to, criticized and condemned, opposed and supported. Our daily lives are scrutinized from abroad and at home by a stream of foreign experts, and the whole world seems to feel free to take part in our politics, liking or disliking our Presidents, our habits, our customs, our arts, and ourselves.

If we have not fully realized what a radical change our world position means to our educational thinking and in the use of our own resources, this is perfectly understandable. The years of rapid change in America's position were years in which educators at home were inundated with the practical problems of expanding radically an inadequate educational system while at the same time reforming its content. The educators were building a system of mass education without having thought first about how they were doing it. So concentrated has been the attention given to the practical problems of enrollment, buildings, and rising budgets, that questions about the world and where it is going have very seldom been raised among working educators. They have tended to do what they have been asked to do, having discovered during the fifties that reforming the science and mathematics curriculum was safe, good and rewarded, while meddling with international issues could turn out to be nasty, brutish, and short. Reforms in the curriculum of world affairs were based on a philosophy of strengthening and rationalizing our side of an ideological conflict with Communism. In the case of foreign visitors and programs to bring them here, the aim was to win friends and allies to our side.

That philosophy has been outdated by events, if it could be said to have had validity in the first place. Our purpose in American education is not to induct our visitors into an American curriculum so that they will appreciate and support America and the West, but to enrich our curriculum and their education with the points of view and knowledge of those from elsewhere around the earth. We should now ask them to join us in teaching ourselves.

First, let us declare that teaching is a form of national and international service. Let us then call the country's youth to that service as volunteers for a national Student Corps. Let us say what is true, that to prepare oneself to teach is to give to liberal education its true meaning—to use knowledge for the improvement of human life—and that the normal expectation for the college graduate is that he should give at least two years of his life to the service of his country by teaching to others what he has learned in college.

We have already begun this in part, by calling upon volunteers for the National Teacher Corps, Head Start, the Domestic Service Corps, the Peace Corps, and the Poverty program, but we have stopped short of making the call for service into a philosophy of education for a democratic society. Let us give our youth a chance to serve.

We should then provide the volunteers with subsistence and tuition, just as we did in an earlier time through the G.I. Bill, when a whole new generation of youth was brought into the main stream of American society. Let us give 50,000 student-teachers a year abroad in practice teaching, foreign languages, and service in communities. Let us assume that foreign service is a natural part of the education of teachers, both for those already teaching and those being prepared. For those at home, let us send 50,000 student volunteers into the Spanish-American, Indian, Puerto Rican, Negro, poor white, and other communities for a "year abroad" in the United States. Let us follow out the implications of the Peace Corps, and think of it as a teacher education program of world dimension by making it mutually international, with 15,000 foreign students brought to America yearly to teach in our schools, help us with our foreign languages, our studies of Asia, Africa, Eastern Europe, South America, to teach us about their countries and join us in our effort to make a world community and a world curriculum.

Let us make of America a meeting-ground for the teachers and peoples of the world, a place where we can pool the world's resources for the benefit of all. Let them bring their instruments and play their music, act their plays, read their poems, dance, sing, compose, paint, and write with us in an all-year, every-year world festival of the arts. Let everyone teach everyone whatever it is he knows. Abroad, we can take the initiative to create, not merely East-West Centers for client countries and potential allies, but World Centers on the seven continents, world centers on our own campuses, where students, teachers, and scholars from everywhere can work together on common tasks.

We would then find ourselves closer to the place we ought to be. Having been handed the leadership of the world as a gift from history, a gift seldom given and quickly taken away, we would have shown that we had chosen to use that gift and our power to secure the peaceable welfare and education of all mankind.

Before these proposals are dismissed as visionary, let me say that they are simply attempts to put into operation the declared intention of the President of the United States and the United States Congress. The proposals deal simultaneously with the problems of producing the Great Society and creating a peaceful world order. Beginning with the President's Smithsonian Institution address of 1965, moving on to his subsequent message on international education to Congress, and the passage of the International Education Act last year, a straight line of argument has developed about the American intention.

For the first time in the history of the United States, a President of this country has called for a conception of American education which makes it part of a world system. The United States has formerly accepted an obligation to share her cultural resources with the world and to advance the cause of education everywhere, in cooperation with "all nations, friend and foe alike," with a wish to "receive as much as we give, to learn as well as to teach." The United States has declared explicitly that we are one among many cultures, willing to do our part in uniting them all. These new developments and the extraordinary opportunities they provide, bring a whole new set of energies, ideas and talents into the work of educating teachers. There is enormous power in the individual acts and singular persons who, in the communities, colleges and schools of America have simply taken it upon themselves to do something and have set about doing it. We are lucky enough to be a nation of volunteers.

The parents of a school child who started the Ogontz plan for foreign students teaching in the schools, the Colorado student who formed an exchange with Brazilian students for community action and education, the faculty at Michigan State who proposed and established an international curriculum at Justin Morrill College, with four hundred students, sixty of whom will be traveling and studying abroad this summer, the dozens of international projects in the colleges of the Midwest, the pilot projects of the member institutions of the Association of Colleges for Teacher Education, the major programs and projects of Stanford, Indiana University, the University of Wisconsin, and the new plans and achievements of Universities in California and New York State—all of these were originally started by the initiative of either a single or just a few persons. The issue of reform in education is not as important as the simple task of taking on the right projects and doing them. After a while, if enough good projects are done, you find that education has been reformed. I call upon all educational institutions to set in motion at least one new project, to appoint at least one faculty member, to make at least one new program in the education of teachers which will help to extend education into the world and the world into education.

I am deeply devoted to the idea of teachers colleges, to the idea that learning to teach is the ultimate liberal art, and that the best way to learn something is to try to teach it. Against the current of contemporary opinions, I deplore the mass movement of educators away from the idea of teachers colleges and toward the multi-purpose university, or toward that alarming and inelegant hybrid, the multiversity. I think I know why the educators have moved that way. They have been dislodged from their belief in the primacy of teaching and learning by those with the power and prestige of the knowledge industry behind them. There can be no genuine multi-purpose university no matter what diversity of clients it claims to serve. In the true university there is a single purpose, the advancement of learning. Learning depends on the capacity and commitment of students to learn, and this, in large part, depends on the talent of scholars to teach.

The powerful social and intellectual force which exists within the new generation of students has been greatly underestimated by educators and the public, who have tended to think of student activists and those concerned with civil rights and world affairs as a general nuisance, a motley group of radical dissidents, draft-dodgers, or young rebels who will soon get over it. On the contrary, what we have is a new and significant national asset. The core of the student protest movement is composed of a serious and informed body of young people who act out of a sense of personal commitment to each other and a sense of compassion for those who have been blocked from a place in society. They care very much for the quality of their own lives and are sensitive to the effects of their acts on the lives of others. They are responsible critics of the society and its educational system, and the best of them have a political sophistication and social energy which is in advance of many of those appointed to educate them. In short, by their acts of engagement and their intellectual commitments, they have shown that they are already teachers. They have trained themselves.

But, as I have talked among them, I have found a curious paradox. The motivations and interests which have brought them into a direct confrontation with the problems of world society and its educational system are exactly those which turn them away from entering the teaching profession. Within their ideas, their persons and their social idealism lies a formidable force for educational change of exactly the kind the country has been calling for. Two hundred and fifty thousand of them are volunteer tutors in the urban and rural slums. Thousands more are at work on educational reform, tens of thousands have volunteered for service in social welfare programs. Yet most of these do not intend to be teachers.

When asked for the reasons, they say two things: they refuse to spend what they think to be wasteful time in taking education courses which they contend are without serious intellectual content or relevance to their own experience as teachers and tutors. They want to work out their own methods and curricula directly with the children and teachers in the school, with such help as they can get from educators who welcome their questions. They then say that once properly certified and installed in a teaching post, they would not be able to teach about the world with any real sense of integrity because the system—the school board, the superintendent, the principal, the other teachers and the community—has a set pattern of political, social and educational attitude in which they would, by conforming, lose their personal identity. To which I have replied, then how do you hope to reform either the society or its educational system if you refuse to get into the game? I usually win the argument while losing the candidate.

The way to win them is to take them seriously. Until we create programs in the undergraduate and graduate colleges of education which can speak to their concerns and yield to them the satisfaction of learning to act in the world and of using their lives in an ideal cause, we will not engage the most promising among them in our profession. We have been going about it backwards. When we should have been creating an education which could enlist their energies, we have been organizing a system which instructs them in how to behave.

A college or university which took seriously the education of teachers would take the world as its campus and move the world into its curriculum and into its student-body and faculty as a perfectly natural thing to do. It would be an example of how liberal education can best be conducted. It would be an institution for the education of students, whether or not they were to become teachers. I use the words, teacher and student, not to describe the people you see in the halls or read about as parts of schools and colleges. By teachers I mean those who have learned, or who know intuitively, how to set the minds of others into motion and who place their own knowledge, whatever it may be, at the disposal of those who are learning.

The college for these teachers and students would be a staging ground for expeditions into the world, a central place where the student could prepare himself, through the study of the arts and sciences, to understand what he would find beyond the campus. As a regular part of his education he would both live in his society and study at the college, bringing to his seminars and courses the information, ideas and insights which he had gathered at first hand. He would become an interne in society, here and abroad, learning from the experience it has to give him. He would be proving to himself that what he learned from his academic colleagues, their books and their imparted knowledge, squared with the facts as he saw them in his experience. The time of the student on the campus would be a time for doing the things which can best be done there, in some cases can *only* be done there, in the science laboratory, the library, the art studio, the theater, the classroom, the seminar.

Some, or most, of the students in a college of this kind would become teachers after graduation, the others would have had the crucial experience of learning through teaching and learning how to create their own education out of the materials at hand. The graduate student would become a partner of the undergraduate in a community where each would help the other. They would all be practice teachers and practice learners at the same time. The faculty, as is so often said, would become colleagues with the students in the enterprise of learning.

There are already models among the experimental colleges for institutions of this kind, as well as colleges and universities where these conceptions are taken with the seriousness which they deserve. Among other examples, I can mention the fascinating developments at San Francisco State College, where both the students and the College of Education have invented new educational forms which take full advantage of the natural capacities for learning and teaching which lie within the student-body. There the faculty is making plans for a World Urban Teaching Center to which educators and education students from a sweep of foreign countries could come together to work on the crucial educational problems of the cities of the world, using the inner city of San Francisco as a laboratory. There the students have formed their own internal Experimental College of more than six hundred students enrolled in courses taught by other students.

There is of course Antioch College, where at a given point in time, a half of the 1800 students are studying and working away from the campus, half of that half are in foreign countries. But what appeals to me most in this idea of a college is the fact that it is central to the tradition of American public education. More than that, it *is* the tradition of the State Colleges whose philosophy is that of the land-grant university, whose origins are in the teachers college movement, the majority of whose students intend to become teachers, where one out of every five American college students is enrolled, and where a very large part of the expanding enrollment in higher education is going to take place.

As the universities, from Berkeley to Harvard, move farther and farther away from the undergraduate education of teachers to concentration on producing what Harvard has called the Missing Elite, the field is left open for a whole new movement of innovation and experiment in the reform of undergraduate education at large and teacher education in particular. It is clear to me, after surveying the field, that the most interesting and imaginative reforms in mass education are now likely to take place in the State Colleges and the urban universities. Pressures for change and reform are coming from a new generation of students with new needs, without cultural antecedents or social inhibitions. Because of their constituency and often because of their location, institutions like these are confronted, directly and daily, with the problems of poverty, cultural deprivation and radical social change.

It is therefore possible to develop a theory of education within such institutions which links them directly to the social and educational innovations represented by the Domestic Service Corps, Head Start, the National Teachers' Corps and, in its world dimension, the Peace Corps. If we were to internationalize the National Teachers Corps by including foreign students and a new curriculum, and were to think of the Peace Corps as a program of teacher education in world affairs, we would have the model we are seeking for a major solution to the problems of the education of teachers in world affairs.

In the present situation I believe that the colleges of education are going to have to take their own initiatives, make their own alliances, invent their own programs, recruit their own scholars, artists, foreign teachers, students, scientists interested in curriculum, sociologists interested in education, and prepare to teach a much more varied student-body of social activists, young poets, composers, internationalists, and others. Only when they do take such initiatives will the students wish to come to them with a sense of commitment to act upon the world by first learning how to act in it.

Death at an Early Age

JONATHAN KOZOL

Stephen is eight years old. A picture of him standing in front of the bulletin board on Arab Bedouins shows a little light-brown person staring with unusual concentration at a chosen spot upon the floor. Stephen is tiny, desperate, unwell. Sometimes he talks to himself. He moves his mouth as if he were talking. At other times he laughs out loud in class for no apparent reason. He is also an indescribably mild and unmalicious child. He cannot do any of his school work very well. His math and reading are poor. In Third Grade he was in a class that had substitute teachers much of the year. Most of the year before that, he had a row of substitute teachers too. He is in the Fourth Grade now but his work is barely at the level of the Second. Nobody has complained about the things that have happened to Stephen because he does not have any mother or father. Stephen is a ward of the State of Massachusetts and, as such, he has been placed in the home of some very poor people who do not want him now that he is not a baby any more. The money that they are given for him to pay his expenses every week does not cover the other kind of expense—the more important kind which is the immense emotional burden that is continually at stake. Stephen often comes into school badly beaten. If I ask him about it, he is apt to deny it because he does not want us to know first-hand what a miserable time he has. Like many children, and many adults too, Stephen is far more concerned with hiding his abased condition from the view of the world than he is with escaping that condition. He lied to me first when I asked him how his eye got so battered. He said it happened from being hit by accident when somebody opened up the door. Later, because it was so bruised and because I questioned him, he admitted that it was his foster mother who had flung him out onto the porch. His eye had struck the banister and it had closed and purpled. The children in the class were frightened to see him. I thought that they also felt some real compassion, but perhaps it was just shock.

Although Stephen did poorly in his school work, there was one thing he could do well. He was a fine artist. He made delightful drawings. The thing about them that was good, however, was also the thing that got him into trouble. For they were not neat and orderly and organized but entirely random and casual, messy, somewhat unpredictable, seldom according to the instructions he had been given, and—in short—real drawings. For these drawings, Stephen received considerable embarrassment at the hands of the Art Teacher. This person was a lady no longer very young who had some rather fixed values and opinions about children and about teaching. Above all, her manner was marked by unusual confidence. She seldom would merely walk into our class but seemed always to sweep into it. Even for myself, her advent, at least in the beginning of the year, used to cause a wave of anxiety. For she came into our class generally in a mood of self-assurance and of almost punitive restlessness which never made one confident but which generally made me wonder what I had done wrong. In dealing with Stephen, I thought she could be quite overwhelming.

The Art Teacher's most common technique for art instruction was to pass out mimeographed designs and then to have the pupils fill them in according to a dictated or suggested color plan. An alternate approach was to stick up on the wall or on the blackboard some of the drawings on a particular subject that had been done in the previous years by predominantly white classes. These drawings, neat and ordered and very uniform, would be the models for our children. The art lesson, in effect, would be to copy what had been done before, and the neatest and most accurate reproductions of the original drawings would be the ones that would win the highest approval from the teacher. None of the new drawings, the Art Teacher would tell me frequently, was comparable to the work that had been done in former times, but at least the children in the class could try to copy good examples. The fact that they were being asked to copy something in which they could not believe because it was not of them and did not in any way correspond to their own interests did not occur to the Art Teacher, or if it did occur she did not say it. Like a number of other teachers at my school and in other schools of the same nature, she possessed a remarkable self-defense apparatus, and anything that seriously threatened to disturb her point of view could be effectively denied.

How did a pupil like Stephen react to a teacher of this sort? Alone almost out of the entire class, I think that he absolutely turned off his signals while she was speaking and withdrew to his own private spot. At his desk he would sit silently while the Art Teacher was talking and performing. With a pencil, frequently stubby and end-bitten, he would scribble and fiddle and cock his head and whisper to himself throughout the time that the Art Teacher was going on. At length, when the art lesson officially began, he would perhaps push aside his little drawing and try the paint and paper that he had been given, usually using the watercolors freely and the paintbrush sloppily and a little bit defiantly and he would come up with things that certainly were delightful and personal and private, and full of his own nature.

If Stephen began to fiddle around during a lesson, the Art Teacher generally would not notice him at first. When she did, both he and I and the children around him would prepare for trouble. For she would go at his desk with something truly like a vengeance and would shriek at him in a way that carried terror. "Give me that! Your paints are all muddy! You've made it a mess. Look at what he's done! He's mixed up the colors! I don't know why we waste good paper on this child!" Then: "Garbage! Junk! He gives me garbage and junk! And garbage is one thing I will not have." Now I thought that that garbage and junk was very nearly the only real artwork in the class. I do not know very much about painting, but I know enough to know that the Art Teacher did not know much about it either and that, furthermore, she did not know or care anything at all about the way in which you can destroy a human being. Stephen, in many ways already dying, died a second and third and fourth and final death before her anger.

Sometimes when the Art Teacher was not present in our classroom, and when no other supervisory person happened to be there, Stephen would sneak up to me, maybe while I was sitting at my desk and going over records or totaling up the milk money or checking a paper, so that I would not see him until he was beside me. Then, hastily, secretly, with mystery, with fun, with something out of a spy movie, he would hand me one of his small drawings. The ones I liked the most, to be honest, were often not completely his own, but pictures which he had copied out of comic books and then elaborated, amended, fiddled with, and frequently added to by putting under them some kind of mock announcement ("I AM THE GREATEST AND THE STRONGEST") which might have been something he had wished. I think he must have seen something special and valuable about comic books, because another thing that he sometimes did was just cut out part of a comic book story that he liked and bring it in to me as a present. When he did this, as with his paintings and drawings, he usually would belittle his gift by crumpling it up or folding it up very tiny before he handed it to me. It was a way, perhaps, of saying that he didn't value it too much (although it was clear that he did value it a great deal) in case I didn't like it.

If the Art Teacher came upon us while he was slipping me a picture he had drawn, both he and I were apt to get an effective lashing out. Although she could be as affectionate and benevolent as she liked with other children, with Stephen she was almost always scathing in her comments and made no attempt at seeming mild. "He wants to show you his little scribbles because he wants to use you and your affection for him and make you pity him but we don't have time for that. Keep him away. If you don't, I'll do it. I don't want him getting near you during class."

For weeks after that outburst, when we had been caught in the act of friendship, he stopped coming near me. He stopped bringing me his drawings. He kept to his seat and giggled, mumbled, fiddled. Possibly he felt that he was doing this for my sake in order not to get me into further trouble. Then one day for a brief second he got up his nerve and darted forward. He crumpled up some paper in his fist and handed it to me quickly and got back into his chair. The crumpled paper turned out to be more funnies that he had painstakingly cut out. Another time he dropped a ball of crunched-up math paper on my desk. On the paper he had written out his age—eight years old—and his birthday—which I seem to remember came at Christmas. I also remember that once he either whispered to me or wrote to me on a note that he weighed sixty pounds. This information, I thought, came almost a little boastfully, even though it obviously isn't a lot to weigh if you are almost nine, and I wondered about it for a time until it occurred to me that maybe it was just one of very few things that he knew about himself, one of the half dozen measurable facts that had anything to do with him in the world, and so—like all people, using as best they can whatever they've got—he had to make the most of it.

I think that much of his life, inwardly and outwardly, must have involved a steady and, as it turned out, inwardly at least, a losing battle to survive. He battled for his existence and, like many defenseless humans, he had to use whatever odd little weapons came to hand. Acting up at school was part of it. He was granted so little attention that he must have panicked repeatedly about the possibility that, with a few slight mistakes, he might simply stop existing or being seen at all. I imagine this is one reason why he seemed so often to invite or court a tongue-lashing or a whipping. Doing anything at all that would make a teacher mad at him, scream at him, strike at him, would also have been a kind of ratification, even if it was painful, that he actually was there. Other times, outside of school, he might do things like pulling a fire alarm lever and then having the satisfaction of hearing the sirens and seeing the fire engines and knowing that it was all of his own doing and to his own credit, so that at least he would have proof in that way that his hands and his arm muscles and his mischievous imagination actually did count for something measurable in the world. Maybe the only way in which he could ever impinge upon other people's lives was by infuriating them, but that at least was something. It was better than not having any use at all.

I remember that the Art Teacher once caught him out in the back, in the hallway, in front of a big floor-length coat-closet mirror. She grabbed him by the arm and pulled him into the classroom and announced to me and to the children in the classroom that he was "just standing there and making faces at himself and staring." While she talked, he looked away and examined the floor with his eyes, as he did so often, because he was embarrassed by being exposed like that. I thought it was needlessly cruel of her to have hauled him before the children in that manner, and surely a little hesitation on her part might have given her a moment to think why he might *like* to see himself in a mirror, even if it was only to see a scratched reflection. I didn't think it was shameful for him to be doing that, even to be making funny faces. It seemed rather normal and explicable to me that he might want to check up on his existence. Possibly it was a desperate act, and certainly a curious one, but I do not think it was unnatural. What did seem to me to be unnatural was the unusual virulence of the Art Teacher's reaction.

Another time, seeing him all curled up in one of the corners, I went over to him and tried to get him to look up at me and smile and talk. He would not do that. He remained all shriveled up there and he would not cry and would not laugh. I said to him: "Stephen, if you curl up like that and will not even look up at me, it will just seem as if you wanted to make me think you were a little rat." He looked down at himself hurriedly and then he looked up at me and he chuckled grotesquely and he said, with a pitiful little laugh: "I *know* I couldn't be a rat, Mr. Kozol, because a rat has got to have a little tail!" I never forgot that and I told it later to a child psychiatrist, whose answer to me made it more explicit and more clear: "It is the absence of a tail which convinces him that he has not yet become a rat." Perhaps that is overly absolute and smacks a bit of the psychiatric dogmatism that seems so difficult to accept because it leaves so little room for uncertainty or doubt; yet in this one instance I do not really think that it carries the point too far. For it is the Boston schoolteachers themselves who for years have been speaking of the Negro children in their charge as "animals" and the school building that houses them as "a zoo." And it is well known by now how commonly the injustices and depredations of the Boston school system have compelled its Negro pupils to regard themselves with something less than the dignity and respect of human beings. The toll that this took was probably greater upon Stephen than it might have been upon some other children. But the price that it exacted was paid ultimately by every child, and in the long run I am convinced that the same price has been paid by every teacher too.

Youth, Change and Violence

KENNETH KENISTON

We often feel that today's youth are somehow "different." There is something about today's world that seems to give the young a special restlessness, an increased impatience with the "hypocrisies" of the past, and yet an open gentleness and a searching honesty more intense than that of youth in the past. Much of what we see in today's students and nonstudents is of course familiar: to be young is in one sense always the same. But it is also new and different, as each generation confronts its unique historical position and role.

Yet we find it hard to define the difference. Partly the difficulty derives from the elusive nature of youth itself. Still this generation seems even more elusive than most—and that, too, may be one of the differences. Partly the problem stems from the sheer variety and number of "youth" in a society where youth is often protracted into the mid-twenties. No one characterization can be adequate to the drop-outs and stay-ins, hawks

Reprinted with permission of the author from "Youth, Change and Violence," pp. 227–245, *The American Scholar*, Spring 1968.

and doves, up-tights and cools, radicals and conservatives, heads and seekers that constitute American youth. But although we understand that the young are as various as the old in our complex society, the sense that they are different persists.

In giving today's American youth this special quality and mood, two movements have played a major role: the New Left and the hippies. Both groups are spontaneous creations of the young; both are in strong reaction to what Paul Goodman calls the Organized System; both seek alternatives to the institutions of middle-class life. Radicals and hippies are also different from each other in numerous ways, from psychodynamics to ideology. The hippie has dropped out of a society he considers irredeemable: his attention is riveted on interior change and the expansion of personal consciousness. The radical has not given up on this society: his efforts are aimed at changing and redeeming it. Furthermore, both "movements" together comprise but a few percent of their contemporaries. But, although neither hippies nor New Leftists are "representative" of their generation, together they are helping to give this generation its distinctive mood. By examining the style of these young men and women, we come closer to understanding what makes their generation "different."

THE STYLE OF POST-MODERN YOUTH

Today's youth is the first generation to grow up with "modern" parents; it is the first "post-modern" generation. This fact alone distinguishes it from previous generations and helps create a mood born out of modernity, affluence, rapid social change and violence. Despite the many pitfalls in the way of any effort to delineate a post-modern style, the effort seems worth making. For not only in America but in other nations, new styles of dissent and unrest have begun to appear, suggesting the slow emergence of youthful style that is a reflection of and reaction to the history of the past two decades.*

In emphasizing "style" rather than ideology, program or characteristics, I mean to suggest that the communalities in post-modern youth groups are to be found in the *way* they approach the world, rather than in their actual behavior, ideologies or goals. Indeed, the focus on process rather than program is itself a prime characteristic of the post-modern style, reflecting a world where flux is more obvious than fixed purpose. Post-modern youth, at least in America, is very much in process, unfinished in its development, psychologically open to a historically unpredictable future. In such a world, where ideologies come and go, and where revolutionary change is the rule, a style, a *way* of doing things, is more possible to identify than any fixed goals or constancies of behavior.

* In the effort to delineate this style, I have been helped and influenced by Robert J. Lifton's concept of Protean Man. For a summary of his views, see *Partisan Review*, Winter 1968.

Fluidity, Flux, Movement

Post-modern youth display a special personal and psychological openness, flexibility and unfinishedness. Although many of today's youth have achieved a sense of inner identity, the term "identity" suggests a fixity, stability and "closure" that many of them are not willing to accept: with these young men and women, it is not always possible to speak of the "normal resolution" of identity issues. Our earlier fear of the ominous psychiatric implications of "prolonged adolescence" must now be qualified by an awareness that in post-modern youth many adolescent concerns and qualities persist long past the time when (according to the standards in earlier eras) they should have ended. Increasingly, post-modern youth are tied to social and historical changes that have not occurred, and that may never occur. Thus, psychological "closure," shutting doors and burning bridges, becomes impossible. The concepts of the personal future and the "life work" are ever more hazily defined; the effort to change oneself, redefine oneself or reform oneself does not cease with the arrival of adulthood.

This fluidity and openness extends through all areas of life. Both hippie and New Left movements are nondogmatic, nonideological, and to a large extent hostile to doctrine and formula. In the New Left, the focus is on "tactics"; amongst hippies, on simple direct acts of love and communication. In neither group does one find clear-cut long-range plans, life patterns laid out in advance. The vision of the personal and collective future is blurred and vague: later adulthood is left deliberately open. In neither group is psychological development considered complete; in both groups, identity, like history, is fluid and indeterminate. In one sense, of course, identity development takes place; but, in another sense, identity is always undergoing transformations that parallel the transformations of the historical world.

Generational Identification

Post-modern youth views itself primarily as a part of a generation rather than an organization; they identify with their contemporaries as a group, rather than with elders, and they do not have clearly defined leaders and heroes. Their deepest collective identification is to their own group or "Movement"—a term that in its ambiguous meanings points not only to the fluidity and openness of post-modern youth, but to its physical mobility, and the absence of traditional patterns of leadership and emulation. Among young radicals, for example, the absence of heroes or older leaders is impressive: even those five years older are sometimes viewed with mild amusement or suspicion. And although post-modern youth is often widely read in the "literature" of the New Left or that of consciousness-expansion, no one person or set of people is central to their intellectual beliefs. Although they live together in groups, these groups are without clear leaders.

Identification with a generational movement, rather than a cross-generational organization or a nongenerational ideology, distinguishes post-modern youth from its parents and from the "previous" generation. In addition, it also creates "generational" distinctions involving five years and less. Within the New Left, clear lines are drawn between the "old New Left" (approximate age, thirty), the New Left (between twenty-two and twenty-eight) and the "new New Left" or "young kids" (under twenty-two). Generations, then, are separated by a very brief span; and the individual's own phase of youthful usefulness—for example, as an organizer—is limited to a relatively few years. Generations come and go quickly; whatever is to be accomplished must therefore be done soon.

Generational consciousness also entails a feeling of psychological disconnection from previous generations, their life situations and their ideologies. Among young radicals, there is a strong feeling that the older ideologies are exhausted or irrelevant, expressed in detached amusement at the doctrinaire disputes of the "old Left" and impatience with "old liberals." Among hippies, the irrelevance of the parental past is even greater: if there is any source of insight, it is the timeless tradition of the East, not the values of the previous generation in American society. But in both groups, the central values are those created in the present by the "Movement" itself.

Personalism

Both groups are highly personalistic in their styles of relationship. Among hippies, personalism usually entails privatism, a withdrawal from efforts to be involved in or to change the wider social world; among young radicals, personalism is joined with efforts to change the world. But despite this difference, both groups care most deeply about the creation of intimate, loving, open and trusting relationships between small groups of people. Writers who condemn the depersonalization of the modern world, who insist on "I-thou" relationships, or who expose the elements of anger, control and sadism in nonreciprocal relationships, find a ready audience in post-modern youth. The ultimate measure of man's life is the quality of his personal relationships; the greatest sin is to be unable to relate to others in a direct, face-to-face, one-to-one relationship.

The obverse of personalism is the discomfort created by any nonpersonal, "objectified," professionalized and, above all, exploitative relationship. Manipulation, power relationships, superordination, control and domination are at violent odds with the I-thou mystique. Failure to treat others as fully human, inability to enter into personal relationships with them, is viewed with dismay in others and with guilt in oneself. Even with opponents the goal is to establish intimate confrontations in which the issues can be discussed openly. When opponents refuse to "meet with" young radicals, this produces anger and frequently demonstrations. The reaction of the Harvard Students for a Democratic Society when Secretary McNamara did not meet with them to discuss American foreign policies is a case in point. Equally important, perhaps the most profound source of personal guilt among post-modern youth is the "hangups" that make intimacy and love difficult.

Nonasceticism

Post-modern youth is nonascetic, expressive and sexually free. The sexual openness of the hippie world has been much discussed and criticized in the mass media. One finds a similar sexual and expressive freedom among many young radicals, although it is less provocatively demonstrative. It is of continuing importance to these young men and women to overcome and move beyond inhibition and puritanism to a greater physical expressiveness, sexual freedom, capacity for intimacy, and ability to enjoy life.

In the era of the Pill, then, responsible sexual expression becomes increasingly possible outside of marriage, at the same time that sexuality becomes less laden with guilt, fear, and prohibition. As asceticism disappears, so does promiscuity: the personalism of post-modern youth requires that sexual expression must occur in the context of "meaningful" human relationships, of intimacy and mutuality. Marriage is increasingly seen as an institution for having children, but sexual relationships are viewed as the natural concomitant of close relationships between the sexes. What is important is not sexual activity itself, but the context in which it occurs. Sex is right and natural between people who are "good to each other," but sexual exploitation—failure to treat one's partner as a person—is strongly disapproved.

Inclusiveness

The search for personal and organizational inclusiveness is still another characteristic of post-modern youth. These young men and women attempt to include both within their personalities and within their movements every opposite, every possibility and every person, no matter how apparently alien. Psychologically, inclusiveness involves an effort to be open to every aspect of one's feelings, impulses and fantasies, to synthesize and integrate rather than repress and dissociate, not to reject or exclude any part of one's personality or potential. Interpersonally, inclusiveness means a capacity for involvement with, identification with and collaboration with those who are superficially alien: the peasant in Vietnam, the poor in America, the nonwhite, the deprived and deformed. Indeed, so great is the pressure to include the alien, especially among hippies, that the apparently alien is often treated more favorably than the superficially similar: thus, the respect afforded to people and ideas that are distant and strange is sometimes not equally afforded those who are similar, be they one's parents or their middle-class values. One way of explaining the reaction of post-modern youth to the war in Vietnam is via the concept of inclusiveness: these young men and women react to events in Southeast Asia much as if they occurred in Newton, Massachusetts, Evanston, Illinois, Harlem, or Berkeley, California: they make little distinction in their reactions to their fellow Americans and those overseas.

One corollary of inclusiveness is intense internationalism. What matters to hippies or young radicals is not where a person comes from, but what kind of relationship is possible with him. The nationality of ideas matters little: Zen Buddhism, American pragmatism, French existentialism, Indian mysticism or Yugoslav communism are accorded equal hearings. Interracialism is another corollary of inclusiveness: racial barriers are minimized or non-existent, and the ultimate expressions of unity between the races, sexual relationships and marriage, are considered basically natural and normal, whatever the social problems they currently entail. In post-modern youth, then, identity and ideology are no longer parochial or national; increasingly, the reference group is the world, and the artificial subspeciation of the human species is broken down.

Antitechnologism

Post-modern youth has grave reservations about many of the technological aspects of the contemporary world. The depersonalization of life, commercialism, careerism and familism, the bureaucratization and complex organization of advanced nations—all seem intolerable to these young men and women, who seek to create new forms of association and action to oppose the technologism of our day. Bigness, impersonality, stratification and hierarchy are rejected, as is any involvement with the furtherance of technological values. In reaction to these values, post-modern youth seeks simplicity, naturalness, personhood, and even voluntary poverty.

But a revolt against technologism is only possible, of course, in a technological society; and to be effective, it must inevitably exploit technology to overcome technologism. Thus in post-modern youth, the fruits of technology—synthetic hallucinogens in the hippie subculture, modern technology of communication among young radicals—and the affluence made possible by technological society are a precondition for a post-modern style. The demonstrative poverty of the hippie would be meaningless in a society where poverty is routine; for the radical to work for subsistence wages as a matter of choice is to *have* a choice not available in most parts of the world. Furthermore, to "organize" against the pernicious aspects of the technological era requires high skill in the use of modern technologies of organization: the long-distance telephone, the use of the mass media, high-speed travel, the mimeograph machine and so on. In the end, then, it is not the material but the spiritual consequences of technology that post-modern youth opposes: indeed, in the developing nations, those who exhibit a post-modern style may be in the vanguard of movements toward modernization. What *is* adamantly rejected is the contamination of life with the values of technological organization and production. It seems probable that a comparable rejection of the psychological consequences of current technology, coupled with the simultaneous ability to exploit that technology, characterizes all dissenting groups in all epochs.

Participation

Post-modern youth is committed to a search for new forms of groups, of organizations and of action where decision-making is collective, arguments are resolved by "talking them out," self-examination, interpersonal criticism and group decision-making are fused. The objective is to create new styles of life and new types of organization that humanize rather than dehumanize, that activate and strengthen the participants rather than undermining or weakening them. And the primary vehicle for such participation is the small, face-to-face primary group of peers.

The search for new participatory forms of organization and action can hardly be deemed successful as yet, especially in the New Left, where effectiveness in the wider social and political scene remains to be demonstrated. There are inherent differences between the often task-less, face-to-face group that is the basic form of organization for both hippies and radicals and the task-oriented organization—differences that make it difficult to achieve social effectiveness based solely on small primary groups. But there may yet evolve from the hippie "tribes," small Digger communities, and primary groups of the New Left, new forms of association in which self-criticism, awareness of group interaction, and the accomplishment of social and political goals go hand in hand. The effort to create groups in which individuals grow from their participation in the group extends far beyond the New Left and the hippie world; the same search is seen in the widespread enthusiasm for "sensitivity training" groups and even in the increasing use of groups as a therapeutic instrument. Nor is this solely an American search: one sees a similar focus, for example, in the Communist nations, with their emphasis on small groups that engage in the "struggle" of mutual criticism and self-criticism.

The search for effectiveness combined with participation has also led to the evolution of "new" styles of social and political action. The newness of such forms of political action as parades and demonstrations is open to some question; perhaps what is most new is the *style* in which old forms of social action are carried out. The most consistent effort is to force one's opponent into a personal confrontation with one's own point of view. Sit-ins, freedom rides, insistence upon discussions, silent and nonviolent demonstrations—all have a prime objective to "get through to" the other side, to force reflection, to bear witness to one's own principles, and to impress upon others the validity of these same principles. There is much that is old and familiar about this, although few of today's young radicals or hippies are ideologically committed to Gandhian views of nonviolence. Yet the underlying purpose of many of the emerging forms of social and political action, whether they be "human be-ins," "love-ins," peace marches or "teach-ins," has a new motive—hope that by expressing one's own principles, by "demonstrating" one's convictions, one can through sheer moral force win over one's opponents and lure them as well into participating with one's own values.

Antiacademicism

Among post-modern youth, one finds a virtually unanimous rejection of the "merely academic." This rejection is one manifestation of a wider insistence on the relevance, applicability and personal meaningfulness of knowledge. It would be wrong simply to label this trend "anti-intellectual," for many new radicals and not a few hippies are themselves highly intellectual people. What is demanded is that intelligence be engaged with the world, just as action should be informed by knowledge. In the New Left, at least amongst leaders, there is enormous respect for knowledge and information, and great impatience with those who act without understanding. Even amongst hippies, where the importance of knowledge and information is less stressed, it would be wrong simply to identify the rejection of the academic world and its values with a total rejection of intellect, knowledge and wisdom.

To post-modern youth, then, most of what is taught in schools, colleges and universities is largely irrelevant to living life in the last third of the twentieth century. Many academics are seen as direct or accidental apologists for the Organized System in the United States. Much of what they teach is considered simply unconnected to the experience of post-modern youth. New ways of learning are sought: ways that combine action with reflection upon action, ways that fuse engagement in the world with understanding of it. In an era of rapid change, the accrued wisdom of the past is cast into question, and youth seeks not only new knowledge, but new ways of learning and knowing.

Nonviolence

Finally, post-modern youth of all persuasions meets on the ground of nonviolence. For hippies, the avoidance of and calming of violence is a central objective, symbolized by gifts of flowers to policemen and the slogan, "Make love, not war." And although nonviolence as a philosophical principle has lost most of its power in the New Left, nonviolence as a psychological orientation is a crucial—perhaps *the* crucial—issue. The nonviolence of post-modern youth should not be confused with pacificism: these are not necessarily young men and women who believe in turning the other cheek or who are systematically opposed to fighting for what they believe in. But the basic style of both radicals and hippies is profoundly opposed to warfare, destruction and exploitation of man by man, and to violence whether on an interpersonal or an international scale. Even among those who do not consider nonviolence a good in itself, a psychological inoculation against violence, even a fear of it, is a unifying theme.

THE CREDIBILITY GAP: PRINCIPLE AND PRACTICE

In creating the style of today's youth, the massive and violent social changes of the past two decades have played a central role. Such social changes are not only distantly perceived by those who are growing up, but are immediately interwoven into the texture of their daily lives as they develop. The social changes of the post-war era affect the young in a variety of ways: in particular, they contribute to a special sensitivity to the discrepancy between principle and practice. For during this era of rapid social change the values most deeply embedded in the parental generation and expressed in their behavior in time of crisis are frequently very different from the more "modern" principles, ideals and values that this generation has professed and attempted to practice in bringing up its children. Filial perception of the discrepancy between practice and principle may help explain the very widespread sensitivity amongst post-modern youth to the "hypocrisy" of the previous generation.

The grandparents of today's twenty-year-olds were generally born at the end of the nineteenth century, and brought up during the pre-World War I years. Heirs of a Victorian tradition as yet unaffected by the value revolutions of the twentieth century, they reared their own children, the parents of today's youth, in families that emphasized respect, the control of impulse, obedience to authority, and the traditional "inner-directed" values of hard work, deferred gratification, and self-restraint. Their children, born around the time of the First World War, were thus socialized in families that remained largely Victorian in outlook.

During their lifetimes, however, these parents (and in particular the most intelligent and advantaged among them) were exposed to a great variety of new values that often changed their nominal faiths. During their youths in the 1920's and 1930's, major changes in American behavior and American values took place. For example, the "emancipation of women" in the 1920's, marked by the achievement of suffrage for women, coincided with the last major change in actual sexual behavior in America: during this period, women began to become the equal partners of men, who no longer sought premarital sexual experience solely with women of a lower class. More important, the 1920's and the 1930's were an era when older Victorian values were challenged, attacked and all but discredited, especially in educated middle-class families. Young men and women who went to college during this period (as did most of the parents of those who can be termed "post-modern" today) were influenced outside their families by a variety of "progressive," "liberal," and even psychoanalytic ideas that contrasted sharply with the values of their childhood families. Moreover, during the 1930's, many of the parents of today's upper middle-class youth were exposed to or involved with the ideals of the New Deal, and sometimes to more radical interpretations of man, society and history. Finally, in the 1940's and 1950's, when it came time to rear their own children, the parents of today's elite youth were strongly influenced by "permissive" views of child-rearing that again contrasted sharply with the techniques by which they themselves had been raised. Thus, many middle-class parents moved during their lifetime from the Victorian ethos in which they had been socialized to the less moralistic, more humanitarian, and more "expressive" values of their own adulthoods.

But major changes in values, when they occur in adult life, are likely to be far from complete. To have grown up in a family where unquestioning obedience to parents was expected, but to rear one's own children in an atmosphere of "democratic" permissiveness and self-determination—and never to revert to the practices of one's own childhood—requires a change of values more total and comprehensive than most adults can achieve. Furthermore, behavior that springs from values acquired in adulthood often appears somewhat forced, artificial or insincere to the sensitive observer. Children, clearly the most sensitive observers of their own parents, are likely to sense a discrepancy between their parents' avowed and consciously held values and their "basic instincts" with regard to child-rearing. Furthermore, the parental tendency to "revert to form" is greatest in times of family crisis, which are of course the times that have the greatest effect upon children. No matter how "genuinely" parents held their "new" values, many of them inevitably found themselves falling back on the lessons of their own childhoods when the chips were down.

In a time of rapid social change, then, a special *credibility gap* is likely to open between the generations. Children are likely to perceive a considerable discrepancy between what their parents avow as their values and the actual assumptions from which parental behavior springs. In many middle-class teen-agers today, for example, the focal issue of adolescent rebellion against parents often seems to be just this discrepancy: the children arguing that their parents' endorsement of independence and self-determination for their children is "hypocritical" in that it does not correspond with the real behavior of the parents when their children actually seek independence. Similar perceptions of parental "hypocrisy" occur around racial matters: for example, there are many parents who in principle support racial and religious equality, but become violently upset when their children date someone from another race or religion. Around political activity similar issues arise. For example, many of the parents of today's youth espouse in principle the cause of political freedom, but are not involved themselves in politics and oppose their children's involvement lest they "jeopardize their record" or "ruin their later career."

Of course, no society ever fully lives up to its own professed ideals. In every society there is a gap between creedal values and actual practices, and in every society, the recognition of this gap constitutes a powerful motor for social change. But in most societies, especially when social change is slow and institutions are powerful and unchanging, there occurs what can be termed *institutionalization of hypocrisy*. Children and adolescents routinely learn when it is "reasonable" to expect that the values people profess will be implemented in their behavior, and when it is not reasonable. There develops an elaborate system of exegesis and commentary upon the society's creedal values, excluding certain people or situations from the full weight of these values, or "demonstrating" that apparent inconsistencies are not really inconsistencies at all. Thus, in almost all societies, a "sincere" man who "honestly" believes one set of values is frequently allowed to ignore them completely, for example, in the practice of his business, in his interpersonal relationships, in dealings with foreigners, in relationships to his children, and so on—all because these areas have been officially defined as exempt from the application of his creedal values.

In a time of rapid social change and value change, however, the institutionalization of hypocrisy seems to break down. "New" values have been in existence for so brief a period that the exemptions to them have not yet been defined, the situations to be excluded have not yet been determined, and the universal gap between principle and practice appears in all of its nakedness. Thus, the mere fact of a discrepancy between creedal values and practice is not at all unusual. But what is special about the present situation of rapid value change is, first, that parents themselves tend to have two conflicting sets of values, one related to the experience of their early childhood, the other to the ideologies and principles acquired in adulthood; and second, that no stable institutions or rules for defining hypocrisy out of existence have yet been fully evolved. In such a situation, children see the Emperor's nakedness with unusual clarity, recognizing the value conflict within their parents and perceiving clearly the hypocritical gap between creed and behavior.

This argument suggests that the post-modern youth may not be confronted with an "objective" gap between parental preaching and practice any greater than that of most generations. But they are confronted with an unusual internal ambivalance within the parental generation over the values that parents successfully inculcated in their children, and they are "deprived" of a system of social interpretation that rationalizes the discrepancy between creed and deed. It seems likely, then, that today's youth may simply be able to perceive the universal gulf between principle and practice more clearly than previous generations have done.

This points to one of the central characteristics of post-modern youth; they insist on taking seriously a great variety of political, personal and social principles that "no one in his right mind" ever before thought of attempting to extend to such situations as dealings with strangers, relations between the races, or international politics. For example, peaceable openness has long been a creedal virtue in our society, but it has never been extended to foreigners, particularly with dark skins. Similarly, quality has long been preached, but the "American dilemma" has been resolved by a series of institutionalized hypocrisies that exempted Negroes from the application of this principle. Love has always been a central value in Christian society, but really to love one's enemies—to be generous to policemen, customers, criminals, servants and foreigners—has been considered folly.

These speculations on the credibility gap between the generations in a time of rapid change may help explain two crucial facts about post-modern youth: first, they frequently come from highly principled families with whose principles they continue to agree; second, that they have the outrageous temerity to insist that individuals and societies live by the values they preach. And these speculations may also explain the frequent feeling of those who have worked intensively with student radicals or hippies that, apart from the "impracticality" of some of their views, these sometimes seem to be the only clear-eyed and sane people in a society and a world where most of us are still systematically blind to the traditional gap between personal principle and practice, national creed and policy, a gap that we may no longer be able to afford.

VIOLENCE: SADISM AND CATACLYSM

Those who are today in their early twenties were born near the end of World War II, the most violent and barbarous war in world history. The lasting imprint of that war can be summarized in the names of three towns: Auschwitz, Hiroshima and Nuremberg. *Auschwitz* points to the possibility of a "civilized" nation embarking on a systematized, well-organized and scientific plan of exterminating an entire people. *Hiroshima* demonstrated how "clean," easy and impersonal cataclysm could be to those who perpetrate it, and how demonic, sadistic and brutal to those who experience it. And *Nuremberg* summarizes the principle that men have an accountability above obedience to national policy, a responsibility to conscience more primary even than fidelity to national law. These three lessons are the matrix for the growth of post-modern youth.

The terror of violence that has hung over all men and women since the Second World War has especially shaped the outlooks of today's youth. In the first memories of a group of young radicals, for example, one finds the following recollections: a dim recall of the end of World War II; childhood terror of the atomic bomb; witnessing the aftermath of a violent riot in the United States; being frightened by a picture of a tank riding over rubble; being violently jealous at the birth of a younger brother; taking part in "gruesome" fights in the school yard. Such memories mean many things, but in them, violence-in-the-world finds echo and counterpart in the violence of inner feelings. The term "violence" suggests both of these possibilities: the *psychological* violence of sadism, exploitation and aggression, and the *historical* violence of war, cataclysm and holocaust. In the lives of most of this generation, the threats of inner and outer violence are fused, each activating, exciting and potentiating the other. To summarize a complex thesis into a few words: *the issue of violence is to this generation what the issue of sex was to the Victorian world.*

Stated differently, what is most deeply repressed, rejected, feared, controlled and projected onto others by the post-modern generation is no longer their own sexuality. Sex, for most of this generation, is much freer, more open, less guilt- and anxiety-ridden. But violence, whether in one's self or in others, has assumed new prominence as the prime source of inner and outer terror. That this should be so in the modern world is readily understandable. Over all of us hangs the continual threat of a technological violence more meaningless, absurd, total and unpremeditated than any ever imagined before. Individual life always resonates with historical change; history is not merely the backdrop for development, but its ground. To be grounded in the history of the past two decades is to have stood upon, to have experienced both directly and vicariously, violent upheaval, violent worldwide revolution, and the unrelenting possibility of worldwide destruction. To have been alive and aware in America during the past decade has been to be exposed to the assassination of a President and the televised murder of his murderer, to the well-publicized slaughter of Americans by their fellow countrymen, and to the recent violence in our cities. To have been a middle-class child in the past two decades is to have watched daily the violence of television, both as it reports the bloodshed and turmoil of the American and non-American world, and as it skillfully elaborates and externalizes in repetitive dramas the potential for violence within each of us.

It therefore requires no assumption of an increase in biological aggression to account for the salience of the issue of violence for post-modern youth. The capacity for rage, spite and aggression is part of our endowment as human beings: it is a constant potential of human nature. But during the past two decades—indeed, starting before the Second World War—we have witnessed violence and imagined violence on a scale more frightening than ever before. Like the angry child who fears that his rage will itself destroy those around him, we have become vastly more sensitive to and fearful of our inner angers, for we live in a world where even the mildest irritation, multiplied a billionfold by modern technology, might destroy all civilization. The fact of violent upheaval and the possibility of cataclysm has been literally brought into our living rooms during the past twenty years: it has been interwoven with the development of a whole generation.

It should not surprise us, then, that the issue of violence is a focal concern for those of contemporary youth with the greatest historical consciousness. The hippie slogan "Make love, not war" expresses their sentiment, albeit in a form that the "realist" of previous generations might deem sentimental or romantic. Although few young radicals would agree with the wording of this statement, the underlying sentiment corresponds to their basic psychological orientation. For them, as for many others of their generation, the primary task is to develop new psychological, political and international controls on violence. Indeed, many of the dilemmas of today's young radicals seem related to their extraordinarily zealous efforts to avoid any action or relationship in which inner or outer violence might be evoked. Distaste for violence animates the profound revulsion many of today's youth feel toward the war in Southeast Asia, just as it underlies a similar revulsion against the exploitation or control of man by man. The same psychological nonviolence is related to young radicals' avoidance of traditional leadership lest it lead to domination, to their emphasis on person-to-person participation and "confrontation," and even to their unwillingness to "play the media" in an attempt to gain political effectiveness. Even the search for forms of mass political action that avoid physical violence —a preference severely tested and somewhat undermined by the events of recent months—points to a considerable distaste for the direct expression of aggression.

I do not mean to suggest that post-modern youth contains a disproportionate number of tight-lipped pacifists or rage-filled deniers of their own inner angers. On the contrary, among today's youth, exuberance, passionateness and zest are the rule rather than the exception. Nor are hippies and young radicals incapable of anger, rage and resentment—especially when their principles are violated. But for many of these young men and women, the experiences of early life and the experience of the postwar world are joined in a special sensitivity to the issue of violence, whether in themselves or in others. This confluence of psychological and historical forces helps explain the intensity of their search for new forms of social organization and political action that avoid manipulation, domination and control, just as it contributes to their widespread opposition to warfare of all kinds.

Yet the position of psychologically nonviolent youth in a violent world is difficult and paradoxical. On the one hand, he seeks to minimize violence, but on the other, his efforts often elicit violence from others. At the same time that he attempts to work to actualize his vision of a peaceful world, he must confront more directly and continually than do his peers the fact that the world is neither peaceful nor just. The frustration and discouragement of his work repetitively reawaken his anger, which must forever be rechanneled into peaceful paths. Since he continually confronts destructiveness and exploitation in the world, his own inevitable potential for destructiveness and exploitiveness inevitably arouses in him great guilt. The young men and women who make up the New Left in America, like other post-modern youth, have far less difficulty in living with their sexual natures than did their parents; but what they continue to find difficult to live with, what they still repress, avoid and counteract is their own potential for violence. It remains to be seen whether, in the movement toward "resistance" and disruption of today's young radicals, their psychological nonviolence will continue to be reflected in their actions.

In pointing to the psychological dimension of the issue of violence, I do not mean to attribute causal primacy either to the experiences of early life or to their residues in adulthood. My thesis is rather that for those of this generation with the greatest historical awareness, the psychological and historical possibility of violence have come to potentiate each other. To repeat: witnessing the acting out of violence on a scale more gigantic than ever before, or imaginatively participating in the possibility of world-wide holocaust activates the fear of one's own violence; heightened awareness of one's inner potential for rage, anger or destructiveness increases sensitivity to the possibility of violence in the world.

This same process of historical potentiation of inner violence has occurred, I believe, throughout the modern world, and brings with it not only the intensified efforts to curb violence we see in this small segment of post-modern youth, but other more frightening possibilities. Post-modern youth, to an unusual degree, remain open to and aware of their own angers and aggressions, and this awareness creates in them a sufficient understanding of inner violence to enable them to control it in themselves and oppose it in others. Most men and women, young or old, possess less insight: their inner sadism is projected onto others whom they thereafter loathe or abjectly serve; or, more disastrously, historically-heightened inner violence is translated into outer aggression and murderousness, sanctioned by self-righteousness.

Thus, if the issue of violence plagues post-modern youth, it is not because these young men and women are more deeply rage-filled than most. On the contrary, it is because such young men and women have confronted this issue more squarely in themselves and in the world than have any but a handful of their fellows. If they have not yet found solutions, they have at least faced an issue so dangerous that most of us find it too painful even to acknowledge, and they have done so, most remarkably, without identifying with what they oppose. Their still-incomplete lives pose for us all the question on which our survival as individuals and as a world depends: Can we create formulations and forms to control historical and psychological violence before their fusion destroys us all?

The Liberal Tradition and Art Education

RALPH A. SMITH

. . . liberalism is not solely a matter of economic or political dimension; it is concerned with the general enrichment of the individual and may relate to his education, his religion, his thinking, his esthetic creativeness and appreciation.[1]

This article examines issues which arise in an attempt to explain the meaning of liberalism in contemporary art education. The occasion for such an essay stems on the one hand from an awareness of contemporary art education's commitment to the ideology of latter-day liberalism and, on the other, from recent criticisms of the liberal tradition of thought and action. Accordingly, the purpose of this essay is (a) to explain the meaning of the term liberalism, (b) to sketch the crisis through which liberalism is passing, (c) to indicate the relations between the general aims of contemporary art education and the ideas of liberalism, and (d) to formulate questions that can be used to help clarify the problems of art education.

Reprinted by permission of the author *Studies in Art Education*, Vol. 4, No. 2, Spring 1963, pp. 35–44, reprinted here with several minor changes, with the permission of *Art Education Journal of the National Art Education Association*.

I

What is the meaning of "liberalism," and in what sense is liberalism experiencing a crisis? A crisis may be characterized as a dramatic shift in the course of events, a crucial "point of no return" in which a decisive change for better or worse is imminent. Darwin's *The Origin of Species* symbolized one such turning point: it marked the beginning of a fundamental change in man's thinking about his relation to the universe.[2] Conceived in slightly different terms, Darwin (and many others after him) posed the dilemma of building anew an accurate conception of personal identity and of the right relation between the self and culture—and it is overwhelmingly clear that it is this sense of crisis that pervades contemporary discourse.

Alfred A. Mavrinac, for example, writes that we are experiencing not only an "evident disruption of communication" but also the "search for ourselves which the sensitive students in our times see as its special characteristic."[3] Nathan A. Scott, Jr., concludes that "nowhere can we find guarantees of security or the promise of any immediate renovation of the present disorder." "Nor has it been possible," he says, "to gain any relief from the outer disorder in the world of society and politics by turning back to the inner world of the private self, for there we discover the real cost that contemporary life exacts in nightmare and neurosis, in fear and remorse and hysteria."[4] Similarly, Lionel Trilling emphasizes that we are witnessing the "progressive deterioration of accurate knowledge of the self and of the right relation between the self and culture," and that this situation constitutes a crisis in our culture.[5]

The crisis of self provides a key to the meaning of liberalism, for in an important sense liberalism may be understood as an interpretation of selfhood and of the proper relation between the self and culture. Moreover, the crisis in liberalism consists in the telling criticism liberals have encountered regarding their views on such matters. And to say that liberalism may be understood as primarily an interpretation of selfhood and of the proper relation between the self and culture is to say that liberalism holds a distinctive view of the drama of history. It is appropriate, then, to examine liberalism from the standpoint of its view of history. Charles Frankel has indicated that the liberal view of history turns on four important beliefs. The first is

. . . the belief that human progress can be measured in secular terms, and that a secular morality, which does not go beyond the sphere of temporal human interests, is sufficient for interpreting human history and for organizing human affairs. The second is the doctrine of "the indefinite perfectibility of man." The third is the belief that it is meaningful to speak of such a thing as objective truth in the study of history and human society, and that intelligence and good will can rise to a level of impartiality that is not wholly limited by personal idiosyncrasy, social status, or historical position; it is therefore meaningful, this thesis holds, to regard progress in social science as an objective possibility, and to expect that such progress might give man increasing power to control his destiny. Finally, there is the belief that a society can be approached in terms of its parts, and that it does not have to be understood or remade all of a piece and all at once.

It is a belief that social progress proceeds by deliberately instituted legislative, judicial, and administrative techniques, and by the piecemeal reconstruction of human institutions—and not by spiritual conversions, moral appeals for a change of heart, or the sudden intervention of external powers.[6]

To expand Frankel's explanation, it may be noted that the insistence on a secular morality for the purposes of organizing and interpreting human history derives primarily from a faith in the spirit and general patterns of natural science as the most effective means available for coming to grips with problems of social and historical change. "Liberals in general have believed in the existence of objective truth," says J. Salwyn Schapiro, "discoverable through reason according to the scientific method of research, experiment, and verification." [7] On the other hand, a belief in "the indefinite perfectibility of man" stems from the positive bent of liberalism in connection with which Max Lerner asserts that "Its credo has been progress, its mood optimist, its view of human nature rationalist and plastic." [8] And it was because the liberal "was capable of the free use of reason, or of thinking out things independently of his particular interests, prejudices, or subconscious drives," states R. R. Palmer, "that liberals favored education." [9] Hence the idea of human perfectibility implied not only a belief about untapped reservoirs of human potentiality, but also that, according to the tenets of a liberal society, persons should be given opportunities to realize their talents and capacities. Such a belief also implied a certain impatience to get on with this job.

The third tenet of the liberal view of history, the belief in intelligence and good will to attain significant levels of impartiality, follows from the notion that it is more fruitful to stress man's capacities for reason and rationality than it is to stress his propensities for error and mistake. Consistent with this outlook is a conception of the openness of the historical process, as opposed to deterministic theories of social change which posit inevitable recurring cycles. Finally, a piecemeal engineering approach to social reform may be interpreted as a position which proposes reconstructing external social arrangements in contradistinction to making dramatic appeals to interior motivation. Indeed, the impression after examining several accounts of liberalism is that there is some consensus after all regarding the meaning of liberalism so that as a descriptive label the term need not be completely discarded. Still, the issue with liberalism is not whether it still provides an effective label, but rather, ought liberalism to have stressed the tenets it did? Did not liberalism err, in other words, in its estimate of human goodness and perfectibility? These are the questions asked by critics. But what, more specifically, is the nature of the crisis in liberalism?

It will be suggested in the second part of this essay that the ideas which characterize the outlook of contemporary art education can be related in large measure to the general goals framed for liberalism by Dewey and other progressives earlier in this century. But important for this section is the commonplace that Dewey's liberalism is out of style and at variance with the contemporary climate of thought. In 1947, for example, Morton G. White could comment that "These are days in which Dewey's views are being replaced by Kierkegaard's in places where once Dewey was king. . . ." [10] And little did White realize (which he acknowledged later) that in a decade the new current of thinking "would soon swell into a powerful effort to discredit the ideas and outlook of some of the most distinguished Americans of the twentieth century." [11] Indeed in 1960 we find Geoffrey Clive writing that Kierkegaard now "ranks as seminal for the understanding of modern consciousness and intellectual life." [12] Dewey's brand of liberalism, however, did loom large in the first half of this century, and it has been remarked that just as the age in which Dewey began to write was no golden age of American liberalism, so the period in which Dewey's thought experienced a decline can be described as the end of the go' 'en age of American liberalism. [13] This testifies to the importance of Dewey's career in the history of American liberalism, and many have urged that we would be wise to understand Dewey before attempting to make sense of the present, or before planning for the future. [14]

The preeminence of antiliberal thought underscores the crisis in liberalism, and Frankel cautions that the significance of this new style of thought should not be underestimated, for it seems to mark a polar swing in the perspective of thinking. At what time in modern history did the crisis in liberalism become acute?

While there are good reasons for preferring 1914 as the end of the great liberal period in history, and while some have cautioned against taking 1929 as a major turning point in modern intellectual history, this year figures prominently in any discussion of the crisis in latter-day liberalism. It was about 1929, for example, that Dewey's style of liberalism began to experience serious difficulty. It was also the year in which The Modern Temper by Joseph Wood Krutch appeared, whose essay "The Tragic Fallacy" described the dilemma of an age of scientific naturalism, psychological determinism, and democratic equalitarianism. [15] And it was, of course, the first year of the Great Depression which contributed notably to a crisis in education. [16] In short, it may be said that in 1929 not only were forces at work undermining certain of liberalism's basic tenets—particularly its belief in human goodness and rationality—but also that a debate was materializing which turned on man's capacity for human dignity in the face of new determinisms.

In connection with the foregoing it may be noted that one current in the critique of liberalism asserts that liberalism lacked a "tragic sense of life." [17] This view holds that liberalism too quickly adopted the idea of the essential goodness and rationality of persons, too willingly accepted the doctrines of progress and human perfectibility, placed too great a faith in reason and the methods of science, with the result that liberals are now either "disillusioned" or "frightened" as the possibilities of nuclear devastation and mass democracy are contemplated. Whether or not liberalism as a tradition of thought interpreting man's relation to the universe was sensitive to the tragic is, of course, a matter for historical and philosophical analysis. But it is not too crucial here whether liberalism did or did not have a "tragic sense of life," whatever this expression may mean. It is sufficient to indicate an increasing "attitude of attentiveness" [18] today toward the tragic aspects in the lives of persons and societies. This is exemplified in part by the judgment that liberalism did not have a tragic sense of life, the implication being that this was therefore an error on the part of liberalism, and by the analysis which holds that pragmatism—certainly a liberal philosophy—actually derives from a recognition of the tragic sense of life, the implication being that pragmatism need not consequently be criticized on this issue.[19] Nor is it necessary to know why so much ambivalence has been generated on this matter, although the notion that the paradoxes in liberalism itself help to explain such ambivalence is suggestive.[20]

In summary, the crisis in contemporary liberalism turns on whether those tenets expressed in its view of history—beliefs in a secular morality to guide human affairs, human perfectibility, the methods of science, and piecemeal engineering reform—are still cogent and have the power to persuade and attract devotees in the face of the developing realities of the twentieth century; that is, those realities which emerge in connection with the appearance of powerful corporate superstructures in which the ends of organization are often anathema to the needs of the individual. We may now turn to some of the ways in which contemporary art education expresses the spirit of liberalism.

II

The question, it may be noted, is not whether contemporary art education expresses the spirit of liberalism. Practically any statement of aims and objectives since the 1920's gives expression to this commitment.[21] True, the term *democracy* was and is often preferred, yet new democratic interpretations of art education resemble, in tone and outlook, the reinterpretations of liberalism undertaken primarily by Dewey in the 1930's. But at this point perhaps a digression might be permitted.

Articles of this type, that is, articles dealing with the intellectual origins of ideas in art education, are not common. Definitions of art education are usually conceived in what might be called a state of "present-mindedness." They usually contain a set of slogans which suggest for art education such outcomes as "self-identification," "self-adjustment," "creative self-expression," "self-realization," "self-discovery," and so on. While the use of such slogans is perfectly valid—so long as practical programs of instruction are not thought to be *logically* derivable from the slogans themselves—and while the use of such slogans is to be understood within the contexts of "democratic" interpretations of arts instruction, the outcomes suggested by such slogans are also consistent with the ends set for liberalism by Dewey. In 1935, for example, Dewey reiterated what he had said so many times, that "the ends of liberalism are liberty and the opportunity of individuals to secure full realization of their potentialities. . . ." [22]

There is no need to document the extent to which this kind of language has dominated educational discourse for the past three decades, so that it may be said that contemporary art education expresses the spirit of liberalism insofar as it has committed itself to achieving the general outcomes of freedom of expression and individual self-fulfillment. Moreover, the scientific or research dimension of art education exemplifies the rational aspect of liberalism in that the purpose of a great deal of research in art education is to develop a core of empirically verifiable knowledge. Perhaps expression of liberal sentiment is most characteristically embodied in the Statement of Beliefs of the National Art Education Association published in 1949, which is still occasionally referred to as appropriate for thinking about the enterprise of art education. It is here quoted in its entirety not only because it is an ideal expression of the kind of thinking that has characterized art education in the immediate past, but also because it is an excellent starting point for a needed re-examination of basic concepts in art education.

Art experiences are essential to the fullest development of all people at all levels of growth because *they promote* self-realization of the whole individual by integrating his imaginative, creative, intellectual, emotional and manual capacities, and social maturity and responsibility through cultivating a deepened understanding of the problems, ideals, and goals of other individuals and social groups.

Art is especially well suited to such growth because it: encourages freedom of expression, emphasizes emotional and spiritual values, integrates all human capacities, and universalizes human expression.

Art instruction should encourage: exploration and experimentation in many media, sharpened perception of aesthetic qualities, increased art knowledge and skills, and the creative experience in significant activities, and the realization that art has its roots in everyday experience.

Art classes should be taught with full recognition that: all individuals are capable of expression in art, individuals vary markedly in motivations and capacities, and art is less a body of subject matter than a developmental activity.

Because art experiences are close to the core of individual and social development and because they pervade all phases of living, The National Art Education Association believes that *all* teachers should have basic training in art.[23]

A sense of present-mindedness may again be invoked to explain why professional art educators have neglected the intellectual foundations of their field.[24] Contemporary art education has placed great stress on providing opportunities for aesthetic experiences. And aesthetic experience, as Philip Phenix has indicated, "has the quality of immediacy, of all-at-once-ness. Each moment of time may bring a new experience, but the aesthetic quality is appreciated in the mode of 'presentness' rather than that of succession." [25] Other factors might also be noted. Aside from the growing pains of any discipline, there is the peculiar yet persistent and overly stressed notion that talking about art destroys it. There was also the discrediting of organized subject matter by certain leading educators during the progressive movement in education.[26] (An element of this still remains in Lowenfeld's statement that "art education may well become the catalyst for a child-centered education in which the individual and his creative potentialities are placed *above* [27] subject matter," which comes out as "art is less a body of subject matter than a developmental activity" in the NAEA Statement of Beliefs.) Perhaps consistent with the discrediting of organized subject matter was the additional failure to distinguish carefully between different modes of thought and action.[28] And finally, because many art educators are themselves more alert to the immediate qualities of things, art education as a field of study has not (understandably) attracted those interested in its historical and philosophical roots.

But now, what are some questions that will help to formulate the meaning of a new liberalism in contemporary art education?

III

Insofar as liberalism is concerned with the right relation between the self and culture, the question of the meaning of liberalism in art education today turns on whether or not art education can contribute toward the building of a significant sense of self. When we ask such a question today, of course, we assume its relevance. But it wasn't always relevant. It would have been nonsensical, for example, to a rural-agrarian American so long as the rigors of farm and frontier had to be dealt with. But the conditions which supported the growth of self in agrarian America have been radically altered by the emergence of a new industrial, metropolitan society. How does a sense of self develop in the modern world? What is the locus of self in a mass technological society? And does contemporary liberal thought provide any enlightment on these questions?

As might be expected in mid-twentieth century America, enlightened liberal thought is first difficult to locate, and second, the choices it offers are not always clear. But it may be suggested that the liberal today sees basically two choices open to persons, and he opts for the first of these. That is to say, liberals tend to see problems as essentially social, political, and institutional, rather than as principally moral and psychological. They place great stress on the reform of organizations to help solve problems, or on the need to create new ones if needed. For as Dewey once remarked, "Liberalism knows that social conditions may restrict, distort and almost prevent the development of individuality. It therefore takes an active interest in the making of social institutions that have a bearing, positive or negative, upon the growth of individuals. . . ." [29]

Now one manifestation of contemporary industrial society is the institution of aesthetic culture, and it now seems as if our civilization will be the first to provide cultural opportunities for a large proportion of its people. Full participation in the life of aesthetic culture, however, requires highly developed aesthetic skills and sensitivities. Such abilities are needed not only to appropriate the meanings of complex works of art, but also to continue the struggle against the dulling of sensitivity by the mass media and the degradation of the environment through mindless expansionism.

Perhaps a start in answering the question of liberalism—that is, the question of the self's right relation to contemporary culture—can be found in the philosophy of education recently articulated in *Education and the New America* by Solon T. Kimball and James E. McClellan, Jr., an anthropologist and a philosopher, respectively.[30] Kimball and McClellan present a philosophy of education in which *commitment* is a key concept. They understand commitment *not* as a condition involving essentially interior and personal feeling states, but rather as "a particular configuration of four structural elements including a person, an external world, the relations between these two, and the symbolic system by which the person can understand the world and his relation to it." [31] The problem of commitment consists of finding an effective configuration of these four elements, for not any configuration at all defines commitment in the modern world. Kimball and McClellan think at least four disciplines of thought and action are relevant to building commitment to modernity, including what they call "the discipline of aesthetic form." [32] Aesthetic form, they hold, is a primordial habit and way of knowing, interpreting, and learning the world, and thus instruction in aesthetic form should, they say, be a part of everyone's education. Otherwise, full participation in contemporary culture is denied, and the self is stunted in its aesthetic growth. The pedagogical question has to do with how the discipline of aesthetic form can be effectively taught in the schools. But this problem cannot be taken up here.

IV

In summary, this article has asked what might be involved in explaining the meaning of liberalism in contemporary art education. It should be clear that I do not think liberalism, as I have discussed it, is wholly beside the point. Liberalism does, however, need to be re-defined in light of new realities. These new realities stem in large from jarring dislocations in the institutional life of modern America. A new liberalism in art education must be cognizant of this and cast its credo in a language that reflects more convincingly the facts and consequences of a changed social order. It was suggested that an analysis of the ways in which art education contributes to a state of commitment might provide a starting point.

NOTES

1. Geiger, George. *John Dewey in Perspective.* New York: Oxford Univ. Press, 1958. p. 177.
2. Jones, Howard Mumford. "1859 and the Idea of Crisis: General Introduc-

tion." *1859: Entering An Age of Crisis*. (Edited by Phillip Appleman and others.) Bloomington: Indiana University Press, 1959. p. 22.

3. "The Liberal Dilemma and the Christian Debt to Liberalism," *Review of Politics*, 22:367; July 1960.

4. *The Tragic Vision and the Christian Faith*. New York: Association Press, 1957. pp. ix–xix.

5. *Freud and the Crisis of Our Culture*. Boston: Beacon Press, 1955. pp. 33–34.

6. *The Case for Modern Man*. New York: Harper & Brothers, 1956. p. 47. Also see Frankel's *The Democratic Prospect*. New York: Harper & Row, 1962.

7. *Liberalism: Its Meaning and History*. Princeton, N.J.: D. Van Nostrand Co., 1958. pp. 11–12.

8. *America as a Civilization*. New York: Albert Schuster, 1957. p. 729.

9. *A History of the Modern World*. New York: Albert A. Knopf, 1950. p. 607.

10. *Social Thought in America*. Boston: Beacon Press, 1957. p. 3.

11. *Ibid.*, p. ix.

12. *The Romantic Enlightenment*. New York: Meridian Books, 1960. p. 9.

13. White, Morton G. *The Origins of Dewey's Instrumentalism*. New York: Columbia University Press, 1943. p. 3; Dworkin, Martin S., editor. *Dewey on Education*. New York: Teachers College, Columbia University, 1959. pp. 3–4.

14. Thus Frankel writes, "To read Dewey's works is to be forced to ask what we ourselves, facing our own problems, really think about progressive education, the welfare state, the moral implications of science, the meaning of liberalism, or almost any of the other contemporary issues around which intellectual controversies rage." *The American Scholar*, 29:314; Summer 1960.

15. For references to Krutch and the debate in question, see Monroe C. Beardsley's *Aesthetics: Problems in the Philosophy of Criticism*. New York: Harcourt, Brace and Co., 1958, p. 441.

16. Shannon, David A. *The Great Depression*. Englewood Cliffs, N.J.: Prentice-Hall, 1960. Chapter 6. For what happened to art education, see p. 99.

17. This notion is implicit in many critiques of liberalism. It is stated explicitly in R. J. Kaufmann's "The Need to Risk Tragedy," *The Nation*, 184:370; April 1957.

18. The expression is from Scott, *op. cit.*

19. Sidney Hook, "Pragmatism and the Tragic Sense of Life." *Commentary*, 30:139–40; August 1960.

20. Lionel Trilling, for example, suggests that ". . . as is true of any other human entity, the conscious and the unconscious life of liberalism are not always in accord. So far as liberalism is active and positive, so far, that is, as it moves toward *organization*, it tends to select the emotions and qualities that are most susceptible to organization. As it carries out its active and positive ends, it unconsciously limits its view of the world to what it can deal with, and it unconsciously tends to develop theories and principles, particularly in relation to the nature of the human mind, that justify its limitations. Its *characteristic paradox* appears again, and in another form, for in the very interests of its great primal act of imagination by which it establishes its essence and existence—in the interests, that is, of its vision and a general enlargement and freedom and rational direction of human

life—it drifts toward a denial of the emotions and the imagination." *The Liberal Imagination*. New York: Doubleday & Co., 1953. pp. 8–9.

21. A few remarks are perhaps needed here. The period referred to was marked by progressivism in education. Not all educators, of course, were progressive, nor was there unanimity among progressives; but art education as it is understood today bears the imprint of the progressives' thought, and the tenor of this thought was essentially liberal stressing the release and development of individual capacities. For a history of the progressive movement in American education, see Lawrence A. Cremin's *The Transformation of the School*. New York: Alfred A. Knopf, 1961. Cremin's account makes it plain that the progressives had no tragic sense of life whatsoever.

22. *Liberalism and Social Action*. New York: G. P. Putnam's Sons, 1935. p. 51.

23. The Association, 1949; as quoted in Italo L. deFrancesco. *Art Education: Its Means and Ends*. New York: Harper & Brothers, 1958. pp. 34–35.

24. The major exception, of course, is Frederick Logan's *Growth of Art in American Schools*. New York: Harper & Brothers, 1954.

25. *Philosophy of Education*. New York: Henry Holt & Co., 1958. p. 428.

26. Cremin, *op. cit.* p. 220.

27. Emphasis added.

28. Woodring, Paul. A *Fourth of a Nation*. New York: McGraw-Hill Book Co., 1957. pp. 42–43.

29. "The Future of Liberalism." *School and Society*, 41:74–75; January 1935.

30. New York: Random House, 1962.

31. *Ibid.*, p. 279.

32. *Ibid.*, pp. 301–303.

The School as a Model of Society

JOSEPH C. GRANNIS

Every school represents to its students a model of society and its possibilities. In the very composition of the students and teachers, in the authority and decision-making structure of the school, in the ways that people talk with one another, learn and work and play together, and in the expectations the school holds for its students—in all these ways, and more, the school instructs about society.

We are accustomed to thinking of content as the most important learning a school conveys to its students. It is the structure of the school, however, that instructs most systematically, and it is this structure that the students respond to first and remember longest.

In this essay we shall look at the schools of the nation today in terms of

Reprinted with the author's permission from *Harvard Graduate School Association Bulletin*, Vol. XII, No. 2, pages 15–27, Fall 1967.

several different models of society that they present to their students. Each of these models is an ideal type, and no single model may fully describe a single school. It will be necessary to think of the schools in terms of different combinations of the models. We shall have to weigh the adequacy of these models for the schools today, and shall then have to examine society to uncover new possibilities for the schools.

The various models of society that we find now in the schools have originated in different sectors of the society as a whole, and at various stages of its historical development. Our capacity to change the schools depends on our understanding not only what they teach about society now, but the process by which they came to represent various views of society.

Three models will serve to describe a great deal of what we can see now in the schools. A "family" model can be most readily associated with preschools and with the primary grades of certain private schools that had their origins in the progressive era. A second model, the "factory" school, is the most prevalent type in the elementary and secondary schools of the nation today. It originated principally in the cities, in the late nineteenth and early twentieth centuries, for the primary purpose of inducting immigrant and rural youth into the working-class life of the industrial system of the times, and secondarily for initiating some youth into the ways of American middle-class life of these times. A third model, the "corporation" school, has been developing most rapidly in the schools of the suburbs during just the last ten years or so. Its primary function seems to be the induction of youth into certain of the ways of a modern, bureaucratically organized society.

Team teaching and nongraded patterns of organization characterize the corporation school, while rigidly graded and horizontally segmented patterns characterize the factory school. These, however, are only the more manifest structural features by which these schools can be identified. Underlying them are significant differences in the attitudes of the schools toward education, toward the work and lives of the students and the teachers in school, and toward life in society itself.

Again we stress that no single model adequately describes all that happens in a single school, especially when we take into account the variations among different classrooms within a school. For example, a teacher in a school patterned like a factory may attempt in certain ways to be a mother or a father with his students, and to treat the class like a family in some of the students' dealings with one another. Nonetheless, each of our three models has a coherent structure and message, and individual schools tend on the whole to represent one model more than another, in their overall organization and in their effects on the students and staff within them.

The "Family" School

It has been observed that the early New England school was instituted in response to the extended family's ceasing to fulfill certain functions in colonial society. We would add that the structure of the colonial school itself reflected certain features of the colonial family, both in the relationships among its pupils, who were of different ages in a given classroom, and in the authority exercised over the pupils by the master of the school.

John Dewey stated most explicitly the idea of the family school as it was developed by the progressives. The model of school that Dewey promulgated in *The School and Society* still governs the conduct of some schools today:

If we take an example from an ideal home, where the parent is intelligent enough to recognize what is best for the child, and is able to supply what is needed, we find the child learning through the social converse and constitution of the family. There are certain points of interest and value to him in the conversation carried on: statements are made, inquiries arise, topics are discussed, and the child continually learns. He states his experiences, his misconceptions are corrected. Again the child participates in the household occupations, and thereby gets habits of industry, order, and regard for the rights and ideas of others, and the fundamental habit of subordinating his activities to the general interest of the household. Participation in these household tasks becomes an opportunity for gaining knowledge. The ideal home would naturally have a workshop where the child could work out his constructive instincts. It would have a miniature laboratory in which his inquiries could be directed. The life of the child would extend out of doors to the garden, surrounding fields, and forests. He would have his excursions, his walks and talks, in which the larger world out of doors would open to him.

Now, if we organize and generalize all of this, we have the ideal school. There is no mystery about it, no wonderful discovery of pedagogy or educational theory. It is simply a question of doing systematically and in a large, intelligent, and competent way what for various reasons can be done in most households only in a comparatively meager and haphazard manner. In the first place, the ideal home has to be enlarged. The child must be brought into contact with more grown people and with more children in order that there may be the freest and richest social life. Moreover, the occupations and relationships of the home environment are not especially selected for the growth of the child; the main object is something else, and what the child can get out of them is incidental. Hence the need of a school. In this school the life of the child becomes the all-controlling aim. All the media necessary to further the growth of the child center there. Learning? certainly, but living primarily, and learning through and in relation to this living. . . . (The School and Society. *Chicago: Phoenix, 1963, 33–46*)

Our terming this a family model emphasizes the intimate manner of the children's learning with and from each other, and the teacher's nurturing role, as one who shares with the children certain interests and occupations, who provides materials and settings for the children's growth, and who facilitates the children's solving of problems that develop essentially out of their own life in the environment created for them.

Dewey meant his Chicago Laboratory School to be a model for all elementary schools. He discussed at length, in *The School and Society*, the difficulty of making meaningful connections among the myriad occupations and enterprises of an industrial society, and he argued that the life of the family, especially the preindustrial or rural family as he had known it in his own Vermont childhood, provided the key to a way that children's experiences in society could be integrated. The family school so construed does not correspond in important ways to life in the family as we know it today. It represents a family where the occupations of the adults were carried on in the home or the near vicinity of the home, and where the children witnessed and participated in the production of all life's necessities.

Since the early 1930's English educators have been working deliberately to develop Dewey's concept of the family school, and today it is in effect in fully half of the English infant schools, the public schools for children from five to seven years old. The passage quoted above reads very much like the descriptions of infant schools that visitors from this country have published. Children in an infant school classroom work spontaneously with all kinds of materials that have been provided for them: clay, wood and tools, musical instruments, Dienes blocks and Cuisenaire rods, cooking equipment, pendulums, books, and on and on. They move freely about the classroom and work in the corridors and outside. Only at the beginning of the day do the children and the teacher all sit together, for "prayers" that often take the form of a little play or some other presentation. During the rest of the day the teacher meets the children individually or in small groups, as she encounters them working on various problems they have set for themselves or forms a small group for reading and discussion. Five-, six-, and seven-year-olds are all placed in the same room. The pupil-teacher ratio in the infant schools is 40 to one.

According to the British government's Plowden Report, English educators now consider that the family model has proved its worth in the infant schools. They plan next to extend the model to the junior schools for children eight to eleven years old.

Some elementary school teachers in this country have tried to implement the family model on a limited basis in their classrooms. On balance, however, the model has had little enduring impact on our elementary schools. This is testimony to the strength of the very forces Dewey discerned in industrial society and wanted to counteract through his vision of schooling. It also points to certain limitations of the model itself, which we shall consider after examining the different models that now prevail in most of this country's schools.

We can further sharpen the concept of the family school by taking note of two current controversies. The first concerns the appropriateness of the family model for lower-class as against middle-class children. Bereiter and Engelmann have observed, correctly, that the private preschools in which the family model has flourished have been largely for middle-class children. Middle-class children, they say, have already learned impulse controls at home, and thus they need a permissive environment in the school to free them up. In contrast, lower-class children, they maintain, have not learned these controls at home, and consequently need a more highly structured and authoritarian school environment.

Whether the distinction between permissive and nonpermissive practices applies so neatly to lower- and middle-class homes is much more questionable than Bereiter and Engelmann indicate. More than this, however, it must be realized that the model of the family school does not stand simply for permissiveness. It has to do with the integrity of the child's self-concept in relation to other individuals and to the world around him, a concern that the schools most readily violate in their dealings with lower-class children. In abandoning the family model altogether for a combination of the factory and corporation models, Bereiter and Engelmann—and the children themselves—may be losing more than they gain.

A second current controversy involves the elementary school's use of team teaching, a characteristic of the corporation school. Some educators have looked askance at team teaching in the elementary school, precisely because they identify the self-contained classroom with the family model and fear that the model's advantages will be lost. We shall see that there is good reason to question the intimacy and spontaneity of relationships among the individuals in a corporation school. At the same time, however, we must recognize that the family model has been overwhelmed by the factory model in most self-contained classrooms today. In fact, it is possible to combine the family and the corporation models to a certain degree, as was evidenced by Dewey's Laboratory School itself, where a variety of teachers and other staff, together with professors from the University, planned and carried out many of the affairs of the school collectively.

THE "FACTORY" SCHOOL

Students in a factory school classroom are generally found working on identical material at a uniform pace. Identical grading standards are presumed to be applied to all the students, though in practice there are great discrepancies in their application to different students, or in their application to different performances by one and the same student on various occasions. Much of the work is assign and recite, and the pattern of dialogue is often rote teaching. Students in the factory school do not get to see the teacher "do things" that matter to the teacher himself, except teach, nor do they see the teacher working on his own questions.

At any given time it is expected either that the students already know what they are to do, or that they can pick it up with a little telling, or that they do not know—the distinctions are never quite clear—but that, in any case, it is the teacher's job to demand the doing of the children and to reward or punish according to the outcome. Thus the students in the factory school learn to think in terms of a crude standardization of products, effort, and reward, and at the same time to expect a certain arbitrariness of the standards by which their work is to be done and judged. They learn to expect the failure of many individuals to meet these standards. Finally, they learn the necessity of repetition, or, eventually, out-and-out withdrawal from the production line when individuals fail to meet the standards that have been laid down for them.

Competition is encouraged among the students in the factory school. However, it is a limited form of competition compared with that which is most likely to be functional in work and society today. The factory school does not foster individual initiative and quality of work, but stresses instead a competition in sheer quantity and rate of production—the best rate being that which is neither too fast nor too slow for the line.

Collaboration too is very limited in the factory school. Elementary school classrooms often have routines in which the students take turns cleaning the boards, taking attendance, and so on, and secondary school students may monitor the halls or manage the bookstore. Students may make a report together or undertake a mural or a skit cooperatively. For the most part, however, one is hard put to find collaboration on difficult problems that require cooperative planning and the varied skills of different individuals, except in the "extracurricular" activities that really depend on collaboration.

A punitive authority pervades the factory school, emanating from the principal's office and delegated to the teachers. In the mix of the factory and the family models, this authority of the school is paternalistic. Certain students are depended on to set the pace and exemplify the standards set down for the group. Often the teachers delegate some of their own authority to these students, and certain students emerge from the ranks to become more identified with their bosses, the teachers. Sometimes, however, the students reject the system. They sit in sullen silence, or they range themselves against the teachers and the school and bring the works to a futile halt.

The students in the factory school are exhorted to listen to the directives of their superiors. They are taught to say the words of a vaguely equalitarian creed, as a way of glossing over or putting up with all kinds of individual inconsistencies and injustices they experience. They learn to punch a clock, and to stay put in their stations, through hours of uninterrupted, or disrupted, monotony and tedium. Their teachers, too, may feel all these effects of a factory way of life in the schools.

We have already noted that the family model mitigates the effects of the factory school for the students and teachers in some classrooms. Another concept of society that functions in a similar way is the idea of a community of scholars. As a model for a whole school, it is perhaps most evident in this country in a few of the private secondary schools that have deliberately imitated the college system of Oxford and Cambridge and the English tradition, in contrast to that of the continent, of a community of scholars and gentlemen. Individual teachers, particularly those with a liberal arts background, sometimes manage to develop this relationship with their students in public schools, especially if the students are bright and come from the middle class. In the face of conditions in the factory school, however, the community of scholars is very difficult to bring off.

That most of our suburban schools retain many features of the factory school has led one visitor from abroad to observe that American schools in the suburbs are a lower-class joke on the middle class. As for the inner-city schools, the notion that they represent middle-class norms and attitudes to the students is a gross oversimplification of what actually happens. It is the norms and attitudes of the middle class *toward* the lower class that are most in effect in our city schools.

The "Corporation" School

The full-fledged corporation school includes both team teaching and non-graded characteristics. In practice, however, these are not always joined together and may be combined with features of other models. Again we resort to the device of a caricature or an ideal type to emphasize its essential features.

Our initial description of the corporation school will appear to be more positive than our account of the factory school, but, as we shall see, the corporation school also raises troublesome questions.

Team teaching in the corporation school recognizes first the different capacities and interests of the teachers themselves. The teachers do not, however, simply divide the labor up among themselves as in the factory school. They plan, conduct, and evaluate the instruction collectively. This pushes the teachers to rationalize much of the teaching that they would otherwise do intuitively or mechanically, and it forces them to adjust their own interests and styles to the requirements of the team as a whole.

While team teaching alone does not necessarily recognize the different interests and capacities of the students, it does do so when combined with a vertically nongraded scheme. This is especially true if the scheme does not simply locate the students along various straight-line continua, but allows them to diverge and to concentrate more in one area of study or another. The corporation school tends to develop an elaborately differentiated scheme for evaluating and reporting students' progress, and it often involves the students themselves in evaluation of their progress. It sets up contracts with individual students for their work. Students and teachers are grouped in numerous ways for various purposes, and complex schedules evolve to allocate the time and resources of the school.

Materials of instruction too are much more specialized than in the factory school, many of them being created by the teachers themselves for specific occasions. Teacher aides facilitate this development of materials, either by working on the materials themselves, or by releasing the teachers from non-instructional duties so that the teachers gain time for planning and development. Again, the corporation school is able to make much greater use of expensive equipment—projectors, computers, teaching machines, tape recorders and headsets, and so on—since the use of this equipment can be rationalized for larger pools of students and teachers.

It is not merely availability of these resources that leads to their use in the corporation school. The whole attitude of the school is oriented toward planning and rationalization and toward the employment of specialized skills and technology.

Change and innovation are institutionalized in the corporate school. This is experienced by the students in the shifting combinations of people and resources to which they are assigned, and in the constantly changing schedule of the school's activities. It is probably experienced by the teachers with even greater force, in the degree that they change their objectives and strategies from year to year or from one month to the next.

There is a highly differentiated hierarchy in the corporation school. The principal, team teachers, regular teachers, and teacher aides all stand above the students, and the authority to make decisions is distributed systematically throughout the hierarchy. Some of the authority reserved to the principal in a factory school is assigned to team leaders in the corporation school, and teams generally have more control over the curriculum than do teachers in the factory school.

Two questions about the corporation school are especially crucial. How much and what kind of control do the students themselves have over their activities? And what kinds of feelings and attachments develop between the students and the teachers and among the students themselves?

It is striking that in some corporation schools the students have even less control over their activities than in the factory schools, where the teacher makes so many decisions spontaneously, and the pupils learn to manipulate, if only by sabotage, the teacher's propensities to their advantage. A couple of factors work against the students' control in the corporation school. The most obvious is that the coordination of a team's various activities and resources may impose more rigid time constraints on the classes than is the case within the self-contained classroom, at least in the elementary school; thus a group cannot so easily persevere in something that is especially rewarding, or break off from an activity they dislike. A second factor is the rationalization of instruction. The teachers may do so much detailed planning collectively that very few decisions are left to be contingent on the immediate circumstances of the ensuing activities. A similar observation can be made about the programmed materials used in the school.

In many corporation schools deliberate provisions have been made for individual students' selection and timing of their studies, often in connection with elaborately constructed study centers and multi-media retrieval systems. Students have been involved in the actual planning of their studies, including quite ambitious individual and group projects, instead of their just being let in on the teachers' plans, as in other corporation schools. All of these variations, however, remain quite distinct from the family model. Both the teachers and the students are more systematically organized, and the instructional process and materials are more highly rationalized.

The feeling relationships between individuals in the corporation school are more detached than in the factory school, again at least at the elementary level, and certainly more detached than in the family school. In the factory school, the different individuals do everything in common, whereas in the corporation school there are many more limited-purpose associations. A class in the factory school tends to develop a relatively stable social system, while the system in the corporation school is very fluid. In the one, a class has "good" students and "bad," trouble-makers, teachers' pets, all in all a familiar backdrop of individuals against which a given student measures himself. The class develops a history of happenings with each of the teachers who has succeeded or failed in molding it to his special inclinations. In the corporation school the students, who are placed in a variety of groups, are constantly reevaluated in different settings, and the groups to which they belong are more diffusely associated with the team or the institution as a whole. Furthermore, the teachers consciously construe their role as more professional and less nurturing, a distinction that has been emphasized in one elementary school system by designating a teacher *aide* as "team mother."

Research conducted by Millie Almy in a corporation school at the elementary level (the only research of this specific nature known to the author) indicated that the children did indeed differentiate among their various teachers, though it did not reveal how much knowledge of a given teacher there was compared to a self-contained classroom. This same research showed that the children were less likely to give responses indicating emotional attachment to the teacher than were the children in self-contained classes in a control school (presumably a family-modified factory school), and that on indirect measures of their perception of teachers the children in the team situation more often saw the teacher as either neutral or punitive, less often as supportive or helpful. Again, while children in this school knew considerably more children by name than did children in the control school, they more often reported that their friendships had been made at home rather than at school.

In all of its characteristics the development of the corporation school parallels the trend in many of our social institutions today, from the more entrepreneurial to more bureaucratic forms of organization. This underlines all the more the import of our questions about the students' control and feelings in the school, for these are questions that are raised by the life of the individual in modern society generally. The corporation school represents to its students a society in which there is greater interdependence, in which there is greater specialization of individuals' tasks and functions, and in which technology and institutionalized processes of change and innovation play a greater part than in the societies of the past. Whether this society is to entail less or more control for individuals and greater or less feeling and empathy in their relationships with others, is a question that has been answered differently by different analysts of the society at large. The answer it is given in the schools depends on choices we make.

Who Are the Disadvantaged?

We know that the poor in our society are disadvantaged, and that somehow inequalities in the schools attended by lower- and middle-class youth play a part in keeping them poor. Understanding just what these inequalities are is much more difficult. Again, we know that Negroes and Puerto Ricans are disadvantaged in our society, and again it is hard to say exactly how the schools contribute to their being disadvantaged.

The problem is compounded when we realize the extent to which all the nation's youth are disadvantaged by the schools, as the schools have stressed getting ahead, or not getting ahead, in narrowly defined and isolated channels. In addressing ourselves first to the effects of the three different models on students' achievement, we are recognizing that all students have to achieve if they are to compete on equal terms in the economy. At the same time, we do not want to think in terms that will just force lower-class students into the tracks that already confine the middle class.

When we ask which of our three models of school is most effective in raising students' performance on standard achievement tests, the answer seems to be extraordinarily simple. At least in the present stage of knowledge about teaching, none of the models is superior to the others. The Plowden Committee in England conducted a major study of the achievement of children in the infant schools organized on the family model and children in conventionally organized infant schools (we do not know whether to call them "factory" schools in the English context) and found slight differences in favor of the conventional schools. However, they found that these differences in achievement disappeared in later school years, and they concluded that the result was explained by the fact that the children in the family-model school had no practice in taking tests. Comparisons of team teaching and self-contained classrooms in this country have not shown consistent differences in the students' achievement.

The results of nongraded instruction are not quite so clear-cut. In particular, it has been found in some programs that allowing students to define their own goals on a contract basis raises achievement, while programs where the teachers have decided what level the students should be working at seem to produce no differences on achievement tests in comparison to graded instruction. The results of programmed and automated instruction are also mixed, but the few programs and devices that appear to show promise are not likely to be available to most schools for many years.

In the last several years, a host of compensatory education programs for lower-class Negro youth has used various combinations of team teaching, individual tutoring, involvment of parents, cultural enrichment, new instructional techniques, and direct appeals to students' aspirations.

The devastating conclusion of the U. S. Commission on Civil Rights' report, *Racial Isolation in the Public Schools,* is that none of these programs has produced lasting gains in the achievement of these youth so long as the students remained segregated from middle-class students. On the other hand, their data show that lower-class students who have been placed in schools with middle-class students, however these have been organized, have made significant gains in achievement. These findings parallel the Coleman Report conclusion that "the social composition of the student body is more highly related to achievement, independently of the student's own social background, than is any school factor."

What are we to make of all this? The first thing we have to recognize is that really not very much is known about teaching *any* students. The lower-class student's achievement in a school with middle-class students is a function of the general level of discourse and expectations that can be maintained in a predominantly middle-class classroom, not any special wizardry of the teachers. As many students of the problem are concluding, this argues strongly for the integration of lower- and middle-class students, and thus for the integration of white and Negro students, since these divisions in our society are so related. It also argues for our persisting in trying to learn more about teaching and learning in relation to all students and thus for our continuing to experiment with different models of instruction.

The second thing that we have to consider is that the proponents of the various models of school, and particularly the advocates of the family and corporation schools, remain convinced of the worth of these models despite their not raising students' levels of achievement. Spokesmen for the family school, beginning with Dewey himself, have always stressed that conventional academic achievement was not the only aim of the school, and that we must be concerned with the whole life of the child. The proponents of the corporation school are very much concerned with achievement, but their not getting significant gains in no way diminishes their ardor. We think the explanation of this is that it is the corporation model of society itself that they prize, perhaps most of all because of the satisfactions it gives the teachers, but also for the way of life that it represents to the students.

Defenders of the factory school can be counted on to rejoin, whenever one questions the authoritarianism or the monotony and failure the students experience, "But isn't that the way life is?"

This brings us back to the point we have been arguing from the beginning. Underlying our debates about teaching are fundamental questions about life and society itself and how the schools should construe the lives of their students and teachers. We think the issues posed by the different models are important and valid, but we want to argue that none of the models is adequate for the schools today.

Contemporary society *does* require more competence in all its members. The basic problem of both the factory and corporation schools is that they are preoccupied with the accumulation and specialization of knowledge and skills, and too little concerned with personal and social integration. Learning is represented to the students as a good to be hoarded for some future day. It is passed down in pieces and subjects from those on high who have already got it, not personally constructed or reconstructed.

The message of the schools is that only students learn, while those who have already made it into the world pursue life's real occupations. Only teachers teach, with all kinds of paraphernalia to assist them in the job.

Awaiting the students outside and in the years to come is a fixed system of slots, and innumerable obstacles have to be hurdled on the way to finding one's predestined place. Students in the corporation school learn that these slots are complexly organized, and that interpersonal skills and adaptability are required for success in the system. Students in the factory school learn that the individual must struggle alone toward these slots, trying to shoulder his way above the average without incurring the wrath of those in the way.

We have addressed these observations to both the factory and the corporation schools. However, there is a crucial sense in which they do not apply equally to all the students in these schools. Lower-class youths are systematically disadvantaged by the factory school. As we have indicated, this is not because it is a less efficient way of raising conventional achievement scores. The factory school, like the plantation of an earlier era, peculiarly lends itself to a perception of the lower class, and especially of black people, as aliens who must learn a menial conception of work and life before they are fit to take their place in society. The place that awaits them is at the bottom of the system.

This interpretation of the way in which the factory school disadvantages lower-class youth reflects our conviction that the expectations exerted by the whole structure of the school, not just individual teachers' expectations, can cripple the students' self-concepts and performance. We need data on the effects of different schools and programs on all aspects of individuals' development, not just on academic achievement alone.

Whether either the factory or the corporation school is more destructive to middle-class youth we do not know, but the toll is high among them, too: school dropouts, cynical youths who despise the system at the same time that they make it in the schools, youths who tune out while they drift through, and hippies who reject the whole society. Some find the system confusing; others find it materialistic, and they play the game or leave it according to their values.

A great paradox lies under all of this. From the outside, modern society can be seen to be a complex, functioning whole—not integrated in every respect, and functioning badly for many purposes, but nonetheless an interconnected whole. From within, it can be felt as fragmented and disconnected. Durkheim applied the term "organic" to *modern*, not primitive, society, in order to distinguish it as a system of interdependent, uniquely functioning parts. Yet it is precisely this differentiation of the parts of modern society that makes it so difficult to experience one's life as a whole, and to have an effect on the society where one wants to change it.

This is again the problem Dewey posed for education in *The School and Society*. His solution has not prevailed, however, and we have to ask why.

Callahan, in *Education and the Cult of Efficiency*, has laid the blame to a business mentality that has dominated educational policy making at the local level in the schools and has tried to apply cost accounting and time-and-effort productivity standards to the myriad decisions of running an "efficient" school system. Newmann and Oliver, in their article "Education and Community," have extended this explanation to include all the ways that the education industry today thinks of learning and the students themselves as products of an essentially economic system. Our own argument goes still further. Educators and taxpayers have taken economic institutions not only as a model for how *they* should operate the schools but as a design for what the *students* are to learn in them.

A second explanation for the failure of Dewey's solution has to do with the family model itself. The author believes that the family model, perhaps with some corporation features, *is* the most appropriate model for the preschool and primary years, but that it becomes increasingly less adequate as we try to apply it to the later years of school. Whether it can be applied in the early years in the same way it has been applied in England depends chiefly on the differences and similarities of family life in England and America, or the norms and expectations developed in the home. This is the same question for research that we noted earlier.

The trouble with the family model as the students get older is its increasing discrepancy with the larger institutions of society that impinge on the students' lives. Dewey himself recognized this insofar as he maintained that a part of education would have to be more formal and disciplined in these later years. He also recognized it in stating that the schools should collaborate with business, science, and other institutions outside the school. However, the conception of disciplined thinking that he most often put forth was a highly individual, common sense problem solving. Similarly, the model of the family school itself so dominated his rationale for schools that the progressives never got beyond it to implement a more viable relationship of the schools to society.

Harold Rugg and the later reconstructionists did concern themselves more with the need for the school's dealing with society's problems, and they envisioned the school's becoming a center for community life. Again, however, they did not come to terms with the nature of the modern community and society, and their proposals lacked incisiveness accordingly.

Society as a Model for Schools

Individuals find meaning and control in modern life, as in the life of any society, by participating in its social institutions—political, economic, artistic, nurturing, and so on—or by rebelling against institutions that they *understand* are stupid or inequitable. Our problem, in essence, is that effective entry into most of the institutions of modern society is a great deal more difficult than was entry into the institutions of pre-industrial society. Not only does it require more technical competence to be effective in any given institution, but initiation into one does not, as it did in pre-industrial society, go hand in hand with initiation into the other. One does not simply enter or participate in *a* community with political, economic, artistic, and other aspects, but, rather, one enters highly differentiated *communities.*

There are two broad implications of this kind of thinking. One is that we must systematically examine the society's institutions for the ways that youth and the schools can participate in them. The second is that the whole question of the "community's" control of the school should be conceived of in terms of a plurality of communities of interest, each having relatively greater control over that part of the school's program which it is competent to, and cares to, participate in. This model of control is not meant simply to replace the egalitarian idea of a school's being controlled by elected representatives (a school board, more or less local as the case may be), but to complement this idea, as it does in the relationship of the formal and informal aspects of our various units of government. In order for this control by interested parties to be possible, the school would have to be open to scrutiny and participation by the various communities of interest. Thus we are talking both about facilitating the entrée of students and the schools into the society's institutions of politics, economics, the arts, nurturing, science, scholarship, and so on, and about making the school itself more hospitable and permeable to persons having these interests.

One can look at a variety of developments in the nation today and see that their potential for education is very large from this point of view.

The confrontation of the schools and inner-city communities today is itself proving to be a political education for all concerned. We need to ask in what ways youth could be involved in this, as indeed they have been in some communities where they have participated in demonstrations. They might be a party to the ongoing dialogue that must ensue between the schools and their constituencies and they could be involved in other political dialogues, for example, debates in surburban communities about fair housing codes, industrial zoning, and recreation. Student governments and civic courses have been a farce on politics, and the students know it. In combination with students' involvement in politics, these activities could be made very potent.

Work-study programs have induced dropouts to continue their education. Could not these opportunities be extended to all students in the secondary schools? At all levels of school, facilities should be developed both by businesses and industry for an active interchange, as students develop questions about the workings of business and industry and about the kinds of satisfactions and problems that men have in different careers. Likewise, ways should be sought to involve the schools and businesses and industry together in community action programs, to improve property or employment possibilities or to develop relationships to other communities. In all of these efforts, and in the schools' participation in other institutions, there must be a deliberate concern with the students' and the general community's sense of control of their fate. No one can have unlimited control, but there are great differences in the control exercised by different individuals in modern society. These stem both from their different resources and their varying sense of the control that they can exert as individuals or in collaboration with others.

The concept of the community school has long included the provision of educational and recreational opportunities for adults and older people. It should be implemented in such a way that there is free traffic between adults and the young in the vicinity of the school, and in a way that allows the old to participate directly in the education of the young, as readers, historians, craftsmen, and so on—more than anything else, perhaps, as people who have watched the times change and have helped create or resisted change. Again, the idea of the community school is being extended today to include the school as a coordinating center for the great variety of social and welfare services that are now becoming available to citizens. Simply getting information about these opportunities is a major problem for many who might benefit from them, and petty but enormously frustrating problems of the law and communication beset many who try to claim new rights. Students could contribute to, and learn much from, these efforts.

Artists and craftsmen are being invited to work and perform in residence in a few schools today. This ought to be a practice of all schools from time to time, and exhibitions of contemporary art and crafts should be staged in the schools. Cultural enrichment programs have reportedly had a negative impact in some cases, as students and teachers have been taken out of their own neighborhoods to the places where art, music, and drama are conventionally offered. It is crucial that the arts be made an integral part of the school community.

A great deal of effort is being expended today to reform the subject offerings of the curriculum, in order to bring them more into line with the disciplines of the sciences and the humanities. It is vital that scholars be concerned with the validity of inquiry in the disciplines, but two problems must be recognized. First, the new curriculum is fast being transformed in practice into the same old message in a new form, as it pours vast new quantities of knowledge into the schools for students to accumulate. The notion that there are certain fixed structures of thought to be mastered in order to have knowledge of the disciplines may well gain the upper hand over the sophisticated entreaties of a few that these structures are man-made and that every individual must make choices and develop his own style within a discipline. The key to this problem too may be to think of the disciplines as social institutions. We might then construe the concepts and procedures of the disciplines in a more social light, and might ask, far more boldly than we have so far, how the quarrels and rivalries of the scholars, their ethical dilemmas, publishing mores, financing ventures, conventions, and so on, can be shared with the students. This is not just a matter of teaching *about* the disciplines as social instructions. Again it is a question of initiation. Teachers must come across to students as persons who themselves seek meaning and control through their disciplines, and who are themselves nourished and constrained by the thoughts and passions of other men present and past. They must not be perceived simply as purveyors of knowledge *or* as manipulators of critical thinking and inductive method, but as men participating in the disciplines for their own ends.

Our second problem stands in the way of all the possibilities we have been considering for the schools. So long as college-bound students, and their teachers, perceive that it is necessary to spend night and day preparing for college, through academic studies, they will be afraid to elect the schools' alternatives, and rightly so. The plain fact of the matter is that these alternatives would prepare students for college, if one must speak of the matter this way, just as well as, if not better than, academic study of the disciplines would alone. This *may* not be so true of the natural sciences and mathematics, but this should not inhibit us from freeing up the curriculum even for mathematics and science concentrators.

The colleges themselves must take the lead in this. It is ironic that a year or more of absence is fast becoming institutionalized in college, to enable students to get their bearings on what college is all about. It is necessary once again, as was done quite successfully in the Progressive Education Association's Eight Year Study, for the colleges and the schools to negotiate a truce that gives the schools more freedom to experiment with their curriculum.

In all of these proposals we have been laying great stress on collective endeavor. This is partly the result of recognizing the specifically corporate nature of so much of man's effort in the world today, but it is more the consequence of the idea that initiation into society's institutions is a prerequisite of understanding them. We would hope at the same time that students would develop some critical perspective on these institutions, and that they would establish their indentity as individuals in some distinction from these institutions. Perhaps in art it is easiest to see how one must both participate and stand apart in order to be an autonomous individual. Somehow this autonomy must be fostered in individuals' relationships to all of society's institutions. Friedenberg, in *The Vanishing Adolescent*, has pointed out how the rebellion of youth today is emasculated by adults' seeming acceptance of youths' opinions and points of view. The problem is to cultivate not only what matters to the students, but what matters to everyone, so that genuine dialogue can ensue among all the parties to any question.

Obviously the structure of the schools will have to change to take advantage of all these needs and possibilities. We envision a combination of formal courses, laboratories, and seminars, involving professional teachers and laymen in different capacities in each setting. Much of the school's endeavor would have to be carried on outside the school proper. The concept of an educational park or complex that is now being explored for the purpose of integrating students of different social backgrounds might especially lend itself to this thinking, if such parks were planned in relation to all of society's resources. However, schools in every community could be suited to these proposals, and it would be necessary to carry some of these out in the students' and their families' neighborhoods.

Let us enter one more suggestion. The schools that would result from these adventures would run the risk of separating students from one another even more than the corporation school does today, as they participated now in one and now in another enterprise with different colleagues. In order to provide the opportunity for the students to see themselves in relation to a stable group of others outside the family during these years of their development, the schools might establish small groups of, say, ten or twelve children, early in the school years, that would continue on into their adolescence. New members could be added to a group as others chose to leave or moved out of the community. These groups would not do everything together, but they would meet on a regular basis, perhaps as clubs, and they would engage in some of the school's activities as a group. A group might be reconstituted if it clearly failed to contribute to the students' development and pleasure. The students themselves might be as wise as educators in deciding how these groups should be set up.

These ideas are just a beginning and are meant to be suggestive, not definitive. Some of them have been suggested by steps that inner-city communities themselves are contemplating for the improvement of their schools, and many more will occur to others who confront the problems. We cannot be very sanguine about how the schools and educators will respond to these problems of youth and society. A number of observers have concluded that the schools are too wedded to the nation's system of economic and social selection, in ways that the schools do not even know, to take seriously the goals of personal and social integration. Some have proceeded to set up private community schools, and others have called for a break from the whole institution of school as we know it. There is merit in both approaches. It seems necessary that education be redesigned, in ways that would change the structure of the schools and schooling fundamentally.

At the same time, school remains the institution that, in the long run, has the greatest potential for focusing society's resources for education. Perhaps the new thinking that inner-city communities are demanding of their schools will someday redound to the advantage of schools in every community. Our awareness of the schools' teaching about society, our sense of larger possibilities for the school, may be greatest at the very points where the system has broken down.

SUGGESTED READINGS

Bereiter, Carl and Engelmann, Siegfried. *Teaching Disadvantaged Children in the Preschool.* Englewood Cliffs, N.J.: Prentice-Hall, 1966.
Callahan, Raymond. *Education and the Cult of Efficiency: A Study of the Social Forces That Have Shaped the Administration of the Public Schools.* Chicago: University of Chicago Press, 1962.
Dewey, John. *The School and Society.* Chicago: University of Chicago, 1900.

Dreeben, Robert. "The Contribution of Schooling to the Learning of Norms." *Harvard Educational Review*, XXXVII, No. 2 (Spring, 1967), 211–238.

Featherstone, Joseph. "The Primary School Revolution in Britain: I. Schools for Children; II. How Children Learn; III. Teaching Children to Think." *The New Republic*, CLVII, August 10, September 2, and September 9, 1967.

Newmann, Fred M. and Oliver, Donald W. "Education and Community." *Harvard Educational Review*, XXXVII, No. 1 (Winter, 1967), 61–106.

Rugg, Harold. *American Life and the School Curriculum.* Boston: Ginn and Company, 1936.

United States Commission on Civil Rights. *Racial Isolation in the Schools.* Vols. I and II (Appendices). Washington: U.S. Government Printing Office, 1967.

"The World Across the Street." Transcript of a radio program developed with WGBH-FM by Robert A. Rosenthal and Bernard Bruce of the Pathways Project. *Harvard Graduate School of Education Association Bulletin*, XI, No. 2 (Fall, 1966), 2–24.

A Revision of Purposes for Art Education

GUY HUBBARD

Great ideas have continually spurred people onward to great achievements. Without great ideas nothing can be achieved. Our own nation is the outgrowth of a great idea: our education today remains the instrument of that idea. And art education is a part of a total educational enterprise that is designed to serve the American people and the American idea.

Of course it is true that art education also goes on through parents, churches, community traditions, college art programs, 4-H Clubs, and Madison Avenue advertisers; but without being unduly presumptuous, we can say that only in the schools is the task likely to be done dispassionately, in the most socially responsible way, and for the greatest number of people. It is within the schools that this power of great ideas may be felt on a massive scale.

Most of us realize the inspiring quality of ideas like these, but most of us are equally aware of how sadly words of inspiration compare with the hard facts of art in public schools. Art teachers have to live and work in a world where their subject is often repressed, or disregarded, or not appreciated and valued as it should be. They know what it means to be rarely, if ever, adequately rewarded for their extra efforts. It is not surprising, therefore, that the morale of art teachers is often low. They lack the inspiration that can come only from leadership—leadership in people and

Reprinted by permission from *Art Education Journal of the National Art Education Association*, Vol. 19, No. 2, February 1966.

leadership in ideas. People and ideas are inseparable: people generate ideas and ideas stimulate people to great achievements and to more and better ideas.

Art exists in the schools but not healthily—this much is evident from two recent studies; [1] but studies like these do not account for the whole sorry picture. What proportion of art teachers, for example, are members of their own professional associations? How many of these people play an active part in their associations? How many read the publications devoted to art education? How many art teachers tolerate written curriculums in their school districts which are unusable? How many are working on curriculum committees to improve the present situation? We must conclude sadly that art educators possess *no great ideas in common* except those which sound important but which no one can define with the approval of the profession: we resort to slogans such as "love of beauty," "self-expression," "the whole child," "process or product."

The only solution to the predicament is for the membership of this profession of art teachers to review the bases of their thinking and to do so against the broad screen of social and cultural needs. Human cultures will always be imperfect, but advances are most likely in those which possess well defined, common goals. We may not like Russia, and yet since the Bolshevik Revolution that nation has leaped from the Middle Ages to the twentieth century. Communism is repulsive to us but it is an idea—*an inspiration*—and it demonstrates the effectiveness of ideas. The vigor of our labor unions during the early years of the century, the present strength of the American Medical Association, and the power of our form of government are all indicators of the irresistible force of ideas in the hands of people with common purposes.

Ideas bind people together and give them the strength necessary for collective action. A well organized, well informed, militant group of intelligent people is invincible. Unhappily, these things have rarely been appropriate statements with reference to art educators.

America today is passing through a period of grave crisis. She is being challenged on all sides. *And so are we being challenged!* But *we* do not possess the political and economic resources that are everywhere apparent in the nation as a whole. The nation may or may not need an intensification of common goals, but we in art education have not merely to intensify our goals: *we need to define them.* We have not done this with reference to the contemporary scene.

Do we have a model to help us? Can we invent one? Probably the best one to follow is that which is most basic. Human beings are all individuals; they all possess unique qualities. People are also molded by the environments in which they live to a considerable extent. The contact between the individual and his environment thus occurs through his various senses. In fact we are able to give meaning to things only through the use we make of our senses—the senses of sight, touch, hearing, taste, and smell. Both individually and collectively we cannot advance ourselves if we are visually illiterate. The manipulation of symbolic forms in reading and mathematics is important: and we all agree that this is so. But to restrict education in this manner is to kowtow to a traditional practice which is no longer appropriate. To cling to tradition however, is a constant weakness among human beings. We may call it economy of effort, although such words as inertia, fear of change, or even laziness are more appropriate. It is true, nevertheless, that teaching an old dog new tricks is difficult and educational traditions are, indeed, deeply entrenched and often have about them the air of old dogs.

We need to direct our thinking, our search for purposes, to what Americans and American society needs now and not only for what the needs are now but for what they will be in the forseeable future. The fundamental question here is not one of asking how we can do things better than we are now doing them: we have to ask ourselves about what is needed. In order to overcome this dilemma we must first look directly to the nation and to its people, and to their educational needs—not to current practices and to traditional habits of thinking about art teaching. We must also define those endeavors in which we are eminently suitable to work. Out of these conclusions may be created an appropriate set of ideas to guide us. And finally, we must recognize that if this is not done and if art teachers do not act forcefully and in union, they will eventually lose all right to be given any time in the school curriculums of the future; they will not be worthy of any public money.

The Need for an Educated Vision

All of us have to meet the circumstances of life in a given society, and the purposes of education are to enable people to do this effectively. One of our most fundamental means of having contact with any events outside the individual is, as we mentioned earlier, through our sense of sight. Deny us our senses of sight and our lives change irrevocably. Is the task of developing vision handled at all systematically in schools—or anywhere else for that matter? No, it is not. Except, that is, if we think of the art teacher and the work he does. Do we find any explicit, detailed statements coming from the art education profession as a whole to the effect that art teachers are dedicated to the goal of systematically developing visual maturity and visual efficiency? No, we do not. The art teacher's curriculum may be focussing, in part, on perceptual awareness but we can only know to what degree if it is explicitly stated. But then, art curriculums themselves are not even commonplace occurrences.

The visual aesthetic indicates a high point of visual excellence or critical judgment relative to a particular way of life, and most art teachers are likely to place great value on this in their private and professional lives. This, also, implies that the lower levels of development which lead to what we might describe as the visual aesthetic have been reached first of all. But we have no grounds for this assumption from what may be observed among our students in the public schools.

Our way of life today, for example, is now too complex for some children simply to begin at the beginning of the educational stream. Culturally deprived children frequently lack many basic visual abilities. Instruction is needed here. But this work is not art for self-expression so much as "adaptive art"[2] for more efficient thinking: it precedes the development of the visual aesthetic, or at least it proceeds concurrently with aesthetic development.

Such an approach as this one need not, however, be limited to unfortunate children. Future classroom teachers usually have some work in the practice of art and some work in art appreciation, but these studies are in art as a study that exists in its own right. This experience is both necessary and excellent, but by itself, it is not likely to meet our needs today in the elementary schools of this country. The sad but true condition is that these young teachers are perceptually disadvantaged themselves in spite of being intelligent and relatively well informed in the common academic areas. They may have learned to handle the techniques and terminology of art modestly, but they have no conception of a much more basic general competency, that of perceptual maturity itself. What is true for students majoring in elementary education is, furthermore, all too often true for those who are planning to work in the secondary schools.

We may believe that teaching art as a subject in its own right is important since art is part of our way of life, but it is every bit as important to teach people to see more effectively, and within this broad context of visual education to include, as one approaches a peak of visual excellence, the concept of art. This is not to suggest neglecting the study of art until the senior high school or college years. The matter is one of emphasis only and this matter of balance should be considered at all levels. From what we know about the transfer of learning, teaching the practice of art will not necessarily do more than sharpen visual perception in those kinds of art that are studied. And for this to be the goal of art within the public schools does not seem to be a satisfactory use of school funds.

Perceptual education—or whatever this area of responsibility might be called—employs behaviors. These behaviors are typically described as artistic or creative. Unless we decide to transform our field completely, we have an obligation to know them and to use them to enhance the maturity of our students. We may hope that we shall improve what is often called the aesthetic sensitivity of the students, but no one yet has been able to define aesthetic sensitivity with sufficient clarity to satisfy more than a handful of people. Such an objective sounds pleasant to our ears, but it is not very practical and teachers have to try and be practical; schools are imperfect enough without compounding the condition. We cannot begin to plan a curriculum for something we cannot describe satisfactorily, and we should not be trying to do so until we have resolved some more fundamental questions about our professional obligations. These obligations include the subject we call art, but at a more fundamental level they include the development of the senses of vision and touch. Art educators are the only people in the schools who are potentially capable of developing these senses in order that students may learn how to use them productively.

The first and the broadest conception we need to establish for a revision of purposes in art education is, therefore, that of perceptual efficiency. To make this known publicly could enhance the status of art instruction, and it could point to an undeniably valuable area of human potential, which has never yet been considered seriously by educators, possibly because educators themselves may not have been asking the right questions in education. At a time in history when we can not know exactly what human potentialities will have to be developed in order to meet the demands of the future we dare not neglect any one of them. This work lies at the very root of all of our objectives and furthermore, lies at the heart of education and *not* at the periphery—which is where we so very often find art education today.

THE NEED FOR CULTURAL IDENTITY

The first of the guiding ideas to be considered in a redefinition of art education is directed toward vision in general: the second one is narrower but is every bit as crucial. A major concern in all educational enterprises is that those who are subjected to instruction will be loyal to the system which established the education. American schools represent American society— the American way of life. Educators devote themselves to too many goals but they must, above all things, try to ensure that their students identify themselves with the standards and values that are central to life in this country.

Once again, it is clearly evident that we live in a society that we can see and touch. One of the functions of the Social Studies curriculum is, for example to cement these allegiances, but no single curricular area is able to do this alone and social studies teachers are not generally likely to possess the interest or the sensory preparation to do this work in a consistent manner—and we are.[3] And aesthetic values, so anthropologists inform us, are invested in things and ideas by a people—that is, by a way of life.[4]

Some readers might suggest, however, that this is not an important issue compared with our social and political history. If all people—or even a majority of people—possessed a scholarly desire for handling abstract verbal conceptions then it might be true that visual, tangible learning would be less important than that which is verbal. But if that were truly the case, then we should find ample prestige granted to scholars and we should also have a plentiful supply of teachers. In fact, the opposite is all too often true. Moreover, we know that among people in this country whose cultural identification is very weak the major means through which they can be reached tends to be through visual, concrete, and physical devices.[5]

In addition, and by no means least, we find those people who are least tolerant of all are the ones who disregard aesthetic values most of all.[6] Tolerance is a priceless quality of civilized man, and we are distressed at the absence of tolerance that has been reported during recent years in this country.

These two topics may seem to be far removed from each other and equally far removed from art education and yet they may be considered as part of the same problem. The fact is, that in order for the people to be emotionally affiliated with a way of life, they have to be educated to belong to it, and that education calls for exposure to the visual aesthetic of that culture for the simple reason that vision is a primary means of interpretation and communication. This is not to imply that students should be exposed to extended historical studies. History has, of course, played an important part in determining our visual culture. More importantly, students need to know what this culture looks like and feels like now in all its sensory manifestations, for art-teaching this includes the arts of painting and drawing and also the arts of freeway engineering and automobile styling.

This country is impressive in its visual imagery and yet native Americans may be blind to it unless they are systematically informed. To some extent people are sensitized through every day exposure but this may often be unbalanced and ineffective. Only through careful instruction can a person be made to feel the impact of American visual culture and not merely have a fuzzy feeling of knowing something—something which so easily drifts into ethnocentric sentimentality.

We do not now do this job at all well in the schools. But if anyone is to do it that person is the art teacher. We need to use every means at our disposal to ensure that students in school are made consciously aware of their visual environment. For many people the verbal abstractions of the American Constitution and the laws of the nation are enough, for many others they are not. Educators dare not neglect any means of reinforcing the cultural identity of students and not merely of those who elect art. In all probability those who do not elect are among those who need this exposure most of all; this is not a pursuit for a few sophisticated individuals but rather the opposite.

Regardless of the obstacles we cannot disregard the challenge of a population that is undergoing catastrophic social change. Large companies move families from point to point like pawns in a game of chess, social unrest is apparent everywhere, hard physical labor is declining and leaving people time and energy for thinking and acting. Extended unemployment is offering fertile conditions for dissatisfaction. Clearly no panacea will be found in any one place. These problems, nevertheless, point directly at the vital concern of cultural identification in the visual domain. It is a challenge art educators have to face and it extends beyond the boundaries of what is conventionally described as art teaching.

The Need to be Prepared for Leisure

The next purpose has to do with the commodity of time. Our days are divided into manageable parts of hours and minutes. For the first time in the history of mankind a dream is about to be realized where everyone will be able to enjoy a life of plentiful leisure. It may never be realized, however, and George Orwell showed us one alternative in his well-known novel *1984*. Adolf Hitler, Josef Stalin, Benito Mussolini, and Mao Tse Tung in this century also have demonstrated how easily tyranny can ruin the possibility of mankind achieving his dreams.

Here in America the electronic age is upon us and with it is emerging a revolutionary redistribution of time in the lives of people. Strangely enough, however, many people today are "moonlighting" in less than desirable work at illegally low wages. In spite of the fact that they frequently receive poor payment for this work, sociologists believe that one of the real reasons for this activity is that these people have not been prepared for the leisure time they now possess. In their dilemma they turn instinctively to what they are used to doing—working.

Education in that mythical age of American history when all that was needed was instruction in the three "R's" has long since passed. Every other aspect of our society has become increasingly complex so it is reasonable to expect that education should also have advanced. The fact is that education has not kept pace in some areas of vital national concern. Two areas have already been described in which art education has a particular investment. A basic premise of the art educator must now be to help equip all people to use time well. Part of this commodity of time will be consumed by gainful employment. Part of it will be taken up with the acts of living—with sleeping, eating, bathing, purchasing clothes, and so on. Researchers who have been studying the distribution of time in people's lives have been predicting that working time will diminish rapidly. But some of the early predictions have been achieved long before they were anticipated. Some people already work less than thirty hours a week.

Will people naturally know what to do with their newly acquired leisure? We might ask whether anyone knows naturally what to do with anything. When people are left to themselves with time on their hands they become unpredictable: why else were the peacetime armies of the past saddled with interminable chores such as polishing brassware. What happens in a classroom at school if a teacher leaves the students to their own devices for an hour? He wouldn't dare do so unless, that is, the students were educated to that level of trust.

Dare we, as educators, leave an entire population to its own devices when it is not gainfully employed? Can we automatically conclude that the unused energies of men will be directed in socially acceptable ways? School drop-outs, for example, have time—it is not *leisure* time, of course, so much as idle time. James Bryant Conant is well aware of the explosive danger among this group of people who are poorly prepared for living in the world of today.[7] Such people are often not very intelligent and not well organized, and yet they create considerable trouble and have already become a social menace of serious proportions. If this is what time can do for one group, what can be expected if an entire population has an abundance of time but does not know how to use it, or more properly stated, has not been educated to use time well. Beside this problem a great many other social problems seem to be of minor significance. Some readers may say that this is not the task of the schools. But what other social agency is there that either is doing something or is likely to do something? We can be sure of one thing and that is that the problem cannot safely be ignored, and wherever and however it is handled the professional art educator will be needed to play an important role.

Since leisure time is increasing dramatically we must plan to educate people to use it wisely. One richly rewarding way of using leisure is through artistic expression—as Winston Churchill and other outstanding men have known very well. The rewarding use of leisure, however, does not come naturally: it is learned. And only the public schools have been established to teach things on a state-wide or national scale. The schools of the future may, of course, change their identity, and in some respects this might be very good, but as things are this challenge lies in the lap of all art educators, since among other things they are the representatives in the schools of this important leisure time pursuit.

THE NEED TO DEVELOP TALENTS

The fourth and final idea that must be included in any revision of purposes in art education relates to the nurturing of talent. In their 1963 study of secondary school art, Reid Hastie and David Templeton of the University of Minnesota reported that pre-professional objectives were of first importance in the eyes of art teachers from the larger secondary schools.[8] We also know that the larger schools are more likely to offer art than the smaller ones for a number of reasons.[9] In spite of this mood among art teachers this objective has in the eyes of this writer, the least right to be considered primary in a public school—or for that matter the least right to be primary in most college art programs. It smacks more of the pursuit of a special interest than education for the public good.

Some readers may conclude that this is an attack both on artistic talent and on those who help develop this talent. This is not true. In all areas of the school curriculum, teachers must do all they can to develop student potentials—potentials of many kinds. The art teacher's responsibilities center on visual matters. He will encounter creative talents of many kinds and many levels of quality among his students, some of which may be aesthetic. Students may, on the other hand, be visually creative but not in the conventionally artistic ways. By all means, when an art teacher discovers a student whose talents are in the image of his own he should nurture them; he will naturally do so. It is infinitely more difficult, however, to perceive and to nurture those talents which fall within the broad area of his teaching responsibility when those talents are *unlike* his own. Art teachers, as we know, tend to be art practitioners in one or more of the fine arts or the artistic crafts, but this is a very narrow interpretation of the visual arts—not to mention the twin focuses of visual maturity and creative development which underly art instruction in the schools.

Art educators have a profound responsibility to help the future art professional but if that goal holds the center of the stage then they are losing the opportunity to take a proud position in the schools. The art educator needs to recognize the breadth of his task in the area of developing talent as being one that calls for art to be used in the future less as an end in itself and more as an instrumental means of developing the kinds of creative, visual behavior that are in demand in all spheres of life and leisure including the world of the Fine Arts.

Four Purposes in Review

Briefly we can summarize these revisions of purpose in art education under four headings. They are as follows:

First, it is imperative that all people should see efficiently. Alternatively they are likely to remain underdeveloped for many human functions—artistic and otherwise.

Second, it is imperative that all people appreciate their common visual values; otherwise they cannot be said truly to belong to this nation.

Third, it is imperative that at a time in history when the dream of leisure for all is about to be realized that people be educated to the point where they can use this time in satisfying ways; and one of these ways is through art. Idleness or passiveness are not simply undesirable; they are social hazards. In the gift of leisure, then, may lie our dream of the good life—or our undoing.

Fourth, it is imperative that all of those whose unique medium of expression is visual should be helped to make the most of their potential and so enhance both their own lives and our way of life in general.

This conception of art education is proposed as one to guide and to unify our profession. Art education lies *at the center* of the education that all people need, but until art educators clarify their own objectives and work toward their own objectives and their realization, nothing is likely to be done. And American life will be the poorer for it!

This paper has been an attempt to present a conception of art education which may serve us well in an uncertain present and in an even more uncertain future. Some readers may reject these statements as fundamentally unsound and also dangerous to the continuing identity of art and of art education. Consideration is due to those who are suspicious of ideas which lead to the overthrow of an established order. *We need to remember*—and the history of art illustrates this very well—*that those ideas which are condemned as outrageous in one generation are commonplace in the next,* and the greatest strength lies with those who can anticipate future needs and demands and are prepared to take risks to realize their objectives.

REFERENCES

1. National Education Association, *Music and Art in the Public Schools*, Research Monograph 1963-M3, Washington, D. C., 1963; Hastie, R. and Templeton, D., *Art Education in the Secondary Schools*, Department of Art Education, Research Report 1-63, University of Minnesota, 1963.
2. Hodges, W. L., McCandless, B. R., and Spicker, H. H., (Indiana University). "The Development and Evaluation of a Diagnostically Based Curriculum for Psychologically Deprived Pre-school Children." A research proposal supported by the U. S. Office of Education, P.L. 88–164.
3. Hubbard, Guy, "Art in the Schools: No Fork in the Road," *Art Education*, Vol. XVII, December, 1964, pp. 10–12.
4. Keesing, Felix, M. *Cultural Anthropology*. New York: Holt, Rinehart and Winston, 1962, p. 348.
5. Reissman, Frank. *The Culturally Deprived Child*. New York: Harper and Brothers, 1962, p. 73.
6. Evans, R. I., "Personal Values as Factors in Anti-Semitism," *Journal of Abnormal and Social Psychology*, Vol. 27, 1952, pp. 749–56.
7. Conant, James Bryant. *Slums and Suburbs*. New York: McGraw-Hill Book Company, 1961.
8. Hastie, Reid and Templeton, David, "Profile of Art in the Secondary Schools: Report of a National Survey," *Art Education*, Vol. XVII, May, 1964, p. 7.
9. "Music and Art in the Public Schools," *Art Education*, Vol. XVI, December, 1963, p. 10.

4

Practice

The Contexts of Teaching Art

IRVING KAUFMAN

At a college commencement address not too long ago, the well-known architect, Philip Johnson, exhorted the graduating seniors to persuade their generation that "beauty, that much neglected, abused, perjorative word is worth money." Mr. Johnson couched his plea in a manner calculated to appeal to the conditioned concerns of Americans and perhaps all other denizens of acquisitive and mass societies. In a society as affluent as twentieth century America he argued that some of the surplus billions of the national product should be spent to make our cities and our homes beautiful (and to quote him further) "if not for posterity and immortality like the Greeks, then for ourselves, for the same selfish reasons we dress prettily, decorate our bedrooms and grow gardens." The argument has a contemporary logic. Yet in a way it is also a philosophical *non sequitur*. Genuine beauty has never

Reprinted with permission from the author.

been limited to or solely created for an intrinsic dollar value or a specific instrumental purpose. Rather, it has inherently expressed the spontaneous aspiring and sympathetic human spirit, despite the fact that the object of beauty can be bought and sold. To sell beauty is not necessarily to relinquish its qualities nor does one genuinely possess beauty simply by buying its concrete form or utilizing it for ends beyond itself. Of course, beauty has many connotations, and great inconsistencies in its shapes and revelations. I use the term generally and I assume Mr. Johnson also did so, to denote the aesthetic shaping of materials into not only pleasurable, but expressive and significant forms—in short—the making of human art as against the comely but gratuitous aspects of nature.

Yet is it sufficient to make our obeisance to Orpheus and to intone the cultural canticle extolling the beauty and art a rich civilization could well afford to provide. Perhaps it should be but is it more than a gesture to address such remarks to a graduating class, whose formal education is finished. The assumption is that education has previously provided the sensibilities with which to appreciate beauty and art. Such an assumption is too easily established. On the other hand if the sensitive awareness of art was already present in the students, then the plea for beauty is redundant. However, Mr. Johnson finds much in our cities and our personal environments either down right ugly or depressingly drab and in so doing, Mr. Johnson's remarks are knowingly addressed to a group in need of special persuasion. A further implication can be drawn that students generally, have not been effectively encouraged in a critical aesthetics. Their previous education has not fully developed the necessary refinement of perceptual and symbolic discrimination, or in even a less salutary fashion, the personal valuing of art and beauty. Despite the remarkable emphasis in the United States upon schooling, can any observer claim for the average citizen including college graduates, more than a cursory assessment of beauty in other than inadequately commonplace ways or an identification with the necessarily cultivated qualities of art in other than blandly innocent, indifferent or even notorious and Philistine terms. It would seem that this average citizen arrived at the end of his formal education without the cultivation and sophistication required for mature, independent insights and the internally felt kinship with beauty and art with which to achieve the "good life." The teaching of art in the schools must bear some responsibility for such lacks. The theory and practice of art teaching possesses more than a cursory relationship.

For the most part, the creative and artistic experiences provided in school are figuratively audited rather than taken for credit. Where there is a felt and affective response to school art programs, yet with the larger disappointments of subsequent cultural anomie and mass capriciousness in the arts, it may be that the programs are superficial and misleading, but more often the pressures of the mass culture and a depersonalizing economy simply are too overwhelming. In any case, confusion, misunderstanding or indifference to the genuine qualities of art are readily reflected in the things we do, the surroundings we create and the values we admire. Such aspects of cultural concern need to be an important part of the awareness of art educators.

Melvin Tumin said sometime ago, "that America and Americans have available to them the resources, both of mind and matter, to build and support the finest culture the world has ever known; that up until now many of these resources have been spent in foolish and sometimes ugly ways; that the resources nevertheless keep growing, and the chance remains." This last phrase "the chance remains" keeps echoing in the minds of all responsible educators, and even in the thinking of those artists and writers who have not completely despaired of the current human and social condition. They continue to ask, what advantages of the continuing opportunities have been taken in any significant way? Within the past decade some small measure of national interest has been awakened in the area of beauty and artistic culture, witness the endowment of the Arts and the Humanities Act of Congress, the admittedly slow yet continuing growth of art education in the schools and the general advance from the taste levels of what Mencken called the Boobocracy. It may be the trappings and surplus of our affluence which prompt these painfully slow changes; there is the need to exert a sense of productive mastery over every facet of existence. Nevertheless, there may also be a genuine reaching out to resolve some of the tensions of the inner life and to touch one remaining source of mystery and magic to counteract Ortega's process of dehumanization. The vague aestheticism of the hippies and the psychedelic vogue are examples of such tendencies.

With these relatively undisciplined recent exceptions it would seem that the typical college graduate still uncritically accepts his physical environment and cultural milieu or suffers them, either not knowing how to change them for the better, or more likely not caring about the "impractical" matters that Tumin's continuing chance may imply. Consequently, it may be somewhat akin to wishful thinking to address our remarks on beauty or by extension, the achievement of a fine and aesthetic culture, to those who have already been shaped by our cultural substance and patterns despite the efforts of education. Whereas art and beauty require intensities of honest passion, intrinsic pleasures and an interior dialogue of subjective states of being, the average American is largely given to outward control, extrinsic satisfactions and an admiration for objective reality. The implications for mass education, especially on the elementary school level, are obvious. They need to be translated into the cues and insights which individual teachers can utilize in significant ways.

I do not mean to take Mr. Johnson to task. I fully support his thesis that a beautiful environment rather than one primarily economical and efficient is required to establish the conditions for graceful and significant living. Though I would add the word artistic to the beautiful simply to indicate that elements other than the purely hedonistic should enter the context. No doubt we have the money, but do we have the compelling need and requisite sensibilities?

THE INFLUENCE OF CULTURE

This leads me to expand the point that, unwittingly or otherwise, prevailing cultural biases of society make themselves felt even in eloquent attempts to alter those same cultural biases and conditions. Such an understanding is, of course, a fundamental tenet in pedagogical theory, but it is not one that is always understood in all of its ramifications. The perquisites of a mass culture and the requirements of a technological society invade education, through the back door as it were, making themselves at home in an easy, effective manner that appears to forestall any serious questioning of their right to be where they are. Like the proverbial weekend guest who moves in, kit and caboodle, the prevailing cultural influences qualify, and in the case of the contemporary conditions of a mass technological society, distort the values of the household. Education, specifically, traditionally linked with the values of humanism, becomes a context for human submission. As Jacques Ellul says, "children are educated to become precisely what society expects of them." These intrusions of culture into education are frequently direct, brooking a no-nonsense attitude, such as inculcating a solid respect for private property in the social sphere, or accepting a rule of objectivity in the philosophical one. But more often than not the influences are a sublimatory nature. They enter into the mainstream of education subconsciously and pervade the activities of teaching without the teachers' or students' overt awareness. The patterns of curriculum construction and the methods of teaching are vitally shaped by these underground but authoritative cultural dispositions, by such forceful elements of society as an overspread technological development, a ubiquitous commercial mass culture and the psychological displacements effected by such influences.

Such basic considerations have more than a passing relevance to the role of art education and vigorously, if surreptitiously, impinge upon the orientation of the art teacher. They bear directly upon the central substance of art teaching—the awareness and validity of significant and expressive symbol making and response. They make themselves felt in both areas of art education—the active development of an individual and aesthetic creativity as demonstrated in the students' personal participation in the processes of art and in the fashioning of the visual surroundings but also in the responses or cultivation of appreciative and discriminating sensibilities vis à vis the heritage of past art or in its contemporary forms. The very qualities that are encouraged, yet little understood in the school art programs are compromised, especially on the levels below college.

Unwittingly and often with a smug assurance that accepts no real criticism the experiences of art are established in ways that are foreign or hostile to the spirit of art. Saint Exupéry has said "we do not discover the truth, we create it." What we do in an existentially, at least in an artistic sense and in the teaching of art, becomes the substance and the limits or the range of "the truth" or teaching focus we know and act upon. In art education, this "doing" energetically creates the truths that are reflected through cultural conditioning particularly to repeat, in the workings of the modern, pervasive factors of standardization and commerce, the restricting reliance upon supposedly factual or pragmatic considerations and the subsequent psychic anxiety that such an imbalance of natural conditions may engender. Fortunately, art educators are becoming much more cognizant of these factors. The newly developing ideas in the field are imbued with pertinent change and genuine ties to viable artistic values. Nevertheless, there is an abundance of art teaching in existence which unfolds in isolation, divorced from contemporary concerns or is sentimental and insipid in its reliance upon peripheral or instrumental values rather than centrally artistic ones.

Confusions in Value

An example may be seen in its derivative working by referring to Mr. Johnson again. His comments could easily be picked up by the unsophisticated or overly zealous teacher as more background material with which they could "sell" art to their classes, ignoring the context within which he spoke. Mr. Johnson deplores the American cherishing of money and utility as goals to be prized above that of beauty. Yet, in his appeal for an emphasis upon beauty he equates its worth, even if only for purposes of argument, with money—the very value objective which may be one of the detriments to the creation of beauty. I am overstating the interpretation, for actually Mr. Johnson is simply telling us that it is to our advantage and pleasure to spend money so as to create and enjoy beauty. However, it is quite possible, at a cursory reading, to make some unwarranted relationships. It is this kind of confusion which dogs the heels of many general educators and even teachers of art who may be considerably less sophisticated and sensitive to aesthetic values than is Mr. Johnson. Perhaps many teachers comprehend our culture in a far more realistic and pragmatic manner than I ever can, recognizing an apparent need to achieve a goal of beauty by utilizing a fundamental climate of opinion which refers to the sacrosanct province of the pocket book. Yet, Mr. Johnson cites example after example, primarily from architecture, of the distressing visual ugliness and ungraceful cost accounting functionalism that has been perpetrated in a city such as New York. He names the oppressive Pan Am Building, the brutal dominance of the river fronts with Consolidated Edison utility plants that stand, willy-nilly, as public monuments simply by their sheer bulk and presence, or he speaks of the proposed General Motors Building which will be (and has become) a "money-making cheapy on our most prestigeous plaza." It would seem in these instances that money and beauty are antipathetic to one another.

I wonder in another context about the publicity surrounding the recent purchase of the Leonardo by this institution (National Gallery in Washington, D.C.). Will the public come to view the work on its intrinsic merits? Or will they come really to see that immense dollar sign superimposed through the prism of the communications media upon the visage of Ginevra dei Benci as the crowds did some years ago to see the two million dollars plus which got in the way of Rembrandt's Aristotle at the Metropolitan Museum of Art. Daniel Boorstin, the historian, informs us that we are in the era of pseudo considerations, the images and events we experience rarely possess the integrity and intensity of original sources. The images we create or experience in indirect ways are narcissistic signs of our own self-seeking ambitions. We test the reality of ourselves and of our culture by these images, and since one of the rock realities of American culture is money, the Leonardo painting despite its magic and magnificence as a work of art will be measured by its price tag. The genius and artistry of the work will largely be extraneously assumed and in all probability neglected as a direct inspiration by the mass of people who will view it. But, it will certainly be admired and respected as a major and proudly expensive acquisition in the pantheon of our culture. But what will occur in the private dreams of the ordinary viewer—teacher or student, beset as he or she is with ballyhoo and internalized values of popular culture which abet a bumptious, yet conforming response?

Such second-hand manipulations of and responses to environment are direct expressions of cultural values, and conscious or not, they reflect a dubious aspect of our national character. It is questionable if a parallel appeal to the instincts of utilitarian acquisitiveness and aesthetic sensibility will produce any affirmation or beneficent creation of beauty, no matter in what advantageous light they are cast. The road to hell is paved with good intentions and if ever there was a maxim that art educators should be aware of, it is this one.

CLASSROOM CONSEQUENCES

Teachers of art require more than good intentions. They require both perceptual and intuitive insight into art and culture as well as the paradox of achieving detachment from that culture even as they are committed to art and to teaching. They cannot engage in cunning strategems or crafty manipulations to "sell" art to their students, no matter how altruistic the aims of the deceptions. The devious artifices of a popularized art teaching and a sentimentalized presentation of creativity and appreciation become, in time if not immediately, the actual substance of the educational experience. Values are inculcated that mitigate against the honest, the sympathetic and the genuinely aesthetic expression and transformation of experience. The erratic nature of expediency that results from a lack of insight cannot provide the natural pulse of spontaneity or the nourishing climate for individual search and the unique creative formulation of inner visions that result in genuine art. The experience in the art class, when it is the contrived face of gimmicks or arbitary cultural imposition emphasizes a collective patterning and a largely predetermined anticipation of results. The student is inexorably led up the path to a confining context of aesthetic security and shallow expressiveness—to a conformity of taste and an abnegation of direct and expanding experiences in art. The resulting and larger social vulgarity of landscape and poverty of spirit belie the fundamental objectives of education. One is to produce an independent citizen, receptive to those life experiences of a significant symbolic and aesthetic nature as well as the more utilitarian and socializing in the narrow sense. The entire process is considerably intensified when teachers are unaware of the vagrant nature of the questionable strategems they employ or the contradictory and digressive values they unwittingly establish. The compelling enthusiasm of a naiveté and the expedient success of a lively artlessness can be devastating in their influence.

The blend of a subliminal, indiscriminate cultural incursion into education and a sentimental teaching innocence, may be one of the most potent factors in creating the tone and the ultimate worth of an art program—or any educational program, for that matter. For instance, it may be one of the reasons that education fails to overcome the widespread rejection of genuinely artistic activity observed in the early adolescent. Along with puberty and junior high school comes a marked diminishing of expressive symbolic behavior transformed into some aesthetically concrete form. It may be argued that the child is progressing into a cognitive mode that is more abstract, more intellectually oriented, and into an organization of training that is vocational in content necessary at this point of a student's career. It may also be noted that there is some concensus accepting child art as separate and different from adult art, running its developmental course during the elementary years. Nevertheless, even if we accept all of these theories to account for the cessation of childish exploration and achievement in art (and some parts of their structure may be open to question), no subsequent activity in the arts, on a more advanced level seems to occur in any great measure. There is little apparent in the average adolescent of a genuinely artistic nature to replace the earlier easy rapport with expressive and aesthetic activity, witness the minor demand for art in the high school. More important, the desire for a sincere and legitimate engagement with art simply does not manifest itself to any significant degree at a later date or as a compelling need. The value commitments simply are not there.

THE NEED FOR CRITICAL DISTINCTIONS

I would assign a good measure of this failing to the inadequacy and the sophistry of the overall art education program in the schools, or should I say in the lack of programs, especially on the lower levels (most particularly there) in their inability to counteract destructive cultural forces. In the greater majority of instances, the elementary schools do not even have the ameliorating presence of an art teacher or consultant. However, it is vital for art teachers on any level to recognize that they may have misread the signs, that their values may be entangled with devious and contrary considerations, that they may be the involuntary channels for cultural imports which they would not knowingly endorse.

Though I recognize the context of his talk and the special nature of his plea, I would still question whether we can encourage or create beauty for the same selfish reasons beyond money that Mr. Johnson enumerates: depressing prettily, decorating our bedrooms or growing our gardens. Each of these activities is valid and they are bound up with elements of beauty. But they are of a different order, if not of a different kind than the beauty that one equates with art. And here we may arrive at one of the core problems in art education—the assessment of the relative worth of the wide variety and many faces of beauty—the realization of the values of the varying aspects of art. To oversimplify, and despite the philosophical thrust of Pop Art, if we make no qualitative and aesthetic distinctions between the choice of a color scheme for a party dress and the color rhythms of a Matisse or the arrangement of a bed in a boudoir and the visual structure of a Gabo, then I wonder if we can arrive at a really pertinent set of theoretical assumptions for a broadly based teaching of art.

The democratic emphasis upon the sharing of cultural wealth may have a salutory ring to it. It may be regarded as the harbinger of that utopian dream, of a land of cultural Cockaigne where leisure, desire, and experience have fabulous sport with art, beauty, and fulfillment. But it may also exist in a vacuum of aesthetic discernment, arbitrarily mixing good with bad, the spurious with the genuine, the superficial with the profound. In the rush and commitment to popularize art, to provide for every man what was once the almost exclusive province of an artistocracy, the criterion of the best, of excellence, may be adulterated if not completely displaced. Certainly, if the art of the hair dresser or of the interior decorator is thought to strike an even balance with the art of a Modigliani, a Henry Moore, or of Mr. Johnson himself, then our understanding of art has undergone a remarkable and not too desirable metamorphosis. Similarly, in a classroom example of equating such as stereotyped holiday drawings that many teachers exact from children with the same children's own bittersweet struggle to symbolize, independently and uniquely, in personal and expressive form some aspect of their confrontation with the world or even their own psyche. If such imperceptive relationships are made, then art education is, indeed, no more than a pleasant, pink-glassed pipeline for the unexamined bric-a-brac of culture rather than an intrinsic experience of meaning and growth existing dynamically within the culture to enrich the individual.

Briefly, we can look upon some of the more potent and pervasive conditions of contemporary culture as these impinge, in my mind undesirably, upon the teaching of art. Perhaps, with this brief probe, you can understand my concern for the relationships that occur between education and culture, especially in the aesthetic area. Though the criticism is not particularly original, it is quite pertinent and deserves a continuing emphasis.

The Influence of Technology

I've alluded to the broader characteristics earlier, such as the authority, or even supremacy of technology and the rampant spread of popular culture. These two social forces have upset many traditional shibboleths, but have created their own in turn. They set up psychologies of human behavior that are distinctive and different from past patterns, sending out long fingers of influence in every part and process of contemporary life, and provoking a broad scope of reaction in individuals and institutions.

First we can refer to the role of technology—the most fundamental force today and some of the attitudes that are engendered in its wake. On one end of the critical spectrum, technology may be seen as the means whereby man takes a far greater and commanding control of his environment. At this point, the limits stretch well beyond his own world and are almost endless in possibility. This growth and mastery of technology can be regarded as freeing man from drudgery, from a slavish dependence upon the fickle and frequently unaccommodating, if not hostile conditions of nature. It makes man healthier, gives him more leisure, permits him to move about almost at his own will. It helps create a remarkable abundance of material and utilitarian products but also is a compulsion to further knowledge and increased mastery of both the inanimate world and human society. Beyond this, technology is, for some observers, the means to literally set man free to seek some greater collective destiny in which the individual may share; it becomes the crowning glory of a rational human creativeness and genius.

Nor is technology confined to an engineering of inanimate things and forces. It is also an accepted approach in the biological and social sciences, so that more frequently of late, one hears about human engineering, meaning the engineering of humans as much as for humans. It is at this point that the other end of the attitude range is heard from. No sane and sensible critic will ask for the "repeal" of technology or seriously offer such counter measures as those William Morris offered a century ago—in effect, to return to the handcrafting and supposedly less spiritually brutal ways of the Middle Ages. However, they will focus on the mechanization of existence that they insist technology has brought about. They will direct our attention to the depersonalization that accompanies the spread and sophistication of technological processes—to the robot-like conformity expected, to the excising of individual differences due to standardization, to the repetitive and tedious processes common to mechanical functioning. They can indicate that in the past, nature seemed to be caught up in chaos and randomness, outside of divine will, while man had a purpose in being alive, no matter how small or circumscribed it may have been. Now it is the machine that possesses the purpose, while man drifts aimlessly about, lacking a secure faith in the larger human goals, eschatological and personal.

Both of these attitudes are, of course, in themselves correct, both provide a grasp of truth, but again with the insight of Saint Exupéry, whichever one we act upon will be the one that creates the truth for us. I am not certain that a middle ground is possible or if compromises can be worked out. The forces unleashed are gigantic and powerful, perhaps beyond our capacities to control in significant and agreed upon ways. But if I had to make some kind of choice I would opt for more music and less clicking, for more bumbling human experience and less mechanical efficiency, even if it means I have to stay home more often or wait in line somewhere. I would like to illustrate my preferences with some slight anecdotes of the relationship of technology to educational administration. One of my colleagues told me recently that his daughter was scheduled for seven periods of Business Arithmetic in her high school even though she was not in a commercial course. It took all of two weeks to get her straightened out. Another. Before my family moved several years ago from the midwest to New York, my son applied for entrance to the local high school. However, we left before he was to enter the following fall. Later, that year, after the first marking period, we were astonished to have forwarded to us my son's marks from that midwestern school, good marks at that, including driver education, despite the fact that he had never attended the reporting high school, not even one day. Of course, you can say it was human, rather than mechanical error, but there is the larger factor of the limits of human capacity and psychological comfort in a mechanical world.

THE DISTORTION OF TECHNICS

More seriously, there is what Lewis Mumford calls "The distortion of technics." He has said, "The world our operationally minded contemporaries prefer to live in is one from which feeling and emotion have been deliberately eliminated; a world in which whatever seems obscure and inward, whatever cannot be reduced to a quantity, is thereby treated as unreal; a world that is, as we say, impersonal, concerned with means and consequences, not with ends and means." A world, in other words, that is objective and external. Along with Mr. Mumford we can deplore the imbalance he reveals in the overdevelopment of technology—in the imbalance between external and internal responses to experience—in the excessive treasuring and esteem of objective qualities to the resultant detriment of the subjective. On a rather profound level, our current society is increasingly relying upon this technological development, developing the complex and esoteric disciplines of systems analysis, cybernetics and automation, all of which promise even greater and more intricate, but for all that, still mechanical and essentially mindless operations.

To conceive of a fantastic idea, many may even be unknowingly preparing the robots, which because of new electronic circuitry and advanced engineering knowledge will transcend their mechanical natures and replace humans upon their coming collective demise. Or perhaps they will be making robots of themselves as the new research in genetic controls and the establishment of built in educational "memory banks" promise. Not too long ago, Russian and American scientists collaborated in predicting the progress that science will make by the not too distant year of 2000 and they held out the likelihood of a "Brave New World" that even Huxley would not have had the temerity to improvise in his moral laden science fiction.

I would like to quote from one more scholar and observer, the seminal French historian and sociologist Jacques Ellul. I do so at some length because of his profound study of technology and his subsequently intense insights and eloquence.

Unfortunately, it (technology) has evolved autonomously in such a way that man has lost all contact with his natural framework and has to do only with the organized technical intermediary . . . he cannot pierce the shell of technology to find again the ancient milieu to which he was adapted for hundreds of thousands of years. . . . It begins to appear with crushing finality that a new necessity is taking over from the old. . . . It is easy to boast of victory over ancient oppression, but what if victory has been gained at the price of an even greater subjection to the forces of the artificial necessity of the technological society which has come to dominate our lives? . . . The further the technical mechanism develops which allows us to escape natural necessity, the more we are subjected to artificial technical necessities,

and so on in an increasingly frightening realization of the monster that is being created. Ellul not only pictures for us the present and predictable horrors of technology but castigates scientists for their amoral attitudes. He will not even grant the distinctions between scientists and technicians that many others do, feeling that the former rarely rise above banal platitudes in areas outside of their specialities. What he cannot forgive them is their alleged lack of critical ability and the randomness with which they unleash enormous power.

PHILOSOPHICAL CHOICE

All of this may seem to be rather removed from an examination of art and education in contemporary culture. Yet, if technology is the overriding constituent and the chief influence in shaping culture, the relationships are obvious. These relationships have to be a basic ingredient in any educational planning, curricula theorizing and teaching methodology, in art as in any other area. Educators need to recognize the innate constraints and intermediary nature of the technological apparatus as it relentlessly coerces human capacities into its own mold. The schools reflect the obdurate divorce of the individual, not only from the harsh and difficult conditions of nature, but ever more frequently, from a direct confrontation with the wider aspects of experience. Max Frisch, the Swiss writer has characterized technology as "the knack of so arranging the world that we do not have to experience it." Such a trenchant criticism should at least have a hearing in the classroom where the techniques of technology are becoming increasingly evident. It intimately touches upon the procedures and the aims of both art and general education, characterizing as it does the cultural conception of experience and its expression in either symbolic form or social behavior. The consequences of an honest assessment may be a logical but also an emotional insight into the twentieth century quality of alienation, a quality of contemporary existence it would be difficult to deny. The alienation may be found to exist on many levels and refer to many situations—the realization of self, the relationships among persons and to the interplay between man and his environment. Unless there is this awareness of the displacement of human capacities and desires within the currently depersonalized contexts of living, education cannot take on its dynamic function. It would merely wear the patina of individualized instruction, but really function as some gigantic machine stamping out the living products of education much as Detroit produces cars.

What is so aggravating is the understanding of the twentieth century that a good part of the alienation is man-made. Man has created this artificial context of technological paternalism and he now stews in it. The formlessness, purposelessness and turmoil of spirit that has now resulted, is self-inflicted— a seemingly deliberate disintegration of, at one end, the scientific-technical-objective and, the other end, social-artistic-subjective balances that have been the natural, human condition. It may appear that the critics I am quoting are castigating change itself, as well as reflecting a similar personal bias on my own part. That would be untrue, for change is intrinsic to existence and is currently recognized as such even by those who are more comfortable in traditional ways. It is the nature and direction of the change that is being questioned and its implications for education.

QUESTIONING THE GUIDEPOSTS

For instance, I continue to have doubts concerning the undue influence of psychological testing in the schools and the related, so-called objective examination of substance and method in education. My uncertainty is even more intense about the efficacy and the pertinency of the narrower psychological investigations into art education, if not the total appropriateness of pseudo-scientific probing and poking into aesthetic and creative matters. I cannot help being struck by the obvious incongruity of utilizing precise instruments and highly rational procedures to uncover the meaning and processes of very unique, imprecise qualities, possessing none of the discursive or logically sequential order that is brought to bear on them. Nor is there more than a cursory understanding that the tools of investigation usually get in the way of the investigator, more often than not, either changing that which is being investigated, especially if it is of a volatile, subjective nature, or that rather inappropriate and foreign conditions are being imposed upon the examined subject. Art and its educational extensions may possess little of formal structure or objective reliability such as mathematics or grammar possess. They do not lend themselves to external analysis and logical patterning which may then be transferred as a contained body of knowledge. If there is a logic in art it is intrinsic, dependent upon its own laws of aesthetics, emotions, expression and imagination—laws different from and probably much more spontaneous than the rigorously formulated concepts of science and scientific methodology. If I may quote from a recent report on curriculum evaluation that I wrote: "Perhaps it would be helpful to say that the arts (and probably most of the humanities) lead to understanding rather than knowledge; that they assert their truths or their realizations, rather than providing information which attempts to persuade or to coerce no matter how altruistic the goal; that the arts contain intrinsic values which are manifest within the created forms and as they are presented, rather than being conveyor belts leading to greater and hortatory truths; that they enhance existence by creating immediate meaning even though this may be subject to personal interpretations rather than establishing an aggrandizement of objective facts"—facts that must be made to fit into conceptualized designs or intellectual pigeon holes. Art is a symbolic transformation of human feeling, not a mechanical response to experience. Genuine art grows out of a viable and changing relationship to life, not out of any deterministic equation. It devours the world as a basis of motivation moving the heavens for inspiration and the more hellish pits of introspection. It consumes all cultures and eventually transcends the self in creating the perceptual forms of experience. To achieve this it engages the imaginative resources of the mind and the spirit, building on fantasy and intuition as well as upon a judgmental intellect. The wonder and delight, the pain and frustration a child feels when he or she is honestly engaged in artistic experience is not too far removed from the more intense conditions I have noted that occur in mature artists. They may seem remarkably romantic and as evanescent fancies when compared to the cold turkey talk of behavioral characteristics, subject disciplines, curriculum theorizing and program planning in the schools. But I would venture to say that any teacher who attempts to create a climate for art without such imaginative philosophical spinning falls far short of an honestly expressive or appreciative experience.

Individual Insight as Standardized Procedures

Given the pervasive influence of technology in the larger social arena and the reliance upon a mechanical, sequential stimulus-response viewpoint, education has followed suit. The procedures may be more complex and sophisticated than I have noted. Education now also relies upon the specialists and the experts, upon an immense body of investigators in the social sciences to tell it what is right and what is wrong, what works and what doesn't and the emphasis is quantitative. The individual teacher becomes more and more merely a technician in an intricate and overblown apparatus, an increasingly less important consideration. The coming flood of mechanical devices and objectively regularized procedures in education is appalling to think of. Art education in taking to the hills of psychology and the other social sciences during the last two decades, has readily found many of its guideposts in correlation coefficients and significant deviations. It is not only the substance of subject area and the mechanics of method that are studied, prodded and evaluated, but the child and all of his dreams as well, especially doting on the social formulation of values through aesthetic means. Yet is the dream, the child or art ever really understood except as it happens in the random contingencies of existence. I do not mean to attack model methodologies categorically. Even if I wanted to it would be an impossibility to lead the white charger up against a force field that is cunningly invisible but impenetrable all the same. And I do feel that all manner of examination, investigation, hypothesizing and experimenting are valid, provided the values of the object being researched are not violated. Much information has resulted from the research that has been carried on so far, though I would continue to question the unity of insight and the permanence of any of the recommendations. I suppose it is the instrumental direction of much of research in education that I object to and its inherent standardization—the fact that too many investigations do not question the amoral or simplistic context within which they operate, the violence they do to the unique and interpretive forces of living or the easy acceptance of pie-in-the-sky values, indiscriminately sprinkled on everyone's educational meal, like salt.

As an example, educators do not fully inquire into the correctness of social science as a tool in itself, but accept it unhesitatingly as a supposedly objective and efficient instrument that may achieve contrary yet desirable subjective results. Or they confuse the means of investigation with ends creating a "myth of methodology." They are not willing to accept the possibility that some research forces the individual or that which he creates, to be regarded as only one subordinate instrument in an imposed grand design of human nature, or conversely, as fractured and fragmented qualities which have almost no bearing to their role in a fully operating and whole experience.

A favorite in art education is the proliferating beliefs that stem from relating creativity and the appreciation of art to democracy. There are the readily accepted tenets that every child not only deserves but needs the experience of art, that it promotes fraternity and democratic sentiments, that it is the obligation of culture to find those common denominators of form and fancy so that the pleasures of art are bestowed upon one and all, that art is the implied panacea for personality problems, and so on. Then the researchers go out and research so as to create these truths. All well and good. But are they really involved with art, with genuine aesthetic symbols or is all that glitters in their mind not gold? Are they kneading and shaping both art and student behavior to conform to the external dictates of what is convenient for culture? Does the art experience really lead to democracy? Should everyone be primed to become Sunday painters and armchair aesthetes? Or from the other end, we may ask if art should be imposed along with the British Minister in charge of England's arts' development who said, "We do not mean to foist Beethoven and Brecht on those whose interest in the arts never gets beyond striptease."

Of course, the enthusiasm, controls and procedures of model methodology on a mass scale may produce an expanded and even vigorous renaissance of art on a common level. But I would be wary. Someone has dubbed psychology as the mechanization of personality; there may be rather undesirable possibilities in the indiscriminate acceptance of those agents of a culture that is itself within the tumult of transition and uncertain of its direction. Some of the smooth metallic or plastic surfaces and the precision of the procedural engineering of technology still give off a tinny tinkle of tinsel. Or they create an awesome and esoteric environment which is decidedly off limits to any but the initiates, and even they have trouble understanding and controlling their creations. Or there is this comment from Herbert Read, one of the most passionately committed of art educators. "It is not a cheerful prospect for the arts, though there will be more and more artists in the sense of the word used by the entertainment industry. It will be a gay world. There will be lights everywhere except in the mind of man, and the fall of the last civilization will not be heard above the incessant din." It would behoove teachers to assess the processes and values of the instruments that are put at their disposal. No doubt, it is necessary to learn from psychology and sociology whatever the teacher can, and to pursue whatever new possibilities they provide in a serious way. However, it is just as necessary to develop a perspective on the techniques of the social sciences and to appraise their worth for education in the classroom. For art education, particularly, it is the actual, not the simulated accomplishments, that are to be judged. Otherwise, not only may we get dubious findings but we may begin to ask irrelevant questions and find that we act upon rather inappropriate assumptions and answers that are dangerous as well as beside the point. The aspiration of integrating the hard dynamism of technology with the nuanced properties of art may come to naught. The visions of Lewis Mumford or Gyorgy Kepes, who would integrate the two areas, may remain just that —fanciful visions.

I fear I have dwelt too long on one aspect of the cultural influences effecting education in the arts. Technology is, however, the fundamental source of most of the other influences; they are secondary and stem from this dynamic but uncertain center of activity. If education is to foster any creative and humanly dimensioned relationship to technology, its administrators, but most particularly its practitioners, the teachers, have an obligation to examine the contexts within which they function. They have to come to grips with the conditions that are shaping their own personalities, that of their students as well as those of the environment. The teachers of art have an extraordinary amount of understanding to do and an especial responsibility. In a way, they are working against the grain. They have to be in a position to comprehend not only the fundamental techniques of technological change but those secondary considerations I mentioned so as to alter the drift to standardization and reassert the worth of creative speculation and the making of art, even at the expense of efficiency.

POPULAR SIGHTS AND SOUNDS

There is not sufficient time to do more than mention some of these current conditions that technology has spawned. One is the development of a mass or popular culture that is manufactured and imposed upon the citizenry. With the endless inventiveness and improvisation resulting from the new world's pragmatic spirit wedded to "the goose that lays the golden egg" of applied science there is a never ending production of sights and sounds that assault the eye, ear and mind. The production is primed at the profit pump. The commercial motivations have to be recognized. Much though there may be of a charm, homiletics and gaiety, it should be recognized that the sights, sounds and shapes of popular culture are essentially of a conforming and superficial character, when they are not of cheap and shoddy appearance. They do not arise out of the necessities and virtues of daily living and vernacular considerations as did folk art, but are put on the market primarily for other than aesthetic or expressive purposes. The resulting "museum without walls" and plethora of commercialized and televised forms create a bold but battering imagery that forces its way into the collective consciousness, finally creating a narcotized or vitiated response. The overwhelming ubiquity of these forms invade every nook and cranny and make themselves felt in dramatic and direct ways in education as well as in the home. Certainly, popular culture has a profound influence upon art education, either in the manner by which teachers incorporate it in their teaching or rebel against it.

COMMUNION AS COMMUNICATION

One other influence I would like to mention, that which Marshall McLuhan has made us so aware of, the new understandings of mass communications which are central to the cultural and educative processes. Just as the printing press redirected cultural behavior and educational procedures some five hundred years ago, so does McLuhan indicate the drastic changes in outlook which will occur, if they have not already, with the advent of electronic circuitry and simultaneous exposure to information from many sources and on many levels. His thinking, though esoteric and uneven, may well have a vital bearing upon the development of education in the arts.

At the very least, even with tongue in cheek, his statement "the medium is the message" has an enormous import for art educators, interested as they should be in symbol formation and the dissemination of feelings and ideas. Beyond this basic concept there is the evergrowing public for the culture of art, geometrically increased as the various media of communication spread. Educators hope that their students will join this vanguard public, as the critic Harold Rosenberg refers to the developing group. Yet one can question the experiences these people seek and the environment they create. Too often, it is the news about the artist that satisfies rather than the work of the artist; there is a strong element of the entertainment mentioned by Herbert Read and of considerations that are more a mockery of art than a realization of it. The artist may be more isolated than ever, despairing of relating to a community of interests akin to his own. The syrupy adulation and the frenetic interest may be the new Philistinism that swallows its victims whole instead of rejecting them. Such a context could hardly be an auspicious one within which to develop healthy natural attitudes toward art through education, unless educators sense the tenor of the times.

I have had no time to mention any of the contemporary happenings in art—to the significant but sometimes uncomfortable and puzzling occurrences that have been dynamically present for a century now. There is the swing between subjectivity and impersonality, the existential cry of anguish against the cool controlled design arrangement, the movement from a sensate to an ideational art, the harkening to the voice in the street and the complementary obscurity of very private and abstract creations, the rejection of the technological context by some artists and its enthusiastic embrace by others, the transient "isms" that have flooded the scene and the passionate groping for artistic truth that characterized all committed artists, the exploration of new media, new materials, new content, no content and old content: film, light creations, found objects, happenings and what have you. Teachers of art particularly below college level, have only been on the periphery of this vast galaxy of creative fervor and artistic expression. It is time that they partook of it in more vital ways, thus carrying some of its immense drive into the class. Though it may be inconsistent, discontinuous, upsetting and obstreperous, it is by far a more pertinent guide to the magic of art than is a library full of statistical charts.

SETTING THE CONTEXT

My final point and the one I have implied all along is that the art experience in education as elsewhere has worth primarily as it is an activity or a condition that is sufficient unto itself. It cannot be regarded as an instrument for purposes other than its own. It is not essentially a tool for psychological rehabilitation or catharsis, personality formation, sheer fun and frolic, cultural aggrandizement or social development. All of these elements are, of course, present in art, but they function as inherent aspects of the processes of art, rather than as narrowly defined characteristics. We need not gild the lily in order to appreciate and benefit from its loveliness. In fact, to extract any one of the isolated attributes of art and to emphasize its nature is probably to thwart its full operation. Art may be said to exist in a state of grace, to possess an ineffable sense of unity and meaning when it is created or perceived with passion, sympathy and an understanding that is more intuitive than deliberately analyzed. We all know what happens to a poem after its analytical dissection and fragmentation. Its symbolic magic evaporates even as an intellectual delineation of the parts is recognized. I do not mean to discount the need of basic analysis, intellectual organization and critical study that should occur during learning in the arts. I would suggest, however, that the critical logic and internal structure of the arts are distinctly different from that of the discursively rational. They require another order of comprehension and procedure. In order to arrive at this kind of comprehension of form and insight into aesthetically symbolic processes, it is necessary that art be accepted as an independent condition. Art has to be recognized as possessing intrinsic qualities which though they may intimately mesh into other "universes of discourses" to use Cassirer's phrase, nevertheless, have a life of their own and give us their own truth. Similarly, the experience of art for students has as its fundamental goal the revelation of self.

Consequently, it is an obligation for art teachers and for education in general to sense and respect the autonomy of art. Without such autonomy there can be no genuine realization of the expressive symbolism or the perceptual significance of art. And in order to understand the character of art as an intrinsic quality, it is necessary to understand the influences that play about it. To reiterate, I would suggest that this understanding will be more fully and honestly achieved if the teacher of art will apply unadorned, the inherent attributes and processes of art to the problem no matter how troublesome and diffuse they may appear rather than relying too heavily on some foreign instrument. The resolution will probably go beyond the simple mechanics of an equation and enter into the realm of art itself. It may even be the means of reintegrating the artistic elements of the environment with those of the social and the technological, creating as much a homogenous culture as man is capable of. For no matter how much we value art, we cannot believe that it will exist in isolation from the other factors of culture, though it requires its own means of nourishment. Conversely, there can be little of a shared human happiness and of personal satisfaction in a technological social machine devoid of the creative mystery of geninue art, without the beauty Mr. Johnson calls for. The two opposing qualities, the objectivity of technics as against the subjectivity of art, can achieve a synthesis in the best interests of man only if there is a mutual sense of respect and understanding, a harmony of contraries and it is the art teacher's great vocation to achieve exactly that.

Advancing Art in U.S. Public Schools

JOHN GOODLAD

The neglect of art in our schools should be a national disgrace; that it seems not to be generally considered such is, indeed, a disgrace. I am not about to launch into a passionate plea for art in the schools; obviously, this is not the place for it.

My own position with respect to art in the schools can be stated quite simply. I believe that art in the curriculum is at least as important as mathematics, and that art holds potentiality for being a satisfying pursuit for a large number of the people inhabiting tomorrow's world.

But I am not going to harangue you in the name of art for our schools; instead, I am going to attempt to do four things. First, I shall identify some present and anticipated curriculum developments in the schools. Second, I shall speculate on the possibilities for art education in these curricular projections. Third, I shall review briefly some aspects of the present status of art in our schools; and finally, I shall make a simple proposal—it may turn out to be a deceptively simple proposal—for strengthening the position of art in schools.

A year ago, in addressing a general session of the Association for Supervision and Curriculum Development Conference, I attempted to trace three cycles of curriculum development, from the 1950's to 2000 A.D. Let me briefly summarize what I believe these three cycles to be. Two of them are projections; one is of the present. There is still underway, quite vigorously, in the United States, a curriculum reform movement that seems to have started in the early 1940's at the University of Chicago with the work of a small group of mathematicians who believed that the fundamental concepts of mathematics were not being adequately treated in secondary education. Some of these ideas were extended by Max Beberman and his associates in the University of Illinois Mathematics Project, the first materials of which appeared about 1951. Since then, we've entered into a curriculum reform movement emphasizing mathematics, the sciences, and foreign languages; a curriculum reform movement in which both the *ends* and *means* of schooling are derived from the academic subjects. The place of these subjects is defined separately in the curriculum: not social studies but history, geography, and economics; not science but biology, chemistry, and physics. Clearly, this has been a discipline-centered curriculum reform movement. It is still vigorous, but already we are realizing that this reform movement is not likely to be the predominant one in the period from now to about 1980.

Reprinted by permission of the author from *Art Education: Journal of the National Art Education Association*, Vol. 21, No. 2, February 1968., pp. 6–8. Reprinted also with permission from the publisher.

Strengthening the existing subjects of the curriculum as separate disciplines does not in itself constitute an adequate answer to our curriculum problems. During the next 15 years or so, we are likely to see a curriculum reform movement emphasizing what might be called the "comprehensive curriculum," a total curriculum in which an effort will be made to fit together subjects which previously have been treated separately. This movement in turn will begin to wane, I think, by 1980 or 1985, and a new set of considerations will begin to enter in, considerations leading to a humanistic curriculum. There will be a shift, I believe, from the important question of what knowledge is of most worth to the even more basic question of what kinds of human beings we wish to produce. We are not now giving much attention to this question at local, state, or federal levels of educational responsibility.

A curriculum properly focused on human interests and human values is a humanistic curriculum, hopefully to be achieved to considerable degree by the turn of the century. I have been told that I am far too pessimistic—that this curriculum will be achieved far earlier. I think, rather, that I am being optimistic, if one reviews where we are today and what humanism in the educative process means.

Here, then, are three overlapping cycles of curriculum reform: 1950 to 1970 and beyond—a discipline-centered curriculum reform movement; 1970 to 1980 or '90—a search for the comprehensive curriculum; and then, already beginning, a search for humanistic considerations in the schools.

What do these cycles have to say about art education? The present revisionary cycle in the disciplines grew out of scholarly concern for inadequacies in mathematics and the natural sciences, revealed primarily in tests during and following World War II. This scholarly concern was not paralleled in art education; in fact, my 1962–63 study in school curriculum reform in the United States [1] found only a trace of this kind of concern in art education. My colleagues and I were little more encouraged by our 1965–66 study.[2] There is not yet an innovative curricular thrust in the field. The curricular movement that began in math and science was spurred and financed out of threat to our national status. I have not known any national crisis that led to a renaissance in the arts. Consequently, we cannot look to a national crisis as a basis for curriculum reform and curriculum change in the art field.

The kind of curriculum reform that has been underway has increased public awareness of mathematics and science. One scarcely picks up a popular magazine these days without finding some reference, for example, to the new math and how important it is that youngsters be exposed soon and substantially. And there have been pleas by subject specialists in these areas for more time in the curriculum, just as there have been pleas for added periods of days or years in the sciences. Does anyone think that the slice for art will be any larger if the school day, or the school week, or the school year is lengthened? I think not. More school time means more curricular time for the well-established fields. The "haves" grow stronger, the "have nots" weaker. During this period, a curriculum dialogue between the scholars of the academic disciplines and the teachers of elementary and secondary education has emerged. If there is such a dialogue of national proportions in regard to the arts curriculum, it was to us in our studies a well-kept family secret. The need for mathematics and the natural sciences as now perceived by the American people approaches the level of cultural imperatives. At best, we can only say that art is a cultural elective.

In summary, then, art has not fared well in the schools during this recent period of curriculum reform. Cycle one has been "strike one" for art in the schools. How shall art fare in cycles two and three? The answer to this question rests in part on the nature of the curriculum reform movement that actually occurs. I have already indicated what I think cycles two and three are likely to be. Cycle two is likely to be one of synthesis. There cannot be 15 or 30 or 45 separate academic disciplines in the kindergarten. There has to be some kind of meaningful synthesis of these various fields. Synthesis is going to be a synthesis of what already is strong in the curriculum. What is weak or left out entirely is not likely to be synthesized: law, political science, psychology, philosophy, and, of course, art. Only a dreamer could be sanguine about the prospective place of art in the curriculum during the next decade.

What about cycle three? On the surface, it would sound as though art will fare better in a search for a humanistic curriculum and, indeed, I believe it will, but this is some time off and will not affect children in today's schools. Furthermore, a generation of young people growing up without adequate involvement in the arts is not likely to be supportive of the arts. And I am not at all sure that tomorrow's adults are going to perceive art as more uniquely humanistic than any other field. Is the teaching of art conducted in such a humanistic fashion that it clearly contributes to humanistic ends? I doubt that art is taught more humanistically than, say, the social studies.

Let me make a few observations about the present status of art in the schools. I concentrate on the elementary level, because here is where the foundation job must be done; here is where the beginning must be made.

My colleagues and I have just finished a nationwide survey of what is going on educationally in the classrooms enrolling children in the first four years of school, kindergarten through grade three. What is the situation? First, we encountered largely self-contained classrooms; that is, classes in which teachers were attempting to be all things to all people. If art was being taught, by and large it was being taught by a classroom teacher prepared primarily in English or one of the social sciences. In some of the school systems we visited, there were badly overworked itinerant art specialists, usually traveling from school to school, spending far too much of their valuable time on the road instead of in classrooms. Much of their time and energy was being expended on activities other than art. Second, we found limited instructional resources in this golden age of instructional materials. We found primarily textbook teaching, a prescribed text being taught in a prescribed manner. Materials included one or two or three easels for a class of 30, some watercolor paints, some small pieces of paper—conditions shockingly similar to those that I experienced in elementary school many years ago.

Further, we discovered that the standards for performance too frequently were set in advance by the teachers. For example, approved work tended to be neat and orderly, as prescribed by the teacher. This situation is not conducive to the free expression we might hope to elicit from children. We did discover, however, much uninhibited art production in the kindergarten, often in spite of impoverished conditions so far as materials and equipment were concerned. However, creative expression appeared to drop off rapidly in the upper elementary years until, by the fourth grade, it had become virtually applied art, primarily in the social studies or sciences. When we queried the teachers, we found, indeed, they taught "art," but largely to enhance some other field. It was not often art for its own sake, art designed to teach the structure and form of the field itself. Clearly, the kind of teaching now being attempted in math, science, and some other fields, teaching designed to develop understanding of the discipline, is not widespread in the art programs of elementary education.

I noted above that expression in art seems to fall off rapidly in the upper elementary years. Much of the open expression evidenced in kindergarten disappears. Sometimes this phenomenon is explained as a factor of increased age, sometimes as a natural characteristic of pre-adolescence. I doubt this. I believe, rather, that we fail to cultivate creative potentialities. A trained person on hand to provide the kind of assistance needed could make a profound difference in the artistic expression of these children in the upper elementary years.

What is the solution to this dilemma of the absence or near absence of art in the schools? The solution is a qualified art teacher in every elementary school. The solution is not continued dependence on art supervisors, however useful such individuals may be. Hitherto, we have assumed that the best we can do, given the cost situation, is to provide supervisors in our more prosperous school districts. This I believe is exactly the wrong solution. Under such conditions art education lives always under threatening clouds. Art supervisors are the first to go in a budget pinch because, in the eyes of the public, removing an art supervisor does not reduce the ratio of teachers to youngsters and appears not to profoundly affect what goes on behind the classroom doors.

To provide a course in art education for every elementary school teacher is not a solution either, however laudable this may be from an educative point of view. The problem is organizational in character and demands an organizational solution. A certain percentage of the staff of each elementary school must be specialized in art. For example, one of ten teachers might be an art specialist. A way to do this, *without adding to the costs of schooling*, is to ride the coat tails of a significant organizational innovation. This is team teaching.

Conventionally, an elementary school is organized like an egg crate, with one teacher and 28½ students in each room, according to the national norm. The teachers, by and large, are prepared as generalists or as specialists in English or the social sciences. The production of elementary school teachers in the natural sciences, mathematics, foreign languages, and art is limited. Therefore we should redesign the elementary school to take care of this reality. Further, we should staff an elementary school systematically, not just assign so many teachers from a central pool.

Suppose we were to take a small school of 300 youngsters and 10 teachers and instead of 10 rooms of 30 pupils each, set up four clusters of 75 children each, with a social studies or English teacher in charge of each group. We have six positions still to fill in a 10-teacher school. A new opportunity for staffing is created.

We moved into such a plan a little at a time at UCLA's University Elementary School. A kindergarten teacher retired and the other kindergarten teacher was given her choice of ways to use the extra salary. We discussed two possibilities: (1) buying all the materials she could use (this would mean she would have 50 children to teach); and (2) hiring one or several part-time teachers. Her final choice was to hire two part-time people, who were then placed under her supervision. Her plan was to teach as a team. She requested that part of a wall be knocked out between the two rooms to enable the students to move back and forth readily. We found we were no longer thinking in terms of two groups of 25 children with one teacher each; we were thinking, instead, of 50 youngsters and two salaries to be distributed according to our plans.

Now, let us return to our hypothetical elementary school of four groups of 75 students each. In charge of each group is what I call a horizontal coordinator, which means an individual whose responsibility is to envision the relationships in the whole program, to see how the parts fit together, to assure that departmentalization does not creep in. I could add one and one-half teachers to each group of 75 and let each team of two and one-half teachers work out team procedures. Or, better, I can add what I call a vertical coordinator, a precious specialist in art. I can then add additional vertical coordinators in other fields: those hard-to-get fields in which we might well hope for one teacher in 10. For a time during the day, my horizontal coordinator would be joined by this vertical coordinator in art, a person who not only understands art but who sees the curriculum in its entirety throughout the school, who works with the children from their early years to the later years in school. When this art teacher comes into the room, the other teachers don't leave; the art teacher becomes the "head" teacher, coordinating the art programs with other teachers assisting. In conventional classrooms, when the art specialist comes in, the regular teacher usually disappears. How are we going to impress on the conventional wisdom of the teaching profession the importance of art unless we involve them in an ongoing program, planned vertically throughout the school.

Through team teaching, then, specialists in fields of short teacher supply are provided for each elementary school. If we are really serious about the importance of art, we must settle for nothing less than a resident art teacher in every elementary school.

In summary, we have a disadvantaged curriculum; it does not consistently and substantially include art. We have disadvantaged schools throughout the United States; few of them, very few of them, include resident art teachers. Curriculum change in tomorrow's world will not automatically take care of these two problems: the disadvantaged curriculum and the disadvantaged school. The problem, it appears to me, is largely organizational and political. We are not going to change the situation by impassioned pleas for more art in the schools because we do not yet have a generation of citizens who are believers; nor do we have a generation of teachers who are believers. They are not prepared in art, they are not prepared in music. Not enough of them see the critical importance of such fields.

Since the problem is, then, in my judgment, largely organizational and political, I have proposed a solution that is largely organizational and political. No doubt, in the process, I have lost home votes from art supervisors who believe that I am out to do away with them. Not at all. Nor am I proposing additional cost to school systems. Rather, I am proposing to take a fraction of the total number of teachers to be assigned to the schools anyway and to be systematic about assuring that one or more in each school is thoroughly prepared in the field of art. Finally, I propose that these specialists be made available throughout the school, from top to bottom, by means of the innovation known as team teaching. By the simple expedient of a resident art teacher in every school, we could revolutionize the teaching of art. And by revolutionizing the teaching of art, we might well enhance significantly the quality of living and the character of our culture.

REFERENCES

1. John Goodlad, *School Curriculum Reform in the United States*. New York: Fund for the Advancement of Education, 1964.
2. John Goodlad (with Renata von Stoephasius and Frances Klein), *The Changing School Curriculum*. New York: Fund for the Advancement of Education, 1966.

Quality Education and Aesthetic Education

HARRY S. BROUDY

In the last decade we have become familiar with the slogans of quality in education or excellence in education. What criteria do people have in mind when they use this slogan?

1. Quality education is the kind that the social elites give their children. For example, if the 400 best families in the United States want a program of liberal studies for their children, then quality education means liberal studies. If the 400 wanted their children to study archery and horseback riding—as they have on occasion—or ichthyology, then these subjects would define excellence in education. This criterion is closely related to the particular schools the elites' children attend, so that attendance at these schools certified one as having a quality education, regardless of what he has been taught there. Thus, the attendance by children of the elite at certain private secondary schools is regarded by C. Wright Mills as perhaps the most significant single factor in the unity and the persistence of the social elites in this country.

The only really important challenge to this criterion was Progressive Education which, in the name of quality as well as equality, dared, on principle, to challenge the type of schooling provided in the schools being attended by the social elites. But the challenge was more in theory than in practice. Despite the Eight Year Study, for example, very few of its implications were implemented in high schools. The comprehensive high school was not really a challenge to elite secondary education, but rather a way of providing under the same roof a less expensive imitation of it to the college-bound, and some other kind of study to youngsters who, for one reason or another, didn't take to the academic subjects. We satisfied our ideal of equality by providing a secondary schooling for everyone, but not of the same quality for everyone. The public comprehensive high school embodied the same contradictions as the social order itself.

I am not saying that the elite secondary schooling or the college versions of it were not good on other criteria as well. On the contrary, elites, if they survive, are not stupid, and what they consistently prefer probably has some shrewd, albeit not always explicit justification. They are no more stupid about education than about power and money.

However, other criteria don't matter too much; the elite take their own standards for granted; aping the elite makes it unnecessary to having standards of one's own. Among the multitudes of parents who are panting to have their

From a paper presented at "Great Speaker Series," Department of Public Instruction, Harrisburg, Pa., April 25, 1968. Reprinted by permission from the author and the Department of Public Instruction, Harrisburg, Pa.

children enter Ivy League Colleges, not one in a thousand has the vaguest notion as to why these colleges are better for their sons and daughters than a half a hundred other colleges. Since 1957, many public school educators have become equally uncritical, basing their judgments of quality in education on programs that are to be found in schools labeled "prestigious," or sponsored by people from prestigious institutions. Thus, quality in education and in life becomes what some "in" group says it is.

2. Another criterion of quality of excellence is scholarly expertise. Men whose major occupation it is to be scholars in a special domain of knowledge, e.g., geography, sociology, physics, Byzantine culture, etc., develop a set of criteria by which to judge the qualifications of their co-workers and their scholarly products. This is the academic specialization. It is one of the tenets of American educational philosophy that it is good for everyone to be a specialist. In non-academic life the principle of the division of labor sees to it that most of us are specialists of one sort or another, and quality consists in being acknowledged by our peers as being competent in that speciality.

On this view of quality, schooling is good to the extent that what is taught in the schools approximates in content, method, and mood that which experts judge as good. Good geography is what the professional geographer judges to be good, and good cooking is what the expert chef says it is, and so on down the line. Many of the curriculum changes since 1957 have used this criterion, so that the "good" physics curriculum, for example was designed by "real" physicists not educationists. Collaboration with the discipline experts in curriculum construction became a sign or criterion of quality, and lack of it a sign of the opposite.

Clearly, this is a valid criterion, indeed about the most valid that we have, *so far as the content within a given domain of knowledge is concerned.* Nobody in his right mind wants children taught inaccurate physics or inaccurate anything else. Unfortunately, we do not carry this argument into the domain of value. There, too, is room for the connoisseur, the expert. His judgements, so far as the school is involved, presumptively takes precedence over other judgments. I shall return to this point when considering the norms of aesthetic education.

The difficulty with the expertise criterion is its narrowness, which is also its strength. It does not follow that what is a good education for the prospective expert or specialist is the same as that designed for nonspecialized use of the knowledge, e.g., the use of chemistry by a chemist as against its use by a lawyer, a business man, or a housewife. Furthermore, it does not follow necessarily that having determined what is good chemistry for either the generalist or the specialist, the way it should be organized for instruction is automatically prescribed. For the order of instruction and learning is not the same as the order of discovery and development within an academic discipline. It is, therefore, quite possible for good chemists not to be experts on the teaching of chemistry. This, indeed, is the main point of dispute between the subject matter specialists and the educationists. Good sense points to the need for active collaboration between them, but *as equals*. There is collaboration, but, unfortunately, not too often between equals. Nor does it follow that good chemistry + good physics ± good literature + . . . add up necessarily to a good education or a good life.

3. Finally, quality in education means that sort of schooling which develops or promises to develop the individual's potential for high-grade human living. This meaning is in the minds of those who argue that all-round education, liberal education, or general education is needed to produce self-realization and self-actualization. They believe that that education is good which leads men on to virtue (the peculiarly human excellences)—justice, temperance, courage, and the unity of them into the great virtue of wisdom. Wisdom is the use of the best knowledge available to make judgments about truth, of goodness, and of beauty. In practice, the cultivation of the virtues constitute the good character and the life style that we call eminently human.

Clearly, these three meanings of quality in education can be related. Education for virtue develops the powers of man for truth, goodness, and beauty, but the materials used for this purpose have to be selected on the basis of what experts of one kind or another, including educational experts, say. Elitehood hopes to be justified by the virtue which its type of schooling has developed in generations of pupils, and this schooling, too, might turn out to be what the experts in various domains of study had approved. As for the criterion of expertise, it might justify itself first by pointing to the good consequences it has produced, but also by asking what other practical criterion —within a given domain of activity—is available to the schools.

Yet our public schools have been unable to unify these criteria. They have shrunk from hoping to provide education for virtue to *all our children*, thus secretly acquiescing to the very dubious claim of elitehood, namely, that virtue is the prerogative of a special class. They have accepted the principle of expertise in the subjects taught for the intellectual virtues but not for the practical—in the cognitive but not the evaluational domains of schooling.

To put it differently, our schools have been concerned and partly successful in the dimension of truth; they have been concerned and quite unsuccessful in the dimension of goodness, and they have been neither much concerned nor very successful in the dimension of the beautiful. To the degree that these are *different* domains of experience but required for human excellence, this imbalance is fatal to quality education. It will be the contention of the remainder of this paper that the balance and quality can be restored by attention to the aesthetic dimension of life and of schooling.

THE ROLE OF THE AESTHETIC IN LIFE

By the aesthetic dimension of life I mean that part of experience concerned with colors, sounds, textures, shapes, and images, i.e., with the way things look, sound, and feel to our perception and to our imagination. In aesthetic experience, attention is drawn to the appearance of things in nature or created by art, and this appearance is interesting on its own account—not because it leads to something else or because it comes from something else. *This* face, *this* shape, *this* gesture, *this* dramatic episode, *this* line in the poem is savored as a particular and for itself. Scientific knowledge, by contrast, is concerned with general laws, and practical life is dominated by finding means for this or that end. Both use particulars as means to ends beyond themselves.

Another characteristic of aesthetic experience is that whatever meaning or quality we experience is seen or heard or felt as being in the object, not in ourselves. The loneliness of the pine tree is seen as being *in the picture*, and the sadness of the music is heard as *being in the music*. Whatever may be the cause of this objectification, that's the way we experience it *as*, i.e., it has a phenomenological objectivity.

Third, the aesthetic experience or the aesthetic object in whatever form or medium, is never strictly true literally. We say that there is a figurative or imaginative or metaphorical element in it. Art, it has been said, makes the familiar seem a little strange. But, in surrendering literal scientific meaning, the aesthetic object gains other types of meanings—often very complicated and almost never translatable into the literal language of common experience. For example, the image of blood is at one and the same time a symbol of life-giving and life-destroying; of bravery and of cruelty. The inner surgings and rhythms of music do not literally describe anything one can find in nature, but they convey directly the images of motion within the movements of human emotion.

I do not propose to explain, even if I could, how or why certain forms of objects are seen or heard as human-import-messages. The fact is that the black swirling clouds are *seen* as ominous and not as the rain, wind, and wreckage that might result from a tornado. The chin is *seen* as stubborn, not as: "Here is a man hard to convince." Import messages, in aesthetic form, are metaphors referring only obliquely to what they are reporting. Or, if you like, they are deceptively clear. For although the lonesome pine is clearly a pine tree, just as clearly it is not lonesome. Aesthetic import messages are patterns of sound or color or movement that we recognize as relevent to human experience, as, for example, strong black strokes in a Rouault painting or the agitated coloring of a Van Gogh. Relevant for what and in what way we are not told, and often we cannot say. That the common man reacts in this genuinely aesthetic way to many objects in his environment, natural and contrived is, I believe, incontrovertible. Experience is one part explication to 99 parts intimation.

I would point to the obvious fact that the fabric of the common man's experience is, to a large extent, aesthetic. Not only is he often absorbed in the appearance of objects, but he not infrequently experiences what the aesthetician says he should: viz., an awareness of "significant form," or "emotion recalled in tranquility," or "archetypal memories," or "repressed

wishes," or "essential natures," or many other things that aestheticians say one experiences or should experience during the aesthetic encounter. What he does not know is that this is what the experience is to be called.

Indeed, the common man takes the aesthetic dimension of life almost too seriously. He tends to rely on aesthetic cues overmuch for knowledge and appraisal. Stubbornness, for example, is not reliably predicted by the conformation of the chin, and the "Anxious face" may be the result of astigmatism. As our scientific knowledge grows, we should rely less on aesthetic clues for weather prediction and more on the weather bureau, and presumably we should rely more on marriage bureaus and computers, and less on our aesthetic hunches in choosing life partners. We are still a long way from being able to dispense with these aesthetic hunches altogether; even the scientific physician notes that the patient does not *look* well, and long before tests are administered and references examined, we size up prospective employees by their appearance.

It ought also to be noted that the common man will often pay a premium for the appearance of appliances and automobiles even when the ornaments or the design does not enhance their utility. As mass-produced objects approach equality in utility per unit of price, appearance becomes a factor in consumer choice. Aesthetic qualities thus achieve economic value on their own merits.

Even if what has been said about the extent and genuineness of aesthetic activity in the common man is granted, one could still raise two important questions. One is, if aesthetic experience is already functioning so freely and well, why bother devoting formal study time and money to it? The second: if aesthetic activity is not a reliable clue to knowledge and action, why should a society bother to cultivate it? Why should it not, on the contrary, diminish its role to providing the private delight that is its own jusification? But this private delight people are already achieving without much formal training, so why the fuss about aesthetic education?

The answers to these questions depend, it seems to me, on the role of art in the culture of the people; in its role as an instrument of social direction and possible social control. This, in turn, depends on the way art operates on individual motivation. So to these questions I now turn.

Perhaps the most important factor in this connection is that value models are so potent in shaping the aspirations of the young. When a way of life or a life-style is translated into an image by art, it becomes a candidate for introjection and identification, or in less technical language, for imitation.

Each age has its own success formula; its own images of what is beautiful, honorable, manly, womanly; it also has its images of failure and despair. When an epoch, such as ours, cannot come up with viable images of the proper life styles we have feelings of insecurity and rebellion—a break up of the common values. For example, no new life style for the contemporary woman has emerged. The roles of wife, prostitute, and casual companion we are familiar with, but what is the proper image for a woman no longer tied to a man and the family structure by the biological link between sex and reproduction? We are in a similar state with respect to war and aggression. Three wars in which the United States has participated in the last 50 years have failed to turn up a convincing heroic life style for the soldier. The glory of battle has been displaced by a dreary resignation. The Vietnam affair is the last stage of disillusionment with military service even among many young men who do not seek to avoid it. That art has been unable to glorify the modern soldier is a surer sign of war's bankruptcy than any logical argument.

If by value education we mean the development of enlightened preferences for one mode of life rather than another, then the role of art in value education is beyond question. It would be hard to overestimate, for example, the potency of the Horatio Alger stories on a generation of American boys, or the novels of Scott Fitzgerald or Sinclair Lewis, on the popular music, fiction, movies and television. I need only mention the James Bond and the Playboy images of life as prime current examples. Yet how does the school utilize the images of value presented by the arts?

Schools do not rely on the mass media, even though they carry much scientific information, to teach our children science, or mathematics. Why not? Because there is a system of ideas to be mastered, and one cannot expect the mass media to give *systematic* instruction.

But in the realms of moral and aesthetic value, we seem to rely on the mores of the community and the mass media almost entirely for instruction. And when within that community the mores are really changed, the school flounders and mumbles about social change and middle-class values.

We seem to be in the grip of something like a muscular spasm in which antagonistic muscles keep a limb rigid and its owner in impotent agony. One is that our ills result from our inability or unwillingness to face reality. The other is that there is no way of distinguishing reality from illusion. Are poverty, discrimination, and riots reality or masks for reality?

The scapegoat of this spasm is the middle-class value syndrome, whatever that is construed to be. But is it the values that make the middle class objectionable or is it the holding of them by the middle class that makes the values bad? The public schools are expected to redeem the disadvantaged, but not, presumably, by imposing middle-class values and demands upon them. But if one asks in what way the disadvantaged are disadvantaged, we are told they lack the means to achieve what seems suspiciously like middle-class values. Now, I think that one can with some consistency hold that class is the criterion of value, as I believe the Marxists do. Or one can maintain that there is a criterion that transcends class and cultural peculiarities. Finally, one can hold to a denial of all value criteria. The school seems to be trying to ride all three horses at once. This makes for an interesting event in the circus, but it makes a circus of the school's efforts in value education.

QUALITY IN AESTHETIC EDUCATION

The problem of quality, both in life and education, therefore, comes down to the possibility of systematic instruction and expertise judgment in the realm of feeling. Today the masses are direct consumers of art, and paying the piper entitles them to call the tune. The taste of the people does become the voice of God as far as the managers of the mass-entertainment media are concerned. Masses of men possessing political power with feelings shaped only by mass media, are as explosive a threat to rational democracy as a people illiterate in science. Considering how closely action and feelings are connected aesthetic illiterates are more dangerous than intellectual ones.

But what does it mean to become aesthetically literate? What can schools do systematically to produce enlightened cherishing, the cultivated forms of feeling?

Aesthetic Sensitivity

First of all, schools can systematically develop aesthetic sensitivity meaning thereby:

a. sensitivity to sensory differences in the work of art,
b. sensitivity to formal properties in the work of art,
c. sensitivity to technical features in the work of art, and
d. sensitivity to expressiveness in the work of art.

Each art medium has its own sensory qualities that are used by the artist to create images which are "interesting to perception": sound patterns, visual shapes, color patterns, textures, gestures, images of all kinds. The connoisseur is the person to whom little differences make a big difference. The first step on the road to aesthetic connoisseurship is, therefore, the sharpening of sensitivity to differences in the sensory manifold exhibited by a work of art. Training is this phase of aesthetic experience is certainly possible and almost prosaically straightforward.

By sensitivity to the formal properties of a work of art I mean the ability to discern and react to patterns of composition, themes and variations, balances, similarities, and the other characteristics comprehended under design. These matters are of first importance to the artist but are often unnoticed by the naive perceiver. Yet sensitivity to formal properties can be improved by instruction.

Little needs to be said about sensitivity to the technical aspects, because when performance is the goal of instruction, technique usually receives its due. However, when appreciation is the goal, there is a tendency to denigrate technique, as if it detracted from enjoyment. This is arguable, to say the least, and I think it is probably false.

The fourth dimension of sensitivity, namely expressiveness, is more troublesome. By expressiveness I mean that elusive quality by virtue of which some works of art display import, albeit never literally or discursively. When, for example, we see a tree painted with inanimate materials *as* "lonely," then the painting is expressive. That is to say, it expresses something other than the visual outlines of a tree. By some peculiarity of human nature, and perhaps of physical nature as well, it is possible to write a poem which expresses loneliness in words and in symbols which are themselves not lonely. The same applies to such qualities as "strength," "energy," "movement," "sublimity," "serenity," and "grace." It is the business of art to create truthful illusions.

Pedagogically, the problem is whether or not sensitivity to expressiveness can be cultivated. That it exists in most human beings is attested to by the universal tendency of children to perceive things "as" something else. The whole strategy of the fairy tale would back-fire if this were not the case. So strong is this tendency that much of the training during the earlier years is directed toward sharpening the difference between reality and fancy in the child's experience. Having "disillusioned" him, we then have to reverse the process and restore his ability to see images as embodiments of feeling, a more mature and fruitful type of illusion. The artistic imagination is to be distinguished and should be distinguishable from the fancies of the child, the scatterbrain, the drug addict, and the lunatic.

One of the stumbling blocks to sensitivity to expressiveness is the relentless pressure on the child to be literal, factual, and scientifically terse. These are indubitably virtues in modern man, and probably he could not survive without them. But if they do not wholly destroy the aesthetic capacities, they do inhibit the receptivity to the figurative, the imaginative, in short, the aesthetic mode of experience; it becomes increasingly awkward to shift into the aesthetic mood; what was simple and natural for the five-year-old is embarrassing to the twelve-year-old. I feel quite sure that we can improve sensitivity to aesthetic expressiveness, but at the moment I am inclined to let it accrue as a by-product rather than to make it a deliberate goal of instruction.

Aesthetic Skills

For a long time now, the elementary school has been expected to give work in music and in art not only for any enjoyment that pupils might derive from these activities but also to develop skill in the use of these media. One might reasonably expect that pupils by the end of the sixth grade will be able to read music, use the voice, play some musical instrument, have had some experience with paint and crayons, and with the writing of prose and poetry that aspires to literary form. Dramatic skills and skills of the dance are less commonly practiced, although our expectations could extend to these also. We could and should be much firmer in asking the school to live up to these expectations, and be less tolerant of the snitching of the time alloted to these activities for other purposes.

However, whether achieved in the elementary school or elsewhere, achieved they must be, if for no other reason than that they force us to perceive an image in detail. How much performance is needed for authentic appreciation I do not know, but I find it hard to believe that one can see as the painter sees or hear as the musician hears without some effort to translate what is seen into painted surfaces or what is heard into music.

Aesthetic Judgment

In addition to sensitivity and skill, connoisseurship or enlightened cherishing requires aesthetic judgment, for it is in aesthetic judgment that we not only know what we like, but can also attempt at giving reasons for liking it. We approach aesthetic maturity when we can say, "I like this music, but it is not good art," or "This music is good art, but I don't like it." Only God and the aesthetically innocent are spared this discrepancy.

One can think of the aesthetic judgment as taking the form of criticism. I shall not go into the anatomy of criticism.* It will be sufficient to indicate some of its ingredients: classification of an art object by style, period, and the like; formal analysis of the aesthetic features in the work of art; application of some sort of standard to arrive at some reasoned evaluation about each dimension of the work and the total effect of all the dimensions.

Some might say about the teaching of appreciation what T.S. Eliot said about the critic:

So the critic to whom I am most grateful is the one who can make me look at something I have never looked at before, or looked at only with eyes clouded with prejudice, set me face to face with it and then leave me alone with it. From that point, I must rely upon my own sensibility, intelligence, and capacity for wisdom.* *

This was fine for T.S. Eliot, who already had a well-developed sensibility, intelligence, and capacity for wisdom, precisely that which the pupil does not yet have. T.S. Eliot, one must suppose, had already introjected models that guided his aesthetic judgments. To what extent T.S. Eliot developed his own models I do not know, but one can safely wager that however much they were his own, they were modifications of standards that were developed from models espoused by critics from Aristotle on.

The introjection of models brings us back to the question of norms and the propriety of forcing them on the young, but the problem is not fundamentally different in the arts than in other areas of instruction, namely, to find the most economical way of inducting the young into a cultural domain.

Paradigm and Revolution

In every domain there are key concepts, modes of inquiry, standards of evidence, and problems to be solved. This is what I take Thomas Kuhn to

---

* For a convenient collection of discussions of this topic, cf. *Aesthetics and Criticism in Art Education*. Ralph A. Smith, ed., Chicago: Rand McNally, 1966, pp. 299–406.
** T. S. Eliot, *On Poetry and Poets*. London: Faber & Faber, 1957, p. 117, quoted by Jerome Stolnitz in *Aesthetics and Philosophy of Art Criticism*. Boston: Houghton Mifflin Co., 1960.

mean by paradigm science. This is what provides the cognitive map for workers in the domain, and learners have to become familiar with it. In every developing domain there is a frontier that goes beyond the map, and every so often a creative explorer makes it imperative to produce a new map. This is what Kuhn would call a scientific revolution.***

Formal schooling, whatever pedagogical devices it may adopt for purposes of motivation, hopes to make the young familiar with the paradigms of art and science. For this purpose it selects a small sample of those works in each epoch that supplied the models *from which the rules and principles were derived.* These might be classed as (a) summating works, (b) bridging works, and (c) anticipatory works.

By summating work of art, I mean one that is considered by experts as somehow bringing together and brilliantly exemplifying trends that had been developing for a period of time. In philosophy the great *Summae* of St. Thomas Aquinas are regarded as summating works. There is a sense also in which some of the dramas of Shakespeare are regarded as summating works with respect to the Elizabethan era.

By a bridging work, I mean one that contains elements of the past, but also introduces elements quite different from them. I take it that this is the sense in which Herman Melville's novels or T.S. Eliot's poetry or Gustav Mahler's music might be called bridging works. Bridging poems, pictures, and dramas are beloved of historians of art, because they provide grist for the mill that grinds out doctoral theses which are intended (and very often do) to show that what claims to be new really isn't.

Finally, the anticipatory works are those that broke sharply with the tradition of their time, that is, with the then current paradigms. The new seemed strange and weird to the then contemporary taste. Revolutionary music, for example, is a bid to scrap the paradigms and force a new one upon composers. Art experiments are challenges to the paradigm, but there is no way of knowing ahead of time which of the challengers will win the field and which will not last out the decade. About all one can do with contemporary art in aesthetic education is to cultivate a tolerance for experimentation and a sensitivity to whatever aesthetic qualities it may create. Aesthetic sensitivity is as far as the school can go with contemporary art; it can hardly be critical about it, for there are no paradigmatic norms that apply to it. It is the duty of an educated public to harbor the new until it has made or failed to make the grade; the fact that some educated people do not like or enjoy the experiments has nothing to do with their aesthetic duty.

In arguing that the quality of general education will be enhanced by aesthetic education I have relied on the principle that a cultivated taste is as important to this form of feeling and doing as a cultivated knowledge to the form of our thinking. However, aesthetic education is no more primary

*** Thomas Kuhn, *The Structure of Scientific Revolutions.* Chicago: Chicago University Press, 1962.

in general education than art is in life itself. High quality education or excellence in education systematically promotes cultivation of all the human powers.

The good life, not science, not the humanities, not the arts, is the purpose of general education. We justify aesthetic education because aesthetic experience does contribute to well-being in a unique way, by giving aesthetic satisfaction and by intensifying and perhaps illuminating every other mode of experience. It is not the business of a composer to preach over the dead, but his requiem mass may help make death vivid and significant as no verbal account can. Nor do we have to agree with Tolstoy's insistence on the moral import of art in order to appreciate the fact that art can and sometimes does exemplify and communicate aesthetically the shape of feeling appropriate to the great moral problems. The aesthetic, cognitive, moral, and religious experience were originally one, is highly probable; the aesthetic as a distinctive domain is a late development of sophisticated abstraction. So there is something to be said for the common man's instinctive demand that the primordial unity be restored. This sentiment will probably have more weight with educators than with artists, but it has too much weight to be shoved aside.

Enlightened cherishing, of paradigm art at least, blends easily with the other ingredients of general education, and yet contributes something other ingredients cannot. This is the direct apprehension of the images by which the most cultivated people of the past perceived their world. This is not the place to argue about the veridicity of these images, but even creative geniuses cannot escape the images of their time. In reading the *Iliad* we do not read the mind of Homer; we do not communicate with Homer or he with us. But more important, perhaps, in reading Homer aesthetically, we share his images. This way of appropriating the ethos of his or any other epoch is permitted only by the arts, and only serious art allows us to share images with the most cultivated spirits of the epoch. If this does not make an important contribution to general education, much of what we have called civilization has been a mistake.

Light as a Creative Medium

GYORGY KEPES

We know that there is a world outside us because our senses tell us so. The flow of sensations that impinges upon our bodies is crystallized by our nervous systems into sensed patterns. As we establish differences among those sensed patterns, we distinguish such separate units of our surrounding environment

Reprinted by permission from *Design Quarterly*, Vol. 68. Copyright: Walker Art Center.

as earth, people, animals, trees, rocks, tables and chairs, and claps of thunder. As we discover similarities among them, we relate one unit to another, build larger unities, and recognize patterns and harmonies.

The senses of hearing, touch, and smell—important though they may be— are far more limited than vision and give fewer, vaguer, and less essential cues. Vision is basic and prior.

Everything that is seen enters the human eye as a pattern of light qualities. We discern forms in space as configurations of brightness and color. The whole visible world, natural and man-made, is a light world. Its heights and depths, its great outlines and intimate details are mapped by light.

When the artist or designer makes forms, he shapes light and the forms themselves become shapes of light.

Any manipulation of a physical substance is inevitably a modulation of light. Paintings and photographic prints are surface patternings of reflected light. Lantern slides and motion pictures are surface patternings of light that are first transmitted and then reflected. When a sculptor models clay, leaving imprints of his fingers, he is actually modeling with light. Each impression of his hand and tool on the pliant substance directs the traffic of light and shade. The traces of pigment left by the painter's brush are devices to catch a certain part of the light that falls upon the canvas. When a painter spreads different pigments on his canvas, he creates areas of different light reflections and absorptions. These, in turn, arouse through our eyes sensations we call colors. The physiochemical microstructures of the pigments, through selective absorption, modulate the illuminating light into different wave lengths, which we sense as different color qualities.

Every architectural form, every building or group of buildings, regardless of the practical purpose or expressive need that formed it—stability, comfort, economy or symbolic meaning—is a visible form built from differences of light qualities, created by the different hues, textures, opacities, and transparencies of its materials. Without our perception of these patterns of light, our distance sense, our appreciation of the qualities of our wider space would completely disappear and our space would shrink to the reach of our fingertips.

There are four fundamental aspects of physical optics: the rectilinear propagation of light, the rereflection of light, the refraction of light, and the diffraction of light. Of these, the first three are basic to ordinary human experience, and therefore to art and design.

Large or small, simple or complex, the unaided work of a craftsman or the co-operative product of a complex team of men and machines, every material object is ultimately a visible object to which light modulation is fundamental.

Carved wood, hammered silver, cast iron, ancient glass, newfangled plastics, poured concrete, oil-ground pigment, compacted snow, woven-and-cut velvet, cut-and-polished diamonds—each of these is a substance worked into a light modulator with a characteristic mode of distributing light. The structures of substances have a certain light-reflecting or light-absorbing capacity. Technical language calls it "reflectance" or "reflective index." There is a major difference in the amount of light returned from the surface of compacted snow and the surface of velvet fabric. Some of the substances are transparent; each of these is a medium through which a significant amount of the light that falls upon it will travel. Light rays change direction as they pass from a medium of one density into a medium of another density, for they follow a path that will take them through the medium in the minimum of time. The light is said to be "refracted;" and each such substance has a "refractive index." Plexiglass, window glass, and diamond crystals bend light at different angles. (Each, in addition, has a different "dispersive index," for each has the power, although not to the same extent, of breaking up white light into the various color frequencies of which white light is composed.) Let us examine three substances markedly different in structure and the ways they modulate ordinary light which travels in a straight line.

The first of these substances is snow which is made up of tiny transparent crystals. The facets of these crystals are highly reflective, so that, in the mass, snow returns all the light rays that strike it, and it becomes uniformly white. Worked into a sphere and exposed to clear sunlight, it gives us a simple, strong, easily readable form. The sun's rays strike that portion of the snowball's surface which faces them; they travel on past that portion of its surface which is turned away. The snowball is blinding white where illuminated; the rest is in shadow and we read it as a spatial volume, as a solid form, not as a flat disk. This dialogue between the substance and the source of light is the key to the snowball's manifest convexity.

Simple modeling by light and shape of a substance substantially uniform in light reflectance has been the central expressive resource of sculptors, from the men who created statues of gods and Pharaohs in ancient Egypt to Aristide Maillol, Naum Gabo and David Smith. After five thousand years, it is still our most effective means for the unequivocal statement of solid forms. The lesson has not been lost on painters: Giambattista Tiepolo, for example, the great eighteenth-century Venetian, employed such simple means in pen-and-wash drawings of the most dazzling sophistication and virtuoso skill.

The second substance is velvet, a textile loomed of silk or wool, with a soft, plushy nap. In cross section, it consists of tufted rows of threads rising from a firm foundation. When light from some source of illumination falls on the velvet, most of the light rays sift through the gaps between threads and are absorbed. Some light rays collide with the standing threads; after many reflections they return to the surface in spent array. The returned rays have the rich, saturated hue of the velvet itself. The extremely few rays that strike the very tips of the pile are not absorbed; they are reflected back to the eye. These rays have the same color as the source of illumination—white if the source gives off white light—and give velvet its familiar glow. Cut velvet is then a light-trapping substance. Its inner formation modulates light in a variety of ways for this substance is not uniform but varied in light reflectance. The reason for velvet's characteristic texture is its lattice of deep, rich color and soft sheen.

Titian, Rembrandt and Van Gogh are painters who not only depict deep, rich, glowing fabrics but create deep, rich, glowing textures physically, with paint. They did this by creating light-trapping substances, structurally similar to the inner information of velvet. Over a dark, coarsely grained canvas, Titian laid an underpainting in broad, heavy strokes of red and gray, but did not cover the canvas completely. Over the underpainting and the canvas background he placed several transparent layers of glazes and scumbles, light over dark, dark over light. Here and there—in depicting a ruffle, perhaps, or a glimpse of shirt—he placed accents of white, loading the paint rather heavily. Light that falls upon the painting from an illuminating source passes through the layers of glaze, and after having been reflected forward and back from layer to layer, returns, spent, to the surface and to the eye. The few returned rays give the paint the rich, saturated hue of the velvet itself. The whole painting thus becomes a marvelous substance, not uniform but varied in light reflectance which gives such works its characteristic texture, its rich color and soft glow. Rembrandt created a visually similar texture by more direct and freer means. He built the surface of a painting in depth, with grooves and striations and modeled strokes, while Van Gogh laid paint on a canvas thickly, developing a corrugated surface of hills and valleys so most of the oncoming light is absorbed in the hollow depths, sending back saturated color rays but no directly reflected white light. The prominent ridges are the only parts of the surface to reflect white light. The overall effect is of velvety, saturated depth, and the physical structure of his surfaces is an analogue of velvet.

The third substance is a diamond crystal, faceted by the lapidary into a characteristic micro-architectural form. The diamond exceeds all other substances in its power to refract light and almost all others in its power to disperse light. Because of the diamond's refractive power, most of the light rays that fall upon the brilliant do not pass through but are reflected back inside by the clean, smooth planes that bound its mass; they travel round and round inside before escaping to the eye. Because of the diamond's dispersion power, the light rays splinter into all the colors of the rainbow. The fiery, brilliant, flashing concentration of light is poles apart from the light modulation accomplished by cut velvet.

The structures of such substances as snowballs, velvet, and diamond brilliants are paralleled on a larger scale in man-made environments. Men have instinctively recognized and made appropriate use of the light-modulating properties of their building materials, and each such material has a certain light reflectance in accordance with its intrinsic molecular grain. There is a major difference in the amount of light returned from a whitewashed wall and from a deep-stained timber. Each reflectance offers qualities to the eye and rules of the game by which the things made from those substances are read as spatial forms.

Many lands where the sun is bright and the sky deep blue have a simple, strong, convincing architecture that takes full advantage of light reflectance. The indigenous white buildings of the Greek islands, for example, play with sunlight. They stand against an unobstructed sky, from which the dazzling light of the sun pours down. The simple, white forms with their strong masses and lucid geometry, cut into this space-filling, luminous substance; and a crisp, strong counterlight—a shadow—reveals each interception of the oncoming light.

This simple and modest architecture owes its gem-like brilliance to the strong light that falls upon it, yet it owes its legibility not to light alone but to counterlight as well. Because the white surfaces are completely uniform in light reflectance, their spatial multiformity is made clear to us by the variations in the amount of light they receive. Those variations depend upon how the buildings and the forms of which they are composed are oriented with respect to the light source. Surfaces set at right angles to the oncoming light rays receive a maximum amount of light. Surfaces set at an angle greater or less than a right angle receive less than the maximum. And those surfaces set at an angle less than the angle of the light rays themselves receive no light at all because the light rays have been intercepted; they are in shadow. Curved surfaces vary continuously in the amount of light they receive as far as the line at which, if their curvature is strong enough, they receive no direct light at all. Shading thus models the forms, and we read meanings in the shapes and values of shadowed areas: what is straight, what is angular, what is convex, what is concave. Cast shadows, which occur when one form interrupts the light that falls upon another, tell us—through their length, their shape, their sharpness of edge—about the spatial extension of forms: where they are located, what are their dimensions. Cast shadows encode space. All too unconsciously, we decode the messages, and build a simple but very precise vocabulary and grammar of the immense variety of spatial character of the architectural forms.

Architects on the most sophisticated level come back again and again to such simple devices of light modulation. Le Corbusier's chapel at Ronchamps is an impressive contemporary example of clarity and strength of form achieved by limiting the space-enclosing surface to one level of light reflectance.

The spatial world is made legible not only by the distribution of light and shadow, but also by the distribution of pigments. Besides the dark accents which are produced by the nearly total absorption of the light incident to the surface, and white, produced by the nearly total reflection of the incident light, there are visible qualities of the environment we call "colors" which are produced by the unabsorbed light reflected by objects. The visible world is, then, woven for us from these two separate effects, similar in appearance but fundamentally different in physical origin.

If we look around us, we discern spatial areas as combinations of the two modes of light modulation. Sometimes one mode dominates, sometimes the other. When we look at a human face, we see total differences among its dark hair, pale skin, blue eyes, and red lips. These differences are inherent in the pigments, and are produced on a miniature scale of light modulation.

The forms of the head, the sculptural shapes of the cranium, of nose, and chin are given to us by the interplay between the surfaces and the incident light.

For various reasons, artists and designers have emphasized one mode or the other in their expressive work. There are great architectural forms that do not exploit light and shadow, but draw or paint space by means of a lucid structuring of the various materials used to enclose it. Rather than one uniform light-reflecting material, two or more materials are chosen, contrasting in light reflectance. The Katsura Palace in Japan is built, physically and visually, of frankly opposing materials. The key units are the deep, dark wooden timbers and the brilliant, white walls. The Katsura Palace exhibits a crisp, clean contrast of near black and white and a crisp, clean contrast of horizontals and verticals. The dominantly rectangular relation of beam to column is repeated as an optical echo in the dominantly angular relation between white and black. In a manner that resembles the gradual merging of form into form in some Greek island buildings, the angular sense of the black-and-white contrasting forms becomes an intermediate step between the horizontal and the vertical sense of the horizontal-vertical-contrasting forms. The space is read as a sequence of white figures with each area clearly defined by its black boundary lines. A creative decision was made to choose a certain set of information that, at the same time, would reveal a tectonic space and provide a rhythm of areas, directions and sizes; the observer does not take in the work with one steady gaze, but explores the space in the way that a person moving through woods explores the rhythmic interplay between tree trunks and leaves. There is hardly any graduation of tone values.

Our eyes often receive documentary information about forms in space from light that does not come directly from the forms themselves. Photographs, motion pictures and television images are light patterns gathered by a lens and recorded on a photo sensitive emulsion of a fluorescent screen. Every such image is a term in a series of light modulations before and after it reaches the human eye.

The lens of the photographic camera collects light patterns from the environment in a focused image. The photosensitive emulsions on the film register this focused image, first as an invisible latent image, then, after chemical processing, as a visible negative pattern. Then the negative is converted into a positive print—an analogue of the original brightness pattern caught by the camera. Finally, the lens of the eye, the photochemistry of the retina, and the electric signals traveling through nerve and conductors to the brain form the imaged space.

The images formed with the assistance of television are the rear guard of an even longer parade of pattern that begins with an event in space, transformed into electronic signals along a complex route, and ends with an event in our brain.

The brain retains its impression of a light signal, that has entered the eye, for a tenth of a second after the signal disappears. Consequently, if the impressions our eyes receive follow one another at appropriate intervals of time, we perceive a series of such impressions continuously as moving pictures. The television camera scans each pattern of light and shade, dissecting it into some 200,000 separate units. The pattern is then reassembled before our eyes, one unit at a time, as a grid of light signals flashing on and off; the events we see are both simultaneous and successive. Thirty pictures are presented in a second, each made up of 200,000 light units every second. Those thronging impacts are processed by the extremely complex human eye. The retina of the eye has some 400 million cone receptors and is connected to the brain by the optic nerve, a rope of a million fibers. The light signals, now transformed into electrical signals by the optic nerve, are woven by the brain into form, meanings and a sense of spatial depth, and into responses to such visual qualities as proportion, rhythm, and melody of line and tone.

Newer Media and the Teaching of Art

VINCENT LANIER

Time: The very near future.
Class: "The Visual Arts in World Cultures."
Place: Any American high school.

At 10:23, Mr. Dobbs, the art teacher, begins his second lecture to the visual arts lecture group of 30 pupils. (Although the Federal Education Act of 1972 restricted class size to a maximum of 18 pupils, lecture groups of up to 40 students are permissible under the law.) Having dealt with primitive habitations and post and lintel construction in architectural design during the first lecture, he is ready to describe the discovery and uses of the arch as a building principle. As he presents his ideas, he presses the button marked "visual" on his wrist-band instrument panel. The room lights dim and the classroom screen glows with 3-D color images of the Coliseum, the Arch of Titus, the aqueduct of Segovia, etc. The silken tones and fine diction of Richard Burton take over the lecture from Mr. Dobbs with a synopsis of factual data about the structures. At the appropriate moment diagram overlays analyzing the directions of stress appear on the screen. At this point several students tap the photo duplication button on their desk instrument panels: the diagrammatic analysis on the screen in color photocopy form will be a useful illustration in their note book projects. By the end of the lecture session each of the students has selected an individual or small group project for the following study period. Several have chosen programmed sequences presenting architectural history in greater detail, to be viewed on their individual desk

Reprinted by permission of the author and the publisher from *Art Education: Journal of the National Art Education Association*, Vol. 19, No. 4, April 1966, pp. 5–8.

units; some will work together on a series of models of arch-structured build-ings, others on group murals; two younger students have elected to prepare a sound 8mm film on the "Uses of the Arch as a Decorative Motif in our Community." Meanwhile, Mr. Dobbs jots down a reminder to request that film clips from the movie set restoration of the Hadrianic Baths at Lepcis Magna (from the Hollywood epic "Goddesses of the Western World") be stored in the school district computer memory banks. Next school quarter, this lecture will be improved by the extra visuals—though without the god-desses, of course, he tells himself.

Fantasy? Science Fiction? Not at all. Simply one imaginative description, among the many possible, of the consistent application of new media tech-nology to the teaching of art. If we can develop a photosensitive crystal the size of a lump of sugar containing the images of a hundred thousand pages (*Newsweek*, January 24, 1966) there is no reason to regard this projection as far fetched.

Whether or not this is a desirable direction for art education to follow is another question and one which can best be answered by the collective judgment of the profession rather than by an individual. There is no doubt in this writer's mind that the direction noted is not only wholesome, but, indeed, essential to the progress of art education. This opinion, however, may not be universal among us, nor even widespread. For it is not unfair to say that of all the curriculum areas, art education has been one of the least successful in exploiting the newer instructional media appearing on the educational scene. The term "media" alone acts as a block to the art educa-tor's understanding of these new techniques of instruction, since media in our field has traditionally meant the techniques or materials of studio pro-duction in art. Thus, water colors, mosaics, charcoal, are media in art, and the use of the word in another context has not only been unfamiliar to the art person, but may have proved to be irritating initially.

Not that art education has not made and is not making use of some in-structional media in the classroom. For many years art history and art appreciation teachers have used slides to supplement lectures. More recently, as materials were developed, films and some filmstrips, closed circuit and broadcast TV have been used as well. It is, after all, difficult for an essentially visual area to totally avoid the audio-visual field. The newest and perhaps most exciting developments in media, however, do not seem to have made the impression on art education which they have already made on many other curriculum areas. Specifically, programmed instruction, television and computer-assisted learning are rarely, if at all, considered in our literature or adapted to our classrooms.

There are a variety of reasons for this condition. One difficulty the art educator has in confronting the functions of media is his present preoccupa-tion with studio production. At least since the 1920's, art education has concerned itself to a major extent with the so-called "creative" aspects of art, subordinating and often virtually eliminating the historical and critical modes of study. This has been in part a result of our applying priority to the psychological or human development values of art activity in education. We have for example, been deeply bitten by the bug of creativity which has infected so many areas in and out of art education. So great has been the spread of this infection in our body of theory and practice that until very recently no other justification was deemed necessary for the existence of art in the school program—at least in many of our publications.

A second, and in one sense corollary, reason for our lack of concern with the newer media is the frequently held view that mechanization, quantification or measurement are in some undefinable but terrifying way destructive to the arts. The clearest illustration of this position, which is essentially anti-rational, can be found in many of the writings of Joseph Wood Krutch.

A third barrier is our self-admitted lack of a coherent body of subject matter which we are committed to teach or consider of value for our pupils to learn. The instrumentation and the programmatization of media seem of little relevance as means when the ends of instruction are ill-defined and problematical. This problem assumes major proportions when we attempt, speculatively, to introduce the logic of programmed learning into art education. Except for factual material in the history of art and skills in the studio areas, the identification of clearly defined behavioral objectives necessary to the task of developing program sequences seems virtually impossible. No doubt we share this difficulty to some extent with other areas in which affective or attitudinal or qualitative ends as well as cognitive or theoretical ends are at issue.

Despite these serious if somewhat fragile barriers, there have been signs that art education is becoming responsive to developments in the technology of instruction. The very existence of the "Uses of Newer Media" project sponsored by the NAEA is, of course, one sign. Another is the new ferment of ideas in the field, particularly the development of ideas generated by inter-disciplinary relationships. Awareness of and use of learning theories, game theories, communication theories, sociology and anthropology and other disciplines signifies an alertness to the impact of heretofore alien thoughts. Some among us are even willing to concede that the individual who is not in his own right a producing or "creative" artist may have much to say about art which merits our attention or may even be able to teach art effectively on one or several levels.

An interesting illustration of our present and recent readiness to accept new ideas, even in the area of technology, occurred during the September, 1965 seminar at the Pennsylvania State University. When Manuel Barkan read his paper, part of which described a programmed art lesson for use in a teaching machine, he anticipated some if only minimal protest at his "mechanization" of the curriculum. There was no protest at all. The seminar participants seemed merely to nod and press on to other issues.

Nevertheless, though this readiness appears to exist, actual steps towards the exploitation of the possibilities of newer media for the teaching of art are limited both in scope and number. There are, of course, several new single and multi-purpose projection devices used in art classes. Both single, and series paperback books on art are more frequently published now. Slides and slide series often with voice on tape or disc or a printed text are appearing in some profusion. The number and quality of filmstrips on art subjects is increasing rapidly. 8mm loop films and transparency sets, while very limited in number, do exist. Many new and fine films on art are now available. Reproductions are more numerous and museum and school district kits with models or copied objects of art have begun to appear in some areas of the nation.

On the other hand, television, which can hardly be classified as a "new" media device any longer, has not yet been examined with any substantial degree of imagination and care. Art teachers have, in some number, made videotapes of and with children in art situations, and the broadcasting industry has prepared and presented programs on art ranging in quality from the superb "The Louvre" to others less fortunate. However, some of the unique virtues of television, namely immediacy (seeing events as they happen) and universality (being able to record less than important as well as significant events at low cost) have not yet been explored properly. For example, it might prove of some value to students to televise the in-process act of an artist's creation, rather than an edited and "canned" version on film. Or, the simultaneous visual and verbal exchange of two art classes working in different parts of the nation, or even in different countries might supply the kind of contemporary excitement and insight so many art classes lack today, despite the best efforts of dedicated teachers.

Another use of this medium might contribute to the training of art teachers and all other teachers, for that matter. Some in teacher training have made voice tape recordings of the student teacher at work with children. Might there not be even greater benefits derived from having the trainee see himself as he teaches his class? With videotapes' capability for erasure and re-recording, the cost for this type of technique is now not prohibitive.

Also, the area of programmed instruction is only beginning to be examined for its contribution to art education. Essentially a program sequence is a method whereby (1) the content to be learned is broken down into the smallest possible self-sufficient bits, (2) these bits are ordered in a developmental sequence, (3) some type of active student response is required upon assimilation of each or a number of these bits, (4) some type of feedback to pupil response, such as confirmation of response, is built into the program, and (5) the program is carefully tested with an appropriate pupil population.

It requires little imagination to envision the application of these principles to art history content and, perhaps, to art criticism as well. It may stretch our innovative abilities to apply them to studio activities, or they may, in fact, not be appropriate to the production of art. But the first exploratory steps must be taken and, undoubtedly, will be taken soon.

Computer-assisted learning, both on a group as well as individual basis, is another media area deserving of some attention. This, of course, is the media frame of reference of the fanciful paragraphs with which this article started. Oddly, or in truth reasonably enough, the technological gadgetry proposed in those paragraphs is the simplest part of the problem. The difficulties lie in making the collective decision to move in this direction, obtaining the money for experimentation and selecting the art data, both in word and picture, worthy of being stored in one or several computers. Today these are hardly insurmountable obstacles.

A less extravagant but thoroughly wholesome concept in the use of media suggests that media themselves are studio devices with an expressive potential in the visual arts for pupils in our classrooms to use. With movie and still cameras and films as inexpensive and easy to use as they are now, the art teacher has still another art medium with which the child, even at a very early age, can create visual statements. There are, of course, those among us whose attitude towards the products of the camera as a visual art form might be called parochial. Their main argument appears to be that the camera, and by inference, other mechanical means of organizing visual elements, merely record what they see and, therefore, are not truly creative implements.

This position has at least two obvious disadvantages, one being that the camera is by no means simply a passive device, but must be or, at least, can be directed by human purpose. The degree of control may well be far less than that of the easel painter or the ceramic sculptor, but it is still an operative factor. The second problem with this attitude is that it presupposes certain definitive conditions for the term art which would be at the very least difficult to defend.

In any case, if we support the point of view that the photographic arts are acceptable partners in the family of visual arts we provide not only an additional expressive, exciting and thoroughly contemporary art production medium for school art, but also a vast source of visual material which is capable of provoking aesthtetic response. For there is no doubt that the products of some newer media can be looked upon as ends in themselves, as visual arts experiences of a higher order.

In addition to the many curricular uses of the newer media in art education, these essentially technological materials offer a qualitative contribution of considerable significance. Still and motion picture photography, television, auto-instructional devices and computers are "of our time". The boys and girls now in our classes have grown up with technology since infancy. They live in a world of speed and change and mechanization. What is quite often incredible to their teachers they can accept as a matter of course! The contemporary quality of the newer media can, in one sense, bring Altamira and Lascaux up to date and confer upon them the honorific aura of technology. Some of us may regret that this is so, that our young people cannot appreciate the work of Massaccio or Motherwell for its own sake. But it would seem that response to art is a complicated process and that there is more to it than simply the recognition and enjoyment of qualitative or formal relationships. We can therefore console ourselves that a positive response to Massaccio for less than the most desirable reasons is better than a negative response or no repsonse at all and that eventually an understanding of what we deem to be the most significant aesthetic elements in that painter's work may be developed out of an unsophisticated beginning reaction.

No review of the impact of newer media upon the teaching of art would be complete without some confrontation of the problem of the interference by technology in teacher purpose and teacher control of educational activity. During the early days of the growth of educational technology popular as well as professional journals contained cartoons and anecdotes whose humor dealt with the replacement of the teacher by the machine, or at least the encroachment on teacher prerogatives by the machine. More recently this issue appears to have all but disappeared from the arenas of public discussion, so pervasive is the advance of technology. However, this is not to say that there no longer remain questions of substance in the matter. In fact, it may be possible that now that we see the directions in which educational media are developing these earlier questions have become even more real and more pertinent.

The fundamental question of course, is the degree to which the development of media devices and the media materials which they project or present, curtail the freedom of the teacher to determine the *what* and the *how* and the *ends* of art education in the schools. It would be unrealistic or ill-advised or even dishonest to claim that such curtailment does not and will not exist in any appreciable amount. Not only does a media unit (a slide, a filmstrip, a television program or a programmed machine sequence) present one subject (and in doing so, exclude others), but it characteristically contains one or a limited number of attitudes towards the subject being presented. For example, the use of a filmstrip on the terminology of design using advertising design as illustrative material, forces the art teacher towards one particular set of definitions and one exemplary context. If the number of available choices of such filmstrips are quite limited, as they are now and may be for some time, the strip as a media unit actually structures both curriculum and teaching method by its use.

It is also rather fruitless to suggest that just because a media item exists one does not have to use it. In any individual case, as in the instance of the "Louvre" program, this may well be true. But the collective weight of educational technology exerts tremendous pressure upon the school system and the teacher for its use. There seems little doubt that what and how we teach will be changed by the advent of this technology. Whether or not our purposes will change has a less obvious answer.

If it is true that the newer media will influence art education, what can be done to channel that influence in what the profession views as a proper direction? Fortunately, there are a number of safety measures which can be and are being employed. In the first place, although media devices and materials are primarily created by commercial organizations which are not necessarily committed to consider the best interests of young people, many of these companies now appear to be aware that responsibility in this area will help with sales. Perhaps never before have manufacturers turned so consistently to the educator for assistance in the design of what is to be used in the schools.

Secondly, the large amounts of governmental and foundation monies now available for the arts ensure that eventually some media will be developed by art educators in a supervisory capacity, as were some of the science film series. Thirdly, the rather surprising and welcome growth in prestige and power of our professional association indicates that developments in art education can at least be monitored and, if necessary, influenced by the profession acting as a whole. Thus, while technology will curtail the art teacher's present curricular and methodological choices in the classroom, art teachers can have a part in shaping the form and content of that technology to their own wishes.

Ultimately, of course, when media like today's magazines, reproductions and textbooks are produced in vast and comprehensive quantities, the numbers of alternatives of subject and attitude will be so great as to provide, in effect, the latitude in choice most of us prefer. Until that time a recognition of the elements involved in what occurs is at least a safeguard.

Finally, the imposing question of when and how to use the newer instructional media remains to be answered. It is not enough to assert that there is insufficient research evidence to support any one or another strategy of media usage, though this is, unfortunately, quite true. Media are being used in art classrooms now and will be used in increasing quantities. Some guidelines to assist the teacher in selecting types of media, such as slide or filmstrip or television, and units of media materials, such as one filmstrip rather than another, should be developed.

In our present situation, it is almost pointless to construct august criteria for this selection process. At the moment, we are reduced to accepting what is available since there is no great reservoir of prepared media from which to make choices. The one area of exception is slides. Here, where the average art teacher does have adequate experience, the standards found in any audio-visual textbook would certainly be relevant: (1) authenticity or visual likeness to the original image, (2) accuracy or informational authenticity, (3) cost and/or accessibility and (4) appropriateness or relationship to the art activity in which they are used.

A summary evaluation of the impact of the newer media on art education, at least from this writer's position, indicates the following general conclusions.

1. The technology of education is recognized by art educators as a group and is being explored in its less revolutionary aspects.
2. Art educators do not seem to be aware of the newest and most innovative technological devices available in the media field, nor is the production

of materials for these devices in adequate quantity to suggest that awareness, interest and experimentation will soon be forthcoming.

3. A theoretical survey of newer media indicates that their exploitation for the teaching of art might provide valuable educational dividends.

4. While the development of newer media will in an obvious sense influence how we teach art and in a more subtle sense the content we teach, its impact on the purposes of art education does not, at the moment appear to be an important concern. The changes in our conception of purpose, such as the increased emphasis on historical and critical modes of art study, seem to have been proposed in our literature well before educational technology became a professional issue.

5. In the light of this brief review, there is every reason to believe that the newer media can be of substantial value in the improvement of the quality and quantity of art education in our schools. What is needed is information and imagination. This journal issue attempts to provide the former. It is up to each reader to supply the latter.

The Science of Art

ROBERT E. MUELLER

The fact that much art depends upon science, or at least upon technology, is acceptable. Painting can profit from optical know-how, the medium of oils requires considerable chemistry, music needs a base in acoustical physics, and most obviously the motion picture required many scientific discoveries and technological developments before it could come into being. Literary or poetical developments, too, have not been without their reaction to science, whether in terms of new modes of description—as when air views were used by novelists to describe a locale or when the scientific spirit informed a particular poem. To suggest that science depends upon art, however, seems nonsensical; but let us not reject the nonsensical without some careful consideration.

It is legend that scientists think that, at their most creative levels of theoretical ideation, they are functioning in the same way that an artist functions. If we try to crack this cliche we begin to suspect the existence of a startling kernel hiding beneath it. Perhaps this esthetic feeling of the scientist is not so much akin to the beautiful of the artistic attitude as it is derived from it.

The felt world, the world of our emotions and intuitions, is generally thought to be the special province of the artist. The scientist, on the other hand, tries to transcend feeling, to become objective in all ways. But if, when he is being most creative, he thinks himself like an artist, then feeling must be playing a very important role in his activity. Perhaps the word "feeling" is another way of expressing "humanness," and here the scientist and the artist are talking about the same thing.

The artist is assumed to deal in the articulation of emotions, but to what extent is this true and to what extent does the scientist actually deal in more objective things? I suspect that both of these notions are exaggerated if not mistaken. The artist deals with a more objective or at least objectified reality than theories which relegate him to a world of pure emotions suggest; the scientist has more "felt" reality as a basis for his theoretical constructs than science admits.

This art-science cycle turns upon the problem of how to generate those new basic art tendencies which can most profoundly influence our intellect. Science depends upon these basic new inroads to perceptual reality. If science is to deepen, we must force our art in the most meaningful directions for the perpetuation of science.

Before we can arrive at the new logic necessary to begin to cope with the many new realities which modern science is uncovering, we must have at our disposal greater realms of art experience that can be pertinent to the articulation of those realities. I feel that all art, from nursery rhymes to science fiction, enters into the scheme of things that leads us toward our future humanness.

To be modernly useful a medium can be ancient, but it must be used in a significant new way. Temperature and taste, for instance, are ancient phenomena that are definitely perceptual, but they are not directly manipulative (except perhaps in environment control and haute cuisine), and thus escape artistic control. Science has not yet come up with the technical wherewithal to provide the artist with definitely controllable temperature and taste media. But when or if it does, they will then be available for the artist's use. A more radical possibility exists, perhaps, within atomic nuclei or even molecular biology dimensions. In the first case one can imagine a magnificent transducer that gives communicative control perhaps over subatomic transition states; and in the latter some way to control DNA encoding so that it can serve as a palette for a future artist to make complex biological variations! And, too, the many hallucinogens may someday have their Mozarts, chemists who learn to harness their powers and form repeatable mind trips with artistic significance.

Informed of the requirements of science, the artist could conceivably take the oldest of art forms and bring forth a new and meaningful logic which could ultimately revolutionize all future science. You may ask how this is possible. The answer is that the human perceptual articulation can be deepened by any art which brings forth new felt relations, new formal developments; and these need not necessarily be couched in new scientific clothes.

The new felt and formal developments in art pertinent to modern science cannot be predicted, of course, but they lie quite obviously in the direction of exploring media possibilities which escaped attention in the past. Art has often experienced this neoclassical revival to bring forth a new and profound sublime creation out of what was thought to be a sterile or even dead art form.

We have not begun to exhaust the creative potential of even the most ancient of media, any more than mathematicians have exhausted the creative potential of pencil and paper. The technical means of art need not be overly complex to support new ideas, although it is another matter if artists are bored with the traditional ones. Color, for instance, has been used for many years, but I feel that it has never really been exhausted to any extent as a creative communication.

There have been many suggestions for such things as color organs to turn music into color, and the experiments with abstract color movies have suggested interesting possibilities in this direction. But no one has yet actually realized a significant creative communication with pure color.

From the fact that scientists have yet to learn how to derive any meaningful expression from our reactions to color, we can suppose that there has not been sufficient articulation by artists for it to be integrated into our humanness to the extent that it generates a meaningful human level of understanding. This may sound vague, and it is to the extent that I am suggesting something as yet not realized; but it is a clear possibility, long sensed by artists.

It is the task of the artist who is inclined toward exploring the interdependency of art and science to ask himself where lie the most meaningful scientific advances that are relevant to his pursuit. The artist of science can, if he wishes, begin with such things as optical phenomena, computer art, automated functionings; but it would be more directly relevant if he were to begin with those scientific discoveries which lend themselves to more obvious communicative manipulation. These scientific developments include such things as the motion picture, television, xerography, lasers, and multiplexing systems. All such explorations require a strong technical know-how, or at least equipment which can be controlled quite easily. Mixed media also are important, since an old medium plus a new one may the more poignantly immerse us in the hot bath of creative communicative revelations. How the artist will actually achieve this next development in art cannot easily be predicted; but that herein lie many new approaches seems clear.

Another example that comes to mind is the possibility of deriving a new logic from such presentational media as holograms or sound spectra used to analyze human speech. The processing of information in the brain may be closer to the extremes of logic which simultaneous modes such as these suggest rather than to the one-simple-choice-at-a-time logic of present-day computers. We must learn to put such multidimensional complexes into artistic order and find out how they can be used in creative communication. Then our modes of thought may advance from the linear process we now follow.

It will be interesting, for instance, to see if deaf people, trained to recognize vowel tones from the visual writing of frequency and amplitude spectra, develop any new way of conceptualizing. We have a negative example of this with blind people who use braille—their concentration on the tactile perceptions gives them an edge in music or perhaps sculpture but it prevents their processing system from including the more comprehensive information which the eye affords.

We have never entertained the possibility that physically handicapped people, because of their individual situations, may be in a better position to detect some of the unconscious assumptions in traditional thought patterns; therefore, we have never encouraged them to try. We are rewarded on occasion by an insight into ontological developments, as when Helen Keller described her first grasp of the significance of the word-concept water.

The art-science cycle is swinging toward a broader comprehension of art and of science and of man who lies in the middle and supports them. We are questioning the claims of scientists that their method is the only way to the truth, although we are not prepared to give up their methodology for an artistic rendering of experience. The two cultures should both be humbled by their failures and their responsibilities in the modern world. Together they brought man out of the darkness into a modern world, but they have saddled mankind with difficulties and terrors beyond anything prehistoric man ever could have imagined.

Not only does the scientist need the artist for those creative inroads to intuition which vital and original art can supply, but mankind needs the sense of humanity and knowledge of the beautiful and articulation of the soul which the most creative artists obtain. The time we live in is forcing man to make fundamental changes in many areas of his life. These changes must be made if we expect to set afoot a new man who can continue to survive as a human.

Meaning in Crafts

EDWARD L. MATTIL

Our language is full of words that have multiple meanings, creating many problems of comprehension. When we speak of *art*, we may be thinking of a single object, or of the creative experience of the adult or of the child. We may, in fact, be considering the entire process of creation. What we think of as art for the child is both products and processes. Perhaps there would be less chance of misunderstanding if another term, such as *creative activity*, replaced the term *art* for the program with children. In the same way that art has a multitude of meanings, so the word *crafts* has many different meanings; in fact, it has almost as many definitions as definers. There is no doubt about the relatedness of crafts in the varied meanings given to the word or about its relatedness to craftsmanship. In this book, crafts are thought of as a process of creative activities for children in which a product is the result or record of the experience.

When we attempt to trace the historical development of crafts, we become engaged in the examination of almost any piece of hand workmanship that might have a claim to beauty, or, for that matter, any piece to which decoration has been applied. If in such a study we should be privileged to visit a native potter in rural India working at his primitive wheel, we might ask him, "Why did you become an artist?" To this he might reply, "I am not an artist. I am a potter, as were my father and grandfather; in fact, my family have always been potters. We are even *called* 'Potter.'" Curiously we may ask, "But isn't pottery art?" To this the potter may return, "No, it is a livelihood, my industry." Yet by our concepts of art and crafts, this potter may well be an artist as well as a craftsman engaging in his little industry, for as Herbert Read says, "The man who makes becomes potentially, or partially, an artist the moment the things he makes express or excite feelings."

We must assume that the first tools and utensils of primitive man were restricted to the considerations of utility. As their efficiency improved, there was a steady evolution of form. Thus there came a point in man's development when the matter of *choice* entered into the picture. He was able to create a variety of clay bowls, each good for holding grain or water. It was here, then, that he engaged in the process of *aesthetic judgment* in determining form and decoration.

This is not unlike some problems basic to the crafts that we must consider in elementary education.

In crafts and art education, we are able to teach procedures—and every child can learn procedures. However, it is while the procedures are being carried out that the child engages in constant choices or judgments. He may decide why one shape is "better" than another, or he may intuitively select or eliminate in order to arrive at the "best" choice. This selection or choice, in which he constantly engages, is aesthetic judgment, which, it can be assumed, cannot be developed without activities that call upon the constant use of these qualities, which are basically the ones that distinguish man.

It is at this very point that there are many disagreements regarding the teaching of arts and crafts, for many teachers are unable to distinguish between procedures and technique. Procedures are the various activities that can be explained within the general framework of the project being introduced. Technique, on the other hand, is the highly individualized use of the materials involved; it is the child's personal "language" or "handwriting" with materials. It is impossible to teach technique, for it simply must grow out of the child's need to express himself. The teacher who believes that technique is something that can be taught may well be only imposing his own technique upon the child. Impositions will ultimately become handicaps. It is safe, then, to say that one can teach procedures and may help the child only to develop his own technique and that aesthetic judgment can develop only when the child has the freedom to make choices in his work.

Our schools cannot limit the teaching of crafts to only a few processes of the artist-craftsman. The constant development of new materials in every industry suggests an ever-widening area in crafts. Surely clay, wood, weaving, needlework, and many others of the "old standards" will maintain their importance, but it is necessary not to become so bound by traditional materials that one excludes the many exciting possibilities of experimentation with new materials and new processes. It is, however, very easy to become lost in the jungle of gimmicks and gadgets and to conduct a crafts program without depth or meaning. This usually becomes what is commonly called the "product-centered program." When such a program is in effect, the child rarely has the time or sufficient skill with tools or materials to carry out fully his imaginative ideas. Instead he seeks shortcuts in craftsmanship and hides behind a shield of indifference.

A truly creative student is not indifferent to what he does. Rather he dips deeply into his imagination, creates new and necessary symbols, develops personal techniques, and uses his tools with the maximum of skill. He discovers order in creative activity, finding pleasure in form, a personal attachment for the object on which he works, and a respect for his tools and materials. It is important that the crafts program be balanced to provide opportunities for fast, short-time projects using a great many materials in a large variety of ways as well as a number of basic arts and crafts experiences that are pursued in depth. This means that throughout the school life of the child, some activities, such as modeling, drawing, and printmaking, are a regular part of the art program at every level. By repeatedly using the tools and materials of a few processes, the child can gain the skill necessary for him to carry out his ideas directly without always having to learn to use the tools first. When the child's attention is focused primarily on the use of a new tool and the discoveries that accompany it, he is generally unable to focus fully on what he wishes to say with the tools. Ideally, the tool or material should become the extension of the child's thinking, not the focus for it.

Although there is a case for depth approaches to crafts teaching, the schools would err if crafts were limited to just a few processes. The school is one of the main instruments for the development of children's potentiality, and it is up to the school to provide the conditions that foster such development. One of the main conditions is opportunity, where materials and facilities are present to try out one's potential. Such a program allows for the opportunity to try one's ability in a variety of activities and to repeat with regularity those activities of special interest to the individual. Another condition is the presence of a mature and sensitive adult, who guides, suggests, evaluates, and encourages the child. Such a teacher grows as the child grows, enjoys as the child enjoys, and *cares*. The teacher creates the environment, whether it be rich or impoverished. It is the teacher who surrounds the child with experiences that keep him feeding on the stuff of learning, growing, and living. People, like snails, will come out of their shells for something enhancing and will stay inside when threatened. The threatening environment is frequently built upon prevention—prevention of waste, prevention of movement, prevention of soiled clothes, prevention of accidents. How terribly uninspiring it is to have a lesson begin with "Now don't make any mistakes; don't soil your tables; don't spill the paint; don't cut your fingers; don't, don't, don't." Equally important as a factor that represses creative work are restrictions on curiosity and manipulativeness. Children are curious by nature. They come to us all perception—ready to smell, touch, taste, feel, look, think, and ask about everything.

Given a chance to develop sensitively, without undue restrictions, the child learns quickly. He not only absorbs everything from his environment, but he also soon restructures what he takes in—in his own symbols, combining it with his imagination and his fantasy. It is unwise for the parent or teacher to try to eliminate fantasy from the child's thinking.

In the same way that our schools cannot limit the teaching of crafts to a few processes, they cannot limit it to a few children. Children may be likened to a handful of seeds from many flowers. At first they may seem similar in many respects. Place these seeds in the earth and nourish them. As they grow and mature, their differences become marked. Some remain small and delicate, while others are large and brilliant; some bloom early and some late. One thing they have in common: under good conditions, they all bloom and have their own beauty. Our classrooms are the earth for these seeds, and when fertile and rich, they bring forth the best. But the classroom can also have the stultifying effect of poor soil in which nothing can grow. This good soil-poor soil analogy can also be applied to the kind of motivations that are used to introduce various crafts. The child may be given the best kind of instruction in procedures and may use the best materials, but if he has nothing to express through the process, it becomes a meaningless, mechanical experience. In crafts, the child is able to organize his thoughts, ideas, feelings, actions, and technique into a product. If the experience or motivation is shallow, the ideas vague, the feelings diffuse or absent, the product will reflect it. In other words, the product is the record of the complete process. The creative arts and crafts of children have the power of reordering thoughts and experience in their image.

With the very young child, the process exceeds the product in importance. For example, the five- or six-year-old child may, day after day, pound out balls or coils of clay, finally joining them into very simple figure concepts. This daily repetition is of prime importance, for it is only through this repetition that the child gains the sureness of achievement that is necessary for growth of confidence. One must then paint to learn to paint, or pound to learn to pound, or assemble to learn to assemble. In these early efforts, which are significant to growth, the teacher is unwise to place undue emphasis upon the products as such. Rather should the emphasis be placed upon continued good experiences with materials and a continued involvement in the process.

The problem of process as it relates to product is a constant topic for discussion. Yet it is a reasonably easy concept to grasp. Both the process and the product are of importance in creative craft activities. However, in the earliest years, when the child's ideas come rapidly and do not remain for long, when interest spans are short and motor skill limited, the emphasis is more upon the process of creating. During this early phase the product is important as a record of the child's involvement, growth, and level of development. We may be sure that occasionally we shall find a veritable gem of child art that we wish to preserve. However, we err when we start with the intention of firing all the ceramic work of a kindergarten class, for here we focus more upon the product than upon the child and his experience in creating a product. The mere fact that the product is made of a permanent or semipermanent material may cause the teacher, consciously or subconsciously, to impose adult concepts and standards on the children's work. This does not mean that the teacher is without standards. Indeed, we all have standards, some high and some unfortunately not so high. But the standards that are applied must relate to the standards that each child must form for himself. This requires that the teacher be critical without being damaging, be selective without being biased, be able to direct without being dogmatic, be inspiring without establishing the ultimate goal, be patient without being indifferent, praise sincerely and freely without being indiscriminate. The truly creative teacher is never sure he is right, never bound by lock-step methods. He has the feeling he is on the right path, but when he is absolutely sure that he is right about all of his teaching, he is in danger of becoming dull and dogmatic. H. L. Mencken once said, "It is the dull man who is sure and the sure man who is dull."

As the child grows older, it is only natural that the product continually gains in importance, until as adults it is no longer possible to do creative work if there are no products to give personal satisfaction. Adults simply cannot be satisfied only by the process.

In early childhood, when imagination is unfettered, crafts serve as a wholesome outlet for the many fantasies that come into the young mind. Every new thing ever created resulted from the imaginative ability of someone who could imagine or dream beyond the realities of his known world. Children need to have the time to wonder, ponder, and dream, and to have a positive outlet for their imaginations. It is just as important that the child develop his powers of imagination as it is for him to develop in social or group activities. It is important for teachers to foster in children the attitude of expecting and liking to work out their own problems, instead of yielding to others who may try to force them into accepting ready-made solutions. At the same time, they must be shown the need for being able to work with others toward common goals, and not to be so self-centered as to be unable to accept criticism and to weigh the ideas of others.

All of us want to see children grow to express themselves clearly—and to have something worth expressing. If we recall the number of misses Johnny made before he learned to coordinate sufficiently to catch a thrown ball, we will have some idea of the struggle each child has to develop a personal concept in arts or crafts. It is only through this struggle with himself that the child truly grows. Think of the child whose parents never let him struggle, but who make every decision for him. When finally on his own and forced to make a decision, he is unable to do so. Crafts teaching, then, becomes not only the teaching of procedures, but also the creating of problems that call for personal solutions. How often we have seen the teacher who has the ready-made solution for art or crafts in the form of hectograph patterns. He carefully directs the group through every step, selecting and deciding for them, only to arrive with thirty identical products that are as unchildlike as they are uncreative. Such activities not only destroy the opportunity for growth through art experiences, but may even affect the child's confidence in his own ability to create.

Happenings In and Out of School:
An Interview with Allan Kaprow

DAVID ECKER

Allan Kaprow, New York artist-dramatist, produced "18 Happenings in 6 Parts" at the Reuben Gallery in 1959, in effect the first large-scale public Happening in New York. (Privately given works were done in 1957–1958; and the first public one was at Douglass College, Rutgers, in 1958.) Since then he, Jim Dine, Red Grooms, Claes Oldenburg, Robert Whitman and others have established Happenings as a new art form which has excited interest and inspired performances in Paris, Cologne, Milan, Osaka, Stockholm, Prague, and elsewhere.

ECKER: Allan, you mentioned that your own children have participated in Happenings—they worked from a script you had created, something to do with little painted boats the rain washed away and so on. Do they also create Happenings?

Reprinted by permission from *School Arts Magazine* March 1966, pp. 23–28. Copyright 1966, Davis Publications, Inc.

KAPROW: Well, yes, in the sense that they have their own games and rituals, those that they invent for themselves as contrasted with, say, hide-and-seek, a traditional game which passes on from generation to generation. But, no, in the sense that a Happening as I would define it is a highly organized structure of events whose nature fluctuates between that of ordinary life and the extraordinary—for example, when my script calls for going to the store and buying handtowels at one time, and at another for women licking a jam-covered car.

Even if these actions were identical to something my child might do, he would not have done the same kind of selecting; nor would he have polarized the ordinary and extraordinary. Children's art works—if one wishes to call their games and rituals art works—have a different origin. They are charming and sometimes very moving to adults; but they come from children's limited experience, from life-conditions they are powerfully compelled by but little understand. I try to make an architectural arrangement of these events and their multi-levels of meaning while maintaining the same apparent simplicity.

ECKER: Isn't an ethical problem involved here? When you enlist children in a Happening for your sophisticated purposes, aren't they being used as a means apart from their own interests?

KAPROW: I don't ask them to do anything which they cannot get meaning from, or which they do not want to do. It seems to me not difficult at all to understand that any child will enjoy painting little boats in the gutter and watching the rain wash them away; because he is told the boats are going to take a little trip to infinity.

ECKER: So it seems that participants in a Happening are not equivalent to actors in a play who are serving the playwright's ends. Could you elaborate on their motives a little more?

KAPROW: Well, obviously, no motives exist pure and simple. But a superficial motive, I think, is that people of all ages get pleasure out of being a part of something they know is unusual. And why not? I like novelty, and the pleasure I get from novelty is indeed a genuine pleasure.

Another motive is simple enjoyment in the sensuality of play, something most people have little time for nowadays. In Happenings there is a sense of vividness which they can't easily get from the kind of play usually available to them, such as a boat trip to the Virgin Islands with canned music, dances, and deck-tennis.

Then there probably exists a deeper, rudimentary motivation. This kind of play is not merely diverting. The images I choose, their function, and the flow of activity from one to the other, the gamuts of time in which they take place, the places where the time is either stretched or collapsed—all or most of them tend to be of a very primitive order; for instance letting the rain wash one's body clean.

ECKER: I'm interested in all the possible roles art might play in the public school, as you know. What would happen if children were encouraged to perform Happenings in a school setting?

KAPROW: The first thing that would come up in the schools is the question of what kinds of probing or emotional touching-off we could permit in Happenings; I don't think any art can be divorced from ethical considerations. Just as I skirt close to hysteria very often, but never permit it, I also am concerned with sexuality. Indeed, I often probe birth and death themes. But I have children, so I have some idea of what one may or may not do with and for them in school. I would not, for instance, ask of children that they hurt themselves either physically, or worse, mentally.

Yet we know that children are fascinated by the bizarre, the cruel or fantastic. Our job is not to eliminate these in our own interests, but perhaps to transmute them into relatively objective states. Art tends to do this generally; and while I admit not knowing all the answers, one answer is not to make Happenings "safe" according to a Good Housekeeping Seal of Approval. Instead, it might be to really allow art for once to discharge the socially destructive energies psychology has credited it with doing. Safe play, as arranged by most institutional guidance, is so pallid that children are forced by default to seek outlets elsewhere. For sometime, I've been interested in the possibility of Happenings arranged just for kids. But they might upset the adults!

ECKER: What might they be like? Let's take a seventh-grade class in junior high and let's say it were possible to have a permissive atmosphere.

KAPROW: Seventh-graders are very hard to work with, if they're treated as children. I'd give them adult things to do. Extremely adult.

Let's take third grade. I've derived much of my basic material from my son, Anton, who is eight-and-a-half. He's a red-headed Huckleberry Finn-type kid. He loves to climb trees and swing on ropes, take clocks apart—the usual. He's gung-ho for any of these things. So whenever I ask him if he'd like to be part of something, I know he'll enjoy it from the beginning. I'm often thinking of such children as he represents when I make the image. It might be making paper men in trees as in this Happening "Raining." He'd love to do that because he feels it's something he's done more or less ordinarily— making little images out of papier-mache at school and then hanging them in the bushes. I remember now that the idea came to me just this way: he compared the leaves that had fallen down into the bush branches in the fall as little people perched in trees. Then he saw some blackbirds and interpreted them as people in the trees (and of course this is mythologically very sound). Historically, it's an image that recurs and recurs and recurs.

ECKER: To what extent can he analyze, can he reflect upon these elements?

KAPROW: Very much, I think. I mention the images now which have a poetic overtone and immediately suggest a world view. If people are like trees or live in trees, this recapitulates the thinking of nature-worship in the past. The tree is seen as yearning up towards the sun from which it gets its sustenance, while its inverted form, its roots, plunge into the darkness of the earth for another kind of sustenance. This is a kind of oneness in the different aspects of existence: things above united with things below, the light with the dark, and so on. And the children intuitively understand that right away.

ECKER: Many people have claimed that children are much closer to a kind of poetic world than adults who have become removed from it, that society imposes rational barriers. . . .

KAPROW: Yes, I don't have to explain at length to children that the little painted boats in the gutter will be washed away on a trip forever and ever. Kids get that pretty quickly from the image. They are intrigued by this. The moat disappears. Where is it going? It goes down the sewer. Where does the sewer go? Out to the sea. And this is very thought-provoking and dreamy for the child, and he wonders what happens out at sea.

ECKER: As you know, there has been a great deal of criticism in the last decade of something called "progressive education," which supposedly has held us back in our race in space with Russia. Some critics have charged that our schools are not concentrating enough on science and engineering and so on. Wouldn't your conception of art education be possible only in a so-called progressive school? To put it another way, wouldn't a traditionally-oriented school be antagonistic to the kind of poetic world which Happenings draw upon and re-create?

KAPROW: Although I spent most of my time in an ordinary grade school, I went to a progressive school as well. I know there is a difference, but the public schools are beginning to catch on fast. I don't think there is any problem here. Fundamentally, of course, art is not technological research. It's not operative in the sense that engineering is. Engineering will permit you to make a better machine. Such knowledge is absolutely necessary. There is no question that we may have lagged in science, not because of art, but because of sloppy scientific education.

Yet, the poetic side of education is more in the nature of comprehension of feelings; not just simple feelings, but rather feelings bound up with our existential purpose or our connection with the world in which we live and breathe every minute. The poetic is a very vague word standing for all those philosophical and sensual experiences which are hard to define and which in the context of the school could be made real only by careful artistry; that is, by what I would call a structuring or patterning of images and situations. The most "engaged" scientists seem to understand this, and suggest it. This could hardly be called permissive. In fact, I'm very, very suspicious of permissiveness.

ECKER: In the sense of a failure of human control:

KAPROW: Yes. An extremely disciplined situation is required for Happenings, where flexibility is often given but built within parameters of movement and time. Occasionally, even the concept of chaos may be expressed by this discipline. In contrast, a really permissive situation would cause just the opposite of chaos. You would have a very rigid set of human cliches operating with everybody falling back on his own resources and no measure anywhere.

ECKER: You once said that you have tried to eliminate all aspects of previous art forms in Happenings. Is this really possible? After all, you do select and reject materials and situations and in that sense you use traditional methods.

KAPROW: Well, at bottom I suppose I work like any artist: I choose and arrange certain images and events into a composition of meaning (verbalizable or not). But beyond this basis, I try to avoid any resemblance to the arts up until now. At least half of my work tends to be given to eliminating such echoes, ranging from subjects like Matissean odalisques on divans, to serialized form-processes a la Schoenberg.

However, because my Happenings come from some sort of human experience, their novelty as a "language" is only a temporary problem for some adults bound by cultural tradition and habit. There is rarely any difficulty with children on this account. The main thing is to convey a world-view, no matter what means are used. Older art-forms are simply useless for what I understand about the life around me.

ECKER: But even if his main drive is toward a world-view as you call it, the artist's materials and imagery surely come from his culture, his stylistic forebears. Even the Happening, as you point out, comes from a variety of sources. The games children play are cultural!—they've got a tradition of their own. You mentioned the impact of Dada on your thinking. I wonder if we could talk a little bit more about this selection and rejection process. There may very well be different methods or techniques involved.

KAPROW: More important than what I choose is choosing what not to choose; rejection involving more than just artistic allusions, is far more crucial to me than the acceptance. I'll hit upon 25 images, but I might reject 24 because they're corny. Corn is a good old American word for anything that once was a carrier of meaning but no longer serves its original purpose. It's not that there's anything wrong with the rose being the symbol of love, though Gertrude Stein wanted people to look at the rose itself for a change. But you can't always erase cliches by commenting on the fact that they are cliches. Only a few people can be critical that way. For those who are not so inclined, and in fact most children are not so inclined, it is finding things which are indeed fresh and unused. We must remember that many of the things which are cornball for us are not so for kids. We cannot editorialize for them in the same way we would for ourselves because the child can use the word "rose" in a poem or paint a rose in a way that we would never be able to do it. As he gets older he may well become acquainted—if the teacher is smart enough—with the fact that it is a corny symbol. I'm beginning to suspect that we may have to develop courses of study in living imagery, or to put it another way, develop critical courses in the cliches of our culture. And this can be done, even on a very elementary or childlike level.

ECKER: I'm particularly interested in the poetry of Bob Dylan. Not all of his stuff is alive; he works quickly and so on. But there's an amazing freshness to some lines: "I met a thousand talkers whose tongues were all broken." He's a twentieth century troubadour.

KAPROW: Yes, he's fine. He's a case in point of a man both original and corny, in turns. I doubt that this combination is his special virtue. He would be better without the corn. I could be misunderstood here, but I think one of the points of departure among school children could be the very honest consideration of all the sentimental crap that makes up The Pledge of Allegiance to the Flag. This is first and foremost an uncritical ritual and not very interesting at that, judging by lack of attention in the kids' faces when they get up to recite this sort of thing. It is secondly, a very lax physical acivity.

ECKER: You use the word "ritual" now in a pejorative sense. Are you contrasting that with your own sense of ritual?

KAPROW: Yes. Conventional rituals have become emptied of meaning and therefore they're not participated in. It may be necessary for us to dream up new ones which, because they're dreamt up, may be more vital. I mean rituals without any ideological strings attached. True ritual cannot be legislated today by official sentiments. I don't feel it's necessary to express what patriotism is, which may be a kind of siblimation of family feelings. Patriotism may be better expressed by buying only American-made cars. . . . I don't feel that it's necessary to mention "Gold Bless America" all the time. It won't help with other countries as hostile as they are.

ECKER: Of course, what we're talking about now is not the role of art in the school but the role of art in society. Your initial analysis may not apply on a larger scale. How do you get a soldier to kill? How do you get people to pay their taxes? How do you keep a large social group from coming unglued?

KAPROW: Perhaps the only connection between killing in war and spanking a child in the home is the Mommy must spank in order to make the child good; and she spanks with love, and presumably the Christian kills with compassion to save souls. I don't know if this in fact motivates any killer in a modern war. I doubt that. He's probably numb at that point—a point where he's not thinking at all. I've never killed anybody so I don't know. Nevertheless, the family structure and society are metaphorically connected;

and insofar as they are, the school situation is a social model for the child who, as he becomes older and takes on more responsibilities, is faced by power struggles, contradictions, and absurdities. After all, the school is supposedly educating the child for going out on the streets later on. The dream-content of art may be a better teacher than all the sermons and moral advice in the world. And the school is as good a place for art as any.

ECKER: Allan, don't you feel that human beings are capable of participating in art at different levels? There might very well be an important educational role for commercial art, for example. Obviously it has provided materials out of which Pop Art has sprung. And it may be that visual cliches satisfy some needs of those who don't fully participate in art at another level.

KAPROW: Certainly the popular arts in American culture now function on practical and poetic levels that were impossible 15 years ago. They have become a marvelous instrument for mass education, far more so than the exclusive historic arts. But what the intellectual sees in them as evidence of powerful fantasy and direct involvement in everyday life, the uncritical man-on-the-street takes for granted. If he is "educated" by the popular arts it is largely unconsciously and submissively. It's interesting that here is a reversal of roles: the ordinary person is taught to go to the fine arts for edification, while the social psychologist and professional painter goes to the commercial variety! Our question always should be: who is educated for what? Overt propaganda in either the fine or applied arts is a touchy problem and I prefer to avoid it in deference to larger values.

ECKER: Social critics have pointed out, to make a parallel case, that radio and television have such a pervasive effect on Americans, that regional speech is disappearing and we're getting a kind of Huntley-Brinkley vocabulary, intonation, syntax, and so on, a kind of modern American language.

KAPROW: Like the landscape. This town (Columbus, Ohio) doesn't look any different to me than Mineola, Long Island.

ECKER: So there are visual and verbal cliches to be rejected. . . .

KAPROW: Preserving local traditions is one's right, if it is at all possible today, but to exclude living and expanding forms of language and landscape from our cultural education seems ridiculous to me. For example, take the way kids in L.A. dress with day-glow color blouses, and the girls with day-glow dust in their platinum hair. And the way they dance, the way they drink, the way they decorate their cars. They transform those rods into something audibly and visually extraordinary. *Esquire* and other magazines refer us to this phenomenon as though it were a marvelous slumming experience for the hippies, informing us on the way the "lower classes" live. But actually, it seems to me, without any sense of indulgence of patronization, this stuff is so explosive and articulate that one can only see it as a genuine expression of a time and place. I also include here the panorama of filling stations and billboards and neon signs all over America, some of which are really extraordinary. Far from ruining our landscape, the best ones are making a new landscape for us. Now, if this "catches on" and pervades America, the initial reason might be its vitality. Then later on, it, too, will become worn out and homogenized. But we will tend to blame the subject matter rather than the consumers and purveyors of it.

ECKER: The teen-age population is a fourth of our population now and soon going up to a third. Their buying power is enormous. What effect do you think this teen-age subculture is having on contemporary art?

KAPROW: Well, it's going to mow the hell out of us all. There's no question about its relentlessness. These kids are not only evolving a culture; but they're also quite aware of how they're killing us—us, who are the old fogies. Surely they're not philosophically reflective at this point. But for artists and art educators to look down at this monster with disdain, is just going to hasten our end and probably result in the abuse of those kids. We owe it to ourselves to pay attention to what is occurring.

ECKER: A young intellectual in the Berkeley riots was overheard advising his fellow students, "Be careful who you talk to—you can't trust anyone over 30." I'm sure he meant the intellectuals both in and out of the Free Speech Front at the University of California. And it seems that teen-agers now are acting as if they didn't trust anyone over 20. When they realize the economic, political, social power they have, they will have the power to change institutions like the schools and even our culture.

KAPROW: It's happening now, and this so-called pop world is the visual evidence of it. Not only are appeals being made to the visual pleasures of teen-agers on box tops and soap boxes and whatever else we buy in the supermarket, but appeals are also being made to their intellectual level— which granted isn't collectively very high.

However, this is our fault because we set neither good nor clear goals for them. Hence they make and impose their own. None of us knows the answers and all of us, teen-agers and adults alike, are scared stiff. But the ones I would trust to do something about it, whether they're 18 or 60 years old, are those who know the enormity of their responsibility but are willing to take risks anyway. It is difficult to demonstrate how the arts can solve problems of such magnitude directly. And I would hesitate to recommend their use only as "symptoms" or "catharsis." But I suspect that if society—and especially the schools—actually affirmed the radical implications of the modern arts, as acts of personal liberation and value-making, then teen-agers might see that at least some adults have understood what they're looking for.

The Mass Media as an Educational Institution

HERBERT J. GANS

When educators talk of the mass media, they usually do so in two ways: how they can use their audio-visual techniques or individual films, TV programs and magazine articles to buttress classroom teaching; or how the mass media are the school's great competitors, taking the children's interests and energy away from their studies and diverting these into frivolous, time wasting, and intellectually or emotionally harmful pursuits. Of these two views of the media, the second is actually more realistic, for in seeing the media as a competitor, educators acknowledge, if only indirectly, that they are an important educational institution. The mass media also teach, and their students learn, even if both the content and the method of instruction differ from those of the school. In fact, in some ways the media are an even more important educational institution than the school, for they outrank it in terms of size of operation and audience, in the amount of time and the intensity of interest devoted by that audience, and in the diversity of its course content.

We do not yet know enough about the impact of the mass media on their audience to judge whether they help or hurt children—or the school. We can, however, look at the mass media as an educational institution, and study it as such, comparing its structure, functions, problems, and teaching effectiveness to those of the school. Such a study can show what each does better and more poorly and why, so as to provide findings that can help shape future policy for both institutions. The purpose of this essay is to develop some hypotheses about teaching and learning in the two institutions, and in this process, to suggest the kinds of research the Center For Urban Education hopes to carry out in the years to come on the mass media and education.

As any comparative analysis, mine will frequently treat the schools and the media as more homogeneous than they really are, and to neglect the variety within each. Indeed, most of my observations pertain to the numerically and culturally most important school and mass medium: the public school that serves urban and suburban lower-middle-class neighborhoods, and network television.

THE STRUCTURE OF THE MEDIA AND THE SCHOOLS

One can begin a parallel analysis of the mass media in terms of how their structure compares to that of the school. It should be apparent immediately

Reprinted by permission from *Television Quarterly*, Vol. VI, No. 2, Spring 1967, pp. 20–37. Copyright: The National Academy of Television Arts and Sciences.

that as the school, the mass media have teachers, but that they bear such names as announcers, commentators, entertainers, and reporters. Similarly, the students are called audiences, viewers, readers, and if they attend regularly, subscribers. Schools and teachers offer courses of study; the mass media provide television programs, films, magazine articles, and the like. The mass media's courses are more varied than the school's, but are often quite similar in subject matter; only the names have been changed. What the school calls social studies or civics, the mass media call news, documentaries and public affairs programming.

Moreover, these courses are also taught through diversion and entertainment. There are occasional TV programs, such as "Daktari," which provide information about geography and biology, but almost all TV programs and magazine fiction teach something about American society. For example, "Batman" is, from this vantage point, a course in criminology that describes how a superhuman aristocrat does a better job eradicating crime than do public officials. Similarly, "The Beverly Hillbillies" offers a course in social stratification and applied economics, teaching that with money, uneducated and uncultured people can do pretty well in American society, and can easily outwit more sophisticated and more powerful middle-class-types. Television series such as "Bonanza," and "The Virginian," and most popular films and fiction are in reality morality plays, that show how a hero confronts a moral dilemma and how he finally makes a moral choice. These dilemmas are often quite contemporary and controversial; I have seen Bonanza, one of the most popular TV programs, deal with questions of racial intolerance and inter-marriage, albeit in a 19th-century Western setting. Programs like "The Law and Mr. Jones," "East Side/West Side," and "The Defenders" have discussed pertinent social issues in contemporary settings, although they have been less popular from a rating standpoint. And even the innocuous family situation comedies such as "Ozzie and Harriet" deal occasionally with ethical problems encountered on a neighborhood level; for example, how to help the socially isolated child or the unhappy neighbor. Although the schools argue that they are the major transmitter of society's moral values, the mass media offer a great deal more content on this topic.

The administrative structure of the two institutions can also be compared. Behind the teacher stands a curriculum developer and, of course, principals, superintendents, and lay boards of education. In the mass media, the teacher is backed up by an editor or a director who prepares the course, and an executive editor or executive director, who is responsible for an entire group of courses. There is a program executive or editor-in-chief, who functions as the academic superintendent, a business manager or publisher who oversees business matters, and a president or publisher who, like the superintendent of schools, runs the operation. Many of these men are likely to be professionals (some trained in professional schools of communication) and like schoolmen, they carry out the policies made by laymen, company boards of directors.

As in the schools, there is frequent conflict between professionals and laymen, and between those who disburse money and those who spend it.

One can also reverse the analysis and see how the schools resemble the media, and how operations found in the media are handled by the schools. The mass media have sponsors or advertisers who pay for putting on the courses; so do the schools, but they are more numerous and are called taxpayers. Since the schools are funded by taxes, there are no tickets to buy, except as ancillary fees, and there are no commercials except for varsity teams that advertise the school, political campaigns to vote in bond issue or school board elections, and of course, the many, many commercials that a teacher inserts in his or her day-to-day instruction in order to persuade the class to buy the product he or she is selling. As do the mass media, the schools offer entertainment as well as information, although in different proportions. The school's entertainment consists of varsity sports, the band, glee and drama clubs; but the people whom these entertain are parents and the general public, that is, the school's sponsors, not the school's regular audience. In fact, there is very little room for entertainment for students in the daily school fare—which may be one of the school's problems. What would happen to the attention and interest of the television student body if it were presented a steady diet of documentaries from 7 A.M. to sign-off time?

It would be wrong to suggest that the two institutions are entirely similar in the system, he or she is given tenure, whereas the mass media teacher's these is in the teacher-student relationship. The school enrolls an involuntary audience that has little choice in selecting its courses and teachers; the mass media attract a voluntary audience that can choose both—and can reject those it dislikes. As a result, mass media teachers, like courses, are selected by their ability to communicate with their students and hold their attention. School teachers, on the other hand, are recruited by "professional" criteria and the teachers' ability to communicate with and hold the attention of the audience is of minor importance. And once the teacher has served some time in the system, he or she is given tenure, whereas the mass media teacher's contract can be cancelled any time his students no longer pay attention to him. In fact, in the media the students grade the teachers—through box office results, ratings, and circulation figures, and through the critic, who regularly reports what was good or bad about last night's course offerings.

Because the students judge the teacher in the mass media, his curriculum and teaching method must differ considerably. Mass media courses are more topical, and more dynamic; the content of an individual course and the courses themselves change constantly; unpopular courses are not retained just because they have always been in the curriculum. Moreover, all the media's courses observe John Dewey's maxim—that one begins with the interests of the student, rather than those of the teacher—much more closely than the schools. The methods of the print media require reading as much as the schools, but all media, print or electronic, avoid lecturing, which is known to drive away the students. Most often, the media use a dramatic method: both in fiction and nonfiction content, they dramatize the issues and topics they present, particularly through characters who are either people like the audience or heroic figures who presumably represent what the audience would wish to be.

Finally, the social environment in which the media's students learn is quite different from the school's. Because school is compulsory, it is able to organize students into artificial groups called classes, and to enforce rules that regulate and restrict student behavior. These rules are intended to aid the school as an institution rather than the learning situation; to keep down costs, to maintain order—and the authority of the teacher—and to reduce individual expression. In the school, the student has the lowest status and is the least powerful member of a hierarchical organization run by a teaching staff; but in the media, the student is free—and more powerful. Because he has to be attracted, he has the right to choose what he wants to learn, and the conditions under which he learns. He can study by himself or with his family or his peers. His behavior is not restricted by rules of decorum; he does not have to remain quiet when he wants to talk, and although he cannot talk back to his media teacher directly, he can write letters to him and criticize his teaching performance. And, since his choices ultimately determine the course content of the media, he is not treated as a person of low status or power. Even children are equals before the TV screen, and often they are more equal than their parents in choosing what is to be viewed.

THE FUNCTIONS OF SCHOOLS AND MASS MEDIA

The two institutions may also be compared in terms of their functions: their manifest and latent purposes. Functions are difficult to analyze because, among other things, every institution has both societal and segmental functions. That is, there are functions for the whole society and for segments of it, and segmental functions vastly outnumber societal ones. For example, mass media exist to make money for stockholders and advertisers; and to provide diversion and information to their audiences. Similarly, the school system provides status, power, and high salaries to its administrators, education to its audience, and aid in child-raising to parents, to name just a few. In this analysis, I will, however, concentrate on some societal functions.

The societal functions of the school include among others: (1) the socialization of children for adult society: to prepare them to be workers, citizens, and law-abiding members of adult society; (2) the sorting of students; to prepare them for the socio-economic stratification of adult society and train them to enter one of its strata; and (3) the perpetuation of American culture.

As the schools, the media socialize children for adult society, although by for anticipatory socialization into adulthood than the school. The media do not train children in specific skills, for they do not teach the three R's. Instead, they provide images of desirable and prestigious occupations and letting children attend adult courses, they give the child a greater opportunity role-models of people who fill these in ideal ways.

Conversely, the media train children more in the realities of citizenship than in the ideals; the news and documentaries of TV tell children more about politics than do school civic courses, which tend to teach an apolitical or antipolitical model of government. In socializing children for citizenship, both institutions depict American society, but in different ways. Both tend to focus on the culture and problems of middle-class, urban-industrial America, although school texts pay more attention to farmers and now, to non-white Americans, than the media. Both institutions play down controversy, although the media less so than the schools because controversy is news. But both select and distort in describing America; the media by emphasizing unusual and dramatic news—when men bite dogs; the schools by stressing the abstract and the traditional. Not only do they teach more about government than about politics, but they spend more time on the past than on current events.

The mass media differ most sharply from the school in that they train children how to consume and play and how to be family members, whereas the schools emphasize the ability to produce and work, and how to be colleagues and citizens. Commercials are a never-ending course about the goods available in the society and how to use them, and both they and the television programs, films and magazines teach children how people behave in their off-hours and with their families. Many TV situation comedies are also courses in parent-child and husband-wife relationships, teaching children how to get around their parents, and wives to outsmart their husbands. The children's media (cartoons and comic books particularly) provide material in which children and young people fight and defeat authority figures (such as parents) and either drain off or stimulate (the data are sparse and the experts in disagreement) hostility toward them. The schools do not deal extensively with familial roles, although home economics and family life courses teach cooking and child-rearing skills somewhat more directly than the media. But both institutions do little to teach children how to handle the most difficult phases of family life: sex and intrafamilial conflict.

The two institutions also handle the incorporation of children into the stratified adult society in different ways. The schools stratify children at an early age, for the neighborhood school and diverse tracking systems effectively support the national class hierarchy. The school tends more toward a merit system than the rest of American society, but for all practical purposes, class membership is assigned early and permanently; the youngster who is bright in the first grade is given a strong push toward the affluent society; the under-achiever is quickly relegated to the lower class.

The mass media stratify more subtly. Magazines and, to a lesser extent, newspapers are written for specific strata, e.g., *The New Yorker* for the upper-middle-class, *True Story* for the working class, although anyone is free to buy either. Television and the movies side-step the existence of class; their dramas and comedies are peopled largely by affluent heroes and heroines whose behavior, however, follows lower-middle and working-class values. The media do not question the present class hierarchy but ignore its existence, and they can do so mostly because they have little power to affect their audiences' class position. They do, however, suggest that one can be well off and still be "ordinary folks" without adopting the aristocratic ways of the very rich or the cosmopolitan ways of the intellectuals, thus discouraging upward social and cultural mobility while favoring economic mobility.

Moreover, both institutions encourage mobility on the part of individuals: the schools by rewarding the poor but bright youngster with academic success and the certification that will help him get ahead; the media by providing models of middle-class behavior. But both institutions discourage upward mobility on the part of groups, particularly through political action. For example, the demands of Northern Negroes for participation in the affluent society have received only lip-service support from the schools and the media and neither has been especially favorable to labor unions. The two institutions are more likely to praise individuals who make good without upsetting the status quo.

Needless to say, both institutions seek to perpetuate American culture, but they differ sharply on the culture they seek to perpetuate. Indeed, one of the reasons for the deep antagonism between the mass media and the school is that they advocate different cultures. The school promotes the 19th-century Protestant lower-middle-class tradition; conservative, asexual "lower-middle-brow" art, music and literature, and lower-middle-class civic and social but non-political community service (or do-gooding)—in short, a small town culture in which home, church, and civic club are the main pillars. The mass media support this culture too, but they also encourage the 20th-century non-Puritan culture of show business, and the latest fashions in dress, music, cars, and even politics, some of which will include working-class and low-brow styles. The school considers mass media fare "uncultured," uncouth, and because of its erotic and violent components, unwholesome; the mass media view school culture as dull, stodgy, and unfashionable. Moreover, the school preaches a culture of production and participation; the media, one of consumption and spectatoring.

THE PROBLEMS OF THE TWO INSTITUTIONS

Another way of comparing the two institutions is to ask what problems each faces, and how, and how effectively it solves them. This kind of analysis brings out the differences much more than the similarities, for the two institutions have quite different problems, and what is problematic for one is not so for the other. The major problems of public education today would seem to me to include the following: how to teach children from low income and poorly educated homes; how to provide equality, that is, education of equal quality to all classes and races; how to adapt to pluralism, that is, to meet the different needs of classes, races, ethnic groups, rural, urban and suburban children, to mention just a few; how to obtain the necessary public funds for the schools; how to attract qualified teachers; and how to cope with the competition from private and parochial schools.

In contrast, the mass media have no difficulty in attracting the poor, poorly prepared, "culturally deprived," or "intellectually disadvantaged" youngster —such words are never used in the media to describe him. Of course, he is neglected by the media perhaps even more than by the school; because of his low purchasing power, there are no television programs about poor people, and few magazines designed for them. However, the poor youngster seemingly does not mind sharing the fare prepared for more affluent audiences. He does not play hooky from this fare, seems not to resent it or the media teachers, and does not seem to suffer from a reduced I.Q. as a result of attending the media. Perhaps this is because mass media fare, being mass-produced, is eminently equal; rich and poor, white and nonwhite can all choose the same films, TV programs and magazines. Nevertheless, the media are as de facto segregated as the schools; the proportion of Negro actors is surely lower than that of Negro teachers, and there are as few TV programs for Negro audiences as there are school courses in Negro history. We do not know how Negro audiences feel about watching "white television," although some data recently gathered by the Center among poor Negro and Puerto Rican New Yorkers suggest that they prefer programs about poor and non-white people to those about rich and white people; and nonwhite actors to white ones, although most of all they prefer integrated programs.* Even so, nonwhite audiences do not seem to be demanding black TV as much as black power or black dignity. As viewers and readers, they are, after all, integrated—and equal; they do not get an inferior or segregated "I Spy" even while they attend inferior and segregated schools.

The media also cater more to pluralism than the schools; they offer fare for all levels and styles of cultural taste, and magazines exist for all age groups, classes, and races, not to mention hobbies and distinctive cultural interests. Also, because the media allow their students freedom of choice, there is no stigma in choosing a Negro magazine as there is in being forced to attend a ghetto school, so that the values of pluralism and equality are served at the same time. The schools are not homogeneous either of course; the education offered in an upper-middle-class neighborhood differs from that in a lower-class one. But here the pluralism is involuntary and unequal; lower-class children cannot obtain an upper-middle-class education because of residential and school segregation, and a lower-class minority in an upper-middle-class school is often scorned and neglected by teachers and fellow students alike. The pluralism of course offerings in the school is more potential than real; the classification of students into grades discourages them from choosing

* Herbert J. Gans, "Audience Preferences for 'Reality' or 'Fantasy' in Mass Media Fare," Center for Urban Education, dittoed.

courses freely. In theory, the division into grades is also a division by age, but the courses of the schools are less designed for the age-related needs of the children than even those of the media. That is the seventh grade curriculum is not designed to meet the needs of the 13-year-old child, but simply to provide a progression from the sixth grade. If the curriculum were designed for age needs, the seventh grade would be offering children some help in dealing with incipient puberty and heterosexual relations.

Unlike the schools, the media have no problem in obtaining funds or qualified personnel; some magazines may be faring more poorly in attracting advertising since the emergence of television, but they do not have to put their students on double or triple sessions. And, they can offer financial, status, and working-condition incentives which keep the supply of staff members well above the demand. Finally, the media have no problem in coping with competition; they are flexible enough to change their courses, teachers, and even their organization. A poor television program does not last beyond 13 weeks these days, but how many schools drop an unpopular or badly taught course or an inadequate teacher at any time?

Compared to the schools, the media have few problems and these tend to be with the other end of the audience spectrum. The mass-circulation magazines, the television networks, and Hollywood have had little success in attracting the highly educated audience and the intellectuals. This does not really worry the media, however, for being commercial enterprises, they do not have to serve the entire population; they can ignore the intellectuals. In fact, perhaps the major problem of the media today is to keep up with the increasing sophistication and the changing demands of its majority audiences; television is currently faced with rising audience dissatisfaction. Old favorites suddenly drop to the bottom of the ratings, and the majority of the new programs fail to survive their first year on the schedule. The schools may encounter the same dissatisfaction, but it is not a problem for them. Although many students are much better informed than their textbooks and teachers believe, when attendance is compulsory and school income is not affected by how students feel about what they are being taught, the schools do not have to pay attention to audience dissatisfaction. In fact, they tend to do so mainly when it affects their property and the welfare of their staff: when slum children turn to vandalism, and become discipline problems.

One can also look at how the two institutions solve problems. The schools have a much harder time, for most of their problems are political. Not only must they persuade external agencies—governments and voters—to increase their budgets and grant them the right to provide equality and integration, but they must fight internal battles with conservative administrators who reject change, and with teachers who do not want to work with low-status students. (The media have a similar problem but solve it by paying higher salaries to those who create content of low prestige.) The school's struggle with external agencies is complicated by its lack of political power. Its direct constituents cannot vote, and its indirect ones, the parents, often are not sufficiently concerned to support the schools politically. Except in upper-middle-class communities, many voters often see the school as an enemy that tries to exact taxes from them for services ("frills") they do not want. Internal struggles are complicated by the fact that the school's employees are tenured professional and can reject change as violating professional norms and privileges.

The mass media do not depend on the political arena for their survival, and when they must obtain FCC licenses or mail privileges, they can generate enough power to get what they want from government. Their power results in part from their affluence; they can provide campaign funds—although they spend somewhat less on lobbying than the National Education Association. But in large part, their power derives from their relationship to their constituents; the students are on their side and the politicians know this. Moreover, every constituent, regardless of age, can vote: by buying or not buying a magazine, supporting or not supporting a sponsor, so that the mass media as a whole are much more responsive to the voters than the schools. They watch voter behavior much more carefully, and they do audience research to make sure that they remain responsive to their constituents. The schools only conduct audience research when the audience misbehaves and causes trouble for the teachers. After all, no one studied the "culturally deprived" until slum children became discipline problems. The mass media are also more effective at reaching their youthful constituents; many children bother their mothers to buy products they have seen advertised on television, but how many children bother their parents to vote for a school bond issue? Moreover, the mass media are better geared to experimentation and innovation; more money is spent on television pilots than on pilot projects in curriculum innovation.

Teaching and Learning in the Two Institutions

The most important issue is, of course, how well the two institutions teach and how well their students learn. But here there are few answers so that the analysis must be restricted mainly to posing questions. It is easy to study empirically how the two institutions develop their curricula and teaching methods. The media draw on box office figures, ratings and audience research to discover what their students want to learn, and although the people who actually create the programs rarely pay attention to audience data, they tend to be sufficiently like their audience to provide material that interests and entertains both teachers and audience. The schools, on the other hand, have seldom taken student demands into account in formulating courses, although current curriculum reforms in social studies, the sciences and mathematics draw on experienced classroom teachers, who know what children care about and are able to learn. They devise new materials, and the new materials are being tested in ways similar to program pretesting in television.

The schools are, however, handicapped in two ways. First, they must prepare their curricula with an eye to the universities, and these have first notions about what must be taught, and what kinds of courses youngsters must have taken in high school in order to matriculate. Powerful constraints on the content of instruction are thus introduced into the public school curriculum. Second, the schools must provide the kinds of education and certification that the adults who control the national power structure and economy think is necessary to create useful citizens and jobholders. Although no empirical evidence exists to support their judgment that children must be taught the three R's and other subjects through a logically integrated curriculum and a process of organized instruction, the schools have not yet offered an alternative approach to preparing youngsters for adulthood. Moreover, the school's function is to teach children, and to teach them what adults think they ought to learn, whereas teaching is only a secondary—and latent—function for the mass media. And, since their student body is not limited to children, they are under no pressure from adults to limit their content to what is good for children, except for the sporadic pressure that comes from those who object to too much sex and violence on TV.

The mass media also have an easier time in perfecting what they teach and the people they hire to teach. Since most of the mass media fare is provided by national organizations which cater to large audiences, they can draw on huge sums for program preparation, and can pay high salaries to attract the best people—who then teach audiences that number in the millions. The schools are locally run, tied to the classroom, and must provide millions of teachers for small audiences. There is no room in the school system for nationally known stars; it must, like local television and newspapers, rely on people with average skills and conventional ideas. Moreover, the schools draw many teachers from teachers' colleges that instruct them in particular educational methods and frequently discourage the use of distinctive methods. In the mass media, method is learned on the job, and no method is sacred; innovators are encouraged, that which works is adopted—and then often copied ad nauseam. If we could measure how well the mass media and the schools teach, we would probably discover that the national media do better than the schools; and the local media, perhaps no better and no worse.

But the most significant and most difficult question is: what do students learn in the two institutions; how well do they learn what these offer them; and how well do they learn what they need to know to live in adult society? These questions can only be asked of the audience, and neither the media nor the schools have tried to ask them with any degree of seriousness. Teachers give tests and have some measure of what students have learned, or at least whether they have learned to give the teacher what he wants, and there have been studies of the impact of different kinds of schooling on I.Q. and other intelligence tests. The media, of course, rarely test their students, although they do ask viewers and readers whether they recall commercials. But none of the research is reliable enough; for example, just when market researchers thought they had found that hard sell and repetition are the most effective in teaching commercial messages, the advertisers began to switch to soft sell and comedy. (Most likely audiences are as diverse as students; some learn better with a hard sell, others with a soft sell, although most seem to learn what they want to learn from the product and not the commercial.) Two decades ago, a number of studies were done on the short-range effects of the media on attitudes, but these proved largely inconclusive, suggesting that people tend to see and hear from media material what they want to see and hear and that consequently, the media tend to reinforce already held attitudes rather than to change them. We know less about the "informational effects" of the media; what people learn in the way of facts and interpretations of fact; and we know almost nothing about the effects of school on student attitudes.

My hunch is that the schools are best in teaching their students basic methods of formal communication, including the three R's, as well as an array of socially and occupationally relevant skills; that the media allow children to learn what is going on in the modern world, politically and culturally, and that in both, students learn many large lumps of often unimportant or irrelevant facts. From the media, children also learn the ideals, basic values and the mood or ethos of the dominant American culture, that of the lower-middle-class, particularly about the details of consumption and having fun. But children probably learn the most important aspects of life neither in the classroom nor in front of the TV set. The schools may lecture them on home economics and family living, and the media will provide highly romantic versions of marital life (which children probably absorb more readily than the lectures), but the most important lessons in the school of socialization are still being taught by the family and the peer group, as well as in the situations in which people find themselves, on the job, in marriage, and at the public meetings in which they appear as citizens. The school's facts and the media's moods provide some raw material with which to prepare for and confront these situations, but their share of all the teaching and learning that go on in society is still relatively small.

Yet students do learn something from both school and mass media, and until we can go beyond hunches, we can only ask questions. Do children today learn more about the world and how to live in it than their television-less predecessors? Do children become better citizens through television documentaries or through civic texts, or are neither as important as what they learn when they become adults and have to act as citizens? Will children learn more about crime as a phenomenon and as a social problem from Batman or from a "crime unit" in social studies? Or, would the best solution be a combination; to have them watch Batman and then show them how inaccurate and unreal a picture of crime it presents? Or would they learn most by studying their community's police department? Is the school really better at teaching reading, writing and other technical skills, or are there ways of using the mass media—and even entertainment programs—for this purpose?

Moreover, we need to know how the learning process takes place in each institution and what components are significant. Is the medium really the message, as Marshall McLuhan insists, and is content almost irrelevant? If this is too extreme a formulation, as I believe it is, what impact does the medium have; how do children learn differently from TV, the movies, the magazine and the comic book? In addition, we need to know which aspects of the media content are significant for learning. If people are more interested in fiction, does this mean that dramatizing "facts" is better than a documentary—or a classroom discussion? And if dramatizing encourages learning, as I suspect it does, what element of the drama is most important for learning. Is it the plot or the characters, or both? If the latter, what kinds of characters are most persuasive? Judging by the emphasis on series and the weekly reappearance of familiar characters in TV, the hero is very important. Even so, we do not know who learns what from what kinds of heroes, and we do not even know whether it is the hero per se, or the hero as played by a particular actor.

We must also determine the learning implications of the context in which the media content is received. What impact does watching TV at home have on learning and what roles does the presence or absence of parents play on the viewing child? Is it true, as some suggest, that children (and people generally) learn more in the darkness and impersonality of the movie theater than in the living room? And if so, what role do the associates with whom most people go to the movies play; does the real learning perhaps take place after the movie, when peers discuss what they have just seen?

Similar questions have already been asked about the school, although not sufficiently to provide firm answers. We still do not know what kinds of children learn what from what kinds of teachers, in what size classrooms, and in what sorts of school climates. What do children learn better from the rote teaching approach of the past; and what from restrictively (or permissively) organized classrooms; from a homogeneous class of students or a heterogeneous one? What are the qualities in the teacher that make him a good teacher—for what kinds of students? Would the mass media serve as a useful model here; would a teacher who resembled Walter Cronkite or David Brinkley, or Ed Sullivan or Jackie Gleason be more successful, and if so, which of these diverse personalities would be the best model for a new teacher?

Some Policy Implications

If a comparative analysis is to be more than an academic exercise, it must ultimately focus on policy. It would be easy to argue that the schools ought to copy some of the more successful techniques of the mass media—and I shall so argue shortly—but it cannot be forgotten that they have a different and a tougher assignment. The mass media's prime function is to entertain that portion of the total audience affluent enough to buy their services and advertised products. They can give these people what they want. The school, on the other hand, is a public institution which must serve all children, and it must teach them not what they want to learn, but what they will need to know in order to become adults. One cannot, therefore expect the schools to be like the mass media; to teach mainly by entertainment and diversion. Similarly, one cannot expect the mass media to become quasi schools; as long as they are profit-seeking firms they must attract an audience and must give that audience what it wants (or what it will accept). However high the "educational potential" of television, it cannot give its viewers the education that they do not want, even if educators think they ought to have it.

It is, of course, possible to be utopian and suggest that some schools could become profit-seeking agencies, which could then offer their students what these (or their parents) want. Similarly, one can suggest that government ought to set up its own mass media outlets and devote these to formal education. There are pros and cons to both alternatives, but both seem to me to be worth trying. It has not yet been proven that children must learn what they are now taught at various ages to become effective adults; perhaps they might benefit from spending the first years of elementary school life in learning what they want to learn—either on the basis of the kindergarten or the mass media model—and to postpone writing, arithmetic and all technical skill training except for reading, until they are older. A good argument can certainly be made for not exposing children to social studies until they are old enough to understand the nature of society and politics, and for postponing teaching of any job-related skills until they have a clearer notion of who they are, what they want to do, where their talents lie and what jobs are available to them in adulthood.

But it is not necessary to propose utopian alternatives; the comparative analysis has a number of implications for the present school system. I shall concentrate on only a few, particularly on the media's demonstrated ability at engaging a child's interest and holding his attention more adequately than the school. This raises a number of questions that deserve answers, both through research and experimentation. Perhaps school learning should not be a compulsory process: could not the voluntary and self-selective approach by which the TV viewer and the magazine reader learn be applied to the classroom as well? Children might learn more, and more effectively, if the teacher had some of the personal qualities of the entertainer or television commentator; and if he or she used some of the media's dramatic and expository methods. They would surely learn more willingly if they were treated more as equals and if they were bound by fewer rules, as in the mass media. Also, they might learn more in natural peer groupings rather than in the formal class; and if the classroom atmosphere were more like the home or the peer group milieu. Most generally, learning would improve if the school became more audience oriented, and if the organization and power structure of the school were more student centered.

But my analysis raises even more fundamental questions: What should children be learning? Should they continue to learn the culture of the schools, or should they be learning more (or all) of the culture of the mass media, even in school? Is the school culture, that child of 19th-century Protestant laissez faire and rural America, of an emerging industrial and urban society and of an economy of scarcity, relevant to the multiethnic, multiracial, and multireligious post-industrial society of today, with its metropolitan and megapolitan settlement pattern and its economy of affluence-with-poverty? Which culture does today's child really need to know?

Such an analysis, which should, of course, be applied to both the school and the mass media, might quickly isolate the anachronistic and otherwise irrelevant or undesirable structures and functions (and content and method) in each institution. It would call for an end to social studies courses that deal more with the Indians than with the Vietnamese; or more with the cow than with the organization of the milk industry—as well as to television programs about the wild West and private eyes in which an individual hero succeeds without the help of organized society. It would certainly suggest that the school's conception of the child, which developed in an era in which there was no democracy or equality for children—or a teenage youth culture —needs to be replaced. It would indicate also that the conception of the teacher as a professional who has a monopoly of knowledge about education, which emerged when the students came from immigrant, rural, and frequently illiterate homes, is no longer applicable in an era when the mass media have informed both children and parents.

Even so, the analysis also suggests that there can be no either-or-solution, no choice between school or mass media, for the two institutions are teaching not only a different content but a different world view. Each represents some cultural, economic and political groups in our pluralistic society, and each is busy trying to dominate the communication channels of that society with its own world view. If the schools are the agents of Protestant lower-middle-class culture, of employers seeking trained workers, and of parents seeking to equip their children with marketable job skills, the mass media are the agents of post-Puritan middle and working-class cultures, of the consumption goods industries, and of parents (and children) who want to consume. And, of course, each institution supports and defends many other interests. In short, both the school and the mass media, are in the broadest sense, political institutions competing for cultural power in the society. Such competition has many advantages, particularly as long as there is no concensus about the ultimate goals of education. But in a pluralist society there will always be such a lack of consensus—and there should be. American democratic tradition teaches that when ultimate agreement is impossible, the best solution is pluralism; as wide a variety of educational institutions with diverse goals— and educational approaches—as possible.

Even if a comparative analysis of the schools and the mass media begins with this pluralistic premise, it is still possible to ask—and to answer—what each institution can do most effectively, and what it should be doing differently. If there is much the schools can learn from the mass media, the media can also learn much from the schools. And, if the analytic net is widened even further, one can ask similar questions about yet other educational institutions in our society; for example, the family, the peer group, the church, the store, and the political process. If the schools want to improve their effectiveness, they might well ask not only what they can learn from the mass media, but also what they can learn from how the family teaches its children, how youthful peer groups educate their members, or how candidates for election teach the voters how to vote for them.

Teacher as Artist and Artist as Teacher

JEROME HAUSMAN

On the face of it, the identification of the teacher as an artist and the artist as a teacher seems obvious and self-evident. We have long accepted the idea that teaching is an art as well as a science; there are many of the elements of artistic behavior involved in teaching: conceiving, structuring, organizing, presenting, responding, evaluating—in short, the good teacher must engage in significantly creative and qualitatively oriented behavior as part of his function in the classroom. In a similar sense, we have long accepted the idea that the depth of experience and personal insights of the artist provides an essential resource for communicating about the creative processes in making art. The oldest and still most practiced tradition in the teaching of art grows from the artist-apprentice relationship. In many cultures other than our own, distinctions are not made between practitioners of a discipline and the teachers in that discipline. A young person in training as an artist would begin an apprenticeship with a master. Along with being educated in skills and techniques of the craft, he would seek to encounter the underlying spirit and feeling for the form being produced. Thus, it is easy to see how we have come to speak of the artistry involved in teaching and the particular qualities and insights that help to make an artist an effective teacher.

Then where is the problem? What confusions arise out of such references as a "teacher as an artist" and an "artist as a teacher?" The difficulty, of course, arises from oversimplifications and overgeneralizations about teaching and the making of art. I am somewhat reminded of my little girl coming home from school and inquiring as to how it could be that "all bugs are

Reprinted by permission of the author and the publisher from *Art Education: Journal of the National Art Education Association*, Vol. 20, No. 4, April 1967, pp. 13–17.

insects, but all insects are not bugs." To be sure, all good teachers demonstrate considerable artistry in the performance of their teaching function; but all who are skilled as artists may not necessarily be effective as teachers. The difficulty is compounded further by the different ways in which the term "artist" is used. When one speaks of the art of teaching, one is making reference to the qualitative controls exercised by an individual in organizing and communicating particular ideas and feelings. Elements such as physical movement and control (modulation of voice, gesture, facial expression) are combined with the selection, organization, and presentation of ideas. There are an infinity of personal styles and techniques that characterize "the art of teaching." By comparison, the "artist" (who may or may not be a teacher) earns his title by virtue of the qualitative and technical means he exercises over a particular medium. His essential relationship is between himself and the form being created (in the visual arts: painting, sculpture, ceramics, graphics, etc.). While the teacher, in relation to his students, can ill afford large gaps in communication and understanding, the artist (so long as he can keep "eating") can afford the luxury of not being understood or "appreciated" by the audience of his own time. His works (given proper care) can survive beyond the time of their being created to a point in the future when the gap of misunderstanding may become closed. My major point, however, is that the skills and insights involved in making paintings, sculptures, and prints do not necessarily extend into the realm of the personal skills and insights required for effective teaching. Thus, to speak of the teacher as an artist and the painter as an artist is to make reference to different kinds of artists. To speak of the artist (referring to painters, sculptors, printmakers, etc.) as a teacher is of a different order; that is, some artists can be effective teachers and some cannot. I would even go one step further to assert that persons who are not themselves practicing artists can be effective teachers of art. The plea that I want to set forth would urge upon us all the avoidance of oversimplification and bias in relation to assertions about "teachers as artists. To speak of the artist (referring to painters, sculptors, printmakers, concerned, it would be well to get off the "label kick" and turn to the real problems involved in the teaching of art.

Any teaching of art must draw its essential content from the very nature of art itself. Merely engaging in manipulative activities (craft activities, oil painting, carving sculptural forms, etc.) does not necessarily lead to understandings and insights about art. We should not mistake "activity" (being busy with tools and materials) with learning about art. I would only observe that some of the strongest and loudest voices that are raised in behalf of conservative (and sometimes reactionary) values in relation to art are those of "Sunday painters" and other such groups that dabble with paints or pastels. Philosophers and aestheticians have devoted lifetimes to the question: what is art? Much as I am tempted to pursue this argument, I will not do so except to assert that making judgments about art is making judgments about quality.

Making such judgments involves the discovery of "ways of seeing" as well as seeing itself. "The more insight the history of art gives us into the necessities that form the artist, the more nearly it liberates us from the temptation of formulas, theories, and fashions, because it shows us that these things, being subject to perpetual change, are relative and vain. The only permanent thing is quality, which cannot be reduced to a formula or a definition." (R. Huyghe, *Ideas and Images in World Art*, p. 438.) Thus, it cannot be so simple a matter as saying: This is what art is and these are the rules by which it is judged—one, two, three, etc. The simple fact is that a Michelangelo sculpture is different from (and related to) a David Smith standing form; a Rubens' painting must be seen for its differences (as well as its similarities) when compared with a Jackson Pollock canvas.

Any definitions of art must account for its open-ended and metaphoric nature. Thus, there is no such thing as an established form of perfection to which all students and artists must strive. Objects become works of art by virtue of their inherent artistic qualities: the manner in which a work is organized to embody the vividness, intensity, and uniqueness of feelings of an idea. In large part, these qualities are only possible when a person engages in his own exploration of reality—the shaping of ideas and feelings in a medium in relation to particular values and purposes. Teachers can help students to see how others have given form to ideas and feelings—how they have used the elements of form, line, color, texture; how they have drawn upon particular symbols to convey meaning; how they have used tools and materials. But finally, each person is faced with finding and embodying his own unique ideas and feelings in a tangible form.

Just as definitions of art must account for its open-ended and metaphoric nature, conceptions of artistic process must recognize the changing relationship between a person and the art form he creates. In the process of a student's forming a painting or a piece of sculpture, the emerging object takes on an identity of its own. The artifact suggests its own form and meaning. The object being created can be said to be the expression of an idea; it is also the means by which the creator is shaped by the artifact itself. This is the thought expressed by Michelangelo in a sonnet:

"Just as cutting away, O Lady, makes/ In stone craggy and rough/ A figure comes to life,/ And grow the larger as the stone grows small,/ In the same way good works/ For the still trembling soul/ Are hidden by the surplus of the flesh,/ Whose cover is rough and coarse./ This from my outer shell/ You only can release;/ In me there is for me no will nor force."

A key factor in the teaching of art, at any level, involves creating conditions in which students can learn the joy and excitement in the search for and discovery of visual ideas, in the investment of their own ideas and feelings toward realizing new forms. Necessarily such teaching would have to help students to court mystery, deal with ambiguity, and on occasion suffer the pain and disappointment of failure. Given the present circumstances of our high school student body, this is a most difficult assignment. The prevailing value structure is "to play it cool," to avoid deep involvements and to hide one's emotions.

The problem of identifying what is to be "taught" in our high school art programs involves us in different kinds of specifics. Obviously, the specifics of a course of art majors should be different from a general required course for all freshmen; a course in the humanities involving the study of art history and criticism should be different from a course involving studio instruction. Moreover, the specifics of programs should vary in relation to geography, cultural emphases, and general experiential backgrounds of the students involved. Overall, the highly personal and subjective nature of art instruction confronts the teacher with a tremendous challenge and opportunity. This wide range of possibility and great latitude for choice is, at once, a problem and a blessing. Above all, the teacher cannot "play it cool." The teaching of art necessarily involves a demonstration by the teacher of the very values and attitudes that are being encouraged. The willingness to be "involved," to venture into the unknown to seek the poetic and the unusual, to tolerate ambiguity—these are qualities that must pervade the teacher's approach to students.

Where does a teacher start? It would seem to me that certain broad areas of purpose and goals need to be brought together. I would here refer you to the work of Benjamin S. Bloom and others who have set forth a taxonomy of educational objectives. Alas, this is an "approach" undertaken by many, many others. Time and again, lists of educational objectives have been developed without any noticeable effect upon the quality of teaching going on in our schools. It may well be that this is another instance of this same failing. There is, however, a compelling fascination for this effort. For one thing, it should be self-evident that effective teaching stems from a teacher who has a clear (not necessarily rigid) idea of what he is trying to accomplish.

In Bloom's work (along with many others),* a threefold division of educational objectives was set forth: (1) Cognitive: "Objectives which emphasize remembering or reproducing something which has presumably been learned, as well as objectives which involve the solving of some intellectual task for which the individual has to determine the essential problem and then record given material or combine it with ideas, methods, or procedures previously learned;" (2) Affective: "Objectives which emphasize a feeling tone, an emotion, or a degree of acceptance or rejection." This category would include interests, attitudes, appreciations, values, and emotional sets or biases; (3) Psychomotor: "Objectives which emphasize some muscular or motor skill, some manipulation of material and objects, or some act which requires a neuromuscular coordination."

* *Taxonomy of Educational Objectives, Handbook I. Cognitive Domain.* Benjamin S. Bloom, editor; Max D. Englehart, Edward J. Furst, Walker H. Hill, David R. Krathwohl. *Taxonomy of Educational Objectives: Handbook II. Affective Domain.* David R. Krathwohl, Benjamin S. Bloom, Bertram B. Masia.

Putting it more simply, a teacher must be able to set forth his ideas as to what knowledge he seeks to generate in the minds of his students; what values and attitudes he wants to encourage and foster; and what physical skills and techniques he wants his students to achieve. It is all too simple to avoid pressing these questions; this is especially the case in the teaching of art. Time can be consumed in an art class with pleasurable activities that may serve as a "relief" from the academic routine. Please be assured that I am not against "pleasure;" moreover, the very nature of art activity (either in a studio or critical type activity) involves both pleasure and pain. My real fear is that the nature of art instruction contains so many variables (and is so misunderstood by others, as art is misunderstood by others) that teachers under pressure of long hours, poor teaching conditions, and an unsympathetic environment will settle for less than the most demanding and critical discipline in their own teaching. Slogans such as "art is creative and expressive," "art activity provides a sense for beauty," and, yes, "the artist is the best teacher of art" cannot be accepted as being obvious and unquestionable truths.

Let me try to be even more specific: in the area of cognitive learning, it would seem to me that art instruction in our secondary schools needs to face certain obvious points: (1) A work of art is a source for a vast amount of information (it is a datum for studying the history of art; it is also a means to understand the context—values, purposes, conditions—within which it was created); (2) A work of art results from a medium and required technique; (3) Often there are significant art forms and documentation (literature, poetry, social and political documents) that are contemporary with the object being studied.

Even more specifically, the teacher must think through and establish various kinds of cognitive learnings for the art class; for example:

1. Students should become aware of specific facts—names, dates, events, places: Rembrandt van Rijn (1606–1669); the influence of middle class Protestant society of Holland; the specific works of the artist: "Dr. Tulp's Anatomy Lesson," "The Syndics of the Amsterdam Cloth Guild," "Rembrandt's Self Portraits;" or Paul Cezanne (1839–1906); his admiration for the work of Poussin; his retirement from Paris to Aix-en-Provence in southern France; his obsession for pictorial structure; works such as "The Great Bathers," "Card Players," "Mont Sainte-Victoire."

2. Students should become aware of trends and sequences; for example: to understand the flowering of Italian painting in the fifteenth and sixteenth centuries, to understand the period known as the Renaissance, the influence of such painters as Giotto must be seen. They effected a revolution in modes of artistic thought that was echoed in major works of pictorial art for hundreds of years; another example, to understand much of contemporary art (assemblage, pop and op art), one can look to roots in the work of dada, surrealist, and constructivist artists of almost 50 years ago.

3. Students should develop a sense for theory and structure; for example: Romanesque builders were unable to realize the effect of height held as being ideal by the northern temperament because they were limited by the semicircular arches usually found in their methods of vaulting. By substituting oblong for square nave bays, the Gothic builder was able to subordinate the horizontal rhythm still present in the Romanesque interior; by using pointed instead of semicircular arches, he could accentuate the effect of upward movement and increase the actual height of his vaults.

4. Students should learn to seek out principles and generalizations; for example: during the first millennium A.D., most Western world painting (as was true for architecture and sculpture) was done in the service of the Church. The principle functions of art were twofold: the decoration and glorification of religious buildings and the physically smaller (but none the less significant) illustration of manuscripts. How different this is from the art of today. By comparison and juxtaposition of images and ideas, students can seek out and develop generalizations about our art forms: painting, sculpture, architecture, as well as the imagery of motion pictures, television, and other forms of our industrialized and technological culture.

In a similar sense, teachers of art must strive for clarity in dealing with subtle nuances of form and meaning in the classroom. Teaching involves qualitative decision making; in short, it involves communication about judgments, attitudes, and values. To the extent that we can attain some clarity in the never-ending search for aesthetic and meaningful forms, we can better understand, control, and communicate about such processes. To be sure, any given teaching act is the resultant of a complex of decisions. A single action may stem from a variety of simultaneous judgments involving intuitive and felt responses. However, the simple point I wish to set forth is that a teacher who is knowledgeable and informed of the multiplicity of factors involved in his own decisions and actions is more likely than not to make qualitatively better decisions.

Having set forth some examples of what I mean by cognitive learnings, let me turn briefly (and all too generally) to some of the factors in the "mix" of teacher decision making in the affective and psychomotor categories:

1. Teachers must be aware of the medium or media being used. Every medium has its own intrinsic qualities. These qualities dictate its potentials for forming—the resiliency and resistancy with which it can be shaped, its permanence as a form. Each medium imposes its own requirements upon its use. For example, working with a water-based clay requires damp storage until the work has been completed; working with plasticene enables continuous reshaping of forms but no permanency. Working with the wire involves certain physical controls—the medium is, by its very nature, linear in quality. Working with cut paper in doing collage affords opportunities for overlapping

shapes and planes; working with pen and ink provides opportunities for descriptive detail. Every medium also imposes its own demands in terms of skills and techniques. Generally, more resistant materials can only be changed by actions having a relatively fixed consequence (cutting into wood, stone, linoleum, etc.); more resilient materials can be reshaped and reworked after an initial action (modeling of clay, moving and replacing collage forms, painting over an already dry tempera form, etc.). A more resistant medium (wood, wire, stone) can lead to frustration on the part of an inexperienced student who seeks to change its form or quality without having developed adequate knowledge of technique or insights into the inherent nature of the material.

2. Teachers must be aware of the dynamic relationship between the medium being used and the ideas being formed. All too often a student is heard to say: "I had a clear picture in my mind, but I just can't get it on my paper." The "clearly formed image" in one's mind is often times the source of frustration when the medium being used does not lend itself to that "image." By fixing an image in one's mind (using the forms of imagination), an inexperienced student can set an unattainable goal in terms of his abilities and the nature of the medium being used. Moreover, by setting such a fixed goal, the student robs himself of the discovery and invention that takes place in the process of working. Rather than starting with a fixed image (an already completed picture in one's mind), students should be helped to see and feel their ideas interact with materials. The starting point for art work must be ideas and images that will lend themselves to change and modification. In the process that follows, the student's hand and mind engage in interaction with a medium. The evolving form is then the resultant of this interaction. The final image is usually not what may have been envisioned at the start. After all, the image "painted" within one's mind has been created in a different "medium" than is the case when one uses paints and brush.

3. Teachers must be aware that creative activity in art (as in any other field) does not involve the creation of a form from "nothing." Creativity in art is not creativity in a mystical or biblical sense. The forms that are created grow out of already existing facts, ideas, and skills. To be sure, each student is unique; to some extent his drawings, paintings, and sculpture can reflect this uniqueness. However, there is a sense in which the capacity to be "creative" is related to the store of skills, images, and ideas that are provided by others. This is what Pasteur meant when he said: "Fortune favors the prepared mind." Thus, good teaching in art introduces a flux of ideas and images and then helps students to uncover, select, rearrange, combine, and synthesize ideas and images drawn from this flux.

By asserting that students can be helped to recognize their own power in giving shape to their ideas and feelings, I am saying that teachers can help them to recognize that they (the students) can and do respond to their visual world. The nature of this response in the art class has to do with dramatic and poetic aspects of seeing and forming visual images; it has to do with fostering creative insights and the way in which such responses are formed. The central problem to be faced in the teaching of art involves attitudes toward adventure and discovery rather than technical skills. It is much more an attitude, a point of view that would allow for the repositioning and re-structuring of ideas. Of equal importance, it is an attitude that would allow for action in terms of these values.

The teacher of art can do certain basic things in relation to the students in his classroom:

1. He can accept and value his students as being creative. Questions and comments can be directed toward the more personalized and unique aspects of what students do in their art work. An attitude of teacher "acceptance" can give greater psychological freedom and security for the projecting of new ideas and forms.

2. Teachers can consciously relate the inventions of one person to what others are doing or have done. One student's drawing may have sur-realistic overtones, while another's effort may be geometric and non-objective. Yet, each suggests roots in the past; each may be inventive in the quality of detail or in the manner in which the medium has been used. By relating the variety of means by which students give form to their ideas, teachers can give support to the differences as well as the similarities in visual forms.

3. Teachers can recognize the importance of feedback, invention, and intuition. By helping their students to see new possibilities through the emerging forms, by encouraging them to talk about their feelings and ideas, and by supporting the willingness to build something different, teachers can set a tone for the exploration of visual forms.

4. Teachers can encourage the making of visual judgments. Much of our communication is based upon verbal and/or mathematical symbols, yet much of our experience is based upon visual symbols. From illustrations in textbooks to mass-produced images in our magazines, on our television and motion picture screens, and on our highways, we are being con-fronted with powerful and pervasive images. Students need to learn to see the world about them; they need to learn to make visual judgments. They can be helped to talk about and evaluate what they see—by comparing and noticing differences and similarities, by becoming aware of shapes, textures, and other visual qualities, and above all, by making judgments as to quality. Judgments of quality are not simple yes-no, good-bad judgments. Students should be helped to develop and refine their own criteria for the judgments they make.

Returning to the theme of this paper, "the teacher as an artist and the artist as a teacher," I trust that I have made myself clear about the significance of education in art in the midst of twentieth century technology. For empha-sis, I would only want to return to one of my very first points: it is the knowledge and insight about art that is critical for the effective teaching of the subject. It is the teacher who structures the ways and means for dealing with the "how, what, and why" of art instruction. What the teacher does is, of course, related to the students in his class; what the teacher does must also draw upon the field of art as a basic resource. The structure of teaching art, at any level, must be done with a sense for a larger body of knowledge and understanding about art itself. The concept of what constitutes an "artistic" problem—its limitations and possibilities—is central to what is to be taught.

In a recent article, Robert M. Hutchins posed the question: "Are we educating our children for the wrong future?" (*Saturday Review*, September, 1965.) Hutchins observes: "The world is new and is getting newer every minute . . . Almost every 'fact' I was taught from the first grade through law school is no longer a fact. Almost every tendency that was proclaimed has failed to materialize. The 'facts' and tendencies of today are those that nobody foresaw 50 years ago." Given the prospect of even greater change, there are far-reaching and profound questions concerning just what it is that can be "taught" to prepare our youngsters for the future. Hutchins concludes that "what education can and should do is help people become human." A teacher is an artist, with a sense for the depth and poetry of visual form, can contribute greatly toward this end. In the visual arts, I would place key emphasis upon developing knowledge and insight about visual symbols and the capacity to give visual form to emerging ideas and feelings. Visual symbols have always been critical to man's thought processes. By educating students to be more sensitive to and knowledgeable about their visual world, we will provide a key avenue for dealing with the future. The knowledge about art to which I am referring is really knowing art as an endeavor that is never satisfied with the obvious and the trivial. Knowing art, in the sense that I use the term, requires newly created visions and insights at every moment of living.

Summary of All Stages

VIKTOR LOWENFELD

AND

LAMBERT BRITTAIN

Art education has tremendous potential for the understanding of children and for the promoting of their creative growth. Every child is unique. Knowing the stages of his creative growth in relation to his general development allows us to motivate him toward his greatest achievement and personal

Summary. Scribbling Stage—Two to Four Years

Characteristics	Human Figure	Space	Color	Design	Motivation Topics	Materials
(1) Disordered. Kinesthetic experience. No control of motions.	None.	None.	No conscious approach. Use of color for mere enjoyment without any intentions.	None.	Through encouragement. Do not interrupt or discourage or divert child from scribbling.	Large black crayon. Smooth paper. Poster paint. Finger paint only for maladjusted children. Clay.
(2) Controlled. Repeated motions, establishment of co-ordination between visual and motor activity. Control of motions. Self-assurance of control through deviations of type of motions.	None.	None, or only kinesthetically.	Same as above.	None.	Same as above.	Same as above.
(3) Naming. Change from kinesthetic to imaginative thinking. Mixing of motions with frequent interruption.	Only imaginatively by the act of naming.	Purely imaginatively.	Color used to distinguish different meanings of scribbling.	None.	In the direction of the child's thinking by continuing the child's story.	Colored crayons. Poster paint. Clay, felt-nibbed pen.

342

Summary. Preschematic Stage—Four to Seven Years

Characteristics	Human Figure	Space	Color	Design	Motivation Topics	Materials
Discovery of *relationship* between drawing, thinking, and environment. Change of form symbols because of constant search for definite concept.	Circular motion for head, longitudinal for legs and arms. Head-feet representations develop to more complex form concept. Symbols depending on active knowledge during the act of drawing.	Self as center, with no orderly arrangement of objects in space: "There is a table, there is a door, there is a chair." Also emotional relationships: "This is *my* doll."	No relationship to nature. Color according to emotional appeal.	No conscious approach.	Activating of passive knowledge related mainly to self (body parts).	Crayons, clay, tempera paints (thick), large bristle brushes, large sheets of paper (absorbent).

343

Summary. Schematic Stage—Seven to Nine Years

Characteristics	Human Figure	Space	Color	Design	Motivation Topics	Materials
Formulation of a definite concept of man and environment. Self-assurance through repetition of form symbols, schemata. In pure schema no intentional experience is expressed, only the thing itself: "the man," "the tree," etc. Experiences are expressed by deviations from schema. Use of geometric lines.	Definite concept of figure depending on active knowledge and personality, through repetition: schema. Deviations expressing experiences can be seen in— (1) Exaggeration of important parts. (2) Neglect or omission of unimportant parts. (3) Change of symbols.	First definite space concept: base line. Discovery of being a part of environment: important for cooperation and reading. Base line expresses— (1) Base. (2) Terrain. Deviations from base line express experiences. Subjective space: (1) Folding over (egocentric). (2) Mixed forms of plan and elevation. (3) X-ray pictures. (4) Space-time representations.	Discovery of relationship between color and object; through repetition: color schema. Same color for same object. Deviation of color schema shows emotional experience.	No conscious design approach.	Best motivation concentrates on action, characterized by *we, action, where.* Topics referring to— (1) Time sequences (journeys, traveling stories). (2) X-ray pictures (inside and outside are emphasized), factory, school, home, etc.	Colored crayons. Colored chalks. Tempera, poster paint. Large paper. Bristle and hair brushes. Clay: (1) Synthetic (2) Analytic.

Summary. Stage of Dawning Realism—Nine to Eleven Years

Characteristics	Human Figure	Space	Color	Design	Motivation Topics	Materials
Gang age. Removal from geometric lines (schema). Lack of cooperation with adults. Greater awareness of the self and of sex differences.	Attention to clothes, (dresses, uniforms), emphasizing difference between girls and boys. Greater stiffness as result of egocentric attitude, and the emphasis on details (clothes, hair, and so forth). Tendency toward realistic lines. Removal from schema.	Removal from base-line expression. Overlapping. Sky comes down to base line. Discovery of plane. Filling in space between base lines. Difficulties in spatial correlations as result of egocentric attitude and lack of cooperation.	Removal from objective stage of color. Emphasis on emotional approach to color. Subjective stage of color. Color is used according to subjective experience.	First conscious approach toward decoration. Acquaintance with materials and their function.	Self-awareness stimulated by characterization of different dresses and suits (professions). Cooperation and overlapping through group work. Subjective cooperation through type of topic: "We are Building a House." Objective cooperation through team work.	Paper cutting. Crayons. Poster paint. Flat, colored chalk. Clay. Papier-mâché. Wood. Collage materials. Metal. Prints.

Summary. Pseudo-Naturalistic Stage—Eleven to Thirteen Years

Characteristics	Human Figure	Space	Color	Design	Motivation Topics	Materials
Developed intelligence, yet unawareness. Naturalistic approach (unconscious). Tendency toward visual- or nonvisual-mindedness. Love for dramatization and action.	Joints. Visual observation of body actions. Proportions. Emphasis on expression by nonvisually minded.	Urge for three-dimensional expression. Diminishing sizes of distant objects. Horizon line (visually minded). Environment only when significant (nonvisually minded).	Changes of color in nature for distance and mood (visually minded). Emotional reaction to color (nonvisually minded).	First conscious approach to stylizing. Symbols for professions. Function of different materials, with related designs.	Dramatic actions in environment. Actions from imagination and posing (with meaning, like scrubbing). Proportions through emphasis on content. Color moods.	Water color. Gouache (water color and tempera). Poster paint. Bristle brush. Hair brush. Clay. Linoleum. Papier-mâché. Textiles. Wood.

Summary. Adolescent Art—Thirteen to Seventeen Years

Characteristics	Human Figure	Space	Color	Design	Motivation Topics	Materials
Ambition. Energy. Romantic ideals. Introspection. Peer-group pressure. Sexual awakenings.	Action. Participation. Self-identification or empathy. Clothing. Costume. Dance and rhythm.	Visual perspective or perspective of value.	Sophisticated. Not necessarily naturalistic.	As integral part of function. (In furniture, clothing, ornament, architecture, home style, landsite, landscaping, interior decoration). Abpreciation. Abstract. Cartoons.	Self, home, community, nature, industry. Explore materials rather than emphasize technical excellence. Develop sensitivity. Excursions.	Any material that contributes to further growth or adult use. All previous materials, plus photography, ceramics, wood (constructing and carving). Natural materials.

347

fulfillment. An attempt has been made to put into outline form some of the factors involved in the development of creative expression. These outlines are simplified and should be used only as a reminder of the differences and similarities existing among children. For every stage are listed certain procedures and media that are most appropriate; these as well as an outline of the progression of creative expression are summarized.

Some of the most important concepts the authors hoped to convey cannot be put into outline form. Sensitivity to children and an understanding of the importance of the creative act need to be experienced rather than memorized. We must recognize that our knowledge is worthless unless we can develop within children the self-confidence to utilize art as a means of imaginative self-expression according to individual needs. Through such creative experiences our youth may lead more unified and better-adjusted lives.

Part III

Critical Analysis and Research:
Contributors to Complete Art Education

"Critical Analysis and Research," Chapters 5 and 6 of this anthology, present readings related to what are perhaps two of the most neglected and misunderstood areas in the field of art education. The class room teacher and art specialist alike are openly criticized for either neglecting these areas completely or approaching them with apprehension and suspicion. And this criticism is justified, because the opportunity for study and involvement in aesthetics and research is nonexistent in the majority of our undergraduate teacher-training institutions. Too often, study in these vital subjects becomes the exclusive domain of a few graduate students and faculty within the isolated university community. It is imperative that graduating teachers in art education become familiar with the problems of critical analysis and be sympathetic to the important role research is to play in guiding the future of art education.

The continually developing sophistication of twentieth-century art has included the radical change from nameable to unnameable forms and the shifting attitudes which accent the polarity between finite art objects and happenings, environments, and other experiential approaches. Because of this shift, the possible discourse on the descriptive aspects of art has now been limited, and as a result the expressive values of the work must be considered. As there is no ready vocabulary to express these values, the problem is compounded.

The problem of dealing with this "new aesthetic" becomes the focal point of the articles in this chapter by Rosenberg, Feldman, and Burnham. Burnham presents some insights into the most recent and perhaps the most difficult art form to subject to prevailing critical analysis. He states, "Transitions between major paradigms may best express the state of present art. Reasons for it lie in the nature of current technological shifts." In keeping with the technological advance of our age, he feels the "unobjects" in which the concepts of many artists today take form, might best be approached through "systems analysis." Although this approach had its origin in national government as it related to the expense and operational complexity of modern warfare, the logic of its approach might possess the key for dealing with art that is no longer concerned with the production of accustomed art objects.

The specific relationship between aesthetics and the problems of the classroom teacher are explored in readings by Child, Smith, and Eisner. In the contribution by Eisner the concern with an ultimate end of critical analysis—evaluation—is considered. The evaluative process in art has always posed a problem for the art teacher inasmuch as evaluation, for the most part, has been concerned with product evaluation and involvement with grades. Those who are totally committed to the singular importance of the "process" in art education are sometimes reluctant to participate in any evaluation of student art work. They feel that any focus on the product will divert the intrinsic creative drive to an extrinsic desire for rewards in the form of grades. This may be an attempt to avoid the problem, because the process and the product are too closely integrated in good teaching to be separated. However, as undesirable as grades may be, the responsibility of the teacher to his students is not fulfilled unless an analysis and ultimate evaluation of their work is completed. A plan for determining the progress the individual student makes toward a more complete aesthetic awareness and the development of artistic skills must be initiated by each teacher. This can be accomplished through a critical dialogue between the student (his goals), the work (its aesthetic qualities in relationship to today's art), and the teacher (his objectives).

The growth and maturity of art education is made evident by its ability to embrace the complex sources which contribute to its make up and still maintain a character of individuality. This attitude has been fostered by the rejection of generalizations in theories which would tend to blur its image, and the drive to find answers to problems supported by evidence, examples, and logic. Research has played a major role in the development of this position.

In the first article in Chapter 6, "Research," Kaufman points to some of the many problems the researcher in the area of art and education may encounter. The use and misuse of research findings are also considered. He cautiously states,

Objective methodologies of art teaching experimentally "proven" to be correct cannot be packaged and handed over to teachers. In the final analysis, it is the teacher himself who has to find the personal resources for good art teaching in his own psychic insights and range of experience.

Although there has been justified criticism lodged against the infant attempts at research in art education, the past decade has seen the contribution of some major findings and the sophistication of the tools of scientific inquiry. A primary concern by those who are "anti-research," is a feeling that research lacks relevance to utilitarian ends and therefore the time and energy would best be expended in other ways. Carroll responds with a three-pointed answer, stating that

(1) the better understanding of phenomena is a legitimate end in itself, (2) the potential of much research cannot always be known immediately, and (3) one cannot predict whether a given scientific investigation will be "successful" even in its own terms . . . sometimes a negative result is a distinct contribution to knowledge because it informs the scientific community that the hypothesis or methodology tried is apparently of no avail.

As no investigatory method is entirely "pure" and free from problems inherent in the nature of its approach, Bakan suggests another look at the process of introspection and its possible new role in research. Although this approach has lost favor with most researchers, he gives examples of the pragmatic usefulness of the knowledge of possibilities, prediction, and control of human behavior, extending it beyond the clinical situation and into the world arena.

The remainder of the articles in this section deal with the specific directions of research in art education. Davis discusses current trends in the field, whereas Stumbo offers an operational base from which research can be approached.

There is no doubt that research in both the arts and the sciences have had their effect on the direction and content of art education. If there is criticism, it is not the research itself that should be under fire, because the right by any individual to seek answers through honest investigation should be encouraged. The problem, and it is fast disappearing through the experience of involvement, lies in the ability to sift and select research information that can help in developing and extending those dimensions of education that have already been embraced.

5

Critical Analysis

Engaging Art in Dialogue

EDMUND B. FELDMAN

Teaching implies learning just as performance implies an audience. Both are dialogic in form. What is said or made or taught is conditioned by what is replied, accepted, or understood. Learning is contingent upon a dialogue in which we feel ourselves addressed and answered, especially in the arts. How do the "voices of silence" develop the capacity for dialogue?

In one sense, dialogue is conversation; it is an *exchange* of views. A good deal of teaching unfortunately is in the form of monologue. It involves no exchange of views because many assume that students have little of value to contribute about something so technical, so recondite, as art. Consequently, preparation for teaching often consists of preparing monologues— thoughtful advice about how to organize information into packages. We spend much of our time getting students ready to take part in dialogues about art. Someday, but not while they are in school, they may be able to participate actively. As yet, they do not possess the cognitive equipment;

Reprinted with permission from *The Saturday Review*, July 15, 1967, pp. 60, 61, 73, and 74. Copyright 1967, Saturday Review, Inc.

they do not know enough. They have had considerable experience as members of human communities, but that does not meet the requirements for dialogue!

Another notion of dialogue is that it is a type of dramatic recitation. An actor recites dialogue—lines in a role. His art seems to consist of interpreting these lines and finding concrete expression for them by skillfully employing his voice, his body, and his gestures. But the dialogue he recites has been established in advance of his performance. He may elaborate and extemporize on his role; essentially, however, he makes manifest those meanings which existed in another symbolic form—in the playwright's book. The dialogue of visual art, however, is of a different order; it relies on an unspoken but nevertheless quite real communion between man and visual form.

It should be understood that art is created as a *result* of dialogue: The artist, like anyone else, is engaged in a continuous series of transactions with the world. His transactions with materials, ideas, styles, and themes have dialogic form; they involve questions or assertions, and replies. The artist talks to himself as he works and also to his colleagues, his models and competitors —all are implicated in an imaginative but nevertheless real conversation. We know it is real because of the palpable art object which results, just as we know that love is real because of the child which is born as the consequence of a prior dialogue of the flesh and the spirit. To regard any art object as a mere collocation of forms, as a type of distant stimulus which initiates the events culminating in perception, is not only an impoverished idea of art from a humanistic standpoint but an untrue one as well. Anyone who has had serious experience with the creation of art knows how intensely he has questioned himself in the course of making the decisions which result in the forms the world sees. So this questioning—of himself and of others—is implicit in the artist's work. Whatever else art is, it is also a record of the artist's dialogue with the world.

Dialogue also occurs when we look at what the artist has created. No one believes any longer that looking at art is an optical operation alone or that understanding what is seen is a passive process—passive in the sense that a photographic plate records light impressions. On the contrary, we recognize the participation of the total organism in acts of esthetic perception. Once perceptual processes have passed beyond our sensing organs, all of our systems are brought into operation. The events which constitute this involvement do not occur with the speed of events in a modern computer, but they occur fast enough for us to be virtually unaware of a time lapse between their successive explosions. That is why visual art requires shaped space in order to govern essentially temporal sequences of excitation in the cells of a person viewing a work of art. By dialogue in the perception of art, therefore, we also mean the neural and physiological responses of an organism to shaped spatial events.

Dialogue occurs in the way visual forms "speak" to their observers. The humanistic tradition of looking at and studying the arts has taught us to regard forms as vehicles of potential meaning. These are not meanings we as viewers project on the forms. They are meanings we can apprehend because of the way visual elements have been organized in an art object. Through research in linguistics, esthetics, and psychology we are growing in our ability to understand formal and symbolic configurations; they do speak; form does constitute a language. And mastery of that language can be gained, both from the standpoint of using it as a mode of expression and reading it as a mode of communication. While the humanities have been traditionally concerned with reading the language of art, however, art education for a good many years has been concerned only with personal expression through that language.

Now reading a work of art means being able to understand its language, and language always occurs in a social context, a context of dialogue. Therefore, reading art means knowing how a work responds to the questions the artist has asked in the course of creating it. It means knowing what questions the artist asked the world as he went about his business of discovering adequate form. Finally, it means addressing the work oneself—asking and getting answers. In this sort of enterprise mere exposure to art objects is not very helpful, nor is the recitation of authoritative interpretations and judgments about art. From the standpoint of reading, that is, of dialogue, such discourse is largely irrelevant and even evasive. Often it is an unwitting effort to sustain attention to art in the absence of anything better.

Let me illustrate the "human dialogue of art" by examining a familiar twentieth-century masterpiece, Picasso's *Guernica*. Everyone knows it was painted as a protest against the Nazi bombing of the Basque town of Guernica during the Spanish Civil War. A reasonably informed teacher can identify the figures and objects in the mural, sketch in the historical background of the work, offer a formal analysis of the visual elements, and allude to the symbolic meaning of the bull, the horse, the fallen statue, and so on. The iconography of the *Guernica* has been thoroughly analyzed by the experts and widely disseminated by the Museum of Modern Art. But for this work to enter into humanistic dialogue it must be perceived as the answer to a series of questions the artist asked. Now it does not matter whether Picasso did, in fact, ask the questions answered in his painting. It is necessary only that the objective visual evidence sustain the questions we see raised in it. They seem to be the following: How can a calamity be portrayed so that we perceive, simultaneously: (1) the bombing of a town; (2) the agony of the bombing's victims; (3) the communication of the event by news media; (4) the comparison of military terror to a bullfight; (5) the meaning of the bombing in the history of war; and (6) the impact of destruction on classical notions of reason and order?

Anyone can point to the work as an example of Picasso's resentment of Franco and his Nazi allies, or as a protest against the inhumanity of war, or as an example of the capacity of art to express anguish. But an act of creative criticism is required to connect the forms one sees with the specific meanings or answers the total work seems to support. These questions are a device,

"We can talk with Picasso's Guernica in terms of what currently worries us, and the painting says something that makes sense and is relevant to existence now."

Picasso, Pablo. Guernica (Mural), 1937. Oil on canvas, 11'6" x 25'8". On extended loan to The Museum of Modern Art, New York, from the artist, M. Picasso.

then, for calling attention to the answers which the formal syntax, the symbols, the drawing, the color, and the pictorial organization of the *Guernica* provide. The last thing one cares about in connection with a discussion of this mural is a definition of Cubism or a disquisition on the principles of design embodied in it.

What are some of the humanistic answers the *Guernica* seems to make? In the context of the whole, it asserts that personal heroism, in war or in peace, is obsolete. It says that God sees all, including carnage, and is indifferent. It raises the current theological question: Is God dead? Was God dead in 1937? Picasso implies that He lives but doesn't care. What do I think, especially if I am a young man who might serve in Vietnam? The *Guernica* maintains that the bombing of civilians is wrong; do I believe that the purpose for which civilians are bombed transcends the meaning of mutilated flesh? Should one permit such questions to be raised now by a painting which was executed, after all, thirty years ago? Would it be better to focus on Picasso's patriotic emotions, his feelings as a Spaniard who sympathized with the Loyalists? Incidentally, does historical explication save one the embarrassment of being personally addressed by Picasso's forms? The work portrays agony, to be sure, but it also tells us what happens when a catastrophe is converted into the monotonous and impersonal gray of newsprint. While he felt anger, Picasso was also fascinated by man's ability to transform terror into tolerable ideas through the agency of the news media, that is, the black, white, and gray of newspapers and motion picture newsreels.

A prominent feature of the *Guernica* is a terrified, classically drawn woman holding out a type of bedroom lamp. Its light is shed on the central portion of the scene. But the total work seems to say, "Isn't light an absurd symbol of reason in this context?" One wants to ask, "Does light clarify human dilemmas or does it merely illuminate human atrocities committed according to the dictates of someone's reason and abetted by the impersonal application of scientific knowledge?"

We are all familiar with the biblical assertion that light is the symbol of the divine. And Picasso has used an eye, presumably the divine eye, to act as a surrogate spectator for humanity. But this divine eye has a light bulb for a pupil. Does the eye receive light, like most eyes, or does it radiate light in some special sense? Here we should recall Dewey's critique of classical theory of knowledge as being founded largely on an optical analogy. That is, classical thought conceived of knowing as a passive act similar to the passive act of receiving light radiation through one's organ of sight. But Dewey and philosophers of science in general conceive of knowing as an active process, a process of interfering with phenomena one wishes to know about. And, of course, modern theories of perception—notably Gestalt—conceive of vision as acting upon what is seen. Accordingly, the Greeks would be wrong, both in their theory of knowledge so far as it was analogous to optics and also in their understanding of perception.

But it is doubtful that Picasso knew formal Greek thought or Dewey's

"The work portrays agony . . . but it also tells us what happens when catastrophe is converted into the impersonal gray of newsprint."
Picasso, Pablo. Detail from Guernica *(Mural), 1937. Oil on canvas, 11'6" x 25'8". On extended loan to The Museum of Modern Art, New York, from the artist, M. Picasso.*

critique of it. One is aware, nevertheless, of a terrible irony in his portrayal of a handsome, classical woman holding a lamp like a beacon over an arena of pitiful slaughter. Somehow the artist has arrived, through his own language, at a critique of classical reason. It is a similar critique to that being currently advanced by the radical theologians. Altizer, Hamilton, Van Buren, and Rubenstein. Was Picasso saying in 1937 what the radical theologians of 1967 are saying—that the old "God language" is dead? Notice that the all-knowing God of Judeo-Christian tradition is symbolized by Picasso as an all-seeing God. But He is essentially a passive observer, in the classical tradition, because seeing and knowing were regarded as passive operations.

Reinhold Niebuhr and the late Paul Tillich would maintain, I believe, that God cannot be contained, cannot be adequately conceptualized, by a particular cultural symbol or formulation; hence the inadequacies of Greek optics, rationalist philosophy, and Judeo-Christian theological formulations are not God's fault. We need better symbols, that is all. The student of art, as opposed to the theologian, can only observe that Picasso has been painfully effective in showing how ironically the old symbols operate. Altizer and company may strike out in their way at the old symbols and the old "God-language" but only art brings them so intimately to bear on our lives.

These musings about a monument of twentieth-century art are not offered as original insights. They are intended to be demonstrations of the sort of dialogue one can have with a significant work of art. As in all conversations, some of the pressing concerns of the participants get into the discussion. The God Is Dead theologians were not around in 1937 when Guernica was bombed; but Freud was not around when Shakespeare explored Hamlet's relationship to his mother. Tchelitchew painted *Hide and Seek* before modern biologists felt they had erased the line between organic and inorganic substances. In other words, important works of art are capable of sustaining a contemporary dialogue, not because of the resourcefulness or imagination of art critics, but because the languages of the humanities are not time-bound as ordinary language is. The languages of the humanities may lack the precision of the languages of science, but they are less prone to obsolescence. We can talk with Picasso's *Guernica* in terms of what currently worries us and the painting "has something to say," something that makes sense and is relevant to existence now.

Here we might distinguish between historical inquiry and humanistic dialogue. History, particularly scientific history, would appear to be concerned with "what happened," and, aside from getting the record straight, this concern is undergirded by an assumption that "what happened" will happen again. But the humanist always asks of phenomena, "How does 'what happened' affect me now—in terms of my present concerns and dilemmas?" The youngster in class asks: "Why are you taking my time to show me the so-called monuments of art when I would rather talk about the Beatles?" The historian seems to have essentially one answer to this question: "Everything that concerns you now is a recurrence of something that happened before. So far as art is concerned, it constitutes a recurrence of earlier art which reappears to us in forms merely altered by recent technology. Today's art cannot really be understood except in terms of the recurrent forms and ideas it embodies." There may be some truth in this view—a partial truth at best—but the emphasis on historical explanation of contemporary art is nevertheless far too heavy in our educational practice. Students are not indifferent to history; they just resent old-fashioned explanations of what they know is uniquely new.

Can we derive any curricular implications from the dialogic idea of art? One is that the chronological organization of art studies is often unfeasible because it is too lengthy, frequently misleading in its underlying assumptions about the recurrence of esthetic phenomena, and occasionally irrelevant because of its focus on art sequences rather than art objects. Furthermore, it may impose a false conception of time on students: Consider that today's cosmopolitan cities have populations of seven or eight million. Did ancient

Athens hold as many as 20,000 souls? Did Renaissance Florence have 40,000 inhabitants? How large was Rome in Raphael's day? If one's definition of art includes everything that man designs (as it should), think of what is being created in megalopolitan centers like New York and Paris today! Museums contain only selections, not necessarily intelligent selections, of art. Their holdings may imply a definition of art and of time which is indifferent to the output of imaginative energy in contemporary civilization.

In teaching, the chronological presentation of slides—from the cave man to Rauschenberg—giving each work an identical budget of time, reconstructing time in terms of equal, separate events called slide projections, is misleading even in terms of its own goals—the comprehensive presentation of man's art. Almost all the scientists who ever lived are alive today. Should one teach a course in the history of science by giving Daedalus, who invented wax wings, as much attention as Isaac Newton, who developed the laws of the conservation of energy? This, in effect, is what is done in many historical surveys. Perhaps, therefore, we should study art by beginning with the present and working back into antiquity.

We might consider anthropology as a source of useful curricular categories. It studies the tools and rituals man uses to satisfy his persistent needs. They are classified according to the cultural and biological crises he must pass through: conception, birth, puberty, marriage, nurture of the young, aging, death, burial, rebirth. These crises have their associated art objects; industrial man has even developed some new ones—ennui, anomie, alienation, and mass hysteria. Such crises, too, have their associated art forms; it is instructive for students to encounter them in the work of Munch, Soutine, Kokoschka, and Bacon. These are the artistic tools and rituals we use to confront ourselves; they are part of our survival equipment.

If the visual arts are ever to join in cooperative relations with the other arts in education, curricular categories drawn from the social sciences will have to be employed along with the period and stylistic divisions, the media classifications, and the geopolitical and ethnic labels we have been using. Humanities courses should not consist of conventional efforts to teach the histories of three or four arts instead of one. That would only compound our pedagogical difficulties. In planning instruction in the humanities we should start with life as it is felt and as we see it lived. Then we can proceed to find out how organized knowledge and the vast body of created art illuminate life. Our blind spots, enthusiasms, and capacities for feeling are also tools of the teaching trade. Personal reactions to paint, line, enclosed space, color, clay, or the emotion of metal surfaces may be worth, pedagogically speaking, several tons of Art Through the Ages or the entire McGraw-Hill Encyclopedia of World Art.

We ought to remember that artistic form is a language which documents merely echo; for those who are initiated materials speak. The materials shaped by our hands, or by the tools our hands and minds devise, always testify to a human dialogue between man-the-maker and the world he discovered but did not make, the world not quite to his liking. The humanities ought to be an account of the world we try to change through that agency of real and symbolic action called art.

Criticism and Its Premises

HAROLD ROSENBERG

The first requirement of art criticism is that it shall be relevant to the art under consideration—how correct are its evaluations of specific art objects is of lesser importance. The accuracy of a critic's judgments cannot be determined by his contemporaries, in any case. But the inflection given by art criticism to the general thinking about art affects not only the responses of appreciators of art but the creative attitudes of artists as well. When this thinking is trivial or beside the point, painting and sculpture become the specialty of feature writers, decorators, dealers and speculators in masterpieces.

It is the contention of this paper that in order to be relevant art criticism today must maintain a continuing sensitivity to certain characteristics peculiar to the modern epoch which affect the situation of art, including the outlook, rituals and objectives of those who create it. A mind blind to the radical material, social and intellectual transformations of the twentieth century and their influence upon its modes of creation can only respond to representative modern works with confusion and bitterness. For such a mind, criticism has one purpose: to provide a defensive barrier against new work and new ideas by applying "values" presumably drawn from the great achievements of the past. Criticism so oriented leads neither to intelligent perusal of individual works nor to genuine debate concerning the cultural losses and gains of modernism. It merely drops a curtain of polemics between the critic and the artist and contributes to the estrangement of the public from all art, past as well as present, since only through responding to present-day creations can the creations of other periods be genuinely appreciated.

The following are propositions which in my opinion ought to be more or less explicitly recognized by contemporary critical thinking as creating new problems for art and for art criticism.

Proposition 1: That creation of art in the twentieth century is an activity within the politico-cultural drama of a world in the process of remaking itself. Modern art is saturated with issues and ideologies which reflect the technological, political, social and cultural revolutions of the past 50 years. Regardless of the degree to which the individual artist is conscious of these issues, he

Reprinted by permission from A *Seminar in Art Education for Research and Curriculum Development*, Cooperative Research Project, No. J-002, The Pennsylvania State University, 1966, Copyright. University Park, Pa.

in fact responds to them in choosing among immediate aesthetic and technical alternatives. If he chooses one mode of handling line and color he will have affiliated himself with an aesthetic that accepts the obligations of art to communicate judgments of the artist's environment, while a different approach will identify him with the concept that for art reality is that which comes into being through the act of painting. Thus choices having to do with method in art become also decisions regarding the future of man.

In this changed relation between art and history, the automatism involved in a heritage of craft skills has been replaced by acts of the mind *occurring at the very beginning of the artist's training*. Whether these acts be acts of the artist or of the teacher, their effect is to remove art from the realm of habit, manual dexterity and traditional taste into that of philosophy. The present Seminar is an excellent example of the new situation in which art emerges from theory. What need would there have been for our programs and speculations when everyone knew who the masters were and how they should be emulated? We shall return to this subject of the new dependence of art upon our ideas in our Proposition 3.

The consciousness of standing in the midst of developing events lends urgency to the painter's meditations on possible courses to follow. In the past a single tradition, rather than a selection among possible futures, determined stylistic affiliation. Modern art tends towards separate concentrations of energy and towards conflicts of will rather than toward homogeneity of style and meaning. The historical consciousness also pervades the art museum, the art gallery, the private collection, in the form of attempts to forecast which trends and personalities in art will survive. Art today shares in the general awareness that tomorrow is being shaped by a natural weeding out of short-lived impulses. On its profounder levels, modern art is acutely aware of itself as a participant in the contest to affect the future—as one of powers engaged in giving form to the unknown.

Proposition 2: That the politico-cultural drama has in our century assumed global dimensions and that the artist now works in an environment unbounded by time and place.

Under the unrelaxing pressure of political, social and intellectual development since World War I, local, regional and national traditions have been steadily dissolving and being absorbed into world-wide systems. The individual artist, whether in Tokyo, New York or Sao Paulo, is confronted by the activity of art everywhere, without the mediation of an inherited outlook or style. He is confronted, too, by the constant unveiling, through anthropological and archaeological research, of the totality of human thought, belief and accomplishment.

The almost simultaneous transmission of works and styles throughout the world by means of film and print has brought into being a universal pictorial vocabulary. This communication, however, is restricted to surface approximations. Lacking the scale and texture of the originals, to say nothing of their physical and cultural settings, the reproductions fall short of conveying the experience that gave rise to the art works themselves. Art in the global interchange tends to appear as consisting of various categories of decoration. The constantly augmented mass of art studied in the form of emotionally vacant images facilitates the rise of new academicism based on abstraction drawn from art history. Contemporary art, especially, is dealt with as if it consisted of designs the emotional and social content of which may be ignored. Also, the description and classification of art as artifacts contributes to the formation of a world-wide bureaucracy with scholarly pretensions concerning creation.

Thus the internationalization of art becomes a factor in the estrangement of art from the artist. The sum of works of all times and places stands against him as an entity with objectives and values of its own. In turn, becoming aware of the organized body of art works as the obstacle to his own aesthetic self-affirmation the artist is pushed toward anti-intellectualism and willful ignorance of the art of the past.

Proposition 3: That with the weakening of traditional attitudes, assumptions and methods of handling, styles now originate in abstract ideas and idea-based art movements.

Aesthetic programs have replaced locally admired art as authority and as inspiration. "Every modern activity," said Paul Valery, "is dominated and governed by *myths* in the form of *ideologies.*" The roots of contemporary creation lie not in Nature nor in earlier works of art but in theoretical interpretations of these. The new relation of art and ideas has imposed upon art the necessity for a self-consciousness that has rendered the craft imitation obsolete. The theoretical content of modern art also imposes new demands upon criticism, primarily for the clear differentiation between what may be analyzed in a painting or sculpture and what must be left to the intuition of the spectator as unique and inaccessible to language.

Proposition 4: That with change established as the norm of present-day life, the capacity for innovation and for the renewal of old forms has become a primary value in art.

The centrality of art in our civilization depends upon its role as testing ground of conditions and methods of creation. Imitation of the art of earlier centuries, as by Picasso or Modigliani, is carried on not in order to perpetuate ancient stands but to experiment with the power of the artist to evoke novelty from familiar forms. In our era, art that ceases to seek the new becomes at once intellectually insignificant, a species of homecraft. The nature of originality is open to debate—in fact, needs desperately to be debated. But no disagreement exists regarding the value of the new in art. On the other hand, the dedication of art to novelty complicates the problem of values and exposes art to sensationalism and influences of fashion and the press.

Proposition 5: That the break between the present and the past makes the future opaque and plunges art into a permanent state of uncertainty.

"No one can say what will be dead or alive tomorrow in literature, philosophy, aesthetics: no one yet knows what ideas and modes of expression will be inscribed on the casualty list, what novelties will be proclaimed."—Valery.

That condition in which the future cannot be depended upon to resemble the past constitutes a state of crisis. Or, if one prefers, a state of permanent expectancy. In such circumstances art takes as its point of departure the effort *to arrive at values* rather than to accommodate itself to existing criteria.

Criticism, too, must seek its values through particular instances—works, artists, art movements—rather than through the application of rules formulated by criticism for its own purposes. The modern mind is tempted to end its suspense by affirming complete systems of value, including aesthetic systems. Thus in totalitarian countries, the future course of events is charted and the duty imposed upon art to help in realizing that future. The means that promise to make art most effective—e.g., the idealization of facial expressions and bodily postures—are translated into aesthetic values. The result has been the ruin of art. The same result on a smaller scale has followed attempts in the West to reduce the risks of the unknown through calculating the future uses of art. The following observation of Valery might be adopted as a critical axiom: "Since, henceforth, we must deal with the *new* of the irreducible type, our future is endowed with *essential unpredictability.*"

Proposition 6: That vast shiftings of population, both geographically (through migrations, exiles, displacements) and vertically (through revolutions, mass education, equalization of opportunity), have destroyed the historically stabilized character of individuals and introduced the problem of identity, personal and collective, as a dominant theme of contemporary cultural forms.

Art movements in the twentieth century have tended to swing back and forth between extremes of individual self-consciousness (Surrealism, Abstract Expressionism), self-identification with groups (Regionalism, Social Realism) and anonymity (Bauhaus, Optical Art). These rhythms of self-affirmation and self-negation belonging to the dialectics of identity stimulate the formation of new modes of art through opposition, overlapping and merger, as in the rise of Pop Art as a counter statement to Action Painting. Impulses toward and away from identity should be recognized by criticism as providing an essential content of modern art, figurative as well as abstract.

Proposition 7: That ours is an epoch of excavations—archaeological, psychoanalytical, philological—which keeps emptying into our culture the tombs of all the ages of man.

Absorbing the flood of past art, art in our time continually reconstitutes itself as a theater of revivals. Styles of earlier periods, far and near, from the funerary carvings of the Aztecs to the realism of Courbet, are re-awakened as experiences and as slogans by contemporary painting and sculpture.

Modern art is at one with radical politics and with psychotherapy in its fascination by the abyss of lost forms and powers. Like other significant modes of present-day action and research, its explorations periodically lead it to the verge of changing into something else. Thus modern art often crosses over into non-art and adopts anti-art attitudes. Besides augmenting consciousness, this negative strain acts as a lightning rod to divert from society and individuals more perilous temptations to self-surrender—totalitarian politics, drugs, mysticism. The negation of forms and their re-awakening seem to have a profound function in a culture of change.

No doubt other propositions regarding the groundwork of contemporary art might be added to the seven I have sketched. My purpose, however, is not to be exhaustive but to give examples of the kind of phenomena which criticism must absorb into its consciousness and its vocabulary if it is to grasp the dynamics of current art production. These are matters which artists think about, and philosophers and men on the street. Unless critical discussion achieves the intellectual scale of our revolutionary epoch, it must be deprived of serious reference and lore the attention of serious minds. In practical fact current writing on art largely consists of opportunistic sponsorship of trivial novelties and of assertions of personal taste for which support is sought pedantic recitals of art history. Mere technical recipes—e.g. shaping of canvases, ways of handling the "edge" of forms—are heralded as if they were ends toward which Giotto and Rembrandt had been striving but with inadequate means. As a result art criticism today is looked down upon by other forms of critical thinking as an unintelligible jargon immersed in an insigificant estheticism. In some measure, this opinion reflects the specialization that has overtaken all learned pursuits in our society. If art and art criticism tended to become ingrown, so have literature, music, philosophy, sociology, history. Thus each feels justified in attacking the others for being excessively engrossed in their own forms. Beyond sharing in this common narrowness, however, art criticism, it must be confessed, consists for the most part of an indescribable compost of bureaucratic promotional copy, theoretical air bubbles, history without perspective, readings of symbols based on gossip and far-fetched associations of ideas, visual analyses which the eye refuses to confirm, exhibitionistic metaphor mongering, set phrases manageable by girl reporters, human-interest coddling of Sunday art-page audiences, in-group name dropping, ritually repeated nonsense.

Against this sum of amateurishness, lack of talent and willful absurdity, the value of values for art criticism must be the effort to re-introduce art into the framework of humanly serious concerns. Such an aim has nothing in common with the popular-culture fallacy that everything concerned with the creation and evaluation of art can be made immediately intelligible to the so-called common reader. The latter is himself a specialist of a sort—a specialist in the lazy intellectual habits cultivated by the mass media—and there is no reason why he should be given consideration denied to other victims of jargon. But art criticism ought to learn to distinguish between writing that deals with the irrationalities, observities, and paradoxes of creation and writing that is merely lacking in sense.

We now come to the "Charge to Art Critic." My remarks may not always be directly responsive to the language in which some of the topics have been formulated, but I shall come as close to them as my way of thinking permits.

The first item of Charge #1 reads as follows:

Identify the range of values and/or categories appropriate to making critical judgments of works of art.

It follows from our premises that the work of art should be evaluated, first of all, as an act performed by a contemporary. It is an energy and skill directed toward the artist's individual appropriation of that in art which continues to be alive or which is susceptible of resurrection. It has the effect also of demolishing styles and images which have turned into visual conventions; in this destructive activity lies its critical and revolutionary role. By displacing works from which vitality has departed, each new painting helps to determine the continuing content of aesthetic culture. It is also an act of unique and perhaps to some degree, original perception; thus, it is an event in the self-development of the artist. To its public it opens connections with other works of art and contributes to an expansion of individual and collective sensibility.

Hence, all categories of experience, past and present, from fetishism to laboratory discipline, are potentially relevant in making critical evaluations. The critic's primary act of judgment consists of choosing the modes of insight—aesthetic, psychological, social, metaphysical—which he regards as significant in the particular instance. For instance, in writing about the paintings of Barnet Newman I found it necessary to dwell upon the quality of his taste, his counter-statement to the abstract art from which he derived, the rigor of his logic, his humor, his metaphysics of the sublime. In connection with Gorky and de Kooning the question of the sublime did not arise, nor did the question of taste seem to merit much discussion. In regard to Jasper Johns, my major emphasis was on his technique and his motifs as responses to Abstract Expressionism and to the presence of the new Vanguard Audience in the U.S. I also noted the changed mood manifested in his later canvases as bearing upon Johns' aesthetics and as a clue to his possible development.

The elements to be taken into account by criticism will vary from artist to artist and from one critic to another. So, too, will the stress placed on those elements and the way all are balanced. Each piece of critical writing represents a synthesising act of the artist in his simultaneous elaboration of form and content. The medium of the critic's synthesis, like that of the artist, is style. The critic demonstrates his competence by his effectiveness in handling his materials, which consists of words and concepts. A critic who writes badly may have deep insights into painting, but not every connoisseur is a critic.

Second item of Charge #1:

What steps might be taken to overcome barriers and confusions in critical language?

In dealing with modern art, criticism is confronted by a flood of new forms, new motives, experimental attitudes. To react intelligently to these, criticism must test itself and develop new forms of insight and expression (e.g., multiple perspectives, a rhetoric hospitable to the ambiguities and paradoxes of art itself).

Reduction of confusion in critical language and of the barriers between criticism and the art to which it is applied should begin in eliminating abstract universals, such as "harmony" or "expressive form," which can presumably be fitted together to provide a handle for art works of every variety. These residues of old systems of essence should be replaced by concrete analyses in a terminology of action, conflict, intention, creative hypothesis. The technical ingredients of painting need to be re-interpreted in accordance with the psychological and aesthetic functions of line, color, form, etc., implied by the practice of modern masters. An outstanding point of reference in this connection are the teachings of Hans Hofmann.

Charge #2:

Within each system or category, identify the specific concepts and methodologies that make possible critical discourse about works of art.

The art critic is the collaborator of the artist in developing the culture of the visible as a resource of human sensibility. His basic function is to extend the artist's act into the realm of meaningful discourse. Art in our time is itself criticism. Each painting embodies a choice in regard to other styles and works, including the previous work of its creator, and to the possibilities arising from it. Into this dialogue of paint the critic interjects a vocabulary of words. Having thus put himself into the act, not by any means at the invitation of the other performers, he assumes the privilege of responding with a trained rhetoric to the pantomime of the artists. To one gesture he assents, another he opposes, in a third he sees unrealized possibilities.

Can the critic be anything more than the intruder that artists have traditionally considered him to be? If he is the mere representative of a social interest, as for example, the reviewer whose opinions are coordinated with the cultural program of a newspaper or other propaganda or profit-making institution, he stands in relation to art as a species of policeman on the lookout for misdemeanors. He will not interpret art's motives, he will endeavor to keep art in line. His criticism will consist largely of reporting delinquencies—the virtues he discovers in paintings will be of the sort that is held up as an example to the wicked. Such a critic has forced himself on art, and he can continue to be a squatter in it only because there is no way of getting rid of him.

The critic who is to be the intellectual collaborator of the artist, not his truant officer, must possess, above all, a mind engaged by the realities that encompass the painter or sculptor. Besides being a judge of art, he must be a judge of those processes by which art and life are being transformed. His must be a mind with a point of view to affirm; it is this point of view that determines which trends, personages, ideas he will support or combat. An interest in pointing may be the result of chance or temperament. The impulse to criticize is inherent in the intelligence that responds energetically to the existing human situation. It is the development and verbal clarification of this impulse that leads to the calling of critic. Knowledge of art is not enough to make one a critic, any more than knowledge of art is enough to make one an artist. The student whose devotion to art arises out of the wish to avoid reflecting upon his condition as a living person will be a mere specialist, a scholar or a connoisseur, but not a critic. For the latter exists through the deeper and curiosity and the widest practice of intellectual freedom.

The art critic is the outpost of the art educator. He has made his way into the wilderness of values in which art originates. If he is to be of use, it will be by opening a route into the collectivity of artists and to their creations, present and past.

Each critic tends to return to certain attitudes and phrases. For example, I have, perhaps even too emphatically, been insisting that certain concepts relating to the character of twentieth century culture are indispensable to discourse about works of art. I should not, however, like to see those concepts, nor any like them, organized into a methodology. No systematic approach is viable in art criticism. Nor, in my opinion, is it desirable for criticism to mimic the techniques or objectives of science. Let the readers of the criticism *find* the "systems" in it, if there be one. The critic who resorts to formulas does so out of laziness, haste, or uneasiness about making himself understood.

Since the past no longer enlightens us about the future, values cannot be abstracted from earlier masterpieces and applied as a measure to current art. By the same token, values cannot be abstracted from current work and held in readiness to classify the art of tomorrow. In our time values must be created alongside the art which they propose to evaluate. The intellectual center of gravity of criticism must be capable of shifting with the emphasis of new art. Dealing with creation, criticism must maintain its openness to innovation.

This does not mean that criticism is forced to abdicate before each manifestation of the unfamiliar. Continuity is inherent in events, including events of creation. It is this objective continuity that makes discourse possible. It provides the ground for acts of judgment which can cohere into a living nucleus of values augmented and made more firm by each new encounter with the unfamiliar. The weakness of methodology is that it tends to circumscribe this process of creating value by neutralizing those areas of the imagination which cannot be readily organized. The effect is to pulverize criticism into neatly spaced piles of rhetorical powder—for example, one has only to look to the products of our "methodologized" academies literary criticism.

There are two items in Charge #3; I shall remark on them together:

Can we assume a continuum of maturity and sophistication in critical insights? If so, what are the elements of such a continuum?

There are no grounds for assuming that any particular intellectual qualities will continue to prevail in criticism, any more than in art itself. Forms, terms, concepts are susceptible to an inner erosion that empties them of meaning or changes their meanings, perhaps even into their opposites. Criticism is in constant danger of losing touch with its object, the work of art, or with its own purpose, enlightenment. It can be significant only through the unforseeable entry into it of interesting minds and of writings addressed to real things. Besides experience, intelligence and talent, it demands also courage and independence—and these, too, cannot be counted upon to answer a roll call.

Today, the outstanding menace to such critical consciousness as has been developed is that in place of an intensification of insights and a deeper awareness of problems there will be substituted a structure of bureaucratic assents. Everyone, will be in agreement, for instance, that Van Gogh is a forerunner of Expressionism, that his heritage is subjectivism, "distortion" and thick paint; and that the value of his paintings is to be found in the fierce efflux of something called "personality." Everyone will agree, too, that Jackson Pollock represents violence and self-abandonment and is thus descended from Van Gogh. On the other hand, there is, we shall be told, an art achieved through the rigors of analytical reason, as with Seurat, Mondrian, Albers. Such a collection of received ideas may represent a continuity of sorts— perhaps it is even "mature" and "sophisticated." Its advantage is that it can be handed on to each incoming group of students and that it makes the meanings of works of art as easy to memorize as a deck of cards. But a credo is the opposite of a critical consciousness—and incidentally, not one of the opinions mentioned holds up under analysis: for instance, Van Gogh's passion to seize the reality of the object has nothing in common with the phantasizing of German Expressionists with whom he is grouped.

Along with the replacement of criticism by bureaucratically supported articles of faith, there comes into being a bureaucratically supported art with its own vocabulary of mystification and double talk. In the past couple of years, artists have appeared, to say nothing of dealers and reviewers, who study the advance schedules of leading New York museums as leads to the kind of art with which to identify themselves.

Critical continuity depends on an ever-deepening comprehension and clarification of the tradition of the new. There is, for instance, important research to be done in bringing to consciousness attitudes taken for granted in the modern practice of art but ignored or denied in art's public relations—

these bear on the issue of the so-called revolutionary or nihilistic nature of twentieth century painting and sculpture. The tradition of the new in art *is* a tradition precisely because it transmits desires, ideas, myths of which the receiver is unaware *and* which he takes for granted as fact. Within this tradition there exists a continuing strain of revolt—against society, against art, against the orders of the mind, against all existing conditions of life and work. This strain, though often submerged, is so fundamental to the integrity of art in our time that when it disappears, as in the Soviet Union, creation ceases, and when it is denied or veiled, as in OP art and much of Pop, its absence is discussed pro and con and even identified as a form of revolt against revolt. For criticism to extend itself into the future as a coherent energy will require not only intellectual apprehension of the elements that make up the tradition of the new but an unillusioned responsiveness to its rebellious spirit.

The three items of Charge #4 are:

What relationship exists (or should exist) between art criticism and art historical knowledge; between art criticism and art theory; between art criticism and statements of intent or biography of the artists?

Art criticism today *is* art history, though not necessarily the art history of the art historian. In discussing a painting the critic reports on an act that falls within the previous acts of the painter and upon an event within the continuity of art. The painter's act could not have taken a place without preceding acts of creation performed by himself and by others; and in estimating the value of the work, the critic considers what it has brought to the history of art, as well as to the experiences communicated by art. It is a truism that all art derives from art. To know what has been derived from whom and in what manner and degree sheds light on the artist's processes of creation, his motives, and the shape of his imagination—not least illuminating is what he chose not to derive from the works that influenced him.

The critic must, then, be familiar with the art of the past; above all, he must have reflected upon it. But art-historical knowledge has for the critic a different function than it has for art historian. The critic is not primarily concerned with tracing the evolution of styles and arranging works within them. He approaches the work not as an act performed in an interval of past time and which is not ready to be set in its niche within an edifice of finished happenings. He sees it rather as a deed that is still in the course of being enacted and which will take shape through the painter's battle with uncertainties, counterforces, temptations. One might say that the critic unrolls the creation of the picture as an intellectual event in time, while keeping an eye on it as a visual object. In this, his approach corresponds to that of a painter looking at a painting by another artist; he sees it as a complex of situations met, resources employed, leaps executed. Without being aware of it, the painter as spectator imagines himself as a performer; he becomes automatically the original artist. The critic stands in the same line of vision as the painter but he stands further back. For him, not only is the painting "to be done again" in mind; the painter too, is something to be done, that is, to be intellectually constituted as an artist acting and choosing within his medium and his culture.

It is to this end, and only to this end, that he may resort to the biography of the artist, to his ideas and to his statements of intent. He reads the artist's words and interprets events in his life solely in relation to his acts on the canvas. Like the painting itself, they are data from which he constructs the fiction that is the author of the work of art and the key to the full range of its meaning. But statements by artists, though frequently of great value to criticism, are to be regarded with suspicion and never taken as the last word on questions of fact or attitude. Jealous of their originality, artists are prone to certain types of deceit; for instance, American artists, especially, tend to deny their indebtedness to other artists and to art movements which have determined their work. For criticism, this denial of indebtedness is not merely a question of demanding undue credit; it has to do with obscuring the transfer of thought within the community of artists and within the culture of the period. Obviously, this question of communication is too important to be left to the vanity of individuals.

It is a prejudice of the critic that he sees art history backwards, from the painting he is studying to works that anteceded it. (On another plane, there is for the critic no earlier and no later.) In any case, he will refuse to concede that a style can produce art through an immanent drive toward the realization of an idea or form. The scandal of art history is its ability and, in many instances, its willingness to dispense with artists. I shall not pursue this question here, since it is a problem for the historians themselves, one which they have begun to attack.

I shall, however, say a few words about writers who lay down the law to art in the name of art history. Art criticism today is crowded with art historians turned inside out to function as prophets of so-called inevitable trends. A determinism similar to that projected into the evolution of past styles is clamped upon art in the making. In this parody of art history, value judgments are deduced, in advance of any actual paintings, from a presumed logic of development, and commands are issued to artists either to accommodate themselves to these values or be banned from the art of the future. An aesthetician founded on art history yields a club of dogma similar to moralistic criticism in the nineteenth century or political criticism in the Soviet Union.

The deterministic approach simplifies the problem of value and for that reason is seductive to authoritarian minds. To predict the future and thus to be able to accommodate oneself to it, whether as artist, critic, art collector or museum director, seems to offer a means for reducing the hazards of being extinguished by it. To assert with assurance what art must become eliminates the need to analyze what art is actually doing—and whether its present behavior constitutes a rise or a fall. For the critic, values based on a theory of an historically determined stylistic evolution eliminates the need to explore the connection between the social, political, psychological realities by which artists are moved and through which the work of art affects the spectator. Instead of problems, metaphors, hypotheses, hints, paradoxes, art criticism comes to consist of certainties.

But, of course, prediction in art is impossible and all forecasts of what will be desirable tomorrow are nonsense, fraud or propaganda. For the nature of art is that it is creation—and the nature of creation is that it contains the unexpected. To predict with certainty what is going to be created one must be in a position to suppress creation. Hitler and Stalin were excellent forecasters of aesthetic trends, so long as their police controlled what was done in the studios. The critic in a free country who maps out the future as if it had already taken place is forced to function with less effective weapons. Yet, even here, prediction in art is not harmless. It is tied to valuation—while valuation in turn calls for the exercise of power. Historical determinism practiced as criticism misapplies the power of the historian to control the past and introduce order into it. For this distortion art history is of course not to blame.

Yet a practical problem does exist in properly defining the uses of art history, in view of the fact that an academic degree in this subject has become the accepted means of accrediting people for all kinds of careers in art, including that of art critic. The study of art history develops in people the professional habit of tracing the forms and imagery of a work to their influences and sources; also the habit of taking it for granted that doing so establishes the *value* of the work. Uncovering sources is an accomplishment of which the historian is justly proud, and it is not unnatural that he should project the value of what he himself has been doing into the painting. It is not unusual to hear a painting praised as if its merit lay in working out a successful campaign for capturing the qualities of earlier works and transferring them into the present.

Perhaps ways can be found to direct art history toward scholarship, and to develop appropriate curricula for other specialties, including that non-specialized specialty criticism. Both art criticism and art history need to scan more thoroughly their philosophical substructures. Both ought to consider, for instance, the difference between the intellectual origins of art in our time and in earlier periods. Art history as the art historian encounters it in other eras scarcely comes into being any more. Art used to wander on its way, responding to the cues given to it by tradition and chance, until the historian pounced upon it and set it into the order of its time. In the twentieth century, art has lost its innocence. Its naivete in regard to its own history had been replaced by a complex sophistication in manipulating that history. Today, the art historian is dealing with an art that is conscious of itself as engaged in making art history and which, intended in many instances to impress the art historian, especially the art historian turned critic, deliberately takes his prejudices into account. The historian is no longer telling a story of raw events; he is repeating a story told to him in the form of ideas and happenings with which he is implicated. The first requirement in such a situation is to know that he is implicated and to what extent. Both the art historian and the art critic must be wary of responding to a mirror held up to them by the artist for the purpose of arousing their admiration for the image of their own outlook. History in our time—and not only *art* history—is history that is being deliberately tempered with by the object of the historian's study, the history makers.

In the case of art, the prime history makers are painters and sculptors. As indicated earlier, there are writers and cultural commissars who wish to dispute this privilege of the artist and to use him as an instrument for their own art-history making. The attempt to appropriate art history brings about a new kind of conflict—between the artist and the professional representatives of his public. This conflict is a phase of the conflict of ideas which has characterized the creation of art for more than a century. The style is the man, but modern man becomes himself, that is, acquires style, in a wrestle with ideas and even ideologies. In our time, art arises out of a dialetical tension between an individual temperament and art movements founded on various theories of art. The work is neither personality nor idea. But to equip the future artist, art critic, art appreciator to understand what is being created, art education must familiarize him not only with works of art but with the alternatives over which the campaigns of modern art have been fought. To grasp art in our time one must, for example, be able to identify ideas, both in art and in matters related to it, that are genuinely antithetical—such as the idea of art as an instrument of the state or of business and the idea of art as individual discovery or creation—and to differentiate such mutually repellant ideas from ideas that only seem to be in opposition but have a similar approach to creation—for example, conventional naturalism and conventional abstraction.

Statements of intent by artists illuminate their work only when interpreted in the context of the continuing struggle of ideas in art itself. Read in isolation from the artist's concrete intellectual situation, they will often appear in reverse and lead criticism up blind alleys. For instance, the painter Malevich once pointed out that in the work of a famous medieval icon painter the hairs of God's beard were exactly the same as the hairs on the Devil's tail. This was intended to prove that what counted for the artists was not *what* but the *how*. The painter cares neither for God nor the Devil but only about painting. All content is a mere pretext for the exercise of skill and the solution of aesthetic problems. Following this logic—and Malevich did, of course, follow it—subject matter can be eliminated entirely, and everything valid in the art of the present or the past can be translated into space, line, color, design. We arrive at what is called "pure" painting.

By the same type of reasoning we arrive also at what might be called "puristic" criticism or formalism, that is, criticism that evaluates paintings exclusively in terms of their formal elements and by formal standards. Such criticism may be coupled with an exposition of the iconography of the works, but its *value* judgments are founded on the handling of the means of painting.

Yet the statement of formal intentions by an artist and the same theory in the hands of a critic move toward widely separated results. The purist objectives of Malevich, or of Mondrian or Albers, have brought into being paintings that vibrate with vigor and sensibility, in a word, with emotional and psychic content. In his act of painting the artist lives inside his idea, and the more he has narrowed it to exclude all but visual essentials the greater the psychic pressure to which it subjects him. This subjective pressure is not, however, comprehended in his formalist scheme. The thinking the artist aims at giving him direction and assurance rather than producing a correct analysis of everything that goes into his work. The artist's ideas are also polemical: he wants the art of painting to have a certain character, and he need not be aware to what extent this partisan wish has become the ruling passion of his work.

The critic, however, who allows himself to be circumscribed by theoretical statements of painters runs the risk of missing the totality of experience embodied in the paintings. The point is underscored by the inadequacy of formalist criticism in dealing with formalist art, i.e. precisely with the art with whose principles it is in full accord. Taking literally the notion that art aims solely at art, the critic participates in the painter's idea—but he misses the qualities brought into being by the act of painting. These qualities arise not from the theory that instigated the painting and determined its mode but from the positive or negative drive of the artist in regard to himself and to the historical moment in which he functions, including the art by which he is confronted. The neo-Plasticism of Mondrian reacting to Cubism and World War I produces a result quite different from that of a hard-edge painter of the sixties reacting to Abstract Expressionism and the a-political art world of New York. Granted that the formal painter paints neither for love of God or from fear of the Devil; that he paints for the sake of painting, perhaps in order to carry art to its next step; that for him art is *the* absolute and that he lives only in order to serve it; that he takes orders from it (not from Nature or his own feelings) as to how he shall serve it and what he shall bring to its altar; that painting has for him a life, a mind and a will of its own; that the chief impulse of this living independent entity is to purge itself of anything not itself and to reduce itself more and more to its own essence—granted all these motives and beliefs, the painter will not succeed in making himself into nothing but a painter, nor his painting into a crystal of immanent relations among the elements of art. As a painter he is *in* the painting—let us say, he is its flaw. Purist painting is work within a human value system, most often the system of the ascetic. It is from the will to order, to purging, to (one adds automatically) salvation that it derives its passion for neatness, for hygiene, for shapes like the square and the rectangle, presumably immune to emotional associations, and its practice of banning tones and restricting itself to hues cleansed of atmosphere. In the end painting for the purist is God (without a beard). At its most intense, pure painting is religious painting. As such it is as "expressionistic" as the most agitated figurative art. When art in this mode is not caught in a religious trance it is mere interior decoration. And what measures whether it is one or the other is the desperation, self-denial and transcendence communicated by the tensions of its vacant shapes and fields of color. Recently, I received a message from Albers by way of a student from California. "Tell Rosenberg" it said, "that *angst* is dead." What message could be more anxious? The best of Albers' cool paintings literally quiver with psychic tensions.

Charge #5:

What definition of style (or definition of style) provides the most useful structure for art critical study? On what bases may be established the limits or extent of a style?

The concept of style must be related to the function assumed by certain modes of handling within the experience of the individual artist and within the history of art. Visual similarities are not sufficient to define the feature of a style or its limit—that is to say, the eye is not sufficient. The emotional and intellectual ends to which the visual means are put are intrinsic to the definition. For example, the stylistic similarities between a Mondrian and a Newman are obvious. But the neo-Plastic style has with the latter assumed a new function, resulting in a deflection from neo-Plasticism and in moods and purposes in opposition to it. Out of the new use of the style come new stylistic possibilities, and these tend to develop in directions visually unrelated to the original mode in the example just given, "pure" abstraction develops into an aspect of Abstract Expressionism. The shifting and transformation of modern styles center on the fact that style in our time originates in ideologies and is cultivated by theory—thus it is constantly affected by changes of meaning and may even undergo a total erosion of meaning. As de Kooning put it several years ago at a panel discussion of artists: "We are all working on the basis of ideas in which we no longer believe."

This brings me to an additional proposition concerning art in our time that ought to be added to the seven with which this paper began. From this proposition No. 8, I shall draw a few concluding remarks about criticism.

Proposition 8: That the ubiquitous presence of the visual mass media, from advertising posters to industrial design, has introduced into painting and sculpture a new factor which art criticism must reckon with—and that to do so, the critic must clarify his position toward contemporary society as a basis for evaluating its substitute products.

Art in the twentieth century, *including the art that has come to us from the past,* is affected by the mass media both directly (e.g., the use of the *Mona Lisa* in an advertisement) and through their impact upon modern culture generally. Especially in the United States, creation in art is accompanied at every step by the gigantic shadow of the commercial art output which mimics and adapts every new style in painting and sculpture, extending it into a totally different context of meaning, feeling and purpose. Thus Pollock inspires the design of dress fabrics, Calder a beer advertisement.

The utilization of art for the objectives of the market causes styles to become widely familiar but without being grasped. Popular museum programs contribute to the same end. The exhibition of the *Mona Lisa* under the auspices of public relations is intellectually equivalent to its reproduction in an ad. The result is that art in America, both new and old, is subjected to a constant process of alienation. The vast pool of skills directed toward specific economic, political and educational ends challenges art to define its own function and to differentiate its products, if any real difference exists, from those whose efficiency is measurable. A mystification of values causes all novelties to seem of equal significance and breeds the widespread belief that the ultimate function of the fine arts is to contribute visual devices to utilitarian design—e.g., the justification of Mondrian by linoleum patterns or by Park Avenue skyscrapers. Raised in this belief, young artists have been bringing painting and sculpture steadily closer to utilitarian ideals. The shift in art training from Bohemian studios to university art departments threatens to accelerate and deepen the trend toward the kind of art whose uses are foreseeable.

What but criticism can tell us what we are doing and if it is what we want to do? What but criticism can indicate other ends, explain what makes those other ends attractive and indicate what must be done to serve them?

Systems Esthetics

JACK BURNHAM

A polarity is presently developing between the finite, unique work of high art, i.e., painting or sculpture, and conceptions which can loosely be termed "unobjects," these being either environments or artifacts which resist prevailing critical analysis. This includes works by some primary sculptors (though some may reject the charge of creating environments), some gallery kinetic and luminous art, some outdoor works, happenings, and mixed media presentations. Looming below the surface of this dichotomy is a sense of radical evolution which seems to run counter to the waning revolution of abstract and non-objective art. The evolution embraces a series of absolutely logical and incremental changes, wholly devoid of the fevered iconoclasm which accompanied the heroic from 1907 to 1925. As yet the evolving esthetic has no critical vocabulary so necessary for its defense, nor for that matter a name or explicit cause.

Reprinted by permission from *Art Forum*, Vol. VII, No. 1, September 1968.

In a way this situation might be likened to the "morphological development" of a prime scientific concept—as described by Thomas Kuhn in *The Structure of Scientific Revolutions* (1962). Kuhn sees science at any given period dominated by a single "major paradigm"; that is, a scientific conception of the natural order so pervasive and intellectually powerful that it dominates all ensuing scientific discovery. In consistent facts arising through experimentation are invariably labeled as bogus or trivial—until the emergence of a new and more encompassing general theory. Transition between major paradigms may best express the state of present art. Reasons for it lie in the nature of current technological shifts.

The economist, J. K. Galbraith, has rightly insisted that until recently the needs of the modern industrial state were never served by complete expression of the esthetic impulse. Power and expansion were its primary aims.

Special attention should be paid to Galbraith's observation. As an arbiter of impending socio-technical changes his position is pivotal. For the Left he represents America's most articulate apologist for Monopoly Capitalism; for the Right he is the socialist *éminence grise* of the Democratic Party. In *The New Industrial State* (1967) he challenges both Marxist orthodoxies and American mythologies premised upon *laissez-faire* Capitalism. For them he substitutes an incipient technocracy shaped by the evolving technostructure. Such a drift away from ideology has been anticipated for at least fifty years. Already in California think-tanks and the central planning committees of each soviet, futurologists are concentrating on the role of the technocracy, i.e., its decision-making autonomy, how it handles the central storage of information, and the techniques used for smoothly implementing social change. In the automated state power resides less in the control of the traditional symbols of wealth than in information.

In the emergent "superscientific culture" long-range decision-making and its implementation become more difficult and more necessary. Judgment demands precise socio-technical models. Earlier the industrial state evolved by filling consumer needs on a piecemeal basis. The kind of product design that once produced "better living" precipitates vast crises in human ecology in the 1960s. A striking parallel exists between the "new" car of the automobile stylist and the syndrome of formalist invention in art, where "discoveries" are made through visual manipulation. Increasingly "products"—either in art or life—become irrelevant and a different set of needs arises: these revolve around such concerns as maintaining the biological livability of the Earth, producing more accurate models of social interaction, understanding the growing symbiosis in man-machine relationships, establishing priorities for the usage and conservation of natural resources, and defining alternate patterns of education, productivity, and leisure. In the past our technologically-conceived artifacts structured living patterns. We are now in transition from an *object-oriented* to a *systems-oriented* culture. Here change emanates, not from *things*, but from *the way things are done*.

The priorities of the present age revolve around the problems of organization. A systems viewpoint is focused on the creation of stable, on-going relationships between organic and non-organic systems, be these neighborhoods, industrial complexes, farms, transportation systems, information centers, recreation centers, or any of the other matrixes of human activity. All living situations must be treated in the context of a systems hierarchy of values. Intuitively many artists have already grasped these relatively recent distinctions, and if their "environments" are on the unsophisticated side, this will change with time and experience.

The major tool for professionally defining these concerns is systems analysis. This is best known through its usage by the Pentagon and has more to do with the expense and complexity of modern warfare, than with any innate relation between the two. Systems analysts are not cold-blooded logicians; the best have an ever-expanding grasp of human needs and limitations. One of the pioneers of systems applications, E. S. Quade, has stated that "Systems analysis, particularly the type required for military decisions, is still largely a form of art. Art can be taught in part, but not by the means of fixed rules. . . ." [1] Thus "The Further Dimensions" [2] elaborated upon by Galbraith in his book are esthetic criteria. Where for some these become the means for tidying up a derelict technology, for Galbraith esthetic decision-making becomes an integral part of any future technocracy. As yet few governments fully appreciate that the alternative is biological self-destruction.

Situated between aggressive electronic media and two hundred years of industrial vandalism, the long-held idea that a tiny output of art objects modify the environment was naive. A parallel illusion existed in that artistic influence prevails by a psychic osmosis given off by such objects. Accordingly lip service to public beauty remains the province of well-guarded museums. Through the early stages of industrialism it remained possible for decorative media, including painting and sculpture, to embody the esthetic impulse; but as technology progresses this impulse must identify itself with the means of research and production. Obviously nothing could be less true for the present situation. In a society thus estranged only the didactic function of art continues to have meaning. The artist operates as a quasipolitical *provocateur*, though in no concrete sense is he an ideologist or a moralist. "*L'art pour l'art*" and a century's resistance to the vulgarities of moral uplift have insured that.

The specific function of modern didactic art has been to show that art does not reside in material entities, but in relations between people and between people and the components of their environment. This accounts for the radicality of Duchamp and his enduring influence. It throws light on Picasso's lesser position as a seminal force. As with all succeeding formalist art, Cubism followed the tradition of circumscribing art value wholly within finite objects.

In an advanced technological culture the most important artist best succeeds by liquidating his position as artist vis-à-vis society. Artist nihilism established itself through this condition. At the outset the artist refused to participate in idealism through craft. "Craft-fetishism," [3] as termed by the critic Christopher Caudwell, remains the basis of modern formalism. Instead the significant artist strives to reduce the technical and psychical distance between his artistic output and the productive means of society. Duchamp, Warhol, and Robert Morris are similarly directed in this respect. Gradually this strategy transforms artistic and technological decision-making into a single activity—at least it presents that alternative in inescapable terms. Scientists and technicians are not converted into "artists," rather the artist becomes a symptom of the schism between art and technics. Progressively the need to make ultrasensitive judgments as to the uses of technology and scientific information becomes "art" in the most literal sense.

As yet the implication that art contains survival value is nearly as suspect as attaching any moral significance to it. Though with the demise of literary content, the theory that art is a form of psychic preparedness has gained articulate supporters.

Art, as an adaptive mechanism, is reinforcement of the ability to be aware of the disparity between behavioral pattern and the demands consequent upon the interaction with the environment. Art is rehearsal for those real situations in which it is vital for our survival to endure cognitive tension, to refuse the comforts of validation by affective congruence when such validation is inappropriate because too vital interests are at stake. . . .[4]

The post-formalist sensibility naturally responds to stimuli both within and outside the proposed art format. To this extent some of it does begin to resemble "theater," as imputed by Michael Fried. More likely though, the label of "theatricality" is a red herring disguising the real nature of the shift in priorities. In respect to Mr. Fried's argument,[5] the theater was never a purist medium, but a conglomerate of arts. In itself this never prevented the theater from achieving "high art." For clearer reading, rather than maintaining Mr. Fried's adjectives, "theatrical" or "literalist" art, or the phrase used until now in this essay, "post-formalist esthetic," the term *systems esthetic* seems to encompass the present situation more fully.

The systems approach goes beyond a concern with staged environments and happenings; it deals in a revolutionary fashion with the larger problem of boundary concepts. In systems perspective there are no contrived confines such as the theater proscenium or picture frame. Conceptual focus rather than material limits define the system. Thus any situation, either in or outside the context of art, may be designed and judged as a system. Inasmuch as a system may contain people, ideas, messages, atmospheric conditions, power sources, etc., a system is, to quote the systems biologist, Ludwig von Bertalanffy, a "complex of components in interaction," [6] comprised of material, energy, and information in various degrees of organization. In evaluating systems the artist is a perspectivist considering goals, boundaries, structure, input, output, and related activity inside and outside the system. Where the object almost always has a fixed shape and boundaries, the consistency of a system may be altered in time and space, its behavior determined both by external conditions and its mechanisms of control.

In his book, *The New Vision*, Moholy-Nagy described fabricating a set of enamel on metal paintings. These were executed by telephoning precise instructions to a manufacturer. An elaboration of this was projected recently by the director of the Museum of Contemporary Art in Chicago, Jan van der Marck, in a tentative exhibition, "Art by Telephone." In this instance the recorded conversation between artist and manufacturer was to *become part of the displayed work of art*. For systems, information, in whatever form conveyed, becomes a viable esthetic consideration.

Fifteen years ago Victor Vasarely suggested mass art as a legitimate function of industrial society. For angry critics there existed the fear of undermining art's fetish aura, of shattering the mystique of craft and private creation. If some forays have been made into serially produced art, these remain on the periphery of the industrial system. Yet the entire phenomenon of reproducing an art object *ad infinitum* is absurd; rather than making quality available to a large number of people, it signals the end of concrete objects embodying visual metaphor. Such demythification is the Kantian Imperative applied esthetically. On the other hand, a systems esthetic *is* literal in that all phases of the life cycle of a system are relevant. There is no end product which is primarily visual, nor does such an esthetic rely on a "visual" syntax. It resists functioning as an applied esthetic, but is revealed in the principles underlying the progressive reorganization of the natural environment.

Various postures implicit in formalist art were consistently attacked in the later writings of Ad Reinhardt. His black paintings were hardly rhetorical devices (nor were his writings) masking Zen obscurities; rather they were the means of discarding formalist mannerism and all the latent illusionism connected with post-realistic art. His own contribution he described as:

> The one work for the fine artist, the one painting, is the painting of the one-sized canvas . . . The single theme, one formal device, one color-monochrome, one linear division in each direction, one symmetry, one texture, one free-hand brushing, one rhythm, one working everything into dissolution and one indivisibility, each painting into one overall uniformity and nonirregularity.[7]

Even before the emergence of the anti-formalist "specific object" there appeared an oblique type of criticism, resisting emotive and literary associations. Pioneered between 1962 and 1965 in the writings of Donald Judd, it resembles what a computer programmer would call an entity's "list structure," or all the enumerated properties needed to *physically* rebuild an object. Earlier the phenomenologist, Maurice Merleau-Ponty, asserted the impossibility of *conceptually* reconstructing an object from such a procedure. Modified to include a number of perceptual insights not included in a "list structure," such a technique has been used to real advantage by the anti-novelist, Alain Robbe-Grillet. A web of sensorial descriptions is spun around the central images of a plot. The point is not to internalize scrutiny in the Freudian sense, but to infer the essence of a situation through detailed examination of surface effects. Similar attitudes were adopted by Judd for the purpose of critical examination. More than simply an art object's list structure, Judd included phenomenal qualities which would have never shown up in a fabricator's plans, but which proved necessary for the "seeing" of the object. This cleared the air of much criticism centered around meaning and private intention.

It would be misleading to interpret Judd's concept of "specific objects" as the embodiment of a systems esthetic. Rather object art has become a stage towards further rationalization of the esthetic process in general—both by reducing the iconic content of art objects and by Judd's candidness about their conceptual origins. However, even in 1965 he gave indications of looking beyond these finite limits.

A few of the more general aspects may persist, such as the work's being like an object or even being specific, but other characteristics are bound to develop. Since its range is wide, three-dimensional work will probably divide into a number of forms. At any rate, it will be larger than painting and much larger than sculpture, which, compared to painting, is fairly particular. . . . Because the nature of three dimension isn't set, given beforehand, something credible can be made, almost anything.[8]

In the 1966 "68th American Show" at the Chicago Art Institute, the sculptor, Robert Morris, was represented by two large, L-shaped forms which were shown the previous year in New York. Morris sent plans of the pieces to the carpenters at the Chicago museum where they were assembled for less than the cost of shipping the originals from New York. In the context of a systems esthetic possession of a privately fabricated work is no longer important. Accurate information takes priority over history and geographical location.

Morris was the first essayist to precisely describe the relation between sculpture style and the progressively more sophisticated use of industry by artists. He has lately focused upon material-forming techniques and the arrangement of these results so that they no longer form specific objects but remain uncomposed. In such handling of materials the idea of *process* takes precedence over end results: "Disengagement with preconceived enduring forms and orders of things is a positive assertion." [9] Such loose assemblies of materials encompass concerns that resemble the cycles of industrial processing. Here the traditional priority of end results over technique breaks down; in a systems context both may share equal importance, remaining essential parts of the esthetic.

Already Morris has proposed systems which move beyond the confines of the minimal object. One work proposed to the City of New York last fall was later included in Willoughby Sharp's "Air Art" show in a Y.M.H.A. gallery in Philadelphia. In its first state Morris's piece involved capturing steam from the pipes in the city streets, projecting this from nozzles on a platform. In Philadelphia such a system took its energy from the steam bath room. Since 1966 Morris's interests have included designs for low relief earth sculptures consisting of abutments, hedges, and sodded mounds, visible from the air and not unlike Indian burial mounds. "Transporting" one of these would be a matter of cutting and filling earth and resodding. Morris is presently at work on one such project and unlike past sculptural concerns, it involves precise information from surveyors, landscape gardeners, civil engineering contractors, and geologists. In the older context, such as Isamu Noguchi's sunken garden at Yale University's Rare Book Library, sculpture defined the environment, with Morris's approach the environment defines what is sculptural.

More radical for the gallery are the constructions of Carl Andre. His assemblies of modular, unattached forms stand out from the works of artists who have comprised unit assembly with the totality of fixed objects. The mundane origins of Andre's units are not "hidden" within the art work as in the technique of collage. Andre's floor reliefs are architectural modifications—though they are not subliminal since they visually disengage from their surroundings. One of Andre's subtler shows took place in New York last year. The viewer was encouraged to walk stocking-footed across three areas, each 12 by 12 feet and composed of 144 one-foot-square metal plates. One was not only invited to see each of these "rugs" as a grid arrangement in various metals, but each metal grid's thermal conductivity was registered through the soles of the feet. Sight analysis diminishes in importance for some of the best new work; the other senses and especially kinesthesis makes "viewing" a more integrated experience.

The scope of a systems esthetic presumes that problems cannot be solved by a single technical solution, but must be attacked on a multileveled, interdisciplinary basis. Consequently some of the more aware sculptors no longer think like sculptors, but they assume a span of problems more natural to architects, urban planners, civil engineers, electronic technicians, and cultural anthropologists. This is not as pretentious as some critics have insisted. It is a legitimate extension of McLuhan's remark about Pop art when he said that it was an announcement that the entire environment was ready to become a work of art.

As a direct descendant of the "found object," Robert Smithson's identifying mammoth engineering projects as works of art ("Site-Selections") [10] makes eminent sense. Refocusing the esthetic away from the preciousness of the work of art is in the present age no less than a survival mechanism. If Smithson's "Site-Selections" are didactic exercises, they show a desperate need for environmental sensibility on a larger than room scale. Sigfried Giedion pointed to specific engineering feats as *objets d'art* thirty years ago. Smithson has transcended this by putting engineering works into their natural settings and treating the whole as a time-bound web of man-nature interactions.

Methodologically Les Levine is possibly the most consistent exponent of a systems esthetic. His environments of vacuum-formed, modular plastic units are never static; by means of an experience's ambulation through them, they consistently alter their own degree of space-surface penetrability. Levine's *Clean Machine* has no ideal vantage points, no "pieces" to recognize, as are implicit in formalist art. One is *processed* as in driving through the Holland Tunnel. Certainly this echoes Michael Fried's reference to Tony Smith's night-time drive along the uncompleted New Jersey Turnpike.[11] Yet if this is theater, as Fried insists, it is not the stage concerned with focused-upon events. That has more to do with the boundary definitions which have traditionally circumscribed classical and post-classical art. In a recent environment by Levine rows of live electric wires emitted small shocks to passersby. Here behavior is controlled in an esthetic situation with no primary reference to visual circumstances. As Levine insists, "What I am after here is physical reaction, not visual concern." [12]

This brings to mind some of the original intentions of the "Group de Recherches d'Art Visuel" in the early 1960s. The Paris-based group had sought to engage viewers kinesthetically, triggering involuntary responses through ambient-propelled "surprises." Levine's emphasis on visual disengagement is much more assured and iconoclastic; unlike the labyrinths of the G.R.A.V., his possesses no individual work of art deflecting attention from the environment as a concerted experience.

Questions have been raised concerning the implicit anti-art position connected with Levine's *disposable* and *infinite* series. These hardly qualify as anti-art as John Perrault has pointed out. Besides emphasizing that the context of art is fluid, they are a *reductio ad absurdum* of the entire market mechanism which controls art through the fiction of "high art." They do not deny art, they deny scarcity as a legitimate correlative of art.

The components of systems—whether these are artistic or functional—have no higher meaning or value. Systems components derive their value solely through their assigned context. Therefore it would be impossible to regard a fragment of an art system as a work of art in itself—as say, one might treasure a fragment of one of the Parthenon friezes. This became evident in December 1967 when Dan Flavin designed six walls with the same alternate pattern of "rose" and "gold" 8-foot fluorescent lamps. This "Broad Bright Gaudy Vulgar System," as Flavin called it, was installed in the new Museum of Contemporary Art in Chicago. The catalog accompanying the exhibition scrupulously resolves some of the important esthetic implications for modular systems.

The components of a particular exhibition upon its termination are replaced in another situation. Perhaps put into non-art as part of a different whole in a different future. Individual units possess no intrinsic significance beyond their concrete utility. It is difficult either to project into them extraneous qualities, a spurious insight, or for them to be appropriated for fulfillment or personal inner needs. The lights are untransformed. There are no symbolic transcendental redeeming or monetary added values present.[13]

Flavin's work has progressed in the past six years from light sources mounted on flat reliefs, to compositions in fluorescent fixtures mounted directly on walls and floors, and recently to totalities such as his Chicago "walk-in" environment. While the majority of other light artists have continued to fabricate "light sculpture"—as if *sculpture* were the primary concern—Flavin has pioneered articulated illumination systems for given spaces.

By the fact that most systems move or are in some way dynamic, kinetic art should be one of the more radical alternatives to the prevailing formalist esthetic. Yet this has hardly been the case. The best publicized kinetic sculpture is mainly a modification of static formalist sculpture composition. In most instances these have only the added bonus of motion, as in the case of Tinguely, Calder, Bury, and Rickey. Only Duchamp's kinetic output managed to reach beyond formalism. Rather than visual appearance there is an entirely different concern which makes kinetic art unique. This is the peripheral perception of sound and movement in a space filled with activity. All too often gallery kinetic art has trivialized the more graspable aspect of motion: this is motion internalized and experienced kinesthetically.

There are a few important exceptions to the above. These include Otto Piene's early "Light Ballets" (1958–1962), the early (1956) water hammocks and informal on-going environments of Japan's *Gutai* group, some works by Len Lye, Bob Breer's first show of "Floats" (1965), Robert Whitman's laser show "Dark" (1967), and most recently, Boyd Mefferd's "Strobe-Light Floor" (1968).

Formalist art embodies the idea of deterministic relations between a composition's visible elements. But since the early 1960s Hans Haacke has depended upon the invisible components of systems. In a systems context, invisibility, or invisible parts, share equal importance with things seen. Thus air, water, steam and ice have become major elements in his work. On both coasts this has precipitated interest in "invisible art" among a number of young artists. Some of the best of Haacke's efforts are shown outside the gallery. These include his *Rain Tree*, a tree dripping patterns of water; *Sky Line*, a nylon line kept aloft by hundreds of helium filled white balloons; a weather balloon balanced over a jet of air; and a large-scale nylon tent with air pockets designed to remain in balance one foot off the ground.

Haacke's systems have a limited life as an art experience, though some are quite durable. He insists that the need for empathy does not make his work function as with older art. Systems exist as on-going independent entities away from the viewer. In the systems hierarchy of control, *interaction* and *autonomy* become desirable values. In this respect Haacke's *Photo-Electric Viewer Programmed Coordinate System* is probably one of the most elegant responsive environments made to date *by an artist* (certainly more sophisticated ones have been conceived for scientific and technical purposes). Boundary situations are central to his thinking.

A "sculpture" that physically reacts to its environment is no longer to be regarded as an object. The range of outside factors affecting it, as well as its own radius of action, reach beyond the space it materially occupies. It thus merges with the environment in a relationship that is better understood as a "system" of interdependent processes. These processes evolve without the viewer's empathy. He becomes a witness. A system is not imagined, it is real.[14]

Tangential to this systems approach is Allan Kaprow's very unique concept of the Happening. In the past ten years Kaprow has moved the Happening from a rather self-conscious and stagy event to a strict and elegant procedure. The Happening now has a sense of internal logic which was lacking before. It seems to arise naturally from those same considerations which have crystalized the systems approach to environmental situations. As described by their chief inventor, the Happenings establish an indivisibility between themselves and everyday affairs; they consciously avoid materials and procedures identified with art; they allow for geographical expansiveness and mobility; they include experience and duration as part of their esthetic format; and they emphasize practical activities as the most meaningful mode of procedure.[15] As structured events the Happenings are usually reversible. Alterations in the environment may be "erased" after the Happening, or as a part of the Happening's conclusion. While they may involve large areas of space, the format of the Happening is kept relatively simple, with the emphasis on establishing a participatory esthetic.

The emergence of a "post-formalist esthetic" may seem to some to embody a kind of absolute philosophy, something which, through the nature of its concerns cannot be transcended. Yet it is more likely that a "systems esthetic" will become the dominant approach to a maze of socio-technical conditions rooted only in the present. New circumstances will with time generate other major paradigms for the arts.

For some readers these pages will echo feelings of the past. It may be remembered that in the fall of 1920 an ideological schism ruptured two factions of the Moscow Constructivists. The radical Marxists, led by Vladimir Tatlin, proclaimed their rejection of art's false idealisms. Establishing themselves as "Productivists," one of their slogans became: "Down with guarding the traditions of art. Long live the constructivist technician." [16] As a group dedicated to historical materialism and the scientific ethos, most of its members were quickly subsumed by the technological needs of Soviet Russia. As artists they ceased to exist. While the Productivist program might have had some basis as a utilitarian esthetic, it was crushed amid the Stalinist anti-intellectualism that followed.

The reasons are almost self-apparent. Industrially underdeveloped, food and heavy industry remained the prime needs of the Soviet Union for the next forty years. Conditions and structural interdependencies which naturally develop in an advanced industrial state were then only latent. In retrospect it is doubtful if any group of artists had either the knowledge or political strength to meaningfully affect Soviet industrial policies. What emerged was another vein of formalist innovation based on scientific idealism; this manifested itself in the West under the leadership of the Constructivist emigres, Gabo and Pevsner.

But for our time the emerging major paradigm in art is neither an *ism* nor a collection of styles. Rather than a novel way of rearranging surfaces and spaces, it is fundamentally concerned with the implementation of the art impulse in an advanced technological society. As a culture producer, man has traditionally claimed the title, *Homo Faber: man the maker* (of tools and images). With continued advances in the industrial revolution, he assumes a new and more critical function. As *Homo Arbiter Formae* his prime role becomes that of *man the maker of esthetic decisions*. These decisions—whether they are made concertedly or not—control the quality of all future life on the Earth. Moreover these are value judgments dictating the direction of technological endeavor. Quite plainly such a vision extends beyond political realities of the present. This cannot remain the case for long.

REFERENCES

1. Quade, E. S. (November 1964) "Methods and Procedures" in *Analysis for Military Decisions* (Santa Monica: The Rand Corp.) p. 153.
2. Galbraith, John Kenneth (1967) *The New Industrial State* (Boston: Houghton Mifflin Co.) pp. 343–353.
3. Caudwell, Christopher (pseud.) (1937) *Illusion and Reality: A Study of the Sources of Poetry* (London: Macmillan and Co.) p. 111.
4. Peckham, Morse (1965) *Man's Rage for Chaos: Biology, Behavior & the Arts* (New York: Schocken Books, 1967) p. 314.
5. Fried, Michael (Summer, 1967) "Art and Objecthood" *Artforum*, p. 15.
6. Bertalanffy, Ludwig von (1967) *Robots, Men and Minds* (New York: George Braziller Inc.) p. 69.
7. Anonymous (September 1, 1967) "Ad Reinhardt, Painter, Is Dead, Reduced Color to Bare Minimum" in *The New York Times*, p. 33.
8. Judd, Donald (1965) "Specific Objects" in *Contemporary Sculpture* (New York: The Arts Digest, Inc.) p. 78.
9. Morris, Robert (April 1968) "Anti Form," *Artforum*, p. 35.
10. Smithson, Robert (Summer 1967) "Towards the Development of an Air Terminal Site" *Artforum*, pp. 36–40.
11. Fried, *op. cit.*, p. 19.
12. Jacobs, Jay (March 1968) "More Les" *the ART gallery* (Ivoryton, Connecticut: Hollycraft Press) p. 27.
13. Flavin, Dan (with introduction by) (December 1967) *Dan Flavin: Pink and Gold*, exhibition catalog, (Chicago: The Museum of Contemporary Art).
14. Haacke, Hans (with statement by) (January 1968) *Hans Haacke*, exhibition catalog (New York: Howard Wise Gallery).
15. Kaprow, Allan (March 1966) "The Happenings are Dead—Long Live Happenings" *Artforum*, pp. 36–39.
16. Gabo, Naum (1957) *Gabo: Constructions, Sculptures, Paintings, Drawings, Engravings* (Cambridge: Harvard University Press) p. 153.

Evaluating Children's Art

ELLIOT W. EISNER

The evaluation of children's art has been and continues to be one of the most vexing problems in the teaching of art. Making judgments about the adequacy of a child's art work is no easy task. Neither the criteria nor the standards to be applied are easily selected. Furthermore, the literature in art education shows no strong consensus concerning the "best" ways to evaluate. Research findings too are inconclusive. Questions about the desirability of art contests, grading art work, displaying all work regardless of quality, lack a definitive answer. The lack of definitive research findings provides no consolation to the classroom teacher facing thirty or more children. Decisions need to be made. Neither the teacher nor the children can wait; the teacher must act.

The problem of determining the best criteria to use in evaluation is not merely a methodological one. Such a problem rests upon a philosophical base. Deciding upon what is best as a means also implies that in the long run the means selected will contribute to the achievement of the larger ends sought. Thus, any method used to evaluate a child's work should be consonant with not only the particular purposes of art education, but also the larger scheme of education of which it is a part.

It is my purpose here to deal with some major ideas regarding evaluation in general, and to relate them specifically to the evaluation of children's art. Evaluating performance is difficult in any curriculum area. It is especially difficult in art because the nature of the field does not lend itself to the neat categories that are more easily applied to other fields.

Evaluation has a fairly specific meaning in education. It is a *judgment of the adequacy of behavior as compared to a set of educational objectives*. This conception of evaluation rests upon the assumption that educational activities are purposefully planned and that they are formulated to achieve specific ends. While this conception of evaluation is commonplace in education, it is not as common in art education. If it was employed in the teaching of art it would require first, a clear formulation of objectives for each activity included in the art curriculum. Second, it would require that the objectives be stated in terms of desired student behavior rather than in terms of behaviors to be displayed by the teacher. Third, it would require that objectives be so clearly stated that they would be useful in determining if the objectives have or have not been achieved. When purposes and objectives are vague or ambiguous one is hard pressed to know exactly to what they refer.

Being clear about one's teaching purposes does not necessarily mean that

Reprinted by permission from *School Arts Magazine*, Vol. 63, No. 1, September 1963, Davis Publications, Inc.

activities be rigid or that standards be tight. Clarity of purpose is more likely to be useful in the selection of activities designed to reach certain ends than purposes which are diffuse. Clarity of purpose and efficiency in means is desired in the academic areas; it seems reasonable to aspire for no less in the teaching of art.

Objectives in teaching art are not always preplanned. What the student produces and what he learns are not always foreseen. The teacher is often faced with the task of trying to exploit the accidental and ephemeral qualities that are displayed in the work. Thus, if a student happens upon an imaginative use of color in a project designed to further knowledge of composition, the teacher may decide to shift his objectives for that student in order to capitalize upon the student's accidental discovery. This implies flexible purposing on the part of the teacher. It is in these unplanned shifts, these flexible modifications, that teaching becomes most artistic. The teacher recognizes that something valuable can be taught, takes advantage of the unique situation to try to teach it, and evaluates the student's performance with the particular objectives he formulated when he decided to make the shift.

The use of clearly formulated objectives in the evaluation process is an important aid to the teacher but objectives alone will not provide evidence that the student has progressed. In order to determine progress and growth the student's work must be compared. The most common method of comparison in American schools is that of comparing individual performance to group performance. The classroom, the grade level, the national norm, all provide a comparative base for making judgments about the student's achievement. While such a method provides valuable data it does not provide evidence of change. Knowing the relative rank of an individual child in a particular classroom tells a great deal about his relation to the others but nothing about his progress. In order to determine progress, past and present performance must be compared.

The lack of standardized achievement tests in the field of art has enabled the field to avoid some of the evaluation practices that characterize many of the academic areas where standardized tests are available. However, with the growth of research in art education we may some day have and use standardized tests in art. While such tests might be useful for comparing large groups they are of little use for evaluating individual achievement. And it is the individual child and not the statistical abstraction that the teacher faces. However, the practice of comparing children's performance has not totally escaped art education. Although art teachers, I believe, have been generally more sensitive to individual performance, the practice of comparing a student's products to those of his classmates is still used as an important method for judging achievement. The use of such a method is reflected in the concept of developmental levels in art. This concept is essentially a statistical one. It says simply that most children at a given age level produce art work having particular characteristics. While developmental levels in art are very useful for making general descriptions of groups, they cannot justifiably be used prescriptively. That is, it is illogical to conclude that a particular child *ought* to perform in a certain way simply because most children of his age do.

As simple and as reasonable as this might sound in theory, it is seldom employed in practice. Assigning grades and evaluating progress on the basis of large scale group comparisons is characteristic of American schools. Parents, teachers, and principals all desire their children, students, and teachers to be above average and somehow overlook the fact that if by some magic all such individuals were improved by eighty per cent, half would still be below average.

Our enchantment with group comparison is clearly reflected in the way grades are assigned. In general, average performance earns an average grade, above average performance, excellent or superior grades. The student is most often graded, in art as elsewhere, on his relative rank in class. His relationship to others determines how well he is doing. Such a system of grading is further confused by sandwiching an absolute description—excellent—between two comparative descriptions—average and superior! Thus, theoretically a student who is excellent has met certain standards; while one that is superior is better than most. Is it any wonder that confusion over grading exists?

Another shortcoming of using a class or grade level comparison as the dominant method for evaluating children's art work is the widely accepted myth that children in the fifth grade, for example, are fifth graders. Our knowledge of individual differences is often put aside in grading and placement practices in the school. The most common criterion for grade placement and achievement expectations is chronological age. Yet, if the same standardized tests are used in a classroom to determine the range of academic achievement, grade levels dissolve into a convenient fiction. For example, on the average, there is a four year range in school readiness in first grade students. In the eighth grade, in the average classroom, there is an eight year range in reading achievement. In the middle of the academic year for any grade level only from fifteen to twenty per cent of the students are achieving at grade level in each academic area. As yet we do not have such data for art performance, but it is reasonable to expect that similar findings will emerge.

What we will probably find is that as children become older, the range of art ability for each age increases. As the range of ability expands through the grades, the need for differentiating the art curriculum increases. Teachers should encourage these differences and plan so that those who are ready and able to move more quickly are provided with the kind of instruction that will make such progress possible. Conversely those who achieve at a slower rate should be provided with instruction that makes provision for their natural learning pace without being concerned with falling behind. In short, I believe, elementary schools should maximize individual differences despite its lock-step grade structure. And since art programs need not impose identical expectations and activities upon students merely because they are of the same age, it follows that criteria used for evaluating performance should also be differentiated. Comparing the child's work to that of his peers need not be the dominant method of evaluation.

There is an alternative to group comparison that might be well to explore. That alternative is one of comparing a student's work to his previous work and to use such a comparison as the *primary basis* for making judgments about growth. Indeed, if growth, in the Deweyian sense, should be the ultimate goal that schools should seek to attain, it is illogical to measure growth by comparing an individual to others. If we want to know if a child has gotten taller it is fruitless to find out if he is above average in height. The analogy holds true for evaluating achievement in art.

Using an individual comparative base is not only desirable on logical grounds, it also serves to improve instruction. It provides opportunities for diagnosing strengths and weaknesses in art performance. With such diagnosis it may be possible to plan activities specifically designed to help individual students.

If schools kept a portfolio of samples of each student's art work throughout the grades it would be possible for teachers to consult these sources in planning art programs designed to meet the needs of particular students. Activities thus planned would rest upon a clear set of educational objectives in art, a longitudinal view of the student's past performance, and empirical evidence concerning the student's weaknesses and strengths in art. Such a portfolio could also be used by the student to help him recognize his own progress. It could present dramatic evidence of change that often goes unrecognized by those students who frequently underestimate their own progress.

The use of art products as the primary data for comparison can be supplemented by material written by the student at intervals during the school year. If the student can be encouraged to indicate his interest, understanding, and general attitude toward his own work the teacher can obtain valuable information about factors that might otherwise go unnoticed. Students who are "doing well in art" in the eyes of the teacher may have serious misgivings about their own work. Such attitudes can build up and can lead to a rejection of art as a satisfying field of human experience. They can convince the student that he has no aptitude for art. How many adults, who are products of older art education programs, are convinced that they have neither talent nor interest in art?

By obtaining short descriptions from the student about his interest and satisfaction in art, the teacher is placed in a position of being able to provide encouragement and support at those strategic moments when they are most in need. All the teacher has to observe is the student's overt behavior and art products. He can only surmise what the student's covert attitudes are. But the student has direct access to his own feelings and can, when student-teacher relations allow, describe how he feels about his own adequacy in art and his satisfaction in it. It would be sad indeed if we overlooked the attitudes that the student develops toward art in our eagerness to enable them to become responsive to and productive in the field.

In suggesting the use of educational objectives for evaluation and individual past performance as a means of determining progress I realize that many practical difficulties might ensue. Traditional expectations are not easy to dismiss. Both children and parents like to know where they stand in relation to others. Such a desire is further fostered by our culture. The use of material symbols works quite well as signs of success. It would be foolhardy to think that values and expectations as pervasive as these can easily be changed. Comparing achievement between groups and individuals is part of our national scene, yet when the schools use it as a primary method for evaluating and grading students it tends to encourage the slow-moving child to disregard his own achievements. Since the school rewards achievement based upon group status there is little reason for him to think highly of his individual progress. The student needs to recognize his own progress in art as well as to recognize the achievements of others. This recognition is more likely to take place when he is encouraged to measure his own achievement in terms of his own growth rather than by limiting his comparison to the work of others.

In the last analysis differentiating the evaluative criteria for children of different abilities is based upon a conception of educational equality. Equality of educational opportunity means not only that all children have access to education but that all children have equal treatment. Equal treatment does not mean sameness of treatment. It means that all students are provided with the kinds of opportunities that are commensurate with their abilities and that expectations in performance be differentiated on the same basis. Providing an equal opportunity in art education, as in education in general, is after all a goal worthy of our aspirations.

The Problem of Objectivity in Esthetic Value

IRVIN L. CHILD

Once it was generally assumed in Western culture that esthetic value is a property somehow inherent in the work of art independently of any viewer. Disagreement about esthetic value need not lead to rejection of this view. To esthetic value as to color, smell, or sound, some people might well be more sensitive than others. A person deficient in color vision might argue with another about a color they were looking at; each might feel some puzzle-

Reprinted with permission of the author from *Penn State Papers in Art Education*, No. 1, October 1966, pp. 5–25. Department of Art Education, The Pennsylvania State University.

ment or confusion without either's realizing that one of them has a sensory deficiency. Just so, disagreements might be expected between people having and lacking esthetic sensitivity on this objective theory of esthetic value.

The assumption of esthetic value as directly inhering in the object not only was once common among the intellectually sophisticated but is perhaps a simple assumption likely to be made spontaneously by anyone not acquainted with recent currents in philosophy and behavioral science. As Piaget has taught us through his careful observation of intellectual development in children, we all naturally assume at an early age that what we experience is objectively there; and only at a high level of development do we come to realize how very different from our own may be the experience of another person in the same situation.

A simple view of esthetic value as completely objective is less likely to be adopted today; many elements in modern life work against it. Our increasing knowledge of cultures alien to our own, and of their very different forms of art; our increased historical perspective, giving awareness of changes in style from generation to generation and even year to year; an application to art of the personal relativism implicit in much of the psychology and sociology of mental hygiene—all these factors join to make more likely today an assumption that there is no objectivity at all in esthetic value. Indeed, since the very term "esthetic value" suggests something consistent and enduring, the mood of today is rather against the assumption that the term has any useful meaning. The concept itself may seem as outmoded as some of the theories which sought to explain it. As one historical scholar remarked when I said I was interested in the problem of esthetic value: "How very 18th century!"

Certainly we are right in rejecting the once-common view that whatever the artistically elite of a society at the time hold to be beautiful or fine has a special natural superiority over other works of art. Into the judgment of any of us must enter a great deal of the time-bound, the culture-bound, the personality-bound. But rejecting in advance the possibility of some objectivity in esthetic value and of the usefulness of that concept seems likely to be an over-correction of former error, leading to the risk of new error.

This over-correction seems attributable in part to the difficulty of looking at things statistically or probabilistically. On topics not commonly thought about in a statistical manner, it is easy for the skeptic to dismiss a trend by citing negative cases, and art seems to be such a topic. The fact that so few of Gauguin's paintings were sold in his early years of painting, that they brought so poor a price, and that hardly any of Van Gogh's were sold until after Van Gogh's death, provide clear cases against the notion that fine works of art have obvious qualities of superiority that must be visible to anyone who looks at them with care. It is not a question of what the artistically naive people in Tahiti or Arles thought of these painters, for the works were seen by fellow artists, dealers, and collectors, and were not generally acclaimed. Beside these cases we can of course set others such as Michelangelo or

Raphael, where evaluation of a man's work was high when it was produced and has generally remained high. Yet Van Gogh and Gauguin are not isolated instances; parallels are frequent in the history of the arts. And I find they are still being used as evidence against the notion that there is an objectivity in esthetic value.

On topics to which a statistical mode of thought has more generally penetrated, a similar situation leads to a different result. Consider the issue of how disease is produced. There was a time when the notion of contagion could be dismissed by citing negative instances—cases where a person was thoroughly exposed to a disease but did not develop it. The negative instances are very real here as in art. If we keep track of all the times we have seen people exposed to illness, we will surely find that most of the exposures do not lead to their getting sick. But the preponderance of negative cases, and recognition that a variety of other factors also influence whether one becomes sick, do not prevent us from recognizing the role of contagion. If we can extend to art the same kind of reasoning we apply in thinking about causes of illness—recognizing the presence of many interacting influences and the absence of complete determination by any one of them—we may be better prepared to consider whether there is any objectivity at all in esthetic value.

People whose mode of thought has been shaped largely by the scientific tradition readily apply statistical reasoning to the question of esthetic value. Factor analysis, for example, one of the techniques of statistical reasoning now widely used in psychology and education, had not been long in existence before its relevance to this question was noted by the American psychologist Beebe-Center, as well as by several British psychologists. Beebe-Center was working with simple sensory stimuli such as odors but believed his work relevant to general problems of esthetics. Let a number of people each rank a set of smells in order of personal preference. There will be great disagreement. But will there, nonetheless, be some degree of agreement? Factor analysis can be used to find out, and to measure the amount of agreement. For the stimuli he was using, Beebe-Center found a definite tendency toward agreement underlying the obvious disagreements and concluded, in effect, that this agreement established that liking or disliking of smells had an objective or constant basis rather than being purely idiosyncratic. Objectivity, for him, was clearly a question of a statistically recognizable tendency toward agreement, not of absolute uniformity or perfect agreement.

This statistical view of the nature of objectivity in esthetic value is at least implicit in many psychological discussions of esthetic problems—notably, for example, in Pratt's essay, "The Stability of Aesthetic Judgments." Perhaps most widely known is the very explicit statement of this view by the British psychologist, Eysenck, both because his research articles have been widely read and because he has presented the statement in a popular book on psychology, the Pelican book entitled *Sense and Nonsense in Psychology*. Here is the straight-forward statement that esthetic value is objective because it is measured by agreement among individuals in esthetic preference. The individuals Eysenck refers to are considered a sample of human beings in general. Let a number of persons look at a set of paintings, for instance, and each rank the paintings in order of personal preference. Each individual will have some idiosyncratic preferences growing out of peculiarities of temperament or background. But if there is any consistent tendency for some of the paintings to be more pleasing and others less pleasing to human beings in general, this will appear as a consistent tendency toward agreement which statistical analysis can detect under the obvious disagreements. The resemblance between the preferences of one person and another may not be very close. If, for example, it is of the degree indicated by an average correlation coefficient of .10 (where 1.0 means perfect agreement), the only fact apparent to the casual observer will be the profound disagreement. But precise analysis will detect the agreement that is nonetheless there. And it is a truly impressive agreement. If we measure the relative appeal of each painting by the average of the ratings given to it by 100 judges who agree with one another only to the slight extent indicated, we will find that we can predict almost perfectly the average rating which will be given by another 100 judges drawn from the same population. Clearly, people who rate paintings are, even in the presence of much disagreement, responding consistently to visible characteristics of the paintings. If we are willing to apply the label "esthetic value" to the characteristics they are responding to, if we are willing to say that the art generally liked has high esthetic value and the art generally disliked has low esthetic value, then we have in this agreement clear evidence of the objectivity of esthetic value.

But a very serious objection may be raised against this view of how esthetic values might be objective. Here the average taste of the majority is being proposed by Beebe-Center and Eysenck as a standard of esthetic value. We are all well aware of the variation in taste among various strata of society and among individuals. Esthetic value of works of art is ordinarily thought of as corresponding to the taste of that small segment of a society which has developed a specialized interest in art. It seems to be true for many nations and times that the majority taste is a taste which esthetically sensitive people consider extremely debased. Under certain special conditions the average preference of unselected people may correspond to more usually accepted criteria of esthetic value. Eysenck, in his own research on esthetic preference, was well aware of the problem and tried to create special conditions. His conditions, it seems to me, were not special enough to create a likelihood that majority taste would correspond with other standards of esthetic value.

Under ordinary conditions, this objection has a solid basis in fact. I asked a number of unselected college students to arrange various sets of paintings (as reproduced on postcards) in order of personal preference, and also had the same paintings arranged for esthetic merit by students of art. The college students showed remarkable agreement in their preferences, and the art students showed even more agreement with one another in their esthetic judgments. But there was very little agreement between the two groups.

More recently, I have been dealing with pairs of slides, each pair showing two similar works of art which differ in esthetic value according to art students and other experts. Again there is good agreement among experts. Very often, too, there is good agreement among non-experts about which picture they prefer in a pair. But just as with the sets of postcards, there is very little relation between the two kinds of evaluation. For these pairs of slides, I have some data which might indicate the preference of a representative sample of the general population. These data consist of the responses of the entire high-school population of two towns. To be sure, there may well be changes in average preference after high-school graduation, though I know of no evidence for this. If we may tentatively take high-school preferences as representative of those of the general adult population, our data indicate that popular taste shows some systematic tendency to disagree with the judgment of experts. Younger children, in elementary school, prefer the work experts consider better only about 40% of the time. This figure rises with children's development, but even by the last year of high school hardly reaches 50%; systematic agreement with experts would be shown only by a figure above 50%.

There is, then, in many works of art some real basis for widespread appeal to a variety of unselected people; the preferences of the general public are not random, but are systematically related to characteristics of the art. Beebe-Center and Eysenck are right in finding in the fact of agreement, then, evidence of objectivity in the bases of personal preference. Yet the objective characteristics that lead to this agreement appear to be not at all the same features that determine evaluation by experts as works of art. Objectivity of something is demonstrated, but the "esthetic value" seems an inappropriate term for what is agreed on by the general public.

Is there, then, no sound application of agreement as a criterion of objectivity in the case of esthetic value? I believe that there is, and that it is to be found by looking to the opinion of experts rather than of unselected people.

It may be instructive in several ways to consider possible parallels in another field, for example, mathematics. Suppose we are confronted with students' examination papers, in some branch of higher mathematics. We have on the one hand problems which have been posed to the students—problems, let us say, in modern abstract algebra. On the other hand we have the answers given by each of a dozen students. Suppose for the sake of argument that you are like me in having no knowledge of modern abstract algebra, so that you could not hope to evaluate the papers yourself. Yet suppose it is important to you as a college dean to know which of these papers indicate good command of the subject, which indicate slightly defective command, and which display complete incompetence. What would you do? Surely you would consult someone who shows by the way he spends his time and earns his living that he is an expert in modern abstract algebra. You would ask him to evaluate the papers, assigning each one a grade. Generally, in educational institutions, we are willing to act upon grades assigned by one person, presumably being confident of his objectivity—unless we have studied psychology or have just received a low grade. If, however, we doubted the objectivity of the grading, we might give the papers separately to several different mathematicians, asking each to make evaluations without any knowledge of those made by his fellows. If there is reasonably good agreement among the grades assigned by the several experts, we would be ready to believe in the objectivity of these evaluations. We would then confidently take whatever action is suitable, even though we ourselves remain completely ignorant of the subject matter. Note, however, that we are likely to find only "reasonably good" agreement among the experts, not perfect accord. Some papers might be assigned decidedly different grades by different readers. But this would not destroy our confidence that the agreement which also appears is truly based on important aspects of the students' work.

Something similar is possible for the social scientist who wishes to study esthetic value, although his motive is different. In imagining ourselves as a college dean, we asked how we could be sure of the objectivity of grades assigned to papers we could not understand. Getting independent evaluation from several experts was a substitute adopted because of our own ignorance. When we turn now to the psychologist or art educator inquiring into esthetic value, there may be no parallel ignorance. We may feel we know perfectly well which works of art are esthetically superior and which are inferior. But we deliberately set aside these judgments of our own because we recognize they do not carry with them—as modern abstract algebra does for the person who has mastered it—their own internal test of logical consistency, and that objectivity here depends upon the criterion of agreement. If we wish to apply to esthetic values the scientific approach—which must be concerned with objectively determinable knowledge—we must start with establishment, not just our own opinions.

We must, then, present a number of works of art to an expert, asking for evaluation of their esthetic merit. We must show the same art to other experts and obtain their independent evaluations. By going to people whose profession indicates them to be alive to problems of esthetic value, to be reacting to works of art as works of art rather than in terms of purely personal appeal of various kinds, we can hope that their judgments are about esthetic value. And to the extent that the various experts agree in their judgments we have evidence that these values are objective, at least within the range of variety of background and perspective found in the particular set of judges we have used.

Now, of course, there is, as I have already implied, an important respect in which this parallel between evaluation of mathematics and of art breaks down. For the mathematics papers, we feel sure that if we were to take several years off to become experts in modern abstract algebra, there are perfectly clear and straightforward rules with absolute validity to guide us in a part of our evaluation. The best papers will be completely rational in the reasoning presented. The worst papers will have erroneous statements, clear errors of deductive reasoning. We do not, in fact, even need an expert to detect these. An electronic computer could be used if the proper program had been worked out in advance. In art, there is nothing comparable to this aspect of objectivity—no rules of derivation of thought by which we can point unerringly to certain works as clearly correct and others as wrong. But here there is a difference in the subject matter. Mathematics is about logical truth and falsehood. Art is not. Agreement in evaluation by experts in the particular subject matter may provide in either case a similar standard or criterion of value which can be used as a basis for studying the correlates of greater or lesser value. When the subject matter is mathematics, we expect truth and error to be major, though by no means the only, elements in determining high value and low value of product. In art, the characteristics associated with very good and very poor work will be of other sorts. But we need not know in advance just what these characteristics will be in order to take agreement between the independent judgments of different experts as indicating objectivity in evaluation, as evidence that their evaluations are dependably related to some real characteristics of the art.

It is of course possible to carry the parallel with mathematics further—to argue that rational analysis should permit an infallible test of esthetic values just as it does of mathematical truth. It is, indeed, this extreme analogy between evaluation in art and in mathematics that is best known. Estheticians offered us this analogy long ago—Hogarth, for example, in his account of the special beauty of the "line of grace" which curves through three-dimensional space. The analogy has even been put in mathematical form—by Birkhoff several decades ago in his "Aesthetic Measure," and more recently by Rashevsky. I would not want to deny all promise of utility to such efforts to find a numerical formula for beauty. Perhaps something important will eventually come from them. But I do not believe it will be what the parallel with mathematics suggests—a rational means of esthetic evaluation which will guide us to accurate judgments more dependably than will the average evaluation by a number of varied experts. And for the present, at any event, agreement of experts is the only basis for objectifying esthetic evaluation. It is the basis, I think, from which any further inquiry needs to start.

But is there any agreement among experts to provide evidence of objectivity? In talking with students of art or art history, I have frequently encountered the view that evaluation of works of art is purely personal and that there will probably be no agreement between one evaluator and another.

This notion has in many ways been congenial to the temper of thought in the United States in recent decades. It has been encouraged by some writings of psychologists on esthetics, and by some research findings. In an earlier stage of the development of psychology, many psychologists thought one of their most useful functions in society was iconoclasm. By breaking up false images in our thinking, they seemed to believe they could provide the basis for eventual construction of new and sounder cultural ideals. One of the images they considered false was that of absolute esthetic value. Proof of the absolute quality of esthetic value, they felt, would require demonstration that art experts show extremely close agreement on judgments about esthetic value. Kate Gordon, in the early 1920's, produced evidence often cited to support the view that experts agree among themselves less than the general public. I am afraid we have here a case of ready acceptance of news we wish to hear. Gordon's results did not, in fact, show anything of the sort. She obtained preferential ratings of a set of reproductions of Oriental rugs from both experts and non-experts. She found that the averaged opinions of a large number of non-experts showed a high degree of consistency and concluded that a stable esthetic standard, an objective measure of esthetic value, is thus expressed in the averaged opinions of people in general. The averaged opinions of experts, Gordon found, showed less agreement; she therefore expressed skepticism about any special sensitivity to esthetic value on the part of the experts. But what she took for lesser agreement of experts was purely a statistical artifact resulting from the much smaller number of experts averaged together in comparison with the number of representatives of the general public. Dr. Gordon was an excellent psychologist, but at the time she was doing her research very limited or primitive statistical techniques were available. When we look at her study with present-day knowledge of statistics, we see that the experts showed no less agreement than the general public, possibly even a bit more.

We must recognize, however, that if Kate Gordon's evidence was not correct, the skeptical attitude she expressed might still have been justified. Some later evidence seems to support it. A recent researcher with the same surname, Donald Gordon, has obtained such evidence; and his is not a statistical artifact. He had ten student oil paintings evaluated both by experts and by non-experts, and found less agreement among the experts than among the general public. The paintings he was using were very limited in number and probably were also limited in the range of esthetic merit while being highly varied in subject matter and technique. But he provides clear evidence that a set of such materials can be put together for which experts agree less than do non-experts in the evaluations they make. Francès and Voillaume, moreover, have reported similar findings with small sets of paintings which are not student work. Most of their material was drawn from the work of renowned artists, and they reduced the variation in subject matter among the paintings to be compared. That they still obtained less agreement among experts than among non-experts shows that such a finding is not restricted to the very special circumstances which obviously favored it in Donald Gordon's study.

More recent research poses the disturbing possibility that what agreement there is among experts might be largely local, representing the standards of a single interacting group and not shared with other groups. The research

I refer to is that being done by the Educational Testing Service as part of a study of creativity in art school students. Skager, Schultz, and Klein have described the outcome of having a number of judges evaluate 191 student drawings made in response to uniform instructions "to do a drawing using specified materials from a vantage point overlooking the city of Providence." Evaluations were made by 24 experts who were faculty members at three different art schools, and by four non-experts. A factor analysis showed that two different sets of criteria could be distinguished as bases for judgments by experts; one of them could be identified with the dichotomy of spontaneous vs. deliberate that has emerged from research at Penn State, and the other was more difficult to define. One set of criteria was found primarily in judgments by the faculty of one art school, and the other set primarily in judgments by faculty members from the two other art schools. Now it is not true that agreement among experts at different schools was altogether lacking. The ratings by every expert judge showed a positive correlation with the ratings by every other expert judge; these positive correlations merely were lower on the average when the two judges were from different faculties. Negative correlations between judges were obtained only when an expert was compared with a non-expert. Still, the findings in this study may usefully remind us at the outset that local expert standards are very important and might at times be the most conspicuous influences. We could probably select art for judging in such a manner that the various works differed mostly in ways relevant to local criteria and not in ways relevant to more universal criteria. We should then find no agreement between faculties of different art schools. Perhaps this is an unlikely event to occur spontaneously, but it is an important possibility to bear in mind.

In trying to answer the question, "Is there any agreement among experts to provide evidence of objectivity?" I have begun with some of the difficulties, with some of the reasons which may be adduced for expecting little or no objectivity. Let's turn to the positive side. In all the studies I have mentioned, and in many others besides, despite challenges of some sort to objectivity, agreement among experts clearly is found, even though it sometimes is less than the agreement among non-experts. In some other instances, however, the agreement among experts is greater than among non-experts. One example is an incidental finding I have already mentioned from some research of my own. I assembled 12 separate sets of 60 postcard-size reproductions of paintings. One set was of portraits of women, another of men, another of landscapes, another of still lifes and so on. I had undergraduates at two universities rate their personal like or dislike of each picture. I then also had each picture rated for esthetic quality by expert judges who were for the most part students in art school or graduate students of art history. For every one of the 12 sets of pictures, the agreement among the experts was greater than the agreement among the unselected students; and for some sets it was very much greater.

Another example of agreement among experts, though not carrying with it any comparison with non-experts, emerges from some other research of mine. Each of the pairs of slides used in the study of esthetic judgment and preference referred to earlier consisted of two works of art, similar in character but differing in esthetic value according to the opinion of the person forming the pair. The various pairs were made up by 24 different people, mostly art school students or graduate students in art history, but some older people with a diversity of backgrounds. Wishing to use only those pairs on which experts would be well agreed about the difference in esthetic quality, I submitted all of the pairs, more than 3,000 in number, to 14 independent judges, again mostly art school students but some graduate students in art history. Though some of the judges doubted that there would be any agreement, there clearly was. On over 400 pairs, all 14 of the judges agreed with the original selector about which was the better work in the pair; on only 4 pairs did all 14 disagree with the original selector. These are extremes, of course. When we ask the number on which a majority of judges agreed or disagreed with the selector, we find that the comparison is between 2,620 pairs on which a majority agreed with the selector and 513 pairs on which a majority disagreed with him.

What are we to conclude then about whether there is evidence of objectivity? I think the conclusion is clearly positive. When works are to be judged which differ widely in esthetic value, the results lead us to believe that there will be substantial though not perfect agreement in judgments by experts. When we fail to find agreement, there are at least two highly probable reasons.

One reason is that the works being compared do not in fact differ greatly in esthetic value. For an analog, consider judgments about how much people weight, made by just looking at them. If the people vary a great deal in weight, we can expect a good correlation between one judge and another. If the people are all between 149 and 151 pounds, we can expect little or no correlation among judges in their attempts to make the very difficult discriminations then required. We approach this situation in judging art if the works judged are all masterpieces or if they are all by beginning students. I suspect something of this sort was responsible for the fact that Kate Gordon's experts did not show very close agreement among themselves. She used published reproductions of rugs, and the original selection of rugs to be reproduced may have been made partly on esthetic grounds.

A second reason for lack of agreement between judges may be that they are distracted from esthetic evaluation by other facts. An example is provided by paintings of Gauguin and Van Gogh, where we recognize that their high evaluation today disagrees with their evaluation by some experts at the time they were painted. The experts of that period may have been poorly prepared by their culture for adopting an esthetic attitude toward anything unconventional, and while believing they were giving an esthetic evaluation, they may instead have been principally rating the unconventionality of the paintings. In our day, experts are more able to take an esthetic attitude toward the new or the exotic. But still, when we try to judge the esthetic value of paintings by Gauguin and Van Gogh, we also may be distracted—but by considerations about market value and historical significance which may push our presumably esthetic evaluations too high. In this respect, judgments of esthetic value are not so different from judgments of other kinds of value. We all know that our moral judgments are notoriously susceptible to influence by facts which ought to be irrelevant, such as whether we are judging our own acts, those of a friend, or those of an enemy. Even our judgments about practical value can readily be led astray by irrelevancies; it's easy to believe that a car with a nicely streamlined body has a more powerful motor.

Some degree of objectivity in esthetic value, then, can be found. But is the agreement just among people who share a single cultural background? We do not raise this kind of question in the case of mathematics, to revert to the parallel I suggested earlier. We feel sure that a mathematician trained in higher algebra in a university whose language is Arabic or Russian will, if he learns English well enough to read the examination papers we were considering, arrive at evaluations which will agree pretty well with those made by Americans. We don't even consider the possibility that his bases for evaluation might be completely different. In art we do need to consider it, since here the common belief is that cultural or national background is very important. Perhaps we find agreement among the experts used in such studies as I have cited, not because the admirable characteristics of some works and the poor qualities of others are apparent to any artistically competent human being. Perhaps the agreement is found only because the people consulted as judges are all participants in a single culture, living in a country with fairly homogeneous standards for art evaluation, at a time when certain definable standards are current. Perhaps art experts in the United States a hundred years ago would have made evaluations radically different from those found today. And perhaps experts within some other culture would likewise show no agreement with the experts used in these researches by American psychologists of recent times.

The increasing homogeneity of culture all over the world makes it difficult to test this issue. The possibility of getting some relevant information still remains, however, and I am trying to encourage anthropological and psychological field workers to do this while there is still time. The most adequate basis for comparison between judgments by American experts and qualified members of other cultures thus far available comes from observations made by Leon Siroto among the BaKwele in West Africa and by Sumiko Iwao in Japan. Preparing for an anthropological field trip, Leon Siroto took with him photographs of all the BaKwele masks available to him in advance (39 in number). He asked individual BaKwele who had made or used masks to express their degree of like or dislike for each of the ones in the photographs. At the same time I obtained ratings of the esthetic quality of these same photographs of masks from art students in New Haven. There definitely are differences in the reactions of the BaKwele and of the art students. But agreement is also definite; a marked similarity between the judgments of the two groups of people is clearly apparent, even though the similarity is greater within each group. A similar result emerges from observations made by Sumiko Iwao on potters in Japan. She took with her photographic prints of paired works of art to show to potters working within old Japanese traditions and not very familiar with current international movements in art. These pairs had been selected from the ones I have already mentioned, on the basis of requiring little or no specific cultural knowledge to understand the art. Again we have a decided tendency toward agreement, this time between the Japanese potters and the judges in New Haven. Here again though, as in the BaKwele study, agreement is much greater within each group than between groups.

Other field workers have obtained smaller bodies of data. Some of these show clear agreement with American judges, and some do not. More research of this sort is desperately needed before everyone in the world interested in art is absorbed into a single international art movement. What the data suggest thus far, though, is that there is some tendency toward trans-cultural agreement in esthetic evaluation. I am not arguing for the old, culturally naive view that esthetic value is directly inherent in the work of art in some simple, immediate, and total way. There seem to be very real differences in evaluation of works of art by people whose interest in art has developed in quite different cultural traditions. These differences are the analog, at a cultural level, of the conspicuous individual differences between evaluation by one judge and another within a single culture. But just as there is an underlying tendency toward agreement among individuals in a single culture, so there seems to be an underlying tendency toward agreement—though perhaps a smaller tendency—across cultural boundaries.

In interpreting these findings as an indication that the old view of simple and complete objectivity was probably wrong, we must exert the kind of caution Carroll Pratt has wisely brought to the discussion of within-culture variation. Some of the disagreement between judges in different cultures must be ascribed to the fact that they are having different experiences, that they are seeing different things, even though they are looking at the same object. Consider the BaKwele masks, for example: The BaKwele judges had had much less experience in looking at a two-dimension photograph and understanding what the represented object would look like when seen in three dimensions than had the Americans. I have no doubt that their visual experience was therefore very different for many of the masks. To take the converse side, some of the masks were conventionalized representations of a gorilla skull rather than of a human head; I have no doubt that the BaKwele, knowing this, saw those masks very differently from the way they were seen by the Americans who interpreted them as human heads. We know that some of the difference in esthetic evaluation must be due to such differences in the experiences being evaluated; we have no way of knowing whether all of it may be.

Besides seeking direct evidence on whether there is some degree of objectivity in esthetic evaluation, I have also been trying to pursue some indirect implications of that issue. For one thing, I have been inquiring into why people differ from one another in their reactions to art, and, in particular, why some of them react like experts and some do not. And I have been experimenting with ways by which evaluations of art might be changed. In the first of these explorations the outcome so far is favorable toward the notion of objectivity; in the second, it is so far unfavorable. Let me tell you briefly about each of these.

The first exploration asks, "In what kinds of people should we especially expect to find personal preferences or esthetic judgments which agree with those of experts?" If experts tend to agree with one another primarily because they independently see the same esthetically valuable or valueless features in the art they are looking at, then you might expect agreement with them in other individuals who can also independently discover what is to be seen in art—people, that is, who explore their environment with care, enjoy the variety of experiences thus gained, and use their own experiences as the basis for formulating judgments. In a study of college students, I measured agreement with experts in response to the pairs I had assembled, and then tried to measure a number of relevant personality characteristics. The characteristics found to be correlated with tendency to agree with experts were on the whole the ones predicted from this hypothesis. Specifically, tendency to agree with experts was positively correlated with tendency toward independent judgment, with tolerance of complexity, and with ability to regress in the service of the ego or be playful. The first two of these correlations were also confirmed in a study of secondary school students in this country. Most recently Sumiko Iwao has obtained comparable data for college students in Japan and has found all three personality variables correlated with tendency to agree with experts, just as in the United States. Here, then, is evidence, and evidence going somewhat beyond our own culture, for believing that people who arrive at judgments agreeing with those of experts do so in part because they are the sort of people who actively explore their visual world and independently arrive at somewhat similar assessments of what they see.

The other exploration is concerned with experimentally produced variations in experience that might lead to increased agreement with experts. To both college students and school children, I have shown long series of pairs of art such as I have described, getting them to guess, after briefly looking at a pair, which work is the one experts consider better and then immediately telling them whether the guess is right or wrong. This opportunity to learn a discrimination between what experts consider better and worse does lead most people to make the discrimination, not very accurately, to be sure, but more accurately than before. The basis for the discrimination varies a great deal from one person to another if we can trust their own impressions about what cues they are using. Many people learn to use superficial cues of little esthetic relevance, such as the observation that experts tend to prefer older works or the works that are less accurately representational. These experiments seem to demonstrate, if demonstration is needed, that a person who wishes to be "in the know," to make the most socially acceptable response to works of art, can learn to do so on a superficial basis.

If such agreement can also be arrived at by independent experience and judgment, however, perhaps for subjects to look at the same works our trainees did, for the same length of time but without being informed about expert judgment, would also lead to increased agreement with experts. Again, both to college students and to school children, I have shown the same long series of pairs, merely asking the subject to say which work in each pair he likes better or considers to be esthetically superior, and giving him no feedback. This experience does not, on the average, lead to any increased agreement with experts. So here a possible implication of the general notion I am putting forth turns out to be wrong. At least wrong so far; it may be that more intensive experience with works of art would lead to development of evaluations resembling those of experts.

These explorations into various indirect implications of the possible objectivity of esthetic value are not, then, decisive. They offer some support, raise some doubts, and suggest that the most direct exploration itself needs to be carried further.

Agreement among the independent responses of different observers, we have seen, was proposed by earlier writers as a test of the objectivity of esthetic evaluation. I have argued that the test is still valid and useful providing the observers are people we can believe are responding in a manner that can be considered esthetic. This belief is most justified for persons to whom art is a major interest, who have become in some way expert in art. Agreement among such people, representing a specialized, expert response to art, is probably of greatest interest to the esthetician. This is because experts' responses are likely to be most pertinent to the distinctive characteristics of art. But let us not forget that among other people besides experts there is agreement about art. The basis of this agreement may at times be irrelevant to, or even the reverse of, those used by experts in arriving at esthetic evaluation.

These other kinds of agreement may be of less interest to the esthetician, but they may be of great interest to the art educator. The art educator may think of his task as partly that of leading students toward esthetic appreciation of art in the way experts appreciate it, believing that only thus can art come to make the fullest possible contribution to their lives. Or he may think of his task as that of making more accessible to each student the art the student seems to prefer and enjoy most. In the first instance, the art educator should understand the student's original approach to art, the better to be able to induce him to change; in the latter instance, he needs to know the student's original approach to art in order to encourage and nourish it. So I would urge that esthetic evaluation of art by experts not absorb our attention exclusively—and by "our" I mean both researchers' and teachers'. We must all seek also to understand the evaluation of art by people whose response seems not at all esthetic.

Aesthetic Criticism:
The Method of Aesthetic Education

RALPH A. SMITH

A work of art requires an intelligent spectator who must go beyond the pleasure of the eyes to express a judgment and to argue the reasons for what he sees— Lucian

The purpose of this article is to present a concept of teaching method appropriate for the emerging period of instruction in the arts and the humanities.[1] The nature of the discussion is consonant with recent statements by educators who urge paying more attention to the problems of value education in the schools in general [2] and with the arguments of aesthetic educators who advocate developing more disciplined capacities for making aesthetic value judgments.[3] The heightened concern with values today is of course a response to the crisis of sensibility and judgment evident everywhere in the contemporary world and especially notable in the aesthetic domain of human experience. Accordingly, the discussion to follow places emphasis on teaching learners how to decide what is aesthetically relevant, valuable, and unique. Emphasis is further placed on the content or subject matter of formal instruction rather than on such aspects of schooling as the socialization of the child. Emphasis on the primacy of content stems from a notion of the school as an institution in which first and above all formal instruction takes place. In this respect the interpretation of aesthetic education presented here differs radically from approaches which place great stress on the process rather than on the content elements of learning.[4] I am not presumptuous enough to claim that the view presented here is the only way of conceiving aesthetic

Reprinted by permission of the author and publisher from *Studies in Art Education*, Vol. 9, No. 3, Spring 1968.

The research reported herein was performed pursuant to a contract with the United States Office of Education, Department of Health, Education, and Welfare, Project Number 3-6-061279-1609, in progress. Parts of this article have been published in "Patterns of Meaning in Aesthetic Education," *Council for Research in Music Education*, Bulletin No. 5, 1965 (mimeographed; revised 1967); and "Aesthetic Education: A Role for the Humanities Program," *Teachers College Record*, January, 1968. Reprinted with permission. I wish to acknowledge the assistance of C. M. Smith in the preparation of this article.

education. But I do think it points in the right direction. Moreover, while my remarks are directed primarily toward teachers in the visual arts, they are intended to be applicable to music and literature education as well.

I. Introduction

The approach to aesthetic education described in this article derives first of all from presuppositions about the role of the aesthetic in human experience and secondly from beliefs about the kinds of curriculum demands imposed by a democratic society undergoing structural changes in its social system. The cultural shocks and dislocations created by new social forms are documented in scores of studies and need not be described here.[5] It is sufficient to note that the changes accompanying the transition from what may be called a communal to a modern mass society have intensified not only the problems of personal identity but also those of asserting popular control over the processes of institutional decision-making. Accordingly, the new shapes societal functions are taking demand a reevaluation of the kinds of knowledge and outlooks schooling should attempt to teach and foster, particularly with regard to the effects of ideas and attitudes on the goals of citizenship and self-cultivation.

Consider, for example, the goal of self-cultivation, currently neglected as an educational objective. Self-cultivation requires a variety of stable and defensible models which not only invite emulation but also serve as standards against which behavior can be judged unambiguously. Now an earlier communal society provided individuals with just such anchor points for comparison and judgment. Ordered around a set of common and shared traditional beliefs and functioning through close-knit groups which relied on practical intelligence to solve problems, a communal society effectively conveyed to the young the sources and signs of value. The situation today, however, is different. A modern mass society is characterized by great change and social mobility, factors which make it less dependent on a body of cohesive and shared beliefs. Moreover, new giant and impersonal forms of organization increasingly require highly specialized intelligence and technology to achieve their ends, thereby transforming older conceptions of work and intelligence and many other traditional roles as well. With the focal points of a society constantly shifting, and with the prospect that social change will accelerate in the decades ahead, it is perhaps inevitable that such a society induces genuine doubts regarding what is valuable and unique.

Nowhere is this confusion more evident than in contemporary debates about the nature of aesthetic quality or artistic merit. One result of such uncertainty is that *de gustibus non est disputandem* ("there is no disputing tastes") gradually becomes an operative principle in the lives of more and more individuals, notwithstanding the fact that tastes can be disputed and good reasons given for judging one taste superior to another. On the other hand, the *de gustibus* stance is not easily dismissed. Efforts to understand the issues in the antinomy of taste have engaged the minds of some of our most noted philosophers and analytical critics. Still, this does not negate the fact that all is not well with the status of aesthetic values in modern life, and the question is, how are individuals to decide what is aesthetically valuable? Since aesthetic values and images play important roles in human thought and aspiration, one way of dealing with this problem is by paying greater attention to aesthetic value education in the schools.

Aesthetic education, or aesthetic learning, may thus be construed as a special form of value education. What is the distinctive outcome of such learning? Aesthetic value education may be described as having enlightened beholding in the aesthetic domain of human experience as its principal aim. Beholding is enlightened whenever a response or judgment is grounded or justified by relevant criteria in terms of which objects are deemed worthy or unworthy of acclaim.

Holding, then, that aesthetic education implies a learner who goes beyond sensuous pleasure to express judgments and give reasons for what he sees, hears, or reads, the next question turns on the distinctive form and content of enlightened beholding. Or, in slightly different terms, granted that the ideal of reflective response in the aesthetic domain involves something like the building of appraisive and evaluative maps on which learners can plot their experience of aesthetic values, in what degree of detail and sophistication should such maps be constructed? Selecting a destination for aesthetic education, or identifying its central and proper business, is a necessary precondition for any intelligible scheme of teaching and learning in the arts. But maps or enterprises can vary considerably in detail and size, and hence in serviceability.

There are, for example, the large-scale maps of life which set such goals as continuous growth and self-realization, or ever-increasing sensitivity to aesthetic values. Then there are the more limited maps of schooling which lead over relatively short and well-marked paths. Ideally, of course, school maps should productively feed into life maps. The point is that irrespective of the way the link between school learnings and their use in adult life is conceived, the efforts of schooling are more properly evaluated by how well it achieves its more limited objectives. Further, learning objectives are likely to be achieved only if one is relatively clear about the kinds of skills and attitudes to be taught. It is also plain that ideas about ways to relate school and post-school behavior are influenced by prevailing social conditions and cultural priorities. The history of this problem cannot be recorded here, but it is necessary to indicate the position this article takes.

First of all, a theory of the curriculum is accepted that is made up of general studies which are common as well. By "general" is meant a program of studies designed for the nonspecialist, and by "common" is intended that the content of schooling—its basic organization of knowledge and skills— does not significantly vary from learner to learner, which is not to deny the possibility that the same content can perhaps be taught at different levels of complexity to pupils differing in speed or style of learning. It is believed that a society characterized by great variability and fluctuation in its cultural norms requires a common general education of all of its prospective citizens so as to achieve an understanding and appreciation of the opportunities, obligations, and costs of modernity.

Once again, it is especially important to understand the aesthetic domain of human endeavor because of the diverse roles artistic images and aesthetic values play in individual and social conduct. For example, if it is true, as so often asserted, that individuals are more likely to see reality through the images of art than they are by attending to reality itself,[6] than ways must be found to understand the proper place of art and its effects in human life. This is so because the messages of art are less than explicit,[7] and a literal and untutored mind will fail to understand the relevance of a mode of awareness that reveals by means of distortion and ambiguity. Furthermore, art is nothing if not persuasive, seducing persons into cherishing and accepting its forms and actions as models for emulation.[8] Accordingly, the effects of art may be either inhibiting or facilitating to human thought and aspiration. A plethora of new media criticism, e.g., asserts that the forms of human behavior presented in the movies and on television are gross distortions, usually over-simplifications, of actuality, and thus may be injurious to growth.[9] Serious art, on the other hand, is said to portray things more as they are, or to present convincing and sometimes radical possibilities. Decisions about the meanings and import of works of art, then, can have practical consequences;[10] and in a democratic society such consequences are best dealt with by educating a large proportion of people to enlightened judgment in the aesthetic domain.

II. The Aesthetic Value Situation

In the effort to justify aesthetic education a positive and educationally relevant function has been assigned to art. A positive function, however, can be conceived as a value. If art has value, the educational question turns on the strategies and tactics through which that value is appropriated.

This article accepts a theory which locates value in the relation between the structure of objects and the structure of human nature. The object and the individual each contribute something to the value situation: the latter a propensity for valuing or cherishing, the former certain objective properties that hold out the possibility of value experience. While the human or attitudinal component of value experience is less tractable to analysis, the object valued submits to scrutiny, judgment, and evaluation.

In other words, knowledge plays a role in aesthetic valuing because it is possible to obtain information about the objects and phenomena which are components in aesthetic value experiences. Increasingly more precise or relevant knowledge about the object of aesthetic valuing is important in aesthetic education because such knowledge may be said to (a) *justify* the immediately and spontaneously felt liking, since certain features of the object, whether it be a visual, auditory, or verbal design, can be identified and evaluated as the sources of aesthetic satisfaction or enjoyment; (b) *intensify* original feelings of enjoyment because analysis would reveal the object to possess more admirable aspects than perfunctory acquaintance had disclosed; and (c) *engender* satisfaction where none was present prior to an appraisal of the object. Reflection recalls numerous cases where individuals have revealed satisfaction in being able to explain the sources of their liking, where such ability has enhanced liking, and where assistance with analysis and perception has developed new interests. The question is whether this is possible for large numbers of individuals, whether the justifying, intensifying, and engendering of the experience of aesthetic value constitute defensible schooling objectives, and if they do, whether there are content, techniques, and procedures which can facilitate such aesthetic enterprise.

To begin with, what kinds of entities are involved in the judgmental phase of aesthetic value experience? For purposes of the present analysis such entities may be characterized as (a) aesthetic objects which are things of any sort whatever, natural or man-made, which are interesting to awareness; and (b) works of art, which are artifacts specially designed to function as aesthetic objects, whether or not they serve any other function.

As is often the case in distinguishing the entities of human experience, the difference between an aesthetic object and a work of art is not always obvious, cannot be measured, and while there are clear-cut there are also border-line cases. Let it suffice to say that if a seashell, for example, is interesting to perception, then it is an aesthetic object. *Hamlet, The Rites of Spring,* and *Guernica,* however, are aesthetic objects which are also works of art since they have a far greater capacity to reward perception. Another way of putting the distinction is to say that a (good) work of art is a specially designed high-grade aesthetic object.

On the view, then, that knowledge is possible in the evaluational part of value experience and that such knowledge has influence—although it is not known for certain precisely what influence—on the attitudinal component, the question becomes: what knowledge can be gained about works of art and aesthetic objects such that response may become more enlightened, intense, and justifiable? Certain difficulties are at once apparent.

First of all, it is accepted educational strategy to look to the parent discipline for paradigms of knowing, that is, to the theory which is unified by having as its object of formal study what the educator is concerned to teach. In the present case, this would mean looking to aesthetics or philosophy of art. Unfortunately, however, it appears that aesthetics does not offer a clear-cut and hence uncontroversial structure for knowing. This is at least partially due to persistent disagreements among aestheticians about the nature of the entities which should be their proper concern. The term "art," of course, has a common-sense referent, but its meaning tends to dissolve under analysis. Just what it is, if anything, that "the arts" have in common is an unresolved issue, a condition that has given rise to diverse judgments and characterizations of aesthetics as a domain of inquiry. But aesthetics is not the only parent discipline of schooling in which controversy reigns and, indeed, aesthetics can be of considerable assistance to the educator if he understands its relevance.

The second difficulty encountered in attempts to gain knowledge of the aesthetic object is that such knowledge is yielded only under special conditions. A work of art is at once a physical and a perceptual or aesthetic object. As a physical object, it has a location in space and time, substance, size, market value, etc. Thus it can be "known" in much the same way that ordinary things are known, and some of this information is not irrelevant to aesthetic awareness. This is customarily called "knowledge about."

But there is a sense in which a work of art "demands" to be attended to in a special way. This kind of attention, or special type of interest, may be called "aesthetic contemplation," an expression that is roughly adequate, even though we do not normally speak of contemplating a symphony, or even a motion picture. By aesthetic contemplation is meant a kind of absorption in a work's visual appearance, or, in the case of music, its sonic structure, and in literature its verbal design. That is, attention is restricted to visual, auditory, and imaginary actions and events, to the exclusion, generally, of thoughts pertaining to an object's price, the materials used to produce it, the character of the artist, etc. Literature may be thought to be an exception to this restriction and, most assuredly, distinctively intellectual activity is more evident in the reading of poetic literature than it is in either looking at paintings or listening to music. But even in literature it is pointed out that "a character is held up, so to speak, before the reader's mind for him to experience as a possible existence"; [11] and the context of the remark makes it clear that there is a kind of direct confrontation of the image held up to the mind's eye. Thus even in literature it is possible to speak analogically of "perceptual" experience, and there would be something odd in saying that a reader was engaging in abstract, logical reasoning while reading, say, a novel by William Faulkner. Also noteworthy is the fact that the language of literary criticism typically employs the language of visual perception.

By "absorption" is meant a willingness to forego momentarily most personal desires and inclinations, including the wish to own the work, or the emotions, reveries, and reminiscences induced by it; and, in addition, a readiness to attend to the work's powers and qualities. Aesthetic contemplation thus understood is not a direct cue to action, in the sense that the perceived qualities of the red or green of a traffic light are, not a case in which the basic intent is that of recognizing what is perceived as an instance of a class of things about which generalizations can be made, and not a cue to memory in the sense of what the object perceived reminds one of. Once again, the tendency to regard literature as radically different in respect of these "ground rules" is tempered somewhat by the notions that "Common sense seems to say that the statements of fiction do not refer to something outside themselves in the sense in which historical statements do" and that "There is something unsatisfactory about taking a play or novel to be pointing to something. . . ." [12]

It may be that the distinction between aesthetic and other types of "perception" will not hold up under strict logical analysis,[13] but it need not be concluded therefore that nothing can be done to help students achieve a proper contemplative posture relevant to works of art. The term "aesthetic," moreover, is most convenient for referring to this posture. As one writer has remarked: "In a suitable context the adjective 'aesthetic' and the adverb 'aesthetically' may well be superfluous, but it is sometimes necessary to introduce one of these words in order to make it clear that when we refer, say, to a person's satisfaction we are not thinking of moral satisfaction, economic satisfaction, personal satisfaction, intellectual satisfaction, or any satisfaction other than aesthetic satisfaction." [14] Once an understanding of the pedagogical corollaries of different theories of aesthetic relevance are grasped by the teacher, it should not be too difficult to identify aesthetically irrelevant responses, such as, e.g., the class of "it looks like" and "it reminds me of" responses, and to point out the consequences of such responses for aesthetic appraisal and evaluation. Observation, practice, and inclination to introspection should give the teacher or learner an adequate notion of when a satisfaction or response is and is not aesthetic.

The third difficulty in gaining knowledge of aesthetic values involves the frequent assertion that the work of art itself appears to make some sort of cognitive claim different from what was previously discriminated as "knowledge about," or propositional knowledge.

But if art provides for many individuals a kind of illumination or enlightenment, can such enlightenment qualify as knowledge? An appeal to the parent discipline of aesthetics again yields no consensus on this question; yet its importance is acknowledged by the belief that the epistemological question is the only thing that keeps aesthetics alive.[15] Given the interest in recent studies in cognitive growth and the logical structure of knowledge, it is perhaps only natural that aesthetic educators today should be interested in what "knowing" might mean in the aesthetic domain.

III. The Meaning of "Aesthetic Knowing"

The characterization of a work of art as an artifact designed principally to function as an aesthetic object, together with the ground rules stipulated for aesthetic contemplation, seems to offer an approach to the problem of knowing in the arts. To say that an object was intended by the artist to be appropriated by others through a special kind of rapport and not through utilitarian use or consumption, makes it at least plausible to hold that an element of communication is involved. Some human concern may be thought to be communicated.

But, it may be asked, concern with what? An uncomplicated response is that works of art express or communicate simply the human concern with objects of this nature. They exhibit and reaffirm, it might be said, man's peculiar bent to find delight and satisfaction in objects with certain properties, power, and qualities. But the persistent quest to discover the meanings and functions of these properties renders uncomplicated responses inadequate. Thus, it has been thought that works of art might symbolize a sort of equilibrium, the homeostatic principle characteristic of the living form, or exhibit for comprehension the logical forms of the life of feeling. And there is ample testimony that some of the greatest works of art have been experienced as significant and highly complex metaphors.

Whatever the character of the states of awareness conveyed by works of art, they emerge within the confines of aesthetic experience, do not principally induce abstract reasoning and conceptual thought in the senses previously mentioned, and hence should not be accorded the status of propositional knowledge. Only science, it is rightly claimed, gives us such "knowledge about," while aesthetic awareness is more properly regarded as "knowledge of." The central issue involved in the problem of knowledge in the arts was put by Ernest Nagel in his oft-quoted criticism of Susanne Langer's theory of art.

The desire of so many lovers of the arts to exhibit the latter as possessing an important cognitive core is symptomatic of the supreme, though perhaps unwitting, value they place upon *knowledge*. But if that desire can be satisfied only by so radically altering the meaning of "cognitive" that in its new use the term has no recognizable continuity with its normal employment, has not the ideal of clarity been sacrificed, and has not a serious disservice been thereby rendered to that which is prized so highly? [16]

Now there would be no problem in dismissing the states of awareness induced by the arts as possessing an important cognitive core were it not for the fact that many persons, including some highly regarded ones, do claim that they have received a kind of enlightenment through aesthetic contemplation and that such enlightenment seems to bear the stamp of objective validity. Nor is there any reluctance on the part of many individuals to talk about the meanings of works of art with all the certitude of warranted assertions. Such individuals rarely preface their remarks with "it seems to me" or "now, I believe." They are more apt to declare, e.g., "this work expresses an image of lonely despair" or "it conveys the feeling of apocalyptic protest." Yet such assertions are not subject to verification in the way that scientific laws and generalizations are subject to empirical checks. As several writers have indicated, such qualities are defined ostensively,[17] i.e., by pointing them out for others to see, such pointing out sometimes being called a kind of "perceptual proof." [18]

Once more, not only will the percipient talk as if he had attained reliable knowledge from the work of art, but he will also seek to furnish some sort of proof for what he believes to be in the art object. It was also said that persons holding certain things to be true about works of art will, when challenged, point to features of the work as evidence in support of their claim, inviting others to see for themselves. Moreover, it is equally true that while such demonstration may not always convince others, it may nonetheless lead them to perceive aspects they had previously overlooked, or to see properties in a new light.

It has thus far been established that, regardless of the dubious cognitive status of the meanings or messages of works of art, intelligent and highly cultivated individuals do talk as if they had knowledge of them and act as if they could verify this knowledge. Since attributing cognitive import to works of art can have tangible social consequences, the question becomes: are there ways of making talk about art more relevant, systematic, coherent, persuasive, efficacious? The issue, in other words, is not so much whether the purported truth claims of works of art are in fact true or false, but whether there are procedures for defending various sorts of statements which ascribe aesthetic qualities or truth claims to works of art. As procedures usually lend themselves to being taught, these questions suggest a more promising approach to the problem of knowing in the arts.

The earlier contention that the discipline of aesthetics does not appear to yield a knowledge structure reliable enough for educational adaptation should now be modified, for the subdomain of the philosophy of criticism affords paradigms of procedural skills for making the most sense out of whatever can be known in a work of art. The person who typically exemplifies these skills, of course, is the art, music, or literary critic. His training, experience, and cultivated sensitivity enable him to make relevant statements about works of art which often help others to have more meaningful aesthetic experiences. While it is not the purpose of aesthetic education to train professional art critics, it is reasonable to assume that ability to communicate knowledgeably about the qualities and meanings of works of art is *prima facie* evidence that the skills of aesthetic criticism have been learned, or that the disposition for enlightened response and justification in the aesthetic domain has been fostered.

To elevate, moreover, some approximation of the critic's expertise into an objective for aesthetic education does not appear illegitimate in view of similar aims frequently proclaimed for other fields of instruction. Educators have been known to propose that the student learn to "think as the scientist does" or "investigate as the historian does."

IV. AESTHETIC CRITICISM:

The Method of Aesthetic Education

But what, more specifically, is the nature of critical activity? A survey of successful critical statements, i.e., those which have released a work's value potential previously inaccessible to untrained sensibilities, discloses little unity. The statements of critics range from crisp, schematic analyses to eloquent literary essays. The description of the phases and techniques of critical activity that follows is therefore neither exhaustive nor definitive, but it does seem to hold potential for formulating and planning defensible educational objectives and experiences.

Critical activity may be described first of all in terms of overlapping phases which contain statements ranging from the cognitively certain to the cognitively less certain, beginning with description and phasing into analysis, interpretation, and evaluation. The division is open to challenge since the terms are used ambiguously and the boundaries between phases are not always precise.[19]

1. *Description.* By and large description involves naming, identifying, and classifying, a kind of taking stock which inventories cognitively establish aspects of a work of art, e.g., knowledge concerning the type of thing an object is: triptych, symphony, or work of prose fiction, information about the materials and techniques used, and knowledge of the extra-aesthetic function of the work when this is relevant. This category would further comprise art-historical data, and in the case of representational works, knowledge of mythology, cultural history, or whatever is required to identify the subject matter depicted.

Descriptive knowledge of the foregoing types is often depreciated because so-called art appreciation courses frequently degenerate to this level, or so it is said. Assuredly, memorization of dates and names, and drills in the identification of period styles and artists fall short of defensible objectives for aesthetic education. Yet descriptive information of the right sort is obviously important and relevant to aesthetic response. Relevant descriptive knowledge interrelates with the other, more properly aesthetic phases of criticism and thus enriches the total critique. It also is conceivable that ability to talk with cognitive assurance about the descriptive elements of works of art, even though they are not necessarily the most aesthetically relevant, may give teacher and student greater confidence to venture into more ambiguous and uncharted territories.

2. *Analysis.* This involves a close look at the components, elements, or details that make up a work, the larger groups or complexes into which they are composed, and the relationships they sustain. Analysis in art is not a mere enumeration or cataloging of components; it cannot be done in a meaningful way, it seems, without at the same time describing and often characterizing what is singled out for inspection. The distinction between "description" and "characterization" introduces different ways in which parts, complexes, and regional properties can be talked about.[20] Such considerations further introduce the complex notion of aesthetic qualities, concepts, or predicates—a topic that invites analysis of the terms, particularly adjectives, often used in critical talk.

a. There is a first group of predicates so matter-of-fact and uncontroversial that it probably is not proper to consider them as aesthetic. A color may have a certain degree of saturation, a musical note a given pitch, a shape a geometric configuration, a word a definite meaning, and so on. These characteristics, which anyone whose sensory and mental apparatus is not impaired should be able to perceive, are literally in the work. Ascription of such characteristics is normally accompanied with the certitude distinctive of propositions cited in support of fundamental knowledge claims. That an element is crimson, circular, cylindrical, or a high C is not usually subject to further confirmation.

b. The next class of predicates typically finds employment in aesthetic contexts but may also be used in other situations, e.g., words such as "harmonious," "delicate," "graceful," and many others. Here agreement among critics is still substantial but by no means unanimous. Some persons may detect subtle rhythms where others utterly fail to do so. Similarly, a feature appearing "graceful" to one critic may appear "flaccid" to another. Indeed, one cannot always decide whether terms like "delicate," "garish," or "harmonious" are used to describe or characterize, or even to evaluate, whether they are closer to the cognitively certain or to the cognitively uncertain end of the critical spectrum. Once more, it is sometimes impossible to maintain sharp and clear distinctions.

c. There is another, more properly aesthetic, group of characterizing predicates which cannot be certified through simple inspection. They have one thing in common: their normal application lies in a different modality of experience; hence to ascribe them to works of art is to use them metaphorically. Thus critics speak of "strident" colors, "luminous" tones, "lugubrious" movements, "taut" story lines, or "stern" passages, to take only a very few simple examples. While often construed as a source of perplexity, it should not be concluded that this kind of talk is imprecise and is to be corrected by recourse to a more accurate and purely descriptive language of criticism. Of matters metaphorical some reasonably certain things can be said.

1. In the first place it is clear that the metaphorical use of terms is predicated on identifiable features in the work of art; aesthetic judgments containing such terms do not (or need not) report gross or idiosyncratic impressions. Although it may be thought that "violent" does not properly characterize a certain component or pervasive regional property, people generally know what is being talked about. Nor is it impossible to develop some understanding of what led an individual to make such an ascription.

2. Furthermore, divergent judgments are usually not poles apart but seem to lie along a qualitative range. For instance an arrangement of elements may be called "restful" by some and "monotonous" by others, but it is highly unlikely that such elements would be characterized as

being "turbulent." And a concept of aesthetic knowing requires only that we can speak intelligently about matters of relevance and appropriateness.

3. It is also pointed out that the use of metaphorical language is neither unnatural nor esoteric. The shift from literal to metaphorical, or quasi-metaphorical, uses of words is due to "certain abilities and tendencies to link experiences, to regard certain things as similar, and to see, explore, and be interested in these similarities. It is a feature of human intelligence and sensitivity that we do spontaneously do these things and that the tendency can be encouraged and developed. It is no more baffling that we should employ aesthetic terms of this sort than that we should make metaphors at all." [21] Moreover, the propensity for metaphor, or what is sometimes called colorful language, is cultivated at an early age by emulating the actions of parents and peers, a fact perhaps fraught with unexplored educational consequences.

Some additional remarks about the analytical phase are in order. In the first place, it should be clear that the characterization of elements and relationships in a work of art already shades over into the next, the interpretive, phase. Furthermore, descriptive and characterizing terms are in many cases normative as well, thus anticipating the evaluative phase. In most contexts words like "harmonious," "unified," and "graceful" tend to have positive connotations, while "shrill," "harsh," "unbalanced," "disjointed," etc., seem to be not only descriptive characterizations but negative judgments as well, though perhaps not always. In a great deal of modern art criticism the judgments "harsh' and "shrill," for example, seem to have positive connotations, owing no doubt to that peculiar tendency of contemporary sensibility to assert intensity of expression as a norm.

3. *Interpretation.* The proper concern of this phase is say something about the meaning of a work of art as a whole, as distinct from any interpretation of its parts. Judgments of this sort are frequently the first ones made of works of art, which is to say they tend not to be preceded by descriptive and formal analysis. But to justify or support interpretations a critic will often resort to description and analysis. Such activity may have the effect of amplifying, modifying, or even radically altering a viewer's, listener's, or reader's own interpretation—or as David Hume said, such activity can correct "a false relish."

Since interpretation is often taken as the most meaningful and enriching phase of transaction between a percipient and a work of art, just what and what not to expect from it should be indicated. Interpretation, it is suggested, should not be attempted where human significance is obviously irrelevant, e.g., in the case of works primarily concerned with pattern and decoration. Further, the impression should be avoided that interpretation is merely a summing up of what is found in analysis. The interpretation of a work of art as "an image of lonely despair" seems to follow logically from the characterization of its components as "somber," "drooping," "mournful," "dark-hued," "slow-paced," etc. But not necessarily. Transvaluation may also occur.

For instance, normative connotations of interpretive ascriptions may be altered when elements characterized negatively as "unbalanced," "top-heavy," or "murky" are perceived as necessary to a forceful expression, say, of "menace" or "impending disaster." Original characterizations may also take on ironic or disturbing twists when, e.g., details which one would normally call "gay" and "sprightly" are seen as essential to a "sinister" or "anxiety-ridden" mood. This is often the mark of significant transitional works. Mannerist works from the sixteenth century come to mind in which traditional forms were used to create powerful new imagery. The delicate color of Hieronymus Bosch is another example, whose *Garden of Delights* incidentally is anything but delightful. Indeed, the modern movement of Surrealism in painting, literature, and now film trades on such devices to create queasy and unsettling qualities. The work of the expressionist composer Schonberg is also said to have used nineteenth-century values of unreality and modish display in the service of an ultimate seriousness. All of this is merely to indicate that while the citing of analytical findings in support of interpretations is required by responsible criticism, the manner in which interpretive judgments emerge from analytical ones is complex and not productive of general agreement. Perhaps this is one reason why certain works of art continue to have universal appeal: their infinitely rich forms continually give rise to new interpretations when seen from a different angle of vision.

If the connection between interpretation and analysis is often ambiguous, the relationship between the subject matter of a representational work and its message or content is even more so. It is probably a good rule to say that a critical response is inadequate if it offers as an interpretation merely a description of subject-matter. Content, on the other hand, is a kind of distillation, abstraction, or compaction of whatever is depicted or portrayed. And often it is in the more significant works that striking discrepancies are found between what the work ostensibly represents and what it is interpreted to be, or what it is said to be a metaphor or image of. A clear-cut case is Masaccio's mural *The Tribute Money* which is impressive not because it depicts a particular biblical episode, in itself not high in the hierarchy of biblical events; rather it is impressive because it shows the dignity of the individual. An aesthetic interpretation of the *The Tribute Money*, then, delivers the judgment that the picture's significance resides in its image of human nobility, such image being the essential import of what is depicted, i.e., its content in contrast to its subject matter.

4. *Evaluation.* The term as used here implies some kind of summation or assessment of the merit of the work of art in question. The simplest kind

of verdict is one saying that the work is good or bad, based on an examination of its aesthetic qualities, say, its degree of unity, complexity, intensity, or some combination of these.

As for import or significance, the only acceptable aesthetic evaluation is one of sufficiency or deficiency. A work may be judged sufficiently expressive to reward contemplation, or, as in the case of certain elaborate and technically brilliant productions, it may be dismissed as shallow, insignificant, not worth the percipient's time. To praise or condemn on the basis of *what* a work says, however, is to make a moral, cognitive, or extra-aesthetic, and not a distinctively aesthetic, evaluation. To condemn or praise a work *because* it depicts, say, moral decadence would be a case in point. But an aesthetic evaluation would arise from an assessment of the work's parts, complexes, relations, and regional aspects, the overall interpretation of which might give rise to the kinds of content statements previously referred to. However, since extra-aesthetic judgments will be made by teachers and learners anyway, it is no use ruling them out of aesthetic education. Indeed, it may be necessary to know how to handle them to understand better what is involved in aesthetic judgments. The only stipulation would seem to be that teachers and learners understand that different sorts of judgments can be made of works of art.[22]

There are at least two ways in which even a work that rates high in expressiveness and is solid and respectable on every other count may yet draw a negative critical assessment. One is to find it derivative and unoriginal; there simply are too many things of this kind around. Secondly, an aesthetically good work may be rejected as poor when it fails to serve what extra-aesthetic functions it may have. Paul Rudolf's Art and Architecture Building at Yale may be a case in point; it is purportedly interesting to perception, yet students are said to complain about working in it.

Another pair of evaluative terms are "successful" and "unsuccessful." Now "successful" and "good" are almost equivalent. But to ascribe lack of success to a work appears to mean that certain expectations were not fulfilled. This could refer to the artist's intentions: he did not achieve what he set out to do. Speculations about what the artist had in mind, however, are sometimes difficult, if not impossible, to verify, and for purposes of aesthetic evaluation it would seem that the work itself provides most of the necessary information. If "unsuccessful" indicates that a work is not quite what it might have been, then some description of what would have constituted success should be expected.

Lastly, critics will frequently sum up their reaction, the nature of their experience with the work, with such terms as "interesting," "impressive," "challenging," "stimulating," "dull," "preposterous," etc.[23] In other words, an assessment of the value possibilities of a work may be rounded off by a statement about the nature or intensity of the liking or valuing, and the latter is not always predictable in light of the former. It is perhaps the mark of the highly educated aesthetic observer that he can recognize a work's value potential, endorse it, and even recommend it wholeheartedly to others, yet say that it is not his cup of tea. This recognition of the irreducible differences in temperament and personality which have no effect on, nor are affected by, the aesthetic evaluation of a work of art is perhaps the highest degree of objectivity one can hope for in art or in aesthetic education. But there are still problems.

Even if the foregoing constitutes a reasonable and acceptable description of critical activity, it does not explicitly prescribe content or procedures for doing criticism. Needed is a comprehensive set of concepts and critical *techniques* as distinct from critical *phases*.

Very briefly, some content that might be used to help develop critical capacities are the concepts (or topics) of medium, form, content, and style. These are some of the more inclusive notions. Regarding *form* we may mention the principles of harmony, balance, centrality, and development, aspects which can be displayed by the devices of recurrence, similarity, gradation, variation, modulation, symmetry, contrast, opposition, equilibrium, rhythm, measure, dominance, climax, hierarchy, progression, etc.[24] In addition, somewhere in instruction such topics as symbol, meaning, truth, intention, and metaphor should be dealt with.[25] The generality of content from one art to another should not, however, be taken for granted lest a spurious unity be imposed on materials. Content as transfigured subject matter, i.e., the subject as presented in the medium of the materials, is an important and accepted idea in the visual arts, but more problematic in music. And it is an open question how to talk about the significance of some examples of nonobjective and abstract painting. Does a Mondrian or a Kandinsky, or a work of "op" art, have either content or subject matter? It depends on how the terms "content" and "subject matter" are used and on how the properties of such works may be construed. Clearly content or expressiveness is minimal in some objects, and the question of the medium presents difficulties in poetry. How important, e.g., is the sound of poetry, the timbre of the spoken word? Should some novels be read aloud? And how, after all, is the term "form" to be used? Does form simply mean structure, or design, i.e., the elements in relation? Or is form a normative concept implying something achieved and valuable, as it is in several theories? Awareness of some of these important differences among the arts has prompted one philosopher to organize his discussion such that painting and music are examined together with respect to their descriptive aspects, separately with respect to problems of interpretation, whereas literature is a separate topic altogether, except in dealing with critical evaluation where most judgments, it is claimed, can be supported by making appeal to a fundamental set of canons.[26]

Regarding critical procedures or techniques, again as distinct from critical phases, recent studies of the critic's activities suggest methods and procedures for teaching. These techniques have been described as involving approximately seven tactics.[27] There is (1) the pointing out of nonaesthetic features.

Examples would be "Notice these flecks of color." "Did you see the figure of Icarus in the Breughel? Notice how he has made use of the central figure." The idea, of course, in mentioning or pointing out nonaesthetic features is that by indicating one thing the learner is encouraged to see something else, presumably more aesthetically relevant. Then there is (2) the pointing out of aesthetic features and qualities. In doing this the critic simply mentions aesthetic qualities. "See how nervous and delicate." "Observe the tension." "Feel the vitality!" Simply mentioning the quality may do the trick, achieve the perception in the learner. There may also be (3) a linking of remarks about aesthetic and nonaesthetic aspects. This, of course, is quite common. "Do you notice how the horizontal give a feeling of tranquility?" "See how the red adds to the intensity of expression." I have already said something about the metaphorical use of terms in criticism, but the (4) use of genuine metaphors and similes may be noted. "The light shimmers, the lines dance, everything is air, lightness, and gaiety." The critic may also (5) make use of contrasts, comparisons, and reminiscences, e.g. "It has the quality of a Rembrandt." "In the Botticelli the edges of forms are stressed as lines, whereas in the Rubens there is a tendency toward fusion and interplay." The (6) use of repetition and reiteration is another tactic, as is (7) making use of expressive gestures. This latter is merely to say that nonverbal behavior may help: a sweep of the arm, a dip of the body, a certain facial expression.

It is important to note that there can be no guarantee that such techniques will be successful in bringing others to see, hear, or feel what is to be experienced, for critical skills and procedures cannot be equated with a method which, when followed conscientiously, ensures success, i.e., a perfect judgment or appraisal: there is no such thing. The teaching of categories, concepts, criteria, and procedures, though seeming to hold out the only hope for making sense of what can be known in a work of art, constitutes no more than elements of heuristic devices, or sets of questions to ask without expectation that each of them will necessarily be revealingly answered.

But, it may be asked, how can it be determined whether a student is genuinely developing as an aesthetic knower? It is suggested that initial evidence of growth in this direction is found in written and oral responses to works of art. With respect to the problem of authenticity two things may be said. First of all, excessive parroting, or what may be called the "replicative" use of learning, can be avoided by selecting works for test responses which are sufficiently different from the ones used in trial demonstration, yet similar enough to allow learnings to be used "interpretively." [28] To deal with the discrepancies that are bound to occur in student responses, clues may be sought in the appropriateness of the reasons given in support of various types of judgments and evaluations. A sense of what is reasonable and appropriate, however, can come only with experience; hence critical dispositions must be fashioned over a relatively long period of time. Actually, what differentiates the very good from the inferior in student responses is not difficult to discern. Once again, one thing to look for is the organization of critical statements, the ways in which descriptive, analytical, interpretive, and evaluative remarks are interrelated. Neither would one want to overlook matters of style and persuasiveness. Thus criteria for assessing student responses are relevance, appropriateness, cohesiveness, and persuasiveness.

V. Conclusion

Exploratory work and research in each of the arts are necessary before aesthetic criticism can be an effective instrument of teaching and learning. In translating the method into classroom practice a word of caution is in order. The method places a great deal of emphasis on formal analysis as a means of rendering aesthetic values accessible. Such a method, however, must be handled with care, especially with young children. Analysis of course can be mechanical, in which case it will surely miss its avowed mark —the perception of the powers and qualities of works of art. There is a proper time and place for analysis, and the ideal is always relevant and appropriate analysis, or analysis well done. My own experience in working with upper-level elementary school children [29] prompts me to say that even with relatively young minds progress can be expected. But a lot of hard work lies ahead in research, curriculum design, and teacher preparation.

References

1. While significant arguments for aesthetic education have appeared regularly in the literature, the formation of an Arts and Humanities Branch of the Office of Education and the passing of the National Foundation on the Arts and the Humanities Act of 1965 may be regarded as initiating a new period in American cultural life and education.
2. For example, Harry S. Broudy, B. Othanel Smith, and Joe R. Burnett, *Democracy and Excellence in American Secondary Education.* Chicago: Rand McNally & Co., 1964.
3. See the selections and bibliography in R. A. Smith (ed.), *Aesthetics and Criticism in Art Education.* Chicago: Rand McNally & Co., 1966.
4. In other words, the emphasis in this article is placed on the more logical, procedural aspects of teaching in aesthetic education than on the process, psychological aspects.
5. See Broudy *et al., Democracy and Excellence* . . ., *op. cit.,* Chapters I, II. The brief analysis presented in this part is taken from this work.
6. For example, in *Jeffersonianism and the American Novel,* Columbia: Teachers College Press, 1967, Howard Mumford Jones writes that the power of fiction in molding the American outlook is one of the most striking things about it. "In vain," he says, "do historians tell us that the frontier, Puritanism, slavery, international society, and American business ethics were or are far more complex than they appear to be in the cases of Leatherstocking, Hester Prynne, Uncle Tom, Isabel Archer, and George Babbit. Fiction creates its own patterns and stamps their image upon the American imagination," p. 9.

7. In *The House of Intellect*, New York: Harper & Brothers, 1959, Jacques Barzun expresses his conviction "that art is miraculously precise and communicative in its own domain of fused spirit and sensation. It awakens knowledge of a kind no other means can reach. But that kind is not the only kind, and the means that art uses are always less than explicit." p. 17.

8. Oscar Wilde's dictum "Nature imitates art" is standard in this context. In a similar vein a contemporary critic writes that "A great poem, a classic novel, press in upon us; they assail and occupy the strong places of our consciousness. They exercise upon our imagination and desires, upon our ambitions and most covert dreams, a strange, bruising mastery. Men who burn books know what they are doing. The artist is the uncontrollable force: no Western eye, since Van Gogh, looks on a cypress without observing in it the start of flame." George Steiner, *Language and Silence*, New York: Atheneum, 1967, p. 10.

9. See the introductory essay and collection of research studies in Wilbur Schramm (ed.), *The Effects of Television on Children and Adolescents*, New York: UNESCO, 1964.

10. Regarding the practical social consequences of calling something a work of art, Paul Ziff notes that, among other things, objects either do or do not get placed in museums, have public funds spent on them, take up people's time who look at them in museums and galleries or as reproductions in books, etc. Thus on the issue of critical disputes about art he writes that "it would be quite absurd to call such disputes merely verbal." "The Task of Defining a Work of Art," in R. A. Smith (ed.), *Aesthetics and Criticism in Art Education, op. cit.*, pp. 107–08.

11. Knox Hill, *Interpreting Literature*, Chicago: University of Chicago Press, 1966, p. 52.

12. *Ibid.*, p. 51.

13. Currently under attack by some aestheticians are the foundational concepts of aesthetics itself. The issues are drawn in two recent articles: Virgil C. Aldrich, "Back to Aesthetic Experience," *Journal of Aesthetics and Art Criticism*, 24:3, 1966, pp. 365–71; and George Dickey, "Attitude and Object: Aldrich on the Aesthetic," *JAAC*, 25:1, 1966, pp. 89–91.

14. J. O. Urmson, "What Makes a Situation Aesthetic?" in Smith, *op. cit.*, pp. 13, 14.

15. F. E. Sparshott, *The Structure of Aesthetics*, Toronto: University of Toronto Press, 1963, p. 262.

16. *Journal of Philosophy*, 40:12, 1943, p. 329.

17. See Monroe C. Beardsley, *Aesthetics: Problems in the Philosophy of Criticism*, New York: Harcourt, Brace & World, Inc., 1958, p. 86, and C. L. Stevenson, "On the 'Analysis' of a Work of Art," *Philosophical Review*, 67:1, 1958, p. 46.

18. Frank Sibley, "Aesthetic and Nonaesthetic," *Philosophical Review*, 74:2, 1965, p. 143.

19. For a similar classification of critical phases, see Edmund B. Feldman, *Art as Image and Idea*, Englewood Cliffs, N. J.: Prentice-Hall, Inc., 1967, Chapter 15. It might be noted that the usual trinity is description, interpretation, and evaluation. Because of the pedagogical importance of formal analysis, however, this phase is isolated. Especially relevant in understanding the

nature of critical activity is Morris Weitz's *Hamlet and the Philosphy of Literary Criticism*, Chicago: University of Chicago Press, 1964. Weitz takes the criticism of *Hamlet* as a paradigm of what criticism is and isolates the following modes: description, explanation, evaluation, and poetics (aesthetics).

20. The distinction between "description" and "characterization" is for convenience. I use "characterization" whenever aesthetic qualities are pointed out; whereas description is restricted to indicating the more literal properties of objects. The characterization of elements, however, may be regarded as a kind of description.

21. Frank Sibley, "Aesthetic Concepts," in Smith, *op. cit.*, p. 339.

22. For a discussion of cognitive, moral, and aesthetic judgments, see Monroe C. Beardsley, *Aesthetics: Problems. . . ., op. cit.*, Chapter 10. Also "Aesthetics and the Classification of Critical Reasons," *Art Education*, 20:3, 1967, pp. 17–20.

23. See the distinction between "emotion-arousal" and "recognition of emotional quality" words made by R. W. Hepburn in "Emotional and Emotional Qualities: Some Attempts at Analysis," *British Journal of Aesthetics*, 1:4, 1961, p. 267.

24. See the discussion of content in Broudy, "The Structure of Knowledge in the Arts," in Smith, *op. cit.*, pp. 37–40.

25. Any standard anthology of aesthetics will reveal a sense of the topics currently structuring the discipline. In this connection, see the collection of articles from the *Journal of Aesthetics and Art Criticism* in *Aesthetic Inquiry*, edited by Monroe C. Beardsley and Herbert M. Schueller, Belmont, Cal.: Dickerson Publishing Co., 1967.

26. Beardsley, *Aesthetics: Problems. . . ., op. cit.* pp. 469–70.

27. Sibley, "Aesthetic Concepts," *op. cit.*, pp. 336–39.

28. For a discussion of four different kinds of learning, associative, replicative, interpretive, and applicative, see Broudy *et al., Democracy and Excellence. . . ., op. cit.*, Chapter III.

29. Office of Education—University of Illinois Aesthetic Exemplar Project, in progress.

6

Research

Limitations of Research in Teaching Art

IRVING KAUFMAN

One may be honestly dubious concerning the worth of writing or talking about art. The words cannot help being tenuous substitutes for the actual object or experience and often are mistakenly accepted as the real thing. As Paul Valery said: "We must always apologize for talking painting." Art communicates and establishes its meanings on its own sensory and perceptual level of form. It is a direct experience, requiring no mediation of words except in a literary form. The immediacy of the individual senses, the distinctive perceptions, and the singularly private emotions of the creator or onlooker precede and outweigh any abstract notions or precisely rational considerations in art. Intuition and internally ordered aesthetics predominate, and these qualities function in other than logically discursive ways. Painting is primarily visual; music, aural; dance, kinesthetic; and so on; each form characteristically orders a felt emotion and an inner vision through an aesthetic awareness expressively merged with the concrete possibilities of the

Reprinted by permission of the author and the publisher from *Art Education: Journal of the National Art Education Association*, Vol. 20, No. 9, December 1967, pp. 3–6.

materials of any particular medium. Art is created and encountered in unique, complex, and contrasting ways, bending any approach in the making or appreciating of its forms to the emerging and imaginative needs of the moment of dialogue existing between the maker and the process of making. This is as true of the child initially exploring the possibilities of paint as it is of Picasso creating "Guernica," though the relative degrees of sophistication, expressive capacity, and preparatory experience are worlds apart.

The teaching of art follows a similar open pattern, remaining for the most part a very personal affair. It exists primarily as an exchange of human nuances and spontaneous relationships, not too amenable to objective analysis. Its loose sequence of happenings and interchanges may focus upon the particulars of expression or craft. But it is also given to an infinite shading of human interests that may be diffusely behaved and disparate in habit. A teaching method is as much a projection of personality as it is a giving over of understanding. It would be difficult, if not basically inexpedient, to suggest any specifically repeatable patterns of teaching art except in the most general terms. To no two people is the experience identical, nor is the context of any one classroom a readily manufactured condition that may be arbitrarily transferred to another.

The processes of uncovering conditions that affect the teaching of art as well as the making and understanding of art cannot always be explicit, simple, or straightforward ones. The elements involved are frequently intangible and, just as often, inconsistent. Art is inherently possessed of many paradoxes and it is difficult to contain or abstract them and interpret them beyond their own forms without the risk of noticeable and undesirable change or even corruption. It is no simple behavioral matter to speak of sensitivity and awareness, to refer to the expressive rhythms, the subjective intensities, and intricate motivations of the creative process. These loosely ordered elements are all basic to the making, appreciating, and the teaching of art, yet they defy a translation of contained analysis. To objectify them for precise pedagogical reasons is to grapple with almost ineffable qualities of human nature and the immediately given properties of art. A mechanistic residue that creates a restricted or even spurious guide seems to be left. The verbal equivalents evaporate into high-blown sophistry as the atomistic findings disperse into their separate and unrelated niches. Because of their fallacious generality and confusing associations organized as an accumulation of fragmentary consideration, there is a tendency toward trite, sentimentalized, and fractured presentation. Yet the very qualities of sensibility which are characterized by a diverse and even uncertain engagement with experience function as a vague parameter in research. Nevertheless, they remain more important as focal considerations than all the obvious skill and technique requisites or specified behavioral patterns which normally function as the objective elements of art education. These latter are the scaffolding built around the structure of art, if art may be said to possess any structure in the narrow definition of that word. The former subjective aspects are the core. The vivid metaphoric images, the vitality of internal visions, the intensity of direct and felt perception, the sensuous richness in the manipulation of materials, the poetic exploration, the critical intuitions, and the expressive symbolic intent of formative process are the very stuff of art. They deserve a focus of discussion in art education and a teaching emphasis in the classroom despite their conceptual elusiveness and ambiguity. The intrinsic aesthetic factors of art education—its transforming nature—need to be stressed over and above the description of appearances and the tight procedures of craft. The teaching of art has to enter into the subjective realms of experience, into seemingly illogical or nonrational but artistically appropriate areas of perception and feeling if it is to function as a genuinely valued integrant of human development and personal understanding. Research in art education must be cognizant of these inherent conditions if it is to provide legitimate insights for teachers.

It is not suggested that the disciplines or the crafts inherent in the making and understanding of art are to be ignored. Possibly the artistic disciplines and the use of craft would be strengthened if they were based on an imaginative and artistically appropriate teaching. The craft would flow from a genuinely expressive involvement with art and all that it entails, rather than from the more common "bag of tricks" or a divorced craftsmanship taught for its own sake. Skills would be developed as the need for them arises naturally in a student's efforts to express himself. The cute projects, the trivial busywork, the awkward composing, and the superficial fun activities also stem from a shallow understanding and blandly naive teaching of art unrelieved as yet by any research findings. They are the leavings of a grossly sentimentalized, blatantly misunderstood, and otherwise meretricious presentation of art. These spurious activities bypass a more demanding commitment to, yet freely exploratory insight into, artistic conditions and values. Too many teachers accept arbitrary and superficial models because they are easily observed, initiated with small effort, and produce popular results. They tend to avoid what is for them the esoteric and seemingly mystical subjectivity of the serious artist and critic, insisting that the latter has little relevance to setting educational goals.

However, the uncovering of artistic experience does lack an objectively logical sequence and its unfolding in the individual may come about through apparently contradictory or seemingly mutually exclusive means. The artist, nevertheless, accepts such ambiguity as a creative point of departure. Art in the classroom, if it is to be guided by a parallel set of germane considerations, consequently cannot accept the rigorous command of abstractly rational and overly systematized procedures, despite a superficial efficacy of operation. The emotions and feelings follow their own peculiarly unique and changing patterns which many behavioral psychologists more often redundantly describe than understand. Emotions and feelings are the underlying elements which propel and shape the forms of art along with an intelligence of sensibilities beyond the scope of an intellectually reasoned set of propositions. Flashes of intuition, flights of fancy, insights that emerge from below the threshold of consciousness, the congruence of sensations and symbols, reveries, and emotional impulses, and even that old rubric of inspiration are some of the subjective means which come more nearly to the heart of artistic process. Though these considerations may necessitate differing, oblique, and circuitous ways of teaching art at times, they are the authentic means inasmuch as one may categorize the authentic in art. They do not block any confrontation with experience as it may appear to the pedantic mind but, on the contrary, lead much more directly to a significant insight and expressive act. Some humanistically oriented psychologists are beginning to sense these creative dynamics, though no undisputed findings have as yet found their way into qualitatively successful guides for teachers in the arts. The trick lies in examining the problems encountered in the teaching of art by their most appropriate points of entry. Any artistic resolution should jibe with both the inherent yet singular conditions of personal expressiveness and the larger aspects of aesthetic integrity which are generic to creative goals. That is, the problems of form and expressive content are to be empirically resolved within a context of formal relationships as they arise during the artistic process. Each work of art, each attempt at expressive form, has its own rationale and independent means of achieving aesthetic order and comprehension, whether it is a child or a mature artist who is creating. Though the work might partake of certain universal artistic elements such as line and color, and principles such as balance and rhythm, such considerations are the means rather than the ends of art. Each individual creative product, if it is to possess any quality of genuine artistry and expressive unity, travels this independent road, joining the paths traveled earlier, but essentially making its own way in the metaphoric landscape. Such an approach to the teaching of art may stumble upon discrepancies. The resulting contradictions, in the abstract, would be calamitous to the logic of intellectual order. But they serve as the empirical means for further discovery in art, guided by the felt qualities of artistic integrity mentioned above and a context of pertinent dialogue which the sensitive teacher creates as a classroom climate. These are points of departure that have always fascinated the artistic mind, which finds in them a logic that is peculiarly its own, differing from formal systems. We can learn from Cezanne, for instance, when he says: "There is a logic of colors, and it is with this alone, and not with the logic of the brain, that the painter should conform." It is within understandings of this nature that the essential value of art and the revealing honesty of its forms lie. They cannot be reasonably provided in a teacher-proof syllabus.

It may be that not every student is capable of sustaining such a disparate or recondite set of conditions, though the fault probably lies more in the insensitive and unknowing quality of a commonplace teaching of art. However, the theorists in art education are now accepting the obvious limitations of a creative art program ostensibly democratically designed to reach every student in the schools. More stress is being put upon aesthetic education or critical evaluation, and I believe rightly so. This development of a critical base and artistically literate background leading to a cultivated appreciation is being recommended widely, without discarding some large measure of actual participation in art along the way. Thus the schools may provide a corollary of personal creativeness insofar as the individual student has the capacity adequately and creatively to express himself through art. Yet the developing of critical faculties and an appreciation for the qualities of art is itself a creative or, one could say, a recreative process. In order to establish a sound basis for responding to, knowing, and valuing art, the student may not require the broad creative paraphernalia necessary to successful personal expression. He need not possess quite the storehouse of vivid imagery or manipulative and exploratory skills, nor the intensity of artistically creative commitment characterizing the initiating artist. However, he does need a correspondingly high degree of sensibility and artistic intelligence, achieved through continuing dialogue and the result of a cultivation of perceptual discrimination, evocative association, and critical sensitivity.

Much of this cultivation falls into the intellectual sphere, though not in any narrow sense. The student has to be nurtured in what educational psychologists now refer to as appropriate "modes of inquiry" or encouraged in the necessary "strategies." These are to be the means by which a mature, independent, and personal vision, critical appraisal, and educated taste are to be developed. Such a desirable development of the student's perceptions and sensibilities has already been damaged by the amorphous mystique of creativity which has prevailed largely unchallenged for several decades. Obviously there has to be a renewed emphasis upon the relevance and growth of mind and in the art evaluative process or even in simple appreciation. This stress need not be convergent in procedure or stereotyped in aim. Research could certainly address itself to such a problem area, examining the means by which students could be encouraged to confidently express their responses to art, the strategies by which the expression of value and judgment could be related to the actual forms of art, the most conducive channels by which the interplay of symbols and perceptions can be synthesized into insightful meanings, and so on.

Some balance of pedagogical elements between the objectively intellectual and subjectively emotional has to be found. There is doubt that this may be resolved by any predetermined set of criteria which frequently degenerates into a "hardening of the categories." Rather, the most appropriate points of entry into the problem area would seem to be in the individual teacher's own enriched background in art, in the cultivated personal resources which offer an educated and dynamic basis for either analytical or intuitive understanding or both as the need may be, guided by the shared understanding of serious practitioners in the arts. The philosopher Croce tells us that art functions as the root of things whether we make it or observe it. "By creating the first representations and by thus inaugurating the life of knowledge, art continually knows within our spirit the aspects of things, which thought has submitted to reflection, and the intellect to abstraction. Thus art perpetually makes us poets again. . . ." Any success in art education, whether through critical appreciation or creative participation would necessarily guide the student to the vital sources—to an unencumbered but enriched encounter with the intrinsic qualities of art; all people are capable of responding to such a natural stimulus, provided their aesthetic intuitions can rest on an educationally "prepared" or openly sensitized mind and spirit. For some magical moment, we may all be poets.

The joining of learning in art to independent awareness and uniqueness, of education to intuition, finds its critics among more structured educators and researchers. They point disparagingly to such ideas—to what they consider to be a mystical core of faith in the spirit of art—in the largely preconscious, spontaneous, and ambiguous nature of its activities. They would insist upon more rigorously structured knowledge, more standardized cognitive models, more objectively controlled procedures, all of which reflect a supposedly scientific methodology and a rational extension of order through educational method. They would further insist upon a clarity of presentation and a relative preciseness of discipline and appreciation, even in art, for otherwise how can one measure what is being learned? Or they may indicate a skepticism of any learning taking place simply because the central elements of the art experience are diffuse and ambiguous. An art teacher may teach not only out of conviction and artistic sophistication, but may also establish a rich yet elusive rapport merging the students with the experience of art. Yet if this rapport or the activities it stimulates is not conducive to categorical structuring, the nagging question remains in too many minds as to whether a worthwhile educational process has occurred; such educators cannot honestly accept the autonomy of the art experience. What is not recognized is the inappropriateness of many of the technologies of research in the social sciences when applied to art. For art, like it or not, *is* possessed of extra rational and uncategorized, unique elements which we sometimes call the magic of poetry or the spiritual gratifications of beauty. Though these phrases may connote innumerable images and responses, the secure and knowing teacher or artist recognizes such qualities when they encounter them. Conversely, it may be only the innocent, untutored, or dogmatic teacher who requires the presumably objective cues and behaviors with which he or she believes art may be efficiently taught, fearful of trusting the emotional contingencies of the freely developing creative process.

Nor do these well-meaning but misguided investigators and teachers sense that they are merely spectators rather than participants in the processes they purport to examine. Recognizing a principle of objectivity, they slavishly follow it even when the experience obviously calls for an "in-dwelling" and totality of involvement. Consequently, the "objective" observer does not have the necessary vantage point of understanding—one that comes intuitively from within. And by its very nature, this understanding from within transcends a mere viewing and analysis to arrive at full artistic realization. As a result, the true-false concepts that are brought to bear upon art by many researchers can be no more than inert, extraneous considerations, especially if they reflect a no-nonsense bias of intellectual logic and observable behavior. Research studies are especially harmful when they fragment the processes and qualities of art in formulating specified behavioral models which then assume the character of prescriptive statements. The sophisticated research techniques or even the crude bold ones cannot offset their cursory comprehension of art. These aesthetic superficialities then act as unwitting influences in determining curricular content and teaching contexts, especially with the gullible teacher. There is no true-false understanding of art really, no counting of its parts, for all genuine art simply IS. And that is the sum of its being. It directly offers us, existentially, meaning on its own terms. It provides vividness and intensity rather than a rigorous clarity, an immediacy and openness of under-standing rather than a sequential accumulation of knowledge, an affirmation and evocation of experience rather than a codifying of an encounter with existence. Of course, there is good and poor art, but that is another matter, once the creative tenor and the individual artistic intention is established. In any case, it should have a natural place in the curriculum, not one contrived from extraneous considerations.

Obviously, we require some measure by which to judge the effectiveness of what we do in the art classroom. We need further understanding as to what and why and when students function in relationship to artistic process and aesthetic insight. We need to know how to further a development of the individual within personally expressive and critically appreciative con-texts. Perhaps, instead of asking thousands of students "What should you see or feel?" in a work of art or in its making, we should ask of ourselves, and of society, "What in our environment prevents a natural seeing and feeling?" Perhaps we should examine a fundamental and influential condition of values, rather than an arbitrary and isolated behavioristic symptom. One then begins with an affirmation, and this is vital if in the final analysis we individually create our truths rather than collectively uncover them by arbi-trarily poking around. There would be no need to probe vicariously into the artistic development of students if the conditions they were taught in or the values their teachers exemplified naturally excited a creative response. Their work and their appreciation of others' work would be manifest. My question presumes a cultural determinism and one may wonder about the relevance of such an inquiry. And so we get on to another round robin of polemics and abstract considerations. Somehow in the process, art values are lost, at least in a mass sense. Perhaps the teachers of art may sense a teaching relevance in what Louis Armstrong said: "If you *have* to ask the question, you ain't never going to know the answer."

Henry Miller, the vital though controversial novelist, also offers a teaching insight, but as an artist, for he has been a watercolorist most of his adult life. He relates that perhaps the real impetus toward his own art, at the time unsuspected, was given to him negatively during the high school art class he attended. He says: "My ineptitude was so flagrant that I was soon informed not to bother attending class . . . As the teacher rightly said, it was hopeless to expect anything of me. I was an aesthetic leper, so to speak. I say that this experience, with its accompanying sense of failure, or inadequacy, probably served me in good stead. Sometimes the wrong thing turns out to be the right thing; sometimes a setback is as good, or better, than a push. We seldom realize how much the negative serves to induce the positive, the bad the good." And so we have this vast contradiction producing a man who can write "To paint is to love again." I wonder what research could make of such topsy-turvy ideas, how rational thinking would have to twist and turn to logically categorize Miller's educational experience so that it could be contained in an abstractly correct methodology to be given over to teachers.

I do not wish to depreciate a careful quest for appropriate teaching methods of art, to belittle the necessary ordering of pedagogical procedures requisite to a significant level of aesthetic excellence in education. I would like to see more passion and sophistication. Research may very well have a vital function to perform in this area; but I would suggest that it is essential to first accept art as it actually and organically functions in human experience, accepting it for its own sake, rather than as an instrument for extrinsic purposes. As important is the need for research to utilize tools and means which are not foreign to art, nor ones which play havoc with its open-ended nature, masquerading it as something it should not or freezing it into something it cannot be. Though it may possess, for instance, certain sociological and psychological adjunctives such as reinforcement of desirable democratic values and therapeutic aspects for the emotionally disturbed, these elements are not particularly central to its nature. As a matter of fact, art is produced and appreciated in the most undemocratic places and there have been more than a few instances when art may have been considered to drive men mad. Art education has to accept its own content as a symbolic means with which to transform feeling into form. It is a way of metaphorically touching, knowing, and feeling the richness of the world through the shaping of apprehension of visual forms. The latter then establishes a natural and intrinsic morality of insight. The "beauty" and the intensity and personal significance of existence are made vivid through art as well as all of the varied feeling aspects of human expressiveness. Art is largely, then, philosophically experienced and accepted as a given quality, much as is the redness of red.

It is necessary that general research and teaching inquiries in art education take their cues from such speculative and other generically varying aspects of art, rather than primarily from the social sciences or from other enclosed research techniques. No matter how discrete or sophisticated the latter are, they are at the most partial, yet essentially irrelevant, in revealing the workings of art. They impose extraneous elements of consideration. They are forced to pose inappropriate questions and seek a necessary constraint in standardized responses and objectively ordered resolutions. When research is undertaken it is necessary that any structuring in the field be subject to the examination of practicing artists or by those critical minds that have been shaped by a vital liaison with art and have seriously cultivated a continuing involvement with art and artists. Of course, not all artists or critics have the patience or predilection, the educational insights, or the broad investigative skills to function in art education. However, for those that do, the undertaking is a natural one. On the other hand, an individual who possesses only the skills of statistics and abstract study techniques with little of the cultivated or innate understanding of the artist or critic is doomed to superficial findings, shallow understandings, and erroneous recommendations. Perhaps the research apparatus of the doctoral programs in art education is askew, as may be many of the premises of methods courses in the field. Just recently, a leading art educator commented that he would much prefer doctoral students in art education who had been previously trained in psychology or the other social sciences rather than in art. I can understand the efficiency, the precision, and the endless enthusiasm for the research studies that may result, but I would be highly skeptical of the activities of such individuals, of their findings and their pertinence to good art teaching, and the dissemination of aesthetic values. As is the case now, the archives would grow full of papers and their prime significance would be to gather dust. Somehow, the higher institutions, regional laboratories, and private foundations have to find additional ways of involving willing artists and critics in the bread-and-butter research projects in art education. Similarly, these same individuals should be employed more fully in the training of art teachers. At the very least, art education researchers should have an artist or critic around on all of their projects, if only as a "reality check," to counteract the oftentime inappropriate directions and straying research designs undertaken by independent investigators or by educational institutions. Hopefully, the humanistically directed psychologists are opening up new research paths along this line of agreement.

Nevertheless, the one ingredient that everyone can agree upon in art teaching is the need for imagination. This needs to be translated into imaginative methods of teaching and in creating imaginative contexts for personal development. There is the parallel aim of directly activating and enriching the imagination of the individual child, at the same time that one values not only the sense of self but the overall personal relationships of the individual to society. One educator, William Walsh, puts such a goal rather well: "It is on the one hand that restless search for release from the confinement of the single image of one self, and on the other a solicitude to keep inviolable the privacy of another self. We do not know of any one correct way to achieve such an aim in education. Indeed, there may be as many ways as the imagination may conjure up. It may very well be disastrous to narrow our sights to a theoretically secure or correct way."

Art teachers have to recognize when bewildering or alien intrusions occur in the art classroom. For instance, in an overly simplified and cursory assessment, we may say that science is predicated upon uncovering uniform laws, upon objective observation, upon extensions of predictability and the establishment of laws. It has a convergent goal to achieve, rules to explicate, procedures to standardize, even when it is most speculative. Art, on the other hand, seeks diversity, is bathed in subjective considerations and seeks out the original, the variant, and the novel, reaching out for uniqueness, vividness, and intensity, rather than anticipating what is already known and repeating it. It would seem that any attempt arbitrarily or even innocently to merge the two whether for research purposes or cultural synthesis would be doomed to cross-purposes, despite the fact that both science and art feed from a universal human motive of creativity. What has to be understood is that once this creativity is activated, art and science essentially take separate paths. A synthesis of understanding does not lie in indiscriminately wedding the diverse disciplines, but in engaging in each in terms of their natural structures, the complementing of one against the other, to paraphrase the philosopher Cassirer's "harmony of contraries." These discriminations and an enriched ability to observe and feel, to see rather than just to look, have to be passed on to the students engendering the more essential and vitalizing value commitments that have always been synonymous with art.

It would seem that there is no right or wrong in art and perhaps in art teaching as well, but there certainly is good and bad. The good and bad is, however, a value function of the individual. Objective methodologies of art teaching experimentally "proven" to be correct cannot be packaged and handed over to teachers. In the final analysis, it is the teacher himself who has to find the personal resources for good art teaching in his own psychic insights and range of experience. The latter must be involved with art on a continuing high level and generate a felt enthusiasm. Further, art has to be regarded as the humanizing source, that element of existence which separates man from the beasts in the field—and possessed of the magic and mystery which beckons and may offer a continuing experience of intrinsic satisfactions. Only the forces of individual personality and artistic form can pass on such a fundamentally human realization. The larger aspects of art education, its most seminal and dynamic theoretical position, can only be achieved by a continuing dialogue between the genuine qualities of art and the inherent functions of education. Both art and education have to be regarded as open and suggestive possibilities for significant experience rather than as definitive representations of a fixed dogma.

Basic and Applied Research in Education: Definitions, Distinctions and Implications

JOHN B. CARROLL

At a time when questions are being raised with particular poignancy about the value of basic research in the social and behavioral sciences,[1] it seems useful to try to clarify some of the issues as they pertain to research in education. After a period of about ten years during which Federal support of educational research increased markedly—a period in which there was a relative lack of concern as to whether the research being supported was "basic" or "applied," as a result of which a considerable amount of research of a fairly "basic" character was supported—recent Congressional actions and corresponding policy decisions in the Bureau of Research of the U. S. Office of Education[2] have tended to put much more weight on the support of "applied" research which would be directed toward the solution of immediately practical problems in education. This state of affairs appears to reflect considerable confusion about the role of basic research in education and what this research may be expected to achieve. This paper will argue not only that it is possible and useful to distinguish between basic and applied research, but also that there is a continuing need for both of these types of research in education. Since funding agencies already give strong support to applied research, an argument in its favor will not be developed.[3] Thus, while recognizing the importance and desirability of applied research, we shall focus attention on the arguments for basic research.

Reprinted by permission of the author and the publisher from *Harvard Educational Review*, Vol. 38, No. 2, Spring 1968, pp. 263–276. Copyright 1968 by the President and Fellows of Harvard College.

[1] House of Representatives, *The Use of Social Research in Federal Domestic Programs*. Parts I-IV. A staff study for the Research and Technical Programs Subcommittee of the Committee on Government Operations (Washington: U. S. Government Printing Office, 1967).

[2] A leading critic of government educational research programs has been Lee J. Cronbach (1966), who states that the U. S. Office of Education Bureau of Research "has thrown its forces heavily on the side of 'practical products' and dissemination." "While the USOE is a passive patron of basic research," he continues, "it has done nothing to formulate and sell to Congress a policy that will promote the healthy development of basic investigation." Further, he points out that the Office "declines to support a research and development center unless it includes a dissemination program from the outset," a fact to which I can personally testify. Nevertheless, there are signs of at least a slight change in USOE policy. In an interview (Robinson, 1966), Richard L. Bright, the Assistant Commissioner for Research in the USOE, voiced his hope that an effective program for "more really *basic* research" could be instituted in the near future.

[3] Indeed, if anything, one might be tempted to argue against the policy of strong support for applied research on the grounds that there are some respects in which its merits are debatable—for example, its tendency towards lack of generalizability.

Education is not the only field in which this question has been raised. A spate of articles and editorials in *Science* on basic *versus* applied research is a sign that the issue is one of great concern to scientists in general, particularly where it involves the relative amounts of monetary support given to the two types of research. Many scientists feel that basic science is nowadays being by-passed in favor of large "mission-oriented" programs of applied science such as the man-on-the-moon effort. Some (e.g., Weinberg, 1961) have phrased the issue in terms of an opposition between "little science"—the activities of isolated scientists in their laboratories—and "big science"—the efforts of large, well-funded teams of workers toiling in special-purpose research organizations. Yet Kidd (1959) finds it difficult to arrive at "operational criteria" by which basic and applied science activities can be distinguished. He avers that it may be easy enough to *describe* the differences between clear cases of each, in terms of the nature of the activities or possibly in terms of the motivations of the scientists involved, but that one cannot apply any rigorous and well-established criteria to decide whether any given research project is of a basic or of an applied character. Thus, he contends that statistics compiled by government organizations on the relative amounts of support given to basic and to applied research are inherently meaningless. As a possible criterion, he suggests that an activity is "basic science" to the extent that it has a high probability of yielding a "new scientific finding." But such a criterion is itself problematical: an eminently practical new invention, arising from "applied science" activity, may often represent "new knowledge." A recent article by Reagan (1967) suggests abandoning, for practical political purposes, any distinction between basic and applied science, preserving only a distinction between "research" and "development." Unfortunately, such a step could have the effect of inhibiting or jeopardizing support for promising basic research whose direct relevance to a specific practical goal or mission cannot immediately be demonstrated, because politicians could always claim they are still supporting "research" even if all the research is mission-oriented.

There have been few attempts to define basic research in education or to specify its role. Clark (1963) puts forth a number of general arguments for basic research, mostly revolving around the claim that such research will have broad applications in improving the educational process, in introducing new educational technology, and in establishing new curricula. Ausubel (1953), on the other hand, believes that educational research should restrict itself to "applied science"—testing out the application of "extrapolated basic science" to its own practitioners. But now that the support of basic research in education is a "political" issue, it is critical to consider what possible role basic science activities may have in educational research and to what extent they merit fiscal support either from the government or from private sources. Before we can do so, however, it is necessary to re-examine some of the issues raised by Kidd, Reagan, and others in the context of a broader view of the nature of scientific inquiry and the sources of its motivation.

THE GOALS OF SCIENTIFIC INQUIRY

There has been much confusion in the literature about the goals of scientific inquiry. Although it may be difficult to consider the motives of individual scientists in pursuing their work, it remains true that science does have goals and that such goals imply motives to achieve those goals. Indeed, the very notion of inquiry contains the notion of questions needing answers. What some writers have failed to recognize, however, is that motives can be structured in a hierarchy—some goals being more ultimate and others more proximate—and that some of the proximate motives in the hierarchy can be "functionally autonomous," to use Gordon Allport's (1937) phrase. That is to say, from a psychological standpoint, some goals may operate as ends in themselves, without reference to the extent to which they may actually serve still other, more remote goals.

Roughly speaking, the usual goals of scientific inquiry can be arranged in such hierarchy. The ultimate goal, and the basis of society's general support for science, is usually said to be the solution of utilitarian, practical problems.[4] Ideally, these goals ought to be well defined, e.g., the building of safer automobiles, the reduction of air pollution, or the elimination of cancer; or in the field of education, the overcoming of handicaps due to mental retardation or due to "social disadvantage," the nourishment of creativity in gifted children, the facilitation of the learning of foreign languages, etc.

Many scientific research projects are immediately in contact with such well-defined practical problems. But in order to feed necessary basic knowledge into such activities, science can be said to have a more general utilitarian aim—utilitarian in the best Benthamist sense—to produce knowledge and understanding of all natural phenomena that are likely to be relevant to human concerns. This general utilitarian aim is ordinarily conceived to be characteristic of basic science—and indeed of all scientific and scholarly activities. That it can also be regarded as a "functionally autonomous" motive is illustrated by Seaborg's (1963) claim that "the motivating force [for basic research] is not utilitarian goals, but a search for a deeper understanding of the universe and of the phenomena within it."

Some scientists also claim that a basic motive for science is a kind of "curiosity." From the standpoint of the individual scientist, according to Teller (1963), pure research "is a game, is play, led by curiosity, by taste, style, judgment, intangibles." The implication is that the scientist is often motivated not by any ultimate utilitarian aim, not even by some duty to produce new knowledge, but merely by the fun and challenge of unanswered questions (like mountains that must be climbed "just because they're there"). This too—this love of intellectual challenge—is a form of autonomous

[4] But, as Professor Israel Scheffler has pointed out to me, perhaps even utilitarian, practical goals may be construed only as instrumental to achieving intrinsically valuable cultural goals such as the attainment of knowledge for its own sake. Thus we would have not a hierarchy but a circular network of goals.

motive, one that is quite legitimate psychologically as a source of persistent creative effort.[5] As a matter of fact, the public at large may be said to possess curiosity about many questions whose relevance to any utilitarian ends is at best remote. Why does the public support the efforts of linguists endeavoring to decipher Mayan hieroglyphic writing? I can think of no tangible reason other than societal curiosity, except perhaps for the light the results might throw on the nature of human writing systems or on the character of Mayan society. Yet we have little hesitation in supporting this and similar scholarly work with foundation grants, fellowships, and the like. We may equally well support work aimed to satisfy our curiosity about interesting, albeit possibly useless, scientific questions like the nesting habits of the dodo.

Thus, we can exhibit a hierarchy of motives, each imperceptibly merging into the next, as follows:

Curiosity → Better understanding → General, undefined → Well-defined
                of natural phenomena   utilitarian aims   practical goals

The questions asked in science can arise from either or both of two sources: (1) our lack of understanding of some given set of phenomena; (2) our inability to achieve some practical goal. Basic science receives its justification both from the fact that better understanding of natural phenomena is a legitimate autonomous motive and from the fact that such understanding has the potential of serving utilitarian aims even though it is not usually possible to define those aims. Applied science derives its justification, obviously, from its orientation towards the achievement of well-defined practical goals. Basic and applied science can thus be roughly distinguished by the types of questions to which they are addressed. Of course, it is frequently the case that applied science must address itself to basic science questions, answers to which are needed to facilitate progress towards the achievement of a practical end. And as Pfaffmann (1965) has pointed out, ". . . often practical problems [and the superficial solutions one finds for them] are symptoms of [and engender] deeper problems that require more basic study and research." But there is no reason why an applied-science research project cannot be broken down into those tasks that are of a basic-science nature and those that are more concerned with testing basic-science knowledge in its application to a specific practical goal.[6]

[5] See the studies of Rossman (1931) and Roe (1952) for evidence on the role of intrinsic motivation in the creative work of inventors and scientists. In Roe's study, indications of humanitarian motives were found only in some social scientists, and very rarely in natural scientists.

[6] For the purposes of this paper, we must rule out the definition of "applied" which is implied by Revelle's (1965) remark that "because the astronomical and earth sciences do not deal with universals, but only with physical laws acting in particular situations, the physicist tends to think of them as applied rather than fundamental sciences." Even if we believe that all phenomena can be explained, reductionistically, by appeal to a small number of physical laws, there is still a place for "basic science" in determining the way in which these physical laws manifest themselves or interact at the higher levels of physical organization represented by biological cells, nervous systems, or social groups.

Although I do not believe that motivation can be wholly ruled out of any attempt to distinguish basic from applied science—precisely because (as I have tried to show above) science starts from questions which are themselves motivating—it is nevertheless possible to decide, on a fairly objective basis, whether a given scientific task is more immediately addressed to the better understanding of phenomena or to the achievement of a specific practical goal. Any well-designed scientific inquiry contains a series of explicit problems, defined variables, and stated procedures. I would venture the guess that a group of experienced and knowledgeable scientists, upon examination of the design of a scientific investigation, could reach a high degree of agreement on the extent to which it is of a basic or an applied character. It would not be necessary for them to hire a psychologist or a psychiatrist to inquire into the inner motives of the scientist (as Seitz [1963] seems to suggest); the motives of the scientist should be manifest in his statement of hypotheses, procedures, and expected results.

Some writers on basic and applied research have attempted to distinguish them with reference to the different reward systems that appear to apply to them. Storer (1964), for example, writes: "Basic research is that which is carried out by a scientist who hopes that his findings will be primarily of interest to his scientific colleagues, while applied research is intended to produce findings which will be of greater interest to the investigator's employer or to the lay public." But Storer's remarks seem simply to point out that there are different ways in which the scientist can, if he chooses, confirm whether his work has the outcomes he himself hopes for it. The basic scientist looks to his scientific colleagues, generally, for affirmation that his work is sound, reasonable, and contributory to the advance of knowledge; the applied scientist gets his signals from his sponsors, who can be expected to reward him in material ways when his discoveries result in useful applications. There will be many scientists, however, for whom these particular reward systems will have little appeal. Fundamentally, the reward system for the scientist or even for a team of scientists is inherent in scientific activity itself. That is, in basic science, effort will be continued until the investigators are rewarded with answers to their questions, while in applied science, efforts will persist until the desired practical ends are achieved.

Public acclaim or disapproval is no criterion either. Both basic and applied scientists will continue their work—as they should, if they are otherwise justified—despite lack of public support. An example of the ridicule that can come from uninformed journalism is to be found in a recent article in the *Reader's Digest* (Schulz, 1967) which holds up to scorn a government-sup-

---

We must also rule out the definition that one might derive from McLane's (1965) statement that "25 years ago symbolic logic was the 'purest' branch of mathematics; today it is heavily applied, as in computers." The fact that a science *has* applications or has *been* applied does not make it an applied science, nor does it exclude the possibility that one can do basic science in such a field. Otherwise we would have to say that theoretical physics, because it spawned the atom bomb, is an applied science!

ported research project entitled "Understanding the slump in fourth-grade creativity"—a project that, it happens, was conducted by a well-respected educational researcher (E. P. Torrance) concerning a problem of practical significance to many teachers and parents.

THE DIMENSION OF "RELEVANCE"

Much has been said about the evaluation of research in terms of its "relevance" to utilitarian ends. Most frequently, this question is raised about "basic" research: Is this research even conceivably relevant to *any* kind of utilitarian end? From the point of view expressed here, this question is thoroughly inappropriate for at least three reasons:

1. The better understanding of phenomena is a legitimate end in itself which can be justified, if necessary, on the ground of the general experience that at least *some* scientific activity addressed solely to fundamental questions has "paid off" in unexpected practical applications.
2. The potential applications of many basic-science researches cannot always immediately be anticipated, even when they do in fact result eventually in practical applications. (The long-delayed application of the discovery of penicillin is a classic case in point.) Often a given scientific finding needs to be further investigated or supplemented before a practical application can be perceived.
3. One can never predict whether a given scientific investigation will be "successful" even in its own terms. We are perhaps unaware of the tremendous amount of scientific activity that is "unsuccessful" in the sense that it fails to yield any new knowledge; further, sometimes a negative result (e.g., the failure to confirm a hypothesis or the failure to find a solution to a problem) is a distinct contribution to knowledge because it informs the scientific community that the hypothesis or methodology tried is apparently of no avail. Thus we should not try to evaluate the relevance of a given scientific investigation in terms of its results. Even in the case of "applied science" investigations, the use of this criterion would not be appropriate, for many such studies fail to achieve practical solutions although they are nonetheless clearly so *directed*. To assess relevance, we must concentrate on evaluating the *process* of scientific investigation—the framing of questions and hypotheses, the research design, the analysis of findings, and so on—and not the results.

In this light, basic-science investigation is *inherently* relevant (at least to the undefined utilitarian aims mentioned above) when it is addressed to questions that the investigator—if he is well-trained and knowledgeable in his field—feels are reasonable and useful to answer, and when in the judgment of his fellow scientists it is properly designed to answer those questions. We shall not insist, however, on the additional qualification that the relevant scientific community also approve the reasonableness of the questions asked because there are a number of cases in the history of science where a lone investigator successfully showed that apparently unreasonable questions were in fact worth pursuing.

We should point out, too, that except for rare cases, a scientist pursues questions *within a fairly well-defined area*—one for which it is possible to specify in a general way the kinds of practical applications that can be foreseen. We know the kinds of applications that have been made of findings in theoretical physics, in chemistry, in biology, in psychology, or in sociology. We could expect, for example, that work on fundamental processes of learning would have applications, if any, mainly in education—and not, say, in civil engineering; work in molecular biology could be expected to have applications both in learning and in the control of genetics. Relevance is therefore specifiable in general terms, even for the purest of basic research; and it is on this basis that the public can justify the support of basic research even when specific applications are not immediately foreseen. If society cannot find any area of relevance for an *area* of research, the case might be different. But one must be careful even here: in Galileo's time, society rejected large areas of science, and for a long period the Soviet government rejected work in Mendelian genetics. More recently, the practical relevance of learning theory has been debated, even by learning theorists.

SOME FURTHER, BUT ROUGHER, DISTINCTIONS

If basic and applied research can be distinguished in terms of the nature of the work, the kinds of questions investigated, the procedures, and the like, it will be useful to expand on some of these points. No one of them, however, can be used as a sole criterion.

With respect to the questions asked, basic research tends to differ from applied research in the fact that it is more concerned with "understanding" and the attainment of knowledge about fundamental variables and their relationships; the prediction of socially important phenomena is of secondary concern, arising solely out of the laws and relationships discovered; and control of phenomena is often of only incidental interest except to verify a finding. Applied research, however, is generally concerned with the control of socially significant phenomena, or if control is difficult or impossible, at least their prediction. It is interested in the "understanding" of phenomena in terms of laws and relationships as a basis for prediction and control. Generally it starts with facts and propositions already established in basic science and proceeds to test them in particular situations and/or in particular combinations such that extrapolation from basic science is risky.

Correlated with this difference is the fact that basic science, in order to gain a better understanding of the workings of phenomena, is more often concerned with detailed, fundamental processes, such as chemical reaction mechanisms, nerve impulses, or isolated learnings; applied research, on the other hand, is more often concerned with gross, higher-order macro-processes like wine fermentation, social attitudes, or scholastic achievements, because these are the phenomena one wants to predict or control. In the behavioral sciences, we say that basic research has often to do with a "molecular" level of behavior, while applied research has to do with a "molar" level of behavior. For example, basic research in learning is concerned with the precise combinations of stimulus and response variables that produce certain effects, whereas applied research might be concerned with the effects, say, of massive doses of positive reward, which for certain groups of school learners might *on the average* produce significantly beneficial effects. The applied researcher would not necessarily worry about why positive reward works, or why it does not always work for all students, whereas the basic research scientist—if he is worth his salt—will push for understanding of the total dynamics of the phenomena he is studying. (As soon as the applied researcher starts worrying about deeper questions, he becomes a basic scientist.)

In its concern for processes on a "molecular" level, basic research relies to a greater extent on models of functional relationship that involve relatively small error components, while applied research tends to use models that are more probabilistic and error-laden. It is not an accident that statistical procedures were first developed in applied fields of research like certain branches of economics, agriculture, and psychological testing, even though these procedures are, of course, extensively used in basic research even in theoretical physics.

Basic research is more often conducted in the laboratory, or in highly controlled situations, in order to observe the effects of particular variables independently of other possibly relevant variables. Applied research tends to be done in situations that are identical to, or closely similar to, those in which one wants to apply the findings. On the other hand, some basic research is done in relatively uncontrolled situations, and some applied research employs rigorous controls. It is not necessary to suppose that research cannot be basic when it is done in live field situations. In fact, in education there are many arguments for doing certain types of research in such situations. But discussion of this point would take us too far afield.

Basic research is more concerned with the development of theory and of all-embracing models for the explanation of phenomena, while applied research either takes for granted previously established theory and extrapolates from it, or avoids theoretical problems altogether. In any case, basic science stands in a relation of logical priority to applied science. Applied science usually relies heavily upon findings in basic science. It is less often the case that basic science takes off from a finding of applied science; in the instance where this occurs, the purpose usually is to explore the deeper rationale of the finding. Although the essential priority of basic science is not as clearcut in the behavioral and social sciences as it is in the natural sciences, much is to be gained, I think, by following the model of the natural sciences in giving emphasis to basic research at points where applied research cannot make progress alone.

BASIC EDUCATIONAL RESEARCH

It is thus doubtful, in educational research, that we can move ahead to effective educational engineering without an adequate base in fundamental research in mathematics, computer science, genetics, physiology, psychology, sociology, anthropology, and other relevant disciplines. Particularly where applied research seems to be yielding diminishing dividends, we must turn to basic research on the phenomena in which we are interested. I would propose that such research be called *basic educational research,* and that it be thought of as a part of basic science.

It can be easily demonstrated that many of the most fruitful developments in applied educational technology would have been well-nigh impossible without an adequate foundation in basic research. At the same time, some of these same developments have now reached a point of decreasing returns such that they need a new infusion of results from basic research. A good example is the history of so-called programed instruction.

Let us consider what has happened in this field since the publication of B. F. Skinner's well-known article, "The Science of Learning and the Art of Teaching" (1954). It was basic research, of an extensive and profound character, that led Skinner to conclude that certain propositions about "reinforcement" (roughly, the reward of responses) and the temporal relationships between stimuli, responses, and reinforcements could be "applied" in a special way to the conduct of instruction. Skinner felt that he needed to make no apologies for proposing to apply results of research with rats and pigeons to teaching human beings. It took Skinner and others about five years of "applied" research, however, to develop instructional materials that would incorporate the principles he had arrived at from animal research. Many of the "programed" courses that resulted from this development phase seemed to be eminently successful, at least under certain conditions. But others, *apparently* using the same principles as the successful ones, were not as effective.

Many investigators who tried to develop programed courses realized that some of Skinner's principles had not been adequately tested in their application to human learning, and began to investigate them more thoroughly. From the studies that have been conducted over the last ten years, reviewed by such writers as Morrill (1961) and Holland (1965), it can be concluded that many of Skinner's original propositions—deriving from his basic research —were not sufficiently precise to guide the development of programed instruction unfailingly. Where it had been claimed that the student must construct his own response, a selective response was often found to be more efficient. Where it had been claimed that reinforcement must be immediate, it was on occasion found that it could sometimes be delayed, or even omitted entirely, without affecting the success of learning. Where it had been claimed that instruction must proceed in small, carefully sequenced steps, it was found that the steps did not always have to be small and that under some conditions it made no difference whether the steps were presented in a "logical" or in a random sequence.

At the present juncture, therefore, our ideas as to exactly how programed instruction ought to be developed are confused. It is apparent that we must return to some quite basic research and theorizing in order to bring the various apparently conflicting results of applied research into line. Without the necessary basic research into the detailed processes of perception, learning, and forgetting that underlie programed instruction, further "engineering" development will make little headway.

One can cite other instances in which basic research on psychological processes is needed to guide developmental efforts in education. Levin, Gibson, and their associates (Levin, 1966) at Cornell University have recognized such a need in the field of reading and have devoted several years of a concentrated effort to investigating fundamental processes in reading and learning to read. Some of Levin's research draws heavily upon recent findings and formulations in linguistics. Although results of many of the studies have no immediate application, they promise to contribute towards a new theory of the reading process that will guide the development of practical materials and procedures for the teaching of reading. In another field, Guilford's (1966, 1967) twenty-year program of research on individual differences in cognitive abilities can be regarded as basic educational research that may have far-reaching implications for the design of curricula. In view of the burgeoning of interest in the teaching of creativity, his explorations of the dimensions of "divergent production" are being watched with interest by applied researchers. Basic research investigations into the nature of creativity have also been conducted by Getzels and Jackson (1962), with close relations to the more applied-science work of Torrance (1962). A good deal of this research has been supported by funds from the U. S. Office of Education.

Of course, it may be observed that there is already much basic-research activity in psychology and other behavioral sciences carried on outside the field of education as such. Experimental psychologists, for example, are now engaged in intensive programs of basic research in processes of perception, learning, motivation, and so forth, supported by such diverse federal agencies as the National Science Foundation, the National Institutes of Health, the Office of Naval Research, and even the National Aeronautics and Space Administration, as well as by various private foundations. Should educational agencies continue to support basic research in educational psychology when the needs are being fairly well met by support from noneducational sources? I believe they should, on the ground that the mission of educational agencies can have a beneficial effect on directing the attention of basic researchers to the problem areas of education, which in turn will lead them to select basic research problems that will have an appreciable probability of "pay-off" in educational developments—not necessarily immediately, but ultimately, after basic scientific development has run its natural course. The history of research in such areas as programed instruction and reading shows that the applied researchers have posed problems for basic research that might never have been posed purely in the context of basic science as such. As has been the case in the natural sciences, applied problems can have a rejuvenating effect on the development of basic science.

Applied research, development, and dissemination programs have a well-recognized place in education. It has been my purpose to argue that basic educational research can be clearly distinguished from applied research, and that it has an equally vital role to play. If the U. S. Office of Education and other funding agencies are to carry out their responsibilities to education, they must support basic educational research in a due proportion. Just what this proportion should be, monetarily, is a complex question involving the availability of research facilities and of qualified researchers, the relative expense of basic and of applied research, the total funding available, and other factors. The answer would probably turn out to be somewhere between 15 and 25 percent. This figure would include the support not only of basic-research programs themselves, but also of the training of basic-research workers in undergraduate and graduate degree programs that would be distinct from, even though possibly allied with, research operations. A clear mandate for basic research should be given to the universities, either as a part of Research and Development Center programs (which ought not to be constrained within narrow problem areas) or in the form of grants for specific projects. Significant amounts of funds would also be made available to public and private research institutions (both nonprofit and profit-making), including Regional Educational Laboratories if they are appropriately staffed, where concentrated and prolonged efforts could be undertaken.

The establishment and steady pursuit, on the part of funding agencies, of a clear policy that would give adequate recognition to basic educational research would be of enormous benefit to education as well as to the discipline of educational research.

REFERENCES

Allport, G. W., *Personality*. New York: Holt, Rinehart & Winston, 1937.
Ausubel, D. P., "The Nature of Educational Research," *Educational Theory*, 1953, 3, 314–320.
Clark, D. L., "Educational Research: A National Perspective," in J. A. Culbertston and S. P. Hencley (eds.), *Educational Research: New Perspectives*. Danville, Ill.: Interstate, 1963, pp. 7–18.
Cronbach, L. J., "The Role of the University in Improving Education," *Phi Delta Kappan*, 1966, 47 (10), 539–545.
Getzels, J. W., and Jackson, P. W., *Creativity and Intelligence: Explorations with Gifted Students*. New York: Wiley, 1962.

Guilford, J. P., "Potentiality for Creativity and its Measurement," in Anne Anastasi (ed.), *Testing Problems in Perspective*. Washington: Amer. Council on Educ., 1966, pp. 429–435.

Guilford, J. P., *The Nature of Intelligence*. New York: McGraw-Hill, 1967.

Holland, J. G., "Research on Programing Variables," in R. Glaser (ed.), *Teaching Machines and Programed Learning, II: Data and Directions*. Washington: Dept. of Audiovisual Instruction, Nat. Educ. Assn., 1965, pp. 66–117.

Kidd, C. V., "Basic Research—Description Versus Definition," *Science*, 1959, *129*, 368–371.

Levin, H., "Reading Research: What, Why and for Whom?" *Elementary English*, 1966 (Feb.), 138–147.

McLane, S., in *Basic Research and National Goals*. Report to the House Committee on Science and Astronautics by the National Academy of Sciences. Washington: U.S. Government Printing Office, 1965, p. 196.

Morrill, C. S., "Teaching Machines: A Review," *Psychol. Bull.*, 1961, 58, 363–375.

Pfaffmann, C., "Behavioral Sciences," *Amer. Psychologist*, 1965, 20, 667–686.

Reagan, M. D., "Basic and Applied Research: A Meaningful Distinction?" *Science*, 1967, *155*, 1383–1386.

Revelle, R., in *Basic Research and National Goals*. Report to the House Committee on Science and Astronautics by the National Academy of Sciences. Washington: U.S. Government Printing Office, 1965, p. 239.

Robinson, Donald W., "The USOE and Research in Education," an interview with Richard Louis Bright. *Phi Delta Kappan*, 1966, 48 (1), 2–5.

Roe, Anne, *The Making of a Scientist*. New York: Dodd, Mead, 1952.

Rossman, J., *The Psychology of the Inventor*. Washington: Inventors Publishing Co., 1931.

Schulz, W., "The Great Research Boondoggle," *Reader's Digest*, 1967 (March), 91–96.

Seaborg, G. T., in *Federal Research and Development Programs*. Hearings before the House Select Committee on Government Research, 88th Congress, 1st Session. Washington: U.S. Government Printing Office, 1963, p. 66.

Seitz, F., in *Government and Science*. Hearings before the Subcommittee on Science, Research, and Development of the House Committee on Science and Astronautics, 88th Congress, 1st Session. Washington: U.S. Government Printing Office, 1963, p. 283.

Skinner, B. F., "The Science of Learning and the Art of Teaching," *Harvard Educational Review*, 1954, 24, 86–97.

Storer, N. W., *Basic versus Applied Research: The Conflict between Means and Ends in Science*. Cambridge, Mass.: Harvard Univer. Press, 1964.

Teller, E., in *Government and Science*. Hearings before the Subcommittee on Science, Research, and Development of the House Committee on Science and Astronautics, 88th Congress, 1st Session. Washington: U.S. Government Printing Office, 1963, p. 115.

Torrance, E. P., *Guiding Creative Talent*. Englewood Cliffs, N. J.: Prentice-Hall, 1962.

Weinberg, A. M., "Impact of Large-Scale Science on the United States," *Science*, 1961, *134*, 161–164.

A Reconsideration of the Problem of Introspection

DAVID BAKAN

The question of the scientific propriety of the method of introspection should be rethought in the perspective of modern times. Two related considerations are involved. The first is a sense of society's need for a psychology more appropriate to its problems. The second is a conviction that, although psychologists should be methodologically careful, they should not afford themselves the luxury of methodological snobbery. There is no investigatory method which is "pure" and which provides an absolute guarantee against the commission of error. It may indeed be, as one of my students once aptly put it, that the correlation between purity and fertility must at least be negative. If errors be committed, we look to the future for their correctives. In the meantime, and perhaps ultimately, we accept a pragmatic criterion.

It is characteristic in the history of ideas that when some notion is rejected, even for adequate cause, many seemingly associated notions get rejected with it. Often these associated notions may be sound. Such has been the case with introspection. In the outright rejection of the method of introspection, much that was of considerable value was rejected.

In spite of the avowed rejection of the method, it has stayed with us, in several disguised forms. As Boring (1953) has indicated, "introspection is still with us, doing its business under various aliases, of which *verbal report* is one." Boring seems relatively uncritical of the manner in which we contemporarily avail ourselves of introspection. The argument here is for a careful and avowed use of introspection.

In less disguised form introspection is with us in contemporary clinical psychology. The method of introspection is the method that the patient uses, although there is little avowed recognition of it as the method of the clinician, except perhaps among the psychoanalysts (for example, Reik, 1948). However, "therapy" is coming to be viewed as appropriate training for the aspirant clinician even in nonpsychoanalytic contexts.

The rejection of the method of introspection is coincident with the inception of behaviorism in America. The first important behavioristic pronunciamento took place in 1913 (Watson, 1913). It is important to understand the immediate antecedents of behaviorism in order to understand the wide popularity it gained. Boring's comprehensive history makes it unnecessary to recount the involved circumstances associated with the death of classical introspection. Boring (1953) believes that it "went out of style . . . because

Reprinted with permission of the author and the publisher from "A Reconsideration of the Problem of Introspection," Chapter nine, in *On Method: Toward a Reconstruction of Psychological Investigation*. San Francisco: Jossey-Bass Publishers, 1968, pp. 94–112.

it had demonstrated no functional use and therefore seemed dull, and also because it was unreliable."

Psychology was in the throes of the Würzburg-Cornell struggle in the first decade of the twentieth century. The Würzburgers had discovered imageless thoughts; and they themselves hardly knew what to do with them. Titchener, at Cornell, sensed the staggering implications of the Würzburg findings, and struggled desperately to reject them (1909).

The psychological literature of the time is in many respects confused, repetitive, and—we might say—anguished. Psychology had, it seemed, got itself into absolutely inextricable difficulties; and there was no one within the introspective movement who had the clarity of vision to go beyond these difficulties. Watson, for all the limitations that we may ascribe to him, had clarity and offered a program psychologists could follow.

Let us briefly examine the nature of some of the Würzburg findings. They discovered that thought was possible without images; and that thought was guided by states variously designated by the terms *Aufgabe, Bewusstseinslage,* and *determinierende Tendenz.* The favored method was the *Ausfragemethode.* Mayer and Orth (1901) use the method of free association to a verbal stimulus, instructing the subject to report *everything* that went on between the hearing of the stimulus word and the making of the response. Messer (1906) finds himself forced to posit *unconscious* processes underlying the processes of thought. Ach (1905) introduces the concept of the will, that is, motivation, as guiding the thought processes; he uses a probing investigatory procedure; and he uses hypnosis. Bühler (1907) indicates that it is important, in the study of the thought processes, to empathize and sympathize with the subjects engaged in this kind of experimentation.

Then the problem is dropped like the proverbial hot potato. Külpe, the leading figure in the Würzburg movement, leaves Würzburg and goes to Bonn in 1909, and the work practically ceases. Bühler posthumously publishes Külpe's lectures which, according to Boring (1950), "contain a pretty complete system of psychology. But the chapter on thought was missing! Bühler said that Külpe had not been lecturing on the topic."

In the light of the foregoing, and in the light of what we have learned from psychoanalysis, a rather simple explanation suggests itself. These investigators were using themselves and each other as subjects. They had struck the unconscious, and particularly unconscious motivation, and had to probe it if they were to make any headway. However, as we know today, probing the unconscious tends to generate anxiety and resistance; and these investigators simply were not prepared to undergo the necessary personal trials involved. Boring (1953) suggests a relationship between the Würzburg school and Freud, but makes little of it.

Psychology had two possible alternatives: either to widen its investigations to take account of and to study the role of unconscious motivation on the thought processes, or to detour. Academic psychology detoured; and detoured in two ways: It detoured by way of behaviorism, completely rejecting (at least avowedly) the whole method of introspection, and it detoured by way of Gestalt psychology. The former dropped the whole concept of mind, conscious and unconscious. The latter adopted as a basic principle that whatever introspection is done should be naive introspection, with no probing and no analysis, thus preventing intrusion upon the unconscious.

Perhaps one of the most important distinctions necessary for the understanding of the nature of introspection is the classical one between the experience and what is experienced. It is the distinction contained in the classical one of *Kundgabe* versus *Beschreibung* (Boring, 1953). It is the distinction the psychoanalyst makes when he concerns himself primarily with a memory, as contrasted with the event to which the memory presumably refers.

The distinction is somewhat difficult to grasp when we deal with perception. Let us consider a simple experience reported as "I see a book." From the point of view of this distinction it is one or another of two reports: "I *see* a book," or "I see a *book*." In the first instance it is a report of experience as experience. In the second instance the reference is to the object rather than to the experience of the object. One may be true, and the other false, as, for example, in a hallucination.

The distinction is easier to make when we consider something like anxiety. It is hard to make when the experience involves an external stimulus. It is of interest that when Washburn (1922) made her presidential address before the American Psychological Association in 1921 she felt that it was necessary to say that introspection is proper only where there is an external stimulus. This, she believed, would endow introspection with "objectivity"—an unfortunate semantic identification of "object" with "objectivity." It is here, probably, when the Watsonian noose was drawing very tight around the neck of introspection, that introspection surrendered the very thing which was its major merit. Introspection has its maximum value on those very experiences for which there may be no conspicuous physical stimuli, such as grief, joy, anxiety, depression, exhilaration, anger, etc.

A major criticism which has been leveled against the method of introspection is that the data of introspection are not public. In the case of overt behavior it is possible, at least in principle, for two observers to observe a given phenomenon simultaneously. This has sometimes been referred to as the criterion of publicity; and it has been said that data are not acceptable unless this criterion has been satisfied (again, at least in principle).

That introspective data are not public in this sense is not to be questioned. What is to be questioned is whether the criterion is essential. What is the value of the criterion of publicity? Its value, presumably, inheres in the conviction that it avoids error and provides for verification. However, can we not have verification without publicity? Let us consider one of the most acceptable kinds of investigatory procedure from this point of view, the conditioning experiment. There is no way of verifying Pavlov's experiments today by having another observer watching them, since, to say the least,

Pavlov's dogs are quite dead. To verify Pavlov's findings we would have to get other dogs. Furthermore, the fact that two people could have stood by to count the number of drops of saliva is quite irrelevant. If the criterion of publicity is not met by introspection, it is not really very serious as long as each scientist has, so to speak, at least one "dog" he can observe directly.

The crisis generated by disparate results from Würzburg and Cornell, with the one finding imageless thoughts and the other not finding them, was hardly adequate reason for the total rejection of introspection. Disparate results from different laboratories are usually provocative of further investigation, rather than the occasion for dropping the problems, the methods, and the fundamental points of view involved. The failure of the introspective method to satisfy this naive criterion of publicity could hardly have been the real reason for the rejection of introspection as a method.

A more important problem is the possibility of publicity, not of the data, but of the report. Even though the process of introspective observation is, in a sense, private, the information gleaned from the observations must be public. This raises the question of language and communication. There are two questions that may be asked in connection with language with respect to introspection: First, if we relate our introspections to one another, would we understand one another? Second, if we do understand one another, how does this come to pass? If the answer to the first question is to any degree affirmative, then to that exent is the criterion of publicity of report satisfied.

For the answer to the first question we appeal, at the very least, to common sense. If we hear a person say, "I am sorry," or "I am worried," or "I feel sick," etc., there is hardly any question but that we understand what he means. There are times when we may not believe him; but the possibility of fraud, intentional or unintentional, or lack of precision exists with respect to any methodology. The fact is, however, that we understand him.

The answer to the second question now becomes a matter for empirical investigation. This is not the place to enter into a detailed discussion of the psychology of language learning. However, it is extremely pertinent to indicate that the theory of language learning implicit in contemporary behavioristics is much more simple than is consistent with the facts. This implicit theory may be roughly characterized as follows:

The teacher holds up a ball and says, "Ball." The learner repeats, "Ball." The learner then, presumably, comes to "know" the meaning of the word. Certainly the theory is stretched to the breaking point when confronted with the fact that we all fairly well understand the meaning of words such as "sorrow," "feeling," "nausea," "if," "but," etc.

Titchener (1921) wrote an essay which, in part, attempted to present to English-speaking readers some of the contributions of Franz Brentano. In the judgment of the writer, Brentano is one of the most important figures in the history of psychology. The major work of Brentano with respect to psychology (1874) has not, as far as could be determined by the writer, been translated into English. Of Brentano and Wundt, Titchener wrote: "The student of psychology, though his personal indebtedness be also twofold, must still make his choice for one or the other. There is no middle way between Brentano and Wundt." For the most part, the choice of the classical introspectionists was for Wundt. Wundt and Brentano published their major psychological works at about the same time. Two major schools of thought issue from Brentano. One is the already mentioned Würzburg school. The other is psychoanalysis, with Brentano having been the only academic psychologist under whom Freud studied (Merlan, 1945; 1949). Psychoanalysis, however, differed from the Würzburgers with respect to a readiness to face the unconscious. It may have been easier for Freud to break through to the unconscious because of some of the special circumstances of Freud's life and career (see Bakan, 1958).

Brentano, Külpe, and Freud conceived of introspection not so much as of the present, but of the past. They took seriously what was then a common observation, that introspection at the moment an experience is taking place changes the character of that experience. If we are interested, say, in anger, then introspection at the moment of anger tends to reduce the anger. It is only when anger is past that it can be properly examined. Using the method of introspection, thus avowedly retrospectively, makes it possible to examine psychological phenomena which cannot readily be elicited in the laboratory, except perhaps with very great ingenuity.

This difficulty of the introspection of Wundt and Titchener was adequately recognized by McDougall (1922), who wrote: "Experimental introspection has obvious limitations. Many of our most vital and interesting experiences, such as grief or joy or fear or moral struggle, cannot be induced at will, except perhaps in very slight degrees. And, under the most favorable conditions, introspection of our more vivid and vital experiences is difficult, because we are apt to be primarily interested in the events of the outer world in which we are taking part, if only as observers. Then again the very act of introspection does to some extent modify the experiences we wish to observe and describe; so that in introspecting we partially defeat our own purposes."

Thus, the type of introspection which was advocated by Titchener, and which was the object of attack by the anti-introspectionists, was a type which, by its nature, could not attack the important aspects and kinds of experience. The cry that a psychology was wanted which would have some usefulness was completely justified when the object of attack was the kind of introspection advocated by Titchener.

A characteristic of good science is that it is ever alert to the possibility of the commission of systematic types of errors. One of the major criticisms leveled against introspection is that its results are untrustworthy.

There is a respect in which introspective observations are more trustworthy than observations made by the use of the sense organs. Sense organs may be defective. Sense organs are subject to illusion. Observations made with the sense organs are subject to the accidents of angle of regard, kind of illumination, noise level, etc. In the last analysis, the sense organs are subject to hallucination. Introspection is a method which does not involve the sense organs in the usual fashion, and therefore all of the error tendencies associated with the sense organs simply do not exist for introspection.

However, introspection has associated with it other sources of error. But even at this date, we have achieved a certain amount of progress in isolating them. We know about the stimulus-error. We are aware of the tendency to suppress data (repression), of the tendency to supply socially acceptable data in place of other data (distortion, rationalization, displacement, etc.). But, insofar as we are aware of these error tendencies, we can take precautions against their commission. In this respect introspection is no different from any other set of methods in science. To be aware, for example, of the tendency toward rationalization stimulates us to challenge our introspective findings to determine whether they have resulted from the rationalization process. It is a matter of time and careful work to discover other error sources. We have discovered suggestion, cultural determination, ethnocentrism, etc.; and the list will probably lengthen as our experience with the method enlarges.

Psychoanalysis has one major limitation with respect to our purpose which was not present in classical introspection. This is that the major objective of psychoanalysis is therapy.[1] The major objective of the classical introspectionists was the acquisition of knowledge. This is a fundamental difference.

Essentially, what is being advocated in this paper is the use of the psychoanalytic method with the objective of the classical introspectionists.

It has been indicated that what is being advocated in this paper is partly on the grounds of the need for a science of psychology with practical implication. However, there is an old lesson in the history of science of which we avail ourselves. Whereas knowledge may have practicality as its ultimate objective, it has been found that we sometimes do better, both practically and theoretically, if we temporarily forsake the practical objective.

In taking the objective from the classical introspectionists, it is necessary to make some modification in the psychoanalytic procedure. Although the investigator should be "free" in his associations, he should not permit himself to wander too far from the subject under investigation. His associations should stay under the influence of the task at hand. Of course, as in any investigation, decisions of relevance have to be made, and sometimes only a dim intuition dictates the nature of these decisions. Although there is no a priori method for determining relevance, the investigator should always attempt to keep in mind that he is serving science primarily and himself secondarily.

In accordance with what has already been said the writer attempted to conduct an investigation of the kind suggested. It is a "miniature" investigation in that it was conducted only over a very short period of time, five days for about an hour and a half each day.

[1] This is true even though Freud (1929) did envisage that "the future will probably attribute far greater importance to psychoanalysis as the science of the unconscious than as a therapeutic procedure."

There were several reasons for the choice of the topic; retention and revelation of secrets. One of these is that the topic seemed more amenable to introspection than to other methods. By its very nature a secret is something that may not reflect itself in overt behavior. Another reason for the choice of the topic is that it seems fundamental for any kind of introspective investigation. It seemed important to obtain information concerning the nature of secret retention and secret revelation before very much progress could be made with other topics. A third reason was that the topic seemed to lie close to the oft-stated objective of psychology as being prediction and control of human behavior.

The procedure simply involved sitting down to the typewriter and typing whatever came, after the decision concerning the topic was made. The choice of the typewriter was made primarily on the basis that the writer has found himself to be more fluent this way than either writing by hand or talking into a recording machine.

By virtue of the nature of the subject chosen, the writer attempted to write "as though" the material would never be released. Under any circumstances, even if this was a myth, the sense of the possibility of editing was not mythical. At the moment the writer does not consider it wise to release the protocol. However, one example will be given. The following is taken from the record with some editing:

. . . What is one of the secrets such as *thee and me* have? I once talked to a professor of zoology at lunch about the academic life. He commented that over the head of every academician hangs a sword on a thin string. No matter how much you do, you never feel that you are doing enough. I am reminded of Freud's dream of Irma's injection. He says, "I am always careful, of course, to see that the syringe is perfectly clean. *For I am conscientious.*" The italics are mine. If he felt that he were really conscientious, if he had no feelings of shortcomings in this connection, why did he have to protest that he *was* conscientious? The guilt of lack of conscientiousness haunts most of my friends. My lack of conscientiousness is my "secret." But here I find myself confessing to lack of conscientiousness. But I was not able to do so until I was able to remember something which would make it possible for me not to have my guilt alone. I brought up the zoology professor. When I wrote the above line about him I hesitated for a moment on the question of whether or not to use quotation marks, or to write it in the way that I did. The quotation marks would have had to come, in all honesty, after the word "string." I wrote on, however, "No matter how much you do, you never feel that you are doing enough." This is what I would have liked him to have said. I added it to give the impression that he had said it, but not quite lying about it.

I think that what has been said above can be generalized. *We are more prone to confess a secret guilt when we can believe that others have the same secret guilt.* . . .

The general pattern involved in this kind of writing is that of an oscillation between a free expressive mood and an analytic mood, with the free expression being the subject of the analysis. The question of what a given item of free expression might mean with respect to the major topic under investigation was repeatedly asked.

In the course of this investigation a series of propositions, including the italicized one above, were formulated. This list can be considered to be the yield of this "miniature" investigation:

1. (Given above.)
2. Persons with a secret guilt tend to create situations in which they can "see" that others have the same secret guilt.
3. A secret is a secret by virtue of the anticipation of negative reactions from other people.
4. A secret is maintained in order to maintain some given perception of one's self in others.
5. Persons who associate with one another in the context of a larger group, who have a secret from that larger group, will create a metaphorical or otherwise cryptographic language in which to discuss the secret.
6. To conceal a secret, one may tend to reveal a fabricated "secret," or a less-secret secret, in order to generate the impression that one is being open and frank.
7. One of the important secret areas in our culture is in connection with our intellectual limitations.
8. When an individual has a secret he will attempt to "protest" that the opposite is the case, if the secret has an opposite.
9. The revelation of a secret may involve the attempt to generate the impression that one is telling a joke, to achieve the double purpose of revelation on the one hand and disbelief on the other.
10. In the revelation of a secret, one may attempt to generate the impression that one degrades one's self in one's own eyes, in order to reduce the degradation that one anticipates will be the reaction of others to the revelation.
11. If A knows a secret about B, and B knows a secret about A, and if A discovers that B has revealed A's secret, than A will be inclined to reveal B's secret.
12. If an individual changes his group identification from Group A to Group B, and if Group A has a secret which it keeps from Group B, that individual will be inclined to reveal Group A's secret to the members of Group B.

The simple fecundity of the method soon became evident. After the decision was made to attempt it and a brief beginning was made, it became apparent that this was, to use a term from the vernacular, a veritable mine of information. Essentially it capitalizes on the fact that the investigator has had twenty or thirty or forty or fifty or sixty or seventy years for the collection of various kinds of information. Certainly one of the defects of this kind of data collection is that it is not systematic in the usual way in which we understand this term. Yet it is the result of years of trial and error, of a kind which most laboratory types of investigation do not generally get. It may be argued that these data have been uncritically gathered. This is a valid point. However, the necessary criticality can be supplied in the course of the investigation itself.

This kind of investigation can be severely hampered by what may be loosely designated as "ethical" considerations. Let us consider, for example, the proposition that a secret is maintained in order to maintain a given perception of one's self in others. By virtue of the intimate connection between ethics, in this larger sense, and the kind of data which may become the subject of an introspective investigation, it is extremely important that the investigator attempt, to the degree that he can, to divest the investigation of ethical considerations. Methodologically this divesture may involve a preliminary investigation of the ethical considerations themselves. Also, it must be added that, for some kinds of problems to be investigated by these methods, less may be required in the way of preliminary investigation than for other problems. However, for the investigation of any problem by these methods, a scientific and objective attitude is prerequisite.

One of the major merits of this kind of approach is that it studies the phenomena of psychology directly, in a manner rarely the case in most psychological investigations. Actually, the kind of material which issues from an introspective investigation such as is being advocated is presupposed in many other psychological investigations. Consider for the moment the "lie" scale of the Minnesota Multiphasic Personality Inventory. The test presumably "gets at" the kind of thing which has been investigated in the investigation on secrets cited above. However, the items of this scale were selected because they would presumably be answered negatively by persons who were trying to put themselves "in the most acceptable light socially" (Hathaway and McKinley, 1951). This presumes, with little qualification, the content of the fourth proposition above, as well as about fifteen preconceptions concerning the meaning of social acceptability. (There are 15 items in the "lie" scale.)

Furthermore, had the makers of the MMPI critically examined the nature of secrets in the way in which it has been begun in the above investigation, they would have seen that there are other dynamics of lying, in addition to the one of which they did avail themselves. For example, proposition 6 indicates that a certain amount of truth-telling may simply be a device for "covering up" one or more other lies. It may well be that the operation of the dynamic indicated by proposition 6 acts to depress the "lie" score when lying is really taking place. A full awareness of the kind of thing that issues from such an investigation can greatly enhance the effectiveness even of pencil-and-paper tests.

From a more theoretical point of view, if we seriously accept the mission of psychology as being that of the prediction and control of human behavior, the psychology of secrets is an important link in the chain of psychological findings and theory. Investigators, no matter what they are investigating, must be cognizant, at the very least, of the possibility of dissemblance when they use human subjects. To predict and control an individual's behavior it is important to know, for example, his group identifications, his objectives, his values, etc. Many of these items of information are secret. They may even be secret to the subject himself. And under any circumstances they are not items which will be revealed readily. Thus, until psychologists develop a rather full understanding of the dynamics of this phenomenon, ignorance of it will stand in the way of other investigations.

The above paragraph would be considerably less cogent if the phenomenon of the secret played only a small role in connection with other phenomena. However, secrets play their most important role in those phenomena which are most vital. A psychology that seeks to understand these vital phenomena must have an appreciation of the phenomena of secret retention and secret revelation. Whether we are interested in the problems of marriage, international affairs, politics, military strategy, litigation, business practices, economics, etc., the psychology of secrets is extremely pertinent. And the psychology of secrets yields most effectively to the method which is being proposed.

Although the psychology of secrets is perhaps a central and basic one associated with the method, investigations could and should be pursued with great profit on other problems. Thus, for example, problem solving and decision making can and should be investigated by the method of retrospective analysis. Investigations on status, power, anxiety, fear, aggression, aesthetic experience, learning, communication, memory, concept formation, perception, judgment, charity, loneliness, betrayal, etc., could and should be carried out to enhance our understanding of these phenomena.

Perhaps the critical question in the mind of the reader up to this point is that of the validity of the findings of an introspective investigation. The problem of validity has already been discussed, but somewhat abstractly.

The propositions which issued from the "miniature" investigation are what may be considered to be hypotheses for investigation by other methods. Thus, at the very least, the method may be recommended as a device for systematically getting hypotheses as contrasted with, say, the casual reaching out for a pair of variables and hypothesizing a relationship between them.

Again, as has already been indicated, it may be used as a method whereby an investigator can bring his presuppositions concerning an investigation to formulation; where he can critically examine his presuppositions; and where he might be helped in conceiving of other presuppositions against which he can contrast the ones he is using. Or the method could be used as a device whereby an investigator, having gotten some experimental results which he cannot understand, provokes his imagination to arrive at some kind of explanation of his results. The deliberate and avowed adoption of the method would be extremely helpful in these respects.

However, the writer believes that the method warrants more than this. As has been indicated, the method has a directness not to be found in any other method of investigation of psychological phenomena. In any investigation each thing lying between the phenomenon and the data is a source of error. These sources of error are minimized by the method being proposed. All errors such as failure of the subject to cooperate (for example, rehearsal when instructed not to do so in studies on reminiscence), dissemblance, failure to comprehend instructions, refusal to believe the expressions of the investigator's avowed intentions, fear of hidden—or manifest—microphones, lack of skill on the part of the subject (like fixating on a point in a vision experiment), refusal to take a "naive" attitude (in Gestalt experiments), the lack of control over human subjects (such as subjects in problem-solving studies already knowing the solutions to problems but not informing the investigator), subjects knowing the intention of the investigator (such as subjects knowing that the experimenter is interested in demonstrating a relation between frustration and aggression, and therefore concealing their felt aggression), etc., are minimized in this kind of investigation.

The propositions which were yielded by the "miniature" investigation also have a certain kind of self-evidence associated with them. They elicit the "of course" response. Some of the propositions may require further specification and further qualification. Nevertheless, they are in some sense obvious. It is the sense of self-evidence which is associated, perhaps, with the axioms of Euclidean geometry. The nature of self-evidence is, of course, an extremely difficult problem and perhaps more properly falls in the province of the philosopher. Or, perhaps, self-evidence is a problem to be investigated by the very methods here proposed. However, whatever the ultimate nature of self-evidence may be, there is a sense in which the results of an introspective investigation are of this type.

Now, of course, the matter of self-evidence may be challenged by the question: Self-evident to whom? In one respect this is a valid question. But in another respect it is not. It is valid in that if we are to know that it is self-evident it must be self-evident to someone. However, when the mathematician uses the term "self-evident" he means something which is intrinsic to the proposition, rather than something dependent upon the reader or the hearer of the proposition. For the mathematician it is the self-evidence of the proposition which makes it possible for the person to see the self-evidence, rather than the reverse. It is this characteristic which is shared by introspective propositions.

As a matter of fact, some of the propositions which issued from the "miniature" investigation seem to partake of greater self-evidence than others. Thus, for example, proposition 4 seems to be quite self-evident, whereas proposition 5 seems to be somewhat less self-evident. And even the seeming self-evidence of proposition 4 may be quite culture-bound. However, what has been reported is only an extremely limited investigation, only a beginning and only a sample. Nevertheless, what has been presented is enough to suggest the possibility of achieving the kind of self-evidence that has been indicated.

Two related, but distinguishable, problems are those of replication and generality. Can such an investigation be replicated? The answer is affirmative, although the difficulties of replication should be recognized and account should be taken of them. If an investigator attempts to replicate his own investigation at another time, he will inevitably be under the influence of what he has already done. In replicating such an investigation, the very replication itself should come under the scrutiny of the investigator. He should challenge, for example, his personal identification with the results he has already obtained, and prepare himself for finding both novelty and contradiction with respect to his earlier investigation. If one investigator is interested in replicating the investigation of another investigator, he should carefully take into account the possibility of suggestion, or of his willingness to accept the results of the earlier investigator (particularly if the first investigator has prestige for the second investigator). He should take careful cognizance of possible motivation for showing the earlier investigator to be in error, etc. In some instances it may be extremely worth while to investigate some topic without reading the results of the earlier investigation until the completion of the second investigation, making a comparison later on. Carefully controlled experimentation to determine possible effects of suggestion, for example, is extremely feasible.

The generality of the results of such an investigation is somewhat more difficult, but the difficulty is not unique to introspective investigation. One investigator's results can be compared with another investigator's results, so that the problem of uniqueness with respect to a single investigator is vitiated. However, one may ask, in the event of consistency of results among a group of investigators, may the findings not be unique to a group of persons, all of whom are introspective investigators? There is no easy answer to this problem. However, we face the same problem in other investigations. May not the results of studies in rote learning be largely unique to college sophomores? May not the results of studies in, say, secondary reinforcement be unique to rats, or more particularly laboratory rats, or even more particularly white laboatory rats, or still more particularly tamed white laboratory rats, etc.? May not all findings concerning mental abnormality be unique to mentally abnormal persons contacted by investigators, and may not these very contacts be a major determinant of the findings?

The answer, of course, to each of these questions is contingent upon some decision concerning relevance, a decision that has to be made in connection with any investigation. Actually, the kind of investigation being advocated has an advantage in this respect over other kinds of investigation. For, in an introspective investigation the very decisions concerning relevance can come under the same scrutiny as the phenomena being investigated.

The argument concerning the validity of the findings from an introspective investigation thus far has been concerned with validity in the usual sense, that is, the argument has been concerned with the truth or falsity of propositions which issue from an introspective investigation.

There is, however, a value to such propositions which is over and beyond their validity. This is their possibility rather than their truth or falsity. The knowledge that a certain dynamic is possible enhances the sensitivity of the psychological observer. To make this point concrete, let us consider the military interrogation situation. Suppose that the interrogator is interested in determining the nature of some supplies which have been moved in by the enemy. Now suppose that the prisoner being interrogated knows what these supplies are but does not wish to reveal the information. The prisoner may avail himself of the dynamic indicated by proposition 6 (the revelation of less-secret secrets in order to generate the impression that he is being open and frank) and inform the interrogator at length about a great number of lesser secrets, but not the nature of the supplies. He may say, "I will tell you everything that I know, but I do not know what was in those trucks." An interrogator who was not aware of the possibility of proposition 6 might be lulled into believing the man. The interrogator might say to himself, "He is evidently telling all that he knows." On the other hand, an interrogator who is aware of the possibility of the action of the dynamic indicated by proposition 6 would be aware of the possibility of this kind of deception and would be less likely to be taken in.

If at least one person can contrive such a device for deception, then such a device is possible, and some other individual may have conceived of it and may be making use of it. The truth of the proposition in this respect becomes quite secondary. What is important, simply, is that someone thought of it; and if one person thought of it, other persons might think of it.

In this respect psychologists can make a major contribution to society not only by rendering to society established truths, but also by rendering to society established possibles with respect to psychological dynamics. In the matter of prediction and control of human behavior, a knowledge of what an individual might possibly do, or possibly feel, or possibly think, places us well on the way toward the achievement of our objective. Given a detailed knowledge concerning the possibilities, we can act in such a fashion as to discourage some from becoming actualities, and to encourage others into becoming actualities. The pragmatic usefulness of knowledge of possibles extends from the clinical situation to world affairs.

As has been suggested, these possibles may indeed turn out to be truths in the larger and more scientific sense. But even if they fail to meet the criteria for general scientific propositions, they have value in the sense indicated above.

Research Trends in Art and Art Education

DONALD JACK DAVIS

At the outset of any discussion on research, it seems necessary to establish a general concept or working definition of what research is. Needless to say, research is not an easy term to define and it is often misused and misunderstood. Although the scientific method of inquiry was first applied to the methodology of the physical sciences, it has also become useful in the study of human behavior. Probably the most commonly used types or classifications of educational research are: (1) historical research—investigating, recording, analyzing, and interpreting the events of the past for the purpose of discovering generalizations that are helpful in understanding the present and in predicting the future; (2) descriptive research—describing, recording, analyzing, and interpreting the present nature, composition, or process of phenomena; (3) experimental research—what will be when certain factors are carefully controlled.[1]

In order to examine and discuss trends in research in art and art education, it seems imperative to establish a broad statement of principle which encompasses all of the many types and levels of research which provide a common base for integration and an opportunity for each type or level to make a contribution to knowledge in accordance with its respective possibilities and limitations. In such a survey, it is not of concern whether any one type or level of research is better, more sophisticated, or more respectable than another. Rather, a broad, general framework or concept of research is needed if a comprehensive examination of research trends in the visual arts is to be made. Such a perspective encompasses research as including all forms of scholarly work which is aimed at discovering new knowledge or at making creative interpretations, organizations, or applications of this knowledge. Therefore, research may involve experiments in the laboratory, clinic, or classroom, requiring considerable apparatus and equipment, or it may be abstract and theoretical, demanding few facilities beyond paper and pencil.[2]

Research activity has become increasingly important in the field of education during recent years. As a vital and integral part of the larger field of education, art education has also experienced a phenomenal interest in research, especially since 1950. A survey and examination of the research literature relating to art and art education reveals some interesting facts and trends. Although the past 15 to 25 years have seen the most vigorous activity in research relating to the visual arts, scientific experiments of interest to artists and art educators were carried on prior to these years. As early as 1890, Wolfe [3] published the results of his investigations concerning the color vo-

Reprinted by permission of the author and the publisher from *Art Education: Journal of the National Art Education Association*, Vol. 20, No. 7, October 1967, pp. 13–16.

cabulary of children. A survey [4] of the research literature made in 1940 reveals that during the 57-year period between 1883 and 1939, approximately 162 scientific investigations relating to art and art education were carried out and published. These investigations were primarily related to four areas of investigation: (1) studies relating to color vision and color preference; (2) studies concerning drawing and/or graphic ability; (3) investigations of picture preferences and appreciation; (4) studies relating to tests and measurements in the field of art knowledge and appreciation and drawing ability.

An examination of this early research relating to the visual arts reveals that much of the research activity was carried on by individuals in disciplines other than art, with many studies being conducted by psychologists and sociologists. In many instances it appears that art was being used only as a means to an end, without preliminary investigations into such vital and foundational areas as aesthetics, creativity, and artistic processes. Consequently, much early research resulted in sporadic and short-term investigations whose direct contributions to art education are questionable. By contrast, a survey [5] of the research literature in art education between 1940 and 1960 revealed an increased interest. Compared to the 162 scientific investigations relating to the visual arts published between 1883 and 1939, 210 scientific investigations relating to the visual arts were published during the 22-year period between 1940 and 1960.

There seem to be two or three significant reasons which account for the increased interest in research and the increased volume of research produced during the past 25 years. First of all, the rapid development of the field of art education has played a major role. It appears that by the 1940's the field of art education had developed to the point that research was necessary if continued growth was to be made. As can be seen in other disciplines, there comes a time when growth can only continue if an organized approach and program of research can be established. As Eisner [6] pointed out, art educators wanted evidence to substantiate the generalities and beliefs so prevalent in the literature. Such questioning of long-accepted ideas has naturally led to scientific research in the visual arts. By the same token, art educators were becoming more cognizant of research investigations and findings in related fields such as education, sociology, psychology, and anthropology. The growth of graduate education in art education has also made a contribution to the surge of interest expressed in art education research. The increased number of masters and doctoral programs in art education has demanded emphasis on research. Eisner [7] points out that between 1960 and 1963, more doctoral programs in art education were begun than were begun in the 10 years prior. A third and important factor which has contributed to the growth of art education research is the support and emphasis given research by the professional organizations. The monetary support has not been great; however, moral support has been excellent. Not only have existing publications been faithfully reporting research in the visual arts, but the past decade has seen the birth of a publication devoted entirely to research: STUDIES IN ART

EDUCATION. Special yearbooks and publications of the National Art Education Association have also been issued. In addition to these, professional art education meetings have been saturated with research-type programs—not just art education research per se, but related research such as general creativity research. In more recent days, the interest and financial support of the federal government in educational research has been a significant factor in the growth of research in the visual arts. All of these and many more factors are responsible for the present interest and emphasis in research in art and art education.

An analysis of the research literature of the past 25 years shows that some interests have been maintained in research areas established prior to 1940: (1) research relating to color vision and color preference; (2) research relating to drawing and graphic ability; (3) research relating to picture preference and appreciation; and (4) research relating to tests and measurements in art.[8] However, major emphasis seems to have shifted in the past 25 years with the development of four additional areas of research interests which have dominated the literature. They are: (1) research relating to the study and teaching of art; (2) research relating to art and the personality; (3) research relating to creativity and art; and (4) research relating to the therapeutic values of art.[9]

The area of research relating to color vision and color preference was of major interest prior to 1940 with 57 major investigations found in the research literature. By contrast, between 1940 and 1960, only 16 major investigations were published. This area of investigation is dominated by studies of color sensitivity and color preference, and seems to be of primary concern to people outside the field of art education, especially psychologists. Investigations have been made in such areas as color and form reaction as a basis of interpersonal relationships, color combinations as indices to personality traits, and abstraction of form and color as a function of the stimulus object.

Research relating to drawing and graphic ability has continued to receive intense interest since 1940; 33 investigations were published between 1940 and 1960. A great deal of work has been done in studying the developmental patterns of children in relation to their drawing and graphic ability. Interest has also been shown in the effect of various factors such as socioeconomic status and different motivational devices upon drawing and graphic ability. Considerable interest is also expressed in comparing the drawings produced by abnormal children and those produced by normal children. This has resulted in some rather interesting implications for providing and improving art programs for mentally retarded children, emotionally disturbed children, and the like.

The nature of a general factor in aesthetic perception has been of primary concern in research relating to picture preference and aesthetic appreciation since 1940. In the 27 investigations published in the literature between 1940 and 1960, there has also been concern and studies made to determine children's preferences for traditional and modern pictures, as well as the influence of various factors such as prestige and age upon picture preference and appreciation.

Research related to tests and measurements in art has been an area of rather interesting activity. Between 1920 and 1940, standardized tests in art enjoyed a great deal of popularity. As early as 1912, "Thorndike's Drawing Scale" was published in an attempt to standardize evaluation and set up criteria for judgment. This was followed by the "Kline-Carey Measuring Scale for Freehand Drawing" in 1922, the "Providence Drawing Scale" in 1928, and others. Aside from the early interest in drawing scales, standardized measurements also appeared in relation to art aptitudes and art appreciation. These early tests were hindered by the fact that there were no working definitions of the factors which were being measured. Fundamental factors such as art appreciation and art aptitude were not adequately investigated and delineated before attempts were made to measure these factors. The usefulness of these tests was further crippled by the lack of use of established statistical methods in constructing and validating the instruments. The result was that many of the tests measured things which they were not constructed to measure and did not measure factors which they were intended to measure.

In general, a lack of interest has prevailed in the last 25 years in the field of art measurement. Since 1940, some attempts have been made to revise the existing tests and to create new ones; however, the research literature has been virtually devoid of any concentrated or serious efforts in this area. By contrast, recent efforts of art educators in testing and measurement have been devoted to the testing and measurement of creativity or creative thinking abilities. This work has not, by any means, been limited to art education; rather some of the most basic and extensive work has been conducted outside the field of art education by psychologists, educational psychologists, and others. Work in this area was stimulated by Dr. J. P. Guilford [10] in his presidential address to the American Psychology Association in 1950, in which he outlined his interests and proposed research program in this area. This address and the subsequent research of Guilford and his associates has provided the basic groundwork upon which measurements of creative thinking have been built. These efforts have been extended by the work of Getzels and Jackson, Taylor, Torrance, et al. In 1964 Torrance [11] pointed out that there were at least 17 groups [12] (most on university campuses) in the United States who indicated a sustained interest in creativity research which should result in the accumulation of knowledge concerning creative thinking and creative behavior.

Although individuals outside the field of art education led the way in this important area of measurement, art educators have not been totally unaware and uninterested. At least one major research center—Pennsylvania State University—has been largely devoted to efforts to measure creative thinking similar to those identified by Guilford. Brittain scanned the literature on creativity and composed a test of 36 sections to cover 17 qualities which he had abstracted. The results of his research indicated that eight of the 36 sections clearly differentiated a more creative from a less creative group as judged by an art faculty. Guilford, working under a grant on aptitudes of high-level talent, used a factor analytical approach to determine whether or not there were stable criteria which significantly measured creativity in the exact and applied sciences. He started with 35 tests and found that eight factors emerged. A comparison of the two studies reveals that six criteria were named identically; one was in content alike, while one in the Brittain study appeared to differ. Upon the basis of similarities noted in these two studies, further research was carried on by Beittel at the Pennsylvania State University in an effort to correlate four tests developed by Brittain. The results of Beittel's work further supported the position that creativeness, whether applied in the arts or in the sciences, has common attributes.[13]

It appears that in contrast to early attempts at the development of measuring devices in art, the more recent attempts to measure creative thinking abilities have been based on a more solid foundation. A more scientific approach has been established, with concerted efforts made to determine what kind of mental operations are involved in creative thinking before attempts were made to measure it. Yet there is a definite need for continued thinking and experimentation with means of measuring the creative thinking abilities, especially artistic creative thinking abilities.

Art educators hoping to develop measures of aesthetic judgment, art aptitudes, and the like can learn much from the basic work done in measuring creativity. With this background, it appears that the field is wide open for more systematic and scientific approaches toward standardized measurement in art. Needless to say, there is a great need in this area.

In addition to attempts to measure creativity, interest has been shown since 1940 in the various effects of different factors on creative thinking in art. Another area of intense interest has been the effect of various methods of instruction upon creative thinking abilities. Efforts have also been made to compare the creative art work of children from different cultures, socioeconomic situations, and the like. Aside from specific research studies involving creative thinking in the arts, general creativity research has contributed much to the field of art education. In light of the philosophy of art education being a vital part of the general education structure, art education must include some of the range of activity called art as well as the fundamental fields from which much of educational practice is derived. McFee[14] points out that it is when art becomes a part of education that a new range of activity takes form. This new activity should include consideration of the implications derived from the sciences and art, because art education is concerned with the nature of the learner, his range of variability, and the subject matter field. Consequently, one of the most pressing research needs in the field of art education is the systematic and documented application of research findings in related fields to art education.

In recent years researchers in art education have shown a great deal of interest in the study and teaching of the visual arts, with 38 investigations published in the literature between 1940 and 1960. Much of the work in this area has been descriptive in nature; nevertheless, it has provided some valuable information and much needed direction for growth in art education; public school art programs—time allotments, motivational techniques, budgets and expenditures; teacher preparation; college art programs; graduate education in art education; teacher supply and demand; and art for special groups such as the mentally retarded and the art gifted.

Considerable interest has also been expressed in research relating to the personality structure of the artist and the effect of various factors on the artistic personality. With most of the work being done since 1940 by psychologists, the most researched area has been the general nature of the artist's personality. The results of these investigations have provided basic knowledge which is fundamental to art education.

The fourth area of research activity in art education, which has been developed since 1940, is that of the therapeutic values of art. Again most of the work in this area has been done by psychologists; however, it does have implications for the visual arts. The use of art work as a projective technique has dominated this area of interest, with figure drawing and finger painting the two media most explored. Twenty-three investigations were published in the literature between 1940 and 1960.

Along with this increased research activity in art and art education, there has come an increased awareness of the many problems associated with research in the visual arts. One of the primary problems hinges around the very subjective nature of art and the creative process. In doing research in the visual arts, it becomes necessary to first define such abstract qualities as the creative process, aesthetic judgment, art aptitude, and the like. Needless to say, this is not an easy task. Volumes have been written concerning such problems. Besides the problem of definition, there is the problem of measuring these qualities. Because measurement in the visual arts is still in a very unrefined state, it frequently becomes necessary to devise and construct instruments in order that measurements of these qualities can be obtained for the purposes of research. In addition to the construction of measuring devices, great amounts of time and energy are necessary to determine the validity and reliability of the instruments.

In addition to these basic methodological problems, the sheer attitudes of persons in the field raise serious problems to be confronted by researchers. There are those people who think that no attempt should be made to examine such personal and abstract qualities as aesthetic judgment, creative thinking, and the like. They fear that it will kill or hamper the very qualities which make it a unique experience.

Still another problem of importance to art educators is the fact that up to this time, much of the research work done in relation to the visual arts has been done by people in other disciplines such as psychology and sociology. Realizing the major contributions which have been made to art education by these individuals, they sometimes merely use art as a means to an end.

Furthermore, much of the research carried on by individuals outside the field of art education suffers from the same problem as much of the research carried on by art educators—a lack of understanding of the real nature of such things as aesthetic experiences, creative thinking, and artistic processes. This, in turn, has resulted in much research whose contributions to art education are questionable. Nevertheless, recent breakthroughs have been made in research in the visual arts. In spite of weaknesses of past and present research studies, research has made significant contributions to learning and instructional practices in the art classroom at all levels.

REFERENCES

1. Best, John W. *Research in Education*. Englewood Cliffs, N.J.: Prentice-Hall, 1959.
2. Hastie, Reid. "Introduction," *Research in Art Education*, Ninth Yearbook of the National Art Education Association, a department of the National Education Association. Kutztown, Pa.: State Teachers College, 1959, pp. vi–ix.
3. Wolfe, H. K. "On the Color Vocabulary of Children," *University of Nebraska Studies*, Vol. 1 (July 1890), pp. 205–234.
4. Strange, Mary. "A *Summary of Scientific Investigations Relating to Art*." (Unpublished masters thesis, Baylor University, Waco, Texas, 1940.)
5. Davis, Donald Jack. "A *Summary of Scientific Investigations Relating to Art, 1940–1960*." (Unpublished masters thesis, Baylor University, Waco, Texas, 1961).
6. Eisner, Elliot W. "American Education and the Future of Art Education," in *Art Education*, the Sixty-fourth Yearbook of the National Society for the Study of Education, Part II. W. Reid Hastie, editor. Chicago: The University of Chicago Press, 1965, pp. 299–325.
7. *Ibid.*
8. Strange, M. *loc. cit.*
9. Davis, D. J. *loc. cit.*
10. Guilford, J. P. "Creativity," *American Psychologist*, 5: 444–454, September 1950.
11. Torrance, E. Paul. "Education and Creativity" in *Creativity: Progress and Potential*. Calvin W. Taylor, editor. New York: McGraw-Hill Book Co., pp. 49–128.
12. University of Southern California; The Pennsylvania State University; University of Utah; Institute of Personality Assessment and Research at the University of California in Berkeley; Ohio State University; The Creative Education Foundation at the University of Buffalo; University of Texas; University of Chicago; Michigan State University; University of Illinois; University of California at Los Angeles; National Merit Scholarship Corporation; Teachers College, Columbia University; University of Delaware; University of Minnesota; Experimental Teaching Center, New York University; Graduate School of Education and Laboratory of Social Relations, Harvard University.
13. Beittel, Kenneth, and Lowenfeld, Viktor. "Interdisciplinary Criteria in the Arts and Sciences: A Progress Report," *Research in Art Education*, Ninth

Yearbook of the National Art Education Association, a department of the National Education Association, Kutztown, Pa.: State Teachers College, 1959, pp. 35–44.
14. McFee, June King. "Visual Arts: Psychological Implications of Individual Differences in the Perception-Delineation Process" (unpublished doctoral dissertation), Stanford University, Palo Alto, California, 1957.

Three Bases for Research and Teaching in the Arts: Subjective, Objective, and Projective

HUGH W. STUMBO

Too often art teachers have received only part of the truth concerning aesthetic experiences. University art teachers seem to exhort their future teachers to direct their students either to sensuous responses to works of art, to emotional responses to works of art, to formal relationships found within works of art, to conventional meanings found within works of art, or to new meanings found in works of art. Seldom does one find an art educator on the university level proposing a combination of the part-truths. When a proposed combination is found, it is most likely a combination of sensuous and emotional responses, referred to as being *subjective*, or to a combination of formal relationships and meanings, referred to as being *objective*. Why is it that little effort is made by art educators to synthesize the two? What would an explication of such a synthesis entail? Realizing that such a synthesis is possible and believing that it is important to the richest kind of aesthetic experience, this writer has attempted to answer this last question.

The present essay states the basic definitions and assumptions upon which a larger study was founded and outlines what was called the three bases of research and teaching in the arts: subjective, objective, and projective. Since the projective basis is the least studied and discussed by art students and teachers, the greatest amount of space will be devoted to an explication of it.

The most important terms of the longer study may be defined as follows: (a) *Evidence* is something which indicates something greater than itself; (b) *Attention* is an awareness of evidence; (c) *Communication* is the process of one person directing the attention of another person or persons; (d) *Education* is a result of communicating; (e) *Art* is evidence of human intelligence (for our purposes art will include drawings, paintings, sculpture, and any variations of these three); (f) *Art education* is the result of communicating art.

Reprinted by permission of the author and the publisher from *Studies in Art Education: A Journal of Issues and Research in Art Education*, National Art Education Association, Vol. 9, No. 2, Winter 1968, pp. 21–30.

Because of memory, intelligence, and knowledge everything that is perceived has meanings which extend beyond just the material features of the thing itself. Thus, it is impossible to attend to a thing as a thing-in-itself. If this is true, then it would follow that there will always be something which is just beyond the reach of human attention—in simplified terms this is what the existentialists refer to as the human condition. But within this human condition it is possible for one person to direct the attention of another person, that is, it is possible to communicate and thereby to educate. In order to educate one must have some notion of what evidence is relevant to the subject matter under consideration and systematically set about directing the attention of others to that evidence. Art education, in the simplest terms, is the product of communicating artistic evidence.

In less abstract terms, what does all of this mean? It means that the phenomenon of *attention* is the key to theorizing in art education and is that which must be understood before significant gains can be made in research and teaching in the arts. The first task of researchers in art education is that of defining the essential features of attention and how it functions in the teaching of art. The method of inquiry that seems most appropriate to this task is one closely related to phenomenology. According to Merleau-Ponty: "Phenomenology is the study of essences; and according to it, all problems amount to finding definitions of essences: the essence of perception, or the essence of consciousness, for example" (Merleau-Ponty, 1962). The concept "attention" as we will be using it is synonymous with the word "consciousness" as used by phenomenologists such as Merleau-Ponty, Husserl, Heidegger, and Sartre. If we take the basic tenet of phenomenology, i.e. "Consciousness is always consciousness of something," and substitute "attention" for "consciousness," we have the basic assumption of this essay, "Attention is always attention to *something*."

Things, however, are never as simple as one might want them to be. There are many features of things to which one can attend. For example, when a sculptor attends to the negative space of a piece of sculpture, part of that attention involves the positive space which defines the negative. Although the sculptor's attention is primarily upon the negative space, one could ask him at a later time, when the piece of sculpture in question is absent, to describe the positive space of the piece of sculpture and chances are he could do it. The features or details of things to which one is attending occupies what might be called "sub-attention." Some of these features of attention are strong enough at times to push forward and attract full attention while others remain as details never to be called forth.

While the sculptor attends to the negative space he cannot at the same time attend to the positive space (although he may attend to both as one thing at another time). Gestalt psychologists have adequately demonstrated the fact that it is impossible to attend to more than one thing at a time. Consider the classic figure-ground demonstration:

If one attends to the dark shape, it takes on the properties of figure and the white shapes take on the properties of ground; but if one attends to the white shapes, they take on the properties of figure and the dark shape takes on the properties of ground. Attention, then, changes with the change of objects.

There are some objects, however, which cannot be attended to as a totality. This kind of object we wish to refer to as an abstraction. It is abstract simply because it cannot be perceived as a unit. The parts can be attended to separately and then added up and even given a name, but it cannot be attended to as a concrete thing. This idea is very similar to what Descartes refers to as "intellection." To make his point Descartes urges the reader to try to imagine a triangle, then a rectangle, then a pentagon, and then a hexagon. With a little extra effort on the last two polygons, most readers can imagine them in their "mind's eye." But then Descartes asks the reader to imagine a chiliagon, a thousand-sided polygon. This the reader cannot do. In fact, if the reader could see one drawn on a piece of paper before him, he could not attend to it as a chiliagon. There is little or no difference between one's attention to a hundred-sided polygon and a thousand-sided one. The triangle can be attended to as a concrete thing but the chiliagon can only be attended to as an abstraction. Attention, then, can be abstract or concrete.

It should be noted, however, that regardless of whether attention is concrete or abstract, it has two poles—the subjective and the objective. Since both poles are a part of attention there seems to be no good reason for omitting either in the teaching of art.

The history of philosophy has made it amply clear that these two features of experience do exist and that one can attend to either or neither of them; but there is a third kind of thing to which one can attend that has not been so clearly explicated. The third kind of thing is a goal that one is striving to achieve. A painter, for example, who desires to achieve in his painting an effect of sunlight upon haystacks at a particular time of the day (as the impressionist painter Monet attempted) attends primarily to the goal, with the physical means and the accompanying psychological states being attended to secondarily. As long as the goal is uppermost in his mind he cannot at the same time directly attend to either the objective or subjective features of that creative undertaking. If the artist could reflect upon the objective and subjective features of the goal-oriented endeavor, he could learn a great deal about the nature of his instinctive or spontaneous reason. Such knowledge would afford insights concerning his style of life as well as his style of painting, drawing, or sculpting, and would allow him to make calculated changes in his future artistic endeavors.

Artists have long expressed the opinion that their most productive projects have been those in which they were completely "engaged," i.e., free from objective controls and self-consciousness. If it is true (1) that this kind of an experience is most suitable for creative activity, (2) that much of the meaning of this kind of activity goes unnoticed by the creator, and (3) that an explication of that meaning would be valuable to the growth of the creative person, then it seems reasonable that the development of a procedure for bringing that meaning to the level of conscious awareness would be a valuable contribution to the field of teaching in the arts.

The purpose of the remaining portions of this short exposition is to describe three independent bases for research and teaching in the arts and to elaborate one of them. Since space will not permit an elaboration of all three, we will devote our attention primarily to the one that is probably the least familiar to art teachers.

All three of these bases are to be found in the most common place available, experience. The first basis is found in the thinking or experiencing agent, the self or the ego. We shall be using the word "subjective" to refer to that part of the human organism that cannot be exposed for public inspection. It will include such phenomena as sensations, intuitions, and emotions. The arts and some forms of psychology and religion have concerned themselves almost exclusively with the subjective features. The second basis is found in anything that can be publicly shared, in objects. The physical sciences have attended almost exclusively to these objective features of the universe. The third basis is found in planned undertakings. Using the verb "project" as being related to that part of the universe to which we wish to refer, it is significant that we can say that a man can project his subjective self into the objective world.

The subjective basis has been employed by all the arts and such parts of psychology and of the social sciences as are concerned with subject matter not open to public verification. The function of the subjective sciences, in this sense of the word, is to establish specific feelings, including intuitions and emotions, with which the science in question is concerned. Such feelings connect together our separately experienced sensations and help us anticipate feelings as yet unformed. In painting, for example, the intense feelings which have been experienced from a series from which other feelings follow, i.e. other feelings appear as existential consequences of a small number of more intense feelings. Feelings are to be understood as states of one's body which other people cannot experience. The function of the subjective sciences is to take specific units of sensations and form them into intuitions or emotions.

The objective basis has been employed by all the natural sciences, and also such parts of psychology and of the social sciences as are concerned with subject matter that is publicly available. The function of the objective sciences, in this sense of the word, is to establish general laws covering the behavior of the public events or objects with which the science in question is concerned. Such general laws allow us to connect together our knowledge of separately known events and to make reliable predictions of events as yet unknown. In physics, for example, the laws which have been established from a hierarchy, in which specific laws appear as logical consequences of a small number of highly general laws expressed in a highly rigorous manner.

The projective basis has been employed by all describing activities in which the principal portion of the describer's attention is not given exclusively to one pole of experience. If one wishes to consider an experience in which he is attending to neither a physical object nor to the feelings of his body but rather to a project which entails both, then he must have access to a logical category which is not ordinarily considered by researchers in art education. Such a category would refer to the blending of the objective and the subjective into something new. The one concept which parallels the ordinary concepts "subject" and "object" and which seems to contain all the essential meanings to which we wish to give our attention is "project." The word "project" will refer to an undertaking in which a person is attending to objects and feelings only as they are part of a flow of activities that are moving to a close. A project in an art classroom, for example, is to be understood as a series of happenings in which the students and teacher are attending to a planned undertaking. As a parallel to an art project, consider a good basketball player who becomes so absorbed in the game that he attends only to the game. When this happens he does not attend to the basketball, the goals, the rules, or his body—he attends to the game that is moving toward a close. If his attention is forced off the game and onto a rule, he loses the game. Or when he sprains his ankle or gets a scratch on his face, he is separated from the game and is no longer a relevant part of it. In fact, if his sprain or scratch is severe enough to cause him to stop functioning altogether, then the game is destroyed, there is literally no game. As soon as he can be taken from the floor and a substitute put in and the play resumes, the game is recreated. It should be understood that he is caught up in a specific undertaking that happens only once. Much the same happens when an artist is engaged in producing a painting. He becomes so absorbed in the painting that he attends only to the painting, not as a physical object or a subjective event but as a blend of the two. He does not attend to the canvas, the paint, the turpentine, rules of composition, or his body. He attends to the painting that is moving toward a close. If his attention is forced off the painting and onto a formula for a glaze that he wants to use, or onto the weariness of his hand holding the brush, he loses the painting. When he is forced to attend to a single part of the undertaking, he is separated from the painting and is no longer a relevant part of it. In fact, if the weariness in his hand is great enough to cause him to stop functioning altogether, then the painting is destroyed—there is literally no painting. As soon as he can step back from the canvas and become a spectator instead of a creator, the painting is recreated. When the artist's attention is engaged neither by the physical objects of his craft nor the subjective events of his body, but rather is engaged in an undertaking which entails both, he is a functioning part of a specific project.

But how can we as students, teachers, and researchers inquire into this kind of a phenomena? It is clear that the first two kinds of research, subjective and objective, are incapable of explicating projects for the reason that each abstracts from projects and concentrates upon parts. This is not to say, however, that both kinds of sciences are useless. It is overwhelmingly obvious that the objective sciences have produced a wealth of knowledge that has allowed us to control objects in desired ways. It is likewise obvious that the subjective sciences have produced a wealth of knowledge that has allowed us to control intuitions and emotions in desired ways. Although no one has successfully demonstrated just how an explication of the blending of the objective and the subjective in research and teaching in art can be accomplished, it seems clear that such an undertaking would be worth the effort.

Teachers of art should be allowed to conduct projective analysis of their teaching and to have their students conduct projective analysis of their learning—the project of the teacher is teaching and the project of the student is learning. Such freedom would assist in the progress of art teaching and learning as well as in a better understanding of what art teachers and students can do. Teaching in art, in this sense of the expression, is to be understood to include projects in analyzing and producing drawings, paintings, and sculpture. Research in art is to be understood as projects in analyzing art teaching and learning which are conjoined with drawings, paintings, and sculpture. The function of research and teaching in art is to explicate meaning inherent in specific projects in which the art class in question is engaged. Knowledge of these meanings enables students to achieve a more complete understanding of their specific art projects and teachers to achieve a more complete understanding of their specific art teaching projects. "Meaning" is the fundamental concept for research and teaching in art and the achievement of such meaning is the fundamental aim.

Words are the necessary tools for projective analysis in art teaching. In order to avoid extended discussions about the meanings of words outside of a project it is necessary to begin with words that can be accepted as reasonably clear and unambiguous. Although meanings in the art class emerge from the use of words in analyzing art projects, it is obvious that art students could not understand those meanings if the teacher uses strange and unclear words to express them. If definitions become necessary in the art class, words being defined should not be defined in such a rigid fashion that their meanings are "set" at the beginning of the class and not allowed to be recombined with other words in other descriptions to reveal other meanings. The words must be living and allowed to adapt to varying artistic events.

Projective statements are never predictive in nature. They are never concerned with what might be the case in some future classroom. They are concerned only with projects that the describer has already experienced. Any system of research and teaching in art which tends to fix the meaning of statements as to how they relate to future projects should be avoided. Statements are composed of sets of naming, describing, and action words that are interrelated through the use of logical and mathematical terms, but their use is controlled more by the projects that are to be described than by the rules of correct grammar or logic. No one statement or set of statements establishes the limits of the description of art projects that are to occur in the process of teaching art. Only the context of meanings and the projects that are to be described may be appealed to as criteria for evaluation. As long as the statements are descriptive of the project in question they will be independent and consistent. Only when an art teacher begins to theorize about the nature of art, the nature of sensations and impressions, or the nature of physical properties of artistic materials does he run the risk of being inconsistent and dependent. The fruitfulness of statements about art projects depends upon the number of meanings that are uncovered through the combining of the statements into a projective description. For example consider a series of statements from Lowenfeld, in his book *Creative and Mental Growth,* in which he is describing a clay figure "Youth Imploring" modeled by a girl who has been blind since birth.

Its most striking characteristic is overemphasis on the imploring hands. We feel the strength of the elemental forces embodied in this figure when we observe the gradual increase in its proportions. It starts from the slender basis of the delicate legs and rising like a hymn to heaven finds in the great hands its mighty closing chord. The base has, as it were, been dematerialized: It is no longer earth-bound, and we have before us only the feeling "I implore!" (Lowenfeld, 1947, p. 265.)

Projective description in art teaching and research is always reflective in that it reconstructs projects that have already been experienced. There are three kinds of description that can take place in the classroom: immediate, mediate, and mixed, i.e. a combination of the first two.

Immediate description entails the presence of the project that is being described, e.g. the art teacher describing his own actions and feelings as he creates some artifact is doing immediate description. The same is true when a student describes his own artifact and his conjoined feelings. As long as the describer is in immediate contact with the project being described it is immediate. When he is only recalling some past project he is doing mediate description.

Mediate description entails the absence of the project being described, e.g. when the art teacher describes his actions and feelings that happened while painting a picture last summer, he is doing mediate description. When a student describes a Picasso drawing which he saw in a museum last summer, or a bull fight which he saw in Mexico, he is describing an undertaking that he is recalling. One might claim that all description is mediate since the description necessarily lags behind the action of the undertaking; that all description is description from memory. One might also say that all description is mediate since the undertaking being described and the person hearing the description are separated by both time and space and are joined only by words, i.e. words mediate the project and the describer, as well as the project and the person hearing the description. This argument is reasonable and points to the fact that any separation between immediate and mediate description is an arbitrary one and is useful only in the more extreme cases. When someone describes a project that occurred last summer, he is obviously describing something that is not present; and when someone describes a project in which all of the components are present while the description is transpiring, he is obviously describing something that is immediate.

In some instances the two kinds of description will be mixed. In a mixed description a teacher might be describing the process he went through to attain the artifact being described. Here the artifact is present but the actions involved in the making of the artifact are not. A student describing his first impressions of the Picasso drawing he saw last summer at the same time he is showing and describing a reproduction of the drawing is likewise giving a mixed description. If the distinction between the two kinds of descriptions is controlled by the describer, the persons hearing the description can be led to experience essentially the same project as the describer. Regardless of which of the three descriptions is being used, the fruitfulness of any one will depend upon the amount of meaning uncovered through the combining of the descriptions into a projective analysis.

Projective analysis in research and teaching in art entails the uncovering of specific meanings between separate teaching and artistic acts, actions, and performances, including both their objective and subjective features. The painting of a single shape on a grey ground, for example, would constitute an act. A description of this act and its conjoined feelings would constitute the simplest kind of description in a projective analysis. The painting of a red and green shape on a grey ground would be an instance of an action. The completion of a painting would be a performance. A description of a performance including the objective and the subjective features would constitute a highly complex example of projective analysis.

In the same sense a description can be an act, action, or performance. A description of a set of brush strokes is an action, and a description of a completed set of actions is a performance. The point of this parallel between descriptions and the events being described is to show that projective analyses are open to projective analyses ad infinitum. It is difficult, however, to imagine how a projective analysis beyond the first level would be fruitful. But regardless of how far beyond the first level the analysis is carried, it would always be an analysis of a specific example of art, art teaching, or describing project and never with a hypothetical example.

Since projective inquiry subsumes both objective inquiry in the physical sciences and subjective inquiry in some of the behavioral sciences, religion and the arts, it should be obvious that a fuller understanding is to be gained from the projective technique than with either of the other two. Since the two main poles of art education are teaching and learning, the most comprehensive analysis of a specific art classroom project would entail both the teacher and the students involved in that project. If we accept the simple premise that the more information one has concerning any project the more he will be able to control future projects of the same nature, and that the greatest amount of information about any project can be gained through a projective analysis, i.e. an analysis of the conjoined subjective and objective features, then it would follow that the ability to control future projects can be increased through projective analyses. Not only this, but the greater the numbers of projective analyses of a specific project, the greater the amount of information gained and, hence, the greater the amount of control over future projects of that kind. If a class of one teacher and six art students wanted to do the most comprehensive analysis of one of their classes, then each of the seven members would perform a projective analysis. This would include six projective analyses of art learning and one projective analysis of art teaching. Each student member of the class would be in a better position to control future art learning projects after having studied each of the other five analyses of art learning and the one analysis of art teaching. In like manner the teacher would be in a better position to control future art teaching projects after having performed his projective analysis and in an even better position after having studied each of the six analyses of art learning.

In closing, one's attention can be directed to three different features of one's universe: the objective, the subjective, or the projective. The projective has been offered here as being the most fruitful of the three for research and teaching in the arts.

REFERENCES

Lowenfeld, Viktor, *Creative and Mental Growth*, New York: Macmillan, 1947, p. 265.

Maurice Merleau-Ponty, *Phenomenology of Perception*, translated by Colin Smith, New York: The Humanities Press, 1962, p. vii.

100.0
P
Anti theft

Pass